taste of home

MORE

classic

RECIPES

taste of home

BOOKS

REIMAN MEDIA GROUP, INC. • GREENDALE, WISCONSIN

taste of home

Reader's Digest

A TASTE OF HOME/READER'S DIGEST BOOK

© 2010 Reiman Media Group, Inc.
5400 S. 60th St., Greendale WI 53129
All rights reserved.

Taste of Home and Reader's Digest are
registered trademarks of The Reader's Digest Association, Inc.

EDITOR IN CHIEF: Catherine Cassidy
VICE PRESIDENT,
EXECUTIVE EDITOR/BOOKS: Heidi Reuter Lloyd
CREATIVE DIRECTOR: Ardyth Cope
U.S. CHIEF MARKETING OFFICER: Lisa Karpinski
FOOD DIRECTOR: Diane Werner RD
SENIOR EDITOR/BOOKS: Mark Hagen
EDITOR: Janet Briggs
PROJECT EDITOR: Julie Schnittka
ART DIRECTORS: Rudy Krochalk, Gretchen Trautman
CONTENT PRODUCTION SUPERVISOR: Julie Wagner
GRAPHIC DESIGN ASSOCIATE: Heather Meinen
PROOFREADERS: Linne Bruskewitz, Amy Glander
RECIPE ASSET SYSTEM: Coleen Martin
PREMEDIA SUPERVISOR: Scott Berger
RECIPE TESTING & EDITING: Taste of Home Test Kitchen
FOOD PHOTOGRAPHY: Taste of Home Photo Studio
ADMINISTRATIVE ASSISTANT: Barb Czysz

THE READER'S DIGEST ASSOCIATON, INC.

PRESIDENT AND CHIEF EXECUTIVE OFFICER:
Mary G. Berner
PRESIDENT, U.S. AFFINITIES:
Suzanne M. Grimes
SVP, GLOBAL CHIEF MARKETING OFFICER:
Amy J. Radin
PRESIDENT/PUBLISHER TRADE PUBLISHING:
Harold Clarke
ASSOCIATE PUBLISHER:
Rosanne McManus
VICE PRESIDENT, SALES AND MARKETING:
Stacey Ashton

For other Taste of Home books and products, visit **shoptasteofhome.com**.

For more Reader's Digest products and information,
visit **rd.com** (in the United States) or see **rd.ca** (in Canada).

International Standard Book Number (10): 0-89821-772-5
International Standard Book Number (13): 978-0-89821-772-8
Library of Congress Control Number: 2009935815

Pictured on the front cover:
Lemonade Meringue Pie (p. 171), Strawberry Spinach Salad (p. 43),
Mango Cranberry Sauce (p. 78) and Maple-Glazed Ribs (p. 96).

Pictured on the back cover:
Garden-Fresh Bruschetta (p. 13) and Sunday Chicken Stew (p. 106).

Printed in China
1 3 5 7 9 10 8 6 4 2

contents

Intro 4

Snacks & Beverages................................6

Salads & Dressings...............................26

Soups & Sandwiches.............................44

Side Dishes & Condiments..................62

Main Dishes...82

Breads, Rolls & Muffins.......................122

Cookies, Bars & Candies.....................140

Cakes & Pies...160

Just Desserts...186

Potluck Pleasers 206

Cooking for One or Two 230

My Mom's Best Meals.........................246

Editor's Meals.......................................280

Meals in Minutes.................................310

Meals on a Budget..............................326

Seasons of Good Taste......................348

Indexes 368

FIVE YEARS AND **617** OF OUR BEST RECIPES EVER
MAKE FOR A CLASSIC COOKBOOK.

It Doesn't Get Any Better Than This!

We're doing it again! Because you loved *The Taste of Home Classic Cookbook* so much, we wanted to give you more of the same. So we've created a second edition that features even more of Taste of Home's best-loved recipes! Welcome to *Taste of Home More Classic Recipes!*

For years, *Taste of Home* has been the world's #1 cooking magazine, and this new cookbook captures 617 of its most popular recipes. In this attractive full-color keepsake, you'll find mouthwatering recipes for any event.

Need an appetizer for a party? Look for yummy ideas in the Snacks & Beverages chapter on page 6. If you're bringing a contribution to a church social, check out Potluck Pleasers on page 206. Regardless of whether you're looking for a dessert, main dish or even an entire meal, everything you need is right here in your own hands.

Take a look inside and you'll find:

GRAND PRIZE WINNERS. Each issue of *Taste of Home* magazine includes the winners of a national recipe contest. We've featured those amazing hand-picked dishes from the last five years, including Grand Prize winners, runners-up and honorable mentions. Fabulous Grand Prize recipes include flavor-packed Curried Beef with Dumplings on page 94 and irresistible Rustic Nut Bars on page 144.

COMPLETE MEALS. Not sure what to serve for dinner tonight? Check out the Meals in Minutes chapter for some no-fuss solutions. You can also save a few pennies with the menus in Meals on a Budget and plan special dinners with the unbeatable lineups in My Mom's Best Meals and Editor's Meals.

SEASONS OF GOOD TASTE. From holidays and special occasions to seasonal specialties and harvest-time favorites, there's always a reason to celebrate. In this chapter, you'll discover recipes for holidays such as Easter, Halloween and Christmas. Your family will love biting into main dishes such as Stuffed Ham with Raisin Sauce on page 351 or Spinach and Sausage Pork Loin on page 364. There are also recipes that utilize the best produce of each season and take full advantage of the earth's bounty, such as Tomato-Cucumber Mozzarella Salad on page 355 and Cranberry Walnut Tart on page 362.

HELPFUL TIPS. Throughout the book, you'll find plenty of useful hints, tips, serving suggestions and kitchen shortcuts. You might even discover that these ideas help you through your already busy day!

With so many scrumptious dishes to choose from in this big, heirloom-quality book, you can make a different recipe from it every day for well over a year! And like all Taste of Home specialties, you can rest assured knowing that our Test Kitchen staff approved each and every dish.

You'll marvel at the vibrant color photographs that accompany almost every recipe, and no doubt you'll be tempted to start cooking from *More Classic Recipes* immediately. So don't waste any time getting started. From Taste of Home to your home, we wish you many happy cooking adventures!

PICTURED CLOCKWISE FROM UPPER LEFT: White Chocolate Berry Dessert (page 196), Mac and Cheese for a Bunch (page 214), Berry Cheesecake Muffins (page 127) and Sprial Ham with Cranberry Glaze (page 84).

Whether you're hosting a special dinner, throwing a casual party for the big game or just looking to satisfy the kids before supper, you'll find the perfect hors d'oeuvres, snacks, thirst-quenchers and more right here!

snacks & beverages

Pork and Shrimp Spring Rolls 8

Crunchy Cucumber Rounds...............................8

Sensational Slush 9

A Touch of Greek Dip 9

Party Meatballs 9

Chicken Fingers with Lemon Sauce..............10

Savory Ham Cheesecake....................................10

Cocoa for a Crowd...11

Roasted Carrot Dip 11

Prosciutto Chicken Kabobs 12

Pineapple Cheese Ball.......................................12

Spiced Orange Pecans..12

Rhubarb Cheesecake Smoothies.....................13

Garden-Fresh Bruschetta 13

Mini Hot Browns 14

Sparkling Ginger Lemonade.............................14

Caramel Fruit Dip..14

Grilled Corn Dip 15

Warm Asparagus-Crab Spread........................15

Chicken Pom-Poms..16

Lemon Cream-Stuffed Grapes 16

Par-Cheesy Pizza 17

Hot Spinach Spread with Pita Chips 17

Very Berry-licious Smoothies...........................17

Mini Sausage Quiches..18

Asparagus Brunch Pockets 18

Cowboy Beef Dip..19

Cinnamon Mocha Coffee 19

Carrot Zucchini Fritters....................................20

Sweetheart Punch...20

Shrimp Toast Cups 21

Smoky Jalapenos 21

Chocolate Wheat Cereal Snacks....................22

Roasted Cumin Cashews 22

Zesty Snack Mix..22

Double Chocolate Fondue 22

Three-Cheese Pesto Pizza.................................23

Asparagus Salsa 23

Hot Wings 23

Shrimp Wrapped in Bacon 24

Rainbow Pepper Appetizers..............................24

Sunrise Slushies..24

Roasted Vegetable Turkey Pinwheels.............25

Chicken Potstickers...25

PICTURED CLOCKWISE FROM UPPER LEFT: Grilled Corn Dip (page 15), Cinnamon Mocha Coffee (page 19), Chicken Fingers with Lemon Sauce (page 10) and Sparkling Ginger Lemonade (page 14).

Pork and Shrimp Spring Rolls

(Pictured above)

PREP: 1 hour **COOK:** 5 min./batch

Give your appetizer table an Asian accent with these tasty spring rolls. The recipe makes a big batch, so guests can enjoy seconds!
—*Debbie Terenzini-Wilkerson, Lusby, Maryland*

      1 **pound ground pork**
      1 **can (14 ounces) bean sprouts, drained**
      1 **can (8 ounces) bamboo shoots, drained and chopped**
  1/2 **pound cooked medium shrimp, peeled, deveined and finely chopped**
      1 **can (4 ounces) mushroom stems and pieces, drained and chopped**
      4 **green onions, chopped**
      1 **tablespoon cornstarch**
      3 **tablespoons soy sauce**
      1 **tablespoon water**
      1 **teaspoon garlic powder**
      1 **teaspoon canola oil**
      2 **packages (12 ounces** *each***) wonton wrappers**
Oil for frying
Sweet-and-sour sauce

In a large skillet, cook pork over medium heat until no longer pink; drain. Stir in the bean sprouts, bamboo shoots, shrimp, mushrooms and onions.

In a small bowl, whisk cornstarch, soy sauce, water, garlic powder and oil until smooth; stir into skillet. Bring to a boil; cook and stir for 1 minute or until thickened. Remove from the heat.

Position a wonton wrapper with one point toward you. (Keep remaining wrappers covered with a damp paper towel until ready to use.) Place 2 heaping teaspoons of filling in the center of wrapper. Fold bottom corner over filling; fold sides toward center over the filling. Roll toward the remaining point. Moisten top corner with water; press to seal. Repeat with remaining wrappers and filling.

In an electric skillet or deep-fat fryer, heat oil to 375°. Fry spring rolls, a few at a time, for 1-2 minutes on each side or until golden brown. Drain on paper towels. Serve warm with sweet-and-sour sauce. **YIELD:** about 5 dozen.

Crunchy Cucumber Rounds

(Pictured below)

PREP/TOTAL TIME: 30 min.

I found the recipe for these crisp and refreshing appetizers in an old cookbook several years ago. Make sure your cucumber slices are dry so the fruit mixture will stick to them.
—*Phyllis Pollock, Erie, Pennsylvania*

      1 **cup finely chopped red apple**
      1 **can (8 ounces) unsweetened crushed pineapple, drained**
  1/4 **cup finely chopped pecans, toasted**
  1/4 **cup reduced-fat sour cream**
  1/8 **teaspoon salt**
      3 **medium cucumbers**

In a small bowl, combine the apple, pineapple, pecans, sour cream and salt. Cover and refrigerate until chilled.

To score cucumbers, cut strips lengthwise through the peel. Cut each cucumber into 16 slices. Blot with paper towels to remove moisture. Spoon 1 teaspoon apple mixture on each slice. **YIELD:** 4 dozen.

Sensational Slush

(Pictured above)

PREP: 25 min. + freezing

Colorful and invigorating, this sweet-tart slush has become a family favorite. I freeze the mix in 2- and 4-cup containers so it can be served to individuals or the whole gang. I also freeze crushed strawberries to make preparation simpler.

—Connie Friesen, Atlona, Manitoba

      1/2 cup sugar
       1 package (3 ounces) strawberry gelatin
       2 cups boiling water
       2 cups sliced fresh strawberries
       1 cup unsweetened pineapple juice
       1 can (12 ounces) frozen lemonade concentrate, thawed
       1 can (12 ounces) frozen limeade concentrate, thawed
       2 cups cold water
       2 liters lemon-lime soda, chilled

In a large bowl, dissolve sugar and gelatin in boiling water. Place the strawberries and pineapple juice in a blender or food processor; cover and process until smooth. Add to the gelatin mixture. Stir in lemonade and limeade concentrates and cold water. Cover and freeze for 8 hours or overnight.

Remove from the freezer 45 minutes before serving: For each serving, combine 1/2 cup slush mixture with 1/2 cup lemon-lime soda; stir well. **YIELD:** 20 servings.

A Touch of Greek Dip

PREP/TOTAL TIME: 10 min.

This pleasing dip gets its Greek-style flavor from feta cheese and lemon peel. Serve it with chips or raw vegetables when friends stop by, or try a spoonful on top of a baked potato.

—Emily Chaney, Blue Hill, Maine

      1/2 cup fat-free milk
      1/2 cup 1% cottage cheese
      1/2 cup crumbled feta cheese
       1 teaspoon dried oregano
      1/4 teaspoon grated lemon peel
Pepper to taste
Assorted fresh vegetables

In a blender, combine the milk, cottage cheese, feta cheese, oregano, lemon peel and pepper; cover and process until smooth. Transfer to a small bowl. Serve with vegetables. **YIELD:** 1-1/4 cups.

Party Meatballs

(Pictured below)

PREP: 30 min. **BAKE:** 1 hour

We served this scrumptious dish at our wedding. It went over so well that it's been served at other weddings and social functions, and the requests keep coming!

—Stefany Blevins, Portsmouth, Ohio

       2 eggs, lightly beaten
       1 can (12 ounces) evaporated milk
       2 cups quick-cooking oats
       1 cup finely chopped onion
       2 teaspoons salt
       2 teaspoons chili powder
      1/2 teaspoon garlic powder
      1/2 teaspoon pepper
       3 pounds ground beef
SAUCE:
       2 cups ketchup
      1-1/2 cups packed brown sugar
      1/2 cup chopped onion

In a large bowl, combine the first eight ingredients. Crumble ground beef over mixture and mix well. Shape into 1-in. balls. Place in three greased 13-in. x 9-in. baking dishes.

Combine the sauce ingredients; pour over the meatballs. Bake, uncovered, at 325° for 1 hour or until meat is no longer pink. **YIELD:** about 7 dozen.

Chicken Fingers with Lemon Sauce

(Pictured below and on page 6)

PREP: 20 min. **COOK:** 5 min./batch

My husband turned up his nose when he saw me making this for the first time, but he absolutely flipped when he tasted it. I like to serve the chicken with an apple rice pilaf salad.

—*Amanda Donnelly, Fairborn, Ohio*

   1 jar (10 ounces) lemon curd
1/4 cup chicken broth
1/2 teaspoon soy sauce
1/4 teaspoon ground ginger
   1 cup buttermilk
   1 tablespoon grated lemon peel
   1 cup all-purpose flour
1/2 cup cornstarch
1-1/4 pounds boneless skinless chicken breasts, cut into strips
Oil for frying

In a small saucepan, combine the lemon curd, broth, soy sauce and ginger. Cook and stir until combined and heated through; keep warm over low heat.

In a shallow bowl, combine buttermilk and lemon peel. In another bowl, combine flour and cornstarch. Dip the chicken strips in buttermilk mixture, then coat with flour mixture.

In an electric skillet, heat oil to 375°. Fry chicken, a few strips at a time, for 2-3 minutes on each side or until golden brown. Drain on paper towels. Serve with lemon sauce. **YIELD:** 4 servings (1-1/4 cups sauce).

Savory Ham Cheesecake

(Pictured above)

PREP: 35 min. **BAKE:** 1 hour + chilling

My mom was the best cook—everything she made was special. She served this elegant cheesecake on Sunday following a Saturday ham dinner. Now my family loves it, too.

—*Shannon Soper, West Bend, Wisconsin*

   3 cups oyster crackers, crushed
   1 cup grated Parmesan cheese
1/3 cup butter, melted
FILLING:
   4 packages (8 ounces *each*) cream cheese, softened
   4 eggs, lightly beaten
   2 cups finely chopped fully cooked ham
   2 cups (8 ounces) shredded Swiss cheese
1/3 cup snipped chives
1/4 cup minced fresh basil
1/4 teaspoon salt
1/4 teaspoon white pepper
Assorted crackers

In a large bowl, combine the cracker crumbs, Parmesan cheese and butter. Set aside 1/4 cup for topping. Press remaining crumb mixture onto the bottom and 2 in. up the sides of a greased 9-in. springform pan. Cover and refrigerate for at least 30 minutes.

In a large bowl, beat the cream cheese until smooth. Add eggs; beat on low speed just until combined (mixture will be thick). Add the ham, Swiss cheese, chives, basil, salt and pepper; beat just until combined. Pour into crust. Sprinkle with reserved crumb mixture.

Place pan on a baking sheet. Bake at 325° for 60-70 minutes or until filling is almost set. Turn oven off. Leave cheesecake in oven with door ajar for 30 minutes.

Cool on a wire rack for 10 minutes. Carefully run a knife around edge of pan to loosen; cool 1 hour longer. Refrigerate overnight. Remove the sides of the pan. Serve cheesecake chilled or at room temperature with crackers. **YIELD:** 24-30 servings.

Cocoa for a Crowd

(Pictured below)

PREP/TOTAL TIME: 15 min.

You'll warm many hearts with this rich, satisfying cocoa. It's the perfect beverage to serve after an ice-skating outing or any winter gathering.

—*Julia Livingston, Frostproof, Florida*

    5 cups baking cocoa
    3 cups sugar
    2 teaspoons salt
    5 quarts water, *divided*
   10 quarts milk
    1 quart heavy whipping cream
    2 tablespoons vanilla extract
Whipped cream and additional baking cocoa

In each of two large stockpots, combine 2-1/2 cups cocoa, 1-1/2 cups sugar and 1 teaspoon salt. Gradually stir 5 cups water into each pot. Bring to a boil; reduce heat. Whisk in the milk, cream and remaining water; heat through. Remove from the heat; stir in vanilla. Garnish with whipped cream and additional cocoa. **YIELD:** 65 (1-cup) servings.

Roasted Carrot Dip

(Pictured above)

PREP: 15 min. **BAKE:** 45 min.

Once you start eating this delicious dip, it is difficult to stop. The smooth texture and sweet carrot flavor go great with the crisp pita wedges.

—*Alana Rowley, Calgary, Alberta*

   10 medium carrots
    5 garlic cloves, peeled
    2 tablespoons olive oil
    6 to 8 tablespoons water
    2 teaspoons white wine vinegar
  1/2 cup mayonnaise
  1/4 cup sour cream
  1/8 teaspoon sugar
  1/8 teaspoon salt
  1/8 teaspoon pepper
    4 to 6 pita breads (6 inches)
    2 to 3 tablespoons butter, melted

Cut carrots in half widthwise; cut lengthwise into 1/2-in.-thick slices. In a bowl, combine the carrots, garlic and oil; toss to coat. Transfer to a greased 15-in. x 10-in. x 1-in. baking pan. Bake, uncovered, at 425° for 20 minutes. Stir; bake 15-20 minutes longer or until carrots are tender. Cool slightly.

In a blender, combine 6 tablespoons water, vinegar, mayonnaise, sour cream, sugar, salt, pepper and carrot mixture; cover and process until smooth. Add additional water if needed to achieve desired consistency. Transfer to a bowl; refrigerate until serving.

Brush both sides of pita breads with butter. Cut in half; cut each half into six wedges. Place on ungreased baking sheets. Bake at 350° for 4 minutes on each side or until lightly browned. Serve pita wedges with carrot dip. **YIELD:** 8-10 servings.

with two basil leaves and a chicken strip. Roll up jelly-roll style, starting with a short side. Thread onto metal or soaked wooden skewers.

Grill, covered, over medium heat for 5 minutes on each side or until chicken juices run clear.

Meanwhile, for the dip, in a small bowl, mash the avocados. Stir in the cilantro, onions, lime juice, mayonnaise, horseradish, garlic and salt. Serve with kabobs. **YIELD:** 12 appetizers.

Pineapple Cheese Ball

PREP: 20 min. + chilling

Pineapple lends a refreshing fruity tang to this fun and tasty appetizer. Instead of one large cheese ball, you could also make two smaller ones.

—Anne Halfhill, Sunbury, Ohio

- 2 packages (8 ounces *each*) cream cheese, softened
- 1 can (8 ounces) unsweetened crushed pineapple, drained
- 1/4 cup finely chopped green pepper
- 2 tablespoons finely chopped onion
- 2 teaspoons seasoned salt
- 1-1/2 cups finely chopped walnuts
Assorted crackers

In a small bowl, beat the cream cheese, pineapple, green pepper, onion and seasoned salt until blended. Cover and refrigerate for 30 minutes. Shape into a ball; roll in walnuts. Cover and refrigerate overnight. Serve with crackers. **YIELD:** 1 cheese ball (3 cups).

Spiced Orange Pecans

PREP: 10 min. **BAKE:** 30 min. + cooling

You won't be able to eat just one of these spicy-sweet nibblers. You'll want to keep them on hand for unexpected company.

—Ruth Peterson, Jenison, Michigan

- 2 egg whites, lightly beaten
- 3 tablespoons orange juice
- 2 cups pecan halves
- 1-1/2 cups confectioners' sugar
- 2 tablespoons cornstarch
- 2 tablespoons grated orange peel
- 1 teaspoon ground cinnamon
- 3/4 teaspoon ground cloves
- 1/4 teaspoon ground allspice
- 1/8 teaspoon salt

In a large bowl, combine egg whites and orange juice. Add pecans and toss to coat; drain. In another large bowl, combine remaining ingredients. Add pecans and toss to coat.

Spread in single layer in greased 15-in. x 10-in. x 1-in. baking pan. Bake at 250° for 30-35 minutes or until dry and lightly browned. Cool completely. Store in an airtight container. **YIELD:** 5 cups.

Prosciutto Chicken Kabobs

(Pictured above)

PREP: 30 min. + marinating **GRILL:** 10 min.

Everyone will think you spent hours preparing these clever grilled wraps, served with a guacamole-like dip. Basil gives the chicken a lovely, fresh herb flavor.

—Elaine Sweet, Dallas, Texas

- 3/4 cup five-cheese Italian salad dressing
- 1/4 cup lime juice
- 2 teaspoons white Worcestershire sauce for chicken
- 1/2 pound boneless skinless chicken breasts, cut into 3-inch x 1/2-inch strips
- 12 thin slices prosciutto
- 24 fresh basil leaves
AVOCADO DIP:
- 2 medium ripe avocados, peeled
- 1/4 cup minced fresh cilantro
- 2 green onions, chopped
- 2 tablespoons lime juice
- 2 tablespoons mayonnaise
- 1-1/2 teaspoons prepared horseradish
- 1 garlic clove, minced
- 1/4 teaspoon salt

In a large resealable plastic bag, combine the salad dressing, lime juice and Worcestershire sauce; add chicken. Seal bag and turn to coat; refrigerate for 1 hour.

Drain and discard marinade. Fold prosciutto slices in half; top each

Rhubarb Cheesecake Smoothies

(Pictured below)

PREP: 20 min. + cooling

We love smoothies, so there isn't much we don't use to make unusual combinations. Cream cheese adds an extra-special touch to this yummy concoction that our family loves.

—Kathy Specht, Cambria, California

- 2 cups diced fresh *or* frozen rhubarb
- 1/4 cup water
- 4 tablespoons honey, *divided*
- 1-1/2 cups vanilla ice cream
- 1 cup milk
- 1 cup frozen sweetened sliced strawberries
- 2 packages (3 ounces *each*) cream cheese, cubed
- 1/2 cup vanilla yogurt
- 1/4 cup confectioners' sugar
- 5 ice cubes

In a large saucepan, bring the rhubarb, water and 2 tablespoons honey to a boil. Reduce heat; cover and simmer for 5-10 minutes or until the rhubarb is tender. Remove from the heat; cool to room temperature.

In a blender, combine the vanilla ice cream, milk, rhubarb mixture, strawberries, cream cheese, vanilla yogurt, confectioners' sugar, ice cubes and remaining honey; cover and process for 1 minute or until smooth. Pour into chilled glasses; serve immediately. **YIELD:** 6 servings.

Garden-Fresh Bruschetta

(Pictured above)

PREP/TOTAL TIME: 30 min.

I like to serve this easy-to-fix bruschetta as either an appetizer or as a colorful side dish.

—Rachel Garcia, Arlington, Virginia

- 1 garlic clove, peeled and halved
- 14 slices French bread (3/4 inch thick)
- 4 medium tomatoes, seeded and diced
- 1/4 cup chopped red onion
- 2 tablespoons olive oil
- 1 tablespoon minced fresh basil
- 1/4 teaspoon salt
- 1/8 teaspoon pepper
- 14 fresh basil leaves

Rub cut side of garlic over one side of each slice of bread. Place bread garlic side down on an ungreased baking sheet. Bake at 350° for 5 minutes on each side or until lightly browned.

In a bowl, combine the tomatoes, onion, oil, minced basil, salt and pepper; spoon about 2 tablespoons onto each toasted bread slice. Top each with a basil leaf. **YIELD:** 14 servings.

seeding tomatoes

To remove the seeds from a tomato, cut it in half horizontally and remove the stem. Holding a tomato half over a bowl, scrape out the seeds with a small spoon or squeeze the tomato to force out the seeds. Then slice or dice as directed.

Mini Hot Browns

(Pictured below)

PREP/TOTAL TIME: 30 min.

My Mini Hot Browns are smaller versions of the famous sand-wich. Guests quickly saddle up for juicy turkey slices and crispy bacon, piled high on toasted rye bread and then topped with a rich cheese sauce.

—Annette Grahl, Midway, Kentucky

 1 teaspoon chicken bouillon granules
1/4 cup boiling water
 3 tablespoons butter
 2 tablespoons all-purpose flour
3/4 cup half-and-half cream
 1 cup (4 ounces) shredded Swiss cheese
18 slices snack rye bread
 6 ounces sliced deli turkey
 1 small onion, thinly sliced and separated into rings
 5 bacon strips, cooked and crumbled
 2 tablespoons minced fresh parsley

In a small bowl, dissolve bouillon in water; set aside. In a small saucepan, melt the butter over medium heat. Stir in the flour until smooth; stir in cream and bouillon. Bring to a boil; cook and stir for 1-2 minutes or until thickened. Stir in cheese until melted. Remove from the heat.

Place the bread slices on two baking sheets. Layer each with turkey, onion and cheese sauce. Sprinkle with bacon. Bake at 350° for 10-12 minutes or until heated through. Sprinkle with parsley. **YIELD:** 1-1/2 dozen.

Sparkling Ginger Lemonade

(Pictured above and on page 6)

PREP: 20 min. + cooling

Chill out with this delightful cooler, which is perfect for spring-time bridal showers or hot summer days on the deck. It's so easy to fix, you'll find yourself stirring together this refreshing lemon-ade time and again.

—Jodi Blubaugh, Eagle Mountain, Utah

2 cups water
1 cup honey
2 tablespoons minced fresh gingerroot
2 cups club soda, chilled
1 cup lemon juice

In a small saucepan, bring the water, honey and ginger to a boil. Remove from the heat; cover and steep for 10 minutes. Strain, discarding ginger. Cool.

Transfer to a pitcher; stir in the soda and lemon juice. Serve immediately over ice. **YIELD:** 5 servings.

Caramel Fruit Dip

PREP/TOTAL TIME: 10 min.

This creamy melt-in-your-mouth dip, served with assorted fruits, makes a delightful accompaniment to a cheese tray.

—Trish Gehlhar, Ypsilanti, North Dakota

2 packages (8 ounces *each*) cream cheese, softened
1 cup packed brown sugar
1/2 cup caramel ice cream topping
Assorted fresh fruit

In a small bowl, beat cream cheese and brown sugar until smooth. Add the caramel topping; beat until blended. Serve with fruit. Refrigerate leftovers. **YIELD:** 3 cups.

Grilled Corn Dip

(Pictured below and on page 6)

PREP: 30 min. **BAKE:** 25 min.

Great for summer, this tasty appetizer is a must-have at weekend family gatherings at our cottage. It's well worth the time it takes to grill the corn and cut it from the cob.

—*Cathy Myers, Monroeville, Ohio*

- 6 medium ears sweet corn, husks removed
- 1 large onion, chopped
- 1 jalapeno pepper, finely chopped
- 2 garlic cloves, minced
- 2 tablespoons butter
- 1 cup mayonnaise
- 1/2 cup sour cream
- 1/2 teaspoon chili powder
- 2 cups (8 ounces) shredded Monterey Jack cheese
- 1 can (2-1/4 ounces) sliced ripe olives, drained
- 2 tablespoons sliced green onions

Tortilla chips

Grill the corn, covered, over medium heat for 10-12 minutes or until tender, turning occasionally.

Cut corn from cobs. In a large skillet, saute the onion, jalapeno and garlic in butter for 2-3 minutes or until almost tender. Add corn; saute 1-2 minutes longer or until vegetables are tender. Remove from the heat.

In a large bowl, combine the mayonnaise, sour cream and chili powder. Stir in cheese and corn mixture. Transfer to a greased 2-qt. baking dish.

Bake, uncovered, at 400° for 25-30 minutes or until bubbly and golden brown. Sprinkle with olives and green onions; serve with chips. **YIELD:** 5 cups.

EDITOR'S NOTE: When cutting hot peppers, disposable gloves are recommended. Avoid touching your face.

Warm Asparagus-Crab Spread

(Pictured above)

PREP/TOTAL TIME: 30 min.

When my children entertain, I like to help them with the cooking, and this dip is always a hit. Cashew nuts give this creamy spread a nice, crunchy texture.

—*Camille Wisniewski, Jackson, New Jersey*

- 1 medium sweet red pepper, chopped
- 3 green onions, sliced
- 2 medium jalapeno peppers, seeded and finely chopped
- 2 teaspoons canola oil
- 1 can (15 ounces) asparagus spears, drained and chopped
- 2 cans (6 ounces *each*) crabmeat, drained, flaked and cartilage removed
- 1 cup mayonnaise
- 1/2 cup grated *or* shredded Parmesan cheese
- 1/2 cup chopped cashews

Assorted crackers

In a large skillet, saute the red pepper, onions and jalapenos in oil until tender. Add the asparagus, crab, mayonnaise and Parmesan cheese; mix well.

Transfer to a greased 1-qt. baking dish. Sprinkle with cashews. Bake, uncovered, at 375° for 20-25 minutes or until bubbly. Serve with crackers. **YIELD:** 3 cups.

EDITOR'S NOTE: When cutting hot peppers, disposable gloves are recommended. Avoid touching your face.

Stir rice, chicken and cheese into the sauce mixture. Combine bread crumbs and paprika in a shallow baking pan. Shape 1/4 cupfuls of chicken mixture into 2-in. balls; roll in crumb mixture. Place 3 in. apart on lightly greased baking sheets.

Bake 400° for 25-30 minutes or until heated through and golden brown. Heat the gravy; serve with pom-poms. **YIELD:** 40-45 servings (2 pom-poms each).

Chicken Pom-Poms

(Pictured above)

PREP: 30 min. + chilling **BAKE:** 25 min.

These golden baked croquettes are a fun and different way to serve chicken to a crowd. My husband and I are hosts at a mission house where we cook for groups of 30 or more each week. This recipe is a favorite with guests.

—Fran Wolfley, St. Mary, Jamaica

      4 celery ribs, chopped
      1 large onion, finely chopped
      1 cup butter, cubed
      2 cups all-purpose flour
      3 teaspoons poultry seasoning
      1 teaspoon salt
      1 teaspoon pepper
      2 cartons (32 ounces *each*) chicken broth
      2 cups nonfat dry milk powder
    1/4 cup chicken bouillon granules
     16 cups cooked long grain rice
     12 cups chopped cooked chicken
      8 cups (32 ounces) shredded cheddar cheese
     10 cups soft bread crumbs
      3 tablespoons paprika
     10 jars (12 ounces *each*) chicken gravy

In a large Dutch oven or stockpot, saute celery and onion in butter until tender. Combine the flour, poultry seasoning, salt and pepper; stir into vegetable mixture until blended. Gradually stir in broth until blended. Add the milk powder and bouillon. Cook and stir until the mixture comes to a boil; cook and stir 1-2 minutes longer or until very thick. Cool. Cover and refrigerate for at least 3 hours.

Lemon Cream-Stuffed Grapes

(Pictured below)

PREP: 35 min. + chilling

This is a refreshing snack on a hot summer day. It's simple, plus it offers a light change from heartier party foods.

—Janis Plourde, Smooth Rock Falls, Ontario

      4 ounces cream cheese, softened
      3 tablespoons confectioners' sugar
    1-1/2 teaspoons lemon juice
    1/2 teaspoon grated lemon peel
      1 pound seedless globe grapes, rinsed and patted dry

In a small bowl, beat cream cheese, confectioners' sugar, lemon juice and peel until blended. Cover and refrigerate for 1 hour.

Cut a deep "X" in the top of each grape to within 1/4 in. of bottom. Carefully spread each grape apart. Transfer cream cheese mixture to a heavy-duty resealable plastic bag; cut a small hole in a corner of bag. Pipe filling into the grapes. Refrigerate until serving. **YIELD:** 3 dozen.

Par-Cheesy Pizza

(Pictured above)

PREP: 45 min. **BAKE:** 15 min.

I have always received great reactions after serving my pizza at parties and get-togethers. It's easy to make and looks fantastic!
—*Leslie Dumm, Cleveland Heights, Ohio*

- 1 pound frozen bread dough
- 4 thin slices salami
- 1 to 2 medium onions
- 1 to 2 large sweet red peppers
- 3/4 cup pizza sauce
- 1-1/2 cups (6 ounces) shredded part-skim mozzarella cheese
- 4 to 6 pimiento-stuffed olives, halved

Thaw dough according to package directions. Cut the salami into 2-1/2-in. rounds. Cut onions and red peppers into 2-in. x 1/2-in. strips.

On a lightly greased baking sheet, roll bread dough into a 12-in. square. Spread with pizza sauce. Sprinkle with cheese. Arrange the salami, onion and pepper over top to resemble a Parcheesi board.

Bake at 400° for 15-20 minutes or until the crust is lightly browned and the cheese is melted. Top pizza with olives. **YIELD:** 6 servings.

Hot Spinach Spread With Pita Chips

PREP: 30 min. **BAKE:** 20 min.

This warm, cheesy spread is absolutely scrumptious served on toasted pita wedges. Its colorful appearance makes it perfect for a holiday buffet.
—*Teresa Emanuel, Smithville, Missouri*

- 2 cups (8 ounces) shredded Monterey Jack cheese
- 1 package (10 ounces) frozen chopped spinach, thawed and squeezed dry
- 1 package (8 ounces) cream cheese, cubed
- 2 plum tomatoes, seeded and chopped

- 3/4 cup chopped onion
- 1/3 cup half-and-half cream
- 1 tablespoon finely chopped seeded jalapeno pepper
- 6 pita breads (6 inches)
- 1/2 cup butter, melted
- 2 teaspoons lemon-pepper seasoning
- 2 teaspoons ground cumin
- 1/4 teaspoon garlic salt

In a large bowl, combine the first seven ingredients. Transfer to a greased 1-1/2-qt. baking dish. Bake, uncovered, at 375° for 20-25 minutes or until bubbly.

Meanwhile, cut each pita bread into eight wedges. Place in two 15-in. x 10-in. x 1-in. baking pans. Combine butter, lemon-pepper, cumin and garlic salt; brush over pita wedges.

Bake for 7-9 minutes or until crisp. Serve with spinach spread. **YIELD:** 16 servings (4 cups spread).

EDITOR'S NOTE: When cutting hot peppers, disposable gloves are recommended. Avoid touching your face.

Very Berry-licious Smoothies

(Pictured below)

PREP/TOTAL TIME: 10 min.

Four berry flavors combine wonderfully in this cool, sweet-tart beverage. It's an ideal complement to any brunch menu, or to sip while enjoying a lazy afternoon on the patio.
—*Colleen Belbey, Warwick, Rhode Island*

- 2 cups cranberry juice
- 4 cups frozen unsweetened strawberries
- 2 cups frozen unsweetened raspberries
- 2 cartons (6 ounces *each*) blackberry yogurt

In a blender, combine half of each of the ingredients; cover and process until well blended. Pour into chilled glasses. Repeat with remaining ingredients. Serve smoothies immediately. **YIELD:** 6 servings.

Mini Sausage Quiches

(Pictured below)

PREP: 25 min. **BAKE:** 20 min.

These bite-size quiches are loaded with sausage and cheese, plus their crescent roll bases make preparation a snap. Serve the savory "muffinettes" at any potluck gathering.

—*Jan Mead, Milford, Connecticut*

- 1/2 **pound bulk hot Italian sausage**
- 2 **tablespoons dried minced onion**
- 2 **tablespoons minced chives**
- 1 **tube (8 ounces) refrigerated crescent rolls**
- 4 **eggs, lightly beaten**
- 2 **cups (8 ounces) shredded Swiss cheese**
- 1 **cup (8 ounces) 4% cottage cheese**
- 1/3 **cup grated Parmesan cheese**

Paprika

In a large skillet, brown sausage and onion over medium heat for 4-5 minutes or until meat is no longer pink; drain. Stir in chives.

On a lightly floured surface, unroll crescent dough into one long rectangle; seal seams and perforations. Cut into 48 pieces. Press onto the bottom and up the sides of greased miniature muffin cups. Fill each with about 2 teaspoons of sausage mixture. In a large bowl, combine the eggs and cheeses. Spoon 2 teaspoonfuls over sausage mixture. Sprinkle with paprika.

Bake at 375° for 20-25 minutes or until a knife inserted in the center comes out clean. Cool for 5 minutes before removing from pans to wire racks. Serve warm. Refrigerate leftovers. **YIELD:** 4 dozen.

Asparagus Brunch Pockets

(Pictured above)

PREP: 20 min. **BAKE:** 15 min.

These tasty bundles are stuffed with a flavorful asparagus-cream cheese mixture. They're wonderful for brunch or as a side dish.

—*Cynthia Linthicum, Towson, Maryland*

- 1 **pound fresh asparagus, trimmed and cut into 1-inch pieces**
- 4 **ounces cream cheese, softened**
- 1 **tablespoon milk**
- 1 **tablespoon mayonnaise**
- 1 **tablespoon diced pimientos**
- 1 **tablespoon finely chopped onion**
- 1/8 **teaspoon salt**

Pinch pepper
- 1 **tube (8 ounces) refrigerated crescent rolls**
- 2 **teaspoons butter, melted**
- 1 **tablespoon seasoned bread crumbs**

In a large saucepan, bring 1/2 in. of water to a boil. Add asparagus; cover and boil for 3 minutes. Drain and set aside.

In a small bowl, beat the cream cheese, milk and mayonnaise until smooth. Stir in the pimientos, onion, salt and pepper.

Unroll crescent dough and separate into triangles; place on an ungreased baking sheet. Spoon 1 teaspoon of cream cheese mixture into the center of each triangle; top with asparagus. Top each with another teaspoonful of cream cheese mixture. Bring three corners of dough together and twist; pinch edges to seal.

Brush dough with melted butter; sprinkle with bread crumbs. Bake at 375° for 15-18 minutes or until golden brown. **YIELD:** 8 servings.

asparagus tips

After rinsing asparagus in cold water, snap off the ends as far down as they will easily break when bent, or cut off the tough white portion. If the stalks are large, peel the tough part from the end to just below the tip.

Cowboy Beef Dip

(Pictured below)

PREP: 20 min. **COOK:** 25 min.

This hearty dip starring ground beef is a winner with my family. It has all kinds of yummy stuff in it, including chopped onion and bell peppers, olives, green chilies, jalapeno and cheese.

—Jessica Klym, Killdeer, North Dakota

- 1 **pound ground beef**
- 4 **tablespoons chopped onion,** *divided*
- 3 **tablespoons chopped sweet red pepper,** *divided*
- 2 **tablespoons chopped green pepper,** *divided*
- 1 **can (10-3/4 ounces) condensed nacho cheese soup, undiluted**
- 1/2 **cup salsa**
- 4 **tablespoons sliced ripe olives,** *divided*
- 4 **tablespoons sliced pimiento-stuffed olives,** *divided*
- 2 **tablespoons chopped green chilies**
- 1 **teaspoon chopped seeded jalapeno pepper**
- 1/4 **teaspoon dried oregano**
- 1/4 **teaspoon pepper**
- 1/4 **cup shredded cheddar cheese**
- 2 **tablespoons sour cream**
- 2 **to 3 teaspoons minced fresh parsley**

Tortilla chips

In a large skillet, cook the beef, 3 tablespoons onions, 2 tablespoons red pepper and 1 tablespoon green pepper over medium heat until meat is no longer pink; drain. Stir in the soup, salsa, 3 tablespoons ripe olives, 3 tablespoons pimiento-stuffed olives, chilies, jalapeno, oregano and pepper. Bring to a boil. Reduce heat; simmer, uncovered, for 5 minutes.

Transfer to a serving dish. Top with the cheese, sour cream and parsley; sprinkle top with the remaining onion, peppers and olives. Serve the dip with tortilla chips. **YIELD:** 3 cups.

EDITOR'S NOTE: When cutting hot peppers, disposable gloves are recommended. Avoid touching your face.

Cinnamon Mocha Coffee

(Pictured above and on page 6)

PREP/TOTAL TIME: 20 min.

One snowy day, my neighbor called and invited me over to try a new beverage. It was delicious! This spiced coffee is a lovely treat any time of year.

—Bernice Morris, Marshfield, Missouri

- 1/2 **cup ground dark roast coffee**
- 1 **tablespoon ground cinnamon**
- 1/4 **teaspoon ground nutmeg**
- 5 **cups water**
- 1 **cup milk**
- 1/3 **cup chocolate syrup**
- 1/4 **cup packed brown sugar**
- 1 **teaspoon vanilla extract**

Whipped cream, optional

In a small bowl, combine coffee grounds, cinnamon and nutmeg; pour into a coffee filter of a drip coffeemaker. Add water; brew according to manufacturer's directions.

In a large saucepan, combine the milk, chocolate syrup and brown sugar. Cook over low heat until the sugar is dissolved, stirring occasionally. Stir in the vanilla and brewed coffee.

Ladle into mugs; garnish with whipped cream if desired. **YIELD:** 6 servings.

For the fritters, place onion and butter in a microwave-safe dish. Cover; microwave on high until onion is tender. Add egg, zucchini and carrot. In a bowl, combine the flour, cheese, cornmeal, salt and pepper; stir in vegetable mixture just until combined.

In a skillet or deep-fat fryer, heat 2 in. of oil to 375°. Drop rounded tablespoonfuls of batter into oil. Fry for 1-2 minutes until deep golden brown, turning once. Drain on paper towels. Serve fritters with dipping sauce. **YIELD:** 1-1/2 dozen fritters, 2/3 cup basil sauce and 1-1/2 cups horseradish sauce.

Sweetheart Punch

(Pictured below)

PREP: 20 min. + chilling

I received this recipe from a friend years ago and have served it at numerous special occasions. As an eye-catching option, use a heart-shaped mold to make the ice ring.

—Gretchen Montgomery, Marietta, Ohio

- **2 cups sliced fresh strawberries,** *divided*
- **6 cups water,** *divided*
- **1 can (12 ounces) frozen pink lemonade concentrate, thawed**
- **1 package (10 ounces) frozen sweetened sliced strawberries, thawed**
- **1 can (6 ounces) frozen orange juice concentrate, thawed**
- **2 liters lemon-lime soda, chilled**

Arrange 1 cup of fresh strawberries in a 4-1/2-cup ring mold; add 2 cups water. Freeze until solid. Top with the remaining fresh strawberries. Slowly pour 1 cup water into mold to almost cover berries. Freeze until solid.

In a punch bowl, combine the lemonade concentrate, thawed strawberries, orange juice concentrate and remaining water. Refrigerate until chilled.

Just before serving, stir in lemon-lime soda. Unmold ice ring by wrapping the bottom of the mold in a damp hot dishcloth; invert onto a baking sheet. Place the fruit side up in punch bowl. **YIELD:** 14 servings (3-1/2 quarts).

Carrot Zucchini Fritters

(Pictured above)

PREP/TOTAL TIME: 25 min.

I'm always looking for flavorful recipes that increase my veggie intake without being saturated in cheese or cream sauces. This one fills the bill. The crispy fritters are delicious and fun to eat with or without the dipping sauces.

—Laura Mize, Waco, Kentucky

- **2/3 cup sour cream plus 1/2 cup sour cream,** *divided*
- **2/3 cup lightly packed fresh basil leaves**
- **1 teaspoon lemon juice**

Salt and pepper to taste

- **1/2 cup mayonnaise**
- **1/2 cup horseradish sauce**

FRITTERS:

- **2 tablespoons finely chopped onion**
- **1 tablespoon butter**
- **1 egg, lightly beaten**
- **2 medium zucchini, shredded and squeezed dry (about 1-1/2 cups)**
- **1 large carrot, shredded**
- **1/3 cup all-purpose flour**
- **1/3 cup grated Parmesan cheese**
- **1 tablespoon cornmeal**
- **1/2 teaspoon salt**
- **1/8 teaspoon pepper**

Oil for frying

In a blender or food processor, place 2/3 cup sour cream, basil, lemon juice, salt and pepper; cover and process until blended. Transfer to a small bowl. In another bowl, combine the mayonnaise, horseradish and remaining sour cream. Cover and refrigerate both sauces.

Shrimp Toast Cups

(Pictured above, left)

PREP: 30 min. **BAKE:** 15 min./batch

These appetizers always disappear quick as a flash. The pretty toast cups lend themselves to other favorite fillings, too!
—Awynne Thurstenson, Siloam Springs, Arkansas

- 24 **slices white bread, crusts removed**
- 1 **cup butter, melted**
- 2 **packages (8 ounces *each*) cream cheese, softened**
- 1/2 **cup mayonnaise**
- 3 **tablespoons sour cream**
- 3 **tablespoons prepared horseradish**
- 3 **cans (6 ounces *each*) small shrimp, rinsed and drained**
- 16 **green onions, sliced**

Fresh dill sprigs, optional

Flatten bread with a rolling pin; cut each slice into four pieces. Place butter in a shallow dish; dip both sides of bread in butter; press into miniature muffin cups. Bake at 325° for 14 minutes or until golden brown. Remove from pans to wire racks to cool.

In a large bowl, beat the cream cheese, mayonnaise, sour cream and horseradish until blended. Just before serving, stir in shrimp and onions; spoon into cups. Garnish the cups with fresh dill sprigs if desired. Refrigerate leftovers. **YIELD:** 8 dozen.

Smoky Jalapenos

(Pictured above, right)

PREP: 25 min. **BAKE:** 20 min.

There are no leftovers when I make these zesty bites. They can also be made with mild banana peppers or yellow chili peppers.
—Melinda Strable, Ankeny, Iowa

- 14 **jalapeno peppers**
- 4 **ounces cream cheese, softened**
- 14 **miniature smoked sausages**
- 7 **bacon strips**

Cut a lengthwise slit in each pepper; remove seeds and membranes. Spread a teaspoonful of cream cheese into each pepper; stuff each with a sausage.

Cut bacon strips in half widthwise; cook in microwave or skillet until partially cooked. Wrap a bacon piece around each pepper; secure the bacon with a toothpick.

Place in an ungreased 13-in. x 9-in. baking dish. Bake, uncovered, at 350° for 20 minutes for spicy flavor, 30 minutes for medium flavor and 40 minutes for mild flavor. **YIELD:** 14 appetizers.

EDITOR'S NOTE: When cutting hot peppers, disposable gloves are recommended. Avoid touching your face.

Chocolate Wheat Cereal Snacks

PREP/TOTAL TIME: 10 min.

This crunchy mix is great for a late night snack, or any gathering. The chocolate-peanut butter combination will satisfy any sweet tooth!

—Tracy Golder, Bloomsburg, Pennsylvania

6 cups frosted bite-size Shredded Wheat
1 cup milk chocolate chips
1/4 cup creamy peanut butter
1 cup confectioners' sugar

Place cereal in a large bowl; set aside. In a small microwave-safe bowl, melt chocolate chips and peanut butter; stir until smooth. Pour over cereal and stir gently to coat. Let stand for 10 minutes.

Sprinkle with confectioners' sugar and toss to coat. Cool completely. Store in an airtight container. **YIELD:** 6 cups.

Roasted Cumin Cashews

(Pictured below)

PREP: 15 min. **BAKE:** 50 min. + cooling

Kick up parties and get-togethers with these well-seasoned nuts. They're sweet, salty, crunchy and oh, so munchable.

—Martha Fehl, Brookville, Indiana

1 egg white
1 tablespoon water
2 cans (9-3/4 ounces *each*) salted whole cashews
1/3 cup sugar
3 teaspoons chili powder
2 teaspoons salt
2 teaspoons ground cumin
1/2 teaspoon cayenne pepper

In a large bowl, whisk egg white and water. Add cashews and toss to coat. Transfer to a colander; drain for 2 minutes. In another bowl, combine the remaining ingredients; add cashews and toss to coat.

Arrange the nut mixture in a single layer in a greased 15-in. x 10-in. x 1-in. baking pan. Bake, uncovered, at 250° for 50-55 minutes, stirring once. Cool on a wire rack. Store in an airtight container. **YIELD:** 3-1/2 cups.

Zesty Snack Mix

PREP: 10 min. **BAKE:** 2-1/2 hours

Pep up a party with this well-seasoned blend of cereal, pretzels and cheese crackers. If you like, alter it by adding mixed nuts.

—Codie Ray, Tallulah, Louisiana

4 cups Corn Chex
4 cups Cheerios
4 cups pretzel sticks
4 cups cheese-flavored snack crackers
1 cup butter, melted
1/2 cup canola oil
3 tablespoons Worcestershire sauce
1 tablespoon garlic powder
1 tablespoon seasoned salt
1 tablespoon chili powder
1 teaspoon cayenne pepper

In a large bowl, combine the cereals, pretzels and crackers. Spread into two ungreased 15-in. x 10-in. x 1-in. baking pans.

Combine the remaining ingredients; pour over the cereal mixture and toss to coat. Bake at 225° for 2 to 2-1/2 hours, stirring every 30 minutes. Store in airtight containers. **YIELD:** 16 cups.

Double Chocolate Fondue

PREP/TOTAL TIME: 20 min.

Thick, rich and luscious, this dip won't last long. You can also use pretzel sticks as dippers. I love it so much I eat spoonfuls right out of the refrigerator!

—Cindy Stetzer, Alliance, Ohio

1 cup sugar
2 cans (5 ounces *each*) evaporated milk, *divided*
1/2 cup baking cocoa
4 squares (1 ounce *each*) unsweetened chocolate, chopped
2 tablespoons butter
1 teaspoon vanilla extract
Cubed pound cake and assorted fresh fruit

In a small saucepan, combine sugar and 1 can evaporated milk. Cook over low heat, stirring occasionally, until the sugar is dissolved.

In a small bowl, whisk the cocoa and remaining milk until smooth. Add to the sugar mixture; bring to a boil, whisking constantly.

Remove from the heat; stir in chocolate and butter until melted. Stir in vanilla. Keep warm. Serve with cake and fruit. **YIELD:** 1-1/3 cups.

1 tablespoon minced fresh cilantro
1 garlic clove, minced
1 teaspoon cider vinegar
1/4 teaspoon salt
Tortilla chips

Place asparagus in a large saucepan; add 1/2 in. of water. Bring to a boil. Reduce heat; cover and simmer for 2 minutes. Drain and rinse in cold water.

In a bowl, combine the asparagus, tomatoes, onion, jalapeno, cilantro, garlic, vinegar and salt. Cover and refrigerate for at least 4 hours, stirring several times. Serve with tortilla chips. **YIELD:** 3 cups.

EDITOR'S NOTE: When cutting hot peppers, disposable gloves are recommended. Avoid touching your face.

Three-Cheese Pesto Pizza

(Pictured above)

PREP/TOTAL TIME: 30 min.

With a ready-made crust, this pizza can be on a serving tray in half an hour. The three-cheese blend will make slices go fast.

—Pat Stevens, Granbury, Texas

   1/2 **cup finely chopped red onion**
   1/2 **cup finely chopped sweet red pepper**
     1 **tablespoon olive oil**
     1 **prebaked Italian bread shell crust (14 ounces)**
   1/2 **cup prepared pesto**
     1 **cup (4 ounces) crumbled feta cheese**
     1 **cup (4 ounces) shredded part-skim mozzarella cheese**
     1 **cup (4 ounces) shredded Parmesan cheese**
     1 **can (4-1/4 ounces) chopped ripe olives**
     1 **medium tomato, thinly sliced**

In a small skillet, saute the onion and red pepper in oil until tender. Remove from the heat; set aside.

Place crust on an ungreased 14-in. pizza pan. Spread pesto to within 1/2 in. of edges. Layer with the cheeses, onion mixture, olives and tomato. Bake at 400° for 15-18 minutes or until cheese is melted. **YIELD:** 16 slices.

Asparagus Salsa

PREP: 20 min. + chilling

Jalapeno pepper and cilantro spice up this refreshing salsa that's made with tomatoes, onion and fresh asparagus. Serve it chilled with tortilla chips—it won't last long.

—Emma Thomas, Rome, Georgia

     1 **pound fresh asparagus, trimmed and cut into 1/2-inch pieces**
     1 **cup chopped seeded tomatoes**
   1/2 **cup finely chopped onion**
     1 **small jalapeno pepper, seeded and finely chopped**

Hot Wings

(Pictured below)

PREP: 15 min. **BAKE:** 1 hour

These appetizers are hearty for a party—with just the right amount of "heat." My family enjoys them so much that I often serve the wings as our main course!

—Coralie Begin, Fairfield, Maine

     7 **to 8 pounds fresh *or* frozen chicken wingettes, thawed**
     4 **cups ketchup**
 2-1/2 **cups packed brown sugar**
 1-1/3 **cups water**
     1 **cup Louisiana-style hot sauce**
   1/3 **cup Worcestershire sauce**
 2-1/2 **teaspoons chili powder**
     2 **teaspoons garlic powder**
   1/2 **teaspoon onion powder**

Place wingettes in two greased 15-in. x 10-in. x 1-in. baking pans. In a large bowl, combine the remaining ingredients. Pour over wings.

Bake, uncovered, at 350° for 1 hour or until chicken juices run clear. Spoon sauce from pans over wings if desired. **YIELD:** about 6 dozen.

Shrimp Wrapped in Bacon

(Pictured above)

PREP: 25 min. **BAKE:** 20 min.

If you're looking for something a little different to serve guests, you can't go wrong with these elegant shrimp bites, pleasantly seasoned with bacon, basil, goat cheese and barbecue sauce.
—Eileen Stefanski, Wales, Wisconsin

- 10 bacon strips
- 20 large fresh basil leaves
- 20 uncooked medium shrimp, peeled and deveined
- 1/4 cup barbecue sauce
- 1/2 cup finely crumbled goat cheese

Cut each bacon strip in half widthwise; set aside. Wrap a basil leaf around each shrimp. Wrap a piece of bacon around each; secure with wooden toothpicks.

Place in a foil-lined 15-in. x 10-in. x 1-in. baking pan. Bake at 375° for 14-16 minutes or until bacon is crisp.

Brush with barbecue sauce; sprinkle with cheese. Bake 2-4 minutes longer or until heated through. **YIELD:** 20 appetizers.

Rainbow Pepper Appetizers

PREP/TOTAL TIME: 20 min.

Company will quickly polish off this colorful pepper medley that showcases crisp-tender sweet peppers topped with chopped olives and Monterey Jack cheese.
—Marion Karlin, Waterloo, Iowa

- 1/2 *each* medium green, sweet red, yellow and orange peppers
- 1 cup (4 ounces) shredded Monterey Jack cheese
- 2 tablespoons chopped ripe olives
- 1/4 teaspoon crushed red pepper flakes, optional

Cut each pepper half into nine pieces. Place the skin side down in an ungreased ovenproof skillet; sprinkle with cheese, olives and pepper flakes if desired.

Broil peppers 3-4 in. from the heat for 5-7 minutes or until the peppers are crisp-tender and the cheese is melted. **YIELD:** 3 dozen.

Sunrise Slushies

(Pictured below)

PREP/TOTAL TIME: 10 min.

My teenage daughters are perpetual dieters, so I worry about their nutrition. I came up with this yummy breakfast beverage full of fruity goodness, and they love it.
—Linda Evancoe-Coble, Leola, Pennsylvania

- 2 cups orange juice
- 1 cup reduced-calorie reduced-sugar cranberry juice
- 1 medium tart apple, coarsely chopped
- 1/2 cup cubed peeled mango
- 2 kiwifruit, peeled, sliced and quartered
- 2 cups halved fresh strawberries
- 8 to 10 ice cubes

In a blender, place half of each ingredient; cover and process until smooth. Pour into chilled glasses. Repeat with the remaining ingredients. Serve immediately. **YIELD:** 8 servings.

Chicken Potstickers

(Pictured below)

PREP: 50 min. **BAKE:** 10 min.

Chicken and mushrooms make up the filling in these potstickers, a traditional Chinese dumpling. Greasing the steamer rack makes it easier to remove them once they're steamed.
—Jacquelynne Stine, Las Vegas, Nevada

- 1 pound boneless skinless chicken thighs, cut into chunks
- 1-1/2 cups sliced fresh mushrooms
- 1 small onion, cut into wedges
- 2 tablespoons hoisin sauce
- 2 tablespoons prepared mustard
- 2 tablespoons sriracha Asian hot chili sauce *or* 1 tablespoon hot pepper sauce
- 1 package (14 ounces) potsticker dumpling wrappers
- 1 egg, lightly beaten

SAUCE:
- 1 cup soy sauce
- 1 green onion, chopped
- 1 teaspoon ground ginger

In a food processor, combine uncooked chicken, mushrooms, onion, hoisin sauce, mustard and chili sauce; cover and process until blended.

Place 1 tablespoon of chicken mixture in the center of each wrapper. (Until ready to use, keep wrappers covered with a damp towel to prevent them from drying out.) Moisten edges with egg. Bring opposite sides together to form a semicircle; pinch to seal.

Place potstickers in a single layer on a large greased steamer basket rack; place in a Dutch oven over 1 in. of water. Bring to a boil; cover and steam for 8-10 minutes or until filling juices run clear.

Meanwhile, in a small bowl, combine sauce ingredients. Serve with potstickers. Refrigerate leftovers. **YIELD:** 4 dozen.

Roasted Vegetable Turkey Pinwheels

(Pictured above)

PREP: 20 min. **BAKE:** 25 min.

These are always a hit and great for any occasion because they can be made ahead of time! I make a double batch of the veggie cream cheese to use on crackers and bagels.
—Kristin Andrews, Gresham, Oregon

- 2 medium yellow summer squash, cut into 1/2-inch slices
- 1 large sweet yellow pepper, cut into 1-inch pieces
- 1 large sweet red pepper, cut into 1-inch pieces
- 2 large carrots, cut into 1/2-inch slices
- 3 garlic cloves, peeled
- 2 tablespoons olive oil
- 2 packages (8 ounces *each*) cream cheese, cubed
- 1/2 teaspoon salt
- 1/2 teaspoon pepper
- 8 flavored tortillas of your choice (10 inches), room temperature
- 1 pound thinly sliced deli turkey
- 4 cups torn Bibb *or* Boston lettuce

Place the squash, peppers, carrots and garlic in a 15-in. x 10-in. x 1-in. baking pan coated with cooking spray. Drizzle with oil; toss to coat. Bake, uncovered, at 450° for 25-30 minutes or until lightly browned and tender, stirring once. Cool slightly.

Place the vegetables, cream cheese, salt and pepper in a food processor; cover and process until blended. Transfer to a bowl; cover and refrigerate for 2-3 hours or until thickened.

Spread 1/2 cup cream cheese mixture over each tortilla; layer with turkey and lettuce. Roll up tightly; wrap each in plastic wrap. Refrigerate for at least 1 hour. Unwrap and cut each into eight slices.
YIELD: 64 appetizers.

Cool and crisp or warm and wonderful, these salads make a memorable meal. The homemade dressings are so good, you'll never use store-bought again.

salads & dressings

Asparagus Berry Salad............................28

Raspberry Vinaigrette 28

Green Goddess Salad Dressing 28

Sunny Carrot Salad 29

Mustard-Sour Cream Salad Dressing............29

Pecan-Pear Green Salad............................29

Crispy Chicken Strip Salad............................30

Southwestern Rice Salad 30

Tomato Corn Salad 31

Apple-Brie Spinach Salad 31

Grilled Apple Tossed Salad............................32

Balsamic Vinegar Dressing............................32

Orange Gelatin Pretzel Salad............................33

Chunky Blue Cheese Dressing............................33

Colorful Turkey Salad Cups............................34

Grilled Steak Caesar Salad............................34

Hawaiian Ham Salad............................34

Greek Seafood Salad............................35

Summer Chicken Salad............................35

Special Sesame Chicken Salad............................36

Fruit and Nut Tossed Salad 37

Dilly Potato Salad 37

Brown Rice Lentil Salad............................38

Mostaccioli Veggie Salad............................38

Crowd-Pleasing Taco Salad............................39

Fruit Salad Dressing 39

Napa Cabbage Slaw 40

Warm Asparagus Spinach Salad............................40

Poppy Seed Fruit Salad............................41

Waldorf Tuna Salad............................41

Grilled Three-Potato Salad............................41

Asparagus-Fennel Pasta Salad............................42

Fancy Bean Salad 42

Garlic Anchovy Salad Dressing............................42

Applesauce-Raspberry Gelatin Mold............43

Strawberry Spinach Salad............................43

PICTURED CLOCKWISE FROM UPPER LEFT: Balsamic Vinegar Dressing (page 32), Tomato Corn Salad (page 31), Fancy Bean Salad (page 42) and Orange Gelatin Pretzel Salad (page 33).

In a bowl, toss asparagus with 1 tablespoon oil. Spread in a single layer in a greased 15-in. x 10-in. x 1-in. baking pan. Sprinkle with salt and pepper. Bake at 400° for 15-20 minutes or until tender.

In a large salad bowl, toss greens, strawberries, onion, walnuts and asparagus. In a small bowl, whisk the vinegar, sugar and remaining oil. Drizzle over salad and toss to coat. **YIELD:** 6-8 servings.

Raspberry Vinaigrette
PREP/TOTAL TIME: 20 min.

When making this sweet vinaigrette, plan on 2 tablespoons of dressing for each 1-cup serving of salad greens.

—Betty Miller, Angola, Indiana

  2 jars (12 ounces *each*) seedless raspberry preserves
1-1/4 cups sugar, *divided*
  1/2 cup water
  1/3 cup chopped sweet onion
  1/4 cup balsamic vinegar
    1 tablespoon dried tarragon
    1 tablespoon curry powder
    1 teaspoon white pepper
    1 teaspoon pepper
    1 cup olive oil
Torn mixed salad greens

In a large saucepan, bring the preserves and 3/4 cup sugar to a boil. Remove from heat; cool slightly. Transfer to a blender. Add water, onion, vinegar, tarragon, curry powder, white pepper, pepper and remaining sugar; cover and process until smooth. While processing, gradually add oil in a steady stream. Serve with salad greens. **YIELD:** about 4 cups.

Asparagus Berry Salad
(*Pictured above*)
PREP/TOTAL TIME: 30 min.

When strawberries and asparagus are at their peak, this salad is sensational! I like to serve it for brunch or dinner. Sometimes I add grilled chicken or salmon to create a refreshing and satisfying main-dish salad.

—Trisha Kruse, Eagle, Idaho

    1 pound fresh asparagus, trimmed and cut
      into 1-inch pieces
    3 tablespoons olive oil, *divided*
1/4 teaspoon salt
1/4 teaspoon coarsely ground pepper
    8 cups spring mix salad greens
    3 cups sliced fresh strawberries
1/2 small red onion, thinly sliced
1/2 cup chopped walnuts, toasted
    2 tablespoons balsamic vinegar
    2 teaspoons sugar

Green Goddess Salad Dressing
PREP/TOTAL TIME: 10 min.

It's no trick to fix this time-honored dressing at home. Made with plenty of fresh ingredients, it's a real treat compared to store-bought dressing.

—Page Alexander, Baldwin City, Kansas

    1 cup mayonnaise
1/2 cup sour cream
1/4 cup chopped green pepper
1/4 cup packed fresh parsley sprigs
    3 anchovy fillets
    2 tablespoons lemon juice
    2 green onion tops, coarsely chopped
    1 garlic clove, peeled
1/4 teaspoon pepper
1/8 teaspoon Worcestershire sauce

Place all ingredients in a blender; cover and process until smooth. Transfer to a bowl or jar; cover and store in the refrigerator. **YIELD:** 2 cups.

Place the first eight ingredients in a blender; cover and process until smooth. While processing, gradually add oil in a steady stream. Transfer to a bowl or pitcher. Cover and refrigerate until serving. **YIELD:** 2-1/2 cups.

Pecan-Pear Green Salad

(Pictured below)

PREP/TOTAL TIME: 15 min.

This lovely salad adds a special touch to any meal. The juicy pear slices, toasted pecans and mixed greens are coated in a tangy vinaigrette dressing that make for a pleasant sweet and crunchy combination.

—Katie Nicklas, Ridgway, Pennsylvania

- 1 **large ripe red pear, sliced**
- 2 **tablespoons butter,** *divided*
- 1/2 **cup coarsely chopped pecans**
- 1/4 **teaspoon salt,** *divided*
- 2 **cups mixed salad greens**
- 2 **tablespoons balsamic vinegar**
- 2 **tablespoons olive oil**

Pepper to taste

In a large skillet, saute the pear in 1 tablespoon butter until lightly browned, about 7 minutes. In another skillet, saute the pecans in remaining butter until lightly browned, about 5 minutes; sprinkle with 1/8 teaspoon salt.

Divide salad greens between two salad plates; arrange pears over greens. Sprinkle with pecans. In a jar with a tight-fitting lid, combine the vinegar, oil, pepper and remaining salt; shake well. Drizzle over salad. **YIELD:** 2 servings.

Sunny Carrot Salad

(Pictured above)

PREP/TOTAL TIME: 10 min.

Almonds and sunflower kernels give a pleasing crunch to this speedy yet delicious variation on traditional carrot-raisin salad. If you prefer a nuttier flavor, use 1/2 cup of sunflower kernels instead of 1/3 cup.

—Barb Hunter, Ponder, Texas

- 3 **cups shredded carrots**
- 2 **cups unsweetened crushed pineapple, drained**
- 1/2 **cup golden raisins**
- 1/3 **cup mayonnaise**
- 1/2 **cup sliced almonds**
- 1/3 **cup unsalted sunflower kernels**

In a large serving bowl, combine carrots, pineapple and raisins. Stir in mayonnaise. Cover and refrigerate until serving. Just before serving, add almonds and sunflower kernels; toss to coat. **YIELD:** 5 servings.

Mustard-Sour Cream Salad Dressing

PREP/TOTAL TIME: 10 min.

This smooth blend with a mild mustard flavor drapes nicely over any salad or bowl of mixed greens…and it makes a big batch.

—Marian Platt, Sequim, Washington

- 1/2 **cup red wine vinegar**
- 1/2 **cup sour cream**
- 1/2 **cup Dijon mustard**
- 2 **teaspoons sugar**
- 2 **garlic cloves, peeled**
- 1/4 **teaspoon salt**
- 1/4 **teaspoon white pepper**
- 1/4 **teaspoon Worcestershire sauce**
- 1-1/2 **cups vegetable oil**

Crispy Chicken Strip Salad

(*Pictured below*)

PREP: 40 min. **COOK:** 10 min.

These chicken strips taste great. Combined with candied pecans, fresh raspberries and greens—and served with store-bought vinaigrette—the salad is easy and delicious.

—*Lillian Julow, Gainesville, Florida*

1	tablespoon butter
1/2	cup pecan halves
2	tablespoons sugar
3/4	cup all-purpose flour
2	tablespoons minced fresh tarragon *or* 2 teaspoons dried tarragon
1	tablespoon grated lemon peel
2	eggs
1	pound boneless skinless chicken breasts, cut into 1-inch strips
2	tablespoons vegetable oil
4	cups spring mix salad greens
1	cup torn Bibb *or* Boston lettuce
1/2	cup raspberry vinaigrette
2	cups fresh *or* frozen unsweetened raspberries

In a small skillet, melt butter. Add pecans and cook over medium heat until nuts are toasted, about 4 minutes. Sprinkle with sugar. Cook and stir for 2-4 minutes or until sugar is melted. Transfer to a greased foil-lined baking sheet; cool completely.

In a large resealable bag, combine the flour, tarragon and lemon peel. In a shallow bowl, beat the eggs. Add the chicken strips to flour mixture in batches; seal and shake to coat. Dip in eggs, then return to bag and coat again.

In a large skillet over medium heat, cook chicken in oil for 6-8 minutes or until no longer pink, turning once.

Break pecans apart. Toss the greens and lettuce with vinaigrette; arrange on individual plates. Top with the raspberries, chicken strips and sugared pecans. **YIELD:** 4 servings.

Southwestern Rice Salad

(*Pictured above*)

PREP/TOTAL TIME: 30 min.

The recipe for this hearty rice salad has been in my family for years. My mother used to bring it to many different functions, and I'm carrying on her tradition.

—*Ruth Bianchi, Apple Valley, Minnesota*

1-1/3	cups water
2/3	cup uncooked long grain rice
3/4	cup chopped green pepper
1/2	cup chopped red onion
1	medium carrot, chopped
3	garlic cloves, minced
1	tablespoon canola oil
1	package (16 ounces) frozen corn, thawed
1	can (15 ounces) black beans, rinsed and drained
2	medium plum tomatoes, chopped
1	cup salted peanuts
1/3	cup minced fresh cilantro
2/3	cup olive oil
1/3	cup lemon juice
1/2	to 1-1/2 teaspoons cayenne pepper
1/2	teaspoon ground cumin

In a large saucepan, bring water and rice to a boil. Reduce heat; cover and simmer for 15 minutes. Remove from the heat. Let stand for 5 minutes or until rice is tender. Rinse rice with cold water and drain. Place in a large bowl.

In a small skillet, saute the green pepper, onion, carrot and garlic in oil until crisp-tender. Add to rice. Stir in the corn, beans, tomatoes, peanuts and cilantro.

In a small bowl, combine the oil, lemon juice, cayenne and cumin. Pour over rice mixture and stir to coat. Cover and refrigerate until serving. **YIELD:** 12 servings.

Tomato Corn Salad

(Pictured below and on page 26)

PREP/TOTAL TIME: 30 min.

Warm and colorful, this tantalizing side dish bursts with refreshing flavor from corn and tomatoes. Fresh herbs and Dijon mustard add lots of pizzazz.

—*Carrie Skiper, Roselle Park, New Jersey*

- 3 large tomatoes, chopped
- 1 small red onion, halved and thinly sliced
- 1/3 cup chopped green onions
- 1/4 cup balsamic vinegar
- 3 tablespoons minced fresh basil
- 1 tablespoon minced fresh cilantro
- 1 teaspoon salt
- 1/2 teaspoon pepper
- 4 cups fresh corn (about 9 ears of corn)
- 3 garlic cloves, peeled and thinly sliced
- 2 tablespoons olive oil
- 1 tablespoon Dijon mustard

In a large bowl, combine the first eight ingredients. In a large skillet, saute corn and garlic in oil until tender; stir in mustard. Add to the vegetable mixture; toss to coat. Serve with a slotted spoon. **YIELD:** 7 servings.

Apple-Brie Spinach Salad

(Pictured above)

PREP/TOTAL TIME: 30 min.

In the heat of summer, I don't like to prepare or eat large meals, so I often make salads. I'm always on the lookout for new and interesting recipes. This one is a winner that I like to make for friends and family.

—*Rhonda Crowe, Victoria, British Columbia*

- 4 large apples, cut into 1/2-inch wedges
- 4 tablespoons maple syrup, *divided*
- 8 cups fresh baby spinach
- 1 round (8 ounces) Brie *or* Camembert cheese, cubed
- 1/2 cup pecan halves, toasted

DRESSING:
- 1/4 cup apple cider *or* juice
- 1/4 cup canola oil
- 3 tablespoons cider vinegar
- 1 teaspoon Dijon mustard
- 1 garlic clove, minced

Place apples on an ungreased baking sheet; brush with 2 tablespoons syrup. Broil 3-4 in. from the heat for 3 minutes. Turn; brush with remaining syrup. Broil 3-5 minutes longer or until crisp-tender.

In a large salad bowl, combine the spinach, cheese, pecans and apples. In a small saucepan, combine the dressing ingredients; bring to a boil. Pour over salad; toss to coat. **YIELD:** 10 servings.

Drain apples, reserving marinade for basting. Thread onto six metal or soaked wooden skewers. Grill apples, covered, over medium heat for 6-8 minutes or until golden brown, basting frequently. Turn and grill 6-8 minutes longer or until golden and tender.

In a large salad bowl, combine the greens, walnuts and blue cheese. Add apples. Drizzle with reserved dressing and toss to coat. **YIELD:** 4 servings.

Balsamic Vinegar Dressing

(Pictured below and on page 26)

PREP/TOTAL TIME: 25 min.

A variety of savory seasonings gives this dressing a tangy kick. It's the perfect complement to a bed of fresh greens.
—*Edgar Wright, Silver Spring, Maryland*

  1 cup balsamic vinegar
  1 cup honey
  2 tablespoons minced fresh basil
  3 teaspoons onion powder
  2 garlic cloves, peeled
  1 teaspoon white pepper
  1 teaspoon dried oregano
  1 teaspoon dried thyme
  1 teaspoon dill weed
  1 teaspoon prepared mustard
  3 cups canola oil

In a blender, combine half of the first 10 ingredients; cover and process until blended. While processing, gradually add half of the oil in a steady stream. Transfer to a 1-1/2-qt. container.

Repeat with remaining ingredients. Cover and refrigerate until serving. **YIELD:** 36 servings (2 tablespoons per serving).

Grilled Apple Tossed Salad

(Pictured above)

PREP: 15 min. + marinating   **GRILL:** 15 min.

The grilled apples in this salad go so well with the blue cheese, walnuts and balsamic dressing. I like to serve it on pink Depression glass dessert plates from my great-grandmother.
—*Paul Soska, Toledo, Ohio*

    6 tablespoons olive oil
1/4 cup orange juice
1/4 cup white balsamic vinegar
1/4 cup minced fresh cilantro
    2 tablespoons honey
1/2 teaspoon salt
1/2 teaspoon chili sauce
    1 garlic clove, minced
    2 large apples, cut into wedges
    1 package (5 ounces) spring mix salad greens
    1 cup walnut halves
1/2 cup crumbled blue cheese

For dressing, in a bowl, combine the first eight ingredients. Pour 1/4 cup into a large resealable plastic bag; add apples. Seal bag and turn to coat; refrigerate for at least 10 minutes. Cover and refrigerate remaining dressing until serving.

Orange Gelatin Pretzel Salad

(Pictured above and on page 26)

PREP: 30 min. + chilling

I adapted this recipe from using strawberries and strawberry gelatin. The pretzels give the refreshing layered salad a nice crunch. It's a favorite in our family.

—Peggy Boyd, Northport, Alabama

 2 **cups crushed pretzels**
 3 **teaspoons plus 3/4 cup sugar,** *divided*
3/4 **cup butter, melted**
 2 **packages (3 ounces** *each***) orange gelatin**
 2 **cups boiling water**
 2 **cans (8 ounces** *each***) crushed pineapple, drained**
 1 **can (11 ounces) mandarin oranges, drained**
 1 **package (8 ounces) cream cheese, softened**
 2 **cups whipped topping**
Additional whipped topping, optional

In a small bowl, combine the pretzels and 3 teaspoons sugar; stir in the butter. Press into an ungreased 13-in. x 9-in. baking dish. Bake at 350° for 10 minutes. Cool on a wire rack.

In a large bowl, dissolve the gelatin in boiling water. Add the pineapple and oranges. Chill until partially set, about 30 minutes.

In a small bowl, beat the cream cheese and remaining sugar until smooth. Fold in whipped topping. Spread over crust. Gently spoon gelatin mixture over the cream cheese layer. Cover and refrigerate for 2-4 hours or until firm.

Cut into squares. Garnish with additional whipped topping if desired. **YIELD:** 15 servings.

Chunky Blue Cheese Dressing

PREP/TOTAL TIME: 10 min.

This flavorful, full-bodied dressing is better than any bottled dressing I've ever tasted…and it's easy to prepare, too! I found the recipe in a church cookbook.

—Leona Luecking, West Burlington, Iowa

1/4 **cup milk**
 3 **cups mayonnaise**
 1 **cup (8 ounces) sour cream**
 4 **ounces crumbled blue cheese**
 2 **teaspoons garlic salt**

Place the milk, mayonnaise, sour cream, blue cheese and garlic salt in a blender. Cover and process until smooth. Refrigerate until serving. **YIELD:** about 4 cups.

Colorful Turkey Salad Cups

(Pictured below)

PREP/TOTAL TIME: 30 min.

Here's a recipe that's perfect for any season. It uses cooked turkey and cranberry sauce in a light and interesting way. Guests always give this recipe two thumbs up no matter when I serve it!

—Janice Elder, Charlotte, North Carolina

- 1/2 cup jellied cranberry sauce
- 2 tablespoons orange marmalade
- 2 tablespoons hoisin sauce
- 1/2 teaspoon crushed red pepper flakes
- 3 cups cubed cooked turkey
- 1 small sweet red pepper, chopped
- 1 small sweet onion, chopped
- 1/2 cup chopped seeded peeled cucumber
- 1 medium mango, peeled and chopped
- 1 medium avocado, peeled and chopped
- 1/4 cup chopped pecans, toasted
- 2 tablespoons finely chopped candied *or* crystallized ginger
- 12 Bibb lettuce leaves
- 1/2 cup fresh mint leaves, thinly sliced
- 1/2 cup fresh basil leaves, thinly sliced

In a small saucepan, combine cranberry sauce, orange marmalade, hoisin sauce and pepper flakes. Cook over medium heat for 2-3 minutes or until blended, stirring occasionally. Cool.

In a large bowl, combine turkey, red pepper, onion, cucumber, mango, avocado, pecans, ginger and cranberry mixture. Spoon onto lettuce leaves; sprinkle with herbs. Refrigerate until serving. **YIELD:** 6 servings.

Grilled Steak Caesar Salad

(Pictured above)

PREP/TOTAL TIME: 30 min.

This salad, with a tangy anchovy dressing, is my version of a delicious dish offered at one of our finer restaurants. My quilting group really enjoys it, served with hard rolls and a fruit dessert.

—Eleanor Froehlich, Rochester Hills, Michigan

- 4 hard-cooked egg yolks
- 4 anchovy fillets *or* 2 tablespoons anchovy paste
- 4 garlic cloves, minced
- 3 tablespoons Dijon mustard
- 2 tablespoons lemon juice
- 2 tablespoons red wine vinegar
- 1 tablespoon Worcestershire sauce
- 2 teaspoons coarsely ground pepper
- 1 teaspoon sugar
- 1 cup olive oil
- 1 boneless beef sirloin steak (about 1-1/4 pounds)
- 1 large bunch romaine, torn
- 2/3 cup shredded Parmesan cheese, *divided*
- 2 medium tomatoes, cut into wedges
- 2 cups Caesar salad croutons

In a blender or food processor, combine the first nine ingredients; cover and process until blended. While processing, gradually add oil in a steady stream. Cover and refrigerate.

Grill steak, covered, over medium heat for 5-7 minutes on each side or until meat reaches desired doneness (for medium-rare, a meat thermometer should read 145°; medium, 160°; well-done, 170°).

In a large bowl, toss the romaine, 1/3 cup Parmesan cheese and salad dressing. Divide among salad plates. Slice the steak and arrange it and the tomatoes on salads. Top with croutons and remaining cheese. **YIELD:** 6 servings.

Hawaiian Ham Salad

PREP: 15 min. + chilling

There's plenty of flavor and crunch in this crispy salad. I like to use both red and green apples, and sometimes I substitute celery for the water chestnuts.

—Vickie Lowrey, Fallon, Nevada

1 can (8 ounces) unsweetened pineapple chunks
3 cups cooked brown rice
2 cups cubed fully cooked ham
1 can (8 ounces) sliced water chestnuts, drained and halved
1/4 cup finely chopped red onion
1/2 cup plain yogurt
1/2 teaspoon salt
1 medium apple, chopped
Lettuce leaves
1/3 cup chopped macadamia nuts, toasted
1/4 cup flaked coconut, toasted

Drain the pineapple, reserving 1 tablespoon juice. In a large bowl, combine the pineapple, rice, ham, water chestnuts and onion. Cover and refrigerate for at least 2 hours.

In a small bowl, combine the yogurt, salt and reserved pineapple juice. Pour over ham mixture and toss to coat. Stir in apple.

Serve on lettuce-lined plates; sprinkle with macadamia nuts and coconut. **YIELD:** 4 servings.

Greek Seafood Salad

PREP: 25 min. + chilling

My husband and I and our six children—and now their spouses—are real seafood lovers, and this pretty combination of ingredients never fails to get "wows." It's great for summer picnics accompanied by a fresh baguette.

—Maryalice Wood, Langley, British Columbia

2 medium cucumbers, peeled, seeded and coarsely chopped
1 large tomato, coarsely chopped
1 large onion, coarsely chopped
1 large green pepper, coarsely chopped
1 large sweet yellow pepper, coarsely chopped
8 ounces frozen cooked small shrimp, thawed
1 can (6 ounces) pitted ripe olives, drained and sliced
1/2 cup cubed part-skim mozzarella cheese
2 cans (6 ounces *each*) chunk tuna, drained
DRESSING:
1/4 cup white vinegar
1/4 cup crumbled feta cheese
2 tablespoons minced fresh parsley
2 tablespoons minced fresh oregano
1 garlic clove, minced
1/4 teaspoon salt
1/4 teaspoon pepper
1/2 cup olive oil

In a large bowl, combine the first eight ingredients. Gently stir in the tuna. In a small bowl, combine the vinegar, feta cheese, parsley, oregano, garlic, salt and pepper. Whisk in the oil. Pour over salad; do not toss. Cover and refrigerate for at least 1 hour. Toss just before serving. **YIELD:** 10 servings.

Summer Chicken Salad

(Pictured below)

PREP: 10 min. **COOK:** 25 min. + chilling

I found this recipe many years ago in a church cookbook. It's special enough for a fancy dinner but easy enough to fix for a light lunch. There's a nice kick to the tangy citrus dressing, which even my picky son enjoys.

—Nancy Whitford, Edwards, New York

4 boneless skinless chicken breast halves (4 ounces *each*)
1 can (14-1/2 ounces) chicken broth
6 cups torn mixed salad greens
2 cups halved fresh strawberries
CITRUS DRESSING:
1/2 cup fresh strawberries, hulled
1/3 cup orange juice
2 tablespoons canola oil
1 tablespoon lemon juice
2 teaspoons grated lemon peel
1 teaspoon sugar
1/2 teaspoon chili powder
1/4 teaspoon salt
1/4 teaspoon pepper
1/4 cup chopped walnuts, toasted

Place chicken in a large skillet; add broth. Bring to a boil. Reduce heat; cover and simmer for 20-25 minutes or until juices run clear. Drain; cover and refrigerate. In a large bowl, combine the greens and sliced strawberries; refrigerate.

For the dressing, in a blender, combine the hulled strawberries, orange juice, oil, lemon juice and lemon peel, sugar, chili powder, salt and pepper. Cover and process until smooth. Pour into a small saucepan. Bring to a boil. Reduce heat; simmer for 5-6 minutes until slightly thickened. Cool slightly.

Drizzle half of the dressing over greens and berries; toss to coat. Divide among four plates. Cut chicken into 1/8-in. slices; arrange over salads. Drizzle remaining dressing over chicken; sprinkle with nuts. **YIELD:** 4 servings.

Special Sesame Chicken Salad

(Pictured above)

PREP: 30 min. + chilling

With its delicious mix of crunchy peanuts, tangy dried cranberries and mandarin oranges, this colorful pasta salad is a definite crowd-pleaser. Water chestnuts and a teriyaki dressing give this main dish its Asian flare.

—Carolee Ewell, Santaquin, Utah

    1 **package (16 ounces) bow tie pasta**
    1 **cup vegetable oil**
  2/3 **cup white wine vinegar**
  2/3 **cup teriyaki sauce**
  1/3 **cup sugar**
  1/2 **teaspoon pepper**
    3 **cans (11 ounces *each*) mandarin oranges, drained**
    2 **cans (8 ounces *each*) sliced water chestnuts, drained**
    2 **cups cubed cooked chicken**
1-1/3 **cups honey roasted peanuts**
    1 **package (9 ounces) fresh spinach, torn**
    1 **package (6 ounces) dried cranberries**

    6 **green onions, chopped**
  1/2 **cup minced fresh parsley**
  1/4 **cup sesame seeds, toasted**

Cook pasta according to package directions; drain and place in a very large bowl.

In a small bowl, combine the oil, vinegar, teriyaki sauce, sugar and pepper. Pour over pasta and toss to coat. Cover and refrigerate for 2 hours.

Immediately before serving, add remaining ingredients; gently toss to coat. **YIELD:** 22 servings (1 cup per serving).

slicing green onions

It's easier and faster to cut green onions with a kitchen scissors than with a knife. If the recipe calls for quite a few, grab a bunch at one time and snip away. No need to wash a cutting board! If you cut more green onions than you need, store the leftovers in a clean glass jar with a lid and refrigerate. They'll last a couple of weeks this way.

Fruit and Nut Tossed Salad

(Pictured below)

PREP: 20 min. **COOK:** 30 min. + cooling

This refreshing salad has plenty of appeal thanks to juicy straw-berries, tangy mandarin oranges and crunchy pecans. It's an at-tractive addition to a festive menu.

—Denise Bitner, Reedsville, Pennsylvania

- 1/4 cup olive oil
- 2 tablespoons plus 2 teaspoons sugar
- 2 tablespoons white vinegar
- 1 tablespoon minced fresh parsley
- 1/4 teaspoon salt
- Dash hot pepper sauce

PECANS:
- 1/3 cup sugar
- 1 cup pecan halves
- 2 tablespoons butter

SALAD:
- 4 cups torn fresh spinach
- 4 cups torn romaine
- 1 can (15 ounces) mandarin oranges, drained
- 2 celery ribs, chopped
- 1 cup sliced fresh strawberries
- 4 green onions, chopped

For dressing, in a small bowl, whisk the oil, sugar, vinegar, parsley, salt and pepper sauce until blended. Cover and refrigerate.

For the pecans, in a large heavy skillet, melt sugar over medium-low heat without stirring until golden brown, about 30 minutes. Add pecans and butter; stir constantly until butter is melted and pecans are coated. Remove from heat. Pour onto a foil-lined baking sheet; cool completely. Break pecans apart if necessary.

For the salad, in a bowl, combine the spinach, romaine, oranges, celery, strawberries and onions. Just before serving, drizzle with dressing; toss to coat. Top with sugared pecans. **YIELD:** 8-10 servings.

Dilly Potato Salad

(Pictured above)

PREP: 40 min. + chilling

Everyone has a favorite potato salad, and this is mine. I hope you will be adventurous and give it a try. I've had lots of com-pliments and requests for the recipe when I make it for summer-time gatherings.

—Angela Leinenbach, Mechanicsville, Virginia

- 4 pounds red potatoes, halved
- 5 hard-cooked eggs
- 1 cup chopped dill pickles
- 1 small onion, chopped
- 1-1/2 cups mayonnaise
- 1 teaspoon celery seed
- 1/2 teaspoon salt
- 1/4 teaspoon pepper
- Paprika

Place the potatoes in a large kettle; cover with water. Bring to a boil. Reduce heat; cover and cook for 20-25 minutes or until tender. Drain and cool.

Cut potatoes into 3/4-in. cubes. Chop four eggs; slice remaining egg for garnish. In a large bowl, combine the potatoes, chopped eggs, pickles and onion.

In a small bowl, combine the mayonnaise, celery seed, salt and pepper. Pour over potato mixture and stir gently to coat. Sprinkle with paprika; garnish with sliced eggs. Cover and refrigerate for at least 2 hours before serving. **YIELD:** 12-14 servings.

Brown Rice Lentil Salad

(Pictured below)

PREP: 10 min. **COOK:** 45 min. + chilling

My family isn't always crazy about trying new recipes. The first time I served this salad, they took tiny helpings just to appease me. But the unanimous verdict was, "It tastes great!"

—DeAnn Howard, Lisbon, Iowa

- 1/2 cup uncooked brown rice
- 1 cup water
- 1 teaspoon chicken bouillon granules
- 1 cup cooked lentils
- 1 medium tomato, seeded and diced
- 1/3 cup thinly sliced green onions
- 1 tablespoon minced fresh parsley
- 2 tablespoons red wine vinegar
- 1 tablespoon olive oil
- 2 garlic cloves, minced
- 2 teaspoons lime juice
- 2 teaspoons Dijon mustard
- 1/2 teaspoon salt
- 1/4 teaspoon pepper

In a small saucepan over medium heat, bring the rice, water and bouillon to a boil. Reduce heat; cover and simmer for 40 minutes or until rice is tender. Cool.

In a large bowl, combine the cooked rice, lentils, tomato, onions and parsley. In a small bowl, combine the remaining ingredients. Pour over the rice mixture; toss to coat. Cover and refrigerate for at least 1 hour. **YIELD:** 7 servings.

Mostaccioli Veggie Salad

(Pictured above)

PREP: 20 min. + chilling

I first sampled this salad at a church potluck several years ago. The mix of pasta, zucchini, summer squash, cucumber, sweet peppers and black olives is coated with a light vinaigrette.

—Julie Sterchi, Harrisburg, Illinois

- 3 cups uncooked mostaccioli
- 1 medium cucumber, thinly sliced
- 1 small yellow summer squash, quartered and sliced
- 1 small zucchini, halved and sliced
- 1/2 cup diced sweet red pepper
- 1/2 cup diced green pepper
- 1/2 cup sliced ripe olives
- 3 to 4 green onions, chopped

DRESSING:
- 1/3 cup sugar
- 1/3 cup white wine vinegar
- 1/3 cup canola oil
- 1-1/2 teaspoons prepared mustard
- 3/4 teaspoon dried minced onion
- 3/4 teaspoon garlic powder
- 1/2 teaspoon salt
- 1/2 teaspoon pepper

Cook the pasta according to package directions. Drain and rinse in cold water. Place in a large bowl; add the cucumber, summer squash, zucchini, peppers, olives and onions.

In a jar with a tight-fitting lid, combine dressing ingredients; shake well. Pour over pasta mixture; toss to coat. Cover and refrigerate for 8 hours or overnight. Toss again before serving. Serve with a slotted spoon. **YIELD:** 10 servings.

Crowd-Pleasing Taco Salad

(Pictured below)

PREP/TOTAL TIME: 30 min.

While this recipe might sound involved, it can be fixed in just 30 minutes. It's a hit at the potluck table—and I don't have to bring leftovers home after the shindig!

—Ann Cahoon, Bradenton, Florida

- 1 pound ground beef
- 1/2 cup ketchup
- 1 teaspoon dried oregano
- 1 teaspoon chili powder
- 1/2 teaspoon salt
- 1/4 teaspoon pepper
- 1 medium head iceberg lettuce, torn
- 2 medium tomatoes, diced
- 1 cup (4 ounces) shredded taco cheese
- 1 can (2-1/4 ounces) sliced ripe olives, drained
- 1/2 cup mayonnaise
- 1/4 cup taco sauce
- 1 package (10-1/2 ounces) corn chips

In a large saucepan, cook beef over medium heat until no longer pink; drain. Stir in ketchup, oregano, chili powder, salt and pepper. Bring to a boil. Reduce heat; cover and simmer for 10 minutes.

In a large bowl, combine the lettuce, tomatoes, cheese, olives and beef mixture. Combine the mayonnaise and taco sauce; pour over salad and toss to coat. Sprinkle with corn chips. Serve immediately. **YIELD:** 14-16 servings.

Fruit Salad Dressing

(Pictured above)

PREP/TOTAL TIME: 15 min.

Served with seasonal fruit, this citrusy dressing makes a refreshing side dish or dessert for your next ladies' luncheon or breakfast buffet. It's a snap to make, too!

—Shirley Haase, Madison, Wisconsin

- 2/3 cup orange juice
- 3 tablespoons lemon juice
- 1 cup sugar
- 1 egg, lightly beaten
Assorted fresh fruit

In a small saucepan, combine juices, sugar and egg. Bring to a boil; cook and stir for 1 minute or until thickened. Strain. Cover and refrigerate until serving. Serve with fresh fruit. **YIELD:** about 1 cup.

a bit about balsamic

Balsamic vinegar is made from sweet white grapes and aged in wooden barrels for at least 10 years. You can substitute balsamic with apple cider vinegar or red wine vinegar. White wine vinegar is much stronger and sharper than balsamic and should be used sparingly.

Warm Asparagus Spinach Salad

(Pictured below)

PREP/TOTAL TIME: 30 min.

Spinach, cashews and pasta are mixed with roasted asparagus in this delightful spring salad. The mixture is topped with a light vinaigrette, seasoned with soy sauce and sprinkled with Parmesan cheese.

—Kathleen Lucas, Trumbull, Connecticut

- 1-1/2 **pounds fresh asparagus, trimmed and cut into 1-inch pieces**
- 2 **tablespoons plus 1/2 cup olive oil,** *divided*
- 1/4 **teaspoon salt**
- 1-1/2 **pounds uncooked penne pasta**
- 3/4 **cup chopped green onions**
- 6 **tablespoons white wine vinegar**
- 2 **tablespoons soy sauce**
- 1 **package (6 ounces) fresh baby spinach**
- 1 **cup coarsely chopped cashews**
- 1/2 **cup shredded Parmesan cheese**

Place the asparagus in a 13-in. x 9-in. baking dish. Drizzle with 2 tablespoons oil; sprinkle with salt. Bake, uncovered, at 400° for 20-25 minutes or until crisp-tender, stirring every 10 minutes. Meanwhile, cook pasta according to package directions; drain.

In a blender, combine onions, vinegar and soy sauce; cover and process until smooth. While processing, gradually add remaining oil in a steady steam.

In a large salad bowl, combine the pasta, spinach and asparagus. Drizzle with the dressing; toss to coat. Sprinkle with the cashews and Parmesan cheese. **YIELD:** 14-16 servings.

Napa Cabbage Slaw

(Pictured above)

PREP/TOTAL TIME: 15 min.

Chow mein noodles and snow peas give a pleasant crunch to this colorful and fresh-tasting salad. It's sure to be popular at parties and potlucks.

—Genise Krause, Sturgeon Bay, Wisconsin

- 4 **cups chopped napa** *or* **Chinese cabbage**
- 1 **can (11 ounces) mandarin oranges, drained**
- 1 **can (8 ounces) sliced water chestnuts, drained**
- 1 **cup fresh snow peas, trimmed and cut into thirds**
- 1/2 **cup chopped sweet red pepper**
- 1 **green onion, chopped**
- 1/4 **cup reduced-fat sesame ginger salad dressing**
- 1/2 **cup chow mein noodles**

In a large bowl, combine first six ingredients. Drizzle with dressing and toss to coat. Just before serving, sprinkle with chow mein noodles. **YIELD:** 8 servings.

In a large bowl, combine the tuna, apple, celery, raisins, dates and walnuts. Combine yogurt and mayonnaise; add to tuna mixture and toss to coat. Serve on lettuce-lined plates; sprinkle with the cheese. **YIELD:** 4 servings.

Poppy Seed Fruit Salad

(Pictured above)

PREP/TOTAL TIME: 15 min.

Toasted almonds add a nutty flavor to this pretty salad that's always a hit when I serve it. It's refreshing and goes with just about anything. The sweet-tart dressing can be used with any combination of fruits.

—Edie DeSpain, Logan, Utah

- 1/4 cup honey
- 1/4 cup limeade concentrate
- 2 teaspoons poppy seeds
- 1 cup halved fresh strawberries
- 1 cup cubed fresh pineapple
- 1 cup fresh blueberries
- 1 cup cubed seedless watermelon
- 1/4 cup slivered almonds, toasted

In a small bowl, combine the honey, limeade concentrate and poppy seeds. In a serving bowl, combine the fruit. Drizzle with dressing; toss gently to coat. Sprinkle with the almonds. Serve with a slotted spoon. **YIELD:** 6 servings.

Waldorf Tuna Salad

PREP/TOTAL TIME: 20 min.

I dress up tuna salad deliciously with apple, raisins, dates and walnuts…then drizzle it all with a tangy yogurt dressing.

—Shirley Glaab, Hattiesburg, Mississippi

- 2 cans (6 ounces *each*) light water-packed tuna, drained and flaked
- 1 large red apple, chopped
- 1/3 cup chopped celery
- 1/3 cup raisins
- 1/3 cup chopped dates
- 1/4 cup chopped walnuts
- 1/2 cup fat-free plain yogurt
- 1/4 cup reduced-fat mayonnaise
- 4 lettuce leaves
- 1/4 cup shredded reduced-fat Monterey Jack cheese

Grilled Three-Potato Salad

(Pictured below)

PREP: 25 min. **GRILL:** 10 min.

Everyone in our extended family loves to cook, so I assembled our favorite recipes in a cookbook to be handed down from generation to generation. This recipe comes from the cookbook. It's a tasty twist on traditional potato salad.

—Suzette Jury, Keene, California

- 3/4 pound Yukon Gold potatoes (about 3 medium)
- 3/4 pound red potatoes (about 3 medium)
- 1 medium sweet potato, peeled
- 1/2 cup thinly sliced green onions
- 1/4 cup canola oil
- 2 to 3 tablespoons white wine vinegar
- 1 tablespoon Dijon mustard
- 1 teaspoon salt
- 1/2 teaspoon celery seed
- 1/4 teaspoon pepper

Place all of the potatoes in a Dutch oven; cover with water. Bring to a boil. Reduce heat; cover and simmer for 15-20 minutes or until tender. Drain and rinse in cold water. Cut into 1-in. chunks.

Place the potatoes in a grill wok or basket. Grill, uncovered, over medium heat for 8-12 minutes or browned, stirring frequently. Transfer to a large salad bowl; add onions.

In a small bowl, whisk the oil, vinegar, mustard, salt, celery seed and pepper. Drizzle over the potato mixture and toss to coat. Serve warm or at room temperature. **YIELD:** 6 servings.

Asparagus-Fennel Pasta Salad

(Pictured below)

PREP: 25 min. **BAKE:** 20 min.

Asparagus delivers delightful spring flavor in this hearty side salad. Served warm, it includes a wonderful mix of fresh-tasting ingredients.

—Linda Lacek, Winter Park, Florida

- 1 pound fresh asparagus, trimmed and cut into 3/4-inch pieces
- 2 medium onions, halved and thinly sliced
- 1 small fennel bulb, sliced
- 2 tablespoons olive oil
- 8 ounces uncooked penne pasta
- 4 medium tomatoes, seeded and diced
- 12 pitted Greek olives, sliced
- 1 cup minced fresh parsley

VINAIGRETTE:
- 1/4 cup olive oil
- 1/4 cup lemon juice
- 2 garlic cloves, minced
- 1/2 teaspoon Dijon mustard
- 1/2 teaspoon salt
- 1/4 teaspoon pepper
- 1 cup (4 ounces) crumbled feta cheese

Place asparagus, onions and fennel in a 15-in. x 10-in. x 1-in. baking pan. Drizzle with oil; toss to coat. Bake at 400° for 20-25 minutes or until lightly browned and crisp-tender, stirring occasionally.

Meanwhile, cook pasta according to package directions. Drain and place in a large serving bowl. Add the tomatoes, olives, parsley and roasted vegetables.

In a small bowl, whisk the oil, lemon juice, garlic, mustard, salt and pepper until blended. Drizzle over salad and toss to coat. Sprinkle with feta cheese. **YIELD:** 14 servings.

Fancy Bean Salad

(Pictured above and on page 26)

PREP/TOTAL TIME: 20 min.

Bursting with beans, corn and cucumber, this salad is a snap thanks to store-bought salad dressing.

—Iola Eagle, Bella Vista, Arkansas

- 1 package (16 ounces) frozen gold and white corn, thawed
- 1 can (16 ounces) kidney beans, rinsed and drained
- 1 can (15 ounces) garbanzo beans *or* chickpeas, rinsed and drained
- 1 can (15 ounces) black beans, rinsed and drained
- 1 medium cucumber, finely chopped
- 1 cup finely chopped sweet onion
- 1 medium sweet red pepper, finely chopped
- 1 cup fat-free honey Dijon salad dressing

In a large bowl, combine the first seven ingredients. Pour salad dressing over mixture and toss to coat. Cover and refrigerate until serving. **YIELD:** 12 servings.

Garlic Anchovy Salad Dressing

PREP/TOTAL TIME: 10 min.

Here's one of my favorite dressings. It's thick, creamy and terrific with greens and vegetables.

—Lois Taylor Caron, Ottawa, Ontario

- 2 tablespoons lemon juice
- 2 tablespoons sour cream
- 2 tablespoons mayonnaise
- 2 to 3 anchovy fillets
- 1/3 cup grated Parmesan cheese

     2 garlic cloves, peeled
 1/4 teaspoon pepper
 1/8 teaspoon hot pepper sauce
 1/8 teaspoon Worcestershire sauce
 1/3 cup canola oil

Place the first nine ingredients in a blender; cover and process until smooth. While processing, gradually add oil in a steady stream. Transfer to a small bowl or jar; cover and store in the refrigerator. **YIELD:** 2/3 cup.

Applesauce-Raspberry Gelatin Mold

(Pictured below)

PREP: 10 min. **BAKE:** 5 min.

The children in our families especially enjoy this tangy, refreshing salad, and its pretty, bright red color makes it a festive addition to a special-occasion meal.

—Kathy Spang, Manheim, Pennsylvania

     3 cups unsweetened applesauce
 1/4 cup orange juice
     2 packages (3 ounces _each_) raspberry gelatin
 1-1/2 cups lemon-lime soda

In a large saucepan, bring applesauce and orange juice to a boil. Remove from the heat; stir in gelatin until dissolved. Slowly add soda.
   Pour into a 6-cup mold coated with cooking spray. Refrigerate until firm. Unmold onto a serving platter. **YIELD:** 10 servings.

Strawberry Spinach Salad

(Pictured above and on cover)

PREP/TOTAL TIME: 1 hour

Berries add a pop of color to this favorite salad that's a regular part of my dinner lineup. My challenge is to keep the family from eating the sugared almonds before I add them!

—Peggy Gwillim, Strasbourg, Saskatchewan

 1/4 cup slivered almonds
     2 tablespoons sugar
     1 package (10 ounces) fresh spinach, torn
     1 cup fresh strawberries, sliced
DRESSING:
     2 tablespoons canola oil
     1 tablespoon raspberry vinegar
     1 green onion, finely chopped
 1-1/2 teaspoons sugar
 1-1/2 teaspoons gluten-free Worcestershire sauce
     1 teaspoon poppy seeds
 1/4 teaspoon salt
Dash paprika

In a large skillet, cook and stir almonds and sugar over low heat until sugar is dissolved and almonds are coated. Spread on foil to cool; break apart.
   In a large salad bowl, combine the spinach, strawberries and almonds. In a jar with a tight-fitting lid, combine the dressing ingredients; shake well. Drizzle over salad; toss gently to coat. Serve immediately. **YIELD:** 10 servings.

Satisfying soups and hearty sandwiches await you! They're sure to elicit plenty of smiles and compliments.

soups & sandwiches

Turkey Muffuletta......................................46

Southwestern Turkey Soup......................46

Spanish Gazpacho....................................46

Gingered Butternut Squash Soup............47

Blue Cheese Clubs...................................47

Colony Mountain Chili.............................48

Swiss Tuna Melts......................................48

Chunky Taco Soup....................................48

Apple and Prosciutto Sandwiches..........49

Lemony Chicken Soup.............................49

Colorful Chicken and Squash Soup........50

Garlic Butternut Bisque...........................50

Minestrone with Italian Sausage.............51

Black Bean and Pumpkin Chili................51

Italian Wedding Soup..............................52

Pizza Meatball Subs.................................52

Hearty Beef Vegetable Soup...................53

Roasted Yellow Pepper Soup..................53

Cheeseburger Paradise Soup..................54

Asparagus Leek Chowder........................54

Cheesy Corn Chowder.............................54

Cuban Pork Sandwiches..........................55

Land of Enchantment Posole...................55

Chicken Soup with Potato Dumplings.....56

Black Bean Burgers..................................56

Golden Seafood Chowder.......................57

Buffalo Chicken Wraps.............................57

Danish Turkey Dumpling Soup................58

Home Run Slugger Sub............................58

Firecracker Burgers..................................59

White Bean Chicken Chili........................59

Chicken Asparagus Soup.........................60

Zesty Vegetarian Wraps..........................60

Shrimp Salad Croissants..........................60

Mushroom Tomato Bisque.......................61

Chicken Broccoli Calzones.......................61

PICTURED CLOCKWISE FROM UPPER LEFT: Cheeseburger Paradise Soup (page 54), Pizza Meatball Subs (page 52), White Bean Chicken Chili (page 59) and Buffalo Chicken Wraps (page 57).

Turkey Muffuletta

(Pictured above)

PREP: 30 min. + chilling

You have to resist the temptation to eat this impressive, multi-layered sandwich immediately! It needs to "rest" at least 30 minutes in the refrigerator to allow the flavors to blend together, but it's worth the wait.

—Gilda Lester, Wilmington, North Carolina

- 1 loaf (1 pound) Italian bread
- 1/3 cup olive oil
- 3 tablespoons balsamic vinegar
- 1 tablespoon minced fresh basil *or* 1 teaspoon dried basil
- 1 garlic clove, minced
- 1/2 teaspoon salt
- 1/4 teaspoon crushed red pepper flakes
- 3/4 pound sliced deli turkey
- 6 ounces provolone cheese, thinly sliced
- 1 jar (7 ounces) roasted sweet red peppers, drained and sliced
- 1/2 cup sliced pimiento-stuffed olives
- 1 large tomato, sliced
- 3 tablespoons shredded Romano cheese
- 1 tablespoon minced fresh oregano *or* 1 teaspoon dried oregano
- 1/4 teaspoon pepper

Cut bread in half lengthwise; carefully hollow out top and bottom, leaving a 1-in. shell (discard removed bread or save for another use).

In a small bowl, combine oil, vinegar, basil, garlic, salt and pepper flakes; brush over cut sides of bread. In the bottom bread shell, layer the turkey, provolone cheese, red peppers, olives and tomato. Sprinkle with Romano cheese, oregano and pepper. Replace bread top.

Wrap in plastic wrap; refrigerate for 30 minutes. Cut into slices. **YIELD:** 6 servings.

Southwestern Turkey Soup

PREP: 20 min. **COOK:** 30 min.

We like this soup really spicy and hot, so we tend to use all three tablespoons of jalapenos...and then some.

—Brenda Kruse, Ames, Iowa

- 1 medium onion, chopped
- 1 tablespoon olive oil
- 1 can (14-1/2 ounces) chicken broth
- 2 to 3 tablespoons diced jalapeno pepper
- 3 teaspoons ground cumin
- 1-1/2 teaspoons chili powder
- 1/4 teaspoon salt
- 1/4 teaspoon cayenne pepper
- 3 cups cubed cooked turkey
- 1 can (15 ounces) black beans, rinsed and drained
- 1 can (10 ounces) diced tomatoes and green chilies, undrained
- 1-1/2 cups frozen corn
- Sour cream, tortilla chips, shredded cheddar cheese and sliced black olives, optional

In a large saucepan, saute the onion in olive oil until tender. Stir in the chicken broth, jalapeno, cumin, chili powder, salt and cayenne. Add the turkey, beans, tomatoes and corn.

Bring to a boil. Reduce heat; cover and simmer for 20-30 minutes or until heated through. Garnish with sour cream, tortilla chips, cheese and olives if desired. **YIELD:** 7 servings.

EDITOR'S NOTE: When cutting hot peppers, disposable gloves are recommended. Avoid touching your face.

Spanish Gazpacho

PREP: 30 min. + chilling

There's a bounty of vegetables in this tantalizing chilled soup. Its refreshing flavor makes it an ideal addition to summer luncheons.

—Dave Schmitt, Hartland, Wisconsin

- 5 pounds tomatoes, peeled and quartered
- 3 medium carrots, quartered
- 1 large cucumber, peeled and quartered
- 1 large sweet red pepper, quartered
- 1 large green pepper, quartered
- 1 sweet onion, quartered
- 2 garlic cloves, minced
- 1/3 cup olive oil
- 3 tablespoons balsamic vinegar
- 1-1/2 teaspoons salt
- 1/2 teaspoon pepper

In batches, place all of the ingredients in a blender or food processor; cover and blend or process until the soup reaches desired consistency. Pour into a large bowl. Cover and refrigerate for 1-2 hours before serving. **YIELD:** 12 servings (3 quarts).

Gingered Butternut Squash Soup

(Pictured above)

PREP: 35 min. **COOK:** 40 min.

Roasting the squash adds a wonderful flavor to this delightful pureed soup. If you want a true vegetarian dish, simply substitute vegetable stock for the chicken broth.

—Kim Pettipas, Oromocto, New Brunswick

- 4 pounds butternut squash, peeled and cubed (about 8 cups)
- 6 teaspoons olive oil, *divided*
- 1 large onion, chopped
- 2 tablespoons butter
- 1 tablespoon minced fresh gingerroot
- 2-1/2 teaspoons curry powder
- 3/4 teaspoon salt
- 1/4 teaspoon pepper
- 3 large potatoes, peeled and cubed
- 6 cups chicken broth
- 1-1/2 cups milk

Sour cream, optional

Place the butternut squash in a greased 15-in. x 10-in. x 1-in. baking pan. Drizzle with 4-1/2 teaspoons oil; toss to coat. Bake, uncovered, at 450° for 30 minutes, stirring every 15 minutes. Bake 5-10 minutes longer or until tender. Set aside.

In a soup kettle, saute onion in butter and remaining oil for 5 minutes or until tender. Stir in the ginger, curry, salt and pepper; cook for 2 minutes. Stir in potatoes; cook 2 minutes longer. Stir in broth. Bring to a boil. Reduce heat; cover and simmer for 15-20 minutes or until potatoes are tender. Cool slightly.

Stir in reserved squash. In a blender, puree soup in batches until smooth. Return to the pan. Stir in milk; heat through. Garnish with sour cream if desired. **YIELD:** 9 servings (about 3 quarts).

Blue Cheese Clubs

(Pictured below)

PREP/TOTAL TIME: 25 min.

These sandwiches look so elegant, but they're actually easy to make. They're loaded with plenty of turkey, and the blue cheese spread offers a nice tang.

—Nancy Jo Leffler, DePauw, Indiana

- 1 package (3 ounces) cream cheese, softened
- 1/2 cup crumbled blue cheese
- 4 tablespoons mayonnaise, *divided*
- 1 teaspoon dried minced onion

Dash salt and pepper

Dash Worcestershire sauce

- 8 slices white bread, toasted
- 8 slices tomato
- 8 slices deli turkey
- 4 slices Swiss cheese
- 4 slices whole wheat bread, toasted
- 8 bacon strips, cooked
- 4 lettuce leaves

In a small bowl, beat the cream cheese. Add the blue cheese, 1 tablespoon mayonnaise, onion, salt, pepper and Worcestershire sauce; beat until combined.

Spread over four slices of white bread; layer with tomato, turkey, Swiss cheese, wheat bread, bacon and lettuce. Spread remaining mayonnaise over remaining white bread; place over lettuce. Secure with toothpicks; cut into triangles. **YIELD:** 4 servings.

Colony Mountain Chili

(Pictured below)

PREP: 25 min. **COOK:** 6 hours

My husband created this chili for a local cooking contest, and it won the People's Choice award. It's loaded with beef, Italian sausage, tomatoes and beans and seasoned with chili powder, cumin and red pepper flakes for zip.

—Marjorie O'Dell, Bow, Washington

    1 pound boneless beef sirloin steak, cut into
      3/4-inch cubes
    4 Italian sausage links, casings removed and cut into
      3/4-inch slices
    2 tablespoons olive oil, *divided*
    1 medium onion, chopped
    3 garlic cloves, minced
    2 green onions, thinly sliced
    2 teaspoons beef bouillon granules
    1 cup boiling water
    1 can (6 ounces) tomato paste
    3 tablespoons chili powder
    2 tablespoons brown sugar
    2 tablespoons Worcestershire sauce
    2 teaspoons ground cumin
    1 to 2 teaspoons crushed red pepper flakes
    1 teaspoon salt
  1/2 teaspoon pepper
    3 cans (14-1/2 ounces *each*) stewed tomatoes, cut up
    2 cans (15 ounces *each*) pinto beans, rinsed and
      drained
Shredded cheddar cheese

In a large skillet, brown the beef and sausage in 1 tablespoon oil; drain. Transfer meat to a 5-qt. slow cooker. In the same skillet, saute the onion, garlic and green onions in remaining oil until tender. Transfer to slow cooker.

   In a small bowl, dissolve bouillon in water. Stir in the tomato paste, chili powder, brown sugar, Worcestershire sauce and seasonings until blended; add to slow cooker. Stir in tomatoes and beans. Cover and cook on high for 6-8 hours or until the meat is tender. Serve with cheese if desired. **YIELD:** 10 servings.

Swiss Tuna Melts

(Pictured above)

PREP/TOTAL TIME: 20 min.

We like these melts served with homemade vegetable soup. You'll love the crunch that celery gives to the creamy tuna filling.

—Karen Owen, Rising Sun, Indiana

    1 can (6 ounces) light water-packed tuna, drained
      and flaked
  3/4 cup shredded Swiss cheese
  1/2 cup sour cream
  1/2 cup mayonnaise
  1/4 cup chopped onion
  1/4 cup chopped celery
Pepper to taste
    8 slices bread
    2 to 3 tablespoons butter, softened

In a bowl, combine the first seven ingredients. Spread over four slices of bread, about 1/2 cup on each; top with remaining bread. Butter the outsides of sandwiches.

   On a griddle or in a large skillet over medium heat, grill the sandwiches for 4-5 minutes on each side or until lightly toasted. **YIELD:** 4 servings.

Chunky Taco Soup

PREP: 20 min. **COOK:** 20 min.

I've gotten great response at our church dinners and senior groups whenever I bring this easy-to-fix soup. I usually take home an empty pot and often receive requests for the recipe.

—Evelyn Buford, Belton, Missouri

  1-1/2 pounds boneless beef sirloin *or* round steak,
        cut into 3/4-inch cubes
      1 medium onion, chopped
      1 tablespoon olive oil
      2 cans (15 ounces *each*) pinto beans, rinsed
        and drained
      2 cans (14-1/2 ounces *each*) diced tomatoes
        and green chilies, undrained

2 cups water
1 can (15 ounces) black beans, rinsed and drained
1 can (14-3/4 ounces) cream-style corn
1 envelope ranch salad dressing mix
1 envelope taco seasoning
1/4 cup minced fresh cilantro

In a large kettle or Dutch oven, brown beef and onion in oil. Add the pinto beans, tomatoes, water, black beans, corn, salad dressing mix and taco seasoning. Bring to a boil. Reduce heat; cover and simmer for 20-30 minutes or until the meat is tender. Sprinkle with cilantro. **YIELD:** 12 servings (about 3 quarts).

Apple and Prosciutto Sandwiches

(*Pictured below*)

PREP/TOTAL TIME: 20 min.

Prepared on an indoor grill, these Italian-style sandwiches are spread with a homemade rosemary pesto. They're wonderful on a cool day with a bowl of butternut squash soup.

—*Elizabeth Bennett, Mill Creek, Washington*

1/4 cup olive oil
1/2 cup chopped walnuts
2 tablespoons grated Parmesan cheese
2 tablespoons minced fresh rosemary
1 loaf (12 ounces) focaccia bread
8 thin slices prosciutto
1 medium apple, sliced
6 ounces Brie cheese, rind removed and sliced

In a blender, combine oil, walnuts, Parmesan cheese and rosemary; cover and process until blended and nuts are finely chopped. With a bread knife, split focaccia into two horizontal layers. Spread the rosemary mixture over cut sides of bread.

On bottom of bread, layer prosciutto, apple and Brie; replace bread top. Cut into quarters.

Cook on an indoor grill for 2-3 minutes or until bread is browned and cheese is melted. To serve, cut each wedge in half. **YIELD:** 8 servings.

Lemony Chicken Soup

(*Pictured above*)

PREP: 5 min. **COOK:** 30 min.

While living in California, I enjoyed a delicious chicken-lemon soup at a local restaurant. When I returned to Texas, I longed for it but never came across a recipe. I experimented with many versions before creating this one.

—*Brenda Tollett, San Antonio, Texas*

1/3 cup butter, cubed
3/4 cup all-purpose flour
6 cups chicken broth, *divided*
1 cup milk
1 cup half-and-half cream
1-1/2 cups cubed cooked chicken
1 tablespoon lemon juice
1/2 teaspoon salt
1/8 teaspoon pepper
Dash ground nutmeg
8 lemon slices

In a soup kettle or large saucepan, melt butter. Stir in flour until smooth; gradually add 2 cups broth, milk and cream. Bring to a boil; cook and stir for 2 minutes or until thickened.

Stir in the chicken, lemon juice, salt, pepper, nutmeg and remaining broth. Cook over medium heat until heated through, stirring occasionally. Garnish each serving with a lemon slice. **YIELD:** 8 servings (2 quarts).

Colorful Chicken and Squash Soup

(*Pictured above*)

PREP: 25 min. **COOK:** 1-1/2 hours

When I turned 40, I decided to live a better lifestyle, which included cooking healthier for my family. I make this nutritious soup every week, and everyone loves it.

—*Trina Bigham, Fairhaven, Massachusetts*

  1 broiler/fryer chicken (4 pounds), cut up
13 cups water
  5 pounds butternut squash, peeled and cubed (about 10 cups)
1-1/4 pounds fresh kale, chopped
  6 medium carrots, chopped
  2 large onions, chopped
  3 teaspoons salt

Place chicken and water in a soup kettle. Bring to a boil. Reduce heat; cover and simmer for 1 hour or until chicken is tender.

Remove chicken from broth. Strain broth and skim fat. Return broth to the pan; add the squash, kale, carrots and onions. Bring to a boil. Reduce heat; cover and simmer for 25-30 minutes or until vegetables are tender.

When chicken is cool enough to handle, remove meat from bones and cut into bite-size pieces. Discard bones and skin. Add chicken and salt to soup; heat through. **YIELD:** 14 servings (5-1/2 quarts).

Garlic Butternut Bisque

(*Pictured below*)

PREP: 40 min. **COOK:** 30 min.

With its pleasant squash and garlic flavor and golden-orange color, this rich and creamy soup is sure to be a hit whether you serve it for an everyday meal or a holiday dinner.

—*Della Clarke, Vista, California*

    2 whole garlic bulbs
    1 teaspoon olive oil
    3 large onions, chopped
3/4 cup chopped carrots
1/2 cup chopped celery
3/4 cup butter, *divided*
    4 pounds butternut squash, peeled, seeded and cubed (about 8 cups)
    6 cups chicken broth
    3 tablespoons chopped fresh sage, *divided*
1/2 cup plus 1 tablespoon heavy whipping cream, *divided*
1-1/2 teaspoons salt
1/4 teaspoon pepper

Remove the papery outer skin from the garlic (do not peel or separate cloves). Cut tops off the bulbs; brush with oil. Wrap each bulb in heavy-duty foil. Bake at 425° for 30-35 minutes or until softened. Cool 10-15 minutes.

Meanwhile, in a Dutch oven or soup kettle, saute the onions, carrots and celery in 1/2 cup butter until tender. Add the squash, broth and 2 tablespoons sage. Bring to a boil. Reduce heat; simmer, uncovered, for 25-30 minutes or until squash is tender.

Squeeze softened garlic into a small bowl; mash with a fork. Stir into squash mixture. Cool slightly. Puree squash mixture in batches in a blender; return to pan. Stir in 1/2 cup cream, salt and pepper and remaining butter; heat through. Garnish with remaining cream and sage. **YIELD:** 9 servings (3 quarts).

1/2 cup uncooked small pasta shells
3 tablespoons minced fresh parsley
1/3 cup grated Parmesan cheese

In a soup kettle, cook sausage and onion over medium heat until meat is no longer pink; drain. Stir in the carrots, celery, leek and garlic; cook for 3 minutes. Add the zucchini and green beans; cook 2 minutes longer.

Stir in broth, tomatoes, cabbage, basil, oregano and pepper. Bring to a boil. Reduce heat; cover and simmer for 45 minutes.

Return to a boil. Stir in garbanzo beans, pasta and parsley. Cook for 6-9 minutes or until the pasta is tender. Serve with Parmesan cheese. **YIELD:** 11 servings (about 3 quarts).

Black Bean and Pumpkin Chili

PREP: 20 min. **COOK:** 4 hours

Our family loves this slow-cooked recipe, especially on cold days. It's a wonderful variation on standard chili. It freezes well and tastes even better as leftovers.

—*Deborah Vliet, Holland, Michigan*

1 medium onion, chopped
1 medium sweet yellow pepper, chopped
3 garlic cloves, minced
2 tablespoons olive oil
3 cups chicken broth
2 cans (15 ounces *each*) black beans, rinsed and drained
2-1/2 cups cubed cooked turkey
1 can (15 ounces) solid-pack pumpkin
1 can (14-1/2 ounces) diced tomatoes, undrained
2 teaspoons dried parsley flakes
2 teaspoons chili powder
1-1/2 teaspoons dried oregano
1-1/2 teaspoons ground cumin
1/2 teaspoon salt

In a large skillet, saute the onion, yellow pepper and garlic in oil until tender. Transfer to a 5-qt. slow cooker; stir in remaining ingredients.

Cover and cook on low for 4-5 hours or until heated through. **YIELD:** 10 servings (2-1/2 quarts).

Minestrone with Italian Sausage

(*Pictured above*)

PREP: 25 min. **COOK:** 1 hour

I make this zippy, satisfying soup all the time, and it's my dad's favorite. The recipe makes a lot, and I have found that it freezes well and tastes just as great reheated.

—*Linda Reis, Salem, Oregon*

1 pound bulk Italian sausage
1 large onion, chopped
2 large carrots, chopped
2 celery ribs, chopped
1 medium leek (white portion only), chopped
3 garlic cloves, minced
1 medium zucchini, cut into 1/2-inch pieces
1/4 pound fresh green beans, trimmed and cut into 1/2-inch pieces
6 cups beef broth
2 cans (14-1/2 ounces *each*) diced tomatoes with basil, oregano and garlic
3 cups shredded cabbage
1 teaspoon dried basil
1 teaspoon dried oregano
1/4 teaspoon pepper
1 can (15 ounces) garbanzo beans *or* chickpeas, rinsed and drained

pumpkin serving bowls

As a clever way to present individual servings of Black Bean and Pumpkin Chili, make "bowls" with fresh pumpkins. Purchase pie pumpkins; wash and dry. Cut a wide circle around the stem of each pumpkin, making a lid. Scrape out each pumpkin. Place pumpkins and lids in a large shallow roasting pan. Cover with foil and bake at 350° for 30 to 50 minutes or just until tender (do not overbake). Cool slightly; fill with chili.

Italian Wedding Soup

(Pictured above)

PREP: 30 min. **COOK:** 45 min.

I sampled a similar soup for lunch at work one day and decided to re-create it at home. I love the combination of meatballs, vegetables and pasta.

—Noelle Myers, Grand Forks, North Dakota

2 eggs, lightly beaten
1/2 cup seasoned bread crumbs
1 pound ground beef
1 pound bulk Italian sausage
3 medium carrots, sliced
3 celery ribs, diced
1 large onion, chopped
3 garlic cloves, minced
4-1/2 teaspoons olive oil
4 cans (14-1/2 ounces *each*) reduced-sodium chicken broth
2 cans (14-1/2 ounces *each*) beef broth
1 package (10 ounces) frozen chopped spinach, thawed and squeezed dry
1/4 cup minced fresh basil
1 envelope onion soup mix
4-1/2 teaspoons ketchup
1/2 teaspoon dried thyme
3 bay leaves
1-1/2 cups uncooked penne pasta

In a large bowl, combine eggs and bread crumbs. Crumble beef and sausage over mixture; mix well. Shape into 3/4-in. balls.

Place the meatballs on a greased rack in a foil-lined 15-in. x 10-in. x 1-in. baking pan. Bake at 350° for 15-18 minutes or until no longer pink. Meanwhile, in a soup kettle or Dutch oven, saute the carrots, celery, onion and garlic in oil until tender. Stir in the broth, spinach, basil, soup mix, ketchup, thyme and bay leaves.

Drain meatballs on paper towels. Bring soup to a boil; add the meatballs. Reduce heat; simmer, uncovered, for 30 minutes. Add pasta; cook 13-15 minutes longer or until tender, stirring occasionally. Discard bay leaves before serving. **YIELD:** 10 servings (2-1/2 quarts).

Pizza Meatball Subs

(Pictured below and on page 44)

PREP: 30 min. **BAKE:** 25 min.

I made these sandwiches one evening for my family, and they were a huge hit with everyone, including the picky eaters. There's plenty of sauce and cheese to complement the baked meatballs.

—Heather Begin, Athens, Maine

1 egg, lightly beaten
1/3 cup steak sauce
1 cup crushed saltines
1 teaspoon onion powder
1/4 teaspoon seasoned salt
1/8 teaspoon pepper
1-1/2 pounds ground beef
6 to 7 tablespoons mayonnaise
6 to 7 submarine buns, split
9 to 11 slices process American cheese, cut into strips
1 jar (14 ounces) pizza sauce
2 cups (8 ounces) shredded part-skim mozzarella cheese

In a large bowl, combine egg, steak sauce, saltines, onion powder, salt and pepper. Crumble beef over mixture and mix well. Shape into 1-1/2-in. balls.

Place meatballs on a greased rack in a shallow baking pan. Bake at 375° for 20-25 minutes or until no longer pink. Drain on paper towels.

Spread mayonnaise over bun bottoms; top each with American cheese, 1 tablespoon pizza sauce, meatballs and remaining pizza sauce. Sprinkle with mozzarella cheese. Place on a baking sheet. Bake for 5-10 minutes or until cheese is melted. **YIELD:** 6-7 servings.

Hearty Beef Vegetable Soup

(Pictured above)

PREP: 20 min. **COOK:** 2 hours

This stew-like soup is loaded with nutritious ingredients but is easy to make. It gets its kick from green chilies. I like to serve oven-fresh bread with it.

—*Sherman Snowball, Salt Lake City, Utah*

- 3 tablespoons all-purpose flour
- 1/2 teaspoon salt
- 1/4 teaspoon pepper
- 1 pound beef stew meat, cut into 1/2-inch cubes
- 2 tablespoons olive oil
- 1 can (14-1/2 ounces) Italian diced tomatoes
- 1 can (8 ounces) tomato sauce
- 2 tablespoons red wine vinegar
- 2 tablespoons Worcestershire sauce
- 3 garlic cloves, minced
- 1 teaspoon dried oregano
- 3 cups hot water
- 4 medium potatoes, peeled and cubed
- 6 medium carrots, sliced
- 2 medium turnips, peeled and cubed
- 1 medium zucchini, halved lengthwise and sliced
- 1 medium green pepper, julienned
- 1 cup sliced fresh mushrooms
- 1 medium onion, chopped
- 1 can (4 ounces) chopped green chilies
- 2 tablespoons sugar

In a large resealable plastic bag, combine the flour, salt and pepper. Add beef, a few pieces at a time, and shake to coat.

In a soup kettle or Dutch oven, brown the beef in oil. Stir in the tomatoes, tomato sauce, vinegar, Worcestershire sauce, garlic and oregano. Bring to a boil. Reduce heat; cover and simmer for 1 hour.

Stir in the remaining ingredients. Bring to a boil. Reduce heat; cover and simmer for 1 hour or until the meat and vegetables are tender. **YIELD:** 8 servings (about 2-1/2 quarts).

Roasted Yellow Pepper Soup

(Pictured below)

PREP: 25 min. **COOK:** 40 min.

We got this recipe from a good friend and Merchant Marine in New Hampshire. My husband and our two small children liked it so much that I grew my own yellow pepper plants just to prepare it. We enjoy the soup in the middle of summer as well as on cool fall days.

—*Amy Spurrier, Wellsburg, West Virginia*

- 6 large sweet yellow peppers
- 1 large onion, chopped
- 1 cup chopped leeks (white portion only)
- 1/4 cup butter, cubed
- 3 small potatoes, peeled and cubed
- 5 cups chicken broth
- 1/2 teaspoon salt
- 1/2 teaspoon pepper

Shredded Parmesan cheese, optional

Halve peppers; remove and discard tops and seeds. Broil peppers 4 in. from the heat until skins blister, about 4 minutes. Immediately place peppers in a bowl; cover and let stand for 15-20 minutes.

Meanwhile, in a large saucepan, saute onion and leeks in butter until tender. Add the potatoes, broth, salt and pepper. Bring to a boil. Reduce heat; cover and simmer for 30 minutes or until the potatoes are tender.

Peel off and discard charred skin from peppers. Finely chop the peppers; add to potato mixture. Cool slightly.

In a blender, cover and process the soup in batches until smooth. Return to the pan; heat through (do not boil). Serve with Parmesan cheese if desired. **YIELD:** 8 cups (2 quarts).

Cheeseburger Paradise Soup

(Pictured above and on page 44)

PREP: 30 min. **COOK:** 25 min.

I've never met a person who didn't enjoy this creamy soup. With ground beef and potatoes, it's hearty enough to serve as a main course with your favorite bread or rolls.

—Nadina Ladimarco, Burton, Ohio

- 6 medium potatoes, peeled and cubed
- 1 small carrot, grated
- 1 small onion, chopped
- 1/2 cup chopped green pepper
- 2 tablespoons chopped seeded jalapeno pepper
- 3 cups water
- 2 tablespoons plus 2 teaspoons beef bouillon granules
- 2 garlic cloves, minced
- 1/8 teaspoon pepper
- 2 pounds ground beef
- 1/2 pound sliced fresh mushrooms
- 2 tablespoons butter
- 5 cups milk, *divided*
- 6 tablespoons all-purpose flour
- 1 package (16 ounces) process cheese (Velveeta), cubed
- Crumbled cooked bacon

In a soup kettle, combine first nine ingredients; bring to a boil. Reduce heat; cover and simmer for 15-20 minutes or until potatoes are tender.

Meanwhile, in a large skillet, cook beef and mushrooms in butter over medium heat until meat is no longer pink; drain. Add to soup. Stir in 4 cups milk; heat through.

In a small bowl, combine flour and remaining milk until smooth; gradually stir into soup. Bring to a boil; cook and stir for 2 minutes or until thickened. Reduce heat; stir in cheese until melted. Garnish with bacon. **YIELD:** 14 servings (about 3-1/2 quarts).

EDITOR'S NOTE: When cutting hot peppers, disposable gloves are recommended. Avoid touching your face.

Asparagus Leek Chowder

PREP/TOTAL TIME: 20 min.

When my family sees this thick, velvety chowder on the table, they know spring has arrived.

—Elisabeth Harders, West Allis, Wisconsin

- 1 pound fresh asparagus, trimmed and cut into 1-inch pieces
- 3 cups sliced fresh mushrooms
- 3 large leeks (white portion only), sliced
- 6 tablespoons butter
- 1/4 cup all-purpose flour
- 1/2 teaspoon salt
- Dash pepper
- 2 cups chicken broth
- 2 cups half-and-half cream
- 1 can (11 ounces) whole kernel corn, drained
- 1 tablespoon chopped pimientos

In a large saucepan, saute the asparagus, mushrooms and leeks in butter for 10 minutes or until tender. Stir in flour, salt and pepper until blended.

Gradually stir in broth and cream. Bring to a boil. Reduce heat; cook and stir for 2 minutes or until thickened. Stir in corn and pimientos; heat through. **YIELD:** 7 servings.

Cheesy Corn Chowder

PREP: 30 min. **COOK:** 30 min.

I've had this chowder recipe for 30 years, and the whole family really savors its cheesy, corn taste. It makes a big pot—enough for seconds!

—Lola Comer, Marysville, Washington

- 6 bacon strips, chopped
- 3/4 cup chopped sweet onion
- 2-1/2 cups water
- 2-1/2 cups cubed peeled potatoes
- 2 cups sliced fresh carrots
- 2 teaspoons chicken bouillon granules
- 3 cans (11 ounces *each*) gold and white corn, drained
- 1/2 teaspoon pepper
- 7 tablespoons all-purpose flour
- 5 cups milk
- 3 cups (12 ounces) shredded cheddar cheese
- 1 cup cubed process cheese (Velveeta)

In a Dutch oven, cook bacon and onion over medium heat until onion is tender. Add water, potatoes, carrots and bouillon; bring to a boil. Reduce heat; cover and simmer for 15-20 minutes or until potatoes are tender.

Stir in corn and pepper. In a large bowl, whisk flour and milk until smooth; add to soup. Bring to a boil; cook and stir for 2 minutes or until thickened. Reduce heat. Add the cheeses; cook and stir until cheeses are melted. **YIELD:** 15 servings (3-3/4 quarts).

Cuban Pork Sandwiches

(Pictured above)

PREP: 30 min. + marinating   **BAKE:** 25 min. + standing

Seasoned pork, sweet red peppers and mozzarella cheese come together in this satisfying sandwich. To make it even more substantial, sometimes I add bread crumbs and Italian seasoning to the meat and vegetables.

—Connie Zangla, Annadale, Minnesota

- 1 small red onion, thinly sliced
- 1 cup water
- 1 jar (7 ounces) roasted sweet red peppers, drained and chopped
- 1/3 cup cider vinegar
- 2 garlic cloves, peeled and halved
- 1/2 teaspoon dried oregano
- 1/4 teaspoon salt
- 1/4 teaspoon pepper
- 1/4 teaspoon ground cumin

SANDWICH:

- 1 garlic clove, minced
- 1 teaspoon ground cumin
- 1/2 teaspoon salt
- 1 pork tenderloin (about 1 pound)
- 1 teaspoon olive oil
- 8 slices sourdough bread
- 8 slices Swiss cheese

For the relish, in a small saucepan over medium heat, bring onion and water to a boil. Cook and stir for 1 minute; drain. Transfer to a bowl; add the roasted peppers, vinegar, garlic, oregano, salt, pepper and cumin. Let stand at room temperature for 1 hour. Discard the garlic. (The relish can be made ahead and stored in the refrigerator for up to 1 week.)

For the sandwich, in a small bowl, mash the minced garlic, cumin and salt. Rub over tenderloin; place in a shallow baking pan. Bake, uncovered, at 425° for 25-30 minutes or until a meat thermometer reads 160°. Let stand for 10 minutes; thinly slice pork.

Heat oil in a large skillet over medium heat. Top four slices of bread with pork, desired amount of relish and two slices of cheese; top with remaining bread. Cook sandwiches for 2-4 minutes on each side or until golden brown. **YIELD:** 4 servings (2 cups relish).

Land of Enchantment Posole

(Pictured below)

PREP: 30 min.   **COOK:** 1 hour

My family named this spicy soup after our state moniker, "New Mexico, Land of Enchantment." We usually make it around the Christmas holiday when we have lots of family over…and we never have leftovers.

—Suzanne Caldwell, Artesia, New Mexico

- 1-1/2 pounds pork stew meat, cut into 3/4-inch cubes
- 1 large onion, chopped
- 2 garlic cloves, minced
- 2 tablespoons canola oil
- 3 cups beef broth
- 2 cans (15-1/2 ounces *each*) hominy, rinsed and drained
- 2 cans (4 ounces *each*) chopped green chilies
- 1 to 2 jalapeno peppers, seeded and chopped, optional
- 1/2 teaspoon salt
- 1/2 teaspoon ground cumin
- 1/2 teaspoon dried oregano
- 1/4 teaspoon pepper
- 1/4 teaspoon cayenne pepper
- 1/2 cup minced fresh cilantro

Tortilla strips, optional

In a soup kettle or Dutch oven, cook the pork, onion and garlic in oil over medium heat until meat is no longer pink; drain. Stir in the broth, hominy, chilies, jalapeno if desired, salt, cumin, oregano, pepper and cayenne.

Bring to a boil. Reduce heat; cover and simmer for 45-60 minutes or until meat is tender. Stir in cilantro. Serve with tortilla strips if desired. **YIELD:** 5 servings.

EDITOR'S NOTE: When cutting hot peppers, disposable gloves are recommended. Avoid touching your face.

Chicken Soup with Potato Dumplings

(Pictured below)

PREP: 25 min.   **COOK:** 40 min.

Our family calls this comforting, old-fashioned soup our "Sunday dinner soup" because it's almost a complete dinner in a bowl. You'll love the taste!

—Marie McConnell, Shelbyville, Illinois

- 1/4 **cup chopped onion**
- 2 **garlic cloves, minced**
- 1 **tablespoon canola oil**
- 6 **cups chicken broth**
- 2 **cups cubed cooked chicken**
- 2 **celery ribs, chopped**
- 2 **medium carrots, sliced**
- 1/4 **teaspoon dried sage leaves**

DUMPLINGS:

- 1-1/2 **cups biscuit/baking mix**
- 1 **cup cold mashed potatoes (with added milk)**
- 1/4 **cup milk**
- 1 **tablespoon chopped green onion**
- 1/8 **teaspoon pepper**

In a large saucepan, saute onion and garlic in oil for 3-4 minutes or until onion is tender. Stir in the broth, chicken, celery, carrots and sage. Bring to a boil. Reduce heat; cover and simmer for 10-15 minutes or until vegetables are tender.

In a small bowl, combine the dumpling ingredients. Drop heaping tablespoonfuls of batter onto simmering soup. Cover and simmer for 20 minutes or until a toothpick inserted in a dumpling comes out clean (do not lift cover while simmering). **YIELD:** 5 servings.

Black Bean Burgers

(Pictured above)

PREP/TOTAL TIME: 25 min.

My son encouraged me to come up with a good veggie burger for him, and he gave this recipe an AAA+! Not only are they moist and flavorful, but they're very easy to freeze. Now, like my son, I prefer them over traditional burgers.

—Clara Honeyager, North Prairie, Wisconsin

- 1 **cup frozen mixed vegetables, thawed**
- 1 **small onion, chopped**
- 1/2 **cup chopped sweet red pepper**
- 1 **can (15 ounces) black beans, rinsed and drained, *divided***
- 1 **tablespoon cornstarch**
- 2 **tablespoons cold water**
- 1 **cup mashed potato flakes**
- 1/4 **cup quick-cooking oats**
- 3 **tablespoons whole wheat flour**
- 2 **tablespoons nonfat dry milk powder**
- 1 **egg, lightly beaten**
- 1/2 **teaspoon salt**
- 1/4 **teaspoon pepper**
- 4 **teaspoons canola oil**
- 6 **kaiser rolls, split**
- 2 **cups shredded lettuce**
- 3/4 **cup salsa**

In a large microwave-safe bowl, combine the mixed vegetables, onion and red pepper. Cover and microwave on high for 2 minutes.

Coarsely mash 3/4 cup of the black beans. In a bowl, combine the cornstarch and water until smooth; stir in the mashed beans, potato flakes, oats, flour, milk powder, egg, salt and pepper. Stir in vegetable mixture and remaining black beans. Shape into six 5/8-in.-thick patties.

In a large nonstick skillet, cook patties in oil for 4-5 minutes on each side or until lightly browned. Serve on rolls with lettuce and salsa. **YIELD:** 6 servings.

EDITOR'S NOTE: This recipe was tested in a 1,100-watt microwave.

Golden Seafood Chowder

(Pictured below)

PREP: 25 min. **COOK:** 25 min.

Packed with crab, shrimp and cheddar cheese, this chowder is so good that I make it weekly. Sometimes I substitute chicken or ham for the seafood and leave out the clam juice. Either way, this pretty soup is a winner.

—Ami Paton, Waconia, Minnesota

- 1/2 cup finely chopped onion
- 1/4 cup butter, cubed
- 1 can (14-1/2 ounces) chicken broth
- 1 cup cubed peeled potato
- 2 celery ribs, chopped
- 2 medium carrots, chopped
- 1/4 cup Clamato juice
- 1/4 teaspoon lemon-pepper seasoning
- 1/4 cup all-purpose flour
- 2 cups milk
- 2 cups (8 ounces) shredded sharp cheddar cheese
- 1 can (6 ounces) crabmeat, drained, flaked and cartilage removed
- 1 cup cooked medium shrimp, peeled and deveined

In a large saucepan, saute onion in butter until tender. Stir in broth, potato, celery, carrots, Clamato juice and lemon-pepper seasoning. Bring to a boil. Reduce heat; cover and simmer for 15-20 minutes or until vegetables are tender.

In a small bowl, whisk the flour and milk together until smooth; add to soup. Bring to a boil; cook and stir for 2 minutes or until thickened. Reduce heat. Add the cheese, crab and shrimp; cook and stir until cheese is melted. **YIELD:** 4 servings.

Buffalo Chicken Wraps

(Pictured above and on page 44)

PREP/TOTAL TIME: 25 min.

Blue cheese dressing and hot pepper sauce enhance these yummy tortilla wraps. Filled with chicken, cheese, lettuce and tomatoes, they're colorful, fun to eat and easy to tote!

—Athena Russell, Florence, South Carolina

- 1 cup all-purpose flour
- 1 teaspoon salt
- 1/4 teaspoon pepper
- 1/2 cup buttermilk
- 4 boneless skinless chicken breast halves
- 1 cup canola oil
- 1/2 cup hot pepper sauce
- 1/4 cup butter, melted
- 4 spinach tortillas (10 inches)
- 1 cup shredded lettuce
- 1 cup (4 ounces) shredded cheddar cheese
- 2/3 cup chopped tomatoes
- 1/2 cup blue cheese salad dressing

In a shallow bowl, combine the flour, salt and pepper. Place the buttermilk in another shallow bowl. Dip chicken in buttermilk, then roll in flour mixture.

In a large skillet, cook the chicken in oil for 8-10 minutes or until the juices run clear. Drain on paper towels; cut into strips.

In a bowl, combine the hot pepper sauce and butter. Dip chicken strips into mixture, coating both sides. Place chicken in the center of each tortilla. Layer with lettuce, cheese and tomatoes; drizzle with salad dressing. Bring up sides of tortillas; secure with toothpicks if desired. **YIELD:** 4 servings.

For dumplings, in a large saucepan, bring water and butter to a boil. Combine the flour, baking powder and salt; add all at once to pan and stir until a smooth ball forms. Remove from heat; let stand for 5 minutes. Add eggs, one at a time, beating well after each addition. Continue beating until the mixture is smooth and shiny. Stir in parsley.

Drop batter in 12 mounds onto simmering soup. Cover and simmer for 20 minutes or until a toothpick inserted in a dumpling comes out clean (do not lift cover while simmering). **YIELD:** 6 servings (about 2 quarts).

Home Run Slugger Sub

(Pictured below)

PREP/TOTAL TIME: 15 min.

Sometimes I trim a long loaf of French bread to make these hearty hoagies look like baseball bats. Then I fill them with cold cuts, veggies and cheese.

—Cathy Runyon, Allendale, Michigan

  1 **French bread baguette (1 pound and 20 inches long)**
1/4 **pound thinly sliced fully cooked ham**
1/4 **pound thinly sliced bologna**
1/4 **pound thinly sliced hard salami**
  4 **romaine leaves**
  6 **slices Swiss cheese**
  6 **slices Colby cheese**
  1 **medium tomato, sliced**

With a sharp knife, cut one end of the baguette into the shape of a baseball bat handle. Slice loaf in half lengthwise.

On the bottom half, layer the ham, bologna, salami, romaine, cheeses and tomato. Replace top. Secure with toothpicks if necessary. Cut into slices. **YIELD:** 8 servings.

Danish Turkey Dumpling Soup

(Pictured above)

PREP: 35 min. **COOK:** 3 hours

This recipe was handed down from my grandmother, who was a Danish caterer. My 100% Italian husband has come to expect this on chilly evenings because it not only warms the body but warms the heart as well.

—Karen Sue Garback-Pristera, Albany, New York

  1 **leftover turkey carcass (from a 12- to 14-pound turkey)**
  9 **cups water**
  3 **teaspoons chicken bouillon granules**
  1 **bay leaf**
  1 **can (14-1/2 ounces) stewed tomatoes, cut up**
  1 **medium turnip, peeled and diced**
  2 **celery ribs, chopped**
  1 **medium onion, chopped**
  1 **medium carrot, chopped**
1/4 **cup minced fresh parsley**
  1 **teaspoon salt**
DUMPLINGS:
1/2 **cup water**
1/4 **cup butter, cubed**
1/2 **cup all-purpose flour**
  1 **teaspoon baking powder**
1/8 **teaspoon salt**
  2 **eggs**
  1 **tablespoon minced fresh parsley**

Place carcass, water, bouillon and bay leaf in a soup kettle. Bring to a boil. Reduce heat; cover and simmer for 1-1/2 hours.

Remove carcass. Strain broth and skim fat; discard bay leaf. Return broth to pan. Add the tomatoes, vegetables, parsley and salt. Remove turkey from bones and cut into bite-size pieces; add to soup. Discard bones. Bring to a boil. Reduce heat; cover and simmer for 25-30 minutes or until vegetables are crisp-tender.

White Bean Chicken Chili

(Pictured below and on page 44)

PREP: 35 min. **COOK:** 3 hours

My sister shared this chili recipe with me. I usually double it and add one extra can of beans, then serve with cheddar biscuits or warmed tortillas. The jalapeno adds just enough heat to notice but not too much for my children.

—*Kristine Bowles, Albuquerque, New Mexico*

> 3/4 pound boneless skinless chicken breasts, cubed
> 1/2 teaspoon salt
> 1/4 teaspoon pepper
> 2 tablespoons olive oil
> 1 medium onion, chopped
> 4 garlic cloves, minced
> 1 jalapeno pepper, seeded and chopped
> 2 teaspoons dried oregano
> 1 teaspoon ground cumin
> 2 cans (15 ounces *each*) white kidney *or* cannellini beans, rinsed and drained, *divided*
> 3 cups chicken broth, *divided*
> 1-1/2 cups (6 ounces) shredded cheddar cheese
> Sour cream and minced fresh cilantro, optional

Sprinkle chicken with salt and pepper. In a large skillet over medium heat, cook chicken in oil for 2 minutes.

Stir in onion, garlic and jalapeno; cook 2 minutes longer. Sprinkle with oregano and cumin; cook 1 minute longer or until chicken is browned and vegetables are tender. Transfer to a 3-qt. slow cooker.

In a small bowl, mash 1 cup of beans. Add 1/2 cup broth; stir until blended. Add to slow cooker with the remaining beans and broth.

Cover and cook on low for 3 to 3-1/2 hours or until chicken juices run clear. Stir before serving. Sprinkle with cheese. Garnish with sour cream and cilantro if desired. **YIELD:** 6 servings.

EDITOR'S NOTE: When cutting hot peppers, disposable gloves are recommended. Avoid touching your face.

Firecracker Burgers

(Pictured above)

PREP: 20 min. **GRILL:** 15 min.

These tasty stuffed burgers are perfect July 4th fare. They're great with a cool, creamy macaroni salad and an icy cold beverage!

—*Kelly Williams, LaPorte, Indiana*

> 1 pound lean ground beef
> 1/4 cup chunky salsa
> 4 frozen breaded cheddar cheese jalapeno peppers, thawed
> 1/4 cup guacamole
> 4 hamburger buns, split and toasted
> 4 lettuce leaves
> 1/4 cup salsa con queso dip
> 1/4 cup sliced plum tomatoes
> 2 tablespoons sliced ripe olives
> 4 thin slices sweet onion

In a bowl, combine beef and salsa. Shape into four patties. Place a jalapeno in the center of each; wrap beef around jalapeno, forming a ball. Reshape into patties, about 3-1/2 to 4 in. in diameter and 1 in. thick.

Grill, covered, over medium-hot heat for 7-8 minutes on each side or until the meat is no longer pink. Spread the guacamole over toasted side of bun tops. On each bun bottom, layer the lettuce, a burger, con queso dip, tomatoes, olives and onion; replace tops. **YIELD:** 4 servings.

hot pepper prep

When handling jalapeno peppers, always wear plastic gloves. If you have to cut a large number, try this quick, safe method: First, cut off the tops of the peppers and slice them in half the long way. Then, using the small end of a melon baller, scrape out the seeds and membranes.

Chicken Asparagus Soup

(Pictured below)

PREP: 1 hour **BAKE:** 45 min.

Asparagus stars in this flavorful soup, a favorite recipe from my Italian grandmother. I have fond memories of chopping veggies and cooking with her as a child.

—Sandy Clayton, Visalia, California

- 2 pounds thin fresh asparagus
- 2 large potatoes, peeled and diced
- 1 large onion, chopped
- 2 celery ribs, chopped
- 1 medium carrot, chopped
- 2 teaspoons dried parsley flakes
- 1 garlic clove, minced
- 2 tablespoons canola oil
- 2 cans (14-1/2 ounces *each*) chicken broth
- 1 teaspoon salt
- 1/2 teaspoon pepper, *divided*
- 1 bay leaf
- 2 cups cubed cooked chicken
- 2 cups half-and-half cream
Shaved Parmesan cheese, optional

Cut tips from asparagus spears; set aside. Place stalks in a large skillet; cover with water. Bring to a boil. Reduce heat; cover and simmer for 40 minutes. Strain, reserving 4 cups cooking liquid. Discard stalks.

In a Dutch oven, saute the potatoes, onion, celery, carrot, parsley and garlic in oil until vegetables are tender. Stir in the broth, salt, 1/4 teaspoon pepper, bay leaf and reserved cooking liquid. Bring to a boil. Reduce heat; simmer, uncovered, for 30 minutes. Discard bay leaf. Cool slightly.

In a blender, cover and puree the soup in batches until smooth. Return to the pan. Add the chicken, cream, remaining pepper and reserved asparagus tips. Bring to a boil. Reduce heat; simmer, uncovered, for 5 minutes or until asparagus is tender. Garnish with Parmesan cheese if desired. **YIELD:** 10 servings (about 2 quarts).

Zesty Vegetarian Wraps

(Pictured above)

PREP/TOTAL TIME: 10 min.

Beautiful in color and very tasty, this vegetarian wrap is filled with crisp veggies, pepper Jack cheese and a zesty sauce.

—Cori Lehman, South Milwaukee, Wisconsin

- 2 tablespoons mayonnaise
- 1 teaspoon lime juice
- 2 to 4 drops Louisiana-style hot sauce
- 2 spinach tortillas *or* flour tortillas of your choice (8 inches)
- 2 lettuce leaves
- 1/2 medium green pepper, julienned
- 2 slices pepper Jack cheese

In a small bowl, combine the mayonnaise, lime juice and hot sauce. Spread over tortillas. Top with lettuce, green pepper and cheese; roll up tightly. **YIELD:** 2 servings.

Shrimp Salad Croissants

PREP/TOTAL TIME: 15 min.

I've had this recipe for years and get raves whenever I make it. It can be served on a bed of lettuce or atop a flaky croissant. Either way, it's perfect for a quick, delicious lunch.

—Molly Seidel, Edgewood, New Mexico

- 1 pound cooked small shrimp
- 2 celery ribs, diced
- 2 small carrots, shredded
- 1 cup mayonnaise
- 1/3 cup finely chopped onion
Dash salt and pepper
- 2 packages (2-1/4 ounces *each*) sliced almonds
- 8 croissants, split

In a large bowl, combine the shrimp, celery, carrots, mayonnaise, onion, salt and pepper. Cover and refrigerate for at least 2 hours. Just before serving, stir in almonds. Serve on croissants. **YIELD:** 8 servings.

Mushroom Tomato Bisque

(Pictured below)

PREP: 30 min. **BAKE:** 10 min.

*After tasting a similar soup in a restaurant, I tinkered around
with a few recipes at home and this was the result. The recipe
might seem complicated, but it's really not. And I love the blend
of ingredients.*
—Connie Stevens, Schaefferstown, Pennsylvania

- 1-1/2 pounds plum tomatoes, halved lengthwise
- 5 tablespoons olive oil, *divided*
- 2 garlic cloves, minced
- 1/2 teaspoon salt
- 1/2 teaspoon dried basil
- 1/2 teaspoon dried oregano
- 1/2 teaspoon pepper
- 1/2 pound sliced fresh mushrooms
- 1/2 cup finely chopped sweet onion
- 1-1/4 cups chicken broth
- 1/3 to 1/2 cup tomato paste
- Pinch sugar, optional
- 3/4 cup heavy whipping cream
- 2 tablespoons grated Parmesan cheese

Place the tomatoes cut side down in a greased 15-in. x 10-in. x 1-in. baking pan. Brush with 3 tablespoons oil. Combine garlic, salt, basil, oregano and pepper; sprinkle over tomatoes. Bake, uncovered, at 450° for 20-25 minutes or until edges are well browned.

Cool slightly. Place tomatoes and pan drippings in a blender. Cover and process until blended; process 1 minute longer.

In a large saucepan, saute mushrooms and onion in remaining oil for 5-8 minutes or until tender. Stir in broth, tomato paste, sugar if desired and tomato puree. Bring to a boil. Remove from the heat; stir in cream. Garnish with Parmesan cheese. **YIELD:** 4 servings.

Chicken Broccoli Calzones

(Pictured above)

PREP: 20 min. **BAKE:** 20 min.

*Smoked mozzarella cheese and golden raisins add to the excellent
flavor of the broccoli and chicken in these easy-to-fix calzones.*
—Iola Egle, Bella Vista, Arkansas

- 3 cups frozen chopped broccoli
- 1/2 teaspoon rubbed sage
- 1 small onion, finely chopped
- 3 garlic cloves, minced
- 1 tablespoon olive oil
- 2 cups shredded cooked chicken breast
- 1/2 pound smoked mozzarella cheese, shredded
- 1/3 cup chopped fresh basil
- 1/3 cup golden raisins
- 1 loaf (1 pound) frozen bread dough, thawed
- 1 egg
- 1 tablespoon water

Cook broccoli according to package directions; drain. Sprinkle with sage; set aside. In a large saucepan, saute onion and garlic in oil until tender. Remove from the heat. Stir in the broccoli, chicken, cheese, basil and raisins; set aside.

On a lightly floured surface, divide dough into four pieces. Roll each piece into a 10-in. circle. Carefully place one circle on a lightly greased baking sheet. Spoon a fourth of the chicken mixture onto half of the circle. Brush edges of dough with water; fold dough over filling and pinch edges to seal. Repeat with remaining dough and filling.

With a sharp knife, make two slashes on each calzone. Beat egg and water; brush over calzones. Bake at 400° for 18-22 minutes or until golden brown. **YIELD:** 4 calzones.

You'll **savor** this luscious lineup
of recipes to go with your favorite foods.
Rounding out meals has never been easier.

side dishes & condiments

Pearl Onion Broccoli Bake 64

Slow-Cooked Bean Medley 64

Duo Tater Bake 65

Springtime Barley 65

Grilled Corn Salsa 66

Ribboned Vegetables 66

Dilly Pickled Asparagus 66

Roasted Squash Medley 67

Cheesy Noodle Casserole 67

German-Style Mashed Potatoes 67

Fried Shoestring Carrots 68

So-Sweet Squash Pickles 68

Tomato and Corn Risotto 69

Maple-Ginger Root Vegetables 69

Rustic Squash Tarts 70

Mexicorn Grits 70

Orange Rhubarb Spread 71

Broccoli with Orange Sauce 71

Curried Butternut Squash Kabobs 71

Grilled Asparagus Medley 72

Crumb-Coated Spaetzle 72

Fresh Corn Medley 72

Tangy Rhubarb Chutney 73

Double Corn Dressing 73

Onion-Bacon Baby Carrots 74

Peas in Cheese Sauce 74

Smoky Grilled Corn 74

Baked Cranberry Sauce 74

Orange-Glazed Acorn Squash 75

Herbed Tomatoes and Green Beans 75

Gnocchi with Thyme Butter 76

German Potato Salad with Sausage 76

Party Carrots 77

Asparagus with Mustard Sauce 77

Cherry Tomato Mozzarella Saute 77

Creamy Vegetable Bow Tie Toss 78

Mango Cranberry Sauce 78

Garlic-Pepper Rub 78

Spaghetti Squash Supreme 79

Loaded Red Potato Casserole 79

Swiss-Almond Floret Bake 80

Green Beans in Lemon Chiffon Sauce 80

Peppery Parsnip Fries 81

Sweet & Sour Brussels Sprouts 81

O'Larry's Skillet Potatoes 81

PICTURED CLOCKWISE FROM UPPER LEFT: Maple-Ginger Root Vegetables (page 69), Rustic Squash Tarts (page 70), Green Beans in Lemon Chiffon Sauce (page 80) and German Potato Salad with Sausage (page 76).

Slow-Cooked Bean Medley

(*Pictured below*)

PREP: 25 min. **COOK:** 5 hours

I often change the variety of beans in this classic side, using whatever I have on hand to total five 15- to 16-ounce cans. The sauce makes any combination delicious!

—Peggy Gwillim, Strasbourg, Saskatchewan

- 1-1/2 cups ketchup
- 2 celery ribs, chopped
- 1 medium onion, chopped
- 1 medium green pepper, chopped
- 1 medium sweet red pepper, chopped
- 1/2 cup packed brown sugar
- 1/2 cup water
- 1/2 cup Italian salad dressing
- 2 bay leaves
- 1 tablespoon cider vinegar
- 1 teaspoon ground mustard
- 1/8 teaspoon pepper
- 1 can (16 ounces) kidney beans, rinsed and drained
- 1 can (15-1/2 ounces) black-eyed peas, rinsed and drained
- 1 can (15-1/2 ounces) great northern beans, rinsed and drained
- 1 can (15-1/4 ounces) whole kernel corn, drained
- 1 can (15-1/4 ounces) lima beans, rinsed and drained
- 1 can (15 ounces) black beans, rinsed and drained

In a 5-qt. slow cooker, combine the first 12 ingredients. Stir in the remaining ingredients. Cover and cook on low for 5-7 hours or until onion and peppers are tender. Discard bay leaves. **YIELD:** 12 servings.

Pearl Onion Broccoli Bake

(*Pictured above*)

PREP: 20 min. **BAKE:** 25 min.

With its smooth white cheese sauce and buttery crumb topping, this dish is great comfort food. If you're looking for a mild way to dress up broccoli, this is the recipe.

—Charles Keating, Manchester, Maryland

- 4 packages (8 ounces *each*) frozen broccoli cuts
- 4 cups frozen pearl onions
- 1/2 cup butter, *divided*
- 1/4 cup all-purpose flour
- 3/4 teaspoon salt
- 1/8 teaspoon pepper
- 2 cups milk
- 2 packages (3 ounces *each*) cream cheese, cubed
- 2 cups soft bread crumbs
- 1 cup (4 ounces) shredded cheddar cheese

In a large saucepan, cook the broccoli in 1 in. of water until almost tender; drain. Cook the pearl onions in 1 in. of water until almost tender; drain.

In a large saucepan, melt 1/4 cup butter; stir in the flour, salt and pepper until smooth. Gradually add milk. Bring to a boil; cook and stir for 1-2 minutes or until thickened. Reduce heat; stir in cream cheese until smooth and blended.

Place the broccoli and onions in a greased 13-in. x 9-in. baking dish. Add the sauce and gently stir to coat. Melt the remaining butter; toss with bread crumbs. Sprinkle crumbs and cheddar cheese over vegetables.

Bake, uncovered, at 350° for 25-30 minutes or until topping is golden brown. **YIELD:** 12-15 servings.

Duo Tater Bake

(Pictured above)

PREP: 40 min. **BAKE:** 20 min. + chilling

I made this creamy and comforting potato dish for Thanksgiving, and it was a winner with my family. They said to be sure to include it at every holiday dinner. It's a keeper!

—Joan McCulloch, Abbotsford, British Columbia

- 4 **pounds russet *or* Yukon Gold potatoes, peeled and cubed**
- 3 **pounds sweet potatoes, peeled and cubed**
- 2 **cartons (8 ounces *each*) spreadable chive and onion cream cheese**
- 1 **cup (8 ounces) sour cream**
- 1/4 **cup shredded Colby-Monterey Jack cheese**
- 1/3 **cup milk**
- 1/4 **cup shredded Parmesan cheese**
- 1/2 **teaspoon salt**
- 1/2 **teaspoon pepper**

TOPPING:
- 1 **cup (4 ounces) shredded Colby-Monterey Jack cheese**
- 1/2 **cup chopped green onions**
- 1/4 **cup shredded Parmesan cheese**

Place the russet potatoes in a Dutch oven and cover with water. Bring to a boil. Reduce heat; cover and cook for 15-20 minutes or until tender.

Meanwhile, place sweet potatoes in a large saucepan; cover with water. Bring to a boil. Reduce heat; cover and cook for 15-20 minutes or until tender. Drain; mash with half of the cream cheese and sour cream and all of the Colby cheese.

Drain russet potatoes; mash with the remaining cream cheese and sour cream. Add the milk, Parmesan cheese, salt and pepper; mix well.

Spread 2-2/3 cups russet potato mixture into each of two greased 11-in. x 7-in. baking dishes. Layer with 4 cups sweet potato mixture. Repeat layers. Spread with remaining russet potato mixture.

Bake, uncovered, at 350° for 15 minutes or until heated through. Combine the topping ingredients; sprinkle over casseroles. Bake 2-3 minutes longer or until cheese is melted. **YIELD:** 2 casseroles (10 servings each).

Springtime Barley

(Pictured below)

PREP/TOTAL TIME: 30 min.

While working as a sorority house mother, I occasionally filled in for the cook. The girls really liked low-fat dishes like this attractive medley.

—Sharon Helmick, Colfax, Washington

- 1 **small onion, chopped**
- 1 **medium carrot, chopped**
- 1 **tablespoon butter**
- 1 **cup quick-cooking barley**
- 2 **cups reduced-sodium chicken broth, *divided***
- 1/2 **pound fresh asparagus, trimmed and cut into 1-inch pieces**
- 1/4 **teaspoon dried marjoram**
- 1/8 **teaspoon pepper**
- 2 **tablespoons shredded Parmesan cheese**

In a large skillet, saute onion and carrot in butter until crisp-tender. Stir in the barley; cook and stir for 1 minute. Stir in 1 cup broth. Bring to a boil. Reduce heat; cook and stir until liquid is absorbed.

Add the asparagus. Cook for 15-20 minutes or until the barley is tender and the liquid is absorbed, stirring occasionally and adding more broth as needed. Stir in marjoram and pepper; sprinkle with Parmesan cheese. **YIELD:** 4 servings.

Fried Shoestring Carrots

(*Pictured below*)

PREP/TOTAL TIME: 25 min.

I came up with these savory snacks as a fun alternative to french fries. We like to serve them hot with ranch-style dressing as a dipping sauce.

—Kim Gammill, Raymondville, Texas

      2   **cups self-rising flour**
  1-1/2   **cups water**
      1   **teaspoon salt,** *divided*
    3/4   **teaspoon cayenne pepper,** *divided*
    1/2   **teaspoon pepper,** *divided*
     10   **cups shredded carrots**
Oil for frying

In a large bowl, whisk the flour, water, 1/2 teaspoon salt, 1/4 teaspoon cayenne and 1/4 teaspoon pepper until smooth. Stir in the carrots. In a small bowl, combine the remaining salt, cayenne and pepper; set aside.

In an electric skillet or deep-fat fryer, heat oil to 375°. Drop spoonfuls of carrot mixture, a few at a time, into oil; cook for 3-4 minutes or until golden brown, stirring frequently. Drain on paper towels; sprinkle with reserved seasoning mixture. **YIELD:** 10 servings.

EDITOR'S NOTE: As a substitute for each cup of self-rising flour, place 1-1/2 teaspoons baking powder and 1/2 teaspoon salt in a measuring cup. Add all-purpose flour to measure 1 cup.

So-Sweet Squash Pickles

(*Pictured above*)

PREP: 30 min. + chilling

These crisp, crunchy slices, seasoned with celery seed and mustard seed, have a sweet-sour taste that everyone is sure to relish! The colorful blend of yellow squash, sweet red pepper and chopped onion makes a beautiful presentation.

—Eleanor Sundman, Farmington, Connecticut

     3   **small yellow summer squash, thinly sliced**
     1   **medium onion, chopped**
     1   **large sweet red pepper, cut into 1/4-inch strips**
     1   **tablespoon salt**
     1   **cup sugar**
   3/4   **cup white vinegar**
   3/4   **teaspoon mustard seed**
   3/4   **teaspoon celery seed**
   1/4   **teaspoon ground mustard**

In a large bowl, combine the squash, onion, red pepper and salt. Cover and refrigerate for 1 hour; drain.

In a large saucepan, combine the remaining ingredients. Bring to a boil. Add squash mixture; return to a boil. Remove from the heat; cool.

Store in an airtight container in the refrigerator for at least 4 days before serving. May be stored in the refrigerator for up to 3 weeks. **YIELD:** 4 cups.

sweet maple syrup

There are four grades of maple syrup available to consumers. Grade A Light Amber is light and mild; Grade A Light Medium is a bit darker with more maple flavor; Grade A Dark Amber is even darker and more flavorful; and Grade B is very dark with a strong maple flavor. Deciding which one to use is simply personal preference.

Tomato and Corn Risotto

(Pictured below)

PREP: 15 min. **COOK:** 35 min.

This is one of my best-loved recipes because it uses items from the garden. Milk and Parmesan cheese give this side dish a creaminess everyone's sure to enjoy.

—*Angela Lively, Baxter, Tennessee*

        2-1/2 cups water
            2 cups milk
            3 tablespoons chicken broth
            1 large onion, finely chopped
            1 garlic clove, minced
            2 tablespoons butter
          3/4 cup uncooked arborio rice
        1-1/3 cups fresh corn (about 5 ears of corn)
            1 medium tomato, peeled, seeded and chopped
          1/2 cup grated Parmesan cheese
          1/2 cup fresh basil leaves, thinly sliced
          1/2 teaspoon salt

Pepper to taste

In a large saucepan, heat the water, milk and broth; keep warm.

In a large skillet, saute onion and garlic in butter until tender. Add rice; cook and stir for 2-3 minutes. Stir in 1 cup hot water mixture. Cook and stir until all liquid is absorbed.

Add remaining water mixture, 1/2 cup at a time, stirring constantly. Allow the liquid to absorb between additions. Cook until the risotto is creamy and the rice is almost tender. (Cooking time is about 20 minutes.) Stir in the remaining ingredients; heat through. **YIELD:** 5 servings.

Maple-Ginger Root Vegetables

(Pictured above and on page 62)

PREP: 35 min. **BAKE:** 45 min.

My family likes this recipe because it brings out the lovely flavors of the vegetables. It's a tasty way to introduce kids to turnips, rutabaga and parsnips—they love the drizzle of maple syrup!

—*Kelli Ritz, Innisfail, Alberta*

            5 medium parsnips, peeled and sliced
            5 small carrots, sliced
            3 medium turnips, peeled and cubed
            1 large sweet potato, peeled and cubed
            1 small rutabaga, peeled and cubed
            1 large sweet onion, cut into wedges
            1 small red onion, cut into wedges
            2 tablespoons olive oil
            1 tablespoon minced fresh gingerroot
            1 teaspoon salt
          1/2 teaspoon pepper
            1 cup maple syrup

Place the first seven ingredients in a large resealable plastic bag; add the oil, ginger, salt and pepper. Seal bag and shake to coat. Arrange the vegetables in a single layer in two 15-in. x 10-in. x 1-in. baking pans coated with cooking spray.

Bake, uncovered, at 425° for 25 minutes, stirring once. Drizzle with syrup. Bake 20-25 minutes longer or until the vegetables are tender, stirring once. **YIELD:** 24 servings.

Unfold pastry sheets on a lightly floured surface. Roll each pastry to 1/8-in. thickness; transfer each to an ungreased baking sheet. Sprinkle with pecan mixture. Arrange squash slices to within 1-1/2 in. of edges, alternating slices of butternut and acorn squash.

Fold up edges of pastry over filling, leaving centers uncovered. Brush pastry with egg. Dot squash with butter. Bake at 375° for 35-40 minutes or until golden brown. **YIELD:** 2 tarts (8 servings each).

EDITOR'S NOTE: This recipe was tested in a 1,100-watt microwave.

Mexicorn Grits

(*Pictured below*)

PREP: 20 min. **BAKE:** 35 min.

I grew up on grits and have fixed them various ways. I decided to put a new twist on them with this recipe, and my husband says it's a keeper. Even the leftovers are sensational.
—*Barbara Moorhead, Gaffney, South Carolina*

  4 cups milk
1/2 cup plus 1/3 cup butter, *divided*
  1 cup quick-cooking grits
  2 eggs
  1 can (11 ounces) Mexicorn, drained
  1 can (4 ounces) chopped green chilies
  1 cup (4 ounces) shredded Mexican cheese blend
  1 teaspoon salt
1/4 teaspoon white pepper
  1 cup shredded Parmesan cheese

In a large saucepan, bring the milk and 1/2 cup butter to a boil. Slowly stir in the grits. Reduce heat; cook and stir for 5-7 minutes.

In a small bowl, whisk the eggs. Stir a small amount of hot grits into eggs; return all to the pan, stirring constantly. Melt remaining butter; stir into grits. Add the corn, chilies, cheese, salt and pepper.

Transfer to a greased 2-qt. baking dish. Sprinkle with Parmesan cheese. Bake, uncovered, at 350° for 35-40 minutes or until a knife inserted near the center comes out clean. **YIELD:** 10 servings.

Rustic Squash Tarts

(*Pictured above and on page 62*)

PREP: 30 min. **BAKE:** 35 min.

This delicious side dish will surprise you. The rustic-looking, flaky pastry shells hold a sweet and spicy pecan layer under squash slices.
—*Ann Marie Moch, Kintyre, North Dakota*

  1 medium butternut squash, peeled, seeded and cut into 1/8-inch slices
  1 medium acorn squash, peeled, seeded and cut into 1/8-inch slices
  2 tablespoons water
1/4 cup olive oil
  1 tablespoon minced fresh thyme
  1 tablespoon minced fresh parsley
1/2 teaspoon salt
1/4 teaspoon pepper
1/2 cup all-purpose flour
1/2 cup ground pecans
  6 tablespoons sugar
1/2 teaspoon ground nutmeg
1/2 teaspoon ground cinnamon
  1 package (17.3 ounces) frozen puff pastry, thawed
  1 egg, lightly beaten
  2 tablespoons butter

In a large microwave-safe bowl, combine squash and water. Cover and cook on high for 5 minutes or until crisp-tender. Drain; transfer to a large resealable plastic bag. Add the oil, thyme, parsley, salt and pepper; seal bag and shake to coat. Set aside. In a small bowl, combine the flour, pecans, sugar, nutmeg and cinnamon; set aside.

2 packages (10 ounce *each*) frozen broccoli spears
1/4 cup butter, cubed
1 teaspoon cornstarch
1/2 cup orange juice
1 tablespoon grated orange peel

Cook broccoli according to package directions. Meanwhile, in a small saucepan, melt butter. Whisk in the cornstarch until smooth. Gradually stir in orange juice; add orange peel. Bring to a boil; cook and stir for 2 minutes or until thickened. Drain broccoli; drizzle with sauce. **YIELD:** 4 servings.

Curried Butternut Squash Kabobs

(Pictured below)

PREP: 30 min. + cooling **GRILL:** 10 min.

These baked squash cubes pick up a mouthwatering grilled taste along with a mild, curry-butter flavor. The pretty orange side dish adds interest to summer entrees.

—*Mary Relyea, Canastota, New York*

1 butternut squash (2 pounds), peeled, seeded and cut into 1-inch cubes
3 tablespoons butter, melted
1 teaspoon curry powder
1/4 teaspoon salt

Place squash in a greased 13-in. x 9-in. baking dish. Combine the butter, curry powder and salt; drizzle over squash and toss to coat.

Bake, uncovered, at 450° for 20-25 minutes or until tender and lightly browned, stirring twice. Cool on a wire rack.

Thread the butternut squash cubes onto 12 metal or soaked wooden skewers. Grill, covered, over medium heat for 3-5 minutes on each side or until heated through. **YIELD:** 12 servings.

Orange Rhubarb Spread

(Pictured above)

PREP: 5 min. **COOK:** 20 min. + standing

This tangy spread is easy to make and tastes especially good on hot, buttered cinnamon toast. The recipe makes enough to have on hand well beyond the rhubarb growing season.

—*Betty Nyenhuis, Oostburg, Wisconsin*

4 cups diced fresh *or* frozen rhubarb
2 cups water
1 can (6 ounces) frozen orange juice concentrate, thawed
1 package (1-3/4 ounces) powdered fruit pectin
4 cups sugar

In a large saucepan, bring rhubarb and water to a boil. Reduce heat; simmer, uncovered, for 7-8 minutes or until rhubarb is tender. Drain and reserve cooking liquid. Cool the rhubarb and liquid to room temperature.

Place the rhubarb in a blender; cover and process until pureed. Transfer to a 4-cup measuring cup; add enough reserved cooking liquid to measure 2-1/3 cups. Return to the saucepan.

Add orange juice concentrate and pectin; bring to a full rolling boil, stirring constantly. Stir in sugar. Return to a full rolling boil; boil and stir for 1 minute. Remove from the heat; skim off foam.

Pour into jars or freezer containers; cool to room temperature, about 1 hour. Cover and let stand overnight or until set, but not longer than 24 hours. Refrigerate or freeze. **YIELD:** 5 half-pints.

Broccoli with Orange Sauce

PREP/TOTAL TIME: 15 min.

As a busy working mother, I was looking for a simple broccoli recipe that didn't take very long to make. This one, adapted from an old cookbook, can be whipped up in a hurry. I think you'll find it complements any meal.

—*Edie DeSpain, Logan, Utah*

Grilled Asparagus Medley

(Pictured above)

PREP/TOTAL TIME: 25 min.

This colorful veggie recipe happened by accident. One evening, I didn't have room on the grill for all the things I wanted to prepare, so I threw two of the dishes together and came up with this medley. It goes well with any grilled meat.
—Pam Gaspers, Hastings, Nebraska

  1 pound fresh asparagus, trimmed
  1 *each* sweet red, yellow and green pepper, julienned
  1 cup sliced fresh mushrooms
  1 medium tomato, chopped
  1 medium onion, sliced
  1 can (2-1/4 ounces) sliced ripe olives, drained
  2 garlic cloves, minced
  2 tablespoons olive oil
  1 teaspoon minced fresh parsley
1/2 teaspoon salt
1/2 teaspoon pepper
1/4 teaspoon lemon-pepper seasoning
1/4 teaspoon dill weed

In a disposable foil pan, combine the vegetables, olives and garlic; drizzle with oil and toss to coat. Sprinkle with parsley, salt, pepper, lemon-pepper and dill; toss to coat.

  Grill, covered, over indirect medium heat for 20-25 minutes or until the vegetables are crisp-tender, stirring occasionally. **YIELD:** 8 servings.

Crumb-Coated Spaetzle

PREP/TOTAL TIME: 20 min.

Spaetzle is a cross between a curly noodle and a small dumpling. It's a traditional German accompaniment to all types of roasts.
—Patricia Rutherford, Winchester, Illinois

  2 cups all-purpose flour
  1 teaspoon salt
  2 eggs, lightly beaten
3/4 cup milk
1/2 cup dry bread crumbs
1/2 cup butter, melted

In a bowl, combine the flour and salt. Stir in the eggs and milk until smooth. Fill a large kettle three-fourths full with water; bring to a boil. With a rubber spatula, press dough through a colander into boiling water. Cook and stir gently for 4-5 minutes or until the spaetzle float and are tender.

  Combine the bread crumbs and butter. With a slotted spoon, transfer spaetzle to a large bowl; add crumb mixture and toss to coat. **YIELD:** 6 servings.

Fresh Corn Medley

PREP: 25 min. **COOK:** 20 min.

Your family will be sweet on this summery side dish that combines corn "off" the cob with green pepper, bacon and cheddar cheese.
—Susan Paden, Mexico, Missouri

  1 medium green pepper, chopped
  1 small onion, chopped
  3 tablespoons butter
  4 cups fresh corn (about 9 ears of corn)
1/4 cup hot water
  1 jar (2 ounces) diced pimientos, drained
  1 tablespoon honey
  1 teaspoon salt
Dash pepper
1/2 cup shredded cheddar cheese
  4 bacon strips, cooked and crumbled

In a large skillet, saute the green pepper and onion in butter until tender. Add the corn, water, pimientos, honey, salt and pepper.

  Bring to a boil. Reduce the heat; simmer, uncovered, for 8-10 minutes or until the corn is tender. Sprinkle with the cheese and bacon. **YIELD:** 5 servings.

simple secret

To remove kernels from corn, stand one end of the cob on a cutting board. Run a sharp knife down the cob, cutting deeply to remove whole kernels.

Double Corn Dressing

(Pictured above)

PREP: 25 min. **BAKE:** 40 min.

I have served this delicious dressing, made with a dry stuffing mix, to many family members and friends, and it always receives compliments. It is wonderful with pork or poultry.

—Berliene Grosh, Lakeland, Florida

- 1 package (12 ounces) unseasoned stuffing cubes
- 1 medium onion, finely chopped
- 1/2 *each* medium green, sweet yellow and red pepper, chopped
- 1 teaspoon garlic powder
- 1/2 teaspoon salt
- 1/4 teaspoon pepper
- 3 eggs, lightly beaten
- 1 can (15-1/4 ounces) whole kernel corn, drained
- 1 can (14-3/4 ounces) cream-style corn
- 1/2 cup butter, melted
- 1/2 to 1 cup chicken broth

In a large bowl, combine the stuffing, onion, sweet peppers and seasonings. Add eggs, corn and butter; toss to coat. Stir in enough broth to achieve desired moistness.

Spoon into a greased 3-qt. baking dish. Cover and bake at 350° for 25 minutes. Uncover; bake 15-20 minutes longer or until golden brown. **YIELD:** 16 servings.

Tangy Rhubarb Chutney

(Pictured below)

PREP: 25 min. **COOK:** 40 min. + chilling

My mother-in-law shared a great chutney recipe that I experiment with by changing the fruits. This version is a bit different, but I love the pear, onion and rhubarb combination. The longer it sets, the better it tastes!

—Barbara Estabrook, Rhinelander, Wisconsin

- 3 cups chopped fresh *or* frozen rhubarb
- 1 cup packed brown sugar
- 1 cup white balsamic vinegar
- 1 cup finely chopped onion
- 3/4 cup golden raisins
- 1 tablespoon Worcestershire sauce
- 2 teaspoons minced fresh gingerroot
- 1 teaspoon salt
- 3/4 teaspoon curry powder
- 1/4 teaspoon ground nutmeg
- 2 medium pears, peeled and diced
- 2 tablespoons minced fresh mint

In a large saucepan, combine the rhubarb, brown sugar, vinegar, onion, raisins, Worcestershire sauce, ginger, salt, curry and nutmeg. Cook and stir until mixture comes to a boil. Reduce heat; simmer, uncovered, for 25-30 minutes or until the rhubarb is tender, stirring occasionally.

Add pears. Simmer, uncovered, 10-15 minutes longer or until pears are tender. Cool to room temperature. Stir in mint. Transfer to a bowl. Cover and refrigerate for at least 6 hours before serving. May be stored in the refrigerator up to 1 week. **YIELD:** 4 cups.

Onion-Bacon Baby Carrots

(Pictured below)

PREP: 35 min. **BAKE:** 45 min.

I came up with this side dish for Thanksgiving, and it was a big hit. Now it has a place at our holiday table as well as impromptu get-togethers with family and friends.

—Diana Morrison Poole, Rock Hill, South Carolina

2	large sweet onions, sliced
1	tablespoon olive oil
2	pounds fresh baby carrots, halved lengthwise
1	teaspoon salt
1/4	teaspoon coarsely ground pepper
1/4	cup maple syrup
2	tablespoons butter
1/2	cup french-fried onions
8	bacon strips, cooked and crumbled
1/4	cup chopped green onions

In a large skillet, cook onions in oil over medium heat for 15-20 minutes or until golden brown, stirring frequently.

In a large bowl, combine the onions, carrots, salt and pepper; toss to combine. Transfer to a greased shallow 3-qt. baking dish. Cover and bake at 400° for 40-45 minutes or until tender.

Stir in the syrup and butter. Sprinkle with french-fried onions and bacon. Bake, uncovered, 5 minutes longer or until fried onions are browned. Sprinkle with green onions. Serve with a slotted spoon. **YIELD:** 8 servings.

Peas in Cheese Sauce

PREP/TOTAL TIME: 20 min.

Mom dresses up convenient frozen peas with this quick-to-fix cheese sauce that our family loves.

—June Blomquist, Eugene, Oregon

4-1/2	teaspoons butter
4-1/2	teaspoons all-purpose flour
1/4	teaspoon salt
1/8	teaspoon white pepper
1-1/2	cups milk
3/4	cup cubed process cheese (Velveeta)
2	packages (10 ounces *each*) frozen peas, thawed

In a large saucepan, melt the butter over low heat. Stir in the flour, salt and pepper until smooth. Gradually add the milk. Bring to a boil; cook and stir for 2 minutes or until thickened. Add the cheese; stir until melted. Stir in the peas; cook 1-2 minutes longer or until heated through. **YIELD:** 8 servings.

Smoky Grilled Corn

PREP: 25 min. **GRILL:** 10 min.

A friend and I cooked up this corn one evening when getting ready to grill. The buttery corn, with its sweet-spicy seasoning, won top honors over our favorite steaks.

—Linda Landers, Kalispell, Montana

2	tablespoons plus 1-1/2 teaspoons butter
1/2	cup honey
2	large garlic cloves, minced
2	tablespoons hot pepper sauce
1/2	teaspoon salt
1/4	teaspoon pepper
1/4	teaspoon paprika
6	medium ears sweet corn, husks removed

In a small saucepan, melt butter. Stir in the honey, garlic, pepper sauce and seasonings until blended; heat through. Brush over corn.

Coat grill rack with cooking spray before starting the grill. Grill, covered, over medium heat for 10-12 minutes or until the corn is tender, turning and basting occasionally. Serve corn with any remaining butter mixture. **YIELD:** 6 servings.

Baked Cranberry Sauce

PREP/TOTAL TIME: 30 min.

We live in cranberry country and are always looking for good recipes to use them. This sauce is a favorite.

—Kathy Olsen, Provincetown, Massachusetts

1	pound fresh *or* frozen cranberries, thawed
1-1/2	cups chopped pecans

1 cup flaked coconut
1 cup orange marmalade
3/4 cup sugar
1/2 cup water

In a large bowl, combine all of the ingredients. Pour into a greased 11-in. x 7-in. baking dish. Bake, uncovered, at 350° for 25-30 minutes or until cranberries are tender. Serve warm or cold. Refrigerate leftovers. **YIELD:** 10 servings.

Orange-Glazed Acorn Squash

(Pictured below)

PREP: 15 min. **BAKE:** 55 min.

This savory side dish gets its lovely taste from orange juice, orange zest and nutmeg. The smooth syrupy sauce is a great complement to the squash. I serve this on Christmas Eve to everyone's delight.

—Joyce Moynihan, Lakeville, Minnesota

4 small acorn squash
2 tablespoons butter
1 cup sugar
1 cup orange juice
1/3 cup orange juice concentrate
1/4 teaspoon salt
1/4 teaspoon ground nutmeg
1/4 teaspoon grated orange peel
1/8 teaspoon pepper

Cut squash in half; discard seeds. Place the squash cut side down in a 15-in. x 10-in. x 1-in. baking pan; add 1/2 in. of hot water. Bake, uncovered, at 350° for 30 minutes.

Meanwhile, in a saucepan, melt butter over medium heat. Stir in the remaining ingredients. Bring to a boil. Reduce heat to medium-low; cook, uncovered, for 30 minutes or until syrupy, stirring occasionally.

Drain water from baking pan; turn squash cut side up. Pour about 2 tablespoons orange glaze into each squash half. Bake 25-30 minutes longer or until squash is tender. **YIELD:** 8 servings.

Herbed Tomatoes and Green Beans

(Pictured above)

PREP/TOTAL TIME: 30 min.

Looking for new ways to dress up fresh-picked green beans? With just the right amount of oregano and parsley, this colorful side dish is seasoned to please.

—Maryalice Wood, Langley, British Columbia

3 green onions, coarsely chopped
2 garlic cloves, minced
2 teaspoons olive oil
1/2 pound fresh green beans, trimmed
1/4 cup chicken broth
2 medium tomatoes, diced
1 tablespoon minced fresh oregano
1 tablespoon minced fresh parsley
1/8 teaspoon salt
1/8 teaspoon pepper

In a small skillet, saute onions and garlic in oil until tender. Add the beans and the broth. Bring to a boil. Reduce heat; cover and simmer for 6-9 minutes or until crisp-tender.

Stir in tomatoes and seasonings; heat through. **YIELD:** 4 servings.

storing fresh herbs

To keep fresh herbs in tip-top shape, snip the ends off, then wash and dry them. A salad spinner works great to remove excess water. Wrap in damp paper towels and store in a resealable plastic bag. Refrigerate, preferably in a crisper drawer.

Creamy Vegetable Bow Tie Toss

(Pictured below)

PREP: 15 min. **BAKE:** 15 min.

You can use any kind of pasta for this creamy toss that is bursting with colorful veggies. It's been a mainstay for about 10 years now and is perfect for potlucks.

—*Lorraine Caland, Thunder Bay, Ontario*

- 12 ounces uncooked bow tie pasta
- 2 cups sliced fresh mushrooms
- 2 cups cut fresh asparagus (about 1/2 pound)
- 2 medium sweet onions, finely chopped
- 2 medium carrots, sliced
- 2 medium zucchini, halved and sliced
- 1 medium sweet yellow pepper, julienned
- 1/3 cup butter, cubed
- 2/3 cup chicken broth
- 1 cup (8 ounces) sour cream
- 1/2 cup prepared ranch dip
- 1/2 cup grated Parmesan cheese
- 1/4 cup minced fresh parsley
- 2 tablespoons minced fresh basil
- 1/2 teaspoon salt

Cook pasta according to package directions. Meanwhile, in a large skillet, saute vegetables in butter for 5 minutes. Stir in broth; cook for 3 minutes or until vegetables are crisp-tender.

In a small bowl, combine the sour cream, dip, Parmesan cheese, parsley, basil and salt; stir into skillet and heat through. Drain pasta; add to the skillet and toss to coat. **YIELD:** 12 servings.

Mango Cranberry Sauce

(Pictured above and on cover)

PREP/TOTAL TIME: 25 min.

We got this recipe from a friend. It's definitely worth the effort if you want to wow your gang at Thanksgiving. The leftovers are delicious with chicken or ham.

—*Robert & Rebecca Littlejohn, Meadow Vista, California*

- 1-1/2 cups whole-berry cranberry sauce
- 3 tangerines, peeled, seeded and chopped
- 1 medium mango, peeled and diced
- 1 cup diced fresh pineapple
- 1/4 cup finely chopped red onion
- 1/4 cup minced fresh cilantro
- 1 jalapeno pepper, seeded and finely chopped

In a large bowl, combine all the ingredients. Cover and refrigerate until serving. **YIELD:** 4-1/2 cups.

EDITOR'S NOTE: When cutting hot peppers, disposable gloves are recommended. Avoid touching your face.

Garlic-Pepper Rub

PREP/TOTAL TIME: 5 min.

This rub adds a tasty mix of garlic, pepper and lemon to any burger. It's a fantastic way to spice up your grilling experience.

—*Ann Marie Moch, Kintyre, North Dakota*

- 6 tablespoons lemon-pepper seasoning
- 2 tablespoons dried thyme
- 2 tablespoons paprika
- 2 teaspoons garlic powder
- 1 teaspoon sugar
- 1/2 teaspoon salt
- 1/4 teaspoon ground coriander
- 1/8 teaspoon ground cumin
- 1/8 teaspoon cayenne pepper

In a large bowl, combine all ingredients; store in a covered container. Rub over meat or poultry; let stand for at least 30 minutes before grilling or broiling. **YIELD:** 2/3 cup.

Spaghetti Squash Supreme

(Pictured below)

PREP/TOTAL TIME: 30 min.

I often use the empty squash shells as serving dishes for this unique side dish. The bacon complements the squash and Swiss cheese combination nicely. It's attractive and fun to eat!

—*Jean Williams, Stillwater, Oklahoma*

- 1 large spaghetti squash (3-1/2 pounds)
- 4 bacon strips, diced
- 3 tablespoons butter
- 1 tablespoon brown sugar
- 1/2 teaspoon salt
- 1/4 teaspoon pepper
- 1/2 cup shredded Swiss cheese

Cut squash in half lengthwise; discard seeds. Place one squash half cut side down on a microwave-safe plate. Cover and microwave on high for 8 minutes or until easily pierced with a fork, turning once. Repeat with second squash half. When cool enough to handle, scoop out squash, separating strands with a fork; set aside.

In a large skillet, cook bacon over medium heat until crisp. Using a slotted spoon, remove to paper towels; drain, reserving drippings. Add the butter, brown sugar, salt and pepper to the drippings. Stir in squash and bacon; heat through. Remove from the heat; stir in cheese just until blended. Serve immediately. **YIELD:** 4 servings.

Loaded Red Potato Casserole

(Pictured above)

PREP: 25 min. **BAKE:** 20 min.

This potato casserole has the same flavor of the potato skins you can order as a restaurant appetizer. It's great to serve at casual dinner parties.

—*Charlane Gathy, Lexington, Kentucky*

- 16 small red potatoes
- 1/2 cup milk
- 1/4 cup butter, cubed
- 1/2 teaspoon pepper
- 1/8 teaspoon salt
- 1-1/2 cups (6 ounces) shredded cheddar cheese, *divided*
- 1/2 cup crumbled cooked bacon
- 1 cup (8 ounces) sour cream
- 2 tablespoons minced chives

Place the potatoes in a Dutch oven and cover with water. Bring to a boil. Reduce heat; cover and cook for 15-20 minutes or until tender. Drain.

Mash potatoes with the milk, butter, pepper and salt. Transfer to a greased 13-in. x 9-in. baking dish. Sprinkle with 1 cup cheese and bacon.

Dollop with sour cream; sprinkle with chives and remaining cheese. Bake, uncovered, at 350° for 20-25 minutes or until cheese is melted. **YIELD:** 9 servings.

Swiss-Almond Floret Bake

(Pictured above)

PREP: 20 min. **BAKE:** 20 min.

This wonderful vegetable dish, with a touch of curry, has been served in our home for the past decade on Thanksgiving and Christmas. Even folks who say they don't like broccoli or cauliflower enjoy this casserole. It's one of my favorites!

—Sandy Christopherson, Bradford, Ontario

  2 cups fresh cauliflowerets
  2 cups chopped fresh broccoli
  2 tablespoons butter
  2 tablespoons all-purpose flour
1-1/4 cups milk
  1/2 cup shredded Swiss cheese
    1 tablespoon apricot jam
  1/4 teaspoon curry powder
  1/8 teaspoon salt
  1/8 teaspoon pepper
TOPPING:
  1/2 cup dry bread crumbs
  1/4 cup sliced almonds, toasted
    2 tablespoons butter, melted

In a large saucepan, bring 1 in. of water, cauliflower and broccoli to a boil. Cover and cook for 3 minutes. Drain and pat dry.

In another large saucepan, melt butter. Stir in flour until smooth; gradually add milk. Bring to a boil; cook and stir for 2 minutes or until thickened. Reduce heat; stir in the cheese, jam, curry, salt and pepper. Cook and stir over low heat until cheese is melted. Remove from the heat.

Place the cauliflower and broccoli in a greased 1-1/2-qt. baking dish. Top with cheese sauce. Combine topping ingredients; sprinkle over sauce.

Bake, uncovered, at 350° for 20-25 minutes or until vegetables are tender. **YIELD:** 4-6 servings.

Green Beans in Lemon Chiffon Sauce

(Pictured below and on page 62)

PREP: 15 min. **BAKE:** 25 min.

A light citrus sauce drapes the garden-fresh green beans in this delicious side dish. It goes well with chicken, turkey or a roast at meals anytime of year.

—Marian Platt, Sequim, Washington

    3 pounds fresh green beans, trimmed
    3 cups water
    1 tablespoon cornstarch
1-1/2 cups chicken broth
    6 eggs, lightly beaten
  1/4 cup grated Parmesan cheese
  1/2 cup butter, cubed
  1/4 cup lemon juice
    2 teaspoons minced fresh parsley
    2 teaspoons chopped green onion

Place beans in a Dutch oven and cover with water. Bring to a boil. Cover and cook for 8-10 minutes or until crisp-tender.

Meanwhile, in a large saucepan, combine the cornstarch, broth, and Parmesan cheese until smooth. Cook and stir over medium-high heat until thickened and bubbly. Reduce heat; cook and stir 2 minutes longer. Remove from the heat. Stir a small amount of hot filling into eggs; return all to pan, stirring constantly. Bring to a gentle boil; cook and stir 2 minutes longer. Add butter, one piece at a time, whisking after each addition until butter is melted.

Remove from the heat. Gently stir in the lemon juice, parsley and onion. Drain beans; top with sauce. **YIELD:** 12 servings.

In a Dutch oven, cook bacon over medium heat until crisp. Using a slotted spoon, remove to paper towels to drain.

In the drippings, saute the brussels sprouts and onion until crisp-tender. Add the vinegar, sugar, salt, mustard and pepper. Bring to a boil. Reduce heat; cover and simmer for 4-5 minutes or until sprouts are tender. Stir in bacon. **YIELD:** 16 servings.

O'Larry's Skillet Potatoes

(*Pictured below*)

PREP: 15 min. **BAKE:** 15 min.

My husband, Larry, uses all fresh ingredients when he prepares his famous potatoes. These zippy potatoes have colorful bits of red pepper.

—*Kerry Barnett-Amundson, Ocean Park, Washington*

> 2 pounds potatoes, cut into 1/2-inch cubes
> 1 medium onion, finely chopped
> 1 medium sweet red pepper, chopped
> 2 garlic cloves, minced
> 1 teaspoon Caribbean jerk seasoning
> 1 teaspoon salt
> 1/4 cup olive oil

Place the potatoes in a large saucepan and cover with water. Bring to a boil. Reduce heat; cover and simmer for 5-10 minutes or until almost tender. Drain.

In a large skillet, saute the onion, red pepper, garlic, jerk seasoning, salt and potatoes in oil until potatoes are golden brown and vegetables are tender. **YIELD:** 10 servings.

Peppery Parsnip Fries

(*Pictured above*)

PREP: 15 min. **BAKE:** 20 min.

Looking for creative ways to use parsnips? These crispy bites are a healthier take on popular french fries.

—*Sandy Abrams, Greenville, New York*

> 8 medium parsnips, peeled
> 1 tablespoon olive oil
> 1/4 cup grated Parmesan cheese
> 1/2 teaspoon salt
> 1/4 teaspoon pepper
> 1/8 teaspoon ground nutmeg

Cut the parsnips lengthwise into 2-1/2-in. x 1/2-in. sticks. In a large resealable plastic bag, combine oil, Parmesan cheese, salt, pepper and nutmeg. Add parsnips, a few sticks at a time, and shake to coat.

Line two 15-in. x 10-in. x 1-in. baking pans with foil; coat the foil with cooking spray. Place parsnips in a single layer in pans. Bake at 425° for 20-25 minutes or until tender, turning several times. **YIELD:** 8 servings.

Sweet & Sour Brussels Sprouts

PREP: 10 min. **BAKE:** 25 min.

This side dish has a nice sweet-and-sour balance, and bacon adds a tasty accent. Sprout lovers will definitely approve of this flavorful treatment.

—*Barbara McCalley, Allison Park, Pennsylvania*

> 1/2 pound sliced bacon, diced
> 4 packages (16 ounces *each*) frozen brussels sprouts, thawed
> 1 medium onion, finely chopped
> 1/3 cup cider vinegar
> 3 tablespoons sugar
> 1-1/2 teaspoons salt
> 1/2 teaspoon ground mustard
> 1/8 teaspoon pepper

The centerpiece of any home-style menu is always the main course...and you'll have the perfect one for any occasion when you turn to the mouthwatering beef, poultry, pork, seafood and meatless creations in this chapter.

main dishes

Orange Chicken with Sweet Potatoes..............84
Spiral Ham with Cranberry Glaze.......................84
Asparagus Sausage Crepes.................................85
Apple-Stuffed French Toast................................85
Dad's Swedish Meatballs.....................................86
Thai Beef Stir-Fry...86
Creamy Ham and Macaroni................................87
Pot Roast with Gravy...87
Bavarian Pork Loin...88
Buckwheat Brunch Crepes.................................88
Butternut Turkey Bake...89
Vegetarian Pasta Sauce......................................89
Pecan Apple Pancakes..89
Chicken and Asparagus Kabobs.......................90
Tasty Pork Ribs..90
Brined Roasting Chicken.....................................91
Waldorf Stuffed Ham...91
Tenderloin in Puff Pastry.....................................92
Vegetarian Stuffed Peppers...............................92
Spicy Nacho Bake...93
Pretty Penne Ham Skillet....................................93
Grilled Asparagus Pizzas....................................94
Curried Beef with Dumplings.............................94
Cornmeal Ham Cakes...95
Shrimp Pasta Primavera.......................................95
Maple-Glazed Ribs..96
Asian Chicken Thighs...96
Indiana Swiss Steak..97
Pecan Chicken with Chutney.............................97
Fiesta Lasagna...98
Lime Shrimp with Asparagus.............................98
Salmon with Polenta..99
Macadamia-Crusted Tilapia................................99
Giant Calzone..100
Stuffed Squash for Two.....................................100
Pepperoni Spinach Quiche...............................101
Steaks with Cucumber Sauce..........................101
Mozzarella-Stuffed Meatballs.........................102
Old-Fashioned Chicken Potpie........................102
Meat Loaf Wellington...103

Grilled Raspberry Chicken.................................103
Pineapple-Stuffed Cornish Hens......................104
Cranberry Ham Loaf...104
Butterflied Pork Chop Dinner..........................105
Chicken Pepper Stir-Fry.....................................105
Sunday Chicken Stew...106
Meatless Mexican Lasagna...............................106
Next Day Turkey Primavera..............................107
Asparagus Crab Omelets..................................107
Turkey Enchiladas...107
Prosciutto-Stuffed Meat Loaf..........................108
Spaghetti Squash with Red Sauce...................108
Braised Short Ribs..109
Bacon-Cheese Topped Chicken.......................109
Cube Steaks Parmigiana....................................110
Pizza Margherita...110
Rosemary Leg of Lamb......................................111
Spinach Crab Chicken..111
Turkey Potpies...112
Curried Shrimp and Apples..............................112
Sweet and Tender Cabbage Rolls....................113
Chicken & Tomato Risotto................................113
Meat Loaf Gyros..114
Creamed Chicken over Biscuits.......................114
Taco Meat Loaves...115
Asian Pot Roast..115
Crab-Stuffed Sole...116
Tropical Lime Chicken..116
Crescent-Topped Turkey Amandine................117
Savory Pumpkin Ravioli.....................................117
Shrimp Quesadillas..118
Artichoke Ham Puffs..118
Reuben Crescent Bake.......................................119
Thai Chicken Fettuccine.....................................119
Rolled-Up Turkey..120
Caesar Orange Roughy......................................120
Brisket in a Bag...121
Turkey Chop Suey...121
Asparagus Beef Stir-Fry.....................................121

PICTURED CLOCKWISE FROM UPPER LEFT: Ceasar Orange Roughy (page 120), Sunday Chicken Stew (page 106), Vegetarian Stuffed Peppers (page 92) and Turkey Potpies (page 112).

Orange Chicken with Sweet Potatoes

(Pictured below)

PREP: 25 min. **COOK:** 3-1/2 hours

Orange peel and pineapple juice lend a fruity flavor to this super chicken and sweet potato combo. Served over rice, this appealing entree is bound to win you lots of praise.

—Vicki Smith, Okeechobee, Florida

- 3 medium sweet potatoes, peeled and sliced
- 2/3 cup plus 3 tablespoons all-purpose flour, *divided*
- 1 teaspoon salt
- 1 teaspoon onion powder
- 1 teaspoon ground nutmeg
- 1 teaspoon ground cinnamon
- 1 teaspoon pepper
- 4 boneless skinless chicken breast halves (5 ounces *each*)
- 2 tablespoons butter
- 1 can (10-3/4 ounces) condensed cream of chicken soup, undiluted
- 3/4 cup unsweetened pineapple juice
- 2 teaspoons brown sugar
- 1 teaspoon grated orange peel
- 1/2 pound sliced fresh mushrooms

Hot cooked rice

Layer sweet potatoes in a 3-qt. slow cooker. In a large resealable plastic bag, combine 2/3 cup flour and seasonings; add the chicken, one piece at a time, and shake to coat.

In a large skillet over medium heat, cook the chicken in butter for 3 minutes on each side or until lightly browned. Arrange chicken over sweet potatoes.

Place remaining flour in a small bowl. Stir in the soup, pineapple juice, brown sugar and orange peel until blended. Add mushrooms; pour over chicken.

Cover and cook on low for 3-1/2 to 4 hours or until a meat thermometer reads 170° and the potatoes are tender. Serve with rice. **YIELD:** 4 servings.

Spiral Ham with Cranberry Glaze

(Pictured above)

PREP: 15 min. **BAKE:** 3 hours

The sweet, tangy glaze that complements this ham looks so pretty, and the cranberry flavor pairs well with the meat. It's been a tradition in my home for as long as I can remember.

—Pattie Prescott, Manchester, New Hampshire

- 1 fully cooked spiral-sliced ham (8 pounds)
- 1 can (16 ounces) whole-berry cranberry sauce
- 1 package (12 ounces) fresh *or* frozen cranberries
- 1 jar (12 ounces) red currant jelly
- 1 cup light corn syrup
- 1/2 teaspoon ground ginger

Place ham on a rack in a shallow roasting pan. Cover and bake at 325° for 2-1/2 hours.

Meanwhile, for glaze, combine the remaining ingredients in a saucepan. Bring to a boil. Reduce heat; simmer, uncovered, until the cranberries pop, stirring occasionally. Remove from the heat; set aside.

Uncover the ham; bake 30 minutes longer or until a meat thermometer reads 140°, basting twice with 1-1/2 cups glaze. Serve the remaining glaze with ham. **YIELD:** 12-16 servings.

Asparagus Sausage Crepes
(Pictured below)

PREP: 20 min. **BAKE:** 20 min.

This was my favorite recipe when I was growing up in western Michigan, where asparagus is a big spring crop. With its sausage-and-cheese filling, tender asparagus and rich sour cream topping, this pretty dish will impress guests.

—Lisa Hanson, Glenview, Illinois

- 1 pound bulk pork sausage
- 1 small onion, chopped
- 1 package (3 ounces) cream cheese, cubed
- 1/2 cup shredded Monterey Jack cheese
- 1/4 teaspoon dried marjoram
- 1 cup all-purpose flour
- 1/2 teaspoon salt
- 1 cup milk
- 3 eggs
- 1 tablespoon canola oil
- 32 fresh asparagus spears (about 1 pound), trimmed

TOPPING:
- 1/4 cup butter, softened
- 1/2 cup sour cream

In a large skillet, cook the sausage and onion over medium heat until the sausage is no longer pink; drain. Stir in cream cheese, Monterey Jack cheese and marjoram; set aside.

In a bowl, combine the flour and salt. Add the milk, eggs and oil; mix well. Heat a lightly greased 8-in. nonstick skillet; pour 2 tablespoons batter into the center of skillet. Lift and tilt the pan to evenly coat bottom. Cook until the top appears dry; turn and cook for 15-20 seconds. Remove to a wire rack.

Repeat with remaining batter, adding oil to skillet as needed. When cool, stack crepes with waxed paper or paper towels in between.

Spoon 2 tablespoons of the sausage mixture onto the center of each crepe. Top with two asparagus spears. Roll up; place in two greased 13-in. x 9-in. baking dishes. Cover and bake at 375° for 15 minutes. Combine the butter and sour cream; spoon over crepes. Bake for 5 minutes longer or until heated through. **YIELD:** 8 servings.

Apple-Stuffed French Toast
(Pictured above)

PREP: 20 min. + chilling **BAKE:** 35 min.

This is a great breakfast to make ahead for the holidays or even Sunday brunch. I run a bed-and-breakfast with a tea room cafe, and this recipe is often requested by customers.

—Kay Clark, Lawrenceburg, Kentucky

- 1 cup packed brown sugar
- 1/2 cup butter, cubed
- 2 tablespoons light corn syrup
- 1 cup chopped pecans
- 12 slices Italian bread (1/2 inch thick)
- 2 large tart apples, peeled and thinly sliced
- 6 eggs
- 1-1/2 cups milk
- 1-1/2 teaspoons ground cinnamon
- 1 teaspoon vanilla extract
- 1/4 teaspoon salt
- 1/4 teaspoon ground nutmeg

CARAMEL SAUCE:
- 1/2 cup packed brown sugar
- 1/4 cup butter, cubed
- 1 tablespoon light corn syrup

In a small saucepan, combine the brown sugar, butter and corn syrup; cook and stir over medium heat until thickened. Pour into a greased 13-in. x 9-in. baking dish; top with half of the pecans, a single layer of bread and then remaining pecans. Arrange apples and remaining bread over the top.

In a large bowl, whisk the eggs, milk, cinnamon, vanilla, salt and nutmeg. Pour over bread. Cover and refrigerate overnight.

Remove from the refrigerator 30 minutes before baking. Bake, uncovered, at 350° for 35-40 minutes or until lightly browned.

For the sauce, in a small saucepan, combine the brown sugar, butter and corn syrup. Cook and stir over medium heat until thickened. Serve with French toast. **YIELD:** 6 servings.

Dad's Swedish Meatballs

(*Pictured above*)

PREP: 30 min. **COOK:** 35 min.

My father used to make these tender meatballs every year for Christmas when I was a kid. Now I carry on the tradition, and everyone still loves them.
—Michelle Lizotte, Cumberland, Rhode Island

        1 egg, lightly beaten
    1/2 cup milk
        1 cup soft bread crumbs
    1/2 cup finely chopped onion
        1 teaspoon salt
    1/4 teaspoon ground nutmeg
    1/4 teaspoon pepper
        1 pound ground beef
    1/2 pound ground pork
    1/4 cup butter, cubed
DILL CREAM SAUCE:
        2 tablespoons all-purpose flour
        1 cup heavy whipping cream
        1 cup beef broth
        1 teaspoon salt
    1/2 teaspoon dill seed

In a large bowl, combine the first seven ingredients. Crumble beef and pork over mixture and mix well. Shape into 1-1/2-in. balls. In a large skillet, cook meatballs in butter in batches until no longer pink. Remove and keep warm.

In a small bowl, combine the sauce ingredients until blended. Stir into skillet. Bring to a boil; cook and stir for 2 minutes or until thickened. Serve with meatballs. **YIELD:** 6 servings.

Thai Beef Stir-Fry

(*Pictured below*)

PREP: 20 min. **COOK:** 20 min.

A distinctive peanut sauce complements this colorful combination of tender sirloin strips, cauliflower, carrots, broccoli and mushrooms. I like to serve it over spaghetti, but you could also use fried noodles.
—Janice Fehr, Austin, Manitoba

    1/2 cup packed brown sugar
        2 tablespoons cornstarch
        2 cups beef broth
    1/3 cup soy sauce
        1 teaspoon onion powder
        1 teaspoon garlic powder
        1 teaspoon ground ginger
    1/4 teaspoon hot pepper sauce
        2 pounds boneless beef sirloin steak,
            cut into thin strips
        6 tablespoons olive oil, *divided*
        2 cups fresh cauliflowerets
  1-1/2 cups julienned carrots
        4 cups fresh broccoli florets
        2 cups sliced fresh mushrooms
    1/4 cup peanut butter
Hot cooked spaghetti
    1/2 cup chopped peanuts

In a bowl, combine the first eight ingredients until smooth; set aside. In a large skillet or wok, stir-fry beef in 3 tablespoons oil until meat is no longer pink. Remove and keep warm.

In the same skillet, stir-fry the cauliflower and carrots in the remaining oil for 5 minutes. Add broccoli; stir-fry for 7 minutes. Add mushrooms; stir-fry 6-8 minutes longer or until the vegetables are crisp-tender.

Stir broth mixture and add to the pan. Bring to a boil; cook and stir for 2 minutes or until thickened. Reduce heat; add beef and peanut butter. Cook and stir over medium heat until peanut butter is blended. Serve over spaghetti. Sprinkle with peanuts. **YIELD:** 6 servings.

Pot Roast with Gravy

(Pictured below)

PREP: 30 min. **COOK:** 7-1/2 hours

My family enjoys this tangy, slow-cooked beef roast with gravy. We always hope for leftovers so we can have tasty sandwiches the next day.

—*Deborah Dailey, Vancouver, Washington*

- 1 beef bottom round roast (5 pounds)
- 6 tablespoons balsamic vinegar, *divided*
- 1 teaspoon salt
- 1/2 teaspoon garlic powder
- 1/4 teaspoon pepper
- 2 tablespoons canola oil
- 3 garlic cloves, minced
- 4 bay leaves
- 1 large onion, thinly sliced
- 3 teaspoons beef bouillon granules
- 1/2 cup boiling water
- 1 can (10-3/4 ounces) condensed cream of mushroom soup, undiluted
- 4 to 5 tablespoons cornstarch
- 1/4 cup cold water

Cut roast in half; rub with 2 tablespoons vinegar. Combine the salt, garlic powder and pepper; rub over meat. In a large skillet, brown roast in oil on all sides. Transfer to a 5-qt. slow cooker.

Place the garlic, bay leaves and onion on the roast. In a small bowl, dissolve bouillon in boiling water; stir in soup and remaining vinegar. Slowly pour over the roast. Cover and cook on low for 7-8 hours or until meat is tender.

Remove roast; keep warm. Discard bay leaves. Whisk cornstarch and cold water until smooth; stir into cooking juices. Cover and cook on high for 30 minutes or until gravy is thickened. Slice roast; return to slow cooker and heat through. **YIELD:** 10 servings.

Creamy Ham and Macaroni

(Pictured above)

PREP: 20 min. **BAKE:** 20 min.

The original comfort food, macaroni and cheese gets a makeover with the addition of cubed ham and grated Parmesan. Kids will love it!

—*Christy Looper, Colorado Springs, Colorado*

- 2 cups uncooked elbow macaroni
- 1/4 cup butter, cubed
- 1/4 cup all-purpose flour
- 2 cups milk
- 4 teaspoons chicken bouillon granules
- 1/4 teaspoon pepper
- 2 cups (8 ounces) shredded cheddar cheese, *divided*
- 1-1/2 cups cubed fully cooked ham
- 1/4 cup grated Parmesan cheese

Cook the macaroni according to the package directions; drain and set aside. In a large saucepan, melt the butter over low heat; whisk in flour until smooth. Whisk in the milk, bouillon and pepper. Bring to a boil; cook and stir for 2 minutes or until thickened. Remove from the heat. Stir in 1 cup cheddar cheese, ham, Parmesan cheese and macaroni.

Transfer to a greased 2-qt. baking dish. Sprinkle with remaining cheddar cheese. Bake, uncovered, at 350° for 20-25 minutes or until bubbly. Let stand for 5 minutes before serving. **YIELD:** 6 servings.

Bavarian Pork Loin

(Pictured below)

PREP: 25 min. **COOK:** 6 hours

I received the recipe for this tender pork roast from an aunt, who made it all the time. What a delicious taste sensation with sauerkraut, carrots, onions and apples.

—Edie DeSpain, Logan, Utah

- 1 boneless whole pork loin roast (3 pounds)
- 1 can (14 ounces) Bavarian sauerkraut, rinsed and drained
- 1-3/4 cups chopped carrots
- 1 large onion, finely chopped
- 1/2 cup unsweetened apple juice
- 2 teaspoons dried parsley flakes
- 3 large tart apples, peeled and quartered

Cut the roast in half; place in a 5-qt. slow cooker. In a small bowl, combine the sauerkraut, carrots, onion, apple juice and parsley; spoon over roast. Cover and cook on low for 4 hours.

Add the apples to slow cooker. Cover and cook 2 to 2-1/2 hours longer or until a meat thermometer reads 160°. Remove roast; let stand for 5 minutes before slicing. Serve with sauerkraut mixture. **YIELD:** 10 servings.

Buckwheat Brunch Crepes

(Pictured above)

PREP: 20 min. + standing **COOK:** 15 min.

My husband and I enjoy these delectable crepes with sweet berry sauce and cream on Saturday mornings. We even have them for dinner with sausage and eggs. They're considered a special treat here, especially when served with maple syrup.

—Sharon Dyck, Roxton Falls, Quebec

- 5 tablespoons heavy whipping cream
- 1/2 cup sour cream
- 1/2 cup milk
- 2 eggs
- 1/3 cup all-purpose flour
- 3 tablespoons buckwheat flour *or* whole wheat flour
- 1/2 teaspoon salt

BERRY SAUCE:
- 1/2 cup sugar
- 1 tablespoon cornstarch

Dash salt
- 1/2 cup water
- 1/3 cup fresh blueberries
- 1/3 cup fresh raspberries
- 4-1/2 teaspoons butter, *divided*
- 1 teaspoon lemon juice

In a small bowl, beat the whipping cream until stiff peaks form; fold into sour cream. Cover and refrigerate.

In a small bowl, combine milk and eggs. Combine the flours and salt; add to milk mixture and mix well. Let stand for 30 minutes.

Meanwhile, for the sauce, in a small saucepan, combine the sugar, cornstarch and salt; stir in water until smooth. Bring to a boil; cook and stir for 1-2 minutes or until thickened. Add berries; cook over medium-low heat until berries burst. Add 1-1/2 teaspoons butter and lemon juice, stirring until butter is melted. Set aside and keep warm.

Melt 1 teaspoon butter in an 8-in. nonstick skillet; pour 2 tablespoons batter into the center of skillet. Lift and tilt pan to evenly coat bottom. Cook until top appears dry; turn and cook 15-20 seconds longer. Remove to a wire rack. Repeat with remaining batter, adding butter to skillet as needed. Stack crepes with waxed paper or paper towels in between and keep warm. Serve crepes with berry sauce and cream mixture. **YIELD:** about 6 crepes.

Butternut Turkey Bake

PREP: 70 min. **BAKE:** 25 min.

Butternut squash adds a little sweetness to this comforting casserole. You can use leftover turkey and even replace the salad croutons with leftover stuffing, if you wish.

—Mary Ann Dell, Phoenixville, Pennsylvania

- 1 medium butternut squash (about 2-1/2 pounds)
- 3/4 cup finely chopped onion
- 2 tablespoons butter
- 2 cups seasoned salad croutons
- 1/2 teaspoon salt
- 1/2 teaspoon poultry seasoning
- 1/2 teaspoon pepper
- 2 cups cubed cooked turkey
- 1 cup chicken broth
- 1/2 cup shredded cheddar cheese

Cut squash in half; discard seeds. Place cut side down in a 15-in. x 10-in. x 1-in. baking pan; add 1/2 in. of hot water. Bake, uncovered, at 350° for 45 minutes.

Drain water from pan; turn squash cut side up. Bake 10-15 minutes longer or until tender. Scoop out pulp; mash and set aside.

In a large skillet, saute onion in butter until tender. Stir in croutons, salt, poultry seasoning and pepper. Cook 2-3 minutes longer or until croutons are toasted. Stir in squash, turkey and broth; heat through.

Transfer to a greased 1-1/2-qt. baking dish. Bake, uncovered, at 350° for 20 minutes. Sprinkle with cheese. Bake 5-10 minutes longer or until edges are bubbly and cheese is melted. **YIELD:** 4 servings.

Vegetarian Pasta Sauce

PREP: 35 min. **COOK:** 2 hours

Loaded with fresh vegetables and herbs, this hearty, meatless pasta sauce is a perfect way for gardeners to make terrific use of their harvest.

—Jerry Tamburino, Sacramento, California

- 3 medium onions, chopped
- 1 medium green pepper, chopped
- 1 medium sweet red pepper, chopped
- 5 garlic cloves, minced
- 2 tablespoons olive oil
- 3 medium zucchini, chopped
- 3 medium yellow summer squash, chopped
- 3 medium tomatoes, chopped
- 1 medium eggplant, peeled and cubed
- 1/2 pound sliced fresh mushrooms
- 2 cans (28 ounces *each*) Italian crushed tomatoes
- 1 can (6 ounces) tomato paste
- 2 cans (2-1/4 ounces *each*) sliced ripe olives, drained
- 1/4 cup minced fresh basil
- 3 tablespoons minced fresh oregano
- 2 tablespoons minced fresh rosemary
- 2 teaspoons Italian seasoning
- 1-1/2 teaspoons salt
- 1/2 teaspoon pepper

In a Dutch oven, saute the onions, peppers and garlic in olive oil until tender. Add the zucchini, summer squash, tomatoes, eggplant and mushrooms; cook and stir for 5 minutes.

Stir in the remaining ingredients. Bring to a boil. Reduce heat; simmer, uncovered, for 1-1/2 to 2 hours or until sauce is thickened. **YIELD:** 14 servings (1 cup each).

Pecan Apple Pancakes

(Pictured below)

PREP: 15 min. **COOK:** 10 min./batch

Weekend breakfasts are a big deal here in Texas, and these sweet, well-spiced pancakes make any breakfast special. So put on your cooking apron and invite the neighbors over!

—Sharon Richardson, Dallas, Texas

- 2 cups all-purpose flour
- 1 cup sugar
- 2 teaspoons baking powder
- 1 teaspoon baking soda
- 1 teaspoon ground cinnamon
- 1/2 teaspoon salt
- 1/2 teaspoon ground ginger
- 1/2 teaspoon ground mace
- 1/2 teaspoon ground cloves
- 2 eggs
- 1-3/4 cups buttermilk
- 3 tablespoons canola oil
- 1-3/4 cups shredded peeled apples
- 1/2 cup chopped pecans

In a large bowl, combine the first nine ingredients. In another bowl, combine the eggs, buttermilk and oil; stir into dry ingredients just until blended. Stir in apples and pecans.

Pour batter by 1/4 cupfuls onto a greased griddle over medium-low heat. Turn when bubbles form on top; cook until second side is golden brown. **YIELD:** 1-1/2 dozen.

Drain and discard marinade. In a large bowl, toss the asparagus with olive oil and salt. On six metal or soaked wooden skewers, alternately thread one chicken piece and two asparagus pieces.

Grill, covered, over medium heat for 4-5 minutes on each side or until chicken juices run clear and asparagus is crisp-tender. Serve with dipping sauce. **YIELD:** 6 servings.

Tasty Pork Ribs

(Pictured below)

PREP: 10 min. **COOK:** 6 hours

I like to serve tender, country-style ribs over rice. The tantalizing aroma and zippy Cajun barbecue sauce are sure to make them a favorite at your house.

—Michelle Rominger, Albia, Iowa

- 8 bone-in country-style pork ribs (8 ounces *each*)
- 1 cup ketchup
- 1 cup barbecue sauce
- 1/4 cup packed brown sugar
- 1/4 cup Worcestershire sauce
- 1 tablespoon balsamic vinegar
- 1 tablespoon molasses
- 1 garlic clove, minced
- 2 tablespoons dried minced onion
- 1 teaspoon Cajun seasoning
- 1 teaspoon ground mustard
- 1/2 teaspoon salt
- 1/4 teaspoon pepper

Place ribs in a 5-qt. slow cooker. Combine remaining ingredients; pour over ribs.

Cover and cook on low for 6-7 hours or until meat is tender. **YIELD:** 8 servings.

Chicken and Asparagus Kabobs

(Pictured above)

PREP: 25 min. + marinating **GRILL:** 10 min.

These Asian-inspired kabobs, served with a tasty dipping sauce, are special enough to make for guests at your next backyard get-together. Sometimes I substitute salmon for the chicken.

—Kelly Townsend, Syracuse, Nebraska

DIPPING SAUCE:
- 2 cups mayonnaise
- 1/4 cup sugar
- 1/4 cup soy sauce
- 2 tablespoons sesame seeds, toasted
- 1 tablespoon sesame oil
- 1/2 teaspoon white pepper

KABOBS:
- 1/4 cup soy sauce
- 2 tablespoons brown sugar
- 2 tablespoons water
- 1 tablespoon sesame oil
- 1 teaspoon crushed red pepper flakes
- 1 teaspoon minced fresh gingerroot
- 1-1/2 pounds boneless skinless chicken breasts, cut into 1-1/2-inch pieces
- 1 pound fresh asparagus, trimmed and cut into 2-inch pieces
- 2 tablespoons olive oil
- 1/2 teaspoon salt

Combine the sauce ingredients. Cover and refrigerate for 2-4 hours.

In a large resealable plastic bag, combine the soy sauce, brown sugar, water, sesame oil, pepper flakes and ginger. Add the chicken; seal bag and turn to coat. Refrigerate for 2 hours, turning occasionally.

Remove chicken to a serving platter and keep warm. Pour the drippings and loosened browned bits into a measuring cup; skim fat and discard. Add enough broth to measure 1 cup. In a small saucepan, combine flour and broth mixture until smooth. Bring to a boil; cook and stir for 2 minutes or until thickened. Serve with the chicken. **YIELD:** 8 servings.

Waldorf Stuffed Ham

(Pictured below)

PREP: 35 min. **BAKE:** 1-1/4 hours + standing

I wanted to try something new with my spiral ham, and this recipe just popped into my head. I served it to my husband, and he said it's a keeper.

—Colleen Vrooman, Waukesha, Wisconsin

- 1-1/2 cups unsweetened apple juice
- 1/4 cup butter, cubed
- 1 package (6 ounces) pork stuffing mix
- 1 medium tart apple, finely chopped
- 1/4 cup chopped sweet onion
- 1/4 cup chopped celery
- 1/4 cup chopped walnuts
- 1 fully cooked spiral-sliced ham (8 pounds)
- 1 can (21 ounces) apple pie filling
- 1/4 teaspoon ground cinnamon

In a large saucepan, bring apple juice and butter to a boil. Remove from the heat; stir in the stuffing mix, apple, onion, celery and walnuts.

Place ham on a rack in a shallow roasting pan. Spoon stuffing by tablespoonfuls between ham slices. Spoon pie filling over ham; sprinkle with cinnamon.

Bake, uncovered, at 325° for 1-1/4 to 1-3/4 hours or until a meat thermometer reads 140°. Let stand for 10 minutes before serving. **YIELD:** 14-16 servings.

Brined Roasting Chicken

(Pictured above)

PREP: 30 min. + marinating **BAKE:** 1 hour 20 min.

I discovered the art of brining turkey a few years ago and transferred the technique to roasting a whole chicken. I guarantee you will have a moist bird and rich gravy from the pan drippings.

—Julie Noyes, Louisville, Kentucky

- 8 cups warm water
- 1/2 cup kosher salt
- 1/4 cup packed brown sugar
- 3 tablespoons molasses
- 1 tablespoon whole peppercorns, crushed
- 1 tablespoon whole allspice, crushed
- 2 teaspoons ground ginger
- 1 roasting chicken (6 to 7 pounds)
- 4 cups cold water
- 1 teaspoon canola oil
- 3/4 to 1 cup chicken broth
- 1 tablespoon all-purpose flour

For brine, combine the first seven ingredients in a large kettle. Bring to a boil; cook and stir until salt is dissolved. Remove from the heat. Cool to room temperature.

Remove the giblets from chicken; discard. Over a large roasting pan, place cold water in a 2-gal. resealable plastic bag; add chicken. Carefully pour the cooled brine into the bag. Squeeze out as much air as possible; seal bag, turn to coat and place in pan. Refrigerate for 3-4 hours, turning several times.

Discard brine. Rinse the chicken with water; pat dry. Use a skewer to close the chicken openings; tie the drumsticks together. Brush chicken with oil; place in a roasting pan. Bake, uncovered, at 350° for 80-90 minutes or until a meat thermometer reads 180°, basting occasionally with pan drippings (cover loosely with foil if chicken browns too quickly).

Tenderloin in Puff Pastry

(Pictured below)

PREP: 20 min. + chilling **BAKE:** 20 min.

I came up with this entree after combining several different recipes. I set each fillet on puff pastry, then top them with a tasty mushroom mixture. It sounds like a lot of work, but it isn't...and it's so elegant.

—Julie Mahoney, St. Edward, Nebraska

- 4 **beef tenderloin fillets (1-3/4 inches thick and about 5 ounces *each*)**
- 1 **tablespoon canola oil**
- 1/2 **pound sliced fresh mushrooms**
- 4 **green onions, chopped**
- 1/4 **cup butter**
- 1/2 **teaspoon salt**
- 1/4 **teaspoon pepper**
- 1 **frozen puff pastry sheet, thawed**
- 1 **egg**
- 1 **tablespoon water**

In a large skillet, brown fillets in oil on both sides. Place a wire rack on a baking sheet. Transfer fillets to wire rack; refrigerate for 1 hour. In the same skillet, saute mushrooms and onions in butter until tender; drain. Stir in the salt and pepper.

On a lightly floured surface, roll pastry into a 13-in. square. Cut into four squares. Place one fillet in the center of each square; top with mushroom mixture. Combine egg and water; brush over pastry.

Bring up corners to center and tuck in edges; press to seal. Place on a parchment paper-lined baking sheet. Cover and refrigerate for 1 hour or overnight.

Bake, uncovered, at 400° for 20-25 minutes or until the pastry is golden brown and the meat reaches desired doneness (for medium-rare, a meat thermometer should read 145°; medium, 160°; well-done, 170°). **YIELD:** 4 servings.

Vegetarian Stuffed Peppers

(Pictured above and on page 82)

PREP: 30 min. **COOK:** 3-1/2 hours

These filling and flavorful peppers are an updated version of my mom's stuffed peppers, which were a favorite when I was growing up in upstate New York. Whenever I make them, I'm reminded of home. Try them at your house tonight.

—Melissa McCabe, Long Beach, California

- 6 **large sweet peppers**
- 2 **cups cooked brown rice**
- 3 **small tomatoes, diced**
- 1 **cup frozen corn, thawed**
- 1 **small sweet onion, diced**
- 1/3 **cup canned red beans, rinsed and drained**
- 1/3 **cup canned black beans, rinsed and drained**
- 3/4 **cup cubed Monterey Jack cheese**
- 1 **can (4-1/4 ounces) chopped ripe olives**
- 4 **fresh basil leaves, chopped**
- 3 **garlic cloves, minced**
- 1 **teaspoon salt**
- 1/2 **teaspoon pepper**
- 3/4 **cup meatless spaghetti sauce**
- 1/2 **cup water**
- 4 **tablespoons grated Parmesan cheese, *divided***

Cut tops off the peppers and remove seeds; set aside. In a large bowl, combine the rice, tomatoes, corn, onion and beans. Stir in the Monterey Jack cheese, olives, basil, garlic, salt and pepper. Spoon into peppers.

Combine spaghetti sauce and water; pour half into an oval 5-qt. slow cooker. Add the stuffed peppers. Top with remaining sauce. Sprinkle with 2 tablespoons Parmesan cheese.

Cover and cook on low for 3-1/2 to 4 hours or until the peppers are tender and the filling is heated through. Sprinkle with remaining Parmesan cheese. **YIELD:** 6 servings.

Spicy Nacho Bake

(Pictured below)

PREP: 1 hour **BAKE:** 20 min.

I made this hearty, layered Southwestern casserole for a dinner meeting once. Now I'm asked to bring it every time we have a potluck. Everybody loves the ground beef and bean filling, and crunchy, cheesy topping.

—Anita Wilson, Mansfield, Ohio

- 2 pounds ground beef
- 2 large onions, chopped
- 2 large green peppers, chopped
- 2 cans (28 ounces *each*) diced tomatoes, undrained
- 2 cans (15-1/2 ounces *each*) hot chili beans
- 2 cans (15 ounces *each*) black beans, rinsed and drained
- 2 cans (11 ounces *each*) whole kernel corn, drained
- 2 cans (8 ounces *each*) tomato sauce
- 2 envelopes taco seasoning
- 2 packages (13 ounces *each*) spicy nacho tortilla chips
- 4 cups (16 ounces) shredded cheddar cheese

In a Dutch oven or large kettle, cook the beef, onions and green peppers over medium heat until meat is no longer pink; drain. Stir in the tomatoes, beans, corn, tomato sauce and taco seasoning. Bring to a boil. Reduce heat; simmer, uncovered, for 30 minutes (mixture will be thin).

In each of two greased 13-in. x 9-in. baking dishes, layer 5 cups of chips and 4-2/3 cups of meat mixture. Repeat layers. Top each with 4 cups of chips and 2 cups of cheese.

Bake, uncovered, at 350° for 20-25 minutes or until golden brown.
YIELD: 2 casseroles (15 servings each).

Pretty Penne Ham Skillet

(Pictured above)

PREP/TOTAL TIME: 30 min.

I enjoy experimenting with herbs and spices to cut down on salt and sugar. This recipe takes advantage of aromatic herbs, such as parsley, basil and oregano.

—Kathy Stephan, West Seneca, New York

- 1 package (16 ounces) penne pasta
- 3 cups cubed fully cooked ham
- 1 large sweet red pepper, diced
- 1 medium onion, chopped
- 1/4 cup minced fresh parsley
- 2 garlic cloves, minced
- 1-1/2 teaspoons minced fresh basil *or* 1/2 teaspoon dried basil
- 1-1/2 teaspoons minced fresh oregano *or* 1/2 teaspoon dried oregano
- 1/4 cup olive oil
- 3 tablespoons butter
- 1 can (14-1/2 ounces) chicken broth
- 1 tablespoon lemon juice
- 1/2 cup shredded Parmesan cheese

Cook pasta according to package directions. Meanwhile, in a large skillet, saute the ham, red pepper, onion, parsley, garlic, basil and oregano in oil and butter for 4-6 minutes or until ham is browned and vegetables are tender.

Stir in the broth and lemon juice. Bring to a boil. Reduce heat; simmer, uncovered, for 10-15 minutes or until liquid is reduced by half. Drain pasta and stir into ham mixture. Sprinkle with Parmesan cheese. **YIELD:** 6 servings.

Brush asparagus with oil; sprinkle with garlic salt and pepper. Grill asparagus, uncovered, over medium heat for 6-8 minutes or until tender, turning every 2 minutes. Cut into 1-inch pieces.

Punch the dough down. Turn onto a floured surface; divide into eight portions. Roll each portion into a 6-in. circle. Place the dough directly on grill.

Grill, uncovered, over medium heat for 1-2 minutes or until bubbles form on top. Place toasted side up on two ungreased baking sheets. Top with pizza sauce, asparagus, ham and cheese. Cover and grill 2-3 minutes longer or until the bottom of the crust is golden brown. **YIELD:** 8 servings.

Curried Beef with Dumplings

(*Pictured below*)

PREP: 30 min. **COOK:** 2-3/4 hours

I like making this robust pot roast in the winter and serve left-overs the next day. It's not only easy to prepare, but the aroma is just wonderful while it's cooking.

—*Janell Schmidt, Athelstane, Wisconsin*

  1 **boneless beef rump roast (3 pounds)**
  2 **tablespoons olive oil**
  6 **medium carrots, cut into chunks**
  1 **can (14-1/2 ounces) diced tomatoes, undrained**
  1 **medium onion, sliced**
  2 **teaspoons curry powder**
  1 **teaspoon sugar**
  2 **teaspoons salt,** *divided*

Grilled Asparagus Pizzas

(*Pictured above*)

PREP: 20 min. + rising **GRILL:** 10 min.

Tired of pepperoni pizza? When we have the grill going, we like to make this recipe. The chewy, from-scratch crust is topped with pizza sauce, mozzarella cheese, asparagus and ham. Made on the grill, it's even better than delivery!

—*Monica Woods, Springfield, Missouri*

1-3/4 **to 2-1/2 cups all-purpose flour**
    1 **package (1/4 ounce) quick-rise yeast**
    1 **tablespoon minced fresh thyme**
    1 **teaspoon salt**
 1/2 **teaspoon sugar**
 3/4 **cup warm water (120° to 130°)**
  24 **asparagus spears, trimmed**
    1 **tablespoon olive oil**
 1/8 **teaspoon garlic salt**
 1/8 **teaspoon pepper**
    1 **cup pizza sauce**
    3 **ounces thinly sliced deli ham, chopped**
    2 **cups (8 ounces) shredded part-skim mozzarella cheese**

In large bowl, combine 1 cup flour, yeast, thyme, salt and sugar. Add water; beat until blended. Stir in enough remaining flour to form a soft dough. Turn onto a floured surface; knead until smooth and elastic, about 6-8 minutes. Place in a greased bowl, turning once to grease top. Cover and let rise in warm place until doubled, about 1 hour.

1 teaspoon Worcestershire sauce
1 cup hot water
1-2/3 cups all-purpose flour
3 teaspoons baking powder
2 tablespoons cold butter
3/4 cup milk
2 tablespoons minced fresh parsley
2 tablespoons chopped pimientos

In a Dutch oven, brown roast in oil on all sides; drain. Combine carrots, tomatoes, onion, curry powder, sugar, 1 teaspoon salt and Worcestershire sauce; pour over roast. Bring to a boil. Reduce heat to low; cover and cook for 2-1/2 hours or until meat and carrots are tender.

Remove roast and carrots; keep warm. Add hot water to pan; bring to a boil. For dumplings, combine flour, baking powder and remaining salt in a large bowl. Cut in butter until mixture resembles fine crumbs. Stir in milk, parsley and pimientos just until moistened.

Drop by tablespoonfuls onto simmering liquid. Cover and cook for 15 minutes or until a toothpick inserted in a dumpling comes out clean (do not lift cover while simmering). Remove the dumplings. Strain the cooking juices and serve with roast, dumplings and carrots. **YIELD:** 8 servings.

Cornmeal Ham Cakes

PREP/TOTAL TIME: 30 min.

These cakes are hearty because of the addition of ham. My husband and I think they are great for breakfast.
—Priscilla Gilbert, Indian Harbour Beach, Florida

1/2 cup all-purpose flour
1/2 cup cornmeal
2 tablespoons sugar
1/2 teaspoon baking powder
1/4 teaspoon baking soda
1/8 teaspoon salt
2 eggs, lightly beaten
1 cup buttermilk
3 tablespoons butter, melted
1 teaspoon vanilla extract
1-1/2 cups diced fully cooked ham
PINEAPPLE MAPLE SYRUP:
1 cup diced fresh pineapple
1/4 teaspoon ground cinnamon
1 tablespoon butter
1 cup maple syrup

In a large bowl, combine the first six ingredients. Combine the eggs, buttermilk, butter and vanilla; stir into dry ingredients until well blended. Fold in the ham. Pour batter by 1/4 cupfuls onto a greased hot griddle. Turn when bubbles form on top; cook until the second side is golden brown.

For syrup, in a small saucepan, saute the pineapple and cinnamon in butter for 4-6 minutes or until pineapple is browned. Stir in maple syrup. Serve with pancakes. **YIELD:** 4 servings.

Shrimp Pasta Primavera

(Pictured above)

PREP/TOTAL TIME: 15 min.

When I invite that special someone to dinner, I like to prepare something equally special. This well-seasoned pasta dish has lots of flavor…and it won't hurt your budget!
—Shari Neff, Takoma Park, Maryland

4 ounces uncooked angel hair pasta
8 jumbo shrimp, peeled and deveined
6 fresh asparagus spears, trimmed and cut into 2-inch pieces
2 garlic cloves, minced
1/4 cup olive oil
1/2 cup sliced fresh mushrooms
1/2 cup chicken broth
1 small plum tomato, peeled, seeded and diced
1/4 teaspoon salt
1/8 teaspoon crushed red pepper flakes
1 tablespoon *each* minced fresh basil, oregano, thyme and parsley
1/4 cup grated Parmesan cheese

Cook angel hair pasta according to package directions. Meanwhile, in a large skillet, saute shrimp, asparagus and garlic in oil for 3-4 minutes or until shrimp turn pink. Add the mushrooms, broth, tomato, salt and pepper flakes; simmer, uncovered, for 2 minutes.

Drain the pasta. Add the pasta and fresh herbs to the skillet; toss to coat. Sprinkle with Parmesan cheese. **YIELD:** 2 servings.

Maple-Glazed Ribs

(Pictured below and on the cover)

PREP: 15 minutes **COOK:** 1-1/2 hours

My family and I love maple syrup, so I gave this recipe a try. It's well worth the effort! I make these ribs often, and I never have leftovers. With two teenage boys who never seem to have enough to eat, this main dish is a real winner.

—Linda Kobeluck, Ardrossan, Alberta

    3 **pounds pork spareribs, cut into serving-size pieces**
    1 **cup maple syrup**
    3 **tablespoons orange juice concentrate**
    3 **tablespoons ketchup**
    2 **tablespoons soy sauce**
    1 **tablespoon Worcestershire sauce**
    1 **tablespoon Dijon mustard**
    1 **teaspoon curry powder**
    1 **garlic clove, minced**
    2 **green onions, minced**
    1 **tablespoon sesame seeds, toasted**

Place ribs, meaty side up, on a rack in a greased 15-in. x 10-in. baking pan. Cover pan tightly with foil. Bake at 350° for 1-1/4 hours or until tender; drain.

Meanwhile, combine the next nine ingredients in a small saucepan. Bring to a boil over medium heat. Reduce heat; simmer, uncovered, for 15 minutes, stirring occasionally.

Coat grill rack with cooking spray before starting the grill. Grill ribs, covered, over medium heat for 15-20 minutes, brushing with glaze twice. Sprinkle with sesame seeds just before serving. **YIELD:** 6 servings.

Asian Chicken Thighs

(Pictured above)

PREP: 15 min. **COOK:** 50 min.

A thick, tangy sauce coats these golden chicken pieces in this savory skillet recipe. I like to serve them over long grain rice or with a helping of ramen noodle slaw.

—Dave Farrington, Midwest City, Oklahoma

    5 **bone-in chicken thighs, skin removed**
    5 **teaspoons olive oil**
  1/3 **cup warm water**
  1/4 **cup packed brown sugar**
    2 **tablespoons orange juice**
    2 **tablespoons soy sauce**
    2 **tablespoons ketchup**
    1 **tablespoon white vinegar**
    4 **garlic cloves, minced**
  1/2 **teaspoon crushed red pepper flakes**
  1/4 **teaspoon Chinese five-spice powder**
    2 **teaspoons cornstarch**
    2 **tablespoons cold water**
Hot cooked rice
Sliced green onions

In a large skillet, brown chicken over medium heat in oil for 18-20 minutes or until juices run clear. Meanwhile, in a jar with a tight-fitting lid, combine the warm water, brown sugar, orange juice, soy sauce, ketchup, vinegar, garlic, pepper flakes and five-spice powder; shake until sugar is dissolved.

Pour over chicken. Bring to a boil. Reduce heat; simmer, uncovered, for 30-35 minutes or until chicken is tender, turning occasionally.

Combine cornstarch and cold water until smooth; gradually stir into skillet. Bring to a boil; cook and stir for 2 minutes or until thickened. Serve with rice. Garnish with green onions. **YIELD:** 5 servings.

Indiana Swiss Steak

(Pictured below)

PREP: 20 min. **COOK:** 1 hour

I entered the Indiana State Beef Contest and won first place with this recipe. A mixture of picante sauce, ketchup, cider vinegar and veggies enhances the tender slices of steak that are served over pasta. I use bow tie pasta, but you could substitute rice.

—Ann Dixon, North Vernon, Indiana

- 1/4 **cup all-purpose flour**
- 1 **teaspoon salt**
- 1/2 **teaspoon pepper**
- 1-1/2 **pounds boneless beef top round steak, cut into serving-size pieces**
- 1 **tablespoon canola oil**
- 1 **medium onion, chopped**
- 3/4 **cup grated carrot**
- 3/4 **cup water**
- 1/2 **cup chopped celery**
- 1/2 **cup chopped green pepper**
- 1/2 **cup ketchup**
- 1/4 **cup picante sauce**
- 1 **tablespoon cider vinegar**

Hot cooked pasta

In a large resealable plastic bag, combine the flour, salt and pepper. Add the beef, a few pieces at a time, and shake to coat. In a large skillet, brown beef in oil.

Combine the onion, carrot, water, celery, green pepper, ketchup, picante sauce and vinegar; pour over beef. Bring to a boil. Reduce heat; cover and simmer for 60-75 minutes or until beef is tender. Serve over the pasta. **YIELD:** 6 servings.

Pecan Chicken with Chutney

(Pictured above)

PREP: 15 min. **COOK:** 20 min.

These zippy, pecan-crusted chicken breasts are so tender, and the easy-fix peach chutney adds a sweet-sour taste. They taste great with rice on the side.

—Carisa Bravoco, Furlong, Pennsylvania

- 3/4 **cup all-purpose flour**
- 1/8 **teaspoon salt**
- 1/8 **teaspoon pepper**
- 2 **eggs**
- 1/3 **cup buttermilk**
- 1/8 **teaspoon hot pepper sauce**
- 1 **cup finely chopped pecans**
- 3/4 **cup dry bread crumbs**
- 6 **boneless skinless chicken breast halves (6 ounces *each*)**
- 2 **tablespoons butter**
- 2 **tablespoons canola oil**

PEACH MANGO CHUTNEY:

- 2 **cups sliced peeled fresh *or* frozen peaches, thawed**
- 1 **cup mango chutney**

In a shallow bowl, combine the flour, salt and pepper. In another shallow bowl, whisk the eggs, buttermilk and hot pepper sauce. In a third bowl, combine the pecans and bread crumbs.

Flatten chicken to 1/4-in. thickness. Coat the chicken with flour mixture, then dip in egg mixture and coat with the pecan mixture.

In a large skillet over medium heat, cook chicken in butter and oil for 8-10 minutes on each side or until juices run clear.

Meanwhile, in a small saucepan, combine peaches and chutney. Bring to a boil. Reduce heat; simmer, uncovered, for 15-20 minutes or until heated through. Serve with chicken. **YIELD:** 6 servings (1-3/4 cups chutney).

In a Dutch oven, cook beef and onion over medium heat until meat is no longer pink; drain. Stir in the beans, tomatoes, salsa, chilies and seasonings.

In a bowl, combine Monterey Jack and mozzarella cheeses; set aside 1 cup. Stir cottage cheese and 3/4 cup sour cream into remaining cheese mixture.

Spread 1 cup of the meat sauce into a greased 13-in. x 9-in. baking dish. Layer with three noodles, and a third of the cottage cheese mixture and meat sauce. Repeat layers twice (dish will be full). Cover and bake at 350° for 1 hour.

Uncover; spread with the remaining sour cream. Sprinkle with reserved cheeses. Bake 10-12 minutes longer or until cheese is melted. Let stand for 20 minutes before serving. **YIELD:** 12 servings.

Lime Shrimp with Asparagus

(Pictured below)

PREP/TOTAL TIME: 15 min.

For this eye-catching main dish, I combine shrimp, asparagus and sweet red pepper and flavor them with lime juice, lime peel, garlic and soy sauce. It may look like it takes a long time to prepare, but it goes together fast in the microwave.

—Peggy Davies, Canon City, Colorado

- 3/4 pound fresh asparagus, trimmed and cut into 2-inch pieces
- 1 garlic clove, minced
- 2 tablespoons water
- 3/4 pound uncooked medium shrimp, peeled and deveined
- 1 medium sweet red pepper, thinly sliced
- 1 jalapeno pepper, seeded and finely chopped
- 1 teaspoon cornstarch
- 2 tablespoons soy sauce
- 1 tablespoon lime juice

Fiesta Lasagna

(Pictured above)

PREP: 25 min. **BAKE:** 70 min. + standing

Loaded with Mexican-style ingredients, this filling lasagna is sure to please the whole gang, whether you make it for your family or take it to a potluck. Every bite is mmm-good!

—Karen Ann Bland, Gove, Kansas

- 1 pound ground beef
- 1/4 cup chopped onion
- 1 can (16 ounces) refried beans
- 1 can (15-1/2 ounces) mild chili beans
- 1 can (14-1/2 ounces) Mexican stewed tomatoes, drained
- 1 cup salsa
- 1 can (4 ounces) chopped green chilies
- 1 envelope reduced-sodium taco seasoning
- 1 teaspoon dried oregano
- 1 teaspoon ground cumin
- 1/4 teaspoon garlic powder
- 1-1/4 cups shredded Monterey Jack cheese
- 1-1/4 cups shredded part-skim mozzarella cheese
- 3/4 cup 4% cottage cheese
- 1-1/4 cups sour cream, *divided*
- 9 lasagna noodles, cooked, rinsed and drained

1/2 teaspoon grated lime peel
Hot cooked rice

Place the asparagus, garlic and water in a 1-1/2-qt. microwave-safe dish. Cover and microwave on high for 3-4 minutes or until the asparagus is crisp-tender. Remove with a slotted spoon; keep warm.

Add the shrimp, red pepper and jalapeno to dish. Cover and cook on high for 3 minutes or until the shrimp turn pink. Remove with a slotted spoon; keep warm.

In a small bowl, whisk cornstarch, soy sauce, lime juice and lime peel until blended; stir into the cooking juices. Microwave, uncovered, on high for 1 minute or until sauce is thickened and bubbly.

Stir in shrimp and asparagus mixtures. Cook, uncovered, on high for 30-60 seconds or until heated through. Serve with rice. **YIELD:** 4 servings.

EDITOR'S NOTE: This recipe was tested in a 1,100-watt microwave. When cutting or seeding hot peppers, use rubber or plastic gloves to protect your hands. Avoid touching your face.

Salmon with Polenta

PREP: 25 min. **COOK:** 20 min.

My husband was of Italian-Swiss descent, and one of his favorite dishes was salmon or bass with tomato sauce served over polenta. I still prepare this recipe for my son and his family.
—Rena Pilotti, Ripon, California

2 celery ribs, chopped
1 medium onion, chopped
2 tablespoons olive oil, *divided*
1 can (28 ounces) diced tomatoes, undrained
1 can (8 ounces) tomato sauce
1/4 cup minced fresh parsley
1-1/2 teaspoons salt, *divided*
1 teaspoon Italian seasoning
1/2 teaspoon dried thyme
1/2 teaspoon dried basil
1/2 teaspoon pepper
6 cups water
2 cups cornmeal
1/4 cup all-purpose flour
6 salmon fillets (6 ounces *each*)

In a Dutch oven, saute the celery and onion in 1 tablespoon oil until tender. Add the tomatoes, tomato sauce, parsley, 1/2 teaspoon salt, Italian seasoning, thyme, basil and pepper. Cover and simmer for 1 hour, stirring occasionally.

In a large heavy saucepan, bring water to a boil. Reduce heat to a gentle boil; slowly whisk in cornmeal. Cook and stir with a wooden spoon for 15-20 minutes or until polenta is thickened and pulls away cleanly from the sides of the pan.

Place flour in a large shallow bowl; coat salmon on both sides. In a large skillet, brown salmon in remaining oil. Transfer salmon to tomato mixture; cook, uncovered, for 3-5 minutes or until fish flakes easily with a fork. Serve salmon and sauce with polenta. **YIELD:** 6 servings.

Macadamia-Crusted Tilapia

(Pictured above)

PREP: 20 min. **BAKE:** 15 min.

A refreshing pineapple salsa complements these crispy, golden fillets. The colorful entree will make an impression with guests. I like to garnish each fillet with whole macadamia nuts.
—Jennifer Fisher, Austin, Texas

2 eggs
1/8 teaspoon cayenne pepper
1 cup all-purpose flour
1-3/4 cups macadamia nuts, finely chopped
4 tilapia fillets (6 ounces *each*)
1 tablespoon butter, melted
PINEAPPLE SALSA:
1 cup cubed fresh pineapple
1/4 cup chopped sweet red pepper
3 tablespoons thinly sliced green onions
2 tablespoons sugar
1 jalapeno pepper, seeded and chopped
1 tablespoon lime juice
1/2 teaspoon minced fresh gingerroot
2 tablespoons minced fresh cilantro

In a shallow bowl, whisk the eggs and cayenne. Place the flour and macadamia nuts in separate shallow bowls. Coat tilapia with flour, then dip in egg mixture and coat with nuts.

Place on a greased baking sheet; drizzle with melted butter. Bake at 375° for 15-20 minutes or until fish flakes easily with a fork.

Meanwhile, for the salsa, combine the pineapple, red pepper, onions, sugar, jalapeno, lime juice and ginger; sprinkle with cilantro. Serve with fish. **YIELD:** 4 servings (1-1/2 cups salsa).

EDITOR'S NOTE: When cutting hot peppers, disposable gloves are recommended. Avoid touching your face.

Giant Calzone

(Pictured below)

PREP: 25 min. + rising **BAKE:** 40 min.

While the filling ingredients for this impressive calzone are our favorites, you could substitute some of your own. You can also make two small calzones instead of one large one. We use the extra sauce for dipping or just freeze it for another time.

—Ronna Anderson, Prague, Oklahoma

- 1-1/2 cups water (70° to 80°)
- 2 tablespoons olive oil
- 2 teaspoons sugar
- 2 teaspoons salt
- 4-1/2 cups all-purpose flour
- 2 teaspoons active dry yeast
- 1 pound bulk Italian sausage
- 1 can (26 ounces) garlic and herb spaghetti sauce, *divided*
- 3 tablespoons grated Parmesan cheese
- 1 jar (4-1/2 ounces) sliced mushrooms, drained
- 1/2 cup finely chopped green pepper
- 1/4 cup finely chopped onion
- 1-1/2 cups (6 ounces) shredded part-skim mozzarella cheese
- 1 egg, beaten

In the bread machine pan, place the first six ingredients in order suggested by manufacturer. Select the dough setting (check dough after 5 minutes of mixing; add 1 to 2 tablespoons of water or flour if needed).

Meanwhile, in a large skillet, cook sausage over medium heat until no longer pink; drain and cool. When bread machine cycle is completed, turn dough onto a lightly floured surface. Roll out to a 15-in. circle. Transfer to a lightly greased baking sheet.

Spread 1/2 cup spaghetti sauce over half of the circle to within 1/4 in. of edges. Sprinkle the sauce with Parmesan cheese, sausage, mushrooms, green pepper, onion and mozzarella cheese. Fold dough over filling and pinch edges to seal.

With a sharp knife, make two slashes in dough; brush with egg. Bake at 350° for 40-45 minutes or until golden brown. Let stand for 5 minutes before cutting into six wedges. Warm remaining spaghetti sauce; serve with calzone. **YIELD:** 6 servings.

Stuffed Squash for Two

PREP: 20 min. **BAKE:** 1-1/2 hours

My husband and I have loved this recipe since we first got married, and we still do. As soon as the weather turns cool, we get hungry for this squash dish, filled with savory ground beef and topped with cheese.

—Barbara Rohlck, Sioux Falls, South Dakota

- 1 medium acorn squash
- 1 tablespoon butter, melted
- 2 tablespoons brown sugar
- 3/4 teaspoon salt, *divided*
- 1/8 teaspoon pepper
- 1/2 pound ground beef
- 3 tablespoons chopped celery
- 3 tablespoons chopped onion
- 2 tablespoons all-purpose flour
- 1/2 teaspoon rubbed sage
- 3/4 cup milk
- 1 cup salad croutons
- 1/4 cup shredded cheddar cheese

Cut squash in half; discard seeds. Place squash cut side down in an 11-in. x 7-in. baking pan; add 1/2 in. of hot water. Bake, uncovered, at 350° for 30 minutes. Drain water from pan; turn squash cut side up. Brush with butter; sprinkle with brown sugar, 1/4 teaspoon salt and pepper. Bake 30-40 minutes or longer or until the squash is tender.

Meanwhile, in skillet, cook the beef, celery and onion over medium heat until meat is no longer pink; drain. Stir in the flour, sage and remaining salt. Gradually stir in the milk. Bring to a boil; cook and stir for 2 minutes or until thickened.

Remove from the heat; stir in croutons. Spoon into squash halves. Sprinkle with cheese. Bake 5 minutes longer or until cheese is melted. **YIELD:** 2 servings.

winter squash

The most common varieties of winter squash are butternut, acorn, hubbard, spaghetti and turban. They should feel heavy for their size and have hard, deep-colored rinds that are free of blemishes. Store in a dry, cool place for up to 1 month.

Pepperoni Spinach Quiche

(Pictured above)

PREP: 25 min. **BAKE:** 25 min.

Several years ago, I had to come up with an appetizer to serve at a party, and this colorful quiche was a hit. You can serve it as an entree, but it's great on an antipasto tray, cut into wedges.
—Elly Townsend, Summerfield, Florida

- 1 tube (8 ounces) refrigerated crescent rolls
- 1 large sweet red pepper, chopped
- 1 garlic clove, minced
- 1 tablespoon olive oil
- 5 eggs, lightly beaten
- 1/2 cup shredded part-skim mozzarella cheese
- 1/2 cup frozen chopped spinach, thawed and squeezed dry
- 1/4 cup sliced pepperoni, cut into strips
- 1/4 cup half-and-half cream
- 2 tablespoons grated Parmesan cheese
- 1 tablespoon minced fresh parsley
- 1 tablespoon minced fresh basil *or* 1 teaspoon dried basil

Dash pepper

Separate the crescent dough into eight triangles; place in an ungreased 9-in. fluted tart pan with removable bottom with the points toward the center. Press onto the bottom and up the sides to form a crust; seal seams. Set aside.

In a small skillet, saute red pepper and garlic in oil until tender. Remove from the heat. In another small bowl, combine remaining ingredients; stir in red pepper mixture. Pour into crust.

Bake at 375° for 25-30 minutes or until a knife inserted near the center comes out clean. Let stand for 5 minutes before cutting. **YIELD:** 8 servings.

Steaks with Cucumber Sauce

(Pictured below)

PREP: 10 min. + marinating **GRILL:** 10 min.

Tender steaks, marinated with teriyaki sauce, are accompanied by a creamy cucumber sauce in this recipe.
—Erika Aylward, Clinton, Michigan

- 4 boneless beef New York strip steaks (8 to 10 ounces *each*)
- 3/4 cup teriyaki sauce
- 1/2 cup chopped seeded peeled cucumber
- 1/2 cup sour cream
- 1/2 cup mayonnaise
- 1 tablespoon minced chives
- 1/2 to 1 teaspoon dill weed
- 1/4 teaspoon salt

Place the steaks in a large resealable plastic bag; add the teriyaki sauce. Seal bag and turn to coat; refrigerate overnight. In a bowl, combine the cucumber, sour cream, mayonnaise, chives, dill and salt. Cover and refrigerate.

Drain and discard marinade. Grill steaks, uncovered, over medium-hot heat for 4-5 minutes on each side or until meat reaches desired doneness (for medium-rare, a meat thermometer should read 145°; medium, 160°; well-done, 170°). Serve with the cucumber sauce. **YIELD:** 4 servings.

Old-Fashioned Chicken Potpie

(Pictured below)

PREP: 1 hour **BAKE:** 15 min.

I use leftover chicken broth to make this comforting family favorite. You can bake your own biscuits, like I do, or simply buy them at the store. I like to bake extra biscuits to eat with butter and jam.

—Liliane Jahnke, Cypress, Texas

  1-1/2 cups sliced fresh mushrooms
     1 cup sliced fresh carrots
    1/2 cup chopped onion
    1/3 cup butter
    1/3 cup all-purpose flour
  1-1/2 cups chicken broth
  1-1/2 cups milk
     4 cups cubed cooked chicken breast
     1 cup frozen peas
     1 jar (2 ounces) diced pimientos, drained
     1 teaspoon salt

BISCUIT TOPPING:
     2 cups all-purpose flour
     4 teaspoons baking powder
     2 teaspoons sugar
    1/2 teaspoon salt
    1/2 teaspoon cream of tartar
    1/2 cup cold butter
    2/3 cup milk

In a large saucepan, saute mushrooms, carrots and onion in butter until tender; sprinkle with flour. Gradually stir in the broth and milk until blended. Bring to a boil; cook and stir for 2 minutes or until thickened. Add the chicken, peas, pimientos and salt; heat through. Pour into a greased shallow 2-1/2-qt. baking dish; set aside.

For the topping, in a large bowl, combine flour, baking powder, sugar, salt and cream of tartar. Cut in butter until mixture resembles coarse crumbs; stir in milk just until moistened. Turn on to a lightly floured surface; knead 8-10 times. Pat or roll out to 1/2-in. thickness. Cut with a floured 2-1/2-in. biscuit cutter.

Place biscuits over chicken mixture. Bake, uncovered, at 400° for 15-20 minutes or until biscuits are golden brown. **YIELD:** 6-8 servings.

Mozzarella-Stuffed Meatballs

(Pictured above)

PREP: 20 min. **COOK:** 15 min.

It's fun to watch my friends eat these meatballs for the first time. They're pleasantly surprised to find melted cheese in the middle. The meatballs are also terrific in a hot sub sandwich.

—Michaela Rosenthal, Woodland Hills, California

     1 egg, lightly beaten
    1/4 cup prepared Italian salad dressing
  1-1/2 cups cubed bread
     2 tablespoons minced fresh parsley
     2 garlic cloves, minced
    1/2 teaspoon dried oregano
    1/2 teaspoon pepper
    1/4 teaspoon salt
    1/2 pound ground pork
    1/2 pound ground sirloin
     3 ounces fresh mozzarella cheese
     2 tablespoons canola oil
     1 jar (26 ounces) marinara sauce
Hot cooked pasta

In a large bowl, combine the first eight ingredients. Crumble the pork and beef over egg mixture; mix well. Cut the mozzarella into eighteen 1/2-in. cubes. Divide the meat mixture into 18 portions; shape each around a cheese cube.

In a large skillet, cook the meatballs in oil in batches until no pink remains; drain. In a large saucepan, heat marinara sauce; add the meatballs and heat through. Serve over pasta. **YIELD:** 6 servings.

Bake, uncovered, at 350° for 1 hour; drain. Unroll crescent dough; seal seams and perforations. Drape dough over meat loaf to cover the top, sides and ends; seal ends. Bake 15-20 minutes longer or until a meat thermometer reads 160° and crust is golden brown. Let stand for 5 minutes.

Using two large spatulas, carefully transfer meat loaf to a serving platter. Sprinkle with remaining cheese. Serve with the remaining spaghetti sauce. **YIELD:** 8 servings.

Grilled Raspberry Chicken

(Pictured below)

PREP: 15 min. + marinating **GRILL:** 30 min.

Raspberry vinaigrette and raspberry jam lend fruity flavor to this moist chicken dish I created. The grill gives the chicken a great taste as well.

—Gloria Warczak, Cedarburg, Wisconsin

  1 **cup plus 4-1/2 teaspoons raspberry vinaigrette,** *divided*
  2 **tablespoons minced fresh rosemary**
    ***or* 2 teaspoons dried rosemary, crushed,** *divided*
  6 **bone-in chicken thighs**
  6 **chicken drumsticks**
1/2 **cup seedless raspberry jam**
1-1/2 **teaspoons lime juice**
1/2 **teaspoon soy sauce**
1/8 **teaspoon garlic powder**

In a large resealable plastic bag, combine 1 cup vinaigrette and half of the rosemary. Add chicken. Seal bag and turn to coat; refrigerate for 1 hour.

In a bowl, combine the jam, lime juice, soy sauce, garlic powder, and remaining vinaigrette and rosemary; set aside.

Drain the chicken and discard marinade. Place the chicken skin side down on grill rack. Grill, covered, over indirect medium heat for 20 minutes. Turn; grill 10-20 minutes longer or until the juices run clear, basting occasionally with the raspberry jam sauce. **YIELD:** 6 servings.

Meat Loaf Wellington

(Pictured above)

PREP: 20 min. **BAKE:** 1-1/4 hours

I took what I liked from a few different recipes and came up with this cheese-stuffed loaf. I make it for neighbors and friends when they're sick. It's a pleaser!

—Janine Talbot, Santaquin, Utah

  1 **egg, lightly beaten**
  1 **cup meatless spaghetti sauce,** *divided*
1/4 **cup dry bread crumbs**
1/2 **teaspoon salt**
1/4 **teaspoon pepper**
1-1/2 **pounds ground beef**
  2 **cups (8 ounces) shredded part-skim mozzarella cheese,** *divided*
  1 **tablespoon minced fresh parsley**
  1 **tube (8 ounces) refrigerated crescent rolls**

In a large bowl, combine the egg, 1/3 cup spaghetti sauce, bread crumbs, salt and pepper. Crumble beef over mixture and mix well.

On a piece of heavy-duty foil, pat the beef mixture into a 12-in. x 8-in. rectangle. Sprinkle 1 cup cheese and parsley to within 1 in. of edges. Roll up jelly-roll style, starting with a long side and peeling foil away while rolling. Seal seam and ends. Place seam side down in a greased 13-in. x 9-in. baking dish.

Pineapple-Stuffed Cornish Hens

(Pictured below)

PREP: 20 min. **BAKE:** 55 min.

My mother brought this recipe back with her from Hawaii about 25 years ago. The tender meat, pineapple-coconut stuffing and sweet-sour sauce made it a favorite of my family and friends.

—Vicki Corners, Rock Island, Illinois

2 Cornish game hens (20 ounces *each*)
1/2 teaspoon salt, *divided*
1 can (8 ounces) crushed pineapple
3 cups cubed day-old bread (1/2-inch cubes), crusts removed
1 celery rib, chopped
1/2 cup flaked coconut
2/3 cup butter melted, *divided*
1/4 teaspoon poultry seasoning
2 tablespoons steak sauce
2 tablespoons cornstarch
2 tablespoons brown sugar
1 cup water
1 tablespoon lemon juice

Sprinkle inside of hens with 1/4 teaspoon salt; set aside. Drain pineapple, reserving juice. In a bowl, combine the pineapple, bread cubes, celery and coconut. Add 6 tablespoons butter; toss to coat.

Loosely stuff hens; tie legs together with kitchen string. Place on a rack in a greased shallow roasting pan. Place remaining stuffing in a greased 1-1/2-cup baking dish; cover and set aside. Add poultry seasoning and the remaining salt to remaining butter. Spoon some butter mixture over hens. Bake, uncovered, at 350° for 40 minutes, basting twice with butter mixture.

Stir the steak sauce and reserved pineapple juice into remaining butter mixture; baste hens. Bake reserved stuffing with hens for 30 minutes; baste hens twice.

Uncover stuffing; baste hens with remaining butter mixture. Bake 15-20 minutes longer or until a meat thermometer reads 185° for hens and 165° for stuffing in hens. Remove the hens from the pan; keep warm.

Pour the drippings into a saucepan; skim fat. Combine cornstarch, brown sugar, water and lemon juice until smooth; add to drippings. Bring to a boil; cook and stir for 1-2 minutes or until thickened. Serve with hens and stuffing. **YIELD:** 2 servings.

Cranberry Ham Loaf

(Pictured above)

PREP: 20 min. **BAKE:** 70 min.

A cranberry sauce topping makes this easy-to-prepare ham loaf festive enough for a holiday meal. I find it's a great way to use up leftover ham.

—Ronald Heffner, Pawleys Island, South Carolina

1 egg, lightly beaten
1 cup milk
2 medium onions, chopped
1 medium green pepper, chopped
1 cup soft bread crumbs
1-1/2 pounds ground fully cooked ham
1 pound bulk pork sausage
1 can (16 ounces) whole-berry cranberry sauce
1/4 cup water
1 tablespoon light corn syrup

In a large bowl, combine the egg, milk, onions, green pepper and bread crumbs. Crumble ham and sausage over mixture; mix well.

Pat into an ungreased 9-in. x 5-in. loaf pan (pan will be full). Place on a baking sheet. Bake, uncovered, at 350° for 70-80 minutes or until a meat thermometer reads 160°.

In a small saucepan, combine cranberry sauce, water and corn syrup. Bring to a boil. Reduce heat; simmer, uncovered, for 5 minutes or until thickened. Remove ham loaf to a serving platter; top with cranberry sauce. **YIELD:** 8 servings.

Butterflied Pork Chop Dinner

(Pictured below)

PREP: 10 min. **COOK:** 35 min.

The sliced apple and sweet potatoes that complement these tender pork chops remind me of a crisp fall day. However, I enjoy this hearty main dish any time of year, and serve it with a salad and dinner rolls.

—Angela Leinenbach, Mechanicsville, Virginia

- 2 **butterflied pork chops (3/4 inch thick)**
- 1 **tablespoon butter**
- 1 **cup apple juice** *or* **cider,** *divided*
- 1 **teaspoon rubbed sage**
- 3/4 **teaspoon salt**
- 1/2 **teaspoon pepper**
- 2 **medium sweet potatoes, peeled and cut into 1/2-inch slices**
- 1 **green onion, thinly sliced**
- 1 **medium tart apple, peeled, cored and cut into 1/4-inch rings**
- 2 **teaspoons cornstarch**

In a skillet, brown pork chops in butter; drain. Remove from skillet and keep warm. In same skillet, combine 3/4 cup apple juice, sage, salt and pepper. Add sweet potatoes and green onion. Bring to a boil. Reduce heat.

Cover and simmer for 10 minutes; add apple rings and pork chops. Cover and simmer for 13-15 minutes or until apple rings and sweet potatoes are tender and meat juices run clear.

With a slotted spoon, remove pork chops, sweet potatoes and apple to serving plates; keep warm.

Combine the cornstarch with the remaining apple juice until smooth. Gradually stir into pan juices. Bring to a boil; cook and stir for 1-2 minutes or until thickened. Serve over pork chops, sweet potatoes and apple. **YIELD:** 2 servings.

Chicken Pepper Stir-Fry

(Pictured above)

PREP/TOTAL TIME: 30 min.

With a few simple ingredients, this colorful and aromatic stir-fry comes together in half an hour. My family loves it when they're craving Chinese takeout.

—Kelly Baumgardt, Seymour, Wisconsin

- 1 *each* **small green, sweet red and sweet yellow pepper, julienned**
- 1 **medium onion, quartered**
- 2 **garlic cloves, minced**
- 4 **tablespoons olive oil,** *divided*
- 3/4 **pound boneless skinless chicken breast halves, cubed**
- 3/4 **teaspoon Cajun seasoning**
- 1/3 **cup packed brown sugar**
- 2 **teaspoons cornstarch**
- 1 **tablespoon water**
- 1 **tablespoon lemon juice**
- 1 **tablespoon honey mustard**
- 1 **teaspoon soy sauce**
- 1 **teaspoon Worcestershire sauce**

Hot cooked rice, optional

In a large skillet, stir-fry the peppers, onion and garlic in 2 tablespoons oil until crisp-tender. Remove and keep warm. In the same skillet, stir-fry chicken and Cajun seasoning in remaining oil until juices run clear.

Combine brown sugar, cornstarch, water, lemon juice, mustard, soy sauce and Worcestershire sauce; pour over chicken. Return the pepper mixture to the pan; cook and stir for 1 minute. Serve with rice if desired. **YIELD:** 3-4 servings.

In a 5-qt. slow cooker, layer the carrots, celery and onion; sprinkle with rosemary. Add the chicken and hot broth. Cover and cook on low for 6-7 hours or until the chicken juices run clear, vegetables are tender and stew is bubbling. Stir in peas.

For dumplings, in a small bowl, combine flour, baking powder, salt and rosemary. Combine the egg and milk; stir into dry ingredients. Drop by heaping teaspoonfuls onto simmering chicken mixture. Cover and cook on high for 25-30 minutes or until a toothpick inserted in a dumpling comes out clean (do not lift the cover while simmering). **YIELD:** 6 servings.

Meatless Mexican Lasagna

(Pictured below)

PREP: 20 min. **BAKE:** 15 min.

Assemble this fun twist on lasagna for dinner, and your family will ask for it again and again. Instead of lasagna noodles, corn tortillas are layered between Mexican-style cheese and a South-western-style corn filling.

—Jean Ecos, Hartland, Wisconsin

  2 cups frozen corn, thawed
  1 can (15 ounces) black beans, rinsed and drained
  1 can (14-1/2 ounces) diced tomatoes with basil, oregano and garlic, undrained
  1 can (4 ounces) chopped green chilies
  3 green onions, sliced
  2 teaspoons dried oregano
  2 teaspoons ground cumin
  4 corn tortillas (6 inches)
1-1/2 cups (6 ounces) shredded Mexican cheese blend
  6 tablespoons plain yogurt

In a large bowl, combine first seven ingredients. Place two tortillas in an 11-in. x 7-in. baking dish coated with cooking spray. Spread with half of the corn mixture; sprinkle with half of the cheese. Repeat layers.

Bake, uncovered, at 400° for 15-20 minutes or until heated through. Let stand for 5 minutes. Garnish each serving with a dollop of yogurt. **YIELD:** 6 servings.

Sunday Chicken Stew

(Pictured above and on page 82)

PREP: 30 min. **COOK:** 6-1/2 hours

I love this recipe because in the morning I can prepare and assemble everything in the slow cooker before I go to church.

—Diane Halferty, Corpus Christi, Texas

1/2 cup all-purpose flour
  1 teaspoon salt
1/2 teaspoon white pepper
  1 broiler/fryer chicken (3 pounds), cut up and skin removed
  2 tablespoons canola oil
  3 cups chicken broth
  6 large carrots, cut into 1-inch pieces
  2 celery ribs, cut into 1/2-inch pieces
  1 large sweet onion, thinly sliced
  1 teaspoon dried rosemary, crushed
1-1/2 cups frozen peas
DUMPLINGS:
  1 cup all-purpose flour
  2 teaspoons baking powder
1/2 teaspoon salt
1/2 teaspoon dried rosemary, crushed
  1 egg, beaten
1/2 cup milk

In a large resealable plastic bag, combine the flour, salt and pepper; add the chicken, a few pieces at a time, and shake to coat. In a large skillet, brown chicken in oil; remove and keep warm. Gradually add broth to the skillet; bring to a boil.

Next Day Turkey Primavera

(Pictured above)

PREP/TOTAL TIME: 30 min.

I make this recipe often around the holidays. It's a wonderful way to use leftover turkey without feeling like it's a "repeat meal." I love pasta, and the creamy sauce in this primavera is so easy to make.

—*Robyn Hardisty, Lakewood, California*

  1 cup uncooked penne pasta
  8 fresh asparagus spears, trimmed and cut into 1-inch pieces
2/3 cup julienned carrot
  3 tablespoons butter
  4 large fresh mushrooms, sliced
1/2 cup chopped yellow summer squash
1/2 cup chopped zucchini
1-1/2 cups shredded cooked turkey
  1 medium tomato, chopped
  1 envelope Italian salad dressing mix
  1 cup heavy whipping cream
1/4 cup grated Parmesan cheese

Cook pasta according to package directions. Meanwhile, in a large skillet, saute asparagus and carrot in butter for 3 minutes. Add the mushrooms, yellow squash and zucchini; saute until crisp-tender.

Stir in the turkey, tomato, dressing mix and cream. Bring to a boil; cook and stir for 2 minutes.

Drain pasta; add to the vegetable mixture and toss to combine. Sprinkle with Parmesan cheese and toss again. **YIELD:** 4 servings.

Asparagus Crab Omelets

PREP/TOTAL TIME: 30 min.

These satisfying omelets are filled with a savory blend of crabmeat, asparagus, tomatoes and provolone cheese...and they're attractive enough to serve guests. Sometimes I top the omelets with hollandaise sauce.

—*Mae Jean Damron, Sandy, Utah*

  6 fresh asparagus spears, trimmed
  4 eggs
Dash salt
Dash pepper
1/2 cup diced plum tomatoes
  2 tablespoons butter, *divided*
  1 can (6 ounces) crabmeat, drained and flaked, cartilage removed
1/2 cup (2 ounces) provolone cheese, shredded

Place asparagus in a steamer basket. Place in a saucepan over 1 in. of water; bring to a boil. Cover and steam for 4-5 minutes or until crisp-tender; set aside. In a small bowl, whisk the eggs, salt and pepper. Stir in tomatoes.

Melt 1 tablespoon butter in a small skillet over medium heat; add half of the egg mixture. As the eggs set, lift the edges, letting the uncooked portion flow underneath. When the eggs are set, spoon half of the crab, asparagus and provolone cheese over one side; fold the omelet over filling. Cover and let stand for 1-2 minutes or until the cheese is melted. Repeat for the second omelet. **YIELD:** 2 servings.

Turkey Enchiladas

PREP: 40 min. **BAKE:** 40 min.

My family likes these enchiladas so much that they request a turkey dinner several times a year just so I'll make this dish. I usually double it because I feed three growing boys—two teenagers and my husband!

—*Beverly Matthews, Pasco, Washington*

  3 cups cubed cooked turkey
  1 cup chicken broth
  1 cup cooked long grain rice
  2 plum tomatoes, chopped
  1 medium onion, chopped
1/2 cup canned chopped green chilies
1/2 cup sour cream
1/4 cup sliced ripe olives
1/4 cup minced fresh cilantro
  1 teaspoon ground cumin
  8 flour tortillas (10 inches)
  1 can (28 ounces) green enchilada sauce, *divided*
  2 cups (8 ounces) shredded Mexican cheese blend, *divided*

In a large saucepan, combine the first 10 ingredients. Bring to a boil. Reduce the heat and simmer, uncovered, for 20 minutes. Remove from the heat.

Place 1/2 cup turkey mixture down the center of each tortilla; top each with 1 teaspoon enchilada sauce and 1 tablespoon cheese. Roll up and place seam side down in a greased 13-in. x 9-in. baking dish. Pour remaining enchilada sauce over top; sprinkle with remaining cheese.

Cover and bake at 350° for 30 minutes. Uncover; bake 8-10 minutes longer or until bubbly. **YIELD:** 8 servings.

In a large skillet, saute onion in oil and butter for 2 minutes. Add garlic; cook 1 minute longer. Add mushrooms; cook 6-8 minutes longer or until mushrooms are tender and no liquid remains. Stir in salt and pepper.

In a large bowl, combine the eggs, bread crumbs, Parmesan cheese, parsley, thyme and mushroom mixture. Crumble beef and sausage over mixture; mix well.

On a large piece of heavy-duty foil, pat beef mixture into a 15-in. x 10-in. rectangle. Layer the prosciutto, Havarti, basil and tomatoes to within 1 in. of edges. Roll up jelly-roll style, starting with a short side and peeling foil away while rolling. Seal seams and ends.

Place seam side down in a greased 13-in. x 9-in. baking dish. Bake, uncovered, at 350° for 75-85 minutes or until no pink remains and a meat thermometer reads 160°. Let stand for 5 minutes. Using two large spatulas, carefully transfer meat loaf to a serving platter. **YIELD:** 6-8 servings.

Spaghetti Squash with Red Sauce

(Pictured below)

PREP: 25 min. **COOK:** 15 min.

This fabulous, meatless main dish is a great way to get the kids to eat lots of vegetables…and a great way for you to use some of the fresh harvest from your garden.

—Kathryn Pehl, Prescott, Arizona

    1 medium spaghetti squash (about 4 pounds)
    2 cups chopped fresh tomatoes
    1 cup sliced fresh mushrooms

Prosciutto-Stuffed Meat Loaf

(Pictured above)

PREP: 45 min. **BAKE:** 1-1/4 hours

An amazing blend of flavors—including prosciutto, sun-dried tomatoes, fresh basil and two kinds of cheese—makes this rolled loaf something special.

—Carole Hermenau, Oviedo, Florida

    1 cup finely chopped red onion
    1 tablespoon olive oil
    1 tablespoon butter
    2 garlic cloves, minced
    1/2 pound whole fresh mushrooms, coarsely chopped
    3/4 teaspoon salt
    1/2 teaspoon pepper
    2 eggs, lightly beaten
1-3/4 cups soft sourdough bread crumbs
    3/4 cup grated Parmesan cheese
    1/3 cup minced fresh parsley
    1 teaspoon minced fresh thyme
1-1/2 pounds lean ground beef
    3/4 pound bulk Italian sausage
FILLING:
    3 ounces thinly sliced prosciutto
    5 ounces thinly sliced Havarti cheese
1-1/4 cups loosely packed basil leaves, cut into thin strips
    1/3 cup oil-packed sun-dried tomatoes, drained and cut into strips

1 cup diced green pepper
1/2 cup shredded carrot
1/4 cup diced red onion
2 garlic cloves, minced
2 teaspoons Italian seasoning
1/8 teaspoon pepper
1 tablespoon olive oil
1 can (15 ounces) tomato sauce
Grated Parmesan cheese, optional

Cut squash in half lengthwise; discard seeds. Place squash, cut side down, on a microwave-safe plate. Microwave, uncovered, on high for 14-16 minutes or until tender.

Meanwhile, in a large skillet, saute the tomatoes, mushrooms, green pepper, carrot, onion, garlic, Italian seasoning and pepper in oil for 6-8 minutes or until tender. Add tomato sauce; heat through.

When squash is cool enough to handle, use a fork to separate strands. Place squash on a serving platter; top with sauce. Sprinkle with Parmesan cheese if desired. **YIELD:** 6 servings.

EDITOR'S NOTE: This recipe was tested in a 1,100-watt microwave.

Braised Short Ribs

PREP: 25 min. **COOK:** 1-1/2 hours

I've been making these delicious ribs for at least 40 years, and they are often served when my husband and I have company for dinner. The allspice and bay leaf come through nicely, and the meat is very tender.

—Mary Gill, Florence, Oregon

3 pounds beef short ribs
1-1/2 teaspoons butter
1-1/2 teaspoons canola oil
1 large onion, thinly sliced
1 cup water
1-1/4 teaspoons salt
1 teaspoon sugar
1/4 teaspoon coarsely ground pepper
2 bay leaves
1 teaspoon whole allspice
1 tablespoon all-purpose flour
1/4 cup water

In a Dutch oven, brown ribs in butter and oil for about 3 minutes on each side; drain. Remove and keep warm. In the same pan, cook and stir the onion for 2 minutes. Add water, salt, sugar and pepper, stirring to loosen browned bits from pan.

Place the bay leaves and allspice on a double thickness of cheesecloth; bring up corners of cloth and tie with kitchen string to form a bag. Place in pan. Return ribs to pan. Bring to a boil. Reduce heat; cover and simmer for 1-1/2 to 1-3/4 hours or until meat is tender.

Remove the ribs and keep warm. Discard the spice bag. Skim fat from pan drippings. Combine flour and cold water until smooth; gradually stir into drippings. Bring to a boil; cook and stir for 2 minutes or until thickened. Serve with ribs. **YIELD:** 4 servings.

Bacon-Cheese Topped Chicken

(Pictured above)

PREP: 40 min. + marinating **BAKE:** 20 min.

Mushrooms, bacon strips and Monterey Jack cheese top these tender marinated chicken breasts. This dish gets compliments whenever I serve it. It's a family favorite.

—Melanie Kennedy, Battle Ground, Washington

1/2 cup Dijon mustard
1/2 cup honey
4-1/2 teaspoons canola oil, *divided*
1/2 teaspoon lemon juice
4 boneless skinless chicken breast halves
1/4 teaspoon salt
1/8 teaspoon pepper
Dash paprika
2 cups sliced fresh mushrooms
2 tablespoons butter
1 cup (4 ounces) shredded Monterey Jack cheese
1 cup (4 ounces) shredded cheddar cheese
8 bacon strips, partially cooked
2 teaspoons minced fresh parsley

Combine the mustard, honey, 1-1/2 teaspoons oil and lemon juice. Pour 1/2 cup into a large resealable plastic bag; add the chicken. Seal the bag and turn to coat; refrigerate for 2 hours. Cover and refrigerate the remaining marinade.

Drain and discard marinade from chicken. In a large skillet over medium heat, brown chicken in remaining oil on all sides. Sprinkle with salt, pepper and paprika. Transfer to a greased 11-in. x 7-in. baking dish.

In the same skillet, saute mushrooms in butter until tender. Spoon reserved marinade over chicken. Top with cheeses and mushrooms. Place bacon strips in a crisscross pattern over chicken.

Bake, uncovered, at 375° for 20-25 minutes or until a meat thermometer reads 170°. Sprinkle with parsley. **YIELD:** 4 servings.

Cube Steaks Parmigiana

(*Pictured below*)

PREP: 20 min. **BAKE:** 40 min.

Are you tired of ordinary chicken fried steak? This recipe dresses up cube steaks Italian-style with cheese, tomato sauce, basil and oregano. My husband and I like this main dish with a side of fettuccine Alfredo.

—Sarah Befort, Hays, Kansas

  3 tablespoons all-purpose flour
1/2 teaspoon salt
1/4 teaspoon pepper
  2 eggs
  3 tablespoons water
1/3 cup finely crushed saltines
1/3 cup grated Parmesan cheese
1/2 teaspoon dried basil
  4 beef cube steaks (1 pound)
  3 tablespoons canola oil
1-1/4 cups tomato sauce
2-1/4 teaspoons sugar
1/2 teaspoon dried oregano, *divided*
1/4 teaspoon garlic powder
  4 slices part-skim mozzarella cheese
1/3 cup shredded Parmesan cheese

In a shallow bowl, combine the flour, salt and pepper. In another bowl, beat the eggs and water. Place the cracker crumbs, grated Parmesan cheese and basil in a third bowl.

Coat the steaks with flour mixture, then dip in egg mixture and coat with crumb mixture. In a large skillet, brown steaks in oil for 2-3 minutes on each side or until golden brown.

Arrange the steaks in a greased 13-in. x 9-in. baking dish. Bake, uncovered, at 375° for 25 minutes. Combine the tomato sauce, sugar, 1/4 teaspoon oregano and garlic powder; spoon over the steaks. Bake 10 minutes longer.

Top each steak with mozzarella cheese; sprinkle with shredded Parmesan cheese and the remaining oregano. Bake 2-3 minutes longer or until the cheese is melted. **YIELD:** 4 servings.

Pizza Margherita

(*Pictured above*)

PREP: 30 min. + rising **BAKE:** 15 min.

This classic pizza starts with a chewy homemade crust topped with tomatoes, mozzarella, oregano, fresh basil and zesty red pepper flakes. It's so scrumptious that you'll be glad the recipe makes two 13-inch pizzas!

—Loretta Lawrence, Myrtle Beach, South Carolina

  3 teaspoons active dry yeast
  1 cup warm water (110° to 115°)
  2 tablespoons olive oil
  1 teaspoon sugar
  1 teaspoon salt
  3 cups bread flour
TOPPINGS:
  2 cans (14-1/2 ounces *each*) diced tomatoes, drained
 20 fresh basil leaves, thinly sliced
  8 cups (2 pounds) shredded part-skim mozzarella cheese
  2 teaspoons dried oregano
1/2 teaspoon crushed red pepper flakes
1/8 teaspoon salt

1/8 teaspoon pepper
2 tablespoons olive oil

In a large bowl, dissolve yeast in warm water. Add the oil, sugar, salt and 1 cup flour. Beat until smooth. Stir in enough remaining flour to form a soft dough.

Turn onto a floured surface; knead until smooth and elastic, about 6-8 minutes. Place in a bowl coated with cooking spray, turning once to coat the top. Cover and let rise in a warm place until doubled, about 1 hour.

Punch the dough down; divide in half. Roll each portion into a 13-in. circle. Transfer to two 14-in. pizza pans coated with cooking spray; build up the edges slightly. Cover and let rest for 10 minutes.

For the toppings, spoon tomatoes over the crusts. Top with basil, cheese, oregano, pepper flakes, salt and pepper. Drizzle with oil. Bake at 450° for 15-20 minutes or until the crust and cheese are golden brown. **YIELD:** 2 pizzas (8 slices each).

Rosemary Leg of Lamb

PREP: 10 min. **BAKE:** 1 hour 30 min.

Before putting the leg of lamb in the oven, I rub on a mixture of garlic, rosemary, salt and pepper, which enhances the naturally delicious flavor.

—Marie Hattrup, The Dalles, Oregon

4 garlic cloves, minced
1 to 2 tablespoons minced fresh rosemary
    or 1 teaspoon dried rosemary, crushed
1 teaspoon salt
1/2 teaspoon pepper
1 bone-in leg of lamb (7 to 9 pounds), trimmed
1 teaspoon cornstarch
1/4 cup beef broth

In a small bowl, combine the garlic, rosemary, salt and pepper; rub over meat. Place on a rack in a large roasting pan. Bake, uncovered, at 350° for 1-1/2 to 2-1/2 hours or until the meat reaches desired doneness (for medium-rare, a meat thermometer should read 145°; medium, 160°; well-done, 170°). Let the roast stand for 10 minutes before slicing.

Meanwhile, pour pan drippings into a small saucepan, scraping browned bits. Skim fat. Combine cornstarch and broth until smooth. Whisk into saucepan. Bring to a boil; cook and stir for 1-2 minutes or until thickened. Serve with lamb. **YIELD:** 10-12 servings.

Spinach Crab Chicken

(Pictured at right)

PREP: 45 min. **COOK:** 40 min.

I altered a friend's recipe for crab-stuffed chicken to include one of my favorite vegetables, spinach. Now my husband requests this elegant entree all the time. Served over rice, it's special enough for company.

—Vicki Melies, Elkhorn, Nebraska

1/2 cup finely chopped onion
1/4 cup chopped fresh mushrooms
1/4 cup finely chopped celery
3 tablespoons butter
3 tablespoons all-purpose flour
1/2 teaspoon salt, *divided*
1 cup chicken broth
1/2 cup milk
4 boneless skinless chicken breast halves (6 ounces *each*)
1/8 teaspoon white pepper
1/2 cup dry bread crumbs
1 can (6 ounces) crabmeat, drained, flaked and cartilage removed
12 fresh spinach leaves, chopped
1 tablespoon minced fresh parsley
1 cup (4 ounces) shredded Swiss cheese

Hot cooked rice

For sauce, in a large skillet, saute the onion, mushrooms and celery in butter until tender. Stir in the flour and 1/4 teaspoon salt until blended. Gradually add the broth and milk. Bring to a boil; cook and stir 1-2 minutes or until thickened. Remove from the heat.

Flatten the chicken to 1/4-in. thickness; sprinkle with pepper and remaining salt. In a large bowl, combine the bread crumbs, crab, spinach and parsley; stir in 1/2 cup sauce. Spoon 1/4 cup down the center of each chicken breast half. Roll up; secure with toothpicks. Place seam side down in a greased 13-in. x 9-in. baking dish. Top with remaining sauce.

Cover and bake at 375° for 35-45 minutes or until the juices run clear. Sprinkle with cheese. Broil 4-6 in. from the heat for 5 minutes or until lightly browned. Discard toothpicks. Serve with rice. **YIELD:** 4 servings.

Cover and freeze one potpie for up to 3 months. Bake the remaining potpie at 375° for 40-45 minutes or until golden brown. Let stand for 10 minutes before cutting. **YIELD:** 2 pies (6 servings each).

TO USE FROZEN POTPIE: Remove from the freezer 30 minutes before baking. Cover edges of crust loosely with foil; place on a baking sheet. Bake at 425° for 30 minutes. Reduce heat to 350°; remove foil. Bake 55-60 minutes longer or until golden brown.

Curried Shrimp and Apples

(*Pictured below*)

PREP/TOTAL TIME: 30 min.

Apples and shrimp, seasoned with curry powder, combine beautifully in this appealing main dish. Sometimes I make it with chicken instead of the shrimp.

—*Lynda Mack, Neptune Beach, Florida*

  1 **medium onion, chopped**
  2 **celery ribs, chopped**
1/4 **cup butter, cubed**
  2 **medium apples, sliced**
  2 **teaspoons all-purpose flour**
3/4 **teaspoon curry powder**
3/4 **cup water**
  1 **teaspoon chicken bouillon granules**
3/4 **pound uncooked medium shrimp, peeled and deveined**
Hot cooked rice

In a large skillet, saute the onion and celery in butter for 2 minutes. Stir in apples; saute 1-2 minutes longer or until crisp-tender.

   Sprinkle with flour and curry powder. Gradually whisk in water and bouillon until smooth. Add shrimp; bring to a boil. Reduce heat; simmer for 2-3 minutes or until shrimp turn pink and sauce is thickened. Serve over rice. **YIELD:** 4 servings.

Turkey Potpies

(*Pictured above and on page 82*)

PREP: 40 min. **BAKE:** 40 min. + standing

With golden brown crust and scrumptious filling, these comforting potpies will warm you down to your toes. Because it makes two large pies, you can eat one now and freeze the other for later. They bake and cut beautifully.

—*Laurie Jensen, Cadillac, Michigan*

  2 **medium potatoes, peeled and cut into 1-inch pieces**
  3 **medium carrots, cut into 1-inch slices**
  1 **medium onion, chopped**
  1 **celery rib, diced**
  2 **tablespoons butter**
  1 **tablespoon olive oil**
  6 **tablespoons all-purpose flour**
  3 **cups chicken broth**
  4 **cups cubed cooked turkey**
2/3 **cup frozen peas**
1/2 **cup plus 1 tablespoon heavy whipping cream, *divided***
  1 **tablespoon minced fresh parsley**
  1 **teaspoon garlic salt**
1/4 **teaspoon pepper**
  1 **package (15 ounces) refrigerated pie pastry**
  1 **egg**

In a Dutch oven, saute the potatoes, carrots, onion and celery in butter and oil until tender. Stir in flour until blended; gradually add broth. Bring to a boil; cook and stir for 2 minutes or until thickened. Stir in the turkey, peas, 1/2 cup cream, parsley, garlic salt and pepper.

   Spoon into two ungreased 9-in. pie plates. Roll out the pastry to fit the top of each pie; place over filling. Trim, seal and flute edges. Cut out a decorative center or cut slits in pastry. In a small bowl, whisk the egg and remaining cream; brush over dough.

Sweet and Tender Cabbage Rolls

(Pictured above)

PREP: 40 min. **COOK:** 7 hours

I've used this recipe for more than 30 years, and the extra time it takes to assemble the rolls is well worth the effort. I always make two batches because they go so fast. You can assemble the rolls the night before and simmer them the next day.

— *Sonja Benz, Carmel, Indiana*

- 1 large head cabbage
- 2 eggs, beaten
- 1/2 cup milk
- 2 cups cooked long grain rice
- 2 jars (4-1/2 ounces *each*) sliced mushrooms, well drained
- 1 small onion, chopped
- 2 teaspoons salt
- 1 teaspoon dried parsley flakes
- 1 teaspoon dried oregano
- 1 teaspoon dried basil
- 1/2 teaspoon pepper
- 2 pounds lean ground beef

SAUCE:
- 2 cans (8 ounces *each*) tomato sauce
- 1/2 cup packed brown sugar
- 2 tablespoons lemon juice
- 2 teaspoons Worcestershire sauce

Cook cabbage in boiling water just until leaves fall off head. Set aside 14 large leaves for rolls. (Refrigerate remaining cabbage for another use.) Cut out the thick vein from the bottom of each reserved leaf, making a V-shaped cut.

In a large bowl, combine the eggs, milk, rice, mushrooms, onion and seasonings. Crumble beef over mixture and mix well. Place about 1/2 cup on each cabbage leaf; overlap cut ends and fold in sides, beginning from the cut end. Roll up completely to enclose the filling.

Place seven rolls, seam side down, in a 5-qt. slow cooker. Combine sauce ingredients; pour half over cabbage rolls. Top with remaining rolls and sauce. Cover and cook on low for 7-8 hours or until a meat thermometer reads 160°. **YIELD:** 7 servings.

Chicken & Tomato Risotto

(Pictured below)

PREP: 25 min. **COOK:** 25 min.

If you're looking for Italian comfort food, this is it! By using store-bought spaghetti sauce, you save time when preparing this creamy dish. You'll enjoy every bite!

— *Lorraine Caland, Thunder Bay, Ontario*

- 3 cups chicken broth
- 1 pound boneless skinless chicken breasts, cut into 1-inch cubes
- 1 tablespoon olive oil
- 1-1/2 cups sliced fresh mushrooms
- 1 medium onion, chopped
- 1 garlic clove, minced
- 2 tablespoons butter
- 1 cup uncooked arborio rice
- 1 cup meatless spaghetti sauce
- 1/4 cup grated Parmesan cheese

In a small saucepan, heat broth and keep warm. In a large skillet, saute chicken in oil until no longer pink. Remove and keep warm.

In the same skillet, saute mushrooms, onion and garlic in butter until crisp-tender. Add rice; cook and stir for 3 minutes. Carefully stir in 1 cup warm broth. Cook and stir until all of the liquid is absorbed.

Add remaining broth, 1/2 cup at a time, stirring constantly. Allow the liquid to absorb between additions. Cook until risotto is creamy and rice is almost tender. (Cooking time is about 20 minutes.)

Stir in the spaghetti sauce, cheese and reserved chicken; cook and stir until thickened. Serve immediately. **YIELD:** 4 servings.

Meat Loaf Gyros

(*Pictured below*)

PREP: 30 min. **BAKE:** 1 hour + chilling

I always wanted to learn to make Greek gyros at home but was intimidated. Then I tried this recipe, and they were great. I slice leftover meat in individual portions and freeze for any time I crave a gyro.

—Sharon Rawlings, Tampa, Florida

- 1 egg, lightly beaten
- 6 garlic cloves, minced
- 3 tablespoons dried oregano
- 1-1/2 teaspoons kosher salt
- 1 teaspoon pepper
- 1 pound ground lamb
- 1 pound ground beef

TZATZIKI SAUCE:
- 1 cup (8 ounces) plain yogurt
- 1 medium cucumber, peeled, seeded and chopped
- 2 tablespoons lemon juice
- 2 garlic cloves, minced
- 1/2 teaspoon salt
- 1/4 teaspoon pepper

GYROS:
- 8 whole gyro-style pitas (6 inches)
- 3 tablespoons olive oil, *divided*
- 16 slices tomato
- 8 slices sweet onion, halved

In a large bowl, combine the egg, garlic, oregano, kosher salt and pepper. Crumble the lamb and beef over mixture; mix well.

Pat into an ungreased 9-in. x 5-in. loaf pan. Bake, uncovered, at 350° for 60-70 minutes or until no pink remains and a meat thermometer reads 160°. Cool completely on a wire rack. Refrigerate for 1-2 hours.

For sauce, in a small bowl, combine the yogurt, cucumber, lemon juice, garlic, salt and pepper. Cover and refrigerate until serving.

For the gyros, brush pita breads with 1 tablespoon oil; heat on a lightly greased griddle for 1 minute on each side. Keep warm. Cut the meat loaf into very thin slices. In a large skillet, fry meat loaf in remaining oil in batches until crisp.

On each pita bread, layer tomato, onion and meat loaf slices; top with some tzatziki sauce. Carefully fold pitas in half. Serve with remaining sauce. **YIELD:** 8 servings.

Creamed Chicken over Biscuits

(*Pictured above*)

PREP/TOTAL TIME: 20 min.

A friend of mine prepared this homey dish for my husband and me after our first son was born. I've made just a few minor modifications over the years. We love all of the heartwarming comfort it offers in every bite.

—Pam Kelley, Uniontown, Ohio

- 1 cup cubed peeled potato
- 1/2 cup diced carrot
- 2 tablespoons butter
- 2 tablespoons all-purpose flour
- 1 cup milk
- 2-1/2 teaspoons chicken bouillon granules
- 1/8 teaspoon pepper
- 1/2 pound boneless skinless chicken breasts, cooked and cubed
- 1/2 cup frozen peas, thawed
- 4 warm buttermilk biscuits

Place potato and carrot in a small saucepan. Cover with water. Bring to a boil. Reduce heat; cover and simmer for 8-10 minutes or until vegetables are tender. Drain and set aside.

In a large skillet, melt the butter. Stir in the flour until smooth. Gradually whisk in milk. Add the bouillon and pepper. Bring to a boil; cook and stir for 2 minutes or until thickened. Stir in the chicken, peas and potato mixture; heat through. Serve over the biscuits. **YIELD:** 2 servings.

Taco Meat Loaves

(Pictured below)

PREP: 25 min. **BAKE:** 1 hour + standing

We live in Texas and love the Southwest's spicy style of cooking. This recipe flavors plain old meat loaf so it tastes like a delicious filling for tacos.

—Susan Garoutte, Georgetown, Texas

  3 eggs, lightly beaten
  2 cups picante sauce, *divided*
  1 can (16 ounces) kidney beans, rinsed and drained
  1 can (11 ounces) Mexicorn, drained
  1 medium onion, chopped
  2 cans (2-1/4 ounces *each*) sliced ripe olives, drained
3/4 cup dry bread crumbs
  1 envelope taco seasoning
  1 teaspoon ground cumin
  1 teaspoon chili powder
  2 pounds ground beef
  2 cups (8 ounces) shredded cheddar cheese
Additional picante sauce, optional

In a large bowl, combine the eggs, 1/2 cup picante sauce, beans, corn, onion, olives, bread crumbs, taco seasoning, cumin and chili powder. Crumble beef over mixture and mix well.

Pat into two ungreased 9-in. x 5-in. loaf pans. Bake, uncovered, at 350° for 50-55 minutes or until no pink remains and a meat thermometer reads 160°.

Spoon remaining picante sauce over each meat loaf; sprinkle with cheese. Bake 10-15 minutes longer or until cheese is melted. Let stand for 10 minutes before slicing. Serve with additional picante sauce if desired. **YIELD:** 2 meat loaves (6 servings each).

Asian Pot Roast

(Pictured above)

PREP: 30 min. **COOK:** 2 hours 35 min.

This pot roast satisfies my cravings for Asian food. The original recipe called for spinach, but I use sugar snap peas and carrots instead. Sometimes I serve the roast, vegetables and pineapple over rice or egg noodles.

—Donna Staley, Randlemn, North Carolina

  1 boneless beef rump roast (3 pounds)
  1 tablespoon canola oil
  1 large onion, chopped
  1 can (20 ounces) pineapple chunks
  3 tablespoons soy sauce
  1 garlic clove, minced
  1 teaspoon ground ginger
  3 celery ribs, sliced
  2 medium carrots, sliced
  1 cup fresh sugar snap peas
  1 cup sliced fresh mushrooms
  1 to 2 tablespoons cornstarch
1/4 cup cold water

In a Dutch oven over medium heat, brown roast in oil on all sides; drain. Add onion. Drain pineapple, reserving juice; set pineapple aside. Combine the pineapple juice, soy sauce, garlic and ginger. Pour over roast. Bring to a boil. Reduce heat; cover and simmer for 2 hours or until meat is almost tender.

Add the celery and carrots. Cover and simmer for 20 minutes or until vegetables are crisp-tender. Add the peas, mushrooms and reserved pineapple. Cover and simmer 15 minutes longer or until the vegetables and meat are tender.

Remove the roast, vegetables and pineapple; keep warm. Skim fat from pan drippings. Combine cornstarch and cold water until smooth; gradually stir into the drippings. Bring to a boil; cook and stir for 2 minutes or until thickened. Slice roast across the grain. Serve meat, vegetables and pineapple with gravy. **YIELD:** 6 servings.

Shrimp Quesadillas

(Pictured below)

PREP: 20 min. **BAKE:** 10 min.

For variety, substitute cooked chicken or ground beef for the shrimp in these simple quesadillas.

—Joan Schroeder, Mesquite, Nevada

- 1 can (28 ounces) diced tomatoes, drained
- 1/2 cup chopped green onions
- 1 can (4 ounces) chopped green chilies
- 3 jalapeno peppers, seeded and chopped
- 1 garlic clove, minced
- 1 tablespoon minced fresh cilantro
- 1 teaspoon salt
- 1/2 teaspoon dried oregano
- 1/2 teaspoon ground cumin

QUESADILLAS:
- 1-1/3 cups shredded Mexican cheese blend
- 1 can (4 ounces) chopped green chilies, drained
- 1/2 cup chopped seeded tomato
- 3 tablespoons sliced green onions
- 1 package (8 ounces) frozen cooked salad shrimp, thawed
- 4 flour tortillas (10 inches)
- 1 tablespoon butter

For salsa, place the first nine ingredients in a blender; cover and process until finely chopped. Transfer to a large bowl; set aside.

Sprinkle the cheese, chilies, tomato, onions and shrimp over half of each tortilla; fold over.

In a large skillet over medium heat, cook quesadillas in butter for 1-2 minutes on each side or until cheese is melted. Cut into wedges. Serve with salsa. Refrigerate leftover salsa. **YIELD:** 2-4 servings (2-1/2 cups salsa).

EDITOR'S NOTE: When cutting hot peppers, disposable gloves are recommended. Avoid touching your face.

Artichoke Ham Puffs

(Pictured above)

PREP: 10 min. **BAKE:** 30 min.

This recipe is wonderful for a special brunch with family or friends. With lots of cheese and chunks of ham, the filling is delicious and satisfying. I serve the puffs with fresh fruit and a sweet bread.

—Suzanne Merrill, Modesto, California

- 6 frozen puff pastry shells
- 1/2 pound sliced fresh mushrooms
- 6 tablespoons butter, *divided*
- 3 tablespoons all-purpose flour
- 1/4 teaspoon ground mustard
- 1/4 teaspoon minced fresh tarragon
- 2 cups milk
- 2-1/2 cups (10 ounces) shredded cheddar cheese
- 1/8 teaspoon coarsely ground pepper
- 3 cups cubed fully cooked ham
- 1 can (14 ounces) water-packed artichoke hearts, rinsed, drained, patted dry and quartered

Bake pastry shells according to package directions. Meanwhile, in a large skillet, saute mushrooms in 2 tablespoons butter for 3-4 minutes or until tender. Add the remaining butter; cook over medium heat until melted.

Stir in flour, mustard and tarragon until blended. Gradually add milk. Bring to a boil; cook and stir for 2 minutes or until thickened.

Reduce heat to low. Add the cheese and pepper; cook and stir for 3-4 minutes or until cheese is melted. Remove from the heat; stir in ham and artichokes. Remove tops from pastry shells; fill with ham mixture. Replace tops. **YIELD:** 6 servings.

Reuben Crescent Bake

(Pictured below)

PREP: 20 min. **BAKE:** 15 min.

This may not be a true Reuben, but the taste is still fantastic and it's easy to make. I like to serve this bake with homemade soup.
—*Kathy Kittell, Lenexa, Kansas*

- 2 tubes (8 ounces *each*) refrigerated crescent rolls
- 1 pound sliced Swiss cheese
- 1-1/4 pounds sliced deli corned beef
- 1 can (14 ounces) sauerkraut, rinsed and well drained
- 2/3 cup Thousand Island salad dressing
- 1 egg white, lightly beaten
- 3 teaspoons caraway seeds

Unroll one tube of the crescent dough into one long rectangle; seal seams and perforations. Press onto the bottom of a greased 13-in. x 9-in. baking dish. Bake at 375° for 8-10 minutes or until golden brown.

Layer with half of the cheese and all of the corned beef. Combine sauerkraut and salad dressing; spread over beef. Top with remaining cheese.

On a lightly floured surface, press or roll second tube of crescent dough into a 13-in. x 9-in. rectangle, sealing seams and perforations. Place over the cheese. Brush with the egg white; sprinkle with the caraway seeds.

Bake for 12-16 minutes or until heated through and crust is golden brown. Let stand for 5 minutes before cutting. **YIELD:** 8 servings.

Thai Chicken Fettuccine

(Pictured above)

PREP: 25 min. **BAKE:** 15 min.

Salsa and peanut butter make a taste-tempting pair in this unique chicken recipe. Its innovative flavor combination, fresh taste and ease of preparation will bowl you over.
—*Michelle Van Loon, Round Lake, Illinois*

- 1 cup salsa
- 1/4 cup creamy peanut butter
- 2 tablespoons orange juice
- 2 tablespoons honey
- 1 teaspoon soy sauce
- 8 ounces uncooked fettuccine
- 3/4 pound boneless skinless chicken breasts, cut into strips
- 1 tablespoon canola oil
- 1 medium sweet red pepper, julienned
- 1/4 cup minced fresh cilantro

For sauce, in a microwave-safe bowl, combine first five ingredients. Cover and microwave on high for 1 minute; stir. Set aside.

Cook fettuccine according to package directions. Meanwhile, in a large skillet, cook chicken in oil over medium heat for 3-5 minutes or until the chicken juices run clear. Add the red pepper; cook and stir until crisp-tender.

Drain fettuccine; top with chicken mixture and sauce. Sprinkle with cilantro. **YIELD:** 4 servings.

EDITOR'S NOTE: This recipe was tested in a 1,100-watt microwave.

Spoon 2 cups stuffing over turkey breast to within 1 in. of edges. Roll up jelly-roll style, starting with a long side. Tie with kitchen string at 1-1/2-in. intervals. Place on a rack in a large shallow roasting pan.

Spoon 1 cup stuffing over each thigh section to within 1 in. of edges. Roll up jelly-roll style, starting with a short side. Tie with kitchen string; place on a rack in another shallow roasting pan.

Brush turkey with oil; sprinkle with pepper and remaining salt. Bake turkey breast at 325° for 2 to 2-1/2 hours or until a meat thermometer reads 170°; bake thighs for 1-1/2 to 1-3/4 hours or until a meat thermometer reads 180° and a meat thermometer reads 165° for stuffing. Let turkey stand for 15 minutes before slicing. **YIELD:** 8 servings.

EDITOR'S NOTE: Ask the butcher to debone the turkey for you.

Caesar Orange Roughy

(Pictured below and on page 82)

PREP: 10 min. **BAKE:** 15 min.

Sprinkled with buttery cracker crumbs, these moist fish fillets are nicely flavored with Caesar salad dressing and cheddar cheese. To top it off, they're speedy and easy to make.

—Mary Lou Boyce, Wilmingon, Delaware

    2 pounds orange roughy fillets
    1 cup creamy Caesar salad dressing
    2 cups crushed butter-flavored crackers
       (about 50 crackers)
    1 cup (4 ounces) shredded cheddar cheese

Place the fillets in an ungreased 13-in. x 9-in. baking dish. Drizzle with salad dressing; sprinkle with cracker crumbs.

Bake, uncovered, at 400° for 10 minutes. Sprinkle with cheese. Bake 3-5 minutes longer or until fish flakes easily with a fork and cheese is melted. **YIELD:** 8 servings.

Rolled-Up Turkey

(Pictured above)

PREP: 30 min. **BAKE:** 2 hours

Whenever I think of this appealing rolled turkey filled with Mom's moist corn bread stuffing, I can almost smell the aroma of it baking in the oven. It's delicious!

—June Blomquist, Eugene, Oregon

      1 turkey (12 pounds), deboned and giblets removed
      1 cup chopped celery
      1 medium onion, chopped
    1/2 cup butter, cubed
      5 cups cubed white bread
  1-1/2 cups coarsely crumbled corn bread
      1 teaspoon salt, *divided*
    1/2 teaspoon rubbed sage
    3/4 to 1 cup chicken broth
      3 tablespoons canola oil
    1/4 teaspoon pepper

Unroll the turkey on a large cutting board. With a sharp knife, remove the wings (save for another use). Flatten the turkey to 3/4-in. thickness. Cut between the turkey breast and thighs to separate into three sections.

In a large skillet, saute celery and onion in butter until tender. In a large bowl, combine bread and corn bread; add celery mixture, 1/2 teaspoon salt and sage. Stir in enough broth to moisten.

Brisket in a Bag

PREP: 15 min. **BAKE:** 2-1/2 hours

This slow-roasted brisket is served with a savory cranberry gravy that's made right alongside the meat. You'll want to serve the tender slices with mashed potatoes just so you can drizzle the succulent sauce over them.

—Peggy Stigers, Fort Worth, Texas

3 tablespoons all-purpose flour, *divided*
1 large oven roasting bag
1 fresh beef brisket (5 pounds), trimmed
1 can (16 ounces) whole-berry cranberry sauce
1 can (10-3/4 ounces) condensed cream of mushroom soup, undiluted
1 can (8 ounces) tomato sauce
1 envelope onion soup mix

Place 1 tablespoon of flour in oven bag; shake to coat. Place the bag in an ungreased 13-in. x 9-in. baking pan; place the brisket in the bag.

Combine the cranberry sauce, soup, tomato sauce, soup mix and remaining flour; pour over beef. Seal bag. Cut slits in top of the bag according to package directions.

Bake at 325° for 2-1/2 to 3 hours or until meat is tender. Let stand for 5 minutes. Carefully remove brisket from bag. Thinly slice meat across the grain; serve with gravy. **YIELD:** 12 servings.

EDITOR'S NOTE: This is a fresh beef brisket, not corned beef.

Turkey Chop Suey

PREP: 10 min. **BAKE:** 10 min.

Leftover turkey is ideal for this fast-to-fix chop suey. Canned bean sprouts and water chestnuts add a nice crunch to the mix.

—Ruth Peterson, Jenison, Michigan

1 small onion, sliced
2 celery ribs, sliced
1 tablespoon butter
2 cups cubed cooked turkey breast
1 can (8 ounces) sliced water chestnuts, drained
1-1/4 cups reduced-sodium chicken broth
2 tablespoons cornstarch
1/4 cup cold water
3 tablespoons reduced-sodium soy sauce
1 can (14 ounces) canned bean sprouts, drained
Hot cooked rice

In a large skillet, saute the onion and celery in butter until tender. Add the turkey, water chestnuts and broth; bring to a boil. Reduce the heat.

In a small bowl, combine the cornstarch, water and soy sauce until smooth; add to turkey mixture. Bring to a boil; cook and stir for 2 minutes or until thickened. Add bean sprouts. Serve with rice. **YIELD:** 4 servings.

Asparagus Beef Stir-Fry

(Pictured above)

PREP: 15 min. **BAKE:** 15 min.

I love Filet Mignon, but not its price! While grocery shopping, I picked up a more affordable beef tenderloin tail. I brought it home and came up with this recipe. Now I cook it once a week, plus my husband loves taking the leftovers to work.

—Linda Flynn, Ellicott City, Maryland

1 pound beef tenderloin roast, cubed
1 green onion, sliced
2 garlic cloves, minced
1/2 teaspoon salt
1/4 teaspoon pepper
1 tablespoon vegetable oil
1 pound fresh asparagus, trimmed and cut into 2-inch pieces
1/2 pound sliced fresh mushrooms
1/4 cup butter, cubed
1 tablespoon soy sauce
1-1/2 teaspoons lemon juice
Hot cooked rice

In a wok or large skillet, stir-fry the beef, onion, garlic, salt and pepper in oil for 3-5 minutes; remove and keep warm.

In the same pan, stir-fry asparagus and mushrooms in butter until asparagus is tender. Return beef mixture to the pan. Stir in soy sauce and lemon juice; heat through. Serve with rice. **YIELD:** 4 servings.

Tempting fresh-baked goods are the perfect accompaniment to any meal. They're also great as snacks or even as special gifts during the holidays.

breads, rolls & muffins

Maple Walnut Rolls 124

Vermont Honey-Wheat Bread 124

Sunshine Sweet Rolls 125

Cheddar Skillet Corn Bread 125

Tricolor Braid.......................................126

Orange-Rhubarb Breakfast Bread 126

Black Raspberry Bubble Ring 127

Berry Cheesecake Muffins................................127

Rich Coffee Cake......................................128

Parker House Dinner Rolls...............................128

Five-Topping Bread.......................................129

White Chocolate Macadamia Muffins 129

Lemon Pound Cake Muffins 129

Fruit and Nut Stollen 130

Pretty Pumpkin Cinnamon Buns 130

Tomato Focaccia 131

Poppy Seed Onion Bread 131

Special Banana Nut Bread................................132

Fruit-Nut Pumpkin Bread...............................132

Honey-Oat Pan Rolls................................132

Pull-Apart Bacon Bread 133

Pecan Lemon Loaf 133

Vanilla Cinnamon Rolls 134

Pumpkin Scones with Berry Butter 134

Cheddar Loaves...135

Feta and Chive Muffins 135

Strawberry Popovers............................136

Parmesan Breadsticks 136

Almond Berry Muffins 137

Christmas Morning Croissants 137

Walnut Raspberry Muffins................................138

Vegetable & Cheese Focaccia.........................138

Mini Maple Cinnamon Rolls............................139

Herbed Popovers.......................................139

Sweet Milk Dinner Rolls...............................139

PICTURED CLOCKWISE FROM UPPER LEFT: Pull-Apart Bacon Bread (page 133), Parker House Dinner Rolls (page 128), Christmas Morning Croissants (page 137) and Lemon Pound Cake Muffins (page 129).

Maple Walnut Rolls

(Pictured below)

PREP: 45 min. + rising **BAKE:** 20 min. + cooling

For old-fashioned flavor, you can't beat this attractive nut roll. The recipe makes four loaves, so you'll have enough to serve family and friends during the holiday season.
—Elleen Oberreuter, Danbury, Iowa

- 6 to 7 cups all-purpose flour
- 3 tablespoons sugar
- 2 packages (1/4 ounce *each*) active dry yeast
- 1 teaspoon salt
- 1 cup (8 ounces) sour cream
- 1 cup butter, softened
- 1/2 cup water
- 3 eggs, lightly beaten

FILLING:
- 3/4 cup butter, melted
- 1/2 cup sugar
- 3 tablespoons maple syrup
- 5 cups ground walnuts

ICING:
- 2 cups confectioners' sugar
- 2 to 3 tablespoons milk

In a large bowl, combine 2 cups flour, sugar, yeast and salt. In a small saucepan, heat sour cream, butter and water to 120°-130°; add to dry ingredients. Beat on medium speed for 2 minutes. Add eggs and 1/2 cup flour; beat 2 minutes longer. Stir in enough remaining flour to form a soft dough.

Turn onto a floured surface; knead until smooth and elastic, 6-8 minutes. Place in a greased bowl; turn once to grease top. Cover and let rise in a warm place until doubled, about 1-1/4 hours. Punch the dough down; divide into four portions. Roll each portion into a 14-in. x 12-in. rectangle.

For the filling, in a large bowl, combine butter, sugar and syrup; stir in walnuts. Sprinkle 1 cup over each rectangle. Roll up jelly-roll style, starting with a long side; pinch seam to seal. Place seam side down on greased baking sheets. Cover and let rise in a warm place until doubled, about 45 minutes.

Bake at 350° for 20-25 minutes or until lightly browned. Remove from pans to wire racks to cool. Combine icing ingredients; drizzle over rolls. **YIELD:** 4 loaves.

Vermont Honey-Wheat Bread

PREP: 30 min. + rising **BAKE:** 30 min. + cooling

You don't have to be a health nut to enjoy this hearty loaf. Made with whole wheat flour, oats and wheat germ, this bread gets its pleasant sweetness from honey and maple syrup.
—Roderick Crandall, Hartland, Vermont

- 2 packages (1/4 ounce *each*) active dry yeast
- 3/4 cup warm water (110° to 115°)
- 1 cup old-fashioned oats
- 1 cup warm buttermilk (110° to 115°)
- 1/3 cup butter, softened
- 1-1/2 cups whole wheat flour
- 1/2 cup maple syrup
- 1/2 cup honey
- 1/3 cup toasted wheat germ
- 2 eggs, beaten
- 1 teaspoon salt
- 3 to 4 cups all-purpose flour

TOPPING:
- 1 egg white
- 1 tablespoon water
- 1/4 cup old-fashioned oats

In a small bowl, dissolve the yeast in warm water. In a large bowl, combine the oats, buttermilk and butter; add yeast mixture. Add the whole wheat flour, syrup, honey, wheat germ, eggs and salt; beat on low speed for 30 seconds. Beat on high for 3 minutes. Stir in enough all-purpose flour to form a firm dough.

Turn onto a floured surface; knead until smooth and elastic, 6-8 minutes. Place in a bowl coated with cooking spray, turning once to coat the top. Cover and let rise in a warm place until doubled, about 1 hour.

Punch the dough down. Shape into two loaves; place each in a 9-in. x 5-in. loaf pan coated with cooking spray. Cover and let rise in a warm place until doubled, about 45 minutes.

Beat egg white and water; brush over the loaves. Sprinkle with oats. Bake at 375° for 30-35 minutes or until golden brown. Cool for 10 minutes before removing from pans to wire racks to cool completely. **YIELD:** 2 loaves.

Cut each into six rolls. Place cut side up in two greased 9-in. square baking pans. Cover and let rise in a warm place until doubled, about 30 minutes. Bake at 350° for 25-30 minutes or until golden brown. Cool on wire racks for 5 minutes. Combine glaze ingredients; drizzle over warm rolls. **YIELD:** 1 dozen.

EDITOR'S NOTE: This recipe was tested in a 1,100-watt microwave.

Sunshine Sweet Rolls

(Pictured above)

PREP: 30 min. + rising **BAKE:** 25 min.

This bread-machine recipe is my new favorite. The cream cheese filling and drizzled icing make these golden brown rolls a special treat for breakfast or snacking.

—Alice Vivian Shepherd, Maryville, Tennessee

- 1-1/2 cups warm water (110° to 115°)
- 1/4 cup canola oil
- 1/4 cup shredded carrot
- 4-1/2 cups all-purpose flour
- 1/4 cup sugar
- 1-1/2 teaspoons salt
- 2 teaspoons active dry yeast

FILLING:
- 1 package (8 ounces) cream cheese, softened
- 1/4 cup sugar
- 1 teaspoon vanilla extract
- 1 package (3 ounces) cook-and-serve vanilla pudding mix
- 1 jar (6 ounces) carrot baby food
- 1 teaspoon ground cinnamon

GLAZE:
- 1/2 cup confectioners' sugar
- 2 to 3 teaspoons orange juice
- 1/2 teaspoon grated orange peel
- 1/4 teaspoon vanilla extract

In bread machine pan, place the first seven ingredients in the order suggested by the manufacturer. Select the dough setting (check the dough after 5 minutes of mixing; add 1 to 2 tablespoons of water or flour if needed).

Meanwhile, for the filling, combine the cream cheese, sugar and vanilla; set aside. In a microwave-safe bowl, combine the pudding mix, baby food and cinnamon. Cover and microwave on high for 2 minutes; stir.

When cycle is completed, turn the dough onto a lightly floured surface. Divide in half; shape each portion into a ball. Roll each into a 9-in. x 8-in. rectangle. Spread the cream cheese mixture to within 1/2 in. of edges; top with the carrot mixture. Roll up jelly-roll style, starting with a long side; pinch seam to seal.

Cheddar Skillet Corn Bread

(Pictured below)

PREP/TOTAL TIME: 30 min.

With their crispy edges, wedges of this corn bread go well with just about any meal. I like to pair it with a hearty bowl of chili or a Southwestern chicken casserole.

—Terri Adrian, Lake City, Florida

- 2 tablespoons butter
- 2 packages (8-1/2 ounces *each*) corn bread/muffin mix
- 2 eggs, beaten
- 1/2 cup milk
- 1/2 cup plain yogurt
- 1 can (14-3/4 ounces) cream-style corn
- 1/2 cup shredded cheddar cheese

HONEY BUTTER:
- 1/2 cup butter, softened
- 2 tablespoons honey

Place butter into a deep 10-in. ovenproof skillet. Place in a 400° oven for 4-6 minutes or until melted.

Meanwhile, in a large bowl, combine the corn bread mix, eggs, milk and yogurt until blended. Stir in corn and cheese. Pour into hot skillet. Bake at 400° for 20-25 minutes or until a toothpick inserted near the center comes out clean. Cut into wedges.

In a small bowl, mix butter and honey together. Serve with warm corn bread. **YIELD:** 12 servings.

For the pumpernickel dough, add cocoa and molasses to third bowl; mix well. Gradually add enough rye flour to make a stiff dough. Turn onto a floured surface; knead until smooth and elastic, 6-8 minutes. Place in a greased bowl, turning once to grease top. Cover and set aside. Let all three bowls rise in a warm place until doubled, about 1 hour.

Punch doughs down; divide each in half. Shape each portion into a 15-in. rope. Place a rope of each dough on a greased baking sheet and braid; seal ends. Repeat with remaining ropes. Cover and let rise until doubled, about 45 minutes. Beat egg white and water together; brush over braids. Bake at 350° for 25-30 minutes or until golden brown. Remove to wire racks to cool. **YIELD:** 2 loaves (12 slices each).

Orange-Rhubarb Breakfast Bread

(Pictured below)

PREP: 20 min. **BAKE:** 55 min. + cooling

I love starting my day with a slice of this fabulous sweet bread alongside eggs, sausage and orange juice. It's full of tangy flavor and crunchy slivered almonds.

—Sonya Goergen, Moorhead, Minnesota

- 1/3 **cup butter, softened**
- 1 **cup sugar**
- 2 **eggs**
- 1 **teaspoon vanilla extract**
- 2 **cups all-purpose flour**
- 1-1/2 **teaspoons baking powder**
- 1/2 **teaspoon baking soda**
- 1/2 **teaspoon salt**
- 1/4 **teaspoon ground ginger**
- 1/4 **teaspoon ground nutmeg**

Tricolor Braid

(Pictured above)

PREP: 1 hour + rising **BAKE:** 25 min. + cooling

This impressive loaf is wonderfully dense and chewy. It takes some time to prepare, but the results are worth the extra effort.

—Cindi Paulson, Anchorage, Alaska

- 2 **packages (1/4 ounce** *each***) active dry yeast**
- 2-1/3 **cups warm water (110° to 115°)**
- 1/4 **cup butter, softened**
- 2 **tablespoons honey**
- 3 **teaspoons salt**
- 3-1/3 to 3-2/3 **cups all-purpose flour**
- **WHEAT DOUGH:**
- 2 **tablespoons toasted wheat germ**
- 2 **tablespoons molasses**
- 1 **cup plus 2 to 5 tablespoons whole wheat flour**
- **PUMPERNICKEL DOUGH:**
- 2 **tablespoons baking cocoa**
- 2 **tablespoons molasses**
- 1 **cup plus 2 to 5 tablespoons rye flour**
- **TOPPING:**
- 1 **egg white**
- 1 **tablespoon water**

In a large bowl, dissolve yeast in warm water. Add butter, honey, salt and 2-1/3 cups all-purpose flour; beat for 2 minutes. Divide evenly among three bowls.

To the first bowl, add enough remaining all-purpose flour to make a stiff dough; mix well. Turn onto a floured surface; knead until smooth and elastic, 6-8 minutes. Place in a greased bowl, turning once to grease top. Cover and set aside.

For the wheat dough, add wheat germ and molasses to the second bowl; mix well. Gradually add enough wheat flour to make a stiff dough. Turn onto a floured surface; knead until smooth and elastic, 6-8 minutes. Place in a greased bowl, turning once to grease top. Cover and set aside.

1/2 cup orange juice
1 cup chopped fresh *or* frozen rhubarb
1/2 cup slivered almonds
2 teaspoons grated orange peel

In a large bowl, cream butter and sugar. Add eggs, one at a time, beating well after each addition. Beat in vanilla.

Combine the flour, baking powder, baking soda, salt, ginger and nutmeg; add to creamed mixture alternately with orange juice. Fold in the rhubarb, almonds and orange peel.

Transfer to a greased 9-in. x 5-in. loaf pan. Bake at 350° for 55-65 minutes or until a toothpick inserted near the center comes out clean. Cool for 10 minutes before removing from pan to a wire rack. **YIELD:** 1 loaf.

EDITOR'S NOTE: If using frozen rhubarb, measure rhubarb while still frozen, then thaw completely. Drain in a colander, but do not press liquid out.

Black Raspberry Bubble Ring

PREP: 35 min. + rising **BAKE:** 25 min.

I first made this pretty bread years ago for a 4-H project. It helped me win Grand Champion for my county. It takes a little prep work, but never fails to really impress.
—*Kila Frank, Reedsville, Ohio*

1 package (1/4 ounce) active dry yeast
1/4 cup warm water (110° to 115°)
1 cup warm milk (110° to 115°)
1/4 cup plus 2 tablespoons sugar, *divided*
1/2 cup butter, melted, *divided*
1 egg
1 teaspoon salt
4 cups all-purpose flour
1 jar (10 ounces) seedless black raspberry preserves
SYRUP:
1/3 cup corn syrup
2 tablespoons butter, melted
1/2 teaspoon vanilla extract

In a large bowl, dissolve yeast in warm water. Add the milk, 1/4 cup sugar, 1/4 cup butter, egg, salt and 3-1/2 cups flour. Beat until smooth. Stir in enough remaining flour to form a soft dough.

Turn onto a floured surface; knead until smooth and elastic, 6-8 minutes. Place in a greased bowl, turning once to grease top. Cover and let rise in a warm place until doubled, about 1-1/4 hours.

Punch dough down. Turn onto a lightly floured surface; divide into 32 pieces. Flatten each into a 3-in. disk. Place about 1 teaspoon of preserves in the center of each piece; bring edges together and seal. Place 16 of the filled dough balls in a greased 10-in. fluted tube pan. Brush with half of the remaining butter; sprinkle with 1 tablespoon sugar. Top with the remaining balls, butter and sugar. Cover and let rise until doubled, about 35 minutes.

Bake at 350° for 25-30 minutes or until golden brown. Combine the syrup ingredients; pour over warm bread. Cool for 5 minutes before inverting onto a serving plate. **YIELD:** 1 loaf.

Berry Cheesecake Muffins

(Pictured below)

PREP: 30 min. **BAKE:** 25 min./batch

I adapted this recipe over the years for my family, and they think it's wonderful. Not only are the muffins delicious, but they're bursting with fantastic color, too.
—*Jeanne Bilhimer, Midland, Michigan*

1/3 cup butter, softened
3/4 cup sugar
2 eggs
1-1/2 cups all-purpose flour
1-1/2 teaspoons baking powder
1 teaspoon ground cinnamon
1/3 cup milk
CREAM CHEESE FILLING:
2 packages (3 ounces *each*) cream cheese, softened
1/3 cup sugar
1 egg
3/4 cup fresh raspberries
3/4 cup fresh blueberries
STREUSEL TOPPING:
1/4 cup all-purpose flour
2 tablespoons brown sugar
1/2 teaspoon ground cinnamon
1 tablespoon cold butter

In a large bowl, cream the butter and sugar until light and fluffy. Add the eggs, one at a time, beating well after each addition. Combine the flour, baking powder and cinnamon; add to the creamed mixture alternately with the milk. Fill greased or paper-lined muffin cups one-third full.

For the filling, beat the cream cheese, sugar and egg together until smooth. Fold in berries. Drop one rounded tablespoonful into the center of the batter for each muffin. (Muffin cups will be full.)

For the topping, combine the flour, brown sugar and cinnamon; cut in the butter until mixture is crumbly. Sprinkle over the batter.

Bake at 375° for 25-30 minutes or until a toothpick comes out clean. Cool for 5 minutes. Remove the muffins and transfer to wire racks. Serve warm. Refrigerate leftovers. **YIELD:** 21 muffins.

Rich Coffee Cake

(Pictured below)

PREP: 30 min. **BAKE:** 1 hour

Cinnamon-pecan swirls and a chocolaty drizzle enhance this delectable coffee cake.

—Gaytha Holloway, Marion, Indiana

- 1 cup butter, softened
- 2 cups sugar
- 2 eggs
- 2 cups all-purpose flour
- 1-1/2 teaspoons baking powder
- 1/2 teaspoon salt
- 1 cup (8 ounces) sour cream
- 1/2 teaspoon vanilla extract

TOPPING:
- 1 cup chopped pecans
- 2 tablespoons sugar
- 1 teaspoon ground cinnamon

CHOCOLATE GLAZE:
- 1/2 cup semisweet chocolate chips
- 1/4 cup butter, cubed

In a large bowl, cream butter and sugar until light and fluffy. Add eggs, one at a time, beating well after each addition. Combine the flour, baking powder and salt. Combine sour cream and vanilla; add to creamed mixture alternately with dry ingredients just until combined.

Combine topping ingredients; sprinkle 2 tablespoons into a greased and floured 10-in. tube pan. For glaze, in a microwave-safe bowl, melt chocolate chips and butter; stir until smooth. Spoon half of the batter over topping; sprinkle with half of remaining topping. Drizzle with half of the glaze. Top with remaining batter; sprinkle with remaining topping.

Bake at 350° for 60-70 minutes or until toothpick inserted near the center comes out clean. Cool for 10 minutes before removing from pan to a wire rack. Warm remaining glaze; drizzle over coffee cake. Serve warm if desired. **YIELD:** 12 servings.

Parker House Dinner Rolls

(Pictured above and on page 122)

PREP: 1 hour + rising **BAKE:** 10 min.

You won't be able to eat just one of my mom's famous yeast rolls. They're light and fluffy with a wonderful flavor…and even more delicious served warm with a little butter.

—Susan Hansen, Auburn, Alabama

- 1/2 cup shortening
- 1/4 cup sugar
- 2 teaspoons salt
- 1-1/2 cups boiling water
- 2 tablespoons active dry yeast
- 1/2 cup warm water (110° to 115°)
- 3 eggs
- 6-3/4 to 7-1/4 cups all-purpose flour
- 1/4 cup butter, melted

In a large bowl, combine shortening, sugar and salt. Stir in boiling water. Cool to 110°-115°. Dissolve yeast in warm water. Add yeast mixture, eggs and 3 cups flour to shortening mixture; mix well. Stir in enough remaining flour to form a soft dough.

Turn onto a floured surface; knead until smooth and elastic, 6-8 minutes. Place in a greased bowl, turning once to grease top. Cover and let rise in a warm place until doubled, about 45 minutes.

Punch the dough down; turn onto a lightly floured surface. Roll the dough to 1/2-in. thickness. Cut with a 2-1/2-in. biscuit cutter. Fold circles in half; press edges to seal. Place 2 in. apart on baking sheets coated with cooking spray. Cover and let rise until doubled, about 30 minutes.

Bake at 400° for 10-12 minutes or until golden brown. Remove to wire racks. Brush with butter. Serve warm. **YIELD:** 3 dozen.

Five-Topping Bread

PREP: 30 min. + rising **BAKE:** 20 min.

You can't go wrong with this recipe. The golden brown loaves have a great combination of seasonings.

—Traci Wynne, Falls Church, Virginia

    1 package (1/4 ounce) active dry yeast
  3/4 cup warm water (110° to 115°)
    1 cup warm milk (110° to 115°)
  1/4 cup sugar
  1/4 cup butter, softened
    1 egg, *separated*
    2 teaspoons salt, *divided*
    4 to 4-1/2 cups all-purpose flour
    1 tablespoon water
    1 teaspoon *each* poppy seeds, sesame seeds
      and caraway seeds
    1 teaspoon dried minced onion

In a large bowl, dissolve yeast in warm water. Add the milk, sugar, butter, egg yolk, 1-1/2 teaspoons salt and 2 cups flour. Beat on medium speed for 3 minutes. Beat until smooth. Stir in enough remaining flour to form a soft dough (dough will be sticky).

Turn onto a floured surface; knead until smooth and elastic, 6-8 minutes. Place in a bowl coated with cooking spray, turning once to coat top. Cover and let rise in a warm place until doubled, about 1 hour.

Punch dough down. Turn onto a lightly floured surface; divide in half. Shape into two round loaves. Place each on a baking sheet coated with cooking spray. Beat egg white and water; brush over the loaves.

Combine the poppy seeds, sesame seeds, caraway seeds, dried onion and remaining salt; sprinkle over the loaves. Cover and let rise in a warm place until doubled, about 30 minutes.

Bake at 375° for 20-25 minutes or until golden brown. Cut the bread into wedges; serve warm. **YIELD:** 2 loaves (10 servings each).

White Chocolate Macadamia Muffins

PREP: 20 min. **BAKE:** 15 min.

I enjoy making muffins because they're so versatile and everyone loves them. These remind me of my favorite cookies.

—Lorie Roach, Buckatunna, Mississippi

  1-3/4 cups all-purpose flour
    3/4 cup sugar
  2-1/2 teaspoons baking powder
    1/2 teaspoon salt
      1 egg
    1/2 cup milk
    1/4 cup butter, melted
    3/4 cup vanilla *or* white chips
    3/4 cup chopped macadamia nuts

GLAZE:
    1/2 cup vanilla *or* white chips
      2 tablespoons heavy whipping cream

In a bowl, combine flour, sugar, baking powder and salt. In another bowl, whisk the egg, milk and butter; stir into dry ingredients just until moistened. Fold in the chips and nuts.

Fill paper-lined muffin cups two-thirds full. Bake at 400° for 15-18 minutes or until a toothpick comes out clean. Cool for 5 minutes before removing from pan to a wire rack.

For glaze, in a small microwave-safe bowl, melt chips with cream; stir until smooth. Drizzle over warm muffins. **YIELD:** 1 dozen.

Lemon Pound Cake Muffins

(Pictured below and on page 122)

PREP: 15 min. **BAKE:** 20 min.

I bake these lemony muffins for all kinds of occasions. My family asks for them often because they're so good!

—Lola Baxter, Winnebago, Minnesota

    1/2 cup butter, softened
      1 cup sugar
      2 eggs
      1 teaspoon vanilla extract
    1/2 teaspoon lemon extract
  1-3/4 cups all-purpose flour
    1/2 teaspoon salt
    1/4 teaspoon baking soda
    1/2 cup sour cream

GLAZE:
      2 cups confectioners' sugar
      3 tablespoons lemon juice

In a large bowl, cream the butter and sugar until light and fluffy. Beat in the eggs and extracts. Combine the flour, salt and baking soda; add to creamed mixture alternately with sour cream.

Fill greased or paper-lined muffin cups three-fourths full. Bake at 400° for 18-20 minutes or until a toothpick comes out clean. Cool for 5 minutes before removing from pan to a wire rack.

Combine the glaze ingredients; drizzle over muffins. Serve warm. **YIELD:** 1 dozen.

Fruit and Nut Stollen

(Pictured below)

PREP: 40 min. + rising **BAKE:** 15 min.

Making this stollen has become a tradition for our family. Everyone looks forward to it at Christmas.

—Rebekah Radewahn, Wauwatosa, Wisconsin

       4 to 4-1/2 cups all-purpose flour
   1/4 cup sugar
     3 teaspoons active dry yeast
     1 teaspoon ground cardamom
   1/2 teaspoon salt
   1-1/4 cups milk
   1/2 cup plus 3 tablespoons butter, softened, *divided*
     1 egg
   1/4 cup *each* raisins and dried cranberries
   1/4 cup *each* chopped dried pineapple and apricots
   1/4 cup *each* chopped pecans, almonds, Brazil nuts and walnuts
   1/2 teaspoon lemon extract

LEMON GLAZE:

     1 cup confectioners' sugar
   4-1/2 teaspoons lemon juice

In a large bowl, combine 2 cups flour, sugar, yeast, cardamom and salt. In a small saucepan, heat milk and 1/2 cup butter to 120°-130°. Add to dry ingredients; beat just until moistened. Add egg; beat until smooth. Stir in enough remaining flour to form a soft dough (dough will be sticky).

Turn onto a floured surface; knead until smooth and elastic, 6-8 minutes. Place in a bowl coated with cooking spray, turning once to coat top. Cover and let rise in a warm place until doubled, about 1 hour. Combine the dried fruits, nuts and extract; set aside.

Punch dough down. Turn onto a lightly floured surface; knead fruit mixture into dough. Divide into thirds. Roll each portion into a 10-in. x 8-in. oval. Melt remaining butter; brush over dough. Fold a long side over to within 1 in. of opposite side; press edges lightly to

seal. Place on baking sheets coated with cooking spray. Cover and let rise until doubled, about 45 minutes.

Bake at 375° for 14-16 minutes or until golden brown. Remove to wire racks. Combine glaze ingredients; drizzle over loaves. **YIELD:** 3 loaves.

Pretty Pumpkin Cinnamon Buns

PREP: 45 min. + rising **BAKE:** 25 min.

I make sticky buns and cinnamon rolls quite often because my husband truly enjoys them. One day I had some fresh pumpkin on hand and decided to try pumpkin cinnamon buns. We loved the results.

—Glenda Joseph, Chambersburg, Pennsylvania

     2 tablespoons active dry yeast
   1/2 cup warm water (110° to 115°)
     4 eggs
     1 cup shortening
     1 cup canned pumpkin
     1 cup warm milk (110° to 115°)
   1/2 cup sugar
   1/2 cup packed brown sugar
   1/3 cup instant vanilla pudding mix
   1/3 cup instant butterscotch pudding mix
     1 teaspoon salt
     7 to 8 cups all-purpose flour

FILLING:

   1/4 cup butter, melted
     1 cup packed brown sugar
     2 teaspoons ground cinnamon

ICING:

     3 tablespoons water
     2 tablespoons butter, softened
     1 teaspoon ground cinnamon
     2 cups confectioners' sugar
   1-1/2 teaspoons vanilla extract

In a large bowl, dissolve the yeast in warm water. Add the eggs, shortening, pumpkin, warm milk, sugars, pudding mixes, salt and 6 cups flour. Beat until smooth. Stir in enough remaining flour to form a soft dough (dough will be sticky).

Turn onto a floured surface; knead until smooth and elastic, 6-8 minutes. Place in a greased bowl, turning once to grease top. Cover and let rise in a warm place until doubled, about 1 hour.

Punch the dough down; divide in half. Roll each portion into a 12-in. x 8-in. rectangle; brush with butter. Combine the brown sugar and cinnamon; sprinkle over the dough to within 1/2 in. of the edges.

Roll up jelly-roll style, starting with a long side; pinch seams to seal. Cut each into 12 slices. Place cut side down in two greased 13-in. x 9-in. baking pans. Cover and let rise until doubled, about 30 minutes.

Bake at 350° for 22-28 minutes or until golden brown. For the icing, in a small bowl, combine the water, butter and cinnamon. Add confectioners' sugar and vanilla; beat until smooth. Spread over buns. Serve warm. **YIELD:** 2 dozen.

Punch the dough down. On a lightly floured surface, roll dough into a 12-in. circle. Place on a greased 12-in. pizza pan. Brush with oil. Combine the Parmesan cheese, rosemary, garlic and salt; sprinkle over dough. Arrange onion rings and tomatoes over top, pressing down lightly.

Bake at 400° for 15-20 minutes or until crust is golden brown. Cut into wedges. **YIELD:** 10 servings.

Poppy Seed Onion Bread

(Pictured below)

PREP: 10 min. **BAKE:** 3-4 hours + cooling

For ease and convenience, I use a bread machine for this golden-crusted savory loaf. It has great onion flavor that tastes wonderful when used to make sandwiches.

—Sue Ashford, Blountville, Tennessee

    1-1/4 cups water (70° to 80°)
        2 tablespoons butter, softened
        2 tablespoons brown sugar
      1/4 cup dried minced onion
    1-1/2 teaspoons salt
        1 teaspoon poppy seeds
      1/2 teaspoon onion powder
      1/2 teaspoon pepper
        3 cups bread flour
        2 tablespoons nonfat dry milk powder
        3 teaspoons active dry yeast

In bread machine pan, place all ingredients in order suggested by manufacturer. Select basic bread setting. Choose crust color and loaf size if available.

Bake according to bread machine directions (check dough after 5 minutes of mixing; add 1 to 2 tablespoons of water or flour if needed). **YIELD:** 1 loaf (1-1/2 pounds).

Tomato Focaccia

(Pictured above)

PREP: 30 min. + rising **BAKE:** 15 min.

What makes this focaccia bread so delicious is the topping. The combination of Parmesan cheese, garlic, rosemary, tomato and onion can't be beat.

—Mary Lou Wayman, Salt Lake City, Utah

    2-1/2 to 3 cups all-purpose flour
        1 teaspoon salt
        1 teaspoon sugar
        3 teaspoons active dry yeast
        1 cup warm water (110° to 115°)
        1 tablespoon olive oil
TOPPING:
        1 tablespoon olive oil
        2 tablespoons grated Parmesan cheese
        1 tablespoon minced fresh rosemary
        2 garlic cloves, minced
      1/4 teaspoon salt
        1 small red onion, thinly sliced and separated
           into rings
        3 to 4 medium plum tomatoes, thinly sliced

In a large bowl, combine 2-1/2 cups flour, salt and sugar. Dissolve the yeast in warm water; stir in olive oil. Add to the dry ingredients; beat until smooth. Stir in enough remaining flour to form a soft dough.

Turn onto a floured surface; knead until smooth and elastic, 6-8 minutes. Place in a greased bowl, turning once to grease top. Cover; let rise in a warm place until doubled, about 30 minutes.

Special Banana Nut Bread

(Pictured above)

PREP: 25 min. **BAKE:** 1 hour + cooling

This extra-special banana bread makes a wonderful gift for friends and neighbors. The recipe makes two loaves, so I can serve one and keep the other one in the freezer. I always have a last-minute gift on hand.

—*Beverly Sprague, Catonsville, Maryland*

- 3/4 **cup butter, softened**
- 1 **package (8 ounces) cream cheese, softened**
- 2 **cups sugar**
- 2 **eggs**
- 1-1/2 **cups mashed ripe bananas (about 4 medium)**
- 1/2 **teaspoon vanilla extract**
- 3 **cups all-purpose flour**
- 1/2 **teaspoon baking powder**
- 1/2 **teaspoon baking soda**
- 1/2 **teaspoon salt**
- 2 **cups chopped pecans,** *divided*

ORANGE GLAZE:
- 1 **cup confectioners' sugar**
- 3 **tablespoons orange juice**
- 1 **teaspoon grated orange peel**

In a large bowl, cream the butter, cream cheese and sugar until light and fluffy. Add eggs, one at a time, beating well after each addition. Beat in bananas and vanilla. Combine the flour, baking powder, baking soda and salt; add to creamed mixture. Fold in 1 cup pecans.

Transfer to two greased 8-in. x 4-in. loaf pans. Sprinkle with remaining pecans. Bake at 350° for 1 to 1-1/4 hours or until a toothpick inserted near the center comes out clean.

Whisk the glaze ingredients together; drizzle over the loaves. Cool for 10 minutes before removing from pans to wire racks. **YIELD:** 2 loaves.

Fruit-Nut Pumpkin Bread

PREP: 30 min. **BAKE:** 1 hour + cooling

My family says our Thanksgiving and Christmas dinner wouldn't be complete without this easy bread.

—*Priscilla Gilbert, Indian Harbour Beach, Florida*

- 2-2/3 **cups sugar**
- 1 **can (15 ounces) solid-pack pumpkin**
- 1 **cup canola oil**
- 4 **eggs**
- 1 **teaspoon vanilla extract**
- 3-1/2 **cups all-purpose flour**
- 1-1/2 **teaspoons ground cinnamon**
- 1 **teaspoon salt**
- 1 **teaspoon baking soda**
- 1/4 **teaspoon ground cloves**
- 1-1/2 **cups coarsely chopped walnuts**
- 2/3 **cup golden raisins**
- 2/3 **cup raisins**
- 2/3 **cup dried cranberries**

CRANBERRY CREAM CHEESE SPREAD:
- 1/2 **cup dried cranberries**
- 1-1/2 **cups boiling water**
- 1 **package (8 ounces) cream cheese, softened**
- 1/3 **cup chopped walnuts**

In a large bowl, beat the sugar, pumpkin, oil, eggs and vanilla until well blended. Combine the flour, cinnamon, salt, baking soda and cloves; gradually beat into pumpkin mixture until blended. Fold in the walnuts, raisins and cranberries.

Transfer to two greased 9-in. x 5-in. loaf pans. Bake at 350° for 60-70 minutes or until a toothpick inserted near the center comes out clean. Cool for 10 minutes before removing from pans to wire racks.

For spread, place cranberries in a small bowl; add boiling water. Let stand for 5 minutes; drain. In a small mixing bowl, beat cream cheese until smooth. Beat in cranberries and walnuts until blended. Serve with bread. **YIELD:** 2 loaves and 1 cup spread.

Honey-Oat Pan Rolls

PREP: 45 min. + rising **BAKE:** 20 min.

Since these delicate rolls require only one rising, they are relatively quick to make. Whole wheat flour and hearty oats make them nutritious, too.

—*Arlene Kay Butler, Ogden, Utah*

- 2-1/2 **to 2-3/4 cups all-purpose flour**
- 3/4 **cup whole wheat flour**
- 1/2 **cup old-fashioned oats**
- 2 **packages (1/4 ounce** *each***) active dry yeast**
- 1 **teaspoon salt**
- 1 **cup water**
- 1/4 **cup honey**

5 tablespoons butter, *divided*
1 egg

In a large bowl, combine 1 cup all-purpose flour, whole wheat flour, oats, yeast and salt. In a small saucepan, heat the water, honey and 4 tablespoons butter to 120°-130°. Add to dry ingredients; beat just until moistened. Add egg; beat until combined. Stir in enough remaining all-purpose flour to form a soft dough.

Turn onto a floured surface; knead until smooth and elastic, 6-8 minutes. Place in a greased bowl, turning once to grease top. Cover and let rise in a warm place until doubled, about 1 hour.

Punch dough down. Turn onto a lightly floured surface; divide into 24 pieces. Shape each into a ball. Place in a greased 13-in. x 9-in. baking pan. Cover and let rise until doubled, about 30 minutes.

Bake at 375° for 20-22 minutes or until golden brown. Melt remaining butter; brush over rolls. Remove from pan to a wire rack. **YIELD:** 2 dozen.

Pull-Apart Bacon Bread

(Pictured below and on page 122)

PREP: 15 min. **BAKE:** 25 min.

I baked this tender and tasty bread for my husband, and he just raved about it! When I'm out of bacon, I substitute bacon bits.
—*Terri Christensen, Montague, Michigan*

12 bacon strips, diced
2 tubes (12 ounces *each*) refrigerated buttermilk biscuits
2 cups (8 ounces) shredded part-skim mozzarella cheese
1 tablespoon Italian salad dressing mix
2 teaspoons olive oil

In a large skillet, cook bacon over medium heat until cooked but not crisp. Using a slotted spoon, remove to paper towels to drain. Separate biscuits; cut each biscuit into quarters.

In a large bowl, combine the mozzarella cheese, dressing mix, olive oil and bacon. Place half of the biscuit pieces in a greased 10-in. fluted tube pan; sprinkle with half of the cheese mixture. Top with remaining biscuit pieces and cheese mixture.

Bake at 375° for 25-30 minutes or until golden brown. Cool for 5 minutes before inverting onto a serving plate. Serve immediately. **YIELD:** 12 servings.

Pecan Lemon Loaf

(Pictured above)

PREP: 20 min. **BAKE:** 50 min. + cooling

A pretty glaze gives this moist, nutty bread an extra boost of lemony flavor. For variety, substitute grated orange peel and orange juice for the lemons.
—*Laura Comitz, Enola, Pennsylvania*

1/2 cup butter, softened
1-1/2 cups sugar, *divided*
2 eggs
2 cups all-purpose flour
1 teaspoon baking powder
1/2 teaspoon salt
3/4 cup sour cream
1 cup chopped pecans, toasted
1 tablespoon grated lemon peel
1/4 cup lemon juice

In a large bowl, cream butter and 1 cup sugar until light and fluffy. Add eggs; mix well. Combine the flour, baking powder and salt; add to creamed mixture alternately with sour cream. Fold in pecans and lemon peel.

Transfer to a greased 9-in. x 5-in. loaf pan. Bake at 350° for 50-60 minutes or until a toothpick inserted near the center comes out clean.

In a small saucepan, combine lemon juice and remaining sugar. Cook and stir over medium heat until sugar is dissolved. Pour over warm bread. Cool completely on a wire rack before removing from pan. **YIELD:** 1 loaf.

Vanilla Cinnamon Rolls

(Pictured below)

PREP: 30 min. + rising **BAKE:** 20 min.

This is the best recipe I have found for cinnamon rolls. They're so tender with a delightful vanilla flavor and yummy frosting. When I serve them to my family, they disappear in no time.

—Linda Martin, Warsaw, Indiana

  2 cups cold milk
  1 package (3.4 ounces) instant vanilla pudding mix
  2 packages (1/4 ounce *each*) active dry yeast
1/2 cup warm water (110° to 115°)
1/2 cup plus 2 tablespoons butter, melted, *divided*
  2 eggs
  2 tablespoons sugar
  1 teaspoon salt
  6 cups all-purpose flour
FILLING:
1/2 cup packed brown sugar
  1 teaspoon ground cinnamon
FROSTING:
  1 cup packed brown sugar
1/2 cup heavy whipping cream
1/2 cup butter, cubed
  2 cups confectioners' sugar

Whisk milk and pudding mix together for 2 minutes; set aside. In a large bowl, dissolve yeast in warm water. Add 1/2 cup butter, eggs, sugar, salt and 2 cups flour. Beat on medium speed for 3 minutes. Add pudding; beat until smooth. Stir in enough remaining flour to form a soft dough (dough will be sticky).

Turn onto a floured surface; knead until smooth and elastic, 6-8 minutes. Place in a greased bowl, turning once to grease top. Cover and let rise in a warm place until doubled, about 1 hour.

Punch the dough down. Turn onto a floured surface; divide in half. Roll each portion into an 18-in. x 11-in. rectangle; brush with the remaining butter. Combine brown sugar and cinnamon; sprinkle over dough to within 1/2 in. of edges.

Roll up jelly-roll style, starting with a long side; pinch seams to seal. Cut each into 16 slices. Place cut side down in two greased 13-in. x 9-in. baking dishes. Cover and let rise until doubled, about 30 minutes. Bake at 350° for 20-25 minutes or until golden brown.

Meanwhile, in a large saucepan, combine the brown sugar, cream and butter. Bring to a boil; cook and stir for 2 minutes. Remove from the heat. Beat in confectioners' sugar with a hand mixer until creamy. Frost rolls. Serve warm. **YIELD:** 32 rolls.

Pumpkin Scones with Berry Butter

PREP: 25 min. + chilling **BAKE:** 15 min.

These delightful scones are perfect on a cold winter day with a steaming hot cup of coffee. They also make a wonderful hostess gift arranged in a basket.

—Judy Wilson, Sun City West, Arizona

  2 tablespoons dried cranberries
1/2 cup boiling water
1/2 cup butter, softened
  3 tablespoons confectioners' sugar
DOUGH:
2-1/4 cups all-purpose flour
1/4 cup packed brown sugar
  2 teaspoons baking powder
1-1/2 teaspoons pumpkin pie spice
1/4 teaspoon salt
1/4 teaspoon baking soda
1/2 cup cold butter
  1 egg
1/2 cup canned pumpkin
1/3 cup milk
  2 tablespoons chopped pecans, optional

Place the cranberries in a small bowl; add boiling water. Let stand for 5 minutes; drain and chop. In a small bowl, beat butter until light and fluffy. Add confectioners' sugar and cranberries; mix well. Cover and refrigerate for at least 1 hour.

In a large bowl, combine the flour, brown sugar, baking powder, pie spice, salt and baking soda. Cut in butter until mixture resembles coarse crumbs. In a small bowl, whisk the egg, pumpkin and milk; add to crumb mixture just until moistened. Stir in pecans if desired.

Turn the dough onto a floured surface; knead 10 times. Pat into an 8-in. circle. Cut into eight wedges; separate wedges and place on a greased baking sheet.

Bake at 400° for 12-15 minutes or until golden brown. Serve warm with berry butter. **YIELD:** 8 scones and about 1/2 cup butter.

Bake at 350° for 35-40 minutes or until golden brown. Remove from pans to wire racks to cool. Refrigerate leftovers. **YIELD:** 2 loaves.

Feta and Chive Muffins

(Pictured below)

PREP: 15 min. **BAKE:** 20 min.

This is a springtime variation on a savory muffin my husband has made for years. It has a light texture, almost like a popover, and is best eaten hot from the oven.

—Angela Buchanan, Boulder, Colorado

   1-1/2 **cups all-purpose flour**
    3 **teaspoons baking powder**
  1/4 **teaspoon salt**
    2 **eggs**
    1 **cup milk**
    2 **tablespoons butter, melted**
  1/2 **cup crumbled feta cheese**
    3 **tablespoons snipped chives**

In a bowl, combine the flour, baking powder and salt. In another bowl, whisk the eggs, milk and butter together; stir into dry ingredients just until moistened. Fold in the feta cheese and the chives.

Fill greased or paper-lined muffin cups two-thirds full. Bake at 400° for 18-22 minutes or until a toothpick comes out clean. Cool for 5 minutes before removing from pan to a wire rack. Serve warm. Refrigerate leftovers. **YIELD:** 1 dozen.

Cheddar Loaves

(Pictured above)

PREP: 25 min. + rising **BAKE:** 35 min. + cooling

Swirls of cheddar cheese give these loaves an exquisite taste. Try a slice or two for sandwiches, toasted for breakfast or served on the side with a Caesar salad.

—Agnes Ward, Stratford, Ontario

    3 **teaspoons active dry yeast**
  1/2 **cup warm water (110° to 115°)**
    2 **cups warm milk (110° to 115°)**
    2 **tablespoons butter, melted**
    2 **eggs**
    3 **teaspoons sugar**
    2 **teaspoons salt**
    6 **to 6-1/2 cups all-purpose flour**
    2 **cups (8 ounces) shredded sharp cheddar cheese**

In a large bowl, dissolve yeast in warm water. Add the milk, butter, eggs, sugar, salt and 6 cups flour. Beat on medium speed for 3 minutes. Stir in enough remaining flour to form a soft dough.

Turn onto a lightly floured surface; knead until smooth and elastic, 6-8 minutes. Place in a greased bowl, turning once to grease top. Cover and let rise in a warm place until doubled, about 1 hour.

Punch dough down. Turn onto a lightly floured surface; knead cheese into the dough. Divide in half; shape each portion into a 6-in. round loaf. Place on greased baking sheets. Cover and let rise until doubled, about 45 minutes.

Strawberry Popovers

(Pictured above)

PREP: 20 min. **BAKE:** 30 min.

These pretty popovers "pop up" nicely in the oven and hold a delicate cream filling dotted with fresh chopped strawberries. If you don't have a popover pan on hand, you can try muffin cups.
—*Sandy Holton-Vanthoff, San Diego, California*

   1 cup heavy whipping cream
1/3 cup sugar
   1 teaspoon vanilla extract
   2 cups chopped fresh strawberries
POPOVERS:
4-1/2 teaspoons shortening
   4 eggs
   2 cups milk
   2 cups all-purpose flour
   1 tablespoon sugar
   1 teaspoon salt

In a medium bowl, beat the cream until it begins to thicken. Add the sugar and vanilla; beat until stiff peaks form. Fold in the chopped strawberries. Cover and refrigerate until serving.

For the popovers, using 1/2 teaspoon shortening for each cup, grease the bottom and sides of nine popover cups. In a small bowl, beat eggs; beat in milk. Add the flour, sugar and salt; beat until smooth (do not overmix). Fill prepared cups half full.

Bake at 450° for 15 minutes. Reduce heat to 350°; bake 15 minutes longer or until very firm. Immediately cut a slit in the top of each popover to allow steam to escape. Spoon strawberry filling into popovers. Serve immediately. **YIELD:** 9 servings.

Parmesan Breadsticks

(Pictured below)

PREP: 40 min. + rising **BAKE:** 10 min.

Breadsticks baking in the oven fill the kitchen with a tempting aroma. They're wonderful served warm. My family tells me I can't make them too often.
—*Gaylene Anderson, Sandy, Utah*

   2 packages (1/4 ounce *each*) active dry yeast
1-1/2 cups warm water (110° to 115°)
1/2 cup warm milk (110° to 115°)
   3 tablespoons sugar
   3 tablespoons plus 1/4 cup butter, softened, *divided*
   1 teaspoon salt
4-1/2 to 5-1/2 cups all-purpose flour
1/4 cup grated Parmesan cheese
1/2 teaspoon garlic salt

In a large bowl, dissolve yeast in warm water. Add the milk, sugar, 3 tablespoons butter, salt and 2 cups flour. Beat until smooth. Stir in enough remaining flour to form a soft dough.

Turn onto a floured surface; knead until smooth and elastic, 6-8 minutes. Place in a greased bowl, turning once to grease top. Cover and let rise in a warm place until doubled, about 45 minutes.

Punch the dough down. Turn onto a floured surface; divide into 36 pieces. Shape each piece into a 6-in. rope. Place 2 in. apart on greased baking sheets. Cover and let rise until doubled, about 25 minutes.

Melt remaining butter; brush over dough. Sprinkle with cheese and garlic salt. Bake at 400° for 8-10 minutes or until golden brown. Remove from pans to wire racks. **YIELD:** 3 dozen.

Almond Berry Muffins

PREP: 20 min. **BAKE:** 20 min.

I brought these moist muffins to the office and they were a hit. If strawberries aren't in season, just substitute with frozen cut strawberries directly from the freezer.

—*Deborah Feinberg, East Setauket, New York*

- 1-1/4 cups sliced almonds, *divided*
- 1 egg white, lightly beaten
- 1-1/2 cups sugar, *divided*
- 1/4 cup shortening
- 1/4 cup butter, softened
- 2 eggs
- 1 teaspoon vanilla extract
- 1/2 teaspoon almond extract
- 2 cups all-purpose flour
- 1 teaspoon baking powder
- 1/2 teaspoon salt
- 1/4 teaspoon baking soda
- 3/4 cup buttermilk
- 1-1/4 cups fresh strawberries, chopped

In a bowl, combine 1 cup almonds and egg white. Add 1/2 cup sugar; toss to coat. Spoon into a greased 15-in. x 10-in. x 1-in. baking pan. Bake at 350° for 9-11 minutes or until golden brown, stirring occasionally.

In a large bowl, cream shortening, butter and remaining sugar until light and fluffy. Add eggs, one at a time, beating well after each addition. Beat in extracts. Combine the flour, baking powder, salt and baking soda; add to creamed mixture alternately with buttermilk. Fold in the strawberries and remaining almonds.

Fill greased or paper-lined muffin cups two-thirds full. Sprinkle with sugared almonds. Bake at 350° for 20-25 minutes or until a toothpick comes out clean. Cool for 5 minutes before removing from pans to wire racks. **YIELD:** 1-1/2 dozen.

Christmas Morning Croissants

(Pictured above right and on page 122)

PREP: 50 min. + chilling **BAKE:** 20 min.

Growing up in France, I often enjoyed buttery croissants with a cup of hot chocolate for breakfast. I re-created this experience for my family with this recipe. Now, it's a Christmas tradition!

—*Tish Stevenson, Grand Rapids, Michigan*

- 2 packages (1/4 ounce *each*) active dry yeast
- 1 cup warm water (110° to 115°)
- 1-1/4 cups cold butter, *divided*
- 5 cups all-purpose flour
- 1/3 cup sugar
- 1-1/2 teaspoons salt
- 3/4 cup evaporated milk
- 2 eggs
- 1 tablespoon water

In a large bowl, dissolve yeast in warm water; let stand for 5 minutes. Melt 1/4 cup butter; set aside. Combine 1 cup flour, sugar and salt; add to yeast mixture. Add the milk, 1 egg and melted butter; beat until smooth.

Place remaining flour in a large bowl; cut in remaining cold butter until crumbly. Add yeast mixture; mix well. Do not knead. Cover and refrigerate overnight.

Punch dough down. Turn onto a lightly floured surface; knead about six times. Divide dough into four pieces. Roll each piece into a 16-in. circle; cut each circle into eight wedges.

Roll up wedges from the wide ends and place croissants point side down and 3 in. apart onto ungreased baking sheets. Curve ends to form crescents. Cover and let rise in a warm place for 1 hour.

Beat water and remaining egg; brush over rolls. Bake at 325° for 20-25 minutes or until lightly browned. Serve warm. **YIELD:** 32 rolls.

yeast know-how

To make sure active dry yeast (not quick-rise yeast) is alive and active before starting your baking, you may want to proof it first. Here's how:

Dissolve one package of yeast and 1 teaspoon sugar in 1/4 cup warm water (110° to 115°). Let stand for 5 to 10 minutes.

If the mixture foams up, the yeast mixture can be used because the yeast is active. If it does not foam, the yeast is dead and should be discarded.

Walnut Raspberry Muffins

(Pictured below)

PREP: 25 min. **BAKE:** 20 min./batch

Raspberries are my favorite berry, so this recipe is tops with me. The walnuts give the muffins a nice crunch. You can dress them up by using foil liners instead of paper.

—Elisa Lochridge, Tigard, Oregon

- 2/3 cup cream cheese, softened
- 1/3 cup butter, softened
- 1-1/2 cups sugar
- 2 egg whites
- 1 egg
- 1-1/2 teaspoons vanilla extract
- 2 cups all-purpose flour
- 1 teaspoon baking powder
- 1/4 teaspoon baking soda
- 1/2 cup buttermilk
- 2 cups fresh *or* frozen raspberries
- 1/4 cup chopped walnuts

In a large bowl, beat the cream cheese, butter and sugar until light and fluffy. Add the egg whites, egg and vanilla; beat well. Combine the flour, baking powder and baking soda; add to creamed mixture alternately with buttermilk. Fold in the raspberries and walnuts.

Fill paper-lined muffin cups three-fourths full. Bake at 350° for 20-24 minutes or until a toothpick comes out clean. Cool for 5 minutes before removing from pans to wire racks. Serve warm. **YIELD:** 1-1/2 dozen.

EDITOR'S NOTE: If using frozen raspberries, do not thaw before adding to batter.

Vegetable & Cheese Focaccia

(Pictured above)

PREP: 20 min. **BAKE:** 30 min.

My family eats up this flavorful bread as fast as I can make it. Sometimes I add different herbs, red onion or crumbled bacon. It's one of my best recipes!

—Mary Cass, Baltimore, Maryland

- 1 cup water (70° to 80°)
- 4-1/2 teaspoons olive oil
- 4-1/2 teaspoons sugar
- 2 teaspoons dried oregano
- 1-1/4 teaspoons salt
- 3-1/4 cups bread flour
- 1-1/2 teaspoons active dry yeast

TOPPING:

- 1 tablespoon olive oil
- 1 tablespoon dried basil
- 2 medium tomatoes, thinly sliced
- 1 medium onion, thinly sliced
- 1 cup frozen chopped broccoli, thawed
- 1/4 teaspoon salt
- 1/4 teaspoon pepper
- 3/4 cup grated Parmesan cheese
- 1 cup (4 ounces) shredded part-skim mozzarella cheese

In bread machine pan, place the first seven ingredients in the order suggested by manufacturer. Select the dough setting (check the dough after 5 minutes of mixing; add 1 to 2 tablespoons of water or flour if needed).

When cycle is completed, turn dough onto a lightly floured surface. Punch dough down. Roll into a 13-in. x 9-in. rectangle; transfer to a 13-in. x 9-in. baking dish coated with cooking spray.

For topping, brush dough with olive oil; sprinkle with basil. Layer with the tomatoes, onion and broccoli; sprinkle with salt, pepper and Parmesan cheese. Cover and let rise in a warm place until doubled, about 30 minutes.

Bake at 350° for 20 minutes. Sprinkle with mozzarella cheese; bake 10-15 minutes longer or until golden brown and cheese is melted. Cut into 16 pieces. **YIELD:** 16 servings.

Mini Maple Cinnamon Rolls

PREP: 20 min. **BAKE:** 20 min.

Maple syrup sweetens these lovely cinnamon buns. I make the dough in my bread machine before popping the rolls in the oven.
—_Juanita Carlsen, North Bend, Oregon_

- 2/3 cup milk
- 1/3 cup maple syrup
- 1/3 cup butter, softened
- 1 egg
- 3/4 teaspoon salt
- 3 cups bread flour
- 1 package (1/4 ounce) active dry yeast

TOPPING:

- 1/2 cup packed brown sugar
- 2 tablespoons bread flour
- 4 teaspoons ground cinnamon
- 6 tablespoons cold butter

MAPLE ICING:

- 1 cup confectioners' sugar
- 3 tablespoons butter, melted
- 3 tablespoons maple syrup
- 1 to 2 teaspoons milk

In bread machine pan, place the first seven ingredients in order suggested by manufacturer. Select the dough setting (check the dough after 5 minutes of mixing; add 1 to 2 tablespoons of water or bread flour if needed).

When the cycle is completed, turn dough onto a lightly floured surface. Roll into two 12-in. x 7-in. rectangles. In a small bowl, combine the brown sugar, flour and cinnamon; cut in butter until mixture resembles coarse crumbs. Sprinkle half over each rectangle. Roll up jelly-roll style, starting from a long side; pinch seam to seal.

Cut each roll into 12 slices. Place cut side down in one greased 13-in. x 9-in. baking pan. Cover and let rise in a warm place until doubled, about 20 minutes.

Bake at 375° for 20-25 minutes or until golden brown. Cool on a wire rack for 5 minutes. Meanwhile, in a small bowl, combine the confectioners' sugar, butter, syrup and enough milk to achieve desired consistency. Spread over warm rolls. **YIELD:** 2 dozen.

EDITOR'S NOTE: We recommend you do not use a bread machine's time-delay feature for this recipe.

Herbed Popovers

PREP: 15 min. **BAKE:** 30 min.

One of my family's favorite meals is roast beef dinner with these delicious popovers.
—_Lorraine Caland, Thunder Bay, Ontario_

- 1 cup all-purpose flour
- 1 teaspoon dried thyme
- 1 teaspoon dried basil
- 1 teaspoon rubbed sage
- 1/4 teaspoon celery salt
- 3 eggs
- 1 cup milk
- 1 tablespoon canola oil

In a large bowl, combine the flour, thyme, basil, sage and celery salt. Combine the eggs, milk and oil; whisk into dry ingredients just until blended. Refrigerate for 30 minutes.

Fill eight greased and floured 6-oz. custard cups half full. Place on a baking sheet.

Bake at 450° for 15 minutes. Reduce heat to 350° (do not open oven door). Bake 15-20 minutes longer or until deep golden brown (do not underbake). Serve immediately. **YIELD:** 8 popovers.

Sweet Milk Dinner Rolls

(Pictured below)

PREP: 20 min. **BAKE:** 35 min.

A hint of sweetness in these tender buns brings in many compliments. Served warm with butter or jam, they're a big hit at any meal. They reheat nicely, too.
—_Merle Dyck, Elkford, British Columbia_

- 1 package (1/4 ounce) active dry yeast
- 2 cups warm milk (110° to 115°)
- 1/2 cup sugar
- 2 tablespoons butter, melted
- 1 teaspoon salt
- 4 to 5 cups all-purpose flour

In a large bowl, dissolve yeast in warm milk. Add the sugar, butter, salt and 3 cups flour. Beat until smooth. Add enough remaining flour to form a soft dough.

Turn onto a floured surface; knead until smooth and elastic, about 6-8 minutes. Place in a greased bowl, turning once to grease top. Cover and let rise in a warm place until doubled, about 1 hour.

Punch dough down. Turn onto a floured surface; divide into 16 pieces. Shape each into a ball. Place 2 in. apart on greased baking sheets. Cover and let rise until doubled, about 30 minutes.

Bake at 350° for 35-40 minutes or until golden brown. Remove from pans to wire racks. Serve warm. **YIELD:** 16 rolls.

Stacking your goodie tray high is a cinch with oodles of decadent recipes at your fingertips. Consider any of these 36 delights when your sweet tooth comes calling.

cookies, bars & candies

Blond Brownies a la Mode 142

Iced Pumpkin Cookies 142

Delicate Mint Thins 143

Lemon Tea Cookies 143

Chocolate Mint Dreams 144

Rustic Nut Bars 144

Lavender Cookies 145

Creamy Cashew Brownies 145

Coconut Pecan Cookies 146

Chocolate Heart Cookies 146

Berry-Cream Cookie Snaps 147

Chocolate Pecan Bars 147

Cookie Dough Truffles 148

Butterscotch Eggnog Stars 148

Pinwheels and Checkerboards 149

Elegant Dipped Cherries 149

Coffee and Cream Brownies 150

Slice and Bake Lemon Gems 150

Almond Sugar Cookies 151

Glazed Peanut Butter Bars 151

Nice and Soft Sugar Cookies 152

Irish Mint Brownies 152

Meringue Fudge Drops 153

Frosted Rhubarb Cookies 153

Hazelnut-Espresso Sandwich Cookies 154

Frosted Cookie Brownies 154

Chocolate Pretzels 155

Dipped Pecan Spritz 155

Door County Cherry Biscotti 156

Peanut Butter Blondies 156

Almond Truffle Brownies 157

Chewy Apple Oatmeal Cookies 157

Homemade Peanut Butter Cups 158

Ranger Cookies 158

Cherry Chocolate Bark 159

Tiramisu Brownies 159

PICTURED CLOCKWISE FROM UPPER LEFT: Berry-Cream Cookie Snaps (page 147), Coffee and Cream Brownies (page 150), Homemade Peanut Butter Cups (page 158) and Frosted Rhubarb Cookies (page 153).

Blond Brownies a la Mode

(Pictured above)

PREP: 25 min. **BAKE:** 25 min. + cooling

We have a lot of church socials and I'm always looking for something new and different to prepare. These brownies, drizzled with a sweet maple sauce, are a sure hit.
—Pat Parker, Chester, South Carolina

- 3/4 cup butter, softened
- 2 cups packed brown sugar
- 4 eggs
- 2 teaspoons vanilla extract
- 2 cups all-purpose flour
- 2 teaspoons baking powder
- 1 teaspoon salt
- 1-1/2 cups chopped pecans

MAPLE CREAM SAUCE:
- 1 cup maple syrup
- 2 tablespoons butter
- 1/4 cup evaporated milk

Vanilla ice cream and chopped pecans

In a large bowl, cream butter and brown sugar until light and fluffy. Add eggs, one at a time, beating well after each addition. Beat in vanilla. Combine the flour, baking powder and salt; gradually add to creamed mixture. Stir in pecans.

Spread into a greased 13-in. x 9-in. baking pan. Bake at 350° for 25-30 minutes or until a toothpick inserted near the center comes out clean. Cool on a wire rack.

For the sauce, combine syrup and butter in a saucepan. Bring to a boil; cook and stir for 3 minutes. Remove from the heat; stir in milk. Cut brownies into squares; cut in half if desired.

Place on dessert plates with a scoop of ice cream. Top with sauce; sprinkle with pecans. **YIELD:** 20 servings.

Iced Pumpkin Cookies

PREP: 45 min. **BAKE:** 15 min./batch + cooling

My young son, Joshua, likes testing, or should I say consuming, these chunky cookies! The combination of dried fruit, nuts, spices and vanilla chips is fantastic.
—Johna Nilson, Vista, California

- 1 cup butter, softened
- 1/2 cup sugar
- 1/2 cup packed brown sugar
- 1 egg
- 1 cup canned pumpkin
- 1 cup all-purpose flour
- 1 cup whole wheat flour
- 1-1/2 teaspoons ground cinnamon
- 1 teaspoon baking powder
- 1 teaspoon ground ginger
- 1/2 teaspoon salt
- 1/2 teaspoon baking soda
- 1/2 teaspoon ground nutmeg
- 1/4 teaspoon ground cloves
- 1 cup granola without raisins
- 1 cup chopped walnuts
- 1 cup vanilla *or* white chips
- 1 cup dried cranberries

ICING:
- 1/4 cup butter, softened
- 2 cups confectioners' sugar
- 3 tablespoons milk

In a large bowl, cream the butter and sugars until light and fluffy. Beat in the egg and pumpkin. Combine the flours, cinnamon, baking powder, ginger, salt, baking soda, nutmeg and cloves; gradually add to the creamed mixture. Stir in the granola, walnuts, chips and cranberries.

Drop by tablespoonfuls 2 in. apart onto greased baking sheets. Bake at 350° for 15-18 minutes or until lightly browned. Remove to wire racks to cool.

In a small bowl, for the icing, combine the butter, confectioners' sugar and milk until smooth. Frost cookies. Store in the refrigerator. **YIELD:** 3 dozen.

light vs. dark brown sugar

Both light and dark brown sugar are a mixture of granulated sugar and molasses. Light brown sugar has a delicate flavor. Dark brown sugar, which has more molasses, has a stronger, more intense, flavor. They can be used interchangeably depending on your personal preference.

Lemon Tea Cookies

(Pictured below)

PREP: 25 min. + chilling **BAKE:** 10 min.

These sandwich cookies have a lovely lemon filling and a rich, buttery flavor. My mother got the recipe from a friend in the 1950s. Mom always made them at Christmas, and now my sister and I do the same.

—Phyllis Dietz, Westland, Michigan

> 3/4 cup butter, softened
> 1/2 cup sugar
> 1 egg yolk
> 1/2 teaspoon vanilla extract
> 2 cups all-purpose flour
> 1/4 cup finely chopped walnuts

FILLING:

> 3 tablespoons butter, softened
> 4-1/2 teaspoons lemon juice
> 3/4 teaspoon grated orange peel
> 1-1/2 cups confectioners' sugar
> 2 drops yellow food coloring, optional

In a large bowl, cream butter and sugar until light and fluffy. Beat in the egg yolk and vanilla. Gradually add flour. Shape into two 14-in. rolls; reshape each roll into a 14-in. x 1-1/8-in. x 1-1/8-in. block. Wrap each in plastic wrap. Refrigerate overnight.

Unwrap and cut into 1/4-in. slices. Place 2 in. apart on ungreased baking sheets. Sprinkle half of the cookies with nuts, gently pressing into dough. Bake at 400° for 8-10 minutes or until golden brown around the edges. Remove to wire racks to cool.

For the filling, in a small bowl, cream the butter, lemon juice and orange peel until fluffy. Gradually add confectioners' sugar until smooth. Tint yellow if desired. Spread about 1 teaspoon on bottom of the plain cookies; place nut-topped cookies over filling. **YIELD:** about 4-1/2 dozen.

Delicate Mint Thins

(Pictured above)

PREP: 20 min. + chilling **BAKE:** 20 min. + cooling

When I was newly married, I needed something fancy to impress my relatives at a reunion and came up with these cookies. I received many compliments on their subtle flavor.

—Kristine McDaniel, Kettering, Ohio

> 1/2 cup butter, softened
> 1/2 cup sugar
> 1 egg yolk
> 1/2 teaspoon vanilla extract
> 1-1/2 cups all-purpose flour
> 1-1/2 teaspoons baking powder
> 1/8 teaspoon salt
> 3 tablespoons milk
> 1 cup fresh mint, finely chopped
> 1-2/3 cups semisweet chocolate chips
> 1 tablespoon shortening

In a large bowl, cream butter and sugar until light and fluffy. Beat in egg yolk and vanilla. Combine the flour, baking powder and salt; add to creamed mixture alternately with milk, mixing well after each addition. Stir in mint. Shape into two 8-in. rolls; wrap each in plastic wrap. Refrigerate for 2 hours or until firm.

Unwrap and cut into 1/4-in. slices. Place 1 in. apart on greased baking sheets. Bake at 350° for 8-12 minutes or until edges are golden. Remove to wire racks to cool.

In a microwave-safe bowl, melt chocolate chips and shortening; stir until smooth. Dip each cookie halfway; allowing excess to drip off. Place on waxed paper; let stand until set. **YIELD:** about 4-1/2 dozen.

Chocolate Mint Dreams

(Pictured below)

PREP/TOTAL TIME: 30 min.

Since chocolate and mint create my favorite flavor combination, I can eat these dainty shortbread-like treats by the dozen. But I manage to save some for guests because they make my cookie trays look so elegant.

—Anne Revers, Omaha, Nebraska

3/4 cup butter, softened
1 cup confectioners' sugar
2 squares (1 ounce *each*) unsweetened chocolate, melted and cooled
1/4 teaspoon peppermint extract
1-1/2 cups all-purpose flour
1 cup miniature semisweet chocolate chips

ICING:
2 tablespoons butter, softened
1 cup confectioners' sugar
1 to 2 tablespoons milk
1/4 teaspoon peppermint extract
1 to 2 drops green food coloring

DRIZZLE:
1/2 cup semisweet chocolate chips
1/2 teaspoon shortening

In a large bowl, cream butter and confectioners' sugar. Beat in chocolate and mint extract. Gradually add flour. Stir in chocolate chips. (Dough will be soft.)

Drop by tablespoonfuls 2 in. apart on ungreased baking sheets. Bake at 375° for 6-8 minutes or until firm. Cool for 2 minutes before removing to wire racks to cool completely.

Meanwhile, combine the icing ingredients; spread over the cooled cookies. Let set. In a microwave, melt the chocolate chips and shortening; stir until smooth. Drizzle over cookies. **YIELD:** 4 dozen.

Rustic Nut Bars

(Pictured above)

PREP: 20 min. **BAKE:** 35 min. + cooling

Everyone will jump with joy when they bite into these chewy, gooey bars. They'll love the cookie crust and the nutty topping.
—Barbara Driscoll, West Allis, Wisconsin

1 tablespoon plus 3/4 cup cold butter, *divided*
2-1/3 cups all-purpose flour
1/2 cup sugar
1/2 teaspoon baking powder
1/2 teaspoon salt
1 egg, lightly beaten

TOPPING:
2/3 cup honey
1/2 cup packed brown sugar
1/4 teaspoon salt
6 tablespoons butter, cubed
2 tablespoons heavy whipping cream
1 cup chopped hazelnuts, toasted
1 cup roasted salted almonds
1 cup salted cashews, toasted
1 cup pistachios, toasted

Line a 13-in. x 9-in. baking pan with foil; grease the foil with 1 tablespoon butter. Set aside.

In a large bowl, combine the flour, sugar, baking powder and salt; cut in remaining butter until mixture resembles coarse crumbs. Stir in egg until blended (mixture will be dry).

Press firmly onto the bottom of prepared pan. Bake at 375° for 18-20 minutes or until edges are golden brown. Cool on a wire rack.

For the topping, in a large heavy saucepan, bring the honey, brown sugar and salt to a boil over medium heat until sugar is smooth, stirring often. Boil without stirring for 2 minutes. Add the butter and cream. Bring to a boil; cook and stir for 1 minute or until smooth. Remove from the heat; stir in the hazelnuts, almonds, cashews and pistachios. Spread over crust.

Bake at 375° for 15-20 minutes or until topping is bubbly. Cool completely on a wire rack. Using foil, lift bars out of pan. Discard foil; cut into squares. **YIELD:** about 3 dozen.

Lavender Cookies

(*Pictured below*)

PREP: 30 min. **BAKE:** 10 min./batch

I am a wedding and event planner and one of my brides who had a lavender-themed wedding served these unusual cookies at her reception. They were so good, I asked her for the recipe.
—*Glenna Tooman, Boise, Idaho*

1/2 **cup shortening**
1/2 **cup butter, softened**
1-1/4 **cups sugar**
2 **eggs**
1 **teaspoon vanilla extract**
1/2 **teaspoon almond extract**
2-1/4 **cups all-purpose flour**
4 **teaspoons dried lavender flowers**
1 **teaspoon baking powder**
1/2 **teaspoon salt**

In a large bowl, cream the shortening, butter and sugar. Add eggs, one at a time, beating well after each addition. Beat in extracts. Combine the flour, lavender, baking powder and salt; gradually add to creamed mixture and mix well.

Drop by rounded teaspoonfuls 2 in. apart onto baking sheets lightly coated with cooking spray.

Bake at 375° for 8-10 minutes or until golden brown. Cool for 2 minutes before removing to wire racks. Store in an airtight container. **YIELD:** about 7 dozen.

Creamy Cashew Brownies

(*Pictured above*)

PREP: 15 min. **BAKE:** 25 min. + chilling

My sister-in-law dubbed me the "dessert queen" because of treats like this that I take to our family get-togethers. The brownies have a fudge-like texture and a rich cream cheese topping.
—*Karen Wagner, Danville, Illinois*

1 **package fudge brownie mix (13-inch x 9-inch pan size)**
1/3 **cup water**
1/4 **cup canola oil**
1 **egg**
1 **cup (6 ounces) semisweet chocolate chips**
TOPPING:
2 **packages (8 ounces *each*) cream cheese, softened**
1-1/2 **cups confectioners' sugar**
1 **teaspoon vanilla extract**
1 **cup salted cashews, coarsely chopped**
1/2 **cup hot fudge ice cream topping, warmed**

In a large bowl, combine the brownie mix, water, oil and egg. Stir in chips. Spread into a greased 13-in. x 9-in. baking pan.

Bake at 350° for 25-27 minutes or until a toothpick inserted near the center comes out clean (do not overbake). Cool on a wire rack.

For topping, in a large bowl, beat the cream cheese, confectioners' sugar and vanilla until smooth. Spread over brownies. Sprinkle with cashews; drizzle with hot fudge topping. Refrigerate before cutting. Store in the refrigerator. **YIELD:** 2 dozen.

Drop by tablespoonfuls 2 in. apart onto ungreased baking sheets. Bake at 350° for 8-10 minutes or until lightly browned. Cool for 10 minutes before removing to wire racks to cool completely.

In a microwave, melt the remaining chocolate chips; stir until smooth. First frost cooled cookies, then drizzle with melted chocolate. **YIELD:** 6-1/2 dozen.

Chocolate Heart Cookies

(*Pictured below*)

PREP: 30 min. **BAKE:** 10 min. + cooling

For an elegant look, I dust dessert plates with cocoa powder, add a dollop of melted raspberry fruit spread and place two of these melt-in-your-mouth cookies in the center.

—*T. Moore, Oaklyn, New Jersey*

   1 **cup butter, softened**
1/2 **cup sugar**
   1 **teaspoon vanilla extract**
   2 **cups all-purpose flour**
1/4 **cup baking cocoa**
   1 **cup vanilla *or* white chips**
   2 **tablespoons shortening, *divided***
1/2 **cup semisweet chocolate chips**

In a small bowl, cream the butter and sugar until light and fluffy. Beat in the vanilla. Combine the flour and cocoa; gradually add to creamed mixture.

On a lightly floured surface, roll out dough to 1/4-in. thickness. Cut with a 3-in. heart-shaped cookie cutter. Place 2 in. apart on ungreased baking sheets. Bake at 375° for 8-10 minutes or until firm. Remove to wire racks to cool.

In a microwave-safe bowl, heat vanilla chips and 1 tablespoon shortening until melted, stirring frequently. Dip both sides of cookies into melted mixture.

In another microwave-safe bowl, heat the chocolate chips and remaining shortening until melted, stirring frequently. Drizzle over the cookies. Place on wire racks to dry. **YIELD:** about 2 dozen.

Coconut Pecan Cookies

(*Pictured above*)

PREP: 30 min. **BAKE:** 10 min. + cooling

With chocolate chips and coconut in the batter and a yummy pecan-coconut frosting, these cookies will remind you of German chocolate cake. A drizzle of chocolate tops them off in a festive way.

—*Diane Selich, Vassar, Michigan*

    1 **egg, lightly beaten**
    1 **can (5 ounces) evaporated milk**
 2/3 **cup sugar**
 1/4 **cup butter, cubed**
1-1/4 **cups flaked coconut**
 1/2 **cup chopped pecans**
COOKIE DOUGH:
    1 **cup butter, softened**
 3/4 **cup sugar**
 3/4 **cup packed brown sugar**
    2 **eggs**
    1 **teaspoon vanilla extract**
2-1/4 **cups all-purpose flour**
    1 **teaspoon baking soda**
    1 **teaspoon salt**
    4 **cups (24 ounces) semisweet chocolate chips, *divided***
 1/4 **cup flaked coconut**

For the frosting, in a large saucepan, combine the egg, evaporated milk, sugar and butter. Cook and stir over medium-low heat for 10-12 minutes or until slightly thickened and mixture reaches 160°. Stir in the coconut and pecans. Set aside.

For the cookie dough, in a large bowl, cream butter and sugars until light and fluffy. Add eggs, one at a time, beating well after each addition. Beat in vanilla. Combine the flour, baking soda and salt; gradually add to creamed mixture. Stir in 2 cups chips and coconut.

Chocolate Pecan Bars

(Pictured below)

PREP: 25 min. **BAKE:** 25 min. + cooling

The chewy, chocolaty bars are great for Thanksgiving or Christmas…and always a big hit with everyone. They're easy to prepare and make a big batch. We find them simply irresistible.

—Carole Fraser, North York, Ontario

> 2/3 cup butter, softened
> 1/3 cup sugar
> 2 cups all-purpose flour

FILLING:

> 6 squares (1 ounce *each*) semisweet chocolate
> 1-1/4 cups light corn syrup
> 1-1/4 cups sugar
> 4 eggs, lightly beaten
> 1-1/4 teaspoons vanilla extract
> 2-1/4 cups chopped pecans

DRIZZLE:

> 4 squares (1 ounce *each*) semisweet chocolate
> 1-1/4 teaspoons shortening

In a small bowl, cream butter and sugar until light and fluffy. Beat in flour. Press into a greased 15-in. x 10-in. x 1-in. baking pan. Bake at 350° for 12-15 minutes or until golden brown.

Meanwhile, for the filling, in a large saucepan, melt chocolate with corn syrup over low heat; stir until smooth. Remove from the heat. Stir in the sugar, eggs and vanilla. Add pecans.

Spread evenly over hot crust. Bake for 25-30 minutes or until firm around the edges. Cool on a wire rack. Melt the chocolate and shortening; stir until smooth. Drizzle over bars. **YIELD:** 4 dozen.

Berry-Cream Cookie Snaps

(Pictured above and on page 140)

PREP: 40 min. + chilling **BAKE:** 30 min. + cooling

My mom and I created this recipe by combining two others. These cute cookies are crispy on the outside and light and fluffy inside. You could also bake the cookies flat and serve the filling as a cookie dip if you like.

—Crystal Briddick, Colfax, Illinois

> 4 ounces cream cheese, softened
> 1/4 cup sugar
> 2 tablespoons seedless strawberry jam
> 1/4 cup heavy whipping cream, whipped
> 1 to 3 drops red food coloring, optional

BATTER:

> 1/2 cup sugar
> 1/3 cup all-purpose flour
> 2 egg whites
> 1/4 teaspoon vanilla extract
> 1/8 teaspoon salt
> 1/4 cup butter, melted and cooled
> 1/2 cup chopped fresh strawberries

Additional sugar

Combine the cream cheese, sugar and jam until blended. Fold in the whipped cream and food coloring if desired. Chill.

For the batter, whisk together the sugar, flour, egg whites, vanilla and salt until smooth. Whisk in butter until blended. Line baking sheets with parchment paper. Preparing four cookies at a time, drop batter by 1-1/2 teaspoonfuls 4 in. apart onto prepared pan. Bake at 400° for 5-8 minutes or until edges are lightly browned.

Immediately remove one cookie at a time from parchment and form into a tube around a greased clean round wooden clothespin. Press lightly to seal; hold until set, about 20 seconds. Remove cookie from clothespin; place on waxed paper to cool. Continue with remaining cookies. If cookies become too cool to shape, return to oven for 1 minute to soften. Repeat with remaining batter.

Just before serving, pipe or spoon filling into cookie shells. Dip end of cookie into strawberries and additional sugar. Refrigerate leftovers. **YIELD:** about 2 dozen.

Cookie Dough Truffles

(Pictured below)

PREP: 1 hour + chilling

The flavorful filling at the center of these yummy candies tastes like genuine chocolate chip cookie dough...without the worry of uncooked eggs. That's what makes them so appealing. Plus, they're easy to make.

—Lanita Dedon, Slaughter, Louisiana

  1/2 cup butter, softened
  3/4 cup packed brown sugar
    1 teaspoon vanilla extract
    2 cups all-purpose flour
    1 can (14 ounces) sweetened condensed milk
  1/2 cup miniature semisweet chocolate chips
  1/2 cup chopped walnuts
1-1/2 pounds semisweet candy coating, chopped

In a large bowl, cream the butter and brown sugar until light and fluffy. Beat in the vanilla. Gradually add the flour, alternately with milk, beating well after each addition. Stir in the chocolate chips and walnuts. Shape into 1-in. balls; place on waxed paper-lined baking sheets. Loosely cover and refrigerate for 1-2 hours or until firm.

In a microwave-safe bowl, melt candy coating; stir until smooth. Dip balls in coating, allowing excess to drip off; place on waxed paper-lined baking sheets. Refrigerate until firm, about 15 minutes. If desired, melt remaining candy coating again and drizzle over the candies. Store in the refrigerator. **YIELD:** 5-1/2 dozen.

Butterscotch Eggnog Stars

(Pictured above)

PREP: 25 min. + chilling **BAKE:** 10 min.

These yellow star-shaped cookies with a "stained-glass" center are almost too pretty to eat! The icing isn't mandatory, but does add a special touch.

—Cheryl Hemmer, Swansea, Illinois

  2/3 cup butter, softened
    1 cup sugar
  1/4 cup eggnog
    1 egg
    2 cups all-purpose flour
  3/4 teaspoon baking powder
  1/4 teaspoon salt
  1/4 teaspoon ground nutmeg
  1/2 cup crushed hard butterscotch candies
OPTIONAL ICING:
1-1/2 cups confectioners' sugar
  1/4 teaspoon rum extract
  2 to 3 tablespoons eggnog
Yellow colored sugar, optional

In a large bowl, cream butter and sugar until light and fluffy. Beat in eggnog and egg. Combine flour, baking powder, salt and nutmeg; gradually add to the creamed mixture and mix well. Divide the dough in half.

On a lightly floured surface, roll out one piece of dough at a time to 1/4-in. thickness. Cut with a floured 3-1/2-in. star cutter. Cut out the centers with a 1-1/2-in. star cutter. Line baking sheets with foil; grease foil.

Place large star cutouts on prepared baking sheets. Sprinkle 1 teaspoon candy in center of each. Repeat with remaining dough; reroll small cutouts if desired. Bake at 375° for 6-8 minutes or until edges are golden. Cool on baking sheets for 5 minutes. Carefully slide foil and cookies from baking sheets onto wire racks to cool.

For icing, beat confectioners' sugar, rum extract and enough eggnog to achieve drizzling consistency. Drizzle over the cooled cookies. Sprinkle with the colored sugar if desired. Let stand until hardened. **YIELD:** about 3 dozen.

EDITOR'S NOTE: This recipe was tested with commercially prepared eggnog.

Pinwheels and Checkerboards

(Pictured below)

PREP: 30 min. + chilling **BAKE:** 10 min.

My mom used to make these cookies every Christmas, and I still love them. They are so colorful…and you can get two kinds of cookies from one dough!

—Jill Heatwole, Pittsville, Maryland

- 1-1/4 **cups butter, softened**
- 1 **cup packed brown sugar**
- 1/2 **cup sugar**
- 2 **eggs**
- 1/4 **teaspoon vanilla extract**
- 4 **cups all-purpose flour**
- 1 **teaspoon baking powder**
- 1 **teaspoon salt**
- 1/4 **teaspoon baking soda**
- **Red and green gel food coloring**
- 1 **square (1 ounce) unsweetened chocolate, melted and cooled**

In a large bowl, cream butter and sugars. Beat in eggs and vanilla. Combine flour, baking powder, salt and baking soda; gradually add to creamed mixture. Divide dough into fourths. Tint one portion red and one portion green. Stir chocolate into another portion. Wrap chocolate and plain portions in plastic wrap; chill for 1 hour or until easy to handle.

For pinwheel cookies, divide red and green portions in half. Roll out each portion between waxed paper into a 9-in. x 6-in. rectangle. Refrigerate for 30 minutes. Remove waxed paper. Place one green rectangle over a red rectangle. Roll up tightly jelly-roll style, starting with a long side; wrap in plastic wrap. Repeat. Chill for 2 hours or until firm.

For checkerboard cookies, divide plain and chocolate portions in half. Roll out each portion between waxed paper into a 6-in. x 4-in. rectangle. Cut each rectangle lengthwise into eight 1/2-in. strips. Stack the strips in groups of four, alternating plain and chocolate strips and forming eight separate stacks. Form a four-stack block by alternating chocolate-topped and plain-topped stacks. Repeat. Press together gently. Wrap in plastic. Chill for at least 2 hours.

Unwrap and cut pinwheel and checkerboard dough into 1/4-in. slices. Place 1 in. apart on ungreased baking sheets. Bake at 375° for 9-11 minutes or until set. Remove to wire racks to cool. **YIELD:** 6 dozen pinwheel and 4 dozen checkerboard cookies.

Elegant Dipped Cherries

(Pictured above)

PREP: 1-1/4 hours + freezing

Here's a sure way to impress holiday guests. These sweet maraschino cherries are wrapped in chocolate, then dipped in melted vanilla chips. A chocolate drizzle dresses them up for serving on a festive plate of sweets.

—Sedora Brown, Waynesboro, Virginia

- 1 **jar (10 ounces) maraschino cherries with stems, well drained**
- 3 **tablespoons butter, melted**
- 2 **tablespoons light corn syrup**
- 1 **square (1 ounce) unsweetened chocolate**
- 2 **teaspoons half-and-half cream**
- 2 **cups confectioners' sugar**
- 1 **cup vanilla *or* white chips**
- 2-1/2 **teaspoons shortening, *divided***
- 1/2 **cup semisweet chocolate chips**

Pat cherries dry with paper towels and set aside. In a large bowl, combine the butter, corn syrup, unsweetened chocolate and cream. Stir in the confectioners' sugar.

Knead until smooth. Roll into 18 balls; flatten each into a 2-in. circle. Wrap each circle around a cherry and lightly roll in hands. Place the cherries, stem side up, in a shallow paper-lined container. Cover and freeze for at least 2 hours.

The day before serving, remove the cherries from freezer. In a microwave-safe bowl, melt the vanilla chips and 1-1/2 teaspoons shortening; stir until smooth.

Holding onto the stem, dip each cherry into vanilla mixture; set on waxed paper to set. Melt chocolate chips and remaining shortening; stir until smooth. Drizzle over the candies. Refrigerate until firm. Store candies in an airtight container. **YIELD:** 1-1/2 dozen.

Coffee and Cream Brownies

(Pictured above and on page 140)

PREP: 25 min. **BAKE:** 25 min. + cooling

A friend gave me the recipe for these rich cake-like brownies. Topped with a creamy, coffee-enhanced filling and a chocolate glaze, I like to garnish each square with a coffee bean.

—Michelle Tiemstra, Lacombe, Alberta

  1/2 **cup butter, cubed**
    3 **squares (1 ounce *each*) unsweetened chocolate, chopped**
    2 **eggs**
    1 **cup sugar**
    1 **teaspoon vanilla extract**
  2/3 **cup all-purpose flour**
  1/4 **teaspoon baking soda**
FILLING:
    1 **tablespoon heavy whipping cream**
    1 **teaspoon instant coffee granules**
    2 **tablespoons butter, softened**
    1 **cup confectioners' sugar**
GLAZE:
    1 **cup (6 ounces) semisweet chocolate chips**
  1/3 **cup heavy whipping cream**

In a saucepan over low heat, melt butter and chocolate; cool slightly. In a small bowl, beat eggs, sugar and vanilla; stir in the chocolate mixture. Combine the flour and baking soda; add to the chocolate mixture. Spread into a greased 8-in. square baking pan. Bake at 350° for 25-30 minutes or until a toothpick inserted near the center comes out clean (do not overbake). Cool on a wire rack.

For the filling, combine cream and coffee granules in a small bowl; stir until coffee is dissolved. In a small bowl, beat the butter and confectioners' sugar. Add coffee mixture; beat until creamy. Spread over brownies.

For the glaze, in a small saucepan, combine chips and cream. Cook and stir over low heat until the chocolate is melted and mixture is thickened. Cool slightly. Carefully spread over the filling. Let stand for 30 minutes or until glaze is set. Cut into squares. Store in refrigerator. **YIELD:** 16 servings.

Slice and Bake Lemon Gems

(Pictured below)

PREP: 25 min. + chilling **BAKE:** 10 min./batch + cooling

Rolled in colorful sprinkles, these citrus-flavored cookies are pretty enough for a party. I make a lot of them for holiday dessert trays and as gifts.

—Delores Edgecomb, Atlanta, New York

  3/4 **cup butter, softened**
  1/2 **cup confectioners' sugar**
    1 **tablespoon grated lemon peel**
    1 **cup all-purpose flour**
  1/2 **cup cornstarch**
  1/4 **cup colored nonpareils**
LEMON ICING:
    1 **cup confectioners' sugar**
    2 **tablespoons lemon juice**
  1/2 **teaspoon grated lemon peel**

In a small bowl, cream the butter and confectioners' sugar until light and fluffy. Beat in the lemon peel. Combine the flour and cornstarch; gradually add to the creamed mixture and mix well. Cover and refrigerate for 1 hour or until easy to handle.

Shape into a 1-3/4-in.-diameter roll; roll in the nonpareils. Wrap in plastic wrap. Refrigerate for 2-3 hours or until firm.

Unwrap and cut into 1/4-in. slices. Place 1 in. apart on ungreased baking sheets. Bake at 375° for 9-11 minutes or until set and edges are lightly browned. Cool for 1 minute before removing to wire racks to cool completely.

In a small bowl, combine icing ingredients. Spread over cookies. **YIELD:** 28 cookies.

Almond Sugar Cookies

(Pictured above)

PREP/TOTAL TIME: 30 min.

It's a tradition in our house to start baking Christmas cookies early in the season. This nutty, glazed melt-in-your-mouth cookie is one of my favorites.

—Lisa Hummell, Phillipsburg, New Jersey

- 1 **cup butter, softened**
- 3/4 **cup sugar**
- 1 **teaspoon almond extract**
- 2 **cups all-purpose flour**
- 1/2 **teaspoon baking powder**
- 1/4 **teaspoon salt**

Additional sugar

GLAZE:
- 1 **cup confectioners' sugar**
- 1-1/2 **teaspoons almond extract**
- 2 to 3 **teaspoons water**

Green food coloring, optional

Sliced almonds, toasted

In a large bowl, cream butter and sugar until light and fluffy. Beat in almond extract. Combine flour, baking powder and salt; gradually add to creamed mixture. Roll into 1-in. balls.

Place 2 in. apart on ungreased baking sheets. Coat bottom of a glass with cooking spray; dip in sugar. Flatten cookies with prepared glass, dipping glass in sugar again as needed.

Bake at 400° for 7-9 minutes or until the edges are lightly browned. Cool for 1 minute before removing to wire racks.

For the glaze, whisk together the confectioners' sugar, almond extract and enough water to achieve glaze consistency. Tint with food coloring if desired; drizzle over cookies. Sprinkle with almonds. **YIELD:** about 4-1/2 dozen.

Glazed Peanut Butter Bars

(Pictured below)

PREP: 15 min. **BAKE:** 20 min. + cooling

Memories of lunchtime at school and my aunt Shelly's kitchen come to mind when I bite into these sweet, chewy bars. My husband is the biggest fan of these peanut butter and chocolate treats.

—Janis Luedtke, Thornton, Colorado

- 3/4 **cup butter, softened**
- 3/4 **cup creamy peanut butter**
- 3/4 **cup sugar**
- 3/4 **cup packed brown sugar**
- 2 **teaspoons water**
- 2 **eggs**
- 1-1/2 **teaspoons vanilla extract**
- 1-1/2 **cups all-purpose flour**
- 1-1/2 **cups quick-cooking oats**
- 3/4 **teaspoon baking soda**
- 1/2 **teaspoon salt**

GLAZE:
- 1-1/4 **cups milk chocolate chips**
- 1/2 **cup butterscotch chips**
- 1/2 **cup creamy peanut butter**

In a large bowl, cream the butter, peanut butter, sugars and water. Beat in eggs and vanilla. Combine the flour, oats, baking soda and salt; gradually add to creamed mixture.

Spread into a greased 15-in. x 10-in. x 1-in. baking pan. Bake at 325° for 18-22 minutes or until lightly browned.

For glaze, in a microwave-safe bowl, melt both kinds of chips with peanut butter; pour over the warm bars and spread evenly. Cool completely on a wire rack before cutting. **YIELD:** 4 dozen.

Divide dough into thirds; flatten each portion into a circle. Wrap each in plastic wrap; refrigerate for 1 hour or until easy to handle.

On a lightly floured surface, roll out one portion of the dough to 1/8-in. thickness. Cut with a floured 1-1/2-in. cookie cutter; place 1/2 in. apart on ungreased baking sheets. Repeat with the remaining dough; chill and reroll scraps.

Bake at 375° for 6-8 minutes or until the edges begin to brown. Remove to wire racks to cool.

For filling, in a small saucepan, bring the cream to a boil. Remove from heat; stir in milk chocolate chips and 3/4 cup semisweet chocolate chips until melted. Transfer to a bowl; refrigerate for 1-1/2 hours or until filling reaches spreading consistency, stirring occasionally.

Spread the filling over the bottom of half of the cookies; top with remaining cookies. Melt the remaining semisweet chips; drizzle over the cookies. Let stand until set. Store in an airtight container in the refrigerator. **YIELD:** 3 dozen.

Frosted Cookie Brownies

PREP: 30 min. **BAKE:** 40 min. + cooling

Years ago, my children and I came up with these bars by combining two of their favorite brownie recipes. With a crisp cookie crust and a fluffy frosting, these brownies are the most requested treats at our house.

—Alicia French, Crestline, California

- 1 tube (18 ounces) refrigerated chocolate chip cookie dough
- 3 cups miniature marshmallows
- 2 cups (12 ounces) semisweet chocolate chips
- 1 cup butter, cubed
- 4 eggs
- 2 teaspoons vanilla extract
- 1 cup all-purpose flour
- 1/2 teaspoon baking powder
- 1/4 teaspoon salt
- 1 cup chopped walnuts

FROSTING:
- 2 cups miniature marshmallows
- 6 tablespoons milk
- 1/4 cup butter, softened
- 2 squares (1 ounce *each*) unsweetened chocolate
- 3 cups confectioners' sugar

Press cookie dough into a greased 13-in. x 9-in. baking pan. Bake at 350° for 10 minutes.

Meanwhile, in a large saucepan, combine the marshmallows, chips and butter; cook and stir over low heat until melted and smooth. Transfer to a large bowl; cool. Beat in eggs and vanilla. Combine the flour, baking powder and salt; stir into marshmallow mixture. Stir in nuts.

Spread over cookie crust. Bake for 30-35 minutes or until a toothpick inserted near the center comes out clean. Cool on a wire rack.

For frosting, in a small saucepan, combine the marshmallows, milk, butter and chocolate. Cook and stir over low heat until smooth. Remove from the heat; beat in confectioners' sugar until smooth. Frost brownies. Cut into bars. **YIELD:** 15 servings.

Hazelnut-Espresso Sandwich Cookies

(Pictured above)

PREP: 45 min. + chilling **BAKE:** 10 min./batch + cooling

The inspiration for this cute cookie came from my sister's description of a hazelnut cookie she tried in Italy. She declared my version to be a wonderful approximation. My family likes to help fill them.

—Cindy Beberman, Orland Park, Illinois

- 1 cup butter, softened
- 1-1/4 cups sugar
- 1 egg
- 1 egg yolk
- 4 teaspoons instant espresso granules
- 2 teaspoons vanilla extract
- 2-1/2 cups all-purpose flour
- 1/2 teaspoon salt
- 1/2 teaspoon baking powder
- 1 cup finely ground hazelnuts

FILLING:
- 1 cup heavy whipping cream
- 1-1/4 cups milk chocolate chips
- 1-3/4 cups semisweet chocolate chips, *divided*

In a large bowl, cream the butter and sugar until light and fluffy. Beat in the egg, yolk, espresso granules and vanilla. Combine the flour, salt and baking powder; gradually add to the creamed mixture and mix well. Stir in the hazelnuts.

Dipped Pecan Spritz

(Pictured below)

PREP: 25 min. **BAKE:** 5 min. + cooling

This is my husband's preferred Christmas cookie. They look lovely at the center of festive holiday cookie plates...and they are always the first to disappear.

—Sylvia Neudorf, Abbotsford, British Columbia

- 1-1/2 cups butter, softened
- 1 cup sugar
- 1 egg
- 1 teaspoon vanilla extract
- 1/2 teaspoon almond extract
- 3 cups all-purpose flour
- 1 cup finely ground pecans
- 1 teaspoon baking powder
- 3/4 cup semisweet chocolate chips
- 1-1/2 teaspoons shortening, *divided*
- 3/4 cup vanilla *or* white chips
- Colored sprinkles

In a large bowl, cream the butter and sugar until light and fluffy; beat in egg and extracts. Combine the flour, pecans and baking powder; gradually add to the creamed mixture.

Using a cookie press fitted with disk of your choice, press the dough 2 in. apart onto ungreased baking sheets. Bake at 375° for 5-7 minutes or until set (do not brown). Remove to wire racks to cool.

In a microwave, melt chocolate chips and 3/4 teaspoon shortening; stir until smooth. Melt the vanilla chips and remaining shortening at 70% power; stir until smooth.

Dip half the amount of cookies halfway in semisweet chocolate mixture; allow excess to drip off. Place on waxed paper to harden. Dip remaining cookies halfway in vanilla mixture; allow excess to drip off. Place on waxed paper and sprinkle coated area with the colored sprinkles. Let harden. **YIELD:** 12-1/2 dozen.

Chocolate Pretzels

(Pictured above)

PREP: 30 min. **BAKE:** 10 min./batch + cooling

A rich, chocolate coating accented with crushed peppermint makes these pretzels hard to resist. My grandkids and I love making them together!

—Karen Nemeth, Calgary, Alberta

- 1/2 cup butter, softened
- 1/2 cup shortening
- 1 cup confectioners' sugar
- 1 egg
- 1-1/2 teaspoons vanilla extract
- 2-1/4 cups all-purpose flour
- 1/2 cup baking cocoa
- 1 teaspoon salt

GLAZE:
- 3 squares (1 ounce *each*) semisweet chocolate
- 3 tablespoons butter
- 3 cups confectioners' sugar
- 5 tablespoons water
- 1/2 cup vanilla *or* white chips

In a large bowl, cream the butter, shortening and confectioners' sugar until light and fluffy. Beat in egg and vanilla. Combine the flour, cocoa and salt; gradually add to creamed mixture.

Shape into 1-in. balls. Roll each into a 7-in. rope. On greased baking sheets, form each rope into a pretzel shape, placing 2 in. apart. Bake at 375° for 8-9 minutes or until firm. Cool for 1 minute before removing to wire racks to cool completely.

For the glaze, in a microwave-safe bowl, melt the chocolate and butter; stir until smooth. Stir in the confectioners' sugar and water until smooth. Dip pretzels in glaze; place on waxed paper. Melt vanilla chips; drizzle over half of the pretzels. Let stand until completely set. Store in an airtight container. **YIELD:** 4 dozen.

Transfer to a cutting board; with a serrated knife, cut each rectangle diagonally into 18 slices. Place cut side down on greased baking sheets. Bake for 20-25 minutes or until firm and crisp, turning once. Remove to wire racks to cool.

In a microwave-safe bowl, melt chocolate chips and 1 tablespoon shortening; stir until smooth. Drizzle over both sides of cookies. Place on waxed paper; let stand until set.

Melt white chocolate and remaining shortening; stir until smooth. Drizzle over both sides of cookies. Place on waxed paper; let stand until set. Store in an airtight container. **YIELD:** 3 dozen.

Peanut Butter Blondies

(*Pictured below*)

PREP: 30 min. **BAKE:** 35 min. + cooling

The kids I babysit for just love these moist, chewy bars. There's plenty of peanut butter flavor and a yummy chocolate frosting.
—Karla Johnson, Tyler, Minnesota

    3/4 cup creamy peanut butter
    2/3 cup butter, softened
      1 cup packed brown sugar
    1/2 cup sugar
      2 eggs
      1 teaspoon vanilla extract
1-3/4 cups all-purpose flour
      1 teaspoon baking powder
    1/3 cup milk
      1 cup peanut butter chips

Door County Cherry Biscotti

(*Pictured above*)

PREP: 40 min. **BAKE:** 50 min. + cooling

With a subtle flavor, these biscotti are just sweet enough, with a hint of almond and good level of cinnamon. Roger, my husband, especially likes to eat them with ice cream.
—Joanne Surfus, Sturgeon Bay, Wisconsin

      3 eggs
    1/2 cup butter, softened
      1 cup plus 3 tablespoons sugar, *divided*
      1 teaspoon almond extract
  3-2/3 cups all-purpose flour
    1/2 teaspoon baking powder
    1/4 teaspoon baking soda
      1 cup dried cherries
      1 cup slivered almonds, toasted
      1 cup (6 ounces) semisweet chocolate chips
      1 tablespoon plus 2 teaspoons shortening, *divided*
      4 squares (1 ounce *each*) white baking chocolate

Separate one egg; set aside. In a large bowl, cream butter and 1 cup plus 2 tablespoons sugar until light and fluffy. Beat in 2 eggs and reserved egg yolk. Beat in extract. Combine the flour, baking powder and baking soda; gradually add to creamed mixture.

Turn onto a floured surface. Knead in the cherries and almonds. Divide the dough in half; shape each portion into a 12-in. x 3-in. rectangle. Transfer to a greased baking sheet. Beat reserved egg white; brush over dough. Sprinkle with remaining sugar. Bake at 350° for 28-30 minutes or until lightly browned. Cool for 10 minutes.

FROSTING:

- 1/4 cup butter, softened
- 1/4 cup baking cocoa
- 2 tablespoons milk
- 1 tablespoon light corn syrup
- 1 teaspoon vanilla extract
- 1-1/2 cups confectioners' sugar
- 1/3 cup peanut butter chips

In a large bowl, cream the peanut butter, butter and sugars. Beat in eggs and vanilla. Combine the flour and baking powder; add to creamed mixture alternately with milk. Stir in chips.

Spread into a greased 13-in. x 9-in. baking pan. Bake at 325° for 35-40 minutes or until a toothpick inserted near the center comes out clean (do not overbake). Cool on a wire rack.

For frosting, in a small bowl, combine butter, cocoa, milk, corn syrup and vanilla. Gradually add confectioners' sugar; beat until smooth. Frost brownies. Sprinkle with chips. Cut into bars. **YIELD:** 2 dozen.

Almond Truffle Brownies

PREP: 15 min. **BAKE:** 25 min. + chilling

This wonderful recipe is one my mom shared with me. These fudgy almond delights take several steps to make, but the extra effort is well worth it!

—*Lynn Snow, Taylors, South Carolina*

- 1 package fudge brownie mix (13-inch x 9-inch pan size)
- 1/2 cup water
- 1/2 cup canola oil
- 1 egg
- 3/4 cup chopped almonds
- 1 teaspoon almond extract

FILLING:

- 1 cup (6 ounces) semisweet chocolate chips
- 1 package (8 ounces) cream cheese, softened
- 1/4 cup confectioners' sugar
- 2 tablespoons milk
- 1/2 teaspoon almond extract

TOPPING:

- 1/2 cup semisweet chocolate chips
- 1/4 cup heavy whipping cream
- 1/2 cup sliced almonds, toasted

In a large bowl, combine the first six ingredients. Pour into a greased 13-in. x 9-in. baking pan. Bake at 350° for 23-25 minutes or until a toothpick inserted near the center comes out clean (do not overbake). Cool on a wire rack.

For the filling, in a microwave, melt the chocolate chips; stir until smooth. In a large bowl, beat cream cheese and confectioners' sugar. Add milk, extract and melted chips; mix well. Spread over brownies. Refrigerate for 1 hour or until firm.

For topping, in a small saucepan, melt chips and cream over low heat, stirring occasionally. Spread over filling. Sprinkle with almonds. Refrigerate at least 1 hour longer before cutting. **YIELD:** 1-1/2 dozen.

Chewy Apple Oatmeal Cookies

(Pictured above)

PREP: 20 min. **BAKE:** 10 min./batch

My family has always loved oatmeal raisin cookies, but I wanted to try a new twist on the classic recipe. We enjoy apples, so I thought the dried fruit would make a good addition.

—*Jan Marshall, Fenton, Missouri*

- 1 cup butter, softened
- 1 cup packed brown sugar
- 1/2 cup sugar
- 2 eggs
- 1 teaspoon vanilla extract
- 1-1/2 cups all-purpose flour
- 2 teaspoons ground cinnamon
- 1 teaspoon baking soda
- 1/4 teaspoon salt
- 3 cups old-fashioned oats
- 1/2 cup chopped dried apples

In a large bowl, cream butter and sugars until light and fluffy. Beat in eggs and vanilla. Combine the flour, cinnamon, baking soda and salt; gradually add to creamed mixture, beating well after each addition. Stir in oats and apples.

Drop by rounded tablespoonfuls 2 in. apart onto ungreased baking sheets. Bake at 350° for 10-12 minutes or until golden brown. Let stand for 1 minute before removing to wire racks. **YIELD:** 4 dozen.

about baking powder

Taste of Home recipes that call for baking powder use double-acting, which contains two types of acid that react differently. The first acid releases gases when mixed with liquid, and the second releases gases when exposed to heat. They work together to give plenty of lift to baked goods.

Homemade Peanut Butter Cups

(Pictured below and on page 140)

PREP/TOTAL TIME: 20 min.

Make a lasting impression on Valentine's Day and beyond with this luscious candy featuring a dark chocolate shell and a gooey peanut butter center. Your sweetie will appreciate the colorful sprinkles on top, too.

—LaVonne Hegland, St. Michael, Minnesota

> 1 cup creamy peanut butter, *divided*
> 4-1/2 teaspoons butter, softened
> 1/2 cup confectioners' sugar
> 1/2 teaspoon salt
> 2 cups (12 ounces) semisweet chocolate chips
> 4 milk chocolate candy bars (1.55 ounces *each*), coarsely chopped
> Colored sprinkles, optional

In a small bowl, combine 1/2 cup peanut butter, butter, confectioners' sugar and salt until smooth; set aside.

In a microwave, melt chocolate chips, candy bars and remaining peanut butter; stir until smooth.

Drop teaspoonfuls of the chocolate mixture into paper-lined miniature muffin cups. Top each with a scant teaspoonful of peanut butter mixture; top with another teaspoonful of chocolate mixture. Decorate with sprinkles if desired. Refrigerate until set. Store in an airtight container. **YIELD:** 3 dozen.

Ranger Cookies

(Pictured above)

PREP: 25 min. BAKE: 10 min.

These golden brown cookies are crispy on the outside and cake-like on the inside. Their tasty blend of oats, rice cereal, coconut and brown sugar have made them a favorite with our family. You won't be able to eat just one.

—Mary Lou Boyce, Wilmington, Delaware

> 1 cup shortening
> 1 cup sugar
> 1 cup packed brown sugar
> 2 eggs
> 1 teaspoon vanilla extract
> 2 cups all-purpose flour
> 1 teaspoon baking soda
> 1/2 teaspoon baking powder
> 1/2 teaspoon salt
> 2 cups quick-cooking oats
> 2 cups crisp rice cereal
> 1 cup flaked coconut

In a large bowl, cream shortening and sugars until light and fluffy. Beat in eggs and vanilla. Combine the flour, baking soda, baking powder and salt; gradually add to creamed mixture and mix well. Stir in the oats, cereal and coconut.

Drop by rounded tablespoonfuls 2 in. apart onto ungreased baking sheets. Bake at 350° for 7-9 minutes or until golden brown. Remove to wire racks. **YIELD:** 7-1/2 dozen.

Cherry Chocolate Bark

(Pictured below)

PREP/TOTAL TIME: 20 min.

This recipe from my daughter caught my eye because it reminded me of a candy bar I liked as a child. I love the fudge-like texture.
—Judith Batiuk, San Luis Obispo, California

- 1 **tablespoon plus 1/2 cup butter, softened,** *divided*
- 2 **cups sugar**
- 12 **large marshmallows**
- 1 **can (5 ounces) evaporated milk**

Dash salt

- 1 **cup vanilla** *or* **white chips**
- 1-1/2 **teaspoons cherry extract**
- 1 **teaspoon vanilla extract**
- 1 **cup semisweet chocolate chips**
- 1/3 **cup creamy peanut butter**
- 1/4 **cup finely chopped dry roasted peanuts**

Line a 15-in. x 10-in. x 1-in. pan with foil. Grease the foil with 1 tablespoon butter; set aside. In a large heavy saucepan, combine the sugar, marshmallows, milk, salt and remaining butter. Bring to a boil; cook and stir for 5 minutes. Remove from the heat. Stir in vanilla chips and extracts until smooth. Pour into prepared pan.

In a microwave-safe bowl, melt chocolate chips; stir until smooth. Stir in peanut butter and peanuts. Drop by tablespoonfuls over first layer; cut through with a knife to swirl. Chill until firm.

Using foil, lift candy out of pan. Discard foil. Break candy into pieces. Store in an airtight container in the refrigerator. **YIELD:** about 2 pounds.

Tiramisu Brownies

(Pictured above)

PREP: 25 min. **BAKE:** 45 min.

Tiramisu and brownies—what a yummy combination! This easy recipe gives you the traditional tiramisu flavor you adore minus the fuss.

—Anna-Maria Carpanzano, Whitby, Ontario

- 12 **squares (1 ounce** *each***) semisweet chocolate**
- 1 **cup butter, softened**
- 1-1/3 **cups plus 1/4 cup sugar,** *divided*
- 8 **eggs**
- 1 **cup cake flour**
- 1/4 **cup instant coffee granules** *or* **espresso powder**
- 2 **cartons (8 ounces** *each***) Mascarpone cheese**
- 2 **teaspoons vanilla extract**
- 1 **teaspoon baking cocoa**

In a large microwave-safe bowl, melt chocolate. Stir until smooth; cool slightly. Beat in butter. Gradually beat in 1-1/3 cups sugar. Add six eggs, one at a time, beating well after each addition.

Combine flour and coffee granules; add to chocolate mixture. Beat on low speed just until combined; set aside.

For filling, in a small bowl, beat the cheese, vanilla and remaining sugar and eggs until smooth.

Pour 4 cups of the chocolate batter into a greased 13-in. x 9-in. baking pan. Spread with the filling. Top with the remaining batter, spreading evenly to completely cover filling.

Bake at 350° for 45-50 minutes or until center is almost set and brownies begin to pull away from sides of pan.

Cool on a wire rack. Dust with cocoa. Cut into squares. Store in the refrigerator. **YIELD:** 3 dozen.

Scrumptious cakes, palate-pleasing pies, cheesecakes and tasty cupcakes make a fabulous finale for everyday suppers or special occasions. Any way you slice it, these sweet treats won't disappoint.

cakes & pies

Chocolate Pecan Ice Cream Torte 162

Layered Carrot Cake...162

Mocha Nut Torte 163

Strawberry Shortbread Pie 163

Rhubarb Swirl Cheesecake 164

Butternut Squash Cake Roll 164

Fresh Cherry Pie..165

Frosty Mocha Pie 165

Elegant Chocolate Torte....................................166

Raspberry Cherry Pie..166

Banana Nut Cake 167

Cream Cheese Blueberry Pie 167

Honey Pecan Pie..168

Butternut Cream Pie 168

Lemony White Chocolate Cheesecake......169

Lemonade Icebox Pie..169

Layered Mocha Cheesecake.............................170

Berry Pinwheel Cake..170

Raspberry Patch Cream Pie 171

Lemonade Meringue Pie....................................171

Mascarpone Cheesecake....................................172

Lemon Chiffon Cake 172

Rhubarb Upside-Down Cake............................173

Summer Celebration Ice Cream Cake 173

Strawberry Swirl Cheesecake 174

Lemon Coconut Cake..174

Frozen Peanut Parfait Pies.................................175

Fresh Fruit Tarts 175

Special Mocha Cupcakes....................................176

Cranberry Zucchini Wedges 176

Rustic Autumn Fruit Tart 177

Walnut Banana Cupcakes...................................177

Chocolate Carrot Cake 178

Crumbleberry Pie...178

Cinnamon Apple Cheesecake 179

Cherry Gingerbread Cupcakes.........................179

Carrot Cheesecake 180

Peaches & Cream Pie..180

Pineapple Upside-Down Cupcakes 181

Fudgy Nut Coffee Pie 181

Peanut Butter Cup Cheesecake 182

Frozen Strawberry Pie 182

Raspberry Peach Cupcakes 183

Caramel-Pecan Apple Pie.................................183

Maple Pumpkin Pie 184

Berry Cheesecake Pie 184

Texas Chocolate Cupcakes.................................185

Classic Red Velvet Cake 185

PICTURED CLOCKWISE FROM UPPER LEFT: Cinnamon Apple Cheesecake (page 179), Raspberry Patch Cream Pie (page 171), Layered Mocha Cheesecake (page 170) and Pineapple Upside-Down Cupcakes (page 181).

Spoon remaining butter pecan ice cream around edge of pan; spread remaining chocolate ice cream in center of pan. Cover and freeze overnight.

Carefully run a knife around edge of pan to loosen; remove sides of pan. Top with remaining pecan halves; drizzle with 2 tablespoons chocolate sauce. Serve with remaining sauce. **YIELD:** 16-20 servings.

EDITOR'S NOTE: This recipe was tested in a 1,100-watt microwave.

Layered Carrot Cake

PREP: 50 min. **BAKE:** 30 min. + cooling

I never liked carrot cake until I tried this one. The rich, moist cake with orange-flavored frosting is now a family tradition for special occasions. Sometimes I stir in cranberries.

—*Anna Morgan, Eatonville, Washington*

- 1 package (18-1/4 ounces) yellow cake mix
- 1 package (3.4 ounces) instant vanilla pudding mix
- 2 teaspoons ground cinnamon
- 4 eggs
- 2/3 cup orange juice
- 1/2 cup canola oil
- 3 cups grated carrots
- 1/2 cup raisins
- 1/2 cup chopped walnuts

ORANGE CREAM CHEESE FROSTING:

- 1 package (8 ounces) cream cheese, softened
- 1/2 cup butter, softened
- 3 cups confectioners' sugar
- 1 to 2 tablespoons orange juice
- 1 tablespoon grated orange peel

In a large bowl, combine the cake mix, pudding mix and cinnamon. Whisk eggs, orange juice and oil together; add to dry ingredients. Beat until well blended. Stir in carrots, raisins and nuts (the batter will be thick).

Pour into two greased and floured 9-in. round baking pans. Bake at 350° for 30-35 minutes or until a toothpick inserted near the center comes out clean. Cool for 10 minutes before removing from pans to wire racks to cool completely.

For frosting, in a large bowl, beat cream cheese and butter until fluffy. Add the confectioners' sugar, orange juice and peel; beat until smooth. Spread frosting between layers and over top and sides of cake. Store in the refrigerator. **YIELD:** 12-14 servings.

Chocolate Pecan Ice Cream Torte

(Pictured above)

PREP: 20 min. + freezing

This delectable dessert layers two of our favorite ice cream flavors, chocolate and butter pecan, on a shortbread crust. Along with chocolate candy pieces, toasted pecans and caramel topping, it never fails to impress our guests.

—*Kelly Arvay, Barberton, Ohio*

- 1 jar (12-1/4 ounces) caramel ice cream topping
- 2 milk chocolate candy bars (1.55 ounces *each*), chopped
- 12 pecan shortbread cookies, crushed
- 3 tablespoons butter, melted
- 1 cup pecan halves, toasted, *divided*
- 1/2 gallon butter pecan ice cream, slightly softened
- 1/2 gallon chocolate ice cream, slightly softened

In a microwave-safe bowl, combine the caramel topping and candy bars. Microwave, uncovered, on high for 1-1/2 minutes or until candy bars are melted, stirring every 30 seconds. Cool.

Combine the cookie crumbs and butter. Press onto the bottom of a greased 10-in. springform pan. Chop 1/2 cup pecans; set aside. Spoon half of the butter pecan ice cream over crust. Drizzle with 2 tablespoons chocolate sauce; sprinkle with 1/4 cup chopped pecans.

Spread half of chocolate ice cream over top. Drizzle with 2 tablespoons chocolate sauce; sprinkle with remaining chopped pecans.

zest for life

Zest (also called grated peel) is the outer rind of citrus fruits. To make zest, use a knife to remove thin strips of the peel, being careful not to include the white membrane; mince finely. Or rub the whole fruit over a hand grater.

soft peaks form. Gradually beat in remaining sugar, about 2 tablespoons at a time, on high until stiff glossy peaks form and sugar is dissolved. Gradually fold into batter just until blended. Divide among prepared pans.

Bake at 375° for 20-25 minutes or until tops spring back when lightly touched. Invert pans; cool for 20 minutes. Remove from pans to wire racks; cool completely. Remove waxed paper.

For the filling, beat cream until it begins to thicken. Add confectioners' sugar and vanilla; beat until stiff peaks form. Cover and refrigerate until assembling.

For the frosting, in a large saucepan, melt butter and chocolate over low heat. Remove from the heat. Stir in coffee, vanilla and enough confectioners' sugar to achieve frosting consistency. Spread filling between layers. Frost top and sides of cake. Garnish with pecans if desired. **YIELD:** 12 servings.

Mocha Nut Torte

(*Pictured above*)

PREP: 40 min. + chilling **BAKE:** 20 min. + cooling

My husband doesn't like chocolate cake, but this spectacular three-layer torte is a favorite of his. I've been using this recipe for special events, such as birthdays, for many years.
—*Megan Shepherdson, Winnipeg, Manitoba*

- 7 eggs, *separated*
- 1 cup sugar, *divided*
- 1 teaspoon vanilla extract
- 1-1/4 cups ground walnuts
- 1-1/4 cups ground pecans
- 1/4 cup dry bread crumbs
- 1 teaspoon baking powder
- 3/4 teaspoon salt, *divided*

FILLING:
- 1 cup heavy whipping cream
- 1/2 cup confectioners' sugar
- 1 teaspoon vanilla extract

MOCHA FROSTING:
- 1/4 cup butter, cubed
- 4 squares (1 ounce *each*) unsweetened chocolate
- 1/2 cup brewed coffee
- 2 teaspoons vanilla extract
- 3 to 3-1/4 cups confectioners' sugar

Pecan halves, optional

Line three 9-in. round baking pans with waxed paper; set aside. Place the egg whites in a large bowl; let stand at room temperature for 30 minutes.

Meanwhile, in another bowl, beat egg yolks until slightly thickened. Gradually add 1/2 cup sugar, beating until thick and lemon-colored. Beat in the vanilla. Combine the nuts, crumbs, baking powder and 1/2 teaspoon salt; stir into yolk mixture until combined.

Add remaining salt to egg whites; beat on medium speed until

Strawberry Shortbread Pie

(*Pictured below*)

PREP: 15 min. + chilling

My husband enjoys this pie so much that I always make an extra one just for him! To save time, use a purchased shortbread crust.
—*Sherry Maurer, Manheim, Pennsylvania*

- 3/4 cup sugar
- 3 tablespoons cornstarch
- 1-1/2 cups water
- 1 package (3 ounces) strawberry gelatin
- 4 cups sliced fresh strawberries
- 1 shortbread crust (9 inches)

In a small saucepan, combine sugar, cornstarch and water until smooth. Bring to a boil; cook and stir for 2 minutes or until thickened. Remove from heat; stir in gelatin powder until dissolved. Transfer to a small bowl. Chill until partially set.

Place sliced strawberries in the crust; pour gelatin mixture over the berries. Cover and refrigerate until set. **YIELD:** 6-8 servings.

Rhubarb Swirl Cheesecake

(Pictured below)

PREP: 40 min. **BAKE:** 1 hour + chilling

I love cheesecake and my husband loves white chocolate, so this is a unique dessert for us. The rhubarb adds a tartness that complements the sweet flavors well.

—*Carol Witczak, Tinley Park, Illinois*

- 2-1/2 cups thinly sliced fresh *or* frozen rhubarb
- 1/3 cup plus 1/2 cup sugar, *divided*
- 2 tablespoons orange juice
- 1-1/4 cups graham cracker crumbs
- 1/4 cup butter, melted
- 3 packages (8 ounces *each*) cream cheese, softened
- 2 cups (16 ounces) sour cream
- 1 tablespoon cornstarch
- 2 teaspoons vanilla extract
- 1/2 teaspoon salt
- 3 eggs, lightly beaten
- 8 squares (1 ounce *each*) white baking chocolate, melted

In a large saucepan, bring rhubarb, 1/3 cup sugar and orange juice to a boil. Reduce heat; cook and stir until thickened and rhubarb is tender. Set aside.

Combine cracker crumbs and butter. Press onto the bottom of a greased 9-in. springform pan. Place on a baking sheet. Bake at 350° for 7-9 minutes or until lightly browned. Cool on a wire rack.

In a large bowl, beat cream cheese, sour cream, cornstarch, vanilla, salt and remaining sugar until smooth. Add eggs; beat just until combined. Fold in white chocolate. Pour half of the filling into crust. Top with half of the rhubarb sauce; cut through batter with a knife to gently swirl rhubarb. Layer with remaining filling and rhubarb sauce; cut through top layers with a knife to gently swirl rhubarb.

Place pan on a double thickness of heavy-duty foil (about 16 in. square). Securely wrap foil around pan. Place in a large baking pan; add 1 in. of hot water to larger pan. Bake at 350° for 60-70 minutes or until center is almost set.

Cool on a wire rack for 10 minutes. Carefully run a knife around edge of pan to loosen; cool 1 hour longer. Cover and chill overnight. Remove sides of pan. Refrigerate leftovers. **YIELD:** 12-14 servings.

EDITOR'S NOTE: If using frozen rhubarb, measure rhubarb while still frozen, then thaw completely. Drain in a colander, but do not press liquid out.

Butternut Squash Cake Roll

PREP: 15 min. **BAKE:** 15 min. + chilling

I love the taste of winter squash, especially in sweet desserts. Filled with sweetened cream cheese, this pretty cake roll is perfect for an autumn special occasion.

—*Elizabeth Nelson, Manning, North Dakota*

- 3 eggs
- 1 cup sugar
- 2/3 cup mashed cooked butternut squash
- 3/4 cup all-purpose flour
- 1 teaspoon baking soda
- 1/2 teaspoon ground cinnamon
- 1 cup finely chopped walnuts, optional
- Confectioners' sugar

FILLING:
- 1 package (8 ounces) cream cheese, softened
- 2 tablespoons butter, softened
- 1 cup confectioners' sugar
- 3/4 teaspoon vanilla extract
- Additional confectioners' sugar, optional

In a large bowl, beat eggs; gradually beat in sugar. Add squash and mix well. Combine the flour, baking soda and cinnamon; add to squash mixture and mix well.

Line a 15-in. x 10-in. x 1-in. baking pan with waxed paper; grease and flour the paper. Spread batter evenly into pan. Sprinkle with walnuts if desired. Bake at 375° for 13-15 minutes or until a toothpick inserted near the center comes out clean. Cool on a wire rack for 10 minutes.

Turn the cake onto a kitchen towel dusted with confectioners' sugar. Gently peel off waxed paper. Roll up cake in the towel, jelly-roll style, starting with a short side. Cool completely on a wire rack.

For the filling, beat the cream cheese, butter, confectioners' sugar and vanilla until smooth. Unroll cake; spread filling evenly over cake to within 1 in. of edges. Roll up again. Cover and refrigerate for 1 hour. Just before serving, dust with confectioners' sugar if desired. **YIELD:** 10 servings.

On a lightly floured surface, roll out larger ball to fit a 9-in. pie plate. Transfer pastry to pie plate; trim even with edge of plate. Add filling. Roll out remaining pastry; make a lattice crust. Trim, seal and flute edges.

Bake at 425° for 10 minutes. Reduce the heat to 375°; bake 45-50 minutes longer or until crust is golden brown. Cool on a wire rack. **YIELD:** 8 servings.

Frosty Mocha Pie

(Pictured below)

PREP: 20 min. + freezing

This pie is so creamy and rich-tasting that no one would guess it's light. The added bonus is that you can make it a day or two ahead and keep it in the freezer until needed.
—*Lisa Varner, Greenville, South Carolina*

   4 ounces reduced-fat cream cheese
1/4 cup sugar
1/4 cup baking cocoa
   1 tablespoon instant coffee granules
1/3 cup fat-free milk
   1 teaspoon vanilla extract
   1 carton (12 ounces) frozen reduced-fat whipped topping, thawed
   1 extra-servings-size graham cracker crust (9 inches)
Reduced-calorie chocolate syrup, optional

In a large bowl, beat the cream cheese, sugar and cocoa until smooth. Dissolve coffee granules in milk. Stir coffee mixture and vanilla into cream cheese mixture; fold in whipped topping.

Pour into crust. Cover and freeze for at least 4 hours. Remove from the freezer 10 minutes before serving. Drizzle with chocolate syrup if desired. **YIELD:** 10 servings.

Fresh Cherry Pie

(Pictured above)

PREP: 25 min. **BAKE:** 55 min. + cooling

This ruby-red treat, with a hint of almond and a good level of cinnamon, has just the right amount of sweetness. The cherries peeking out of the lattice crust make it pretty, too.
—*Josie Bochek, Sturgeon Bay, Wisconsin*

1-1/4 cups sugar
 1/3 cup cornstarch
   1 cup cherry juice
   4 cups fresh tart cherries, pitted *or* frozen pitted tart cherries, thawed
 1/2 teaspoon ground cinnamon
 1/4 teaspoon ground nutmeg
 1/4 teaspoon almond extract
PASTRY:
   2 cups all-purpose flour
 1/2 teaspoon salt
 2/3 cup shortening
   3 to 4 tablespoons cold water

In a large saucepan, combine sugar and cornstarch; gradually stir in cherry juice until smooth. Bring to a boil; cook and stir for 2 minutes or until thickened. Remove from the heat. Add the cherries, cinnamon, nutmeg and extract; set aside.

For the pastry, in a large bowl, combine flour and salt; cut in shortening until crumbly. Gradually add cold water, tossing with a fork until a ball forms. Divide pastry in half so that one ball is slightly larger than the other.

Elegant Chocolate Torte

(Pictured above)

PREP: 50 min. **BAKE:** 30 min. + cooling

When I want to serve a really special dessert, I turn to this recipe time and again. The tender, four-layer chocolate cake has a yummy, pudding-like filling.

—Lois Gallup Edwards, Woodland, California

   1/3 cup all-purpose flour
     3 tablespoons sugar
     1 teaspoon salt
 1-3/4 cups milk
     1 cup chocolate syrup
     1 egg, lightly beaten
     1 tablespoon butter
     1 teaspoon vanilla extract

BATTER:
   1/2 cup butter, softened
 1-1/4 cups sugar
     4 eggs
     1 teaspoon vanilla extract
 1-1/4 cups all-purpose flour
   1/3 cup baking cocoa
   3/4 teaspoon baking soda
   1/4 teaspoon salt
 1-1/2 cups chocolate syrup
   1/2 cup water

FROSTING:
     2 cups heavy whipping cream
   1/4 cup chocolate syrup
   1/4 teaspoon vanilla extract

In a small saucepan, combine flour, sugar and salt. Stir in the milk and syrup until smooth. Bring to a boil over medium heat, stirring constantly; cook and stir for 1-2 minutes or until thickened.

Remove from heat. Stir a small amount of hot mixture into egg; return all to the pan, stirring constantly. Bring to a gentle boil; cook and stir for 2 minutes. Remove from heat; stir in butter and vanilla. Cool to room temperature, stirring often.

For the batter, in a large bowl, cream butter and sugar until light and fluffy. Add eggs, one at a time, beating well after each. Stir in the vanilla. Combine the dry ingredients; add to creamed mixture alternately with syrup and water. Beat just until combined.

Pour into two greased and floured 9-in. round baking pans. Bake at 350° for 30-35 minutes or until a toothpick comes out clean. Cool for 10 minutes; remove from pans to wire racks to cool.

Cut each cake in half horizontally. Place one bottom layer on a serving plate; spread with a third of the filling. Repeat layers twice. Top with remaining cake layer. Beat the frosting ingredients together until stiff peaks form; spread or pipe over top and sides of cake. **YIELD:** 16 servings.

Raspberry Cherry Pie

PREP: 20 min. **BAKE:** 1 hour + cooling

No one can resist a slice (or two!) of this tart "cherry-berry" pie. Growing up, my sister and I requested this treat for our birthdays instead of cake. Now it's a favorite of my own family.

—Mari Anne Warren, Milton, Wisconsin

 1-1/2 cups sugar
     3 tablespoons quick-cooking tapioca
     2 cups fresh *or* frozen unsweetened raspberries
     1 cup fresh, frozen *or* canned tart cherries
     1 teaspoon lemon juice

PASTRY:
     3 cups all-purpose flour
     2 teaspoons sugar
 1-1/2 teaspoons salt
   1/2 teaspoon baking powder
     1 cup shortening
     1 egg
     5 to 6 tablespoons cold water
     1 teaspoon white vinegar
     1 tablespoon butter

In a bowl, combine sugar and tapioca. Add raspberries, cherries and lemon juice; toss to coat. Let stand for 15 minutes. Meanwhile, for the pastry, in a large bowl, combine flour, sugar, salt and baking powder; cut in shortening until crumbly. Combine egg, water and vinegar. Gradually add to flour mixture, tossing with a fork until dough forms a ball.

Divide the dough in half. On a lightly floured surface, roll out one portion to fit a 9-in. pie plate. Place pastry in plate; trim even with edge.

Spoon filling into pastry. Dot with butter. Roll out the remaining pastry to fit top of pie. Make decorative cutouts with water; place on top of pie. Cover edges loosely with foil. Bake at 350° for 60-70 minutes or until golden brown. Cool on a wire rack. Store in the refrigerator. **YIELD:** 8 servings.

In a large bowl, cream butter and sugar together. Add eggs, one at a time, beating well after each addition. Stir in vanilla. Combine the flour, baking soda and salt; add to creamed mixture, beating just until combined. Fold in banana and pecans.

Pour into a greased 8-in. square baking dish. Bake at 350° for 30-35 minutes or until a toothpick inserted near the center comes out clean. Cool on a wire rack.

For frosting, beat the butter until light and fluffy. Beat in the milk, vanilla, salt and enough confectioners' sugar to achieve spreading consistency. Stir in the toasted pecans. Frost the cake. Garnish with additional pecans if desired. **YIELD:** 9 servings.

Cream Cheese Blueberry Pie

(Pictured below)

PREP: 20 min. + cooling

Fresh blueberries and a rich cream cheese layer are combined in this fruity and refreshing pie.

—*Lisieux Bauman, Cheektowaga, New York*

- 4 ounces cream cheese, softened
- 1/2 cup confectioners' sugar
- 1/2 cup heavy whipping cream, whipped
- 1 pastry shell (9 inches), baked
- 2/3 cup sugar
- 1/4 cup cornstarch
- 1/2 cup water
- 1/4 cup lemon juice
- 3 cups fresh *or* frozen blueberries

In a bowl, beat the cream cheese and confectioners' sugar until smooth. Fold in the whipped cream. Spread into pastry shell.

In a large saucepan, combine the sugar, cornstarch, water and lemon juice until smooth; stir in the blueberries. Bring to a boil over medium heat; cook and stir for 2 minutes or until thickened. Cool. Spread over the cream cheese layer. Refrigerate until serving. **YIELD:** 6-8 servings.

Banana Nut Cake

(Pictured above)

PREP: 20 min. **BAKE:** 30 min. + cooling

Sweet, buttery frosting and a sprinkling of chopped nuts top this cake that's loaded with banana and pecan flavor. Serve it with a hot cup of coffee or a cold glass of milk.

—*Marlene Saunders, Lincoln, Nebraska*

- 1/2 cup butter, softened
- 1 cup sugar
- 2 eggs
- 1/2 teaspoon vanilla extract
- 1-1/4 cups all-purpose flour
- 3/4 teaspoon baking soda
- 1/2 teaspoon salt
- 3/4 cup mashed ripe banana
- 1/2 cup chopped pecans, toasted

BUTTER PECAN FROSTING:
- 1/2 cup butter, softened
- 1/4 cup milk
- 1 teaspoon vanilla extract

Dash salt
- 2 to 2-1/2 cups confectioners' sugar
- 1 cup finely chopped pecans, toasted

Additional chopped pecans, optional

Honey Pecan Pie

(Pictured above)

PREP: 25 min. **BAKE:** 45 min. + cooling

Looking for a sweet ending to a holiday meal? This attractive pecan pie is bound to please with its traditional filling and honey-glazed pecans.

—Cathy Hudak, Wadsworth, Ohio

    4 **eggs**
    1 **cup chopped pecans**
    1 **cup light corn syrup**
1/4 **cup sugar**
1/4 **cup packed brown sugar**
    2 **tablespoons butter, melted**
    1 **teaspoon vanilla extract**
1/2 **teaspoon salt**
    1 **unbaked pastry shell (9 inches)**
TOPPING:
    3 **tablespoons butter**
1/3 **cup packed brown sugar**
    3 **tablespoons honey**
1-1/2 **cups pecan halves**

In a large bowl, combine the eggs, pecans, corn syrup, sugars, butter, vanilla and salt. Pour into pastry shell. Bake at 350° for 30 minutes.

In a small saucepan, melt butter over medium heat. Stir in brown sugar and honey until combined. Stir in pecan halves until coated. Spoon over pie.

Bake 15-20 minutes longer or until bubbly and golden brown. Cool completely on a wire rack. Refrigerate leftovers. **YIELD:** 8 servings.

Butternut Cream Pie

(Pictured below)

PREP: 35 min. + chilling

Last fall, my garden was loaded with squash. I enjoy experimenting with recipes, so I came up with this creamy pie. It really went over well at Thanksgiving dinner.

—Sandra Kreuter, Burney, California

    1 **medium butternut squash (about 2 pounds)**
1/4 **cup hot water**
    1 **package (8 ounces) cream cheese, softened**
1/4 **cup sugar**
    2 **tablespoons caramel ice cream topping**
    1 **teaspoon ground cinnamon**
1/2 **teaspoon salt**
1/2 **teaspoon ground ginger**
1/4 **teaspoon ground cloves**
    1 **package (5.1 ounces) instant vanilla pudding mix**
3/4 **cup milk plus 2 tablespoons milk**
    1 **pastry shell (9 inches), baked**
Whipped cream and toasted flaked coconut

Cut the squash in half; discard the seeds. Place the squash cut side down in a microwave-safe dish; add hot water. Cover and microwave for 13-15 minutes or until tender. When cool enough to handle, scoop out pulp and mash. Set aside 1-1/2 cups squash (save remaining squash for another use).

In a bowl, beat the cream cheese until smooth. Stir in the squash until blended. Add sugar, caramel topping, cinnamon, salt, ginger and cloves; beat until blended. Add the pudding mix and milk; beat on low speed for 2 minutes.

Spoon into pastry shell. Refrigerate for at least 3 hours. Garnish with whipped cream and coconut. **YIELD:** 6-8 servings.

Lemony White Chocolate Cheesecake

(Pictured above)

PREP: 30 min. **BAKE:** 65 min. + chilling

Although it takes some time to prepare this eye-catching cheese-cake, the combination of tangy lemon and rich white chocolate is hard to beat. It's always a huge hit!

—*Marlene Schollenberge, Bloomington, Illinois*

- 1-1/4 **cups all-purpose flour**
- 2 **tablespoons confectioners' sugar**
- 1 **teaspoon grated lemon peel**
- 1/2 **cup cold butter, cubed**

FILLING:
- 4 **packages (8 ounces *each*) cream cheese, softened**
- 1-1/4 **cups sugar**
- 2 **tablespoons all-purpose flour**
- 2 **tablespoons lemon juice**
- 2 **tablespoons heavy whipping cream**
- 2 **teaspoons vanilla extract**
- 4 **eggs, lightly beaten**
- 10 **squares (1 ounce *each*) white baking chocolate, melted and cooled**
- 2 **teaspoons grated lemon peel**

Place a 9-in. springform pan on a double thickness of heavy-duty foil (about 18 in. square). Securely wrap foil around pan; set aside.

In a small bowl, combine the flour, confectioners' sugar and lemon peel; cut in butter until crumbly. Press onto the bottom and 1 in. up the sides of prepared pan. Place on a baking sheet. Bake at 325° for 25-30 minutes or until golden brown. Cool on a wire rack.

For filling, in a large bowl, beat the cream cheese, sugar, flour, lemon juice, cream and vanilla until well blended. Add the eggs; beat on low speed just until combined. Stir in the white chocolate and lemon peel. Pour into the crust.

Place pan in a large baking pan; add 1 in. of hot water to larger pan. Bake at 325° for 65-85 minutes or until center is just set and top appears dull.

Remove pan from the water bath. Cool on a wire rack for 10 minutes. Carefully run a knife around the edge of pan to loosen; cool 1 hour longer. Refrigerate overnight. Remove sides of pan before slicing. **YIELD:** 12 servings.

Lemonade Icebox Pie

PREP: 15 min. + chilling

This dessert comes to mind immediately when I put together my favorite summer meal. High and fluffy, it has a creamy, smooth consistency and a refreshing lemonade flavor.

—*Cheryl Maczko, Eglon, West Virginia*

- 1 **package (8 ounces) cream cheese, softened**
- 1 **can (14 ounces) sweetened condensed milk**
- 3/4 **cup lemonade concentrate**
- 1 **carton (8 ounces) frozen whipped topping, thawed**

Yellow food coloring, optional
- 1 **graham cracker crust (9 inches)**

In a large bowl, beat the cream cheese until smooth. Gradually beat in the milk until blended. Beat in the lemonade concentrate. Fold in the whipped topping and food coloring if desired. Pour into the crust. Cover and refrigerate until set. **YIELD:** 8 servings.

Combine cookie crumbs and butter; press onto the bottom of a greased 9-in. springform pan. In a small bowl, combine the coffee granules, water and cinnamon; set aside.

In a large bowl, beat cream cheese, sugar and flour until smooth. Add eggs; beat on low speed just until combined. Stir in vanilla. Divide batter in half. Stir melted chocolate into one portion; pour over crust. Stir coffee mixture into remaining batter; gently spoon over chocolate layer.

Place pan on a double thickness of heavy-duty foil (about 16 in. square). Securely wrap the foil around pan. Place in a large baking pan; add 1 in. of hot water to larger pan.

Bake at 325° for 45-50 minutes or until center is just set and top appears dull. Remove springform pan from water bath. Cool on a wire rack for 10 minutes. Carefully run a knife around edge of pan to loosen; cool 1 hour longer. Refrigerate overnight.

In a microwave-safe bowl, melt chocolate chips and butter; stir until smooth. Spread over cheesecake. Remove sides of pan. Garnish with coffee beans if desired. Refrigerate leftovers. **YIELD:** 16 servings.

Berry Pinwheel Cake

PREP: 30 min. **BAKE:** 10 min. + chilling

Perfect for special meals, this lovely chiffon cake is a nice change from strawberry pie or shortcake. It's easier to make than you think. Plus, the waxed paper-lined pan makes cleanup a breeze!
—Becky Ruff, Monona, Iowa

        4 **egg yolks**
        2 **eggs**
    1/2 **cup sugar**
  4-1/2 **teaspoons water**
        2 **teaspoons canola oil**
        1 **teaspoon vanilla extract**
        1 **cup cake flour**
        1 **teaspoon baking powder**
    1/2 **teaspoon salt**
Confectioners' sugar
FILLING:
        1 **cup heavy whipping cream**
        1 **tablespoon sugar**
        3 **tablespoons lemon curd**
        2 **cups chopped fresh strawberries**

In a large bowl, beat egg yolks, eggs and sugar until thick and lemon-colored. Beat in water, oil and vanilla. Combine flour, baking powder and salt; gradually add to egg mixture. Grease a 15-in. x 10-in. x 1-in. baking pan and line with waxed paper; grease and flour the paper. Spread batter into pan.

Bake at 375° for 10-12 minutes or until cake springs back when lightly touched. Cool for 5 minutes. Turn cake onto a kitchen towel dusted with confectioners' sugar. Peel off waxed paper. Roll up cake in towel jelly-roll style, starting with a short side. Cool on a wire rack.

For filling, beat cream until soft peaks form; add sugar, beating until stiff. Fold in lemon curd; gradually fold in strawberries. Unroll cake; spread filling evenly to within 1/2 in. of edges. Roll up again; dust with confectioners' sugar. Cover and chill for 1 hour before serving. Refrigerate leftovers. **YIELD:** 8 servings.

Layered Mocha Cheesecake

(Pictured above and on page 160)

PREP: 30 min. **BAKE:** 45 min. + chilling

In my search for the perfect mocha cheesecake, I ended up combining a few of my favorite recipes to create this delicious version. It's as much a feast for the eyes as for the palate!
—Sue Gronholz, Beaver Dam, Wisconsin

  1-1/2 **cups cream-filled chocolate sandwich cookie crumbs**
    1/4 **cup butter, melted**
FILLING:
        2 **tablespoons plus 1-1/2 teaspoons instant coffee granules**
        1 **tablespoon boiling water**
    1/4 **teaspoon ground cinnamon**
        4 **packages (8 ounces *each*) cream cheese, softened**
  1-1/2 **cups sugar**
    1/4 **cup all-purpose flour**
        4 **eggs, lightly beaten**
        2 **teaspoons vanilla extract**
        2 **cups (12 ounces) semisweet chocolate chips, melted and cooled**
GLAZE:
    1/2 **cup semisweet chocolate chips**
        3 **tablespoons butter**
Chocolate-covered coffee beans, optional

Raspberry Patch Cream Pie

(Pictured below and on page 160)

PREP: 35 min. + chilling

Our family loves raspberries, and this pie keeps the flavor and firmness of the berries intact. The terrific combination of the berry-gelatin and cream cheese layers has everyone coming back for seconds.

—Allison Anderson, Raymond, Washington

 1 cup graham cracker crumbs
 1/2 cup sugar
 5 tablespoons butter, melted
FILLING:
 1 package (8 ounces) cream cheese, softened
 1/4 cup confectioners' sugar
 2 teaspoons milk
 1 teaspoon vanilla extract
TOPPING:
 3/4 cup sugar
 3 tablespoons cornstarch
 1-1/3 cups cold water
 1/4 cup raspberry gelatin powder
 3 cups fresh raspberries

Combine the cracker crumbs, sugar and butter. Press onto the bottom and up the sides of an ungreased 9-in. pie plate. Bake at 350° for 9-11 minutes or until set. Cool on a wire rack.

For filling, combine the cream cheese, confectioners' sugar, milk and vanilla. Carefully spread over crust.

For topping, in a small saucepan, combine the sugar, cornstarch and water until smooth. Bring to a boil; cook and stir for 2 minutes or until thickened. Remove from the heat; stir in gelatin until dissolved. Cool to room temperature. Refrigerate until slightly thickened.

Arrange the raspberries over filling. Spoon the gelatin mixture over the berries. Refrigerate until set. **YIELD:** 6-8 servings.

Lemonade Meringue Pie

(Pictured above and on the cover)

PREP: 30 min. **BAKE:** 15 min. + chilling

Lemonade concentrate and lemon juice give this pretty pie an excellent citrus taste. I also like to add some lemon zest on top of the meringue.

—Kay Seiler, Greenville, Ohio

 3 eggs, *separated*
 1 package (4.6 ounces) cook-and-serve vanilla pudding mix
 1-1/4 cups milk
 1 cup (8 ounces) sour cream
 1/3 cup lemonade concentrate
 1 teaspoon lemon juice
 1/4 teaspoon cream of tartar
 6 tablespoons sugar
 1 pastry shell (9 inches), baked

Place egg whites in a small bowl; let stand at room temperature for 30 minutes. Meanwhile, in a large saucepan, combine the pudding mix, milk and sour cream until smooth. Cook and stir over medium heat until thickened and bubbly, about 5 minutes. Reduce heat; cook and stir 2 minutes longer.

Remove from the heat. Gradually whisk 1 cup hot filling into egg yolks; return all to the pan. Bring to a gentle boil; cook and stir for 2 minutes. Remove from heat. Gently stir in lemonade concentrate; keep warm.

Add the lemon juice and cream of tartar to egg whites; beat on medium speed until soft peaks form. Gradually beat in the sugar, 1 tablespoon at a time, on high until stiff glossy peaks form and the sugar is dissolved.

Pour warm filling into pastry shell. Spread meringue over filling, sealing edges to pastry.

Bake at 350° for 15-20 minutes or until meringue is golden brown. Cool on a wire rack for 1 hour. Refrigerate for at least 3 hours before serving. **YIELD:** 6-8 servings.

Mascarpone Cheesecake

(Pictured below)

PREP: 30 min. **BAKE:** 50 min. + chilling

This rich dessert is sure to delight with its creamy filling, whipped topping and sweet caramel drizzle. It is a perfect dessert for a weekend dinner or potluck contribution.
—*Deanna Polito-Laughinghouse, Raleigh, North Carolina*

   3/4 cup graham cracker crumbs
     3 tablespoons sugar
     3 tablespoons butter, melted
FILLING:
     2 packages (8 ounces *each*) cream cheese, softened
     2 cartons (8 ounces *each*) Mascarpone cheese
     1 cup sugar
     1 tablespoon lemon juice
     1 tablespoon vanilla extract
     4 eggs, lightly beaten
TOPPING:
     1 envelope whipped topping mix
     1 tablespoon caramel ice cream topping

Place a greased 9-in. springform pan on a double thickness of heavy-duty foil (about 18 in. square). Securely wrap foil around pan.

Combine cracker crumbs and sugar; stir in butter. Press onto the bottom of prepared pan. Place pan on a baking sheet. Bake at 325° for 10 minutes. Cool on a wire rack.

For filling, in a large bowl, beat the cheeses, sugar, lemon juice and vanilla until smooth. Add eggs; beat on low speed just until combined. Pour over crust. Place springform pan in a large baking pan; add 1 in. of hot water to larger pan.

Bake at 325° for 50-60 minutes or until center is just set and top appears dull. Remove springform pan from water bath. Cool on a wire rack for 10 minutes. Carefully run a knife around the edge of pan to loosen; cool 1 hour longer.

Refrigerate overnight. Remove sides of the pan. Before serving, prepare topping mix according to the package directions. Garnish the cheesecake with whipped topping; drizzle with caramel. Refrigerate leftovers. **YIELD:** 12 servings.

Lemon Chiffon Cake

(Pictured above)

PREP: 25 min. **BAKE:** 50 min. + cooling

This moist, airy cake was my dad's favorite. My mom revamped the original recipe to include lemons. I'm not much of a baker, so I don't make it very often—but it's well worth the effort.
—*Trisha Kammers, Clarkston, Washington*

     7 eggs, *separated*
     2 cups all-purpose flour
 1-1/2 cups sugar
     3 teaspoons baking powder
     1 teaspoon salt
   3/4 cup water
   1/2 cup canola oil
     4 teaspoons grated lemon peel
     2 teaspoons vanilla extract
   1/2 teaspoon cream of tartar
LEMON FROSTING:
   1/3 cup butter, softened
     3 cups confectioners' sugar
 4-1/2 teaspoons grated lemon peel
Dash salt
   1/4 cup lemon juice

Let eggs stand at room temperature for 30 minutes. In a large bowl, combine the flour, sugar, baking powder and salt. In another bowl, whisk the egg yolks, water, oil, lemon peel and vanilla; add to dry ingredients. Beat until well blended.

In another large bowl, beat egg whites and cream of tartar on medium speed until soft peaks form; fold into batter. Gently spoon into an ungreased 10-in. tube pan. Cut through batter with a knife to remove air pockets.

Bake on the lowest oven rack at 325° for 50-55 minutes or until top springs back when lightly touched. Immediately invert the pan; cool completely, about 1 hour.

Run a knife around the side and center tube of pan. Remove cake to a serving plate. Combine the frosting ingredients; beat until smooth. Spread over top of cake. **YIELD:** 12-16 servings.

Rhubarb Upside-Down Cake

(Pictured below)

PREP: 30 min. **BAKE:** 40 min. + cooling

This buoyant yellow cake is tender but not too sweet, and the caramelized rhubarb topping adds tangy flavor and eye appeal. We like it served with strawberry ice cream.

—Joyce Rowe, Stratham, New Hampshire

- 2/3 cup packed brown sugar
- 3 tablespoons butter, melted
- 2-1/4 cups diced fresh *or* frozen rhubarb
- 4-1/2 teaspoons sugar

BATTER:
- 6 tablespoons butter, softened
- 3/4 cup sugar
- 2 eggs, *separated*
- 1 teaspoon vanilla extract
- 1 cup plus 2 tablespoons all-purpose flour
- 1-1/2 teaspoons baking powder
- 1/2 teaspoon salt
- 1/4 cup milk
- 1/4 teaspoon cream of tartar

Whipped cream, optional

Combine brown sugar and butter. Spread into a greased 9-in. round baking pan. Layer with rhubarb; sprinkle with sugar. Set aside.

In a large bowl, cream butter and sugar. Beat in egg yolks and vanilla. Combine the flour, baking powder and salt; add to creamed mixture alternately with milk.

Beat egg whites and cream of tartar on medium speed until stiff peaks form. Gradually fold into creamed mixture, about 1/2 cup at a time. Gently spoon over rhubarb (pan will be full, about 1/4 in. from top of pan).

Bake at 325° for 50-60 minutes or until cake springs back when lightly touched. Cool for 10 minutes before inverting onto a serving plate. Serve warm with whipped cream if desired. **YIELD:** 10-12 servings.

EDITOR'S NOTE: If using frozen rhubarb, measure rhubarb while still frozen, then thaw completely. Drain in a colander, but do not press liquid out.

Summer Celebration Ice Cream Cake

(Pictured above)

PREP: 15 min. **BAKE:** 20 min. + freezing

I wanted to make my youngest son an ice cream cake one year for his summer birthday. He picked the flavors and I decided to try my best brownie recipe as a crust. It worked!

—Krista Frank, Rhododendron, Oregon

- 1 cup sugar
- 3 tablespoons butter, melted
- 3 tablespoons orange yogurt
- 1 egg
- 1 teaspoon grated orange peel
- 1 teaspoon vanilla extract
- 3/4 cup all-purpose flour
- 1/3 cup baking cocoa
- 1 cup (6 ounces) semisweet chocolate chips
- 1-3/4 quarts vanilla ice cream, softened
- 4 to 6 squares (1 ounce *each*) semisweet chocolate
- 1 tablespoon shortening

Mixed fresh berries

Line an 8-in. square baking dish with foil and grease the foil; set aside. In a large bowl, combine sugar, butter, yogurt, egg, orange peel and vanilla until blended. Combine the flour and cocoa; stir into sugar mixture. Add chocolate chips.

Spread into prepared dish. Bake at 325° for 20-25 minutes or until a toothpick inserted near the center comes out with moist crumbs. Cool on a wire rack.

Spread the ice cream over cake. Cover and freeze for 3 hours or until firm.

Remove from freezer 10 minutes before serving. In a microwave-safe bowl, melt chocolate and shortening; stir until smooth. Using foil, lift the dessert out of dish; gently peel off foil. Cut into squares. Garnish with berries and drizzle with chocolate. **YIELD:** 9 servings.

For the filling, in a large bowl, beat the cream cheese, sugar, flour and cream until smooth. Add the eggs; beat on low speed just until combined. Beat in the lemon juice and vanilla just until blended. Pour 2-1/2 cups of the batter into a bowl; set aside.

Stir 3/4 cup pureed strawberries and food coloring if desired into remaining batter. Pour into crust. Place pan on a double thickness of heavy-duty foil (about 16 in. square). Securely wrap foil around pan. Place in a large baking pan. Add 1 in. of hot water to larger pan. Bake for 35 minutes.

Carefully pour reserved batter over the bottom layer. Spoon the remaining pureed berries over batter in three concentric circles. Carefully cut through top layer only with a knife to swirl. Bake 40-50 minutes longer or until center is almost set. Remove pan from water bath. Cool on a wire rack for 10 minutes. Carefully run a knife around edge of pan to loosen; cool 1 hour longer. Refrigerate overnight. **YIELD:** 12 servings.

Lemon Coconut Cake

PREP: 1 hour + cooling **BAKE:** 20 min. + cooling

If you're pressed for time, use a white cake mix and dress it up with the filling and frosting from this recipe. This is a lovely dessert for spring and summer.
—*LaDonna Reed, Ponca City, Oklahoma*

    5 **egg whites**
  3/4 **cup shortening**
1-1/2 **cups sugar**
1-1/2 **teaspoons vanilla extract**
    2 **cups all-purpose flour**
    2 **teaspoons baking powder**
    1 **teaspoon salt**
    1 **cup milk**
FILLING:
  3/4 **cup sugar**
    2 **tablespoons cornstarch**
Dash salt
  3/4 **cup cold water**
    2 **egg yolks**
    3 **tablespoons lemon juice**
    1 **tablespoon butter**
FROSTING:
  3/4 **cup shortening**
3-3/4 **cups confectioners' sugar**
    1 **teaspoon vanilla extract**
  1/3 **cup water**
1-1/4 **cups flaked coconut**

Place the egg whites in a bowl; let stand at room temperature for 30 minutes. In a large bowl, cream shortening and sugar until light and fluffy. Beat in vanilla. Combine flour, baking powder and salt; add to creamed mixture alternately with milk. Beat egg whites until stiff peaks form; fold into creamed mixture.

Pour into three greased and floured 9-in. round baking pans. Bake at 350° for 18-20 minutes or until a toothpick comes out clean. Cool for 10 minutes; remove from pans to wire racks to cool completely.

Strawberry Swirl Cheesecake

(Pictured above)

PREP: 1 hour **BAKE:** 1-1/4 hours + chilling

This dessert is doubly delicious with two creamy layers…one strawberry, one vanilla. To avoid cracking, run the knife just through the very top when swirling the strawberry puree.
—*Mary Ellen Friend, Ravenswood, West Virginia*

1-1/4 **cups all-purpose flour**
    1 **tablespoon sugar**
    1 **teaspoon grated lemon peel**
  1/2 **cup cold butter**
FILLING:
    4 **packages (8 ounces *each*) cream cheese, softened**
1-1/3 **cups sugar**
    2 **tablespoons all-purpose flour**
    2 **tablespoons heavy whipping cream**
    4 **eggs, lightly beaten**
    1 **tablespoon lemon juice**
    2 **teaspoons vanilla extract**
    1 **cup pureed fresh strawberries, *divided***
    8 **to 10 drops red food coloring, optional**

In a small bowl, combine flour, sugar and lemon peel; cut in butter until crumbly. Pat dough onto the bottom and 1 in. up the sides of a greased 9-in. springform pan. Place on a baking sheet. Bake at 325° for 15-20 minutes or until lightly browned. Cool on a wire rack.

For filling, in a heavy saucepan, combine the sugar, cornstarch and salt. Stir in water until smooth. Cook and stir over medium-high heat until thickened. Reduce heat; cook and stir 2 minutes longer. Remove from heat. Stir a small amount of filling into the egg yolks; return all to pan, stirring constantly. Bring to a boil; cook and stir 2 minutes longer. Remove from heat. Stir in lemon juice and butter. Cool, without stirring, to room temperature.

For frosting, in a large bowl, cream shortening and confectioners' sugar until light and fluffy; beat in the vanilla. Gradually add water, beating until smooth. Spread filling between cake layers. Frost top and sides of cake; sprinkle with coconut. **YIELD:** 12-14 servings.

Frozen Peanut Parfait Pies

(Pictured below)

PREP: 20 min. + freezing

This crowd-pleasing dessert will be the hit of any potluck or party. And although it seems like a lot of trouble to make these luscious pies, with only six ingredients, they're actually very easy.
—Anne Powers, Munford, Alabama

> 1 package (8 ounces) cream cheese, softened
> 1 can (14 ounces) sweetened condensed milk
> 1 carton (16 ounces) frozen whipped topping, thawed
> 1 jar (11-3/4 ounces) hot fudge ice cream topping, warmed
> 2 cups dry roasted peanuts
> 2 pastry shells (9 inches), baked

In a large bowl, beat cream cheese and condensed milk until smooth; fold in whipped topping. Spread a fourth of the mixture into each pie shell. Drizzle each with a fourth of the fudge topping; sprinkle each with 1/2 cup peanuts. Repeat layers.

Cover and freeze for 4 hours or overnight. Remove from the freezer 5 minutes before cutting. **YIELD:** 2 pies (6-8 servings each).

Fresh Fruit Tarts

(Pictured above)

PREP: 20 min. + chilling **BAKE:** 15 min. + cooling

These luscious tarts are the jewels of the party whenever I serve them. You can bake the shells ahead and freeze them, then fill and decorate the tarts the day of the gathering.
—Dona Erhart, Stockbridge, Michigan

> 1-1/2 cups all-purpose flour
> 1/4 cup sugar
> 1/4 teaspoon salt
> 1/2 cup cold butter, cubed
> 1 egg, lightly beaten

FILLING:
> 4 ounces cream cheese, softened
> 1/4 cup sweetened condensed milk
> 2 tablespoons lemon juice

Assorted fresh berries
> 2 tablespoons apricot preserves

In a large bowl, combine the flour, sugar and salt. Cut in butter until mixture resembles coarse crumbs. Add egg; mix with a fork until blended. Shape dough into a ball. Cover and refrigerate for 1 hour or until easy to handle.

Divide dough into six portions. Press each portion into a greased 4-1/2-in. tart pan. Bake at 350° for 15-20 minutes or until edges are lightly browned. Cool for 10 minutes before removing from pans to wire racks to cool completely.

For the filling, beat the cream cheese until smooth. Beat in the sweetened condensed milk and lemon juice. Spoon 2 rounded tablespoonfuls into each cooled tart shell. Arrange berries over filling.

In a small saucepan, melt preserves over medium heat; stir until smooth. Brush over berries. **YIELD:** 6 servings.

Special Mocha Cupcakes

(Pictured below)

PREP: 25 min. **BAKE:** 20 min. + cooling

Topped with a fluffy frosting and chocolate sprinkles, these extra-rich, extra-delicious cupcakes smell wonderful while baking and taste even better!

—Mary Bilyeu, Ann Arbor, Michigan

     1-1/2 cups all-purpose flour
         1 cup sugar
       1/3 cup baking cocoa
         1 teaspoon baking soda
       1/2 teaspoon salt
         2 eggs
       1/2 cup cold brewed coffee
       1/2 cup canola oil
         3 teaspoons cider vinegar
         3 teaspoons vanilla extract

MOCHA FROSTING:
         3 tablespoons milk chocolate chips
         3 tablespoons semisweet chocolate chips
       1/3 cup butter, softened
         2 cups confectioners' sugar
    1 to 2 tablespoons brewed coffee
       1/2 cup chocolate sprinkles

In a small bowl, combine the flour, sugar, cocoa, baking soda and salt. In a small bowl, whisk the eggs, coffee, oil, vinegar and vanilla. Add to dry ingredients; mix well.

Fill paper-lined muffin cups three-fourths full. Bake at 350° for 20-25 minutes or until a toothpick inserted in center comes out clean. Cool for 10 minutes before removing from pan to a wire rack to cool.

For the frosting, in a small microwave-safe bowl, melt the chips; stir until smooth. Add butter; beat until blended. Gradually beat in the confectioners' sugar and coffee. Pipe frosting onto cupcakes. Top with sprinkles; gently press down. **YIELD:** 1 dozen.

Cranberry Zucchini Wedges

(Pictured above)

PREP: 15 min. **BAKE:** 30 min. + cooling

These cake wedges have wonderful flavor and a tender texture. They're great for brunch. With bits of pineapple, cranberries and zucchini, they're also pretty.

—Redawna Kalynchuk, Waskatenau, Alberta

         1 can (20 ounces) pineapple chunks
         3 cups all-purpose flour
     1-3/4 cups sugar
         1 teaspoon baking powder
         1 teaspoon baking soda
         1 teaspoon salt
         3 eggs
         1 cup canola oil
         2 teaspoons vanilla extract
         1 cup tightly packed shredded zucchini
         1 cup fresh *or* frozen cranberries, halved
       1/2 cup chopped walnuts

Confectioners' sugar

Drain the pineapple, reserving 1/3 cup juice (save the remaining juice for another use). Place the pineapple and reserved juice in a blender; cover and process until smooth. Set aside.

In a bowl, combine the flour, sugar, baking powder, baking soda and salt. In a bowl, whisk eggs, oil, vanilla and pineapple mixture; beat into the dry ingredients until blended. Fold in the zucchini, cranberries and nuts.

Pour into two greased and floured 9-in. round baking pans. Bake at 350° for 30-35 minutes or until a toothpick inserted near center comes out clean. Cool for 10 minutes before removing from pans to wire racks to cool completely. Just before serving, dust with confectioners' sugar. **YIELD:** 2 cakes (8 wedges each).

Rustic Autumn Fruit Tart

(Pictured below)

PREP: 25 min. **BAKE:** 40 min.

This impressive dessert was a hit at my house. It's fast, easy and delectable! An apricot jam glaze lends a pretty sheen to the buttery pastry that envelopes tender apple and pear slices.

—Jennifer Richards, Pine Beach, New Jersey

- 1/2 cup butter, softened
- 4 ounces cream cheese, softened
- 1-1/2 cups all-purpose flour
- 2 large apples, peeled and thinly sliced
- 1 medium pear, peeled and thinly sliced
- 4-1/2 teaspoons cornstarch
- 1/2 teaspoon ground cinnamon
- 1/4 teaspoon ground cardamom
- 1/4 teaspoon ground nutmeg
- 1/4 cup orange juice
- 1/3 cup packed brown sugar
- 1/2 cup apricot jam, warmed

In a small bowl, beat the butter and cream cheese until smooth. Gradually add flour, beating just until mixture forms a ball. Cover and refrigerate for 1 hour.

In a large bowl, combine the apples and pear. In a small bowl, combine cornstarch and spices; stir in orange juice until smooth. Stir in brown sugar until blended. Add to apple mixture and stir gently to coat.

On a lightly floured surface, roll out dough into a 14-in. circle. Transfer to a parchment paper-lined baking sheet. Spoon filling over the pastry to within 2 in. of edges. Fold up the edges of pastry over filling, leaving center uncovered.

Bake at 375° for 40-45 minutes or until crust is golden and filling is bubbly. Spread with apricot jam. Using parchment paper, slide tart onto a wire rack to cool. **YIELD:** 6 servings.

Walnut Banana Cupcakes

(Pictured above)

PREP: 25 min. **BAKE:** 20 min. + cooling

What makes these moist banana cupcakes extra special is the nutmeg, but make sure it's fresh. They're amazingly good; I get requests for them all the time.

—Rachel Krupp, Perkiomenville, Pennsylvania

- 1/4 cup butter, softened
- 3/4 cup sugar
- 2 eggs
- 1/2 cup mashed ripe banana
- 1 teaspoon vanilla extract
- 1 cup all-purpose flour
- 1/2 teaspoon baking soda
- 1/2 teaspoon ground nutmeg
- 1/4 teaspoon salt
- 1/4 cup sour cream

CREAM CHEESE FROSTING:
- 4 ounces cream cheese, softened
- 1/2 teaspoon vanilla extract
- 1-3/4 cups confectioners' sugar
- 3 tablespoons chopped walnuts

In a small bowl, cream butter and sugar. Add the eggs, one at a time, beating well after each addition. Add banana and vanilla; mix well. Combine the flour, baking soda, nutmeg and salt; add to creamed mixture alternately with sour cream.

Fill paper-lined muffin cups half full. Bake at 350° for 18-22 minutes or until a toothpick comes out clean. Cool for 10 minutes before removing from pan to a wire rack to cool completely.

For the frosting, in a small bowl, combine cream cheese and vanilla. Gradually beat in confectioners' sugar. Frost cupcakes; sprinkle with walnuts. Store in the refrigerator. **YIELD:** 1 dozen.

For the frosting, in a large bowl, beat cream cheese and butter until smooth. Beat in confectioners' sugar, cocoa and vanilla until smooth. Place one cake layer on a serving plate; spread with half of the frosting. Repeat layers. Sprinkle with walnuts and chocolate chips. **YIELD:** 12-16 servings.

Crumbleberry Pie

(*Pictured below*)

PREP: 15 min. **BAKE:** 50 min.

Pear slices and blueberries add wonderful flavor to this simple-to-make pie. The almonds in the filling add just the right touch of nutty goodness.

—*Maria Regakis, Somerville, Massachusetts*

Pastry for single-crust pie (9 inches)
    6 **tablespoons butter, softened**
  1/2 **cup sugar**
    2 **eggs**
    1 **cup finely ground almonds**
  1/4 **cup all-purpose flour**
    1 **large pear, peeled and thinly sliced**
TOPPING:
  3/4 **cup all-purpose flour**
  1/3 **cup packed brown sugar**
  1/4 **teaspoon almond extract**
  1/3 **cup cold butter**
    1 **cup fresh *or* frozen blueberries**

Line a 9-in. pie plate with pastry; set aside. In a small bowl, cream butter and sugar until light and fluffy. Add the eggs, one at a time, beating well after each addition. Stir in almonds and flour.

Spread into pastry shell. Arrange pear slices over filling. Bake at 350° for 25-30 minutes or until light golden brown.

For the topping, combine the flour, brown sugar and extract; cut in butter until crumbly. Sprinkle blueberries over pears; sprinkle with crumb topping.

Bake 25-30 minutes longer or until golden brown. Serve warm. Refrigerate leftovers. **YIELD:** 6-8 servings.

EDITOR'S NOTE: If using frozen blueberries, do not thaw before adding to filling.

Chocolate Carrot Cake

(*Pictured above*)

PREP: 35 min. **BAKE:** 25 min. + cooling

Finely shredding the carrots gives this cake nice texture. The walnuts sprinkled on top add crunch, but you can leave them off if you prefer.

—*Pamela Brown, Williamsburg, Michigan*

    2 **cups all-purpose flour**
    2 **cups sugar**
  1/2 **cup baking cocoa**
    1 **teaspoon baking soda**
  1/2 **teaspoon salt**
    4 **eggs**
 1-1/4 **cups canola oil**
    3 **cups finely shredded carrots**
FROSTING:
    1 **package (8 ounces) cream cheese, softened**
  1/2 **cup butter, softened**
 3-3/4 **cups confectioners' sugar**
  1/4 **cup baking cocoa**
    3 **teaspoons vanilla extract**
  1/4 **cup chopped walnuts**
  1/4 **cup semisweet chocolate chips**

Line two 9-in. round baking pans with waxed paper; grease the paper and set aside. In a large bowl, combine the flour, sugar, cocoa, baking soda and salt. Add eggs, oil and carrots; beat until combined. Pour into prepared pans.

Bake at 350° for 25-30 minutes or until a toothpick inserted near the center comes out clean. Cool for 10 minutes before removing from pans to wire racks to cool completely.

Place on a baking sheet. Bake at 325° for 10 minutes or until set. Cool on a wire rack.

In a large bowl, beat cream cheese until fluffy. Beat in milk and apple juice concentrate until smooth. Add eggs; beat on low speed just until combined (batter will be thin). Pour into crust.

Return pan to baking sheet. Bake at 325° for 40-45 minutes or until center is almost set. Cool on a wire rack for 10 minutes. Carefully run a knife around edge of pan to loosen; cool 1 hour longer. Refrigerate overnight.

For the topping, in a large skillet, cook and stir apples in butter over medium heat until crisp-tender, about 5 minutes. Cool to room temperature. Arrange over the cheesecake.

In a small saucepan, combine the cornstarch, cinnamon and apple juice concentrate until smooth. Bring to a boil. Reduce heat; cook and stir for 1 minute or until thickened. Immediately brush over apples. Refrigerate for 1 hour or until chilled. Remove sides of pan. Refrigerate leftovers. **YIELD:** 12 servings.

Cinnamon Apple Cheesecake

(Pictured above and on page 160)

PREP: 40 min. **BAKE:** 40 min. + chilling

An attractive topping of cinnamon-spiced apple slices and a home-made oat-and-walnut crust make this creamy dessert a definite showstopper.

—*Emily Ann Young, Edmond, Oklahoma*

- 1/2 cup butter, softened
- 1/4 cup packed brown sugar
- 1 cup all-purpose flour
- 1/4 cup quick-cooking oats
- 1/4 cup finely chopped walnuts
- 1/2 teaspoon ground cinnamon
- 2 packages (8 ounces *each*) cream cheese, softened
- 1 can (14 ounces) sweetened condensed milk
- 1/2 cup apple juice concentrate
- 3 eggs, lightly beaten

TOPPING:
- 2 medium apples, peeled and sliced
- 1 tablespoon butter
- 1 teaspoon cornstarch
- 1/4 teaspoon ground cinnamon
- 1/4 cup apple juice concentrate

In a small bowl, cream butter and brown sugar until light and fluffy. Gradually add flour, oats, walnuts and cinnamon until well blended. Press onto the bottom and 1-1/2 in. up the sides of a greased 9-in. springform pan.

Cherry Gingerbread Cupcakes

PREP: 30 min. **BAKE:** 20 min. + cooling

A maraschino cherry in the center and frosting with a hint of lemon complement these little spice cakes. Making them is a surefire way to get my dad to come over for a cup of coffee.

—*Laura McAllister, Morganton, North Carolina*

- 1/2 cup shortening
- 1 cup sugar
- 2 eggs
- 1 cup molasses
- 3 cups all-purpose flour
- 1 teaspoon baking soda
- 1 teaspoon ground ginger
- 1 teaspoon ground cinnamon
- 1 cup buttermilk
- 1/2 cup chopped walnuts
- 24 maraschino cherries, well drained

LEMON CREAM CHEESE FROSTING:
- 4 ounces cream cheese, softened
- 1/4 cup butter, softened
- 1 teaspoon vanilla extract
- 1 teaspoon grated lemon peel
- 1-3/4 to 2 cups confectioners' sugar

In a large bowl, cream the shortening and sugar until light and fluffy. Add the eggs and molasses; mix well. Combine the flour, baking soda, ginger and cinnamon; add to the creamed mixture alternately with buttermilk. Stir in the walnuts.

Fill paper-lined muffin cups two-thirds full; place a maraschino cherry in the center of each. Bake at 375° for 20-24 minutes or until a toothpick inserted in the centers comes out clean. Cool for 10 minutes before removing from pans to wire racks to cool completely.

For the frosting, in a small bowl, beat cream cheese and butter until smooth; add vanilla and lemon peel. Gradually beat in confectioners' sugar. Frost cupcakes. **YIELD:** 2 dozen.

Carrot Cheesecake

(Pictured below)

PREP: 25 min. **BAKE:** 65 min. + chilling

My family can't wait to dig into this luscious make-ahead dessert. Unlike traditional cheesecake, a streusel topping is sprinkled over the filling.

—Misty Wellman, Scottsdale, Arizona

2 cups graham cracker crumbs
1/4 cup sugar
1/3 cup butter, melted

FILLING:

3 packages (8 ounces *each*) cream cheese, softened
1-1/4 cups sugar
2 tablespoons brown sugar
3 eggs, lightly beaten
1/4 cup heavy whipping cream
2 tablespoons cornstarch
1 tablespoon sour cream
1-1/2 teaspoons vanilla extract
1 teaspoon lemon juice
1/2 teaspoon ground cinnamon
1-1/3 cups chopped carrots, cooked and pureed

TOPPING:

1 cup graham cracker crumbs
2 tablespoons brown sugar
1-1/2 teaspoons ground cinnamon
1/4 cup butter, melted

Combine crumbs and sugar; stir in butter. Press onto the bottom and 2 in. up the sides of a greased 9-in. springform pan. Place on a baking sheet. Bake at 350° for 6-8 minutes. Cool on a wire rack.

For the filling, in a large bowl, beat cream cheese and sugars until smooth. Add eggs; beat on low speed just until combined. Stir in the cream, cornstarch, sour cream, vanilla, lemon juice and cinnamon. Fold in carrots.

Pour into crust. Place pan on a double thickness of heavy-duty foil (about 16 in. square). Securely wrap foil around pan. Place in a larger baking pan. Add 1 in. of hot water to larger pan. Bake at 350° for 55-60 minutes until center is just set.

Combine the topping ingredients; sprinkle over the filling. Bake 7-10 minutes longer. Remove the pan from water bath. Cool on a wire rack for 10 minutes. Carefully run a knife around the edge of pan to loosen; cool 1 hour longer. Refrigerate overnight. Remove sides of pan. **YIELD:** 10-12 servings.

Peaches & Cream Pie

PREP: 20 min. **BAKE:** 1 hour + cooling

This eye-catching pie packed with juicy peaches is irresistible. Its creamy, fruity filling is a refreshing change of pace from ordinary peach pie.

—Emma Rea, Columbia, South Carolina

3 cups all-purpose flour
1 teaspoon salt
1 cup plus 2 tablespoons cold butter
1 egg
1 teaspoon cider vinegar
5 to 7 tablespoons ice water

FILLING:

5 cups sliced peeled peaches
1 teaspoon lemon juice
3/4 cup plus 1 tablespoon sugar, *divided*
3 tablespoons all-purpose flour
3/4 teaspoon ground cinnamon
1/4 teaspoon salt
1/2 cup heavy whipping cream
1 tablespoon butter

In a bowl, combine the flour and salt; cut in butter until the mixture resembles coarse crumbs. Combine egg and vinegar; add to flour mixture. Add water, 1 tablespoon at a time, until dough forms a ball.

Divide dough in half. Roll out one portion to fit a 9-in. pie plate; transfer to pie plate. Trim pastry even with edge; set aside.

For the filling, in a large bowl, combine the peaches and lemon juice. In another bowl, combine 3/4 cup sugar, flour, cinnamon and salt; stir in cream. Pour over the peaches; gently toss to coat. Spoon into the crust. Dot with butter.

Roll out remaining pastry; make a lattice crust. Seal and flute edges. Sprinkle with remaining sugar. Cover edges loosely with foil.

Bake at 425° for 15 minutes. Reduce heat to 350°; bake for 45-50 minutes or until peaches are tender and crust is golden brown. Cool on a wire rack. **YIELD:** 6-8 servings.

In a large bowl, beat the eggs and sugar until thickened and lemon-colored. Beat in the oil, sour cream and vanilla until smooth. Combine the flour, baking powder, baking soda and salt. Add to egg mixture; mix well.

Fill muffin cups two-thirds full. Bake at 350° for 28-32 minutes or until a toothpick comes out clean. Cool for 5 minutes before inverting onto wire racks to cool completely. Garnish with whipped topping if desired. **YIELD:** 1 dozen jumbo cupcakes.

Fudgy Nut Coffee Pie

(Pictured below)

PREP: 15 min. + freezing

My mother served this pretty pie for my birthday dinner one year, and now it's one of my favorites. Sometimes I garnish the pie with dollops of whipped cream.

—Amy Theis, Billings, Montana

> 1-1/2 cups confectioners' sugar
> 1/2 cup heavy whipping cream
> 6 tablespoons butter, cubed
> 3 squares (1 ounce *each*) unsweetened chocolate
> 3 tablespoons light corn syrup
> Dash salt
> 1 teaspoon vanilla extract
> 1 chocolate crumb crust (9 inches)
> 3/4 cup coarsely chopped pecans, *divided*
> 3 pints coffee ice cream, softened

In a small saucepan, combine confectioners' sugar, cream, butter, chocolate, corn syrup and salt. Cook and stir over low heat until smooth. Remove from the heat. Stir in vanilla. Cool completely.

Spread 1/2 cup cooled fudge sauce over the crust. Sprinkle with 1/4 cup pecans. Freeze for 20 minutes or until set. Spread with half of the ice cream. Freeze for 1 hour or until firm. Repeat layers. Cover and freeze for 4 hours or until firm.

Just before serving, drizzle the remaining fudge sauce over the pie and sprinkle with remaining chopped pecans. **YIELD:** 8 servings.

Pineapple Upside-Down Cupcakes

(Pictured above and on page 160)

PREP: 30 min. **BAKE:** 30 min. + cooling

I have baked cupcakes for years since I acted as a room mother for my three children. These easy-to-prepare, jumbo treats make an attractive dessert for special occasions or everyday.

—Barbara Hahn, Park Hills, Missouri

> 6 tablespoons butter, cubed
> 1 cup packed light brown sugar
> 2 tablespoons light corn syrup
> 1 small pineapple, peeled, cored and cut into 1/2-inch slices
> 12 maraschino cherries, well drained
> 3 eggs
> 2 cups sugar
> 1 cup canola oil
> 1 cup (8 ounces) sour cream
> 2 teaspoons vanilla extract
> 2-1/2 cups all-purpose flour
> 1/2 teaspoon baking powder
> 1/2 teaspoon baking soda
> 1/2 teaspoon salt
> Whipped topping, optional

Line greased jumbo muffin cups with waxed paper; grease the paper and set aside. In a small saucepan, melt butter over low heat; stir in brown sugar and corn syrup. Cook and stir over medium heat until sugar is dissolved. Remove from the heat. Spoon 1 tablespoonful into each muffin cup; top each with a pineapple slice and a cherry.

Peanut Butter Cup Cheesecake

(Pictured above)

PREP: 20 min. **BAKE:** 55 min. + chilling

After I volunteered to bring dessert to a holiday party many years ago, I brought this pie. It not only tastes delicious, but it looks great, too!

—Dawn Lowenstein, Hatboro, Pennsylvania

```
1-1/4  cups graham cracker crumbs
  1/4  cup crushed cream-filled chocolate sandwich
       cookies
  1/4  cup sugar
    6  tablespoons butter, melted
  3/4  cup creamy peanut butter
```
FILLING:
```
    3  packages (8 ounces each) cream cheese,
       softened
    1  cup sugar
    1  cup (8 ounces) sour cream
    3  eggs, lightly beaten
1-1/2  teaspoons vanilla extract
    1  cup hot fudge ice cream topping, divided
    6  peanut butter cups, cut into small wedges
```

In a bowl, combine the cracker crumbs, cookie crumbs, sugar and butter. Press onto the bottom and 1 in. up the sides of a greased 9-in. springform pan. Place on a baking sheet.

Bake at 350° for 7-9 minutes or until set. Cool on a wire rack. In a microwave-safe bowl, heat peanut butter on high for 30 seconds or until softened. Spread over crust to within 1 in. of edges.

For the filling, in a large bowl, beat the cream cheese, sugar and sour cream until smooth. Add eggs; beat on low speed just until combined. Stir in vanilla. Pour 1 cup into a bowl; set aside. Pour the remaining filling over peanut butter layer.

In a microwave-safe bowl, heat 1/4 cup fudge topping on high for 30 seconds or until thin; fold into reserved cream cheese mixture. Carefully pour over filling; cut through with a knife to swirl.

Place the pan on a baking sheet. Bake at 350° for 55-65 minutes or until the center is almost set. Cool on a wire rack for 10 minutes. Carefully run a knife around the edge of the pan to loosen; cool 1 hour longer.

Microwave remaining fudge topping for 30 seconds or until warmed; spread over cheesecake. Garnish with peanut butter cups. Refrigerate overnight. Remove sides of pan. Refrigerate leftovers. **YIELD:** 12-14 servings.

EDITOR'S NOTE: Reduced-fat or generic brands of peanut butter are not recommended for this recipe.

Frozen Strawberry Pie

(Pictured below)

PREP: 25 min. + freezing

I work full-time, so I like the fact that these yummy, attractive pies can be made ahead. I serve each slice with a dollop of whipped cream, a strawberry and chocolate curls.

—Awynne Thurstenson, Siloam Springs, Arkansas

```
    1  package (8 ounces) cream cheese,
       softened
    1  cup sugar
    1  teaspoon vanilla extract
    4  cups chopped fresh strawberries
    1  carton (12 ounces) frozen whipped
       topping, thawed
  1/2  cup chopped pecans, toasted
    2  chocolate crumb crusts (9 inches)
```

In a large bowl, beat the cream cheese, sugar and vanilla extract until smooth. Beat in the strawberries. Fold in the whipped topping and pecans. Pour into crusts. Cover and freeze for 3-4 hours or until firm. Remove from the freezer 15-20 minutes before serving. **YIELD:** 2 pies (6 servings each).

Raspberry Peach Cupcakes

(Pictured above)

PREP: 25 min. **BAKE:** 15 min. + cooling

These easy cupcakes, which start with a cake mix, have an appealing combination of fresh fruit and white chocolate. The luscious, lemon buttercream frosting adds a citrus tang to the sweet treats.

—Arlene Kay Butler, Ogden, Utah

  1 **cup vanilla *or* white chips**
  6 **tablespoons butter, cubed**
  1 **package (18-1/4 ounces) white cake mix**
  1 **cup milk**
  3 **eggs**
  1 **teaspoon vanilla extract**
  1 **cup fresh raspberries**
1/2 **cup chopped peeled fresh peaches *or* frozen unsweetened peach slices, thawed and chopped**
LEMON FROSTING:
1/2 **cup butter, softened**
  3 **cups confectioners' sugar**
  2 **tablespoons lemon juice**
Fresh raspberries and peach pieces, optional

In a microwave-safe bowl, combine the chips and butter. Microwave at 70% power until melted; stir until smooth. In a large bowl, combine the cake mix, milk, eggs, vanilla and melted chips; beat on low speed for 30 seconds. Beat on medium for 2 minutes. Fold in raspberries and peaches.

Fill paper-lined muffin cups three-fourths full. Bake at 350° for 15-20 minutes or until a toothpick comes out clean. Cool for 10 minutes before removing from pans to wire racks to cool completely.

For the frosting, in a small bowl, beat the butter, confectioners' sugar and lemon juice until smooth. Frost cupcakes. Top with fruit if desired. **YIELD:** 2 dozen.

Caramel-Pecan Apple Pie

(Pictured below)

PREP: 45 min. **BAKE:** 55 min. + cooling

The wonderful smell of this pie takes me back to my Granny's table in Virginia. Its scrumptious taste will put smiles on everybody's faces.

—Gloria Castro, Santa Rosa, California

  7 **cups sliced peeled tart apples**
  1 **teaspoon lemon juice**
  1 **teaspoon vanilla extract**
3/4 **cup chopped pecans**
1/3 **cup packed brown sugar**
  3 **tablespoons sugar**
4-1/2 **teaspoons ground cinnamon**
  1 **tablespoon cornstarch**
1/4 **cup caramel ice cream topping, room temperature**
  1 **unbaked pastry shell (9 inches)**
  3 **tablespoons butter, melted**
STREUSEL TOPPING:
3/4 **cup all-purpose flour**
2/3 **cup chopped pecans**
1/4 **cup sugar**
  6 **tablespoons cold butter**
1/4 **cup caramel ice cream topping, room temperature**

In a large bowl, toss apples with lemon juice and vanilla. Combine the pecans, sugars, cinnamon and cornstarch; add to apple mixture and toss to coat. Pour caramel topping over bottom of pastry shell; top with apple mixture (shell will be full). Drizzle with butter.

For streusel topping, combine the flour, pecans and sugar. Cut in butter until mixture resembles coarse crumbs. Sprinkle over filling.

Bake at 350° for 55-65 minutes or until filling is bubbly and the topping is browned. Immediately drizzle with caramel topping. Cool on a wire rack. **YIELD:** 8 servings.

Maple Pumpkin Pie

(Pictured below)

PREP: 25 min. **BAKE:** 1 hour

Tired of the usual pumpkin pie? The maple syrup in this special pie provides a subtle but terrific enhancer.

—Lisa Varner, Greenville, South Carolina

        2 **eggs**
        1 **can (15 ounces) solid-pack pumpkin**
        1 **cup evaporated milk**
      3/4 **cup sugar**
      1/2 **cup maple syrup**
        1 **teaspoon pumpkin pie spice**
      1/4 **teaspoon salt**
Pastry for single-crust pie (9 inches)
MAPLE WHIPPED CREAM:
        1 **cup heavy whipping cream**
        2 **tablespoons confectioners' sugar**
        1 **tablespoon maple syrup**
      1/4 **teaspoon pumpkin pie spice**
Chopped pecans, optional

In a large bowl, combine the first seven ingredients; beat until smooth. Pour into crust.

Bake at 425° for 15 minutes. Reduce heat to 350°. Bake 45-50 minutes longer or until crust is golden brown and top of pie is set (cover edges with foil during the last 15 minutes to prevent over-browning if necessary). Cool on a wire rack for 1 hour. Refrigerate overnight or until set.

In a small bowl, beat the cream, confectioners' sugar, syrup and pumpkin pie spice until stiff peaks form. Pipe or dollop onto pie. Sprinkle with pecans if desired. Refrigerate leftovers. **YIELD:** 8 servings.

Berry Cheesecake Pie

(Pictured above)

PREP: 20 min. **BAKE:** 35 min.

Since I don't care for traditional pie crust, I usually eat only the filling of pie. That changed when I discovered this recipe. Boasting a luscious cheesecake flavor, this pretty pie gets creative with phyllo dough.

—Deanne Causey, Midland, Texas

        8 **sheets phyllo dough (14 inches x 9 inches)**
        6 **tablespoons butter, melted**
        2 **packages (8 ounces *each*) cream cheese, softened**
      1/2 **cup sugar**
        1 **teaspoon vanilla extract**
        2 **eggs, lightly beaten**
        2 **cups fresh *or* frozen blueberries**
      1/2 **cup strawberry jelly**
        1 **cup whipped topping**
Sliced fresh strawberries and additional blueberries, optional

Place one phyllo sheet in a greased 9-in. pie plate; brush with butter. Repeat seven times; trim edges. (While working with each sheet, keep remaining phyllo covered with plastic wrap and a damp towel to prevent it from drying out.)

Bake at 425° for 6-8 minutes or until edges are lightly browned (center will puff up). Cool on a wire rack.

For filling, in a small bowl, beat the cream cheese, sugar and vanilla until smooth. Add eggs; beat on low speed just until combined. Fold in blueberries. Spoon into crust.

Bake at 350° for 10 minutes; cover edges with foil to prevent over-browning. Bake 23-27 minutes longer or until center is almost set. Cool on a wire rack for 1 hour. Refrigerate until chilled.

In a small bowl, beat jelly until smooth; spread over filling. Spread with whipped topping. Garnish with strawberries and additional blueberries if desired. **YIELD:** 6-8 servings.

EDITOR'S NOTE: If using frozen blueberries, do not thaw before adding to batter.

Texas Chocolate Cupcakes

(Pictured below)

PREP: 30 min. **BAKE:** 15 min. + cooling

My husband remembers his mother making "little black cupcakes with caramel icing." I never thought about putting caramel icing on chocolate cupcakes, but boy, was I wrong. It's to die for!
—Cathy Bodkins, Dayton, Virginia

    2 cups all-purpose flour
    2 cups sugar
    1 teaspoon salt
  1/2 teaspoon baking soda
  1/4 cup baking cocoa
    1 cup water
    1 cup canola oil
  1/2 cup butter, cubed
    2 eggs
  1/3 cup buttermilk
    1 teaspoon vanilla extract

CARAMEL ICING:

    1 cup packed brown sugar
  1/2 cup butter, cubed
  1/4 cup milk
    2 to 2-1/4 cups confectioners' sugar

In a large bowl, combine the flour, sugar, salt and baking soda. In a large saucepan over medium heat, bring cocoa, water, oil and butter to a boil. Gradually add to dry ingredients; mix well. Combine eggs, buttermilk and vanilla; gradually add to batter and mix well (batter will be very thin).

Fill paper-lined muffin cups three-fourths full. Bake at 350° for 15-20 minutes or until a toothpick comes out clean. Cool for 10 minutes before removing from pans to wire racks to cool completely.

For the icing, in a heavy saucepan, combine brown sugar, butter and milk. Cook and stir over low heat until sugar is dissolved. Increase heat to medium. Do not stir. Cook for 3-6 minutes or until bubbles form in center of mixture and syrup turns amber. Remove from the heat; transfer to a small bowl. Cool to room temperature. Gradually beat in confectioners' sugar. Spread over cupcakes. **YIELD:** 2 dozen.

Classic Red Velvet Cake

(Pictured above)

PREP: 25 min. **BAKE:** 20 min.

This ruby-red cake with it's lovely cream cheese frosting has become my signature dessert. I can't go to any family function without it. The cake is very moist with a buttery chocolate taste.
—Katie Sloan, Charlotte, North Carolina

  1/2 cup shortening
1-1/2 cups sugar
    2 eggs
    1 bottle (1 ounce) red food coloring
    3 teaspoons white vinegar
    1 teaspoon butter flavoring
    1 teaspoon vanilla extract
2-1/2 cups cake flour
  1/4 cup baking cocoa
    1 teaspoon baking soda
    1 teaspoon salt
    1 cup buttermilk

FROSTING:

    1 package (8 ounces) cream cheese, softened
  1/2 cup butter, softened
3-3/4 cups confectioners' sugar
    3 teaspoons vanilla extract

In a large bowl, cream shortening and sugar until light and fluffy. Add eggs, one at a time, beating well after each addition. Beat in the food coloring, vinegar, butter flavoring and vanilla. Combine flour, cocoa, baking soda and salt; add to creamed mixture alternately with buttermilk.

Pour into three greased and floured 9-in. round baking pans. Bake at 350° for 20-25 minutes or until a toothpick inserted near the center comes out clean. Cool for 10 minutes before removing from pans to wire racks to cool completely.

In a large bowl, combine frosting ingredients; beat until smooth and creamy. Spread between layers and over top and sides of cake. **YIELD:** 12 servings.

For some folks, dessert is the best part of the meal! With these favorite recipes for crisps, cobblers, candies, puddings, ice cream and more, no dessert fan will ever have to do without.

just desserts

Strawberry Crepes 188

Chocolate Chip Mousse 188

Praline Chocolate Dessert 189

Pumpkin Rice Pudding 189

Rocky Road Ice Cream 190

Grandmother's Bread Pudding 190

Caramel Chocolate Trifle 191

Ladyfinger Lemon Torte 191

Blueberry Cornmeal Cobbler 192

Cappuccino Cherry Trifle 192

Butter Pecan Ice Cream 193

Peach Ice Cream 193

Chocolate Ice Cream Sandwiches 193

Cranberry-Topped Lemon Tarts 194

Chocolate-Covered Cheesecake
    Squares 194

Rich Hot Fudge Sauce 195

Strawberry Puff Pastry Dessert 195

Raisin Pecan Baklava 196

White Chocolate Berry Dessert 196

Peach Rhubarb Crisp 197

Tiramisu Cheesecake Dessert 197

Apple Crumble 198

Raspberry Pear Crisp 198

Cinnamon-Raisin Soft Pretzels 198

Double-Berry Crisp 199

Strawberry Cheesecake Ice Cream 199

Apple Pizza 200

Strawberry Tartlets 200

Lemon Cheesecake Dessert 201

Gingerbread Pudding Cake 201

Mixed Nut Chocolate Tart 202

Banana Split Brownie Pie 202

Fluffy Lemon Squares 203

Three-Fruit Sundae Sauce 203

Cherry Ice Cream Cake 204

Peaches 'n' Cream Cups 204

Lemon Rice Pudding Brulee 205

Apple Dumplings 205

PICTURED CLOCKWISE FROM UPPER LEFT: Cranberry-Topped Lemon Tarts (page 194), Cherry Ice Cream Cake (page 204), Gingerbread Pudding Cake (page 201) and Double-Berry Crisp (page 199) .

In a large bowl, combine milk, eggs, butter and extract. Combine flour, sugar and salt; add to milk mixture and beat until smooth. Cover and refrigerate for 1 hour.

Heat a lightly greased 8-in. nonstick skillet. Stir the batter; pour 2 tablespoons into center of skillet. Lift and tilt pan to evenly coat bottom. Cook until top appears dry; turn and cook 15-20 seconds longer. Remove to a wire rack. Repeat with the remaining batter, greasing skillet as needed. When cool, stack crepes with waxed paper or paper towels in between.

For the topping, in a small saucepan, combine the sugar and cornstarch; stir in water and lemon juice until smooth. Bring to a boil over medium heat; cook and stir for 1 minute or until thickened. Stir in extract and food coloring if desired. Cool. Add strawberries.

For the filling, in a small bowl, beat the cream until stiff peaks form; set aside. In a large bowl, beat the cream cheese, confectioners' sugar and vanilla until smooth; fold in the whipped cream. Spoon 2 rounded tablespoons of filling down the center of each crepe; roll up. Top with strawberry topping. **YIELD:** 22 crepes.

Strawberry Crepes

(*Pictured above*)

PREP: 25 min. + chilling **COOK:** 1 hour

I feel like a French chef when I serve these pretty crepes. Although they take a little time to prepare, they're well worth the effort. My guests are always impressed.
—*Debra Latta, Port Matilda, Pennsylvania*

  1-1/2 **cups milk**
     3 **eggs**
     2 **tablespoons butter, melted**
   1/2 **teaspoon lemon extract**
  1-1/4 **cups all-purpose flour**
     2 **tablespoons sugar**
Dash salt
TOPPING:
   1/2 **cup sugar**
     2 **tablespoons cornstarch**
   3/4 **cup water**
     1 **tablespoon lemon juice**
     1 **teaspoon strawberry extract**
   1/4 **teaspoon red food coloring, optional**
     4 **cups sliced fresh strawberries**
FILLING:
     1 **cup heavy whipping cream**
     1 **package (8 ounces) cream cheese, softened**
     2 **cups confectioners' sugar**
     1 **teaspoon vanilla extract**

Chocolate Chip Mousse

(*Pictured below*)

PREP/TOTAL TIME: 15 min. + cooling

Chocolate always makes for a wonderful dessert. For your special occasion, turn to this recipe for a rich and creamy chocolate mousse. Your family will be so delighted.
—*Taste of Home Test Kitchen, Greendale, Wisconsin*

     1 **cup (6 ounces) semisweet chocolate chips**
     1 **package (8 ounces) cream cheese, softened**
     1 **teaspoon vanilla extract**
     1 **carton (8 ounces) frozen whipped topping, thawed**

In a microwave or heavy saucepan, melt chocolate chips; stir until smooth. Cool for 20 minutes.

Meanwhile, in a small bowl, beat cream cheese and vanilla until smooth; beat in melted chocolate. Fold in whipped topping. Spoon into dessert dishes. Refrigerate until serving. **YIELD:** 4 servings.

In a large bowl, beat the filling ingredients until smooth. Spread over praline layer. Refrigerate for 1-2 hours or until set.

For ganache, in a microwave-safe bowl, melt the chocolate chips with cream; stir until smooth. Cool slightly; spread over the filling. Refrigerate for 1-2 hours or until set. Carefully run a knife around edge of pan to loosen; remove the sides of the pan. Garnish with pecan halves. Refrigerate leftovers. **YIELD:** 14-16 servings.

Pumpkin Rice Pudding

(Pictured below)

PREP: 15 min. **BAKE:** 25 min.

Rice pudding is the queen of comfort foods! This version is smooth and spicy and smells incredible while baking. What a great way to use up leftover rice.

—*Dee Falk, Stromsburg, Nebraska*

 4 cups milk
 1 can (15 ounces) solid-pack pumpkin
 3/4 cup sugar
 1 teaspoon ground cinnamon
 1/2 teaspoon salt
 1/2 teaspoon ground ginger
 1/4 teaspoon ground cloves
 2 eggs, beaten
 3 cups cooked rice
 1/2 teaspoon vanilla extract
Vanilla ice cream, optional

In a large saucepan, combine the first seven ingredients. Bring to a boil over medium heat, stirring constantly. Gradually stir a small amount of milk mixture into the eggs; return all to the pan. Bring to a gentle boil, stirring constantly. Remove from the heat. Stir in rice and vanilla.

Pour into a greased 13-in. x 9-in. baking dish. Bake, uncovered, at 375° for 25-30 minutes or until a knife inserted near the center comes out clean. Serve warm with ice cream if desired. Refrigerate leftovers. **YIELD:** 8 servings.

Praline Chocolate Dessert

(Pictured above)

PREP: 25 min. + chilling **BAKE:** 10 min. + cooling

A cookie crumb crust, luscious layers of praline and cream cheese, and a chocolate glaze make this dessert a true showstopper. It freezes well, too.

—*Korrie Bastian, Clearfield, Utah*

 2 cups cream-filled chocolate sandwich cookie crumbs
 1/2 cup butter, melted
 1 cup chopped pecans
PRALINE:
 1-1/2 cups butter, cubed
 1 cup packed brown sugar
 1 teaspoon vanilla extract
FILLING:
 2 packages (8 ounces *each*) cream cheese, softened
 1/2 cup confectioners' sugar
 1/3 cup packed brown sugar
GANACHE:
 1 cup (6 ounces) semisweet chocolate chips
 1/2 cup heavy whipping cream
Pecan halves

In a small bowl, combine cookie crumbs and butter. Press onto the bottom of a greased 9-in. springform pan. Place on a baking sheet. Bake at 350° for 10 minutes. Cool on a wire rack. Sprinkle with the pecans.

For the praline, in a large saucepan over medium heat, bring the butter and brown sugar to a boil, stirring constantly. Reduce heat; simmer, uncovered, for 10 minutes. Remove from the heat; stir in vanilla. Pour over pecans. Refrigerate for 1-2 hours or until set.

Rocky Road Ice Cream

(Pictured below)

PREP: 15 min. + cooling **FREEZE:** 30 min.

My daughters like it when I put this ice cream in cones. We especially enjoy the marshmallows, chocolate chips and chopped pecans. Sometimes we even add extra chips on top…and a dollops of whipped cream, too!

—Dale Langford, Atwater, California

        3   cups milk
        3   cups half-and-half cream
        9   squares (1 ounce *each*) semisweet chocolate
    2-3/4   cups sugar
      3/4   teaspoon salt
        6   cups heavy whipping cream
        3   cups miniature marshmallows
    2-1/4   cups miniature semisweet chocolate chips
    1-1/2   cups chopped pecans
        6   teaspoons vanilla extract

In a large saucepan, combine the milk and half-and-half; heat to 175°. Add the chocolate, sugar and salt; stir until chocolate is melted and sugar is dissolved.

Remove from the heat. Cool quickly by placing pan in a bowl of ice water; stir for 2 minutes. Cool completely. Transfer to a large bowl; stir in the remaining ingredients. Cover and refrigerate for at least 30 minutes.

Fill cylinder of ice cream freezer two-thirds full; freeze according to the manufacturer's directions. Refrigerate the remaining mixture until ready to freeze. When the ice cream is frozen, transfer to a freezer container; freeze for 2-4 hours before serving. **YIELD:** about 4-1/2 quarts.

Grandmother's Bread Pudding

(Pictured above)

PREP: 10 min. **BAKE:** 45 min.

Comforting is the best way to describe this lovely, flavorful bread pudding. And the drizzle of tangy lemon sauce offers a little zing!

—Edna Butler, Los Fresnos, Texas

        5   eggs
        3   cups milk
    1-1/4   cups sugar
        1   cup half-and-half cream
      1/4   cup butter, melted and cooled
        2   teaspoons vanilla extract
        1   teaspoon almond extract
      1/2   teaspoon ground nutmeg
        4   cups cubed day-old white bread
        4   cups cubed day-old wheat bread
      1/3   cup raisins
SAUCE:
    1-1/2   cups sugar
      1/3   cup cornstarch
      1/4   teaspoon salt
    2-1/4   cups cold water
        3   egg yolks, beaten
      1/3   cup lemon juice
        2   tablespoons butter

In a large bowl, combine the first eight ingredients. Stir in the bread cubes and raisins. Transfer to a greased 13-in. x 9-in. baking dish. Bake, uncovered, at 350° for 45-55 minutes or until a knife inserted near the center comes out clean.

For the lemon sauce, combine the sugar, cornstarch, salt and water in a large saucepan until smooth. Bring to a boil over medium heat, stirring constantly. Remove from the heat.

Stir a small amount of hot filling into the egg yolks; return all to the pan, stirring constantly. Bring to a gentle boil; cook and stir for 2 minutes.

Remove from the heat; gently stir in lemon juice and butter. Serve with bread pudding. Refrigerate leftovers. **YIELD:** 12-15 servings.

Caramel Chocolate Trifle

(Pictured below)

PREP: 20 min. **BAKE:** 20 min. + cooling

Every year at our family reunion we have a dessert competition, as well as dishes that have been passed down from generation to generation. This recipe is a family favorite.

—*Barb Hausey, Independence, Missouri*

- 1 package (9 ounces) devil's food cake mix
- 2 packages (3.9 ounces *each*) instant chocolate pudding mix
- 1 carton (12 ounces) frozen whipped topping, thawed
- 1 jar (12-1/4 ounces) caramel ice cream topping
- 1 package (7-1/2 *or* 8 ounces) English toffee bits *or* almond brickle chips

Prepare and bake cake according to package directions for an 8-in. square baking pan. Cool on a wire rack. Prepare pudding according to package directions.

Cut the cake into 1-1/2-in. cubes; place half of the cubes in a 3-qt. trifle bowl or large glass serving bowl; lightly press down to fill in gaps. Top with half each of the whipped topping, pudding, caramel topping and toffee bits; repeat layers. Cover and refrigerate until serving. **YIELD:** 16 servings.

Ladyfinger Lemon Torte

(Pictured above)

PREP: 30 min. + chilling + freezing

Golden ladyfingers frame the luscious custard filling of this lovely frozen dessert. Everyone enjoys the yummy combination of sweetness and lemony zest.

—*Mrs. J. H. Carroll, Ottawa, Ontario*

- 5 egg yolks, lightly beaten
- 1-1/2 cups sugar, *divided*
- 3/4 cup lemon juice
- 2 egg whites
- 1 tablespoon grated lemon peel
- 2 cups heavy whipping cream
- 2 packages (3 ounces *each*) ladyfingers, split

Lemon peel and fresh mint leaves

In a heavy saucepan, combine egg yolks, 1-1/4 cups sugar, lemon juice and egg whites. Bring to a boil over medium heat; cook and stir for 8-10 minutes or until mixture reaches 160° or is thick enough to coat a metal spoon. Remove from heat. Cool quickly by placing pan in a bowl of ice water; stir for 2 minutes. Stir in lemon peel. Transfer to a bowl, press the plastic wrap onto the surface of custard. Chill for 2-3 hours or until partially set.

In a large bowl, beat the cream on medium speed until soft peaks form. Gradually beat in the remaining sugar, 1 tablespoon at a time, on high until stiff peaks form. Gradually fold whipped cream into the cooled lemon mixture.

Arrange 24 ladyfingers around the edge of an ungreased 9-in. springform pan. Arrange 16 ladyfingers on bottom of pan. Spread with half of lemon mixture. Arrange remaining ladyfingers over lemon mixture; top with remaining lemon mixture.

Cover and freeze overnight. Remove from the freezer 5 minutes before cutting. Remove sides of the pan. Garnish with lemon peel and mint. **YIELD:** 12 servings.

Blueberry Cornmeal Cobbler

(Pictured above)

PREP: 20 min. + standing **BAKE:** 35 min.

Corn bread, blueberries and maple syrup butter give this special dessert a taste that's different from any cobbler you've had before. I came across the yummy recipe many years ago.
—Judy Watson, Tipton, Indiana

      4 cups fresh blueberries
      1 cup plus 2 tablespoons sugar
      1 tablespoon quick-cooking tapioca
      2 teaspoons grated lemon peel
      1 teaspoon ground cinnamon
    1/4 to 1/2 teaspoon ground nutmeg
TOPPING:
    1/2 cup butter, softened, *divided*
      1 cup confectioners' sugar
      1 egg
      1 cup all-purpose flour
    1/2 cup cornmeal
      2 teaspoons baking powder
    1/2 teaspoon baking soda
    1/2 teaspoon salt
    3/4 cup buttermilk
      2 tablespoons maple syrup

In a large bowl, combine the blueberries, sugar, tapioca, lemon peel, ground cinnamon and nutmeg. Let stand for 15 minutes. Pour into a greased 11-in. x 7-in. baking dish.

For topping, in a small bowl, beat 1/4 cup butter and confectioners' sugar. Add the egg; beat well. Combine the flour, cornmeal, baking powder, baking soda and salt; add to the creamed mixture alternately with buttermilk, beating just until combined. Pour over berry mixture. Bake at 375° for 35-40 minutes or until a toothpick inserted near the center comes out clean.

In a small saucepan, melt remaining butter over low heat. Remove from the heat; stir in the syrup. Brush over corn bread. Broil 4-6 in. from the heat for 1-2 minutes or until bubbly. Serve warm. **YIELD:** 12 servings.

Cappuccino Cherry Trifle

(Pictured below)

PREP: 20 min. **COOK:** 15 min. + chilling

This is a rich dessert that's as pretty to look at as it is good to eat. The combination of dark sweet cherries, chocolate and homemade coffee custard is a real winner.
—Katie Sloan, Charlotte, North Carolina

      3/4 cup sugar
      1/4 cup cornstarch
        2 tablespoons instant coffee granules
        1 tablespoon baking cocoa
    1-1/2 cups milk
        2 tablespoons water
        4 egg yolks, beaten
        2 teaspoons vanilla extract
    2-3/4 cups heavy whipping cream
        2 loaves (10-3/4 ounces *each*) frozen pound cake, thawed and cut into 1-inch cubes
        1 can (15 ounces) pitted dark sweet cherries
        1 cup (6 ounces) semisweet chocolate chips

For the custard, combine the sugar, cornstarch, coffee granules and cocoa in a large saucepan. Stir in milk and water until smooth. Bring to a boil over medium heat; cook and stir for 1-2 minutes or until thick and bubbly.

Remove from the heat. Stir a small amount of hot mixture into yolks; return all to the pan, stirring constantly. Bring to a gentle boil; cook and stir 2 minutes longer. Remove from the heat; gently stir in vanilla. Refrigerate until cool.

In a large bowl, beat cream until stiff peaks form. Fold 2-1/2 cups whipped cream into cooled custard. Set aside the remaining whipped cream for garnish.

Place half of the cake cubes in a 3-qt. trifle bowl. Drain cherries, reserving juice; sprinkle cake with 3-4 tablespoons cherry juice. Top with half of the cherries, 1/3 cup chocolate chips and half of the custard mixture. Repeat layers. Garnish with reserved whipped cream and remaining chocolate chips. **YIELD:** 12-14 servings.

Butter Pecan Ice Cream

PREP: 15 min. + chilling **FREEZE:** 30 min.

This thick, buttery ice cream sure beats store-bought versions. And with its pretty color and plentiful pecan crunch, it's nice enough to serve guests at a summer party.

—Jenny White, Glen, Mississippi

- 1/2 **cup chopped pecans**
- 1 **tablespoon butter**
- 1-1/2 **cups half-and-half cream**
- 1 **cup packed brown sugar**
- 2 **eggs, lightly beaten**
- 1/2 **cup heavy whipping cream**
- 1 **teaspoon vanilla extract**

In a small skillet, toast pecans in butter for 5-6 minutes or until lightly browned. Cool.

In a heavy saucepan, heat half-and-half to 175°; stir in the brown sugar until dissolved. Whisk a small amount of hot cream mixture into the eggs; return all to the pan, whisking constantly. Cook and stir over low heat until mixture reaches at least 160° and coats the back of a metal spoon.

Remove from the heat. Cool quickly by placing pan in a bowl of ice water; stir for 2 minutes. Stir in whipping cream and vanilla. Press plastic wrap onto the surface of custard. Refrigerate for several hours or overnight. Stir in toasted pecans.

Fill cylinder of ice cream freezer two-thirds full; freeze according to the manufacturer's directions. Refrigerate the remaining mixture until ready to freeze. Allow to ripen in the ice cream freezer or firm up in the refrigerator freezer for 2-4 hours before serving. **YIELD:** 1 quart.

Peach Ice Cream

PREP: 15 min. + chilling **FREEZE:** 30 min.

When peaches are in season, this recipe is at the top of my list. The pureed fruit lends a fresh taste to the silky-smooth ice cream. You'll have to make it more than once, though, because the first batch never lasts long!

—Toni Box, Weaver, Alabama

- 2 **cups half-and-half cream**
- 3-1/2 **cups sugar**
- 3/4 **teaspoon salt**
- 6 **eggs, beaten**
- 4 **cups heavy whipping cream**
- 2 **teaspoons vanilla extract**
- 6 **to 8 medium peaches, peeled and sliced *or* 4 cups frozen unsweetened peach slices**

In a saucepan, heat half-and-half to 175°; stir in the sugar and salt until dissolved. Whisk a small amount of hot cream mixture into the eggs. Return all to the pan, whisking constantly. Cook and stir over low heat until the mixture reaches at least 160° and coats the back of a metal spoon.

Remove from heat. Cool quickly by placing pan in a bowl of ice water; stir for 2 minutes. Stir in whipping cream and vanilla. Press plastic wrap onto surface of custard. Refrigerate for several hours or overnight.

In a blender or food processor, puree peaches. Stir into custard. Fill cylinder of ice cream freezer two-thirds full; freeze according to manufacturer's directions.

Refrigerate the remaining mixture until ready to freeze, stirring before freezing each batch. Allow to ripen in an ice cream freezer or firm up in the refrigerator freezer for 2-4 hours before serving. **YIELD:** about 3 quarts.

Chocolate Ice Cream Sandwiches

(Pictured below)

PREP: 20 min. **BAKE:** 10 min. + cooling

These cute, chewy cookies made with two kinds of chocolate form a perfect sandwich for vanilla ice cream…or any variety you prefer. I really enjoy making desserts for my family, and this one hits the spot on hot Texas days.

—Michelle Wolford, San Antonio, Texas

- 1/3 **cup butter, softened**
- 1/3 **cup sugar**
- 1/3 **cup packed brown sugar**
- 1 **egg**
- 1/2 **teaspoon vanilla extract**
- 3/4 **cup plus 2 tablespoons all-purpose flour**
- 1/4 **cup baking cocoa**
- 1/2 **teaspoon baking powder**
- 1/4 **teaspoon baking soda**
- 1/4 **teaspoon salt**
- 1/2 **cup semisweet chocolate chips**
- 1 **pint vanilla ice cream**

In a bowl, cream the butter and sugars. Beat in the egg and vanilla. Combine the flour, cocoa, baking powder, baking soda and salt; add to creamed mixture and mix well.

Drop by rounded tablespoonfuls 2 in. apart onto greased baking sheets, forming 16 cookies. Flatten slightly with a glass. Sprinkle with chocolate chips. Bake at 375° for 8-10 minutes or until set. Remove to wire racks to cool.

To assemble sandwiches, place 1/4 cup ice cream on the bottom of half the cookies. Top with the remaining cookies. Wrap each in plastic wrap. Freeze overnight. **YIELD:** 8 ice cream sandwiches.

For the topping, in a large saucepan, combine the cranberries, sugar and water. Cook over medium heat until berries have popped, about 20 minutes.

Meanwhile, for the filling, in a small saucepan, whisk eggs. Stir in the sugar, lemon juice, butter and lemon peel. Cook and stir over medium heat for 20-25 minutes or until filling is thickened and reaches 160°. Transfer to a small bowl; cover and refrigerate for 1 hour. Transfer berry topping to another bowl; refrigerate until serving.

Spoon filling into tart shells. Chill, uncovered, until set. For garnish, in a small saucepan, bring lemon slices, sugar and water to a boil. Reduce heat; simmer, uncovered, for 20-25 minutes or until lemon is tender. Cut slices in half; chill.

Just before serving, spoon cranberry topping over tarts. Garnish with lemon slices. **YIELD:** 8 servings.

Chocolate-Covered Cheesecake Squares

PREP: 1 hour **BAKE:** 35 min. + freezing

Satisfy your cheesecake craving with these bite-sized treats. Dipped in chocolate, the sweet, creamy delights are party favorites. But be warned…you won't be able to eat just one!
—*Esther Neustaeter, La Crete, Alberta*

    1 **cup graham cracker crumbs**
  1/4 **cup finely chopped pecans**
  1/4 **cup butter, melted**
FILLING:
    2 **packages (8 ounces *each*) cream cheese, softened**
  1/2 **cup sugar**
  1/4 **cup sour cream**
    2 **eggs, lightly beaten**
  1/2 **teaspoon vanilla extract**
COATING:
  24 **squares (1 ounce *each*) semisweet chocolate**
    3 **tablespoons shortening**

Line a 9-in. square baking pan with foil and grease the foil. In a small bowl, combine the graham cracker crumbs, pecans and butter. Press into prepared pan; set aside.

For the filling, in a large bowl, beat cream cheese, sugar and sour cream until smooth. Add eggs; beat on low just until combined. Stir in vanilla. Pour over crust.

Bake at 325° for 35-40 minutes or until the center is almost set. Cool on a wire rack. Refrigerate until chilled. Freeze overnight.

In a microwave-safe bowl, melt chocolate and shortening, stirring occasionally until smooth. Cool slightly. Using foil, lift cheesecake out of pan. Gently peel off foil; cut into 49 squares. Remove a few pieces at a time for dipping; keep remaining squares refrigerated until ready to dip.

Using a toothpick, completely dip the squares, one at a time, in melted chocolate. Place on waxed paper-lined baking sheets; spoon about 1 teaspoon of the chocolate over each. (Reheat chocolate if needed to finish dipping.) Let stand for 20 minutes or until set. Store in an airtight container in the refrigerator or freezer. **YIELD:** 49 servings.

Cranberry-Topped Lemon Tarts

(Pictured above and on page 186)

PREP: 45 min. + chilling **BAKE:** 20 min. + cooling

The delicious combination of colors and tangy-sweet flavors makes this a very pretty, very special dessert. You'll receive a ton of compliments on your culinary expertise.
—*Ruth Lee, Troy, Ontario*

    2 **cups all-purpose flour**
    3 **tablespoons sugar**
  3/4 **teaspoon salt**
    1 **cup cold butter**
TOPPING:
    3 **cups fresh *or* frozen cranberries**
1-1/4 **cups sugar**
  1/4 **cup water**
FILLING:
    5 **eggs**
1-1/2 **cups sugar**
  3/4 **cup lemon juice**
  1/3 **cup butter, softened**
    4 **teaspoons grated lemon peel**
GARNISH:
    1 **medium lemon, cut into 1/4-inch slices**
  1/2 **cup sugar**
  1/4 **cup water**

In a bowl, combine the flour, sugar and salt; cut in butter until mixture resembles coarse crumbs. Stir until dough forms a ball. Divide into eight portions; press each onto the bottom and up the sides of eight 4-in. tart pans.

Cover and refrigerate for 20 minutes. Bake at 350° for 20-25 minutes or until golden brown. Cool on wire racks.

Rich Hot Fudge Sauce

(Pictured below)

PREP/TOTAL TIME: 30 min.

I've made this scrumptious topping ever since the early 1980s. It always turns out smooth and yummy. The dark chocolate flavor, with a hint of rum extract, is not overly sweet but still satisfies a chocoholic's cravings.

—Carol Hunihan, Ann Arbor, Michigan

> 1 cup heavy whipping cream
> 3/4 cup butter, cubed
> 1-1/3 cups packed brown sugar
> 1/4 cup sugar
> Pinch salt
> 1 cup baking cocoa
> 1/2 cup plus 2 tablespoons light corn syrup
> 2 squares (1 ounce *each*) unsweetened chocolate
> 3 teaspoons vanilla extract
> 1 to 2 teaspoons rum extract

In a heavy saucepan, combine the cream and butter. Cook and stir over medium-low heat until butter is melted. Add the sugars and salt; cook and stir until sugar is dissolved, about 4 minutes. Stir in the cocoa and corn syrup; cook and stir for 3 minutes or until cocoa is blended.

Add the chocolate; cook and stir 3-4 minutes longer or until chocolate is melted. Reduce heat to low. Simmer for 12-16 minutes or until desired thickness is reached, stirring constantly. Remove from the heat; stir in extracts. Cool slightly. Serve warm over ice cream. Refrigerate leftovers. **YIELD:** about 3-1/2 cups.

Strawberry Puff Pastry Dessert

(Pictured above)

PREP: 30 min. **BAKE:** 15 min. + cooling

My failed attempt to make a triple-layer strawberry malt mousse resulted in this scrumptious confection. I don't use puff pastry often, but it was simple to work with. My husband declared it one of the best desserts ever.

—Anna Ginsberg, Austin, Texas

> 1 package (17.3 ounces) frozen puff pastry
> 5 cups sliced fresh strawberries, *divided*
> 6 squares (1 ounce *each*) white baking chocolate
> 1 package (8 ounces) cream cheese, softened
> 1 teaspoon vanilla extract
> 1 cup confectioners' sugar
> 1/3 cup malted milk powder
> 2 cups heavy whipping cream, whipped
> Strawberry syrup, optional

Thaw one puff pastry sheet (save remaining sheet for another use). Unfold pastry; cut lengthwise into three 3-in.-wide strips. Cut each strip into thirds, making nine squares. Place 1 in. apart on ungreased baking sheets. Bake at 400° for 11-13 minutes or until golden brown. Remove to wire racks to cool.

Place 2-1/2 cups strawberries in a blender; cover and puree. Set aside. In a large microwave-safe bowl, melt the white chocolate; cool slightly. Add cream cheese and vanilla; beat until smooth. Beat in the confectioners' sugar and malted milk powder until smooth. Stir in the puree. Fold in whipped cream.

Split pastry squares in half horizontally. Line an ungreased 13-in. x 9-in. dish with bottom pastry halves, cut side up; spread with 3-1/2 cups strawberry cream. Top with 1 cup of sliced berries. Cover with pastry tops, cut side down.

Spread with the remaining strawberry cream. Sprinkle with the remaining berries. Drizzle with strawberry syrup if desired. Refrigerate leftovers. **YIELD:** 12 servings.

Raisin Pecan Baklava

(Pictured below)

PREP: 30 min. **BAKE:** 20 min. + cooling

This lightened-up version of traditional baklava is to die for, and it looks beautiful on a goody tray. The toasted pecans really stand out, and the Grape-Nuts add wonderful crunch without very many calories.

—Liv Vors, Peterborough, Ontario

- 1/3 **cup sugar**
- 1/4 **cup water**
- 3 **tablespoons honey**
- 4-1/2 **teaspoons lemon juice**
- 1/2 **cup chopped pecans, toasted**
- 1/2 **cup Grape-Nuts cereal**
- 1/2 **cup raisins**
- 1/3 **cup packed brown sugar**
- 1/2 **teaspoon ground cinnamon**
- 8 **sheets phyllo dough (14 inches x 9 inches)**

In a small saucepan, combine the sugar, water, honey and lemon juice. Bring to a boil; cook and stir until sugar is dissolved. Remove from the heat.

Combine the pecans, cereal, raisins, brown sugar and the cinnamon. Stir in 3 tablespoons of honey mixture; set aside.

Stack phyllo sheets on a flat work surface; trim 1 in. from the 9-in. side. Cut in half lengthwise, forming 8-in. x 7-in. rectangles. Overlap two pieces in a greased 8-in. square baking dish; spray with cooking spray. Repeat three times.

Spread nut mixture over top. Overlap two pieces of phyllo to cover nut mixture; spray with cooking spray. Repeat with remaining phyllo. Using a sharp knife, cut into 24 rectangles, about 2-1/2 in. x 1 in.

Bake, uncovered, at 350° for 20-25 minutes or until golden brown. Reheat reserved honey mixture; pour over hot baklava. Cool completely on a wire rack. **YIELD:** 2 dozen.

White Chocolate Berry Dessert

(Pictured above)

PREP: 35 min. **BAKE:** 40 min. + cooling

After creating this recipe and fine-tuning it a little bit, I knew I had a hit! The sweet flavor of white chocolate combined with strawberries can't be beat.

—Sarah Gwyn, Orlando, Florida

- 8 **squares (1 ounce *each*) white baking chocolate**
- 6 **tablespoons butter, cubed**
- 2 **eggs**
- 1/2 **cup sugar**
- 3 **teaspoons vanilla extract**
- 1 **cup all-purpose flour**
- 1/4 **teaspoon salt**

FILLING:
- 1 **package (8 ounces) cream cheese, softened**
- 3 **squares (1 ounce *each*) white baking chocolate, melted and cooled**
- 1 **egg, lightly beaten**
- 1/3 **cup sugar**
- 1/3 **cup sour cream**
- 1 **teaspoon vanilla extract**

TOPPING:
- 1 **carton (8 ounces) frozen whipped topping, thawed**
- 4 **squares (1 ounce *each*) white baking chocolate, melted and cooled**
- 1 **pint fresh strawberries, sliced**

In a microwave-safe bowl, melt white chocolate and butter at 70% power; stir until smooth. Cool.

In a large bowl, beat eggs and sugar until lemon-colored. Beat in melted chocolate mixture and vanilla. Combine flour and salt; beat into egg mixture. Spread into a greased 13-in. x 9-in. baking dish; set aside.

For filling, in a small bowl, beat cream cheese and white chocolate. Beat in egg, sugar, sour cream and vanilla just until combined. Carefully spread over bottom layer. Cut through filling with a knife to swirl.

Bake at 350° for 40-45 minutes or until a toothpick inserted near the center comes out clean. Cool on a wire rack.

Just before serving, fold whipped topping into white chocolate. Fold in strawberries; spread over dessert. Cut into squares. Refrigerate leftovers. **YIELD:** 15 servings.

Peach Rhubarb Crisp

PREP: 20 min. **BAKE:** 30 min.

When a visit to the local farmers market left me with an abundance of quickly ripening peaches and several stalks of rhubarb, I created this wonderful dessert recipe.
—Sandy Kimble, Salinas, California

- 3/4 cup sugar
- 3 tablespoons all-purpose flour
- 1/2 teaspoon ground nutmeg
- 1/2 teaspoon grated lemon peel
- 1/8 teaspoon salt
- 3 cups sliced fresh *or* frozen rhubarb
- 2-1/2 cups chopped peeled fresh peaches *or* frozen unsweetened peach slices, chopped

TOPPING:
- 1/2 cup all-purpose flour
- 1/2 cup old-fashioned oats
- 1/2 cup packed brown sugar
- 3/4 teaspoon ground cinnamon
- 1/8 teaspoon salt
- 5 tablespoons cold butter

In a large bowl, combine sugar, flour, nutmeg, lemon peel, salt, rhubarb and peaches. Transfer to a greased 11-in. x 7-in. baking dish.

In a bowl, combine the flour, oats, brown sugar, cinnamon and salt. Cut in butter until mixture resembles coarse crumbs; sprinkle over fruit. Bake at 375° for 30-35 minutes or until bubbly and fruit is tender. Serve warm or cold. **YIELD:** 6-8 servings.

EDITOR'S NOTE: If using frozen rhubarb, measure rhubarb while still frozen, then thaw completely. Drain in a colander, but do not press liquid out.

cocoa powder

There are two types of unsweetened cocoa powder: natural and Dutch-processed. Natural cocoa powder tastes bitter and imparts an intense chocolate flavor. Dutch processed is alkalized, which neutralizes the cocoa's acidity; it has a milder flavor and is easier to dissolve in liquids.

Tiramisu Cheesecake Dessert

(*Pictured above*)

PREP: 20 min. **BAKE:** 40 min. + chilling

I wasn't a big fan of tiramisu until I tried this recipe with its distinctive cheesecake- and coffee-flavored layers. It's one of my favorite desserts to make during the fall.
—Christie Nelson, Taylorville, Illinois

- 1 package (12 ounces) vanilla wafers
- 5 teaspoons instant coffee granules, *divided*
- 3 tablespoons hot water, *divided*
- 4 packages (8 ounces *each*) cream cheese, softened
- 1 cup sugar
- 1 cup (8 ounces) sour cream
- 4 eggs, lightly beaten
- 1 cup whipped topping
- 1 tablespoon baking cocoa

Layer half of the wafers in a greased 13-in. x 9-in. baking dish. In a small bowl, dissolve 2 teaspoons of the coffee granules in 2 tablespoons of hot water. Brush the wafers with half of the coffee; set remaining mixture aside.

In a large bowl, beat the cream cheese, sugar and sour cream until smooth. Add eggs; beat on low speed just until combined. Divide batter in half. Dissolve remaining coffee granules in remaining hot water; stir into one portion of batter. Spread over wafers. Layer with the remaining wafers; brush with reserved coffee. Top with the remaining batter.

Bake at 325° for 40-45 minutes or until center is almost set. Cool on a wire rack for 10 minutes. Carefully run a knife around edge of dish to loosen; cool 1 hour longer. Refrigerate overnight.

Spread with whipped topping; dust with cocoa. Refrigerate leftovers. **YIELD:** 12 servings.

Meanwhile, for the apple topping, in a large skillet, cook and stir the apples in butter over medium heat for 2 minutes. Combine the sugar, flour and cinnamon; stir into skillet. Cook 3 minutes longer. Reduce heat to low; cook, uncovered, for 4-6 minutes or until the apples are tender, stirring frequently.

In a small bowl, combine the cheese topping ingredients. For the streusel, in a small bowl, combine the flour and sugar; cut in butter until crumbly.

Pat dough onto a greased 14-in. pizza pan, building up edges slightly. Spread with cheese topping, then apple topping. Sprinkle with streusel. Bake at 375° for 20-25 minutes or until crust is golden brown. Serve warm or cold. **YIELD:** 10-12 servings.

Apple Pizza

(*Pictured above*)

PREP: 40 min. **BAKE:** 20 min.

Pizza is a favorite at our house, so when I had some apples to use up, I started searching for an apple-pizza recipe. I tailored this one to fit my family's tastes.
—Brenda Mowrey, Taylors, South Carolina

   2-1/3 to 3 cups all-purpose flour
       3 tablespoons sugar
       1 package (1/4 ounce) active dry yeast
   1/2 teaspoon salt
   1/2 cup water
   1/4 cup milk
   1/4 cup butter, cubed
APPLE TOPPING:
       4 cups sliced peeled Granny Smith apples
       2 tablespoons butter
   1/2 cup sugar
       2 tablespoons all-purpose flour
       1 teaspoon ground cinnamon
CHEESE TOPPING:
       4 ounces cream cheese, softened
   1/4 cup packed brown sugar
       2 tablespoons caramel ice cream topping
STREUSEL:
   2/3 cup all-purpose flour
   1/3 cup sugar
   1/4 cup cold butter, cubed

In a large bowl, combine 1-1/2 cups flour, sugar, yeast and salt. In a saucepan, heat water, milk and butter to 120°-130°. Add to the dry ingredients; beat for 2 minutes. Stir in enough remaining flour to form a firm dough. Turn onto a floured surface; cover and let rest for 15 minutes.

Strawberry Tartlets

(*Pictured below*)

PREP: 25 min. **BAKE:** 10 min. + cooling

This elegant-looking dessert is easy to prepare, and the cute won-ton "cups" can be made in advance. They're a different way to present fresh strawberries when entertaining.
—Joy Van Meter, Thornton, Colorado

      12 wonton wrappers
       3 tablespoons butter, melted
   1/3 cup packed brown sugar
   3/4 cup Mascarpone cheese
       2 tablespoons honey
       2 teaspoons orange juice
       3 cups fresh strawberries, sliced
Whipped cream and fresh mint, optional

Brush one side of each wonton wrapper with butter. Place brown sugar in a shallow bowl; press buttered side of wontons into sugar to coat. Press wontons sugared side up into greased muffin cups. Bake at 325° for 7-9 minutes or until the edges are lightly browned. Remove to a wire rack to cool.

In a bowl, combine the cheese, honey and orange juice. Spoon about 1 tablespoon into each wonton cup. Top with strawberries. Garnish with whipped cream and mint if desired. **YIELD:** 1 dozen.

Gingerbread Pudding Cake

(Pictured below and on page 186)

PREP: 20 min. **COOK:** 2 hours + standing

A handful of spices and a half cup of molasses give this delightful dessert a comforting, old-fashioned flavor. It's pretty, too, with a dollop of whipped cream and a mint sprig on top.
—Barbara Cook, Yuma, Arizona

- 1/4 cup butter, softened
- 1/4 cup sugar
- 1 egg white
- 1 teaspoon vanilla extract
- 1/2 cup molasses
- 1 cup water
- 1-1/4 cups all-purpose flour
- 3/4 teaspoon baking soda
- 1/2 teaspoon ground cinnamon
- 1/2 teaspoon ground ginger
- 1/4 teaspoon salt
- 1/4 teaspoon ground allspice
- 1/8 teaspoon ground nutmeg
- 1/2 cup chopped pecans

TOPPING:
- 6 tablespoons brown sugar
- 3/4 cup hot water
- 2/3 cup butter, melted

In a large bowl, cream butter and sugar until light and fluffy. Beat in egg white and vanilla.

Combine molasses and water until blended. Combine the flour, baking soda, cinnamon, ginger, salt, allspice and nutmeg; add to creamed mixture alternately with molasses mixture, beating well after each addition. Fold in pecans.

Pour into a greased 3-qt. slow cooker. Sprinkle with brown sugar. Combine hot water and butter; pour over batter (do not stir).

Cover and cook on high for 2 to 2-1/2 hours or until a toothpick inserted near the center of cake comes out clean. Turn off heat. Let stand for 15 minutes. Serve warm. **YIELD:** 6-8 servings.

Lemon Cheesecake Dessert

(Pictured above)

PREP: 25 min. **BAKE:** 30 min. + chilling

Everyone will know spring has arrived when you serve these yummy yellow cheesecake squares. Cool and refreshing, this dessert cuts easily and keeps for several days in the refrigerator.
—Patty Auxier, Royalton, Kentucky

- 2 cups graham cracker crumbs
- 1/4 cup sugar
- 1/2 cup butter, melted

FILLING:
- 4 packages (8 ounces *each*) cream cheese, softened
- 1-1/4 cups sugar
- 1 package (3 ounces) lemon gelatin
- 1 teaspoon lemon extract
- 5 eggs, lightly beaten

SAUCE:
- 1 package (2.9 ounces) cook-and-serve lemon pudding mix
- 1/4 cup sugar
- 2-1/2 cups cold water

In a small bowl, combine cracker crumbs, sugar and butter. Press onto the bottom and 1 in. up the sides of a greased 13-in. x 9-in. baking dish. Refrigerate.

For the filling, in a large bowl, beat cream cheese and sugar until smooth. Add dry gelatin and lemon extract; beat 3 minutes longer. Add eggs; beat on low speed just until combined. Pour into crust.

Bake at 325° for 30-40 minutes or until center is almost set. Cool on a wire rack for 1 hour. Cover and refrigerate overnight.

For the lemon sauce, in a small saucepan, combine the pudding mix and sugar. Gradually stir in water. Cook and stir over medium heat until the mixture comes to a boil. Cook and stir 1-2 minutes longer or until thickened. Transfer to a bowl. Cover the surface with waxed paper; refrigerate until chilled. Serve with dessert. **YIELD:** 12 servings (2 cups sauce).

Mixed Nut Chocolate Tart

(Pictured below)

PREP: 20 min. **BAKE:** 35 min. + cooling

A buttery shortbread crust holds a delectable filling made with chocolate and a mix of chopped pistachios, almonds and pecans. It's impressive yet easy to prepare. I guarantee it will become one of your most requested desserts.

—Debbie Cross, Sharon, Pennsylvania

> 1-1/2 cups all-purpose flour
> 1/4 cup sugar
> 1/2 cup plus 1 tablespoon cold butter
> 6 tablespoons heavy whipping cream
> 1-1/2 teaspoons vanilla extract

FILLING:

> 1 cup pistachios
> 1 cup pecan halves
> 3/4 cup unblanched almonds
> 3 eggs
> 3/4 cup light corn syrup
> 1/4 cup packed brown sugar
> 1/4 cup butter, melted
> 1-1/2 teaspoons almond extract
> 1 teaspoon vanilla extract
> 1 cup milk chocolate chips

Whipped cream

In a small bowl, combine flour and sugar; cut in butter until mixture resembles fine crumbs. Add cream and vanilla, tossing with a fork until dough forms a ball. Press onto the bottom and up the sides of an ungreased fluted 11-in. tart pan with removable bottom; set aside.

For the filling, place nuts in a food processor; cover and process until chopped. In a large bowl, whisk the eggs, corn syrup, brown sugar, butter and extracts until smooth. Stir in chocolate chips and nut mixture; pour into crust.

Place the pan on a baking sheet. Bake at 350° for 35-40 minutes or until center is set. Cool on a wire rack. Store in the refrigerator. Garnish with whipped cream. **YIELD:** 12-14 servings.

Banana Split Brownie Pie

(Pictured above)

PREP: 30 min. + freezing **BAKE:** 30 min. + freezing

I often use Neapolitan in place of three different ice cream flavors to make this luscious confection. Days ahead, you can bake the brownie crust, top it with the ice cream and freeze until you need it.

—Tanna Walker, Salina, Kansas

> 4 ounces German sweet chocolate, chopped
> 1/2 cup butter, cubed
> 3 eggs
> 1 cup sugar
> 1/2 teaspoon vanilla extract
> 1/2 cup all-purpose flour
> 1-1/3 cups vanilla ice cream
> 1-2/3 cups chocolate ice cream
> 1-2/3 cups strawberry ice cream
> 2 medium firm bananas, sliced
> 1 cup fresh strawberries, sliced
> 1/2 to 3/4 cup hot fudge ice cream topping, warmed
> 1/2 to 3/4 cup strawberry ice cream topping
> 1/4 to 1/2 cup toffee bits *or* almond brickle chips

Whipped cream and sliced almonds

In a microwave, melt chocolate and butter; stir until smooth. Cool. In a small bowl, beat the eggs, sugar, vanilla and cooled chocolate mixture. Gradually add flour until well blended. Spread into a greased 9-in. springform pan.

Bake at 350° for 30-35 minutes or until a toothpick inserted near the center comes out clean. Cool on a wire rack. Cover and freeze until firm.

Using 1/3 cup for each scoop, place four scoops of vanilla ice cream, five scoops of chocolate ice cream and five scoops of strawberry ice cream on a waxed paper-lined baking sheet. Freeze until firm. Place vanilla scoops in center of brownie crust; alternate scoops of chocolate and strawberry around edge. Cover and freeze until firm.

Just before serving, remove sides of pan. Arrange bananas and strawberries over ice cream. Drizzle with hot fudge and strawberry toppings. Sprinkle with toffee bits. Garnish with whipped cream and almonds. Cut into wedges. **YIELD:** 10 servings.

Fluffy Lemon Squares

(Pictured below)

PREP: 25 min. + chilling

These rich bars, with a vanilla wafer crust, get their sweet-tart flavor from lemon gelatin, pudding mix and sherbet. They're not only fun to make with my grandchildren, but they're delicious, too.
—Joyce Speerbrecher, Grafton, Wisconsin

- 1-1/2 cups crushed vanilla wafers (about 45 wafers)
- 1/3 cup chopped pecans
- 6 tablespoons butter, melted
- 1/2 cup heavy whipping cream
- 2 packages (3 ounces *each*) lemon gelatin
- 1-1/4 cups boiling water
- 1 package (3.4 ounces) instant lemon pudding mix
- 1 pint lemon sherbet, softened

In a small bowl, combine the wafer crumbs, pecans and butter; set aside 1/4 cup for topping. Press the remaining crumb mixture into an ungreased 11-in. x 7-in. dish. Cover and refrigerate for 30 minutes.

Meanwhile, in a small bowl, beat cream until stiff peaks form; set aside. In a large bowl, dissolve gelatin in boiling water. Add pudding mix; beat on low speed for 2 minutes. Add sherbet; beat on low for 1 minute or until soft-set. Gently fold in whipped cream.

Spread over the crust; sprinkle with the reserved crumb mixture. Refrigerate for 1 hour or until set. **YIELD:** 12 servings.

Three-Fruit Sundae Sauce

(Pictured above)

PREP: 10 min. **COOK:** 55 min. + chilling

I dreamed up this bright-red sauce that blends rhubarb with strawberries, oranges, cinnamon and lemon peel. It's wonderful over vanilla ice cream.
—Sharon Trefren, Grand Bay, Alabama

- 2 cups sugar
- 2 tablespoons cornstarch
- 6 cups chopped fresh rhubarb *or* frozen rhubarb
- 2 cups fresh *or* frozen sweetened sliced strawberries
- 2 medium navel oranges, peeled and sectioned
- 1 teaspoon grated lemon peel
- 3 cups water
- 1 cinnamon stick (3 inches)

Vanilla ice cream

In a large saucepan, combine sugar, cornstarch, rhubarb, strawberries, oranges and lemon peel until blended. Stir in the water and cinnamon stick. Bring to a boil; cook and stir for 2 minutes.

Reduce heat; simmer, uncovered, for 50-60 minutes or until thickened. Discard cinnamon stick. Cool. Place in refrigerator until chilled. Serve over ice cream. **YIELD:** 7 cups.

EDITOR'S NOTE: If using frozen rhubarb, measure rhubarb while still frozen, then thaw completely. Drain in a colander, but do not press liquid out.

oh, nuts!

Nuts can turn rancid over time, so to prevent this, it's best to store them in the freezer. To thaw for a recipe, spread them in a pie plate and place in the oven for a few minutes as the oven preheats. Let cool and chop them to use in baked goods.

Spread with 3/4 cup chocolate sauce; freeze for 20 minutes. Top with remaining cherry ice cream; sprinkle with 1 cup cookie crumbs. Cover and freeze for 4 hours. Transfer the remaining sauce to a microwave-safe dish; cover and refrigerate.

Remove dessert from freezer 10 minutes before serving. Using plastic wrap, remove dessert from pan; discard plastic wrap. Press the remaining cookie crumbs into sides. Using a serrated knife, cut into 12 slices. Warm reserved sauce in a microwave; serve with ice cream cake. **YIELD:** 12 servings (1-1/4 cups sauce).

EDITOR'S NOTE: Reader used crisp Italian macaroons instead of shortbread cookies.

Peaches 'n' Cream Cups

(Pictured below)

PREP/TOTAL TIME: 10 min.

For a no-fuss dessert that's as cool and refreshing as a summer breeze, try these tasty treats with a gingersnap crust and creamy yogurt filling.

—Suzanne Cleveland, Lyons, Georgia

   1 **gingersnap cookie, crumbled**
1/4 **teaspoon ground ginger**
   1 **carton (6 ounces) peach yogurt**
1/4 **cup cream cheese, softened**
1/4 **teaspoon vanilla extract**
1/3 **cup sliced peaches, drained and chopped**

In a small bowl, combine crumbs and ginger; set aside. In a small bowl, beat the yogurt, cream cheese and vanilla until smooth. Fold in peaches.

Spoon into two 6-oz. custard cups; cover and refrigerate for 1 hour. Just before serving, sprinkle with reserved crumb mixture. **YIELD:** 2 servings.

Cherry Ice Cream Cake

(Pictured above and on page 186)

PREP: 15 min. BAKE: 15 min.

A friend shared this recipe, which has become an all-time favorite of mine. It's so versatile—I've substituted different cookies (macaroons or chocolate chip), ice cream and chips with terrific results.

—Kathy Kittell, Lenexa, Kansas

2/3 **cup heavy whipping cream**
  2 **tablespoons butter**
  1 **package (11 ounces) milk chocolate chips**
  1 **teaspoon vanilla extract**
ICE CREAM CAKE:
  2 **pints cherry *or* cherry vanilla ice cream, softened, *divided***
  3 **cups crushed shortbread cookies, *divided***
  1 **pint vanilla ice cream, softened**

In a small saucepan, heat the cream and butter over low heat until butter is melted; remove from the heat. Add the chips; let stand for 1 minute. Whisk until sauce is smooth. Stir in the vanilla. Cool for 30 minutes, stirring occasionally.

Meanwhile, line the bottom and sides of a 9-in. x 5-in. loaf pan with plastic wrap. Spread 1 pint cherry ice cream into prepared pan; sprinkle with 1 cup cookie crumbs. Top with vanilla ice cream. Freeze for 20 minutes or until firm.

Lemon Rice Pudding Brulee

(*Pictured above*)

PREP: 30 min. **BAKE:** 5 min.

You can make the lemonade from frozen concentrate to speed up the assembly of this delicious and easy rice pudding and creme brulee hybrid.

—Helen Conwell, Fairhope, Alabama

- 1-1/3 **cups lemonade**
- 1/2 **cup uncooked long grain rice**
- 1 **teaspoon grated lemon peel**
- 1/3 **cup plus 3 tablepoons sugar,** *divided*
- 1 **tablespoon all-purpose flour**
- 1/2 **teaspoon salt**
- 2 **cups milk**
- 2 **eggs, lightly beaten**
- 1/4 **cup dried cranberries**
- 3 **tablespoons brown sugar**
- 1/3 **cup chopped pecans, toasted**

In a small saucepan, bring the lemonade and rice to a boil. Reduce heat; cover and simmer for 20 minutes. Remove from the heat; stir in the lemon peel. Cover and let stand for 5 minutes. Cool to room temperature.

In a large saucepan, combine 1/3 cup sugar, flour and salt. Stir in the milk until smooth. Cook and stir over medium-high heat until thickened and bubbly. Reduce heat; cook and stir 2 minutes longer.

Remove from the heat. Stir a small amount of hot filling into eggs; return all to the pan, stirring constantly. Bring to a gentle boil; cook and stir 2 minutes longer. Remove from the heat. Gently stir in cranberries and cooled rice.

Divide among six 8-oz. ramekins. Place on a baking sheet. Combine brown sugar and remaining sugar; sprinkle over pudding. Broil 3-4 in. from the heat for 3-5 minutes or sugar is melted and bubbly. Sprinkle with pecans. Serve warm. **YIELD:** 6 servings.

Apple Dumplings

(*Pictured below*)

PREP: 10 min. **BAKE:** 50 min.

Covered in a luscious caramel sauce, these dumplings are great served alone or with a generous scoop of vanilla ice cream. Kids of all ages cannot resist the warm and comforting apple flavor.

—Robin Lendon, Cincinnati, Ohio

- 3 **cups all-purpose flour**
- 1 **teaspoon salt**
- 1 **cup shortening**
- 1/3 **cup cold water**
- 8 **medium tart apples, peeled and cored**
- 8 **teaspoons butter**
- 9 **teaspoons cinnamon-sugar,** *divided*

SAUCE:
- 1-1/2 **cups packed brown sugar**
- 1 **cup water**
- 1/2 **cup butter, cubed**

In a large bowl, combine the flour and salt; cut in shortening until crumbly. Gradually add water, tossing with a fork until dough forms a ball. Divide into eight portions. Cover and refrigerate for at least 30 minutes or until easy to handle.

Roll each portion of dough between two lightly floured sheets of waxed paper into a 7-in. square. Place an apple on each square. Place 1 teaspoon butter and 1 teaspoon cinnamon-sugar in the center of each apple.

Gently bring up corners of pastry to each center; pinch edges to seal. If desired, cut out apple leaves and stems from the dough scraps; attach to dumplings with water. Place in a greased 13-in. x 9-in. baking dish. Sprinkle with remaining cinnamon-sugar.

In a large saucepan, combine sauce ingredients. Bring just to a boil, stirring until blended. Pour over apples.

Bake at 350° for 50-55 minutes or until the apples are tender and pastry is golden brown, basting occasionally with sauce. Serve warm. **YIELD:** 8 servings.

The line at the buffet table is sure to form fast when you contribute any of the large-quantity dishes served up here. Cooking for a crowd has never been easier!

potluck pleasers

Forgotten Jambalaya..208

Chunky Apple Cake 208

Meatballs in Plum Sauce 209

Apple and Carrot Slaw 209

Mini Chicken Salad Croissants.........................210

Coconut Pecan Cupcakes 210

Cashew-Pear Tossed Salad...............................211

Onions Neptune..211

Tamales 212

Red Potato Salad 212

Peanut Butter Pudding Dessert.......................213

Hint of Mint Fruit Salad 213

Watermelon Basket 214

Mac and Cheese for a Bunch 214

Rhubarb Cranberry Cookies 215

Tossed Salad with Lemon Vinaigrette 215

Shredded Beef and Slaw Sandwiches...........215

Peanut Butter Chocolate Cupcakes 216

Scalloped Potatoes and Ham...........................216

Spicy Pork Chili..217

Layered Summertime Salad..............................217

Festive Rice Salad 218

Meaty Pasta Casseroles 218

Slow-Cooked Pork and Beans 219

Peanut Lover's Brownies 219

Ham Bundles 220

Dilly Zucchini Dip..220

Cranberry Gelatin Squares 221

Corn Tortilla Chicken Lasagna 221

Cran-Apple Crisp...222

Biscuit-Topped Lemon Chicken......................222

Buffalo Chicken Dip...223

Cheddar Ham Strata 223

Cheese Enchiladas 224

Tex-Mex Dip 224

Vanilla Pudding Dessert....................................224

Cinnamon-Sugar Rhubarb Cake 225

Tortellini Spinach Casserole 225

Spiral Pepperoni Pizza Bake............................226

Sweet Pea Salad 226

Blue Cheese Deviled Eggs...............................226

Red Cream Soda Punch 227

Apple Streusel Muffins 227

Broccoli Chicken Supreme 228

Deluxe Breakfast Bake 228

Meatball Calzones...229

Salsa for a Crowd..229

PICTURED CLOCKWISE FROM UPPER LEFT: Meaty Pasta Casseroles (page 218), Chunky Apple Cake (page 208), Tortellini Spinach Casserole (page 225) and Shredded Beef and Slaw Sandwiches (page 215).

Forgotten Jambalaya

(Pictured above)

PREP: 35 min. **COOK:** 4-1/4 hours

During the winter, I fix this jambalaya at least once a month. It's so easy…just chop the vegetables, dump everything in the slow cooker and forget it! Even my sons, who are picky about spicy things, like this dish.

—Cindi Coss, Coppell, Texas

   1 can (14-1/2 ounces) diced tomatoes, undrained
   1 can (14-1/2 ounces) beef *or* chicken broth
   1 can (6 ounces) tomato paste
   2 medium green peppers, chopped
   1 medium onion, chopped
   3 celery ribs, chopped
   5 garlic cloves, minced
   3 teaspoons dried parsley flakes
   2 teaspoons dried basil
1-1/2 teaspoons dried oregano
1-1/4 teaspoons salt
 1/2 teaspoon cayenne pepper
 1/2 teaspoon hot pepper sauce
   1 pound boneless skinless chicken breasts, cut into 1-inch cubes
   1 pound smoked sausage, halved and cut into 1/4-inch slices
 1/2 pound uncooked medium shrimp, peeled and deveined
Hot cooked rice

In a 5-qt. slow cooker, combine the tomatoes, broth and tomato paste. Stir in the green peppers, onion, celery, garlic and seasonings. Stir in chicken and sausage.

Cover and cook on low for 4 hours or until chicken is tender. Stir in shrimp. Cover and cook 15-30 minutes longer or until shrimp turn pink. Serve with rice. **YIELD:** 11 servings.

Chunky Apple Cake

(Pictured below and on page 206)

PREP: 20 min. **BAKE:** 40 min. + cooling

This tender cake is full of old-fashioned comfort, and the yummy brown sugar sauce makes it special. For a festive occasion, top individual slices with a dollop of whipped cream and some mint.

—Debi Benson, Bakersfield, California

 1/2 cup butter, softened
   2 cups sugar
 1/2 teaspoon vanilla extract
   2 eggs
   2 cups all-purpose flour
1-1/2 teaspoons ground cinnamon
   1 teaspoon ground nutmeg
 1/2 teaspoon salt
 1/2 teaspoon baking soda
   6 cups chopped peeled tart apples
BUTTERSCOTCH SAUCE:
 1/2 cup packed brown sugar
 1/4 cup butter, cubed
 1/2 cup heavy whipping cream

In a large bowl, cream butter, sugar and vanilla. Add eggs, one at a time, beating well after each addition. Combine flour, cinnamon, nutmeg, salt and baking soda; gradually add to creamed mixture and mix well (batter will be stiff). Stir in apples until well combined.

Spread into a greased 13-in. x 9-in. baking dish. Bake at 350° for 40-45 minutes or until top is lightly browned and springs back when lightly touched. Cool for 30 minutes before serving.

Meanwhile, for the sauce, in a small saucepan, combine the brown sugar and butter. Cook over medium heat until butter is melted. Gradually add the cream. Bring to a slow boil over medium heat, stirring constantly. Remove from the heat. Serve with cake. **YIELD:** 12-14 servings.

In a large skillet, brown meatballs in oil in batches. Drain on paper towels. Place in a greased 13-in. x 9-in. baking dish.

In a small bowl, dissolve bouillon in water. Stir the flour into pan drippings until blended; add bouillon mixture, jam and chili sauce. Bring to a boil; cook and stir for 1-2 minutes or until thickened. Pour over meatballs.

Cover and bake at 350° for 30-45 minutes or until the meat is no longer pink and the sauce is bubbly. **YIELD:** 10-12 servings.

Apple and Carrot Slaw

(Pictured below)

PREP/TOTAL TIME: 30 min.

This crispy, tasty slaw is a true crowd-pleaser at any picnic or church gathering. The apples add color and a touch of sweetness.
—Julia Livingston, Frostproof, Florida

   4 **large heads cabbage, shredded**
   1 **pound carrots, shredded**
   6 **medium red apples, finely chopped**
   3 **cups mayonnaise**
1/2 **cup sugar**
1/4 **cup white vinegar**
   3 **teaspoons salt**
   2 **teaspoons pepper**

In a very large bowl, combine the cabbage, carrots and apples. In a large bowl, combine mayonnaise, sugar, vinegar, salt and pepper. Pour over cabbage mixture and toss to coat. Cover and refrigerate until serving. **YIELD:** 42 servings (3/4 cup each).

Meatballs in Plum Sauce

(Pictured above)

PREP: 1 hour **BAKE:** 30 min.

Plum jam and chili sauce beautifully coat these moist meatballs. You'll want to make sure the delightful appetizers are on your holiday menus.

—Mary Poninski, Whittington, Illinois

1/2 **cup milk**
   1 **cup soft bread crumbs**
   1 **egg, lightly beaten**
   1 **tablespoon Worcestershire sauce**
   1 **medium onion, finely chopped**
1/4 **teaspoon salt**
1/4 **teaspoon pepper**
1/8 **teaspoon ground cloves**
1/2 **pound lean ground beef**
1/2 **pound ground pork**
1/2 **pound ground veal**
   2 **tablespoons canola oil**
1/2 **teaspoon beef bouillon granules**
1/2 **cup boiling water**
   3 **tablespoons all-purpose flour**
   1 **cup plum jam**
1/2 **cup chili sauce**

In a large bowl, pour the milk over bread crumbs; let stand for 10 minutes. Add the egg, Worcestershire sauce, onion, salt, pepper and cloves. Crumble beef, pork and veal over mixture and mix well (mixture will be soft). Shape into 1-in. balls.

Mini Chicken Salad Croissants

(Pictured below)

PREP: 20 min. + chilling

Fresh-tasting and great for a get-together, this popular chicken salad could also be served on lettuce or alongside a slice of cantaloupe or honeydew melon. For kids, I use halved red seedless grapes instead of the peppers.

—Patricia Tjugum, Tomahawk, Wisconsin

- 1/3 cup sour cream
- 1/3 cup mayonnaise
- 4 teaspoons lemon juice
- 1 teaspoon salt
- 1/4 teaspoon pepper
- 3 cups cubed cooked chicken
- 4 celery ribs, thinly sliced
- 1 cup chopped fresh mushrooms
- 1/4 cup chopped green pepper
- 1/4 cup chopped sweet red pepper
- 4 bacon strips, cooked and crumbled
- 1/2 cup chopped pecans, toasted
- 20 lettuce leaves
- 20 miniature croissants, split

In a small bowl, combine the sour cream, mayonnaise, lemon juice, salt and pepper. In a large bowl, combine the chicken, celery, mushrooms and peppers; stir in sour cream mixture until combined. Cover and refrigerate for at least 4 hours.

Just before serving, stir in bacon and pecans. Spoon 1/4 cup chicken salad onto each lettuce-lined croissant. **YIELD:** 20 sandwiches.

Coconut Pecan Cupcakes

(Pictured above)

PREP: 50 min. **BAKE:** 20 min. + cooling

Pecan lovers have lots to cheer about with these cupcakes. I created the recipe for my best friend, who loves Italian cream cake but doesn't want a whole cake. They have a wonderful aroma and fabulous flavor.

—Tina Harrison, Prairieville, Louisiana

- 5 eggs, *separated*
- 1/2 cup butter, softened
- 1/2 cup shortening
- 2 cups sugar
- 3/4 teaspoon vanilla extract
- 1/4 teaspoon almond extract
- 1-1/2 cups all-purpose flour
- 1/4 cup cornstarch
- 1/2 teaspoon baking soda
- 1/2 teaspoon salt
- 1 cup buttermilk
- 2 cups flaked coconut
- 1 cup finely chopped pecans

FROSTING:

- 1 package (8 ounces) cream cheese, softened
- 1/4 cup butter, softened
- 1/2 teaspoon vanilla extract
- 1/4 teaspoon almond extract
- 3-3/4 cups confectioners' sugar
- 3/4 cup chopped pecans

Let eggs stand at room temperature for 30 minutes, then separate. In a large bowl, cream the butter, shortening and sugar until light and fluffy. Add the egg yolks, one at a time, beating well after each addition. Stir in extracts. Combine the flour, cornstarch, baking soda and salt; add to the creamed mixture alternately with buttermilk, beating well after each addition.

In a small bowl, beat the egg whites on high speed until stiff peaks form. Fold into the batter. Stir in the coconut and pecans.

Fill paper-lined muffin cups three-fourths full. Bake at 350° for 20-25 minutes or until a toothpick comes out clean. Cool 10 minutes; remove from pans to wire racks to cool completely.

In a large bowl, combine the frosting ingredients until smooth; frost cupcakes. Store in the refrigerator. **YIELD:** 2 dozen.

Cashew-Pear Tossed Salad

(Pictured below)

PREP/TOTAL TIME: 15 min.

A friend who does a lot of catering fixed this salad for our staff Christmas party several years ago, and we all asked for the recipe. The unexpected sweet-salty mix and lovely dressing make it a hit with everyone.

—*Arlene Muller, Kingwood, Texas*

  1 bunch romaine, torn
  1 cup (4 ounces) shredded Swiss cheese
  1 cup salted cashews
  1 medium pear, thinly sliced
1/2 cup dried cranberries
POPPY SEED VINAIGRETTE:
2/3 cup olive oil
1/2 cup sugar
1/3 cup lemon juice
  2 to 3 teaspoons poppy seeds
  2 teaspoons finely chopped red onion
  1 teaspoon prepared mustard
1/2 teaspoon salt

In a large salad bowl, combine the romaine, Swiss cheese, cashews, pear and cranberries. In a jar with a tight-fitting lid, combine the vinaigrette ingredients; shake well. Drizzle over salad and toss to coat. Serve immediately. **YIELD:** 15 servings.

Onions Neptune

(Pictured above)

PREP: 20 min. BAKE: 35 min.

I serve this dish as an appetizer and often add whatever ingredients I have handy, such as mushrooms or sun-dried tomatoes. Whether I serve it as is or jazz it up, it's always delicious.

—*Todd Noon, Galloway, New Jersey*

  5 to 6 medium sweet onions, sliced and
     separated into rings
1/2 cup butter, softened, *divided*
  2 cans (6 ounces *each*) lump crabmeat,
     drained, *divided*
  3 cups (12 ounces) shredded Swiss cheese
  1 can (10-3/4 ounces) condensed cream of
     mushroom soup, undiluted
1/2 cup evaporated milk
1/2 teaspoon salt
1/4 teaspoon pepper
12 to 16 slices French bread (1/4 inch thick)

In a large skillet, saute onions in 1/4 cup butter until tender. Remove from the heat; gently stir in half of the crab. Spread into a greased 13-in. x 9-in. baking dish. Top with remaining crab. Combine the cheese, soup, milk, salt and pepper; spoon over crab.

Spread remaining butter over one side of each slice of bread; place buttered side up over casserole. Bake, uncovered, at 350° for 35-45 minutes or until golden brown. **YIELD:** 12 servings.

Place the first eight ingredients in a Dutch oven. Cover and bake at 325° for 3-4 hours or until meat is very tender.

Meanwhile, place corn husks in a large kettle; cover with cold water and soak for at least 2 hours.

Remove roast and shred meat with two forks; set aside and keep warm. Skim fat from pan juices; discard chilies. Bring to a boil; cook until liquid is reduced to 4 cups.

For the filling, in a large bowl, combine the cornmeal, baking powder and salt; beat in water, 2 cups of the pan juices and shortening just until combined (bowl will be full). Refrigerate the remaining pan juices.

Drain the corn husks and pat dry. (Until ready to use, keep the husks covered with plastic wrap and a damp towel to prevent them from drying out.) Spread 3 tablespoons of the filling over each husk to within 1/4 in. of the edges. Top each with 1/4 cup pork and another 3 tablespoons of the filling. Using the husk to lift one long side, roll up the filling. Enclose the filling with the husk; fold bottom end of husk over the top.

In a large steamer basket, position tamales upright with folded bottoms down. Place basket in a Dutch oven over 1 in. of water. Bring to a boil; cover and steam for 25-30 minutes or until cornmeal peels away from husk, adding water to pan as needed. Warm the reserved pan juices; serve with tamales. Remove the husks before eating. **YIELD:** 32 tamales.

Tamales

(Pictured above)

PREP: 4-1/4 hours **COOK:** 25 min.

Tamales are bundles of corn dough with a savory or sweet filling, typically wrapped in corn husks or banana leaves. Because they take a while to make, they are often served for special occasions and holidays.

—Jacquelynne Stine, Las Vegas, Nevada

     1 **boneless pork shoulder roast (4 pounds)**
     4 **cups water**
     1 **cup finely chopped onion**
  1/3 **cup adobo sauce**
  1/4 **cup chili sauce**
     2 **dried guajillo chilies**
  1/4 **cup lime juice**
     4 **garlic cloves, peeled**
    32 **corn husks**
FILLING:
     7 **cups maseca cornmeal**
     9 **teaspoons baking powder**
     3 **teaspoons salt**
     4 **cups warm water (110° to 115°)**
1-1/2 **cups butter-flavored shortening**

Red Potato Salad

PREP: 40 min. + chilling

No picnic is complete without potato salad. In my favorite version, red potatoes and hard-cooked eggs add heartiness. The creamy mayonnaise dressing—seasoned with pickle relish and mustard—provides great flavor.

—Margaret Blomquist, Newfield, New York

     5 **pounds medium red potatoes, halved**
     5 **hard-cooked eggs, chopped**
     1 **celery rib, finely chopped**
  1/2 **medium onion, finely chopped**
1-1/2 **cups mayonnaise**
  1/4 **cup sweet pickle relish**
     3 **tablespoons sugar**
     2 **tablespoons dried parsley flakes**
     2 **teaspoons prepared mustard**
     1 **teaspoon salt**
     1 **teaspoon cider vinegar**
  1/8 **teaspoon pepper**

Place the potatoes in a large kettle; cover with water. Bring to a boil. Reduce heat; cover and cook for 20-25 minutes or until tender. Drain and cool. Cut the potatoes into 3/4-in. cubes.

In a large bowl, combine the potatoes, eggs, celery and onion. In a small bowl, combine the mayonnaise, relish, sugar, parsley, mustard, salt, vinegar and pepper. Pour over potato mixture and stir gently to coat. Cover and refrigerate for 6 hours or overnight. **YIELD:** 17 servings (3/4 cup each).

Peanut Butter Pudding Dessert

(Pictured below)

PREP: 25 min. **BAKE:** 25 min. + chilling

Here's a fun, layered dessert that will appeal to all ages. If you want it even nuttier, you can use chunky peanut butter. If you're not a fan of cashews, substitute your favorite nut.

—Barbara Schindler, Napoleon, Ohio

- 1 cup all-purpose flour
- 1/2 cup cold butter, cubed
- 1-1/2 cups chopped cashews, *divided*
- 1 package (8 ounces) cream cheese, softened
- 1/3 cup creamy peanut butter
- 1 cup confectioners' sugar
- 1 carton (12 ounces) frozen whipped topping, thawed, *divided*
- 2-2/3 cups cold milk
- 1 package (3.9 ounces) instant chocolate pudding mix
- 1 package (3.4 ounces) instant vanilla pudding mix
- 1 milk chocolate candy bar (1.55 ounces), coarsely chopped

Place flour and butter in a food processor; cover and process until mixture resembles coarse crumbs. Add 1 cup cashews; pulse a few times until combined.

Press into a greased 13-in. x 9-in. baking dish. Bake at 350° for 25-28 minutes or until golden brown. Cool completely on a wire rack.

In a small bowl, beat the cream cheese, peanut butter and confectioners' sugar until smooth. Fold in 1 cup whipped topping. Spoon over crust.

In another bowl, whisk milk and both pudding mixes for 2 minutes. Let stand for 2 minutes or until soft-set. Spread over cream cheese layer. Top with remaining whipped topping. Sprinkle with chopped candy bar and remaining cashews. Cover and refrigerate for at least 1 hour before serving. **YIELD:** 12-16 servings.

Hint of Mint Fruit Salad

(Pictured above)

PREP: 20 min. + chilling

I love making herbal syrups like the simple dressing for this colorful fruit salad. It definitely adds pizzazz to Easter dinner and other spring gatherings.

—Sue Gronholz, Beaver Dam, Wisconsin

- 1 cup sugar
- 1 cup water
- 1 cup loosely packed mint sprigs
- 2-1/2 cups chopped apples
- 2-1/2 cups chopped ripe pears
- 2 cups cubed fresh pineapple
- 2 cups sliced fresh strawberries
- 1 cup fresh blueberries
- 1 cup mayonnaise

In a large saucepan, bring sugar and water to a boil. Reduce heat; simmer, uncovered, for 4 minutes. Remove from the heat. Add mint; cover and steep for 20 minutes. Strain and discard mint. Transfer syrup to a small bowl; refrigerate until chilled.

Just before serving, combine apples, pears, pineapple, strawberries and blueberries in a large bowl. Stir mayonnaise into mint syrup until blended; pour over fruit and toss to coat. **YIELD:** 12 servings.

wild about berries

Fresh berries should be stored covered in the refrigerator and washed just before using. Use within 10 days of purchase. To wash, place a few berries at a time in a colander in the sink. Gently spray with water and pat dry on paper towels.

Watermelon Basket

(Pictured below)

PREP: 30 min. + chilling

I cut a watermelon into a basket shape, then fill it with melon balls to serve with a creamy dip. It makes an attractive center-piece at parties as well as a delicious fruit salad.

—Christine Johnson, Ricetown, Kentucky

  1 large watermelon (10 pounds)
  1 medium honeydew, cut into balls
  3 cups white cranberry juice
  1 cup light corn syrup
  2 tablespoons lime juice
FRUIT DIP:
  1 package (8 ounces) cream cheese, softened
  1/4 cup milk
  3 tablespoons sugar
  3 tablespoons lemon juice
  3/4 teaspoon ground cardamom

Cut a thin slice from the bottom of watermelon with a sharp knife so it sits flat. Mark a horizontal cutting line 2 in. above the center and around the melon.

For the handle, score a 1-1/2-in.-wide strip across the top of the melon, connecting both sides to the horizontal line. With a long sharp knife, cut all the way through the rind above the cutting line in a zigzag pattern.

Carefully lift off the side pieces. Remove fruit from both sections and cut into balls. Refrigerate the basket.

In a large bowl, combine the watermelon and honeydew balls. In another bowl, whisk cranberry juice, corn syrup and lime juice until blended; pour over melon balls. Cover and chill for 3 hours.

Drain; spoon melon into watermelon basket. For the dip, in a small bowl, beat the cream cheese and milk until smooth. Beat in sugar, lemon juice and cardamom; serve with melon. **YIELD:** 32 servings.

Mac and Cheese for a Bunch

(Pictured above)

PREP: 30 min. **BAKE:** 35 min.

You'll satisfy many taste buds with my comforting dish. This tender macaroni is first covered in a creamy, homemade cheese sauce, and then topped with golden bread crumbs. A true crowd-pleaser!

—Dixie Terry, Goreville, Illinois

  3 packages (two 16 ounces, one 7 ounces)
    elbow macaroni
1-1/4 cups butter, *divided*
  3/4 cup all-purpose flour
  2 teaspoons salt
  3 quarts milk
  3 pounds sharp cheddar cheese, shredded
1-1/2 cups dry bread crumbs

Cook macaroni according to package directions until almost tender. Meanwhile, in a large soup kettle, melt 1 cup butter. Stir in flour and salt until smooth. Gradually stir in milk. Bring to a boil; cook and stir for 2 minutes or until thickened. Reduce heat. Add cheese, stirring until melted. Drain macaroni; stir into sauce.

Transfer to three greased 13-in. x 9-in. baking dishes. Melt remaining butter; toss with bread crumbs. Sprinkle over casseroles. Bake, uncovered, at 350° for 35-40 minutes or until golden brown. **YIELD:** 36 servings (1 cup each).

Rhubarb Cranberry Cookies

PREP: 30 min. **BAKE:** 10 min./ batch + cooling

I like the hint of sweetness when you bite into the white choco-late in these cookies. It really complements the tart flavor from the rhubarb and cranberries.

—Elaine Scott, Lafayette, Indiana

- 1 cup butter, softened
- 1 cup packed brown sugar
- 1/2 cup sugar
- 2 eggs
- 1 teaspoon vanilla extract
- 1-1/2 cups all-purpose flour
- 1 teaspoon baking soda
- 1/2 teaspoon salt
- 1/2 teaspoon ground cinnamon
- 2-1/2 cups old-fashioned oats
- 1-1/2 cups diced frozen rhubarb
- 1 cup vanilla *or* white chips
- 1 cup dried cranberries
- 4 squares (1 ounce *each*) white baking chocolate

In a large bowl, cream the butter and sugars. Beat in the eggs and vanilla. Combine flour, baking soda, salt and cinnamon; gradually add to creamed mixture. Stir in oats, rhubarb, chips and cranberries.

Drop by tablespoonfuls 2 in. apart onto parchment paper-lined baking sheets. Bake at 350° for 10-12 minutes or until set. Remove to wire racks to cool.

In a microwave-safe bowl, melt white chocolate; stir until smooth. Drizzle over cookies; let stand until set. Store in an airtight container. **YIELD:** about 5-1/2 dozen.

Tossed Salad with Lemon Vinaigrette

PREP/TOTAL TIME: 25 min.

I often take this dressed-up Caesar salad to church functions or family reunions. Its interesting blend of flavors is a hit with everyone, so I often come home with an empty bowl.

—Teresa Otto, Hartwell, Georgia

- 1 bunch romaine, torn
- 1 medium head iceberg lettuce, torn
- 10 bacon strips, cooked and crumbled
- 2 cups cherry tomatoes, halved
- 1 cup slivered almonds
- 1 cup shredded Parmesan cheese
- 1 cup salad croutons

VINAIGRETTE:
- 3 tablespoons lemon juice
- 3 tablespoons grated Parmesan cheese
- 2 garlic cloves, minced
- 1/2 teaspoon salt
- 1/4 teaspoon pepper
- 2/3 cup olive oil

In a large salad bowl, combine first seven ingredients. For vinaigrette, in a small bowl, combine lemon juice, grated Parmesan cheese, minced garlic, salt and pepper. Gradually whisk in the olive oil. Drizzle over salad and toss to coat. Serve immediately. **YIELD:** 21 servings.

Shredded Beef and Slaw Sandwiches

(Pictured below and on page 206)

PREP: 20 min. **COOK:** 2-3/4 hours

I have often served these tangy, hearty sandwiches for family gatherings and to many work crews. They have always gone over quite well.

—Mary Johnson, Whitehouse, Ohio

- 4 pounds beef stew meat, cut into 1-inch cubes
- 2 cups water
- 2 cups ketchup
- 1/2 to 3/4 cup Worcestershire sauce
- 2 tablespoons lemon juice
- 2 tablespoons prepared horseradish
- 1 tablespoon prepared mustard
- 2 teaspoons salt
- 8 cups shredded cabbage
- 30 sandwich buns, split

In a Dutch oven, bring the beef and water to a boil. Reduce heat; cover and simmer for 2 hours or until tender.

Remove the beef with a slotted spoon; shred with two forks and set aside. Skim fat from the cooking liquid. Stir in the ketchup, Worcestershire sauce, lemon juice, horseradish, mustard and salt. Add the shredded beef and cabbage. Bring to a boil. Reduce heat; cover and simmer for 45 minutes or until cabbage is tender.

Spoon 1/3 cup onto each sandwich bun. **YIELD:** 30 sandwiches.

Festive Rice Salad

(Pictured below)

PREP: 30 min. + cooling

I once had a similar salad at a friend's house and was determined to re-create it at home. After several tries, I came up with this sweet-tart concoction. It's easy to prepare and colorful, too.
—*Terri Simpson, Palm Harbor, Florida*

    3/4 cup uncooked long grain rice
      1 package (10 ounces) frozen peas, thawed
      1 small sweet red pepper, chopped
    3/4 cup chopped green onions
    1/2 cup dried cranberries
DRESSING:
    1/2 cup canola oil
    1/3 cup white vinegar
      3 tablespoons sugar
    1/2 teaspoon dill weed
    1/4 teaspoon salt
    1/4 teaspoon ground mustard
    1/8 teaspoon pepper

Cook rice according to package directions; cool. In a large bowl, combine the rice, peas, red pepper, onions and cranberries. In a small bowl, whisk the dressing ingredients. Drizzle over salad and toss to coat. Refrigerate until serving. **YIELD:** 12 servings.

Meaty Pasta Casseroles

(Pictured above and on page 206)

PREP: 45 min. **BAKE:** 35 min.

I love this recipe because it makes two robust casseroles. Every time I fix it, I add something different, such as extra garlic, to give it a flavor boost.
—*Debra Butcher, Decatur, Indiana*

      1 package (16 ounces) penne pasta
      1 pound ground beef
      1 pound bulk Italian pork sausage
1-3/4 cups sliced fresh mushrooms
      1 medium onion, chopped
      1 medium green pepper, chopped
      2 cans (14-1/2 ounces *each*) Italian diced tomatoes
      1 jar (25.6 ounces) Italian sausage and garlic
         spaghetti sauce
      1 jar (16 ounces) chunky mild salsa
      1 package (8 ounces) sliced pepperoni, chopped
      1 cup (4 ounces) shredded Swiss cheese, *divided*
      4 cups (16 ounces) shredded part-skim
         mozzarella cheese, *divided*
1-1/2 cups shredded Parmesan cheese, *divided*
      1 jar (26 ounces) three-cheese spaghetti sauce

Cook pasta according to package directions. Meanwhile, in a Dutch oven, cook the beef, sausage, mushrooms, onion and green pepper over medium heat until meat is no longer pink; drain.

Drain the pasta; add to the meat mixture. Stir in the tomatoes, sausage and garlic spaghetti sauce, salsa and pepperoni.

Divide half of pasta mixture between two greased 13-in. x 9-in. baking dishes. Sprinkle each with 1/4 cup Swiss cheese, 1 cup mozzarella cheese and 1/3 cup Parmesan cheese. Spread 3/4 cup of three-cheese spaghetti sauce over each. Top with the remaining pasta mixture and three-cheese spaghetti sauce. Sprinkle with the remaining cheeses.

Cover and freeze one casserole for up to 3 months. Cover and bake remaining casserole at 350° for 25 minutes. Uncover; bake 10 minutes longer or until cheese is melted. **YIELD:** 2 casseroles (6 servings each).

TO USE FROZEN CASSEROLE: Thaw in the refrigerator overnight. Remove from the refrigerator 30 minutes before baking. Cover and bake at 350° for 45 minutes. Uncover; bake 10 minutes longer or until cheese is melted.

Slow-Cooked Pork and Beans

PREP: 15 min. **COOK:** 6 hours

I like to get this dish started before leaving for work in the morning. When I get home, my supper's ready!
—_Patricia Hager, Nicholasville, Kentucky_

      1 **boneless whole pork loin roast (3 pounds)**
      1 **medium onion, sliced**
      3 **cans (15 ounces _each_) pork and beans**
1-1/2 **cups barbecue sauce**
   1/4 **cup packed brown sugar**
      1 **teaspoon garlic powder**

Cut roast in half; place in a 5-qt. slow cooker. Top with onion. Combine the beans, barbecue sauce, brown sugar and garlic powder; pour over meat. Cover and cook on low for 6 hours or until meat is tender.

Remove roast; shred with two forks. Return meat to slow cooker; heat through. **YIELD:** 12 servings.

Peanut Lover's Brownies

(_Pictured above right_)

PREP: 30 min. + cooling **BAKE:** 30 min. + chilling

Peanut butter lovers won't be able to eat just one of these delectable dessert squares. With a chocolate brownie layer, a graham cracker crust and peanut butter mousse, they're irresistible!
—_April Phillips, Lafayette, Indiana_

1/2 **cup butter, softened**
3/4 **cup all-purpose flour**
1/2 **cup graham cracker crumbs**
1/4 **cup sugar**
1/2 **cup salted peanuts, chopped**
BROWNIE LAYER:
   3/4 **cup butter, cubed**
      4 **squares (1 ounce _each_) unsweetened chocolate, chopped**
      4 **eggs**

      2 **cups sugar**
      2 **teaspoons vanilla extract**
      1 **cup all-purpose flour**
PEANUT CREAM TOPPING:
      1 **cup creamy peanut butter**
      1 **carton (12 ounces) frozen whipped topping, thawed**
    12 **miniature peanut butter cups, coarsely chopped**

Line a 13-in. x 9-in. baking pan with foil; grease the foil. In a small bowl, combine the butter, flour, cracker crumbs and sugar; press into prepared pan. Bake at 350° for 10-12 minutes or until set. Cool on a wire rack. Sprinkle peanuts over crust.

For the brownie layer, in a microwave, melt butter and chocolate; stir until smooth. In a bowl, combine the eggs, sugar, vanilla and chocolate mixture. Gradually add flour. Spread over crust. Bake for 30-40 minutes or until a toothpick inserted near the center comes out clean. Cool on a wire rack.

For topping, warm peanut butter for 30 seconds in a microwave. Gradually fold in whipped topping; spread over the brownies. Refrigerate for 1 hour. Sprinkle with chopped peanut butter cups. Using foil, lift brownies out of pan; remove foil. Cut into bars. Store in the refrigerator. **YIELD:** 2 dozen.

cup o' peanut butter

Here's an easy, nonstick way to measure peanut butter: If measuring 1 cup, fill a 2-cup measuring cup with 1 cup of cold water. Add enough peanut butter to raise the water level to the 2-cup mark, making sure the peanut butter is completely immersed. Then pour off all of the water.

Meanwhile, for the filling, in a large skillet, saute onion in 2 table-spoons butter until tender. Add ham and mix well; set aside.

Punch dough down. Turn onto a lightly floured surface; divide into thirds. Roll each portion into a 16-in. x 8-in. rectangle. Cut each rectangle into eight squares. Place a tablespoonful of ham mixture in the center of each square. Add the bacon, olives and/or cheese if desired. Fold up corners to center of dough; seal edges.

Place 2 in. apart on greased baking sheets. Cover and let rise in a warm place until doubled, about 45 minutes.

Melt the remaining butter; brush over dough. Bake at 350° for 16-20 minutes or until golden brown and filling is heated through. Refrigerate leftovers. **YIELD:** 2 dozen.

Dilly Zucchini Dip

(Pictured below)

PREP: 15 min. + chilling

This thick and chunky dip will keep your guests wanting more. When paired with colorful vegetables, it's an appetizer that is pleasing to the eye and the palate.

—*Edna Hoffman, Hebron, Indiana*

        1 cup finely shredded zucchini, squeezed dry
        1 cup (4 ounces) shredded sharp cheddar cheese
      3/4 cup mayonnaise
      1/2 cup chopped walnuts
        1 teaspoon lemon juice
      1/2 teaspoon dill weed
      1/4 teaspoon pepper
Assorted fresh vegetables

In a large bowl, combine the first seven ingredients. Cover and refrigerate for 1 hour or until chilled. Serve with vegetables. **YIELD:** 2 cups.

Ham Bundles

(Pictured above)

PREP: 55 min. + rising **BAKE:** 20 min.

Whenever I serve ham, I can't wait for the leftovers so I can make these ham buns. My husband often warms them up for breakfast, or you could bring them to your next potluck.

—*Chris Sendelbach, Henry, Illinois*

        1 package (1/4 ounce) active dry yeast
      1/4 cup warm water (110° to 115°)
      3/4 cup warm milk (110° to 115°)
      1/2 cup shortening
        3 eggs, lightly beaten
      1/2 cup sugar
    1-1/2 teaspoons salt
    4-1/2 to 4-3/4 cups all-purpose flour
FILLING:
        1 large onion, finely chopped
        5 tablespoons butter, *divided*
        4 cups cubed fully cooked ham, coarsely ground
        4 bacon strips, cooked and crumbled, optional
      1/4 to 1/3 cup sliced pimiento-stuffed olives, optional
      1/2 to 3/4 cup shredded cheddar cheese, optional

In a large bowl, dissolve the yeast in warm water. Add the milk, short-ening, eggs, sugar, salt and 2 cups flour; beat until smooth. Add enough remaining flour to form a soft dough.

Turn onto a lightly floured surface; knead until smooth and elastic, about 8 minutes. Place in a greased bowl, turning once to grease top. Cover and let rise in a warm place until doubled, about 1 hour.

Cranberry Gelatin Squares

(Pictured above)

PREP: 30 min. + chilling

This festive gelatin treat is full of cranberries, pineapple and pecans. It's a great recipe to serve on a holiday buffet table.
—*Lucile Cline, Wichita, Kansas*

  2 cans (8 ounces *each*) crushed pineapple
  2 packages (3 ounces *each*) strawberry gelatin
3/4 cup cold water
  1 can (16 ounces) jellied cranberry sauce
1/3 cup chopped pecans
  1 tablespoon butter
1/2 cup cold milk
1/2 cup heavy whipping cream
  1 package (3.4 ounces) instant vanilla pudding mix
  1 package (3 ounces) cream cheese, softened

Drain the pineapple, reserving juice in a 1-cup measuring cup. Add enough water to measure 1 cup. Set pineapple aside.

In a small saucepan over medium heat, bring the pineapple juice mixture to a boil. Remove from heat; stir in gelatin until dissolved. Stir in cold water; transfer to a bowl. Cover and refrigerate until partially set.

In a small bowl, combine cranberry sauce and reserved pineapple; stir into the gelatin mixture. Pour into a 9-in. square dish; cover and refrigerate until firm.

Place pecans and butter in a shallow baking pan. Bake at 350° for 8 minutes or until golden brown, stirring occasionally; cool.

In a small bowl, whisk milk, cream and pudding mix for 2 minutes. In a small bowl, beat cream cheese until smooth. Add the pudding mixture; beat on low speed just until combined. Spread over gelatin. Sprinkle with toasted pecans. Chill until firm. **YIELD:** 12 servings.

Corn Tortilla Chicken Lasagna

(Pictured below)

PREP: 40 min. **BAKE:** 35 min. + standing

This Southwest-style lasagna will satisfy a hungry crowd. It can be "stretched" with extra beans, and it's super-easy to put together. People love it!
—*Susan Seymar, Valatie, New York*

 36 corn tortillas (6 inches)
  6 cups cubed cooked chicken breast
  2 cans (one 28 ounces, one 16 ounces) kidney beans, rinsed and drained
  3 jars (16 ounces *each*) salsa
  3 cups (24 ounces) sour cream
  3 large green peppers, chopped
  3 cans (3.8 ounces *each*) sliced ripe olives, drained
  3 cups (12 ounces) shredded Monterey Jack cheese
  3 cups (12 ounces) shredded cheddar cheese

In each of two greased 13-in. x 9-in. baking dishes, arrange six tortillas. Top each with 1 cup chicken, 2/3 cup kidney beans, 1 cup salsa, 1/2 cup sour cream, 1/2 cup green pepper, about 1/3 cup olives, 1/2 cup Monterey Jack cheese and 1/2 cup cheddar cheese. Repeat layers twice.

Cover and bake at 350° for 25 minutes. Uncover; bake 10-15 minutes longer or until the cheese is melted. Let stand for 10 minutes before serving. **YIELD:** 2 casseroles (12 servings each).

Cran-Apple Crisp

(Pictured below)

PREP: 30 min. **BAKE:** 35 min. + cooling

An eggnog sauce gives this crunchy, oat-topped crisp a distinctive flavor. The apples and cranberries make it a natural for autumn celebrations and holiday get-togethers.

—Mary Lou Timpson, Colorado City, Arizona

- 2 snack-size cups (4 ounces *each*) vanilla pudding
- 1 cup eggnog
- 3/4 cup sugar
- 2 tablespoons all-purpose flour
- 5 cups thinly sliced peeled tart apples
- 2 cups fresh *or* frozen cranberries, thawed

TOPPING:
- 1 cup quick-cooking oats
- 3/4 cup packed brown sugar
- 2/3 cup all-purpose flour
- 1/2 teaspoon ground cinnamon
- 1/2 cup cold butter

In a small bowl, combine the pudding and eggnog until blended; cover and refrigerate until serving. In a large bowl, combine the sugar and flour. Add apples and cranberries; toss to coat. Transfer to an ungreased 13-in. x 9-in. baking dish.

For the topping, in a large bowl, combine the oats, brown sugar, flour and cinnamon; cut in butter until crumbly. Sprinkle over the fruit mixture.

Bake at 375° for 35-40 minutes or until filling is bubbly and the topping is golden brown. Cool for 10 minutes. Serve with eggnog sauce. **YIELD:** 12-14 servings.

EDITOR'S NOTE: This recipe was tested with commercially prepared eggnog.

Biscuit-Topped Lemon Chicken

(Pictured above)

PREP: 40 min. **BAKE:** 35 min.

This homey recipe combines two of my favorite things—hot, crusty biscuits and a flavorful lemon-pepper sauce. I've taken it to potlucks and given it as gifts.

—Pattie Ishee, Stringer, Mississippi

- 2 large onions, finely chopped
- 4 celery ribs, finely chopped
- 2 garlic cloves, minced
- 1 cup butter, cubed
- 8 green onions, thinly sliced
- 2/3 cup all-purpose flour
- 1/2 gallon milk
- 12 cups cubed cooked chicken
- 2 cans (10-3/4 ounces *each*) condensed cream of chicken soup, undiluted
- 1/2 cup lemon juice
- 2 tablespoons grated lemon peel
- 2 teaspoons pepper
- 1 teaspoon salt

CHEDDAR BISCUITS:
- 5 cups self-rising flour
- 2 cups milk
- 2 cups (8 ounces) shredded cheddar cheese
- 1/4 cup butter, melted

In a Dutch oven, saute the onions, celery and garlic in butter. Add green onions. Stir in flour until blended; gradually add milk. Bring to a boil; cook and stir for 2 minutes or until thickened.

Add the chicken, soup, lemon juice and peel, pepper and salt; heat through. Pour into two greased 13-in. x 9-in. baking dishes; set aside.

For the biscuits, in a large bowl, combine self-rising flour, milk, cheese and butter just until moistened. Turn onto a lightly floured surface; knead 8-10 times. Pat or roll out to 3/4-in. thickness. With a floured 2-1/2-in. biscuit cutter, cut out 30 biscuits.

Place over the chicken mixture. Bake, uncovered, at 350° for 35-40 minutes or until golden brown. **YIELD:** 15 servings (30 biscuits).

EDITOR'S NOTE: As a substitute for each cup of self-rising flour, place 1-1/2 teaspoons baking powder and 1/2 teaspoon salt in a measuring cup. Add all-purpose flour to measure 1 cup.

Buffalo Chicken Dip

(*Pictured below*)

PREP/TOTAL TIME: 30 min.

This is a great, no-fuss dip my family loves for holiday and Super Bowl parties. Everywhere I take it, people ask me for the tasty recipe.

—*Peggy Foster, Florence, Kentucky*

> 1 package (8 ounces) cream cheese, softened
> 1 can (10 ounces) chunk white chicken, drained
> 1/2 cup buffalo wing sauce
> 1/2 cup ranch salad dressing
> 2 cups (8 ounces) shredded Colby-Monterey Jack cheese

Tortilla chips

Spread cream cheese into an ungreased shallow 1-qt. baking dish. Layer with chicken, buffalo wing sauce and ranch dressing. Sprinkle with cheese.

Bake, uncovered, at 350° for 20-25 minutes or until cheese is melted. Serve warm with tortilla chips. **YIELD:** about 2 cups.

Cheddar Ham Strata

(*Pictured above*)

PREP: 20 min. + chilling **BAKE:** 1 hour + standing

I prepare this ham and egg dish on Christmas Eve and refrigerate it overnight. Then, while we open presents on Christmas morning, I pop it in the oven for breakfast. It's a family tradition.

—*Ann Pool, Jerome, Idaho*

> 10 slices day-old bread, crusts removed and cubed
> 1 medium onion, finely chopped
> 4 medium fresh mushrooms, finely chopped
> 1/4 cup butter, cubed
> 4 cups (16 ounces) shredded cheddar cheese
> 2 cups cubed fully cooked ham
> 2 tablespoons all-purpose flour
> 8 eggs
> 3 cups milk
> 2 tablespoons prepared mustard
> 1 teaspoon garlic powder
> 1/2 teaspoon salt

Place the bread cubes in a greased 13-in. x 9-in. baking dish. In a small skillet, saute onion and mushrooms in butter; spoon over bread. Sprinkle with cheese, ham and flour. In a large bowl, whisk the eggs, milk, mustard, garlic powder and salt. Pour over ham and cheese. Cover and refrigerate overnight.

Remove from the refrigerator 30 minutes before baking. Bake, uncovered, at 350° for 60-70 minutes or until a knife inserted near the center comes out clean. Let stand for 10 minutes before serving. **YIELD:** 12 servings.

Spiral Pepperoni Pizza Bake

(Pictured below)

PREP: 30 min. **BAKE:** 40 min.

My grandmother used to fix this yummy dish for my Girl Scout troop when I was growing up. Now, I make it for my stepdaughters' scout troop. It's easy to prepare, and the girls always beg me to make it.

—Kimberly Howland, Fremont, Michigan

  1 package (16 ounces) spiral pasta
  2 pounds ground beef
  1 large onion, chopped
  1 teaspoon salt
1/2 teaspoon pepper
  2 cans (15 ounces *each*) pizza sauce
1/2 teaspoon garlic salt
1/2 teaspoon Italian seasoning
  2 eggs
  2 cups milk
1/2 cup shredded Parmesan cheese
  4 cups (16 ounces) shredded part-skim
     mozzarella cheese
  1 package (3-1/2 ounces) sliced pepperoni

Cook pasta according to package directions. Meanwhile, in a Dutch oven, cook the beef, onion, salt and pepper over medium heat until meat is no longer pink; drain. Stir in the pizza sauce, garlic salt and Italian seasoning; remove from the heat and set aside.

In a small bowl, combine eggs, milk and Parmesan cheese. Drain pasta; toss with egg mixture. Transfer to a greased 3-qt. baking dish. Top with beef mixture, mozzarella cheese and pepperoni.

Cover and bake at 350° for 20 minutes. Uncover; bake 20-25 minutes longer or until golden brown. **YIELD:** 12 servings.

Sweet Pea Salad

(Pictured above)

PREP: 30 min. + chilling

This high-yield salad goes over well at potluck dinners. It combines vegetables with pasta, all in a sweet-and-sour dressing.

—Betty Otten, Tea, South Dakota

    5 pounds uncooked bow tie pasta
    1 pound carrots, shredded
    1 package (16 ounces) frozen peas, thawed
  10 celery ribs, diced
    1 small onion, finely chopped
    5 cups mayonnaise
    4 cups sweetened condensed milk
2-1/2 cups sugar
  3/4 cup cider vinegar
  3/4 cup buttermilk
    2 teaspoons salt
    1 teaspoon pepper

Cook pasta according to package directions; drain. In three large bowls, combine the pasta, carrots, peas, celery and onion. In a large bowl, combine the remaining ingredients. Stir a third of the dressing into each bowl of pasta mixture. Cover and refrigerate until chilled. **YIELD:** 58 servings.

Blue Cheese Deviled Eggs

PREP: 30 min. + chilling

I hope you'll agree that blue cheese and a hint of hot pepper in the filling puts these deviled eggs a step above the ordinary. Folks are delighted to find them on the buffet table.

—Nina Hall, Spokane, Washington

24 hard-cooked eggs
1 cup (4 ounces) crumbled blue cheese
2/3 cup mayonnaise
2 tablespoons minced fresh parsley
1 teaspoon hot pepper sauce
1/2 teaspoon celery seed
1/2 teaspoon pepper
Diced celery

Cut eggs in half lengthwise. Remove yolks; set whites aside. In a large bowl, mash yolks. Add the blue cheese, mayonnaise, parsley, hot pepper sauce, celery seed and pepper; stir until well blended. Stuff or pipe into egg whites. Refrigerate until serving. Sprinkle with celery. **YIELD:** 4 dozen.

Red Cream Soda Punch

(Pictured below)

PREP: 5 min. + chilling

The bright coral color and sweet citrusy flavor of this fizzy punch make it an instant hit with thirsty guests. Don't worry…there'll be plenty to go around!
—*Naomi Cross, Millwood, Kentucky*

4 quarts cold water
2 cans (12 ounces *each*) frozen orange juice concentrate, thawed
1 can (12 ounces) frozen lemonade concentrate, thawed
1/2 cup sugar
1 bottle (2 liters) red cream soda, chilled

In a large punch bowl or several pitchers, combine the water, concentrates and sugar; stir until the sugar is dissolved. Refrigerate for 2 hours or until chilled. Just before serving, stir in the cream soda. **YIELD:** about 7 quarts.

Apple Streusel Muffins

(Pictured above)

PREP: 20 min. **BAKE:** 15 min. + cooling

My husband and children enjoy these tender coffee cake-like muffins as a quick breakfast or snack on the run.
—*Dulcy Grace, Roaring Spring, Pennsylvania*

2 cups all-purpose flour
1 cup sugar
1 teaspoon baking powder
1/2 teaspoon baking soda
1/2 teaspoon salt
2 eggs
1/2 cup butter, melted
1-1/4 teaspoons vanilla extract
1-1/2 cups chopped peeled tart apples
STREUSEL TOPPING:
1/3 cup packed brown sugar
1 tablespoon all-purpose flour
1/8 teaspoon ground cinnamon
1 tablespoon cold butter
GLAZE:
1-1/2 cups confectioners' sugar
1 to 2 tablespoons milk
1 teaspoon butter, melted
1/4 teaspoon vanilla extract
1/8 teaspoon salt

In a bowl, combine the flour, sugar, baking powder, baking soda and salt. In another bowl, whisk the eggs, butter and vanilla; stir into dry ingredients just until moistened (batter will be stiff). Fold in apples.

Fill greased or paper-lined muffin cups three-fourths full. For the topping, combine the brown sugar, flour and cinnamon; cut in the butter until crumbly. Sprinkle over the batter.

Bake at 375° for 15-20 minutes or until a toothpick comes out clean. Cool for 5 minutes before removing from pan to a wire rack to cool completely. Combine glaze ingredients; drizzle over muffins. **YIELD:** 1 dozen.

Stir a small amount of hot mixture into egg yolks. Return all to the pan; cook and stir until mixture reaches 160° and coats the back of a metal spoon. Remove from the heat; stir in lemon juice and nutmeg.

Pour 3 cups sauce over the large casserole and remaining sauce over the small casserole; sprinkle with almonds. Bake, uncovered, at 375° for 20-25 minutes or until bubbly and heated through. **YIELD:** 12 servings.

Deluxe Breakfast Bake

(Pictured below)

PREP: 15 min. **BAKE:** 1 hour 5 min.

My husband and three sons love this rich and creamy egg bake because it is so filling. I like it because it's so versatile (you can alter the ingredients) and you can prepare it ahead of time.

—LaVonne Hegland, St. Michael, Minnesota

- 1 package (6 ounces) onion and garlic salad croutons
- 2 cups (8 ounces) shredded cheddar cheese
- 1-1/2 cups cubed fully cooked ham
- 4 eggs
- 2-3/4 cups milk, *divided*
- 3/4 teaspoon ground mustard
- 1 can (10-3/4 ounces) condensed cream of mushroom soup, undiluted
- 1 package (26 ounces) frozen shredded hash brown potatoes, thawed
- 1/2 teaspoon paprika
- 1/4 teaspoon pepper

Place croutons in a greased 3-qt. baking dish. Sprinkle with cheese and ham. In a large bowl, whisk eggs, 2-1/4 cups milk and mustard; pour over ham and cheese. Cover and refrigerate overnight.

Remove from the refrigerator 30 minutes before baking. Combine soup and remaining milk until blended; spread over casserole. Top with hash browns; sprinkle with paprika and pepper.

Cover and bake at 350° for 30 minutes. Uncover; bake 35-40 minutes longer or until edges are browned. Let stand for 10 minutes before serving. **YIELD:** 12 servings.

Broccoli Chicken Supreme

(Pictured above)

PREP: 30 min. **BAKE:** 20 min.

This saucy, comforting casserole will draw compliments when it's served at your next potluck dinner. You can also use the sauce over leftover meats, fish or vegetables.

—Vi Neiding, South Milwaukee, Wisconsin

- 6 cups fresh broccoli florets
- 3 cups sliced fresh mushrooms
- 1 tablespoon butter
- 6 cups cubed cooked chicken
- 3 cans (8 ounces *each*) sliced water chestnuts, drained

SUPREME SAUCE:
- 6 tablespoons butter, cubed
- 1/2 cup plus 1 tablespoon all-purpose flour
- 1-1/2 teaspoons seasoned salt
- 1/8 teaspoon pepper
- 3 cups chicken broth
- 1 cup heavy whipping cream
- 6 egg yolks, lightly beaten
- 3/4 teaspoon lemon juice
- 1/8 teaspoon ground nutmeg
- 3/4 cup slivered almonds, toasted

Place broccoli in a steamer basket; place in a large saucepan over 1 in. of water. Bring to a boil; cover and steam for 5-7 minutes or until crisp-tender. Meanwhile, in a large skillet, saute the mushrooms in butter until tender.

In a greased 13-in. x 9-in. baking dish, layer 4 cups chicken, two-thirds of the mushrooms, two cans of water chestnuts and 4 cups broccoli. In a greased 8-in. square baking dish, layer the remaining chicken, mushrooms, water chestnuts and broccoli.

In a large saucepan over medium heat, melt butter. Stir in the flour, seasoned salt and pepper until smooth. Gradually add the broth and cream. Bring to a boil; cook and stir for 2 minutes or until thickened and bubbly. Remove from the heat.

Salsa for a Crowd

(Pictured below)

PREP/TOTAL TIME: 30 min.

When planning your next fiesta, look no further than this hearty, pretty salsa. Succulently seasoned with coriander, cumin, garlic and cilantro, your crowd will definitely say, "Ole!"
—*Betsy Sams, Jamesville, New York*

  4 **cans (14-1/2 ounces *each*) diced tomatoes**
  4 **large tomatoes, chopped**
  2 **cups frozen corn, thawed**
  1 **can (15 ounces) black beans, rinsed and drained**
  1 **medium sweet onion, finely chopped**
1/3 **cup lime juice**
1/4 **cup minced fresh cilantro**
  2 **tablespoons cider vinegar**
  2 **tablespoons hot pepper sauce**
  1 **garlic clove, minced**
  1 **tablespoon coriander seeds, crushed**
  1 **tablespoon ground cumin**
  1 **teaspoon salt**
  1 **teaspoon coarsely ground pepper**
Chopped jalapeno pepper, optional
Corn chips *or* tortilla chips

Place two undrained cans of tomatoes in a large bowl; drain the two remaining cans and add tomatoes to the bowl.

Stir in the chopped fresh tomatoes, corn, beans, onion, lime juice, cilantro, vinegar, pepper sauce, garlic and seasonings. Stir in jalapeno if desired. Cover and refrigerate until serving. Serve with chips.
YIELD: 56 servings (1/4 cup each).

EDITOR'S NOTE: When cutting hot peppers, disposable gloves are recommended. Avoid touching your face.

Meatball Calzones

(Pictured above)

PREP: 1 hour 30 min. **BAKE:** 25 min.

My family can't get enough of this savory entree. We need to have it at least once a month, or everyone goes through withdrawal. Leftovers freeze well for a quick meal later.
—*Cori Cooper, Flagstaff, Arizona*

  3 **eggs, lightly beaten**
  1 **cup seasoned bread crumbs**
  1 **cup grated Parmesan cheese**
  3 **teaspoons Italian seasoning**
  2 **pounds ground beef**
  3 **loaves (1 pound *each*) frozen bread dough, thawed**
  3 **cups (12 ounces) shredded part-skim mozzarella cheese**
  1 **egg white, lightly beaten**
Additional Italian seasoning
  1 **jar (14 ounces) spaghetti sauce, warmed**

In a large bowl, combine the eggs, bread crumbs, Parmesan cheese and Italian seasoning. Crumble beef over mixture and mix well. Shape into 1-in. balls.

Place the meatballs on a rack in a shallow baking pan. Bake, uncovered, at 400° for 10-15 minutes or until no longer pink. Drain on paper towels. Reduce heat to 350°.

On a floured surface, roll each portion of dough into an 18-in. x 12-in. rectangle. Spoon a third of the meatballs and mozzarella cheese down the center of each rectangle. Fold dough over filling; press edges firmly to seal.

Place seam side down on greased baking sheets. Brush tops with egg white; sprinkle with Italian seasoning. Let stand for 15-30 minutes. Bake for 25-30 minutes or until golden brown. Serve with spaghetti sauce. **YIELD:** 3 calzones (4 servings each).

Love to cook but don't like leftovers?
You've come to the right spot! Each of the sensational
dishes featured here is just perfect for small households.

cooking for one or two

Stuffed Pork Tenderloin 233

Baked Garlic Green Beans 233

Mixed Fruit Shortcakes..233

Berry Banana Smoothies...234

Fruity French Toast 234

Bacon-Egg English Muffin 234

Valentine Cakes 236

Cheese-Stuffed Potatoes 236

Sweetheart Steaks 237

Honey-Mustard Chicken 238

Sweet Herbed Carrots 238

Almond-Lemon Pound Cake 238

Baked Bananas in Orange Sauce..................................241

Salisbury Steak 241

Tomato Rice Pilaf...241

Minty Ice Cream Shamrocks 242

Corned Beef Supper...242

Irish Soda Muffins..242

Grapefruit Lettuce Salad 245

Holiday Game Hens 245

Toffee Apple Crunch..245

PICTURED CLOCKWISE FROM UPPER LEFT: Fruity French Toast (page 234), Corned Beef Supper (page 242), Almond-Lemon Pound Cake (page 238) and Holiday Game Hens (page 245).

Stuffed Pork Tenderloin

(Pictured at left)

PREP: 20 min. **BAKE:** 50 min.

My grandmother often prepared this dish for Sunday dinner. She loved to cook and eat, especially when she had someone to share her food with.

—Mary Ann Marino, West Pittsburg, Pennsylvania

   1 pork tenderloin (3/4 to 1 pound)
1/2 cup chopped onion
   2 tablespoons butter
   1 cup soft bread crumbs
1/4 cup minced fresh parsley
1/4 teaspoon rubbed sage
1/4 teaspoon dried rosemary, crushed
1/4 teaspoon salt
1/8 teaspoon pepper
   1 egg, lightly beaten
   1 bacon strip

Make a lengthwise slit about three-fourths of the way through tenderloin; open tenderloin so it lies flat. Flatten to 1/4-in. thickness; set aside.

In a small skillet, saute onion in butter until tender. Add bread crumbs; saute until crumbs are golden brown. Remove from the heat. Stir in the parsley, sage, rosemary, salt, pepper and enough egg to moisten the ingredients.

Spread stuffing on one long side of tenderloin to within 1/4 in. of edges. Close meat and place bacon on top; tie with kitchen string. Place on a rack in a shallow roasting pan.

Bake, uncovered, at 350° for 50-60 minutes or until a meat thermometer reads 160°. Let stand for 5 minutes before slicing. **YIELD:** 2 servings.

Baked Garlic Green Beans

(Pictured at left)

PREP/TOTAL TIME: 20 min.

This flavorful dish dresses up frozen green beans with onion, cheese, bread crumbs and garlic. It's easy enough to serve any day of the week, yet special enough for fancy occasions.

—Marilyn Farmer, Centerville, Utah

    1 tablespoon olive oil
1-1/2 teaspoons cider vinegar
    1 teaspoon dried minced onion
    1 garlic clove, minced
  1/4 teaspoon salt
Dash pepper
1-1/2 cups frozen cut green beans, thawed
    1 tablespoon dry bread crumbs
    1 tablespoon grated Parmesan cheese
    1 teaspoon butter, melted

In a small bowl, combine oil, vinegar, onion, garlic, salt and pepper. Add beans; toss to coat. Transfer to a greased 3-cup baking dish.

Combine bread crumbs, Parmesan cheese and butter; sprinkle over beans. Bake, uncovered, at 350° for 10-15 minutes or until heated through. **YIELD:** 2 servings.

Mixed Fruit Shortcakes

(Pictured below)

PREP/TOTAL TIME: 30 min.

This delightful, downsized recipe makes just two biscuit-like shortcakes. Fill them with fresh fruit of your choice and top with whipped cream for an impressive dinner finale.

—Sue Ross, Casa Grande, Arizona

   1 cup mixed fresh berries
1/2 cup sliced fresh peaches *or* nectarines
   4 teaspoons sugar, *divided*
1/2 cup all-purpose flour
3/4 teaspoon baking powder
1/8 teaspoon salt
   2 tablespoons shortening
   3 tablespoons milk
Whipped cream

In a large bowl, combine berries, peaches and 2 teaspoons sugar; set aside. In another large bowl, combine flour, baking powder and salt; cut in shortening until mixture is crumbly. Stir in milk just until moistened. Drop by 1/3 cupfuls 2 in. apart onto an ungreased baking sheet. Flatten into 2-1/2-in. circles. Sprinkle with remaining sugar.

Bake at 425° for 10-12 minutes or until golden brown. Remove to a wire rack to cool. Split shortcakes in half horizontally. Spoon fruit onto bottoms; replace tops. Garnish with whipped cream. **YIELD:** 2 servings.

Berry Banana Smoothies

(Pictured at far right)

PREP/TOTAL TIME: 15 min.

My mother gave me this quick-to-fix, nutritious smoothie, which is thick, frothy and offers a refreshing fruit flavor. I fix it for breakfast or a bedtime snack.

—Linda Barker, Mohawk, Michigan

  1-1/2 cups vanilla *or* plain yogurt
    2/3 cup orange juice
     2 medium ripe bananas, cut into chunks
     1 cup halved fresh strawberries
     2 teaspoons honey

In a blender, combine all ingredients; cover and process until smooth. Pour into chilled glasses; serve immediately. **YIELD:** 2 servings.

Fruity French Toast

(Pictured at far right and on page 230)

PREP/TOTAL TIME: 15 min.

My son begged me to try making the stuffed French toast we enjoyed when our family visited Walt Disney World. His encouragement resulted in this easy, delicious breakfast that's a favorite on Saturday morning.

—Nancy Hawthorne, Gettysburg, Pennsylvania

    1 medium firm banana, sliced
    4 slices Texas toast
    2 teaspoons confectioners' sugar, *divided*
    2 large strawberries, sliced
    1 egg
  1/2 cup milk
  1/2 teaspoon vanilla extract
  1/4 teaspoon ground cinnamon
    2 teaspoons butter
Maple syrup

Place banana slices on two slices of toast. Sprinkle each with 1/2 teaspoon confectioners' sugar. Top with strawberries and remaining toast. In a shallow bowl, whisk the egg, milk, vanilla and cinnamon. Dip toast in egg mixture, coating both sides.

In a large skillet, melt the butter over medium heat; cook the toast for 2-4 minutes on each side or until golden brown. Sprinkle with the remaining confectioners' sugar. Serve with maple syrup. **YIELD:** 2 servings.

Bacon-Egg English Muffin

(Pictured above)

PREP/TOTAL TIME: 15 min.

I stack cheese, Canadian bacon and poached eggs on an English muffin to make an appealing entree. Perfect for one, this delicious open-face sandwich is special enough for guests, too.

—Terry Kuehn, Waunakee, Wisconsin

    2 eggs
    1 tablespoon cream cheese, softened
    1 English muffin, split and toasted
    2 slices process American cheese
    2 slices Canadian bacon

In a large skillet, saucepan or omelet pan with high sides, bring 2-3 in. water to a boil. Reduce heat; simmer gently. Break cold eggs, one at a time, into a custard cup or saucer. Holding the dish close to the surface of the water, slip eggs, one at a time, into the water. Cook, uncovered, until whites are completely set and yolks begin to thicken, about 3 minutes.

Meanwhile, spread cream cheese over muffin halves. Top with cheese slices; set aside. In a small skillet, cook Canadian bacon until heated through; place over cheese. Using a slotted spoon, place eggs over bacon. **YIELD:** 1-2 servings.

Bake at 350° for 15-20 minutes or until a toothpick inserted near center comes out clean. Cool for 10 minutes before removing from pan to a wire rack to cool completely.

For the frosting, in a small bowl, beat the confectioners' sugar, cocoa, milk, butter and vanilla until smooth; set aside. Transfer cake to a work surface. Using a 3- to 3-1/2-in. heart-shaped cookie cutter, gently cut out four heart-shaped cakes (set cake scraps aside for another use).

Place one heart on a serving plate; spread with some frosting. Top with a second cake; frost top and sides. Repeat with remaining cakes and frosting. Decorate with icing and candies. **YIELD:** 2 servings.

Valentine Cakes

(*Pictured above*)

PREP: 30 min. **BAKE:** 15 min. + cooling

These individual chocolate layer cakes are a sweet way to say "I love you" even when it's not Valentine's Day.

—Dixie Terry, Goreville, Illinois

  3/4 **cup all-purpose flour**
  1/4 **cup sugar**
  1/4 **cup packed brown sugar**
    3 **tablespoons baking cocoa**
  1/2 **teaspoon baking soda**
  1/8 **teaspoon salt**
  1/2 **cup water**
    3 **tablespoons canola oil**
  1/2 **teaspoon white vinegar**
  1/2 **teaspoon vanilla extract**
FROSTING:
  1-1/3 **cups confectioners' sugar**
    2 **tablespoons baking cocoa**
    2 **to 3 tablespoons milk**
    2 **tablespoons butter, melted**
  1/4 **teaspoon vanilla extract**
Decorating icing and confetti candies

In a large bowl, combine the first six ingredients. Add the water, oil, vinegar and vanilla. Coat an 8-in. square baking dish with cooking spray and dust with flour; add batter.

Cheese-Stuffed Potatoes

(*Pictured at right*)

PREP: 15 min. **BAKE:** 1 hour

Cottage cheese is the "secret" ingredient in this creamy side dish. I make myself two potatoes—one for dinner and one for lunch the next day.

—Janet English, Pittsburgh, Pennsylvania

  2 **medium baking potatoes**
  1 **small onion, finely chopped**
  2 **tablespoons water**
  1/2 **cup 4% cottage cheese**
  1/4 **cup buttermilk**
  3 **tablespoons grated Parmesan cheese**
Salt and pepper to taste
  2 **tablespoons thinly sliced green onions**

Bake potatoes at 400° for 1 hour or until tender. Cut a thin slice off the top of each potato and discard. Scoop out pulp, leaving a thin shell. In a small mixing bowl, mash pulp; set aside.

In a small skillet, cook and stir the onion in water for 2-3 minutes or until tender. Add the mashed potatoes, cottage cheese, buttermilk, Parmesan cheese, salt and pepper. Stir until blended and heated through. Spoon into potato shells. Sprinkle with green onions. **YIELD:** 2 servings.

simple substitute

Don't have the buttermilk called for in Cheese-Stuffed Potatoes? Don't worry! You can still serve up their comforting goodness tonight.

You can always substitute the buttermilk in this recipe with 1/4 cup of plain yogurt, but there are a few different substitutes for buttermilk you can mix up on your own.

For instance, mix 1 tablespoon of white vinegar or lemon juice with enough milk to measure 1 cup. Stir the mixture, then let it stand for 5 minutes before using. You could also mix 1-3/4 teaspoons cream of tartar into 1 cup of milk.

Sweetheart Steaks

(Pictured above)

PREP: 10 min. **COOK:** 50 min.

I created this recipe when I was planning a steak dinner and wanted a barbecue sauce to go with it. Try the sauce on pork and chicken, too.

—Dolores Jensen, Arnold, Missouri

- 3 tablespoons Catalina salad dressing
- 3 tablespoons honey
- 3 tablespoons apricot preserves
- 3 tablespoons grape jelly
- 2 tablespoons minced chives
- 2 tablespoons balsamic vinegar
- 2 tablespoons olive oil
- 2 tablespoons ketchup
- 1 tablespoon soy sauce
- 3 garlic cloves, minced
- 1 teaspoon ground mustard
- 1 teaspoon Worcestershire sauce
- 1/2 teaspoon salt
- 1/2 teaspoon crushed red pepper flakes
- 1/4 teaspoon pepper
- 2 beef tenderloin steaks (1-1/2 to 2 inches thick)

In a small saucepan, combine first 15 ingredients. Bring to a boil. Reduce heat; simmer, uncovered, for 30 minutes; stirring occasionally. Set aside 1/4 cup sauce for serving and keep warm.

Place steaks on a broiler pan; top with some of the remaining sauce. Broil 4-6 in. from the heat for 10-16 minutes on each side or until the meat reaches desired doneness (for medium-rare, a meat thermometer should read 145°; medium, 160°; well-done, 170°), basting occasionally with remaining sauce. Serve with reserved sauce. **YIELD:** 2 servings.

Honey-Mustard Chicken

(Pictured at far right)

PREP/TOTAL TIME: 30 min.

This entree combines my husband's love for mustard with my love for anything sweet, like honey.

—Lisa Varner, Greenville, South Carolina

- 1/4 **cup honey**
- 2 **tablespoons butter, melted**
- 2 **tablespoons Dijon mustard**
- 1 **tablespoon orange juice**
- 1/8 **teaspoon curry powder**
- 2 **boneless skinless chicken breast halves**
- 1 **tablespoon canola oil**
- 1/8 **teaspoon salt**
- 1/8 **teaspoon pepper**

Combine honey, butter, mustard, orange juice and curry powder. Spoon half of the mixture into a greased 8-in. baking dish.

In a skillet, brown chicken in oil. Sprinkle with salt and pepper. Place chicken over sauce in baking dish; turn to coat.

Bake, uncovered, at 350° for 15 minutes. Drizzle with remaining sauce. Bake 5-10 minutes longer or until a meat thermometer reads 170°. **YIELD:** 2 servings.

Sweet Herbed Carrots

(Pictured at far right)

PREP/TOTAL TIME: 25 min.

The original recipe, which my mother acquired over 45 years ago, called for two bunches of small carrots so I had to guess how much to use. I eventually got the recipe amounts worked out to my liking.

—Beverly Christofferson, Sioux City, Iowa

- 2 **tablespoons butter**
- 1/4 **teaspoon sugar**
- 2 **cups sliced fresh carrots**
- 3 **to 4 lettuce leaves**
- 2 **tablespoons water**
- 2 **tablespoons minced fresh parsley**
- 2 **tablespoons heavy whipping cream**
- 1 **tablespoon minced fresh tarragon**
  or 1 **teaspoon dried tarragon**
- 1/4 **teaspoon salt**
- 1/8 **teaspoon pepper**

In a large skillet, cook and stir the butter and sugar over medium heat until butter is melted and sugar is dissolved. Stir in carrots; cover with lettuce leaves. Sprinkle with water. Cover and simmer for 15-20 minutes or until carrots are crisp-tender.

Discard lettuce. Stir in the parsley, cream, tarragon, salt and pepper. Bring to a boil. Reduce heat; simmer, uncovered, for 1-2 minutes or until heated through. Serve with a slotted spoon. **YIELD:** 2 servings.

Almond-Lemon Pound Cake

(Pictured at right and on page 230)

PREP: 20 min. **BAKE:** 40 min. + cooling

This is the first cake I learned to bake more than 30 years ago, and it's still a favorite of mine. You can freeze any leftovers for another time.

—Michaela Rosenthal, Woodland Hills, California

- 1 **teaspoon plus 3/4 cup butter, softened,** *divided*
- 2 **teaspoons confectioners' sugar**
- 1 **cup slivered almonds**
- 1 **cup sugar**
- 2 **eggs**
- 1/3 **cup sour cream**
- 1 **tablespoon grated lemon peel**
- 1 **cup cake flour**
- 1 **teaspoon baking powder**
- 1/4 **cup lemon juice**

TOPPING:
- 1 **cup** *each* **frozen unsweetened raspberries, strawberries and blueberries**
- 1/4 **cup sugar**
- 2 **tablespoons lemon juice**
- 2 **tablespoons confectioners' sugar**

Grease the bottom and sides of 9-in. round baking pan with 1 teaspoon butter. Sprinkle with the confectioners' sugar; set aside. Place the almonds and sugar in blender or food processor. Cover; process until finely ground.

In a small bowl, cream remaining butter; beat in almond mixture until combined. Add eggs, one at a time, beating well after each addition. Stir in sour cream and lemon peel. Combine the flour and baking powder; add to creamed mixture alternately with lemon juice. Pour into prepared pan.

Bake at 350° for 40-45 minutes or until toothpick inserted near center comes out clean. Cool on wire rack for 10 minutes. Invert onto rack to cool completely.

For topping, in a heavy saucepan, combine the berries, sugar and lemon juice. Cook and stir over medium-low heat for 10 minutes or until mixture begins to thicken. Sprinkle cake with confectioners' sugar. Serve with berry topping. **YIELD:** 6 servings.

perfect pound cake

Making a terrific-tasting pound cake is easy if you follow some simple secrets.

First, bring all of the ingredients to room temperature. Cream butter until fluffy; gradually add sugar. Add eggs one at a time, beating 1 minute after each. Combine dry ingredients; add alternately with liquid in three stages. Do not overbeat.

    1 **egg**
1/4 **cup milk**
1/4 **cup dry bread crumbs**
    1 **envelope brown gravy mix,** *divided*
    1 **teaspoon dried minced onion**
1/2 **pound lean ground beef**
1/2 **cup water**
    1 **tablespoon prepared mustard**

In a large bowl, whisk egg and milk. Add bread crumbs, 1 tablespoon gravy mix and onion. Crumble beef over mixture and mix well. Shape into two patties, about 3/4 in. thick.

    Broil 3-4 in. from the heat for 6-7 minutes on each side or until meat is no longer pink and a meat thermometer reads 160°.

    Place the remaining gravy mix in a small saucepan; stir in the water and mustard. Bring to a boil; cook and stir until thickened. Serve with patties. **YIELD:** 2 servings.

Tomato Rice Pilaf

(Pictured at far left)

PREP/TOTAL TIME: 25 min.

Parsley, green onion and tomato add festive color to this mild rice dish. I serve the pilaf quite often with a variety of meats as a change of pace from potatoes.

—*Carole Fraser, North York, Ontario*

    2 **teaspoons butter**
1/2 **cup uncooked long grain rice**
    1 **small onion, sliced**
1-1/4 **cups chicken broth**
    2 **tablespoons chopped green onion**
    2 **tablespoons chopped tomato**
    2 **tablespoons minced fresh parsley**

In a 3-cup microwave-safe dish, melt butter. Stir in the rice and onion. Microwave, uncovered, on high for 2-3 minutes or until rice is lightly browned and onion is tender, stirring once. Add broth.

    Cover and cook on high for 13-15 minutes or until liquid is absorbed. Stir in the green onion, tomato and parsley. **YIELD:** 2 servings.

EDITOR'S NOTE: This recipe was tested in a 1,100-watt microwave.

Baked Bananas in Orange Sauce

(Pictured above)

PREP/TOTAL TIME: 30 min.

This simply luscious dessert is wonderful served with a scoop of vanilla ice cream. Plus, it looks pretty enough to serve for a special occasion.

—*Gusty Crum, Dover, Ohio*

    2 **medium firm bananas**
    2 **teaspoons butter, melted**
1/4 **cup orange juice**
    2 **tablespoons brown sugar**
    2 **teaspoons grated orange peel**
Vanilla ice cream

Cut each banana in half lengthwise; place cut side down in a greased 8-in. square baking dish. Brush with butter. Bake, uncovered, at 350° for 10 minutes.

    Combine the orange juice, brown sugar and orange peel; pour over bananas. Bake 10 minutes longer. Serve with ice cream. **YIELD:** 2 servings.

Salisbury Steak

(Pictured at left)

PREP/TOTAL TIME: 30 min.

Sometimes I forget about this favorite recipe, so my husband will say, "How about Salisbury Steak for dinner?" He really likes it.

—*Toni Martin, Byron Center, Michigan*

a timely tip

Tomato Rice Pilaf was tested with a 1,100-watt microwave. If your microwave wattage is lower than that, you can still prepare the pilaf using the time-saving device. Simply start with a cook time that is one-third longer than what is called for in the recipe, testing for doneness regularly.

Minty Ice Cream Shamrocks

(Pictured above)

PREP: 30 min. + chilling **BAKE:** 10 min. + freezing

With a soft, chewy chocolate cookie and festive mint green ice cream, these fun desserts are a sweet delight. Cut out the cookie wafers in any shape, and use any flavor ice cream you choose.

—*Beverly Coyde, Gasport, New York*

       6 **tablespoons butter, softened**
    3/4 **cup sugar**
       1 **egg**
  1-1/2 **teaspoons milk**
    3/4 **teaspoon vanilla extract**
  1-1/3 **cups all-purpose flour**
    1/4 **cup baking cocoa**
  1-1/4 **teaspoons baking powder**
    1/4 **teaspoon salt**
  1-1/2 **to 2 cups mint chocolate chip ice cream, softened**

In a small bowl, cream butter and sugar. Add egg, milk and vanilla; mix well. Combine flour, cocoa, baking powder and salt; gradually add to creamed mixture just until blended. Divide dough into two portions; flatten. Wrap in plastic wrap and refrigerate for 1 hour or until firm.

On a lightly floured surface, roll out the dough to 1/8- to 1/4-in. thickness. Cut with a floured 3-in. shamrock cookie cutter. Place 2 in. apart on parchment paper-lined baking sheets. Prick with a fork if desired.

Bake at 350° for 7-10 minutes or until set. Cool for 2 minutes before removing from pans to wire racks to cool completely.

Spread 1/4 to 1/3 cup ice cream over the bottom of six cookies; top with remaining cookies. Wrap individually in plastic wrap; freeze. May be frozen for up to 2 months. **YIELD:** 6 servings.

Corned Beef Supper

(Pictured at right and on page 230)

PREP: 25 min. **COOK:** 3 hours 50 min.

What better way to celebrate St. Patty's Day than with this one-pot meal? The beef, potatoes and carrots are full-flavored.

—*Dawn Fagerstrom, Warren, Minnesota*

       1 **small onion, sliced**
       4 **small carrots, cut into chunks**
       2 **medium potatoes, cut into chunks**
       1 **corned beef brisket with spice packet (1 pound)**
    1/3 **cup unsweetened apple juice**
       2 **whole cloves**
       1 **tablespoon brown sugar**
    1/2 **teaspoon grated orange peel**
    1/2 **teaspoon prepared mustard**
       2 **cabbage wedges**

Place onion in a 3-qt. slow cooker. Top with carrots, potatoes and brisket. Combine the apple juice, cloves, brown sugar, orange peel, mustard and contents of spice packet; pour over brisket. Cover and cook on high for 3-1/2 to 4 hours.

Add cabbage; cover and cook 20-30 minutes longer or until meat and vegetables are tender. Strain and discard the cloves; serve the pan juices with the corned beef and vegetables. **YIELD:** 2 servings.

Irish Soda Muffins

(Pictured at right)

PREP/TOTAL TIME: 30 min.

Who says muffins have to be boring? These little gems are always a hit. When blueberries are in season, I use them instead of raisins.

—*Camille Wisniewski, Jackson, New Jersey*

       1 **cup plus 2 tablespoons all-purpose flour**
    1/4 **cup plus 1 teaspoon sugar,** *divided*
       1 **teaspoon baking powder**
    1/4 **teaspoon baking soda**
    1/4 **teaspoon salt**
    1/2 **cup sour cream**
       2 **tablespoons canola oil**
       2 **tablespoons beaten egg**
    1/3 **cup raisins**

In a small bowl, combine the flour, 1/4 cup sugar, baking powder, baking soda and salt. In another bowl, whisk the sour cream, oil and egg; stir into dry ingredients just until moistened. Fold in raisins.

Fill six greased or paper-lined muffin cups half full. Sprinkle with remaining sugar. Bake at 400° for 15-18 minutes or until a toothpick comes out clean. Cool for 5 minutes before removing to a wire rack. Serve warm. **YIELD:** 6 muffins.

Grapefruit Lettuce Salad

(Pictured at left)

PREP/TOTAL TIME: 15 min.

A light vinaigrette flavored with cilantro and grapefruit juice drapes this tangy salad. You can make the dressing ahead because it keeps well in the refrigerator.

—Vivian Haen, Menomonee Falls, Wisconsin

2 tablespoons pink grapefruit juice
1 tablespoon olive oil
1-1/2 teaspoons red wine vinegar
1/2 teaspoon honey
1-1/2 teaspoons minced fresh cilantro
2 cups torn Bibb _or_ Boston lettuce
1 medium pink grapefruit, peeled and sectioned

In a small bowl, whisk the grapefruit juice, oil, vinegar and honey; stir in cilantro. In a salad bowl, toss lettuce and grapefruit. Drizzle with dressing; gently toss to coat. **YIELD:** 2 servings.

Holiday Game Hens

(Pictured at left and on page 230)

PREP: 40 min. **BAKE:** 40 min.

These golden brown birds are tender and juicy, and stuffed with a savory mixture of pork, apple and raisins. I've had this recipe for some time, and it always makes a great meal. The recipe is easy to double. Everyone feels special with a pretty bird adorning their plate.

—Delia Kennedy, Deer Park, Washington

2 Cornish game hens (20 ounces _each_)
1 medium lemon, cut in half
1/2 teaspoon salt
1/4 teaspoon pepper
1 bacon strip, diced
1/4 pound ground pork
1/2 cup finely chopped apple
1 tablespoon raisins
1 tablespoon chicken broth

Rub each Cornish hen inside and out with cut lemon. Sprinkle each cavity with salt and pepper; set aside. In a small skillet, cook the bacon over medium heat until crisp. Remove to paper towels; drain, reserving drippings.

In a saucepan, cook the pork over medium heat until no longer pink; drain. Stir in the apple, raisins, broth and bacon. Loosely stuff into hens; skewer openings and tie drumsticks together.

In the reserved drippings, brown hens on all sides. Place on a rack in a shallow roasting pan. Tuck wings under hens. Bake, uncovered, at 425° for 40-45 minutes or a meat thermometer reads 180°. **YIELD:** 2 servings.

Toffee Apple Crunch

(Pictured above)

PREP/TOTAL TIME: 15 min.

You'll be licking your lips after one bite of this crunchy combination of apple, toffee bits and pecans topping a cool scoop of vanilla ice cream.

—Ray Butler, Greenville, Texas

1 medium tart apple, peeled and cubed
1 tablespoon butter
1/8 teaspoon ground cinnamon
TOPPING:
2 tablespoons all-purpose flour
1 tablespoon brown sugar
1 tablespoon butter, softened
2 tablespoons finely chopped pecans
1 tablespoon English toffee bits _or_ almond brickle chips
Dash ground cinnamon
Vanilla ice cream

In a microwave-safe bowl, combine the apple, butter and cinnamon; cover and microwave on high for 2 minutes. Stir; cover and set aside.

In another microwave-safe bowl, combine flour and brown sugar. Stir in butter. Add the pecans, toffee bits and cinnamon. Microwave, uncovered, on high for 1-1/2 to 2 minutes, stirring twice. Spoon apple mixture over ice cream; sprinkle with topping. **YIELD:** 1 serving.

EDITOR'S NOTE: This recipe was tested in a 1,100-watt microwave.

Many delicious memories are shared by *Taste of Home* readers who fondly recall their mothers' cooking. Here are eight stories with tempting recipes so you can create these treasured meals.

mom's best meals

Cornish Game Hens Menu 248
Hens with Apricol Rice Stuffing • Bacon Squash Saute
• Orange and Red Onion Salad • Banana Cream Pie

Pork Tenderloin Dinner 252
Pork Tenderloin with Stuffing • Zuccini Apple Salad
• Parsnip Pancakes • Raspberry Squares

Delightful Holiday Celebration 256
Holiday Spiral Ham • Candied Carrots
• Corn Pudding • Pineapple Sour Cream Pie

Southern-Style Supper 260
Down-Home Chicken • Poached Corn
• Freezer Coleslaw • Gingerbread Boy Cookies

Fish Fry Feast 264
Mom's Fried Fish • Crunchy Floret Salad
• Parsley Red Potatoes • Mom's Apple Crisp

Cooking with a French Flair 268
Turkey with Mushrooms and Cream • Hazelnut Vegetable Salad
• Poppy Seed Torte • Yummy Yeast Rolls

Elegant Salmon Meal 272
Puff Pastry Salmon Bundles • Comforting Broccoli Casserole
• Strawberry Spinach Salad • Ice Cream Cookie Dessert

A Yuletide Menu 276
Roast Christmas Goose • Mixed Herb Salad Dressing
• Creamed Fresh Spinach • Apple Plum Streusel Dessert

PICTURED CLOCKWISE FROM UPPER LEFT: Pork Tenderloin with Stuffing (page 254), Freezer Coleslaw (page 263), Raspberry Squares (page 255) and Comforting Broccoli Casserole (page 274).

Her Italian mom's
made-from-scratch
dinners had mass
appeal and left
a legacy of love.

By Jodi Grable, Springfield, Missouri

Cooking for a crowd came naturally for my mom, Antoinette DeGear (above). She grew up in an Italian family in Iowa, the youngest of six kids. And she raised eight kids of her own. (I'm the youngest.)

With such a large family, huge gatherings were the norm. Mom loved to entertain, and we often had dinner parties for 30 people or more. Whether she was serving family or guests, she always set a beautiful table.

When I was a child, Mom was always cooking. My favorite days were when she was making homemade spaghetti sauce. I'd often eat a bowl of it like soup!

My mother has always cooked from scratch, and since she was a child of the Depression, she learned to be creative with garden produce and leftovers.

My favorite meal has to be her Hens with Apricot Rice Stuffing, Bacon Squash Saute, Orange and Red Onion Salad and Banana Cream Pie.

We all love apricots, so Mom tried to work them into any recipe she could, including her tender stuffed hens. The sweet apricots and sauteed mushrooms make the wild rice stuffing so moist and flavorful.

Bacon Squash Saute is a delicious way to use up home-grown squash and zucchini. And Mom's pretty onion salad is a pleasing mix of sweet and tangy.

Cream pies are my mom's specialty, and Banana Cream Pie, with sliced almonds on top, is the best. My late husband requested this pie often.

Mom still cooks every day, but now for fewer people (her children, grandchildren and great-grandchildren are scattered across the country). She and my stepfather live near me and my son, Kirsch. The four of us eat together on weekends.

For Mom's 75th birthday, I compiled a cookbook of her recipes and gave copies to her and my siblings. The cookbook wouldn't have been complete without these recipes.

PICTURED AT LEFT: Hens with Apricot Rice Stuffing, Bacon Squash Saute, Orange and Red Onion Salad and Banana Cream Pie (recipes are on the next page).

Bacon Squash Saute

(Pictured below)

PREP/TOTAL TIME: 20 min.

6 bacon strips, diced
2 small zucchini, cut into 1/4-inch slices
2 small yellow summer squash, cut into 1/4-inch slices
1 medium onion, thinly sliced

In a large skillet, cook bacon over medium heat until crisp; remove to paper towels. Drain, reserving 2 tablespoons of the drippings. In the drippings, saute the zucchini, yellow summer squash and onion for 6-8 minutes or until crisp-tender. Sprinkle with bacon. **YIELD:** 4 servings.

Orange and Red Onion Salad

(Pictured at right)

PREP/TOTAL TIME: 15 min.

4 cups torn romaine
2 medium navel oranges, peeled and sectioned
1 small red onion, sliced and separated into rings
1/4 cup olive oil
3 tablespoons red wine vinegar
1 teaspoon sugar
1/4 teaspoon salt
1/8 teaspoon pepper

Hens with Apricot Rice Stuffing

(Pictured above)

PREP: 25 min. **BAKE:** 2 hours

1 cup sliced fresh mushrooms
3/4 cup chopped pecans
1/2 cup chopped onion
6 tablespoons butter, *divided*
1 cup cooked wild rice
1/2 cup chopped dried apricots
1 tablespoon minced fresh parsley
1/2 teaspoon salt
1/4 teaspoon pepper
1/8 teaspoon cayenne pepper
4 Cornish game hens (20 ounces *each*)
1/2 cup apricot preserves
1 tablespoon white vinegar

In a large skillet, saute mushrooms, pecans and onion in 4 tablespoons butter until tender. Stir in rice, apricots, parsley, salt, pepper and cayenne.

Spoon about 3/4 cup of the rice mixture into each hen; tie legs together. Place hens, breast side up, on a rack in a shallow roasting pan. Melt the remaining butter; drizzle over hens.

Bake, uncovered, at 350° for 1-3/4 to 2 hours or until a meat thermometer reads 180° for hens and 165° for stuffing. In a small saucepan, warm preserves and vinegar; spoon over the hens. Bake 15 minutes longer. **YIELD:** 4 servings.

Remove from the heat. Gently stir in the butter and vanilla. Press the plastic wrap onto surface of custard; cover and refrigerate for 30 minutes.

Slice the bananas into pastry shell; pour custard over top. Spread with whipped cream; sprinkle with almonds. Chill for 6-8 hours or overnight. Refrigerate leftovers. **YIELD:** 6-8 servings.

banana basics

The more ripe a banana becomes, the sweeter it will taste. That's because the starch in bananas turns to sugar as the fruit ripens.

Green-tipped bananas are best for cooking, while yellow are great for salads, cereals or immediate eating. Fully ripe bananas with brown-speckled peels are perfect for baking in breads or mashing into fruit smoothies.

Cooler temperatures slow down the ripening process of bananas, while warmer temperatures speed it up. To make a banana ripen quickly, place it in a brown paper bag with either an apple or tomato and leave it overnight.

On a serving platter, arrange the romaine, oranges and onion. In a jar with a tight-fitting lid, combine the remaining ingredients; shake well. Drizzle over salad; serve immediately. **YIELD:** 4 servings.

Banana Cream Pie

(Pictured at right)

PREP: 10 min. **COOK:** 15 min. + chilling

- 1 **cup sugar**
- 1/4 **cup cornstarch**
- 1/2 **teaspoon salt**
- 3 **cups milk**
- 2 **eggs, lightly beaten**
- 3 **tablespoons butter**
- 1-1/2 **teaspoons vanilla extract**
- 2 **large firm bananas**
- 1 **pastry shell (9 inches), baked**
- 1 **cup heavy whipping cream, whipped**
- 1 **tablespoon sliced almonds, toasted**

In a large saucepan, combine the sugar, cornstarch, salt and milk until smooth. Cook and stir over medium-high heat until thickened and bubbly. Reduce heat; cook and stir 2 minutes longer. Remove from the heat. Stir a small amount of hot filling into eggs; return all to the pan. Bring to a gentle boil; cook and stir 2 minutes longer.

Stuffed pork roasts were the centerpiece of her mom's special Sunday noontime meals.

By Lois Frazee, Gardnerville, Nevada

I've spent part of my life teaching college-level nutrition classes and taste-testing for a federal research lab. But my fondest food-related memories center on my mother's kitchen.

My mom, Sarah Catterson (above), taught school for a short time before I was born. From then on, she was devoted, full-time, to taking care of her family—me, brother Donald and our dad, Frehn, who was a chemical engineer.

There weren't a lot of convenience foods back then, so Mom made everything from scratch. I liked to help her, and I learned to cook in the process.

On Sundays, our big meal was always at noon, and Mom often served a roast. Her best was Pork Tenderloin with Stuffing, Zucchini Apple Salad, Parsnip Pancakes and Raspberry Squares.

Pork Tenderloin with Stuffing was so special-looking that Mom served it for company, too. If you like, prepare it with her stuffing or use one of your own favorite recipes.

I think she came up with her refreshing Apple Zucchini Salad because the colors looked so pretty in a glass bowl.

Mom liked parsnips, so she sometimes substituted them in her potato pancake recipe to make Parsnip Pancakes. Parsnips, rutabaga and other root vegetables were plentiful in Winnipeg, Manitoba, where we lived at the time.

A friend gave Mom the recipe for Raspberry Squares. She'd make them when neighbors came to play bridge.

It was the Depression era, so Mom made the most of the food we had. She'd grind up leftover roast from Sunday dinner with gravy for sandwiches.

I inherited Mom's love of cooking and still enjoy preparing meals when my own children visit. I have two daughters, a son and five grandchildren.

I hope you'll share Mom's menu with your family and enjoy it as much as we have.

PICTURED AT LEFT: Pork Tenderloin with Stuffing, Zucchini Apple Salad, Parsnip Pancakes and Raspberry Squares (recipes are on the next page).

In a small skillet, saute the celery and onion in butter until tender. In a bowl, combine the bread cubes, celery mixture, salt and pepper; set aside.

Cut a lengthwise slit down the center of each tenderloin to within 1/2 in. of the bottom. Open tenderloins so they lie flat; cover with plastic wrap. Flatten to 1/2-in. thickness. In a large skillet, brown pork in oil on both sides over medium-high heat.

Spoon stuffing onto one tenderloin. Top with the second tenderloin; tie with kitchen string. Place on a rack in a shallow roasting pan.

Bake, uncovered, at 350° for 50-60 minutes or until a meat thermometer inserted into meat reads 160°. Let stand for 5 minutes before slicing. **YIELD:** 6 servings.

Zucchini Apple Salad

(Pictured below)

PREP/TOTAL TIME: 10 min.

> 2 medium red apples, chopped
> 2 small zucchini, chopped
> 1/2 cup coarsely chopped walnuts
> 2/3 cup Italian salad dressing

In a serving bowl, toss apples, zucchini, walnuts and salad dressing. **YIELD:** 6 servings.

Pork Tenderloin with Stuffing

(Pictured above and on page 246)

PREP: 20 min. **BAKE:** 50 min.

> 4 celery ribs, chopped
> 1 small onion, chopped
> 2 tablespoons butter
> 6 cups cubed day-old bread (1/2-inch cubes)
> 1/2 teaspoon salt
> 1/4 teaspoon pepper
> 2 pork tenderloins (1 pound *each*)
> 2 tablespoons canola oil

cooking with pork

Sealed, prepacked fresh cuts of pork can be refrigerated for 2 to 4 days. If you plan to keep it longer than this, wrap it well and store it in the freezer for up to 6 months. Thaw the pork overnight in the refrigerator before cooking.

Fresh pork cooks quickly and needs only to be cooked to an internal temperature of 160° and until the juices run clear. Boneless pork roasts may still be slightly pink in the center.

Unlike beef, cuts of pork have less variation in tenderness. Use dry-heat cooking methods, such as broiling, grilling, pan-broiling, roasting or stir-frying, when a firm texture is desired.

Raspberry Squares

(Pictured below and on page 246)

PREP: 20 min. + chilling **BAKE:** 10 min. + cooling

- 1 cup all-purpose flour
- 1/2 cup finely chopped pecans
- 1/4 cup packed brown sugar
- 1/2 cup butter, melted
- 2 packages (8 ounces *each*) cream cheese, softened
- 3/4 cup sugar
- 1 carton (8 ounces) frozen whipped topping, thawed
- 2 packages (3 ounces *each*) raspberry gelatin
- 2 cups boiling water
- 2 cups cold water

In a large bowl, combine the flour, pecans and brown sugar; stir in butter until crumbly. Press into an ungreased 13-in. x 9-in. x 2-in. baking dish. Bake at 350° for 10-13 minutes or until lightly browned. Cool on a wire rack.

In a large bowl, beat cream cheese and sugar until smooth; fold in whipped topping. Spread over the crust. Cover and refrigerate for 1 hour.

In a small bowl, dissolve gelatin in boiling water; stir in cold water. Spoon over cream cheese layer. Chill until firm. Cut into squares. **YIELD:** 12-16 servings.

Parsnip Pancakes

(Pictured above)

PREP/TOTAL TIME: 30 min.

- 2 pounds parsnips, peeled
- 1 teaspoon salt
- 1/2 cup chopped onion
- 1/4 cup all-purpose flour
- 1 egg, lightly beaten
- 1 tablespoon minced chives
- 2 to 4 tablespoons canola oil

Place the parsnips in a large saucepan and cover with water; add salt. Bring to a boil over medium-high heat. Reduce heat; cover and cook for 15-20 minutes or until tender.

Drain and place parsnips in a large bowl; mash. Stir in the onion, flour, egg and chives.

Heat 2 tablespoons of oil in a large nonstick skillet over medium heat. Drop the batter by 1/4 cupfuls into oil. Fry in batches until golden brown on both sides, using the remaining oil as needed. Drain on paper towels. **YIELD:** 6 servings.

Her mom's kitchen
was overflowing
with home-cooked,
delicious dishes for
family and friends.

By P. Lauren Fay-Neri, Syracuse, New York

It didn't matter if you were a relative, a neighbor or a friend. When you came to our house, my mother, Madeline Fay (above), would always ask, "Did you eat? Sit down and have a bite!"

If you didn't eat at our house, she'd send you home with a container of food. Mom liked to take care of everyone.

When my four brothers and I were growing up, the house was filled with tasty foods, from soups to desserts. We enjoyed Mom's great home-cooked meals as well as her delicious cookies and cakes. Everything was prepared from scratch; she never used packaged mixes.

One of our favorite meals featured beautiful Holiday Spiral Ham, Candied Carrots, Corn Pudding and Pineapple Sour Cream Pie for dessert.

Mom served the ham, with cranberry-apple relish and pineapple wedges, for holiday dinners. Although I preferred plain carrots to the Candied Carrots, everyone else enjoyed the sweet brown sugar glaze. Her Corn Pudding is delicious served warm. I also like the leftovers served cold.

Pineapple Sour Cream Pie is a refreshing alternative to traditional favorites like apple and pumpkin. Sometimes, instead of preparing meringue, I'll top the pie with fresh whipped cream. I make the pie a day ahead of time and add the whipped cream just before serving.

I'd call my mother a "natural" cook. She'd follow a recipe at first, but then substituted different ingredients. She memorized much of what she did.

I still have my mom's worn, wallpaper-covered cookbook. The envelopes inside are stuffed with recipes she gathered during her lifetime.

Because she didn't write down many of her own recipes, I don't often make a lot of Mom's dishes. But I think of her each night when I put together our meal. I hope you like this special menu.

PICTURED AT LEFT: Holiday Spiral Ham, Candied Carrots, Corn Pudding and Pineapple Sour Cream Pie (recipes are on the next page).

Candied Carrots

(Pictured below)

PREP/TOTAL TIME: 30 min.

2 pounds carrots, cut into sticks
1/4 cup butter
1/4 cup packed brown sugar
1/4 teaspoon salt
1/8 teaspoon white pepper

Place the carrots in a large saucepan; add 1 in. of water. Bring to a boil. Reduce heat; cover and simmer for 8-10 minutes or until crisp-tender. Drain and set aside.

In the same pan, combine butter, brown sugar, salt and pepper; cook and stir until butter is melted. Return carrots to the pan; cook and stir over medium heat for 5 minutes or until glazed. **YIELD:** 8 servings.

Corn Pudding

(Pictured at right)

PREP: 20 min. **BAKE:** 45 min.

1/2 cup butter, softened
1/2 cup sugar
2 eggs
1 cup (8 ounces) sour cream
1 package (8-1/2 ounces) corn bread/muffin mix
1/2 cup milk
1 can (15-1/4 ounces) whole kernel corn, drained
1 can (14-3/4 ounces) cream-style corn

Holiday Spiral Ham

(Pictured above)

PREP: 30 min. **BAKE:** 1-1/2 hours + standing

1 fully cooked spiral-sliced ham (8 pounds)
1 fresh pineapple, peeled, cored and cut into four wedges
1 package (12 ounces) fresh *or* frozen cranberries
3 medium apples, peeled and cubed
1-1/4 cups sugar
1 medium navel orange, peeled and cut into chunks
3 tablespoons lemon juice

Place ham on a rack in a shallow roasting pan. Arrange pineapple wedges around ham. Cover and bake at 325° for 1 to 1-1/2 hours.

Meanwhile, in a large saucepan, combine cranberries and apples. Cook over medium heat until the berries pop, about 15 minutes. Add the sugar, orange chunks and lemon juice. Cook and stir until sugar is dissolved. Remove from the heat.

Spoon half of the cranberry relish over ham. Bake 30 minutes longer or until a meat thermometer reads 140°. Let stand for 10 minutes before serving. Cut pineapple wedges into large chunks; serve with ham and remaining relish. **YIELD:** 12-16 servings.

Remove from the heat. Stir a small amount of hot filling into egg yolks; return all to the pan, stirring constantly. Bring to a gentle boil; cook and stir 2 minutes longer. Remove from the heat. Pour into pastry shell.

For the meringue, in a small bowl, beat the egg whites, vanilla and cream of tartar on medium speed until soft peaks form. Gradually beat in sugar, 1 tablespoon at a time, on high until stiff glossy peaks form and sugar is dissolved. Spread evenly over hot filling, sealing edges to crust.

Bake at 350° for 15-18 minutes or until meringue is golden brown. Cool on a wire rack for 1 hour. Refrigerate for at least 3 hours before serving. Refrigerate leftovers. **YIELD:** 8 servings.

quick ham hints

- Purchase ham that has a rosy pink color. Also, the meat should feel firm to the touch, not mushy, when pressed with your fingertips.
- Freezing deteriorates ham quality. But if you must freeze, wrap the ham tightly. It can be stored in the freezer for up to 2 months.
- If you're cooking more than one ham, make sure there is uniform space around the hams in the oven so they will cook evenly. They should not touch.
- Leftover cooked ham should be wrapped tightly and put in the refrigerator within 1 to 2 hours after cooking. Ham may be stored this way for up to 4 days.

In a large bowl, cream butter and sugar until light and fluffy. Add eggs, one at a time, beating well after each addition. Beat in sour cream. Gradually add muffin mix alternately with milk. Fold in both cans of corn.

Pour into a greased 3-qt. baking dish. Bake, uncovered, at 325° for 45-50 minutes or until set and lightly browned. **YIELD:** 8 servings.

Pineapple Sour Cream Pie

(Pictured at right)

PREP: 35 min. **BAKE:** 15 min. + chilling

- 1/2 cup sugar
- 2 tablespoons all-purpose flour
- 1 can (20 ounces) crushed pineapple, undrained
- 1 cup (8 ounces) sour cream
- 3 egg yolks, lightly beaten
- 1 pastry shell (9 inches), baked

MERINGUE:
- 3 egg whites
- 1/2 teaspoon vanilla extract
- 1/4 teaspoon cream of tartar
- 6 tablespoons sugar

In a large saucepan, combine the sugar and flour. Stir in pineapple and sour cream until combined. Cook and stir over medium-high heat until thickened and bubbly. Reduce the heat; cook and stir 2 minutes longer.

Poached Corn

(Pictured below)

PREP/TOTAL TIME: 20 min.

- 5 cups fresh *or* frozen corn
- 2 cups milk
- 4 teaspoons sugar
- 1 tablespoon butter
- 3/4 teaspoon salt
- 1/2 teaspoon pepper

In a large saucepan, combine all the ingredients. Cook over low heat

Down-Home Chicken

(Pictured above)

PREP: 30 min. **COOK:** 40 min.

- 1/2 cup all-purpose flour
- 1 teaspoon salt
- 1/2 teaspoon pepper
- 1 broiler/fryer chicken (3 to 4 pounds), cut up
- 1/4 cup canola oil
- **SAUCE:**
- 2/3 cup lemon juice
- 2/3 cup ketchup
- 2/3 cup molasses
- 1/3 cup canola oil
- 1/4 cup Worcestershire sauce
- 1 teaspoon ground cloves
- 1/2 teaspoon salt
- 1/4 teaspoon pepper
- **Hot cooked rice**

In a large resealable plastic bag, combine the flour, salt and pepper. Add chicken, a few pieces at a time, and shake to coat.

In a large skillet, heat oil. Brown chicken in oil on all sides; remove to paper towels. Drain drippings and return chicken to the pan.

For the sauce, combine the lemon juice, ketchup, molasses, oil, Worcestershire sauce, cloves, salt and pepper; pour over chicken. Bring to a boil. Reduce heat; simmer, uncovered, for 35-40 minutes or until chicken juices run clear. Serve with rice. **YIELD:** 6 servings.

sweet 'n' spicy cloves

Through the centuries, cloves have been used to freshen breath, relieve toothaches and even ward off the plague. Nowadays, many people rely on aromatic cloves to spice up ham, pumpkin pie or a hot holiday punch.

Cloves also flavor salad dressings, cookies, baked beans and chili as well as Indian, Chinese and German foods.

Whatever the dish, cloves add a fresh, sweet and spicy taste when used sparingly. Use too much and the pungent flavor can easily overpower a recipe.

Reach for ground cloves to prepare terrific Down-Home Chicken (recipe at left).

Gingerbread Boy Cookies

(Pictured below)

PREP: 1 hour + chilling **BAKE:** 10 min./batch

- 1/2 **cup butter, cubed**
- 1/2 **cup sugar**
- 1/2 **cup molasses**
- 2 **teaspoons white vinegar**
- 1 **egg, lightly beaten**
- 3 **cups all-purpose flour**
- 1/2 **teaspoon baking soda**
- 1/2 **teaspoon ground ginger**
- 1/2 **teaspoon ground cinnamon**
- 1/4 **teaspoon salt**

In a saucepan, combine the butter, sugar, molasses and vinegar; bring to a boil, stirring constantly. Remove from the heat; cool to lukewarm. Stir in egg. Combine the flour, baking soda, ginger, cinnamon and salt; stir into molasses mixture to form a soft dough.

Divide dough into thirds. Shape each portion into a disk; wrap in plastic wrap. Refrigerate for at least 2 hours or until easy to handle.

On a lightly floured surface, roll dough to 1/4-in. thickness. Cut with a floured 3-in. gingerbread boy cookie cutter. Place on greased baking sheets. Bake at 375° for 7-9 minutes or until edges are firm. Remove to wire racks. **YIELD:** 3-4 dozen.

Freezer Coleslaw

(Pictured above and on page 246)

PREP: 25 min. + freezing

- 1 **medium head cabbage (about 2 pounds), shredded**
- 1 **teaspoon salt**
- 2 **cups sugar**
- 1 **cup cider vinegar**
- 1/4 **cup water**
- 1 **teaspoon celery seed**
- 1 **teaspoon mustard seed**
- 1 **large carrot, shredded**
- 1/2 **cup finely chopped green pepper**

In a large bowl, combine cabbage and salt; let stand for 1 hour.

In a large saucepan, combine the sugar, vinegar, water, celery seed and mustard seed. Bring to a boil; boil for 1 minute. Remove from the heat; cool.

Add carrot, green pepper and vinegar mixture to the cabbage mixture; stir to combine. Transfer to large freezer bags; seal and freeze for up to 2 months.

Remove from the freezer 2 hours before serving. Serve with a slotted spoon. **YIELD:** 10 servings.

She's hooked on her mom's delicious family fish-fry menu served on Friday evenings at the lake.

By Julie Jahnke, Green Lake, Wisconsin

My mom, Margaret Peterson (above), from Bloomington, Minnesota, never has to fish for compliments when she cooks a meal...especially when we are away on vacation.

Every year, our family spends a week at a lake in northern Minnesota. We've been doing this for 16 years. With my brother and four sisters as well as all our spouses and children, there are now 14 of us.

We all enjoy fishing because my dad taught us when we were young. So the finale of the week is, appropriately, a fish fry. Dad used to say Mom's Fried Fish was the finest he'd ever tried. Sadly, he is no longer with us, but we share fond memories of Dad during our stay at the lake.

Once the fresh fish is cleaned, Mom dips it in an egg wash and rolls it in crushed crackers. My brother, Jim, cooks it outdoors in a deep fryer to a delicious golden brown.

Mom also prepares her tartar sauce and Parsley Red Potatoes. I help her by peeling and slicing the potatoes. The easy-to-prepare spuds cook up tender and buttery on top of the stove.

She makes Crunchy Floret Salad the night before so the creamy dressing marinates the vegetables. The pretty combination always gets raves.

Mom's Apple Crisp rounds out this satisfying meal. The aroma of baking apples and cinnamon always brings everyone to her cabin. We like this dessert best when served warm, topped with mounded clouds of whipped cream.

Family is so important to my mom. She did her best to have all eight of us at the dinner table every evening when we were growing up.

I'm in awe of how much my mom has done for us over the years. I've told her many times that if I can be half the mother she has been, I'll consider myself a success. I hope her fish-fry menu inspires you to gather your friends around the table as well.

PICTURED AT LEFT: Mom's Fried Fish, Crunchy Floret Salad, Parsley Red Potatoes and Mom's Apple Crisp (recipes are on the next page).

Crunchy Floret Salad

(Pictured below)

PREP/TOTAL TIME: 20 min.

- 3 cups fresh broccoli florets
- 1-1/2 cups fresh cauliflowerets
- 1/2 pound sliced bacon, cooked and crumbled
- 1 cup mayonnaise
- 2 to 3 tablespoons sugar
- 2 tablespoons cider vinegar
- 1/4 teaspoon salt
- 1-1/2 cups (6 ounces) shredded cheddar cheese

In a large bowl, combine the broccoli, cauliflower and bacon. In a small bowl, whisk the mayonnaise, sugar, vinegar and salt. Pour over salad and mix well. Cover and refrigerate until serving. Stir in the cheese. **YIELD:** 6-8 servings.

Mom's Fried Fish

(Pictured above)

PREP/TOTAL TIME: 30 min.

- 2 eggs, beaten
- 1-1/2 cups crushed saltines (about 45 crackers)
- 2 pounds whitefish fillets, cut in half lengthwise
- Oil for frying
- TARTAR SAUCE:
- 1 cup mayonnaise
- 2 tablespoons sweet pickle relish
- 1 tablespoon finely chopped onion

Place eggs and cracker crumbs in separate shallow bowls. Dip fillets into eggs, then coat with crumbs. Let stand for 5 minutes.

In an electric skillet or deep-fat fryer, heat oil to 375°. Fry fillets, a few at a time, for 2 minutes on each side or until fish is golden brown and flakes easily with a fork. Drain on paper towels.

In a small bowl, combine the tartar sauce ingredients. Serve with fish. **YIELD:** 6 servings.

In a large bowl, combine the apples, 1/4 cup sugar and 1 teaspoon cinnamon. Transfer to a greased 8-in. square baking dish.

In a small bowl, combine the flour, baking powder, salt and remaining sugar; cut in butter until crumbly. Sprinkle over apples, pressing down to smooth top.

Slowly pour the water over the top; sprinkle with the remaining cinnamon. Bake, uncovered, at 400° for 40-45 minutes or until the apples are tender. Serve warm. **YIELD:** 8 servings.

deep frying

To allow for bubbling up and splattering, the pot in which you deep fry should be filled no more than halfway with oil.

The temperature of the oil is important and can mean the difference between success and disaster. If the oil isn't hot enough, food will absorb it and become greasy; if it's too hot, the food will burn. The most accurate method of testing the temperature is with a deep-frying thermometer.

It's best to fry food in small batches. Large amounts of food will lower the oil temperature, which means it's more likely to soak into the food.

Parsley Red Potatoes

(Pictured above)

PREP/TOTAL TIME: 25 min.

> 2 pounds red potatoes
> 1-1/2 teaspoons salt
> 1/3 cup butter, cubed
> 2 tablespoons minced fresh parsley

Peel off a strip around each potato if desired. Place in a large saucepan; cover with water. Add salt. Bring to a boil; reduce heat. Cover and cook for 15 minutes or until tender; drain. Add butter and parsley; toss until butter is melted. **YIELD:** 6 servings.

Mom's Apple Crisp

(Pictured at right)

PREP: 25 min. **BAKE:** 40 min.

> 5 medium tart apples, peeled and sliced
> 1-1/4 cups sugar, *divided*
> 1-3/4 teaspoons ground cinnamon, *divided*
> 1 cup all-purpose flour
> 1 teaspoon baking powder
> 1/2 teaspoon salt
> 1/2 cup cold butter, cubed
> 1 cup water

Turkey with a French accent is the highlight of her mother's
best dinner menu...and gets the family reminiscing
about the memorable flavors of France.

By Emma Rea, Hermann, Missouri

My mom, Diana Rea (above), never learned to cook while growing up. Her mother wasn't much into cooking, so she didn't pass on a love for it to her daughters. But through many experiments, some flops and hard work, my mom has become a fantastic cook!

After getting married, she and my dad, Tom, moved to France as missionaries. During the 12 years they lived and worked there—and raised a family—my mother developed a real appreciation for good, wholesome food.

She learned to prepare so many mouthwatering dishes from scratch that it was difficult to choose one meal I consider her best. But Turkey with Mushrooms and Cream has to be one of the best authentic French dishes she makes.

The original turkey recipe, *Dinde a la Crème et Champignons,* uses white wine instead of apple juice, but either way, this main dish is absolutely scrumptious. Mom often serves it for Easter, Christmas and other celebrations.

As an accompaniment, crunchy Hazelnut Vegetable Salad can't be beat. Mom doesn't always add the asparagus spears, but I think the steamed spears make this colorful combination twice as good.

No one passes up Mom's golden brown Yummy Yeast Rolls, served warm with butter. To shape them, we cut them out of the rolled dough with a drinking glass, and they always turn out great.

Layered Poppy Seed Torte, featuring a sweet, nutty filling and creamy mocha frosting, makes an impressive finale for any occasion. It takes a little time to prepare, but everyone agrees that it's worth the effort!

While living in France, our family entertained almost weekly. Often on Sunday afternoons, we would have friends over for a five-course meal that lasted several hours. In true French style, Mom would serve an appetizer, salad, main dish, cheese and dessert...each as a separate course. Each course was accompanied by crusty baguettes from the bakery.

For birthdays, she'd serve a dish called *raclette.* It's a special melted cheese poured over potatoes, served with pickled baby onions and tiny dill pickles.

Mom's style hasn't changed much since we moved back to the United States in 2000. She still cooks and bakes from scratch for our family, which now numbers 10. I'm the oldest of eight children; we're home-schooled by Mom and Dad, who's the pastor of a local church.

Every other week, Mom goes to the grocery store, which is 45 minutes away. We grind our own flour, so she buys 50 to 100 pounds of wheat berries at a time. She also buys 25 pounds of pasta and popcorn. (We love popcorn...in France, you sprinkle sugar on it!) We plant a huge garden in the summer with about 60 tomato plants.

My three sisters and I have always helped Mom in the kitchen, so we have a lot of cooking experience. Sometimes we'll make lunch or dinner by ourselves to give her a break. My brothers dry the dishes, take out the garbage and lick the spoons! They leave the cooking to us.

I am about to start college in South Carolina, and one of the first things I plan to do is join the university's kitchen club so I can continue making my mom's fantastic recipes.

I'm sure you'll like them, too. *Bon appetit!*

PICTURED AT LEFT: Turkey with Mushrooms and Cream, Hazelnut Vegetable Salad, Poppy Seed Torte and Yummy Yeast Rolls (recipes are on the next page).

rolls like mom made

It's not difficult to treat your family to a batch of made-from-scratch, golden brown rolls like Yummy Yeast Rolls (recipe on page 271) for dinner. Want to know the keys to making successful yeast rolls? Follow these guidelines the next time you're in the kitchen:

• When mixing dough, always start with a minimum amount of flour until the dough reaches the desired consistency.

• Do not use light or whipped butter, diet spread or tub margarine in place of the butter, stick margarine (with at least 80% oil) or shortening that a recipe calls for.

• Knead dough only until it doesn't tear easily when stretched.

• Let dough rise in a warm (80° to 85°) draft-free area. Proper rising helps in the development of the texture.

Meanwhile, in another skillet, combine the remaining butter, water and bouillon; cook and stir over medium heat until the bouillon is dissolved. Add mushrooms; cook for 10 minutes or until liquid has evaporated. Serve the turkey over rice; top with cream sauce and mushrooms. **YIELD:** 4 servings.

Hazelnut Vegetable Salad

(Pictured below)

PREP/TOTAL TIME: 25 min.

- 1/4 cup olive oil
- 2 tablespoons lemon juice
- 2 teaspoons cider vinegar
- 2 teaspoons honey
- 1/4 teaspoon salt
- 1/4 teaspoon coarsely ground pepper
- 1/2 pound sliced fresh mushrooms
- 1/2 medium sweet red pepper, julienned
- 2 celery ribs, julienned
- 3 tablespoons minced chives
- 4 lettuce leaves
- 8 asparagus spears, cooked and drained
- 2 tablespoons chopped hazelnuts

For the dressing, in a small bowl, whisk the first six ingredients. In a large bowl, combine the mushrooms, red pepper, celery and chives. Drizzle with dressing and toss to coat. Refrigerate until serving.

Place the lettuce on salad plates; top with the asparagus and mushroom mixture. Sprinkle with hazelnuts. **YIELD:** 4 servings.

Turkey with Mushrooms and Cream

(Pictured above)

PREP/TOTAL TIME: 30 min.

- 1 package (17.6 ounces) turkey breast cutlets
- 1 tablespoon canola oil
- 3 tablespoons butter, *divided*
- 3/4 cup water, *divided*
- 1/4 cup unsweetened apple juice
- 2 teaspoons chicken bouillon granules, *divided*
- 1/4 teaspoon pepper
- 1 cup (8 ounces) sour cream
- 1 pound fresh mushrooms, chopped

Hot cooked rice

In a large skillet over medium-high heat, cook the turkey in oil and 2 tablespoons butter until golden brown and no pink remains; drain. Remove and keep warm.

In the same skillet, combine 1/2 cup water, apple juice, 1 teaspoon bouillon and pepper; cook and stir over medium heat until bouillon is dissolved. Stir in sour cream; heat through.

For the filling, in a heavy saucepan, combine the sugar, sour cream and egg yolks. Cook and stir over low heat just until mixture begins to simmer and reaches 160°. Remove from the heat; add nuts and vanilla. Transfer to a bowl; cover with plastic wrap and refrigerate until completely cooled.

For the frosting, in a small bowl, beat butter, confectioners' sugar and cocoa until blended. Add coffee, 1 tablespoon at a time, until mixture achieves spreading consistency.

Place one cake layer on serving plate; spread with filling. Top with second layer; spread with frosting. Store in the refrigerator. **YIELD:** 10-12 servings.

Yummy Yeast Rolls

(Pictured below)

PREP: 25 min. + rising **BAKE:** 15 min.

- 2 to 2-1/2 cups all-purpose flour
- 3 tablespoons sugar
- 1 package (1/4 ounce) quick-rise yeast
- 1/2 teaspoon salt
- 3/4 cup warm water (120° to 130°)
- 2 tablespoons butter, melted

In a large bowl, combine 1-1/2 cups flour, sugar, yeast and salt. Add water and butter; beat on medium speed for 3 minutes or until smooth. Stir in enough remaining flour to form a soft dough.

Turn onto a well floured surface; knead until smooth and elastic, about 4-6 minutes. Cover and let rest for 10 minutes. Roll dough to 3/8-in. thickness; cut with a lightly floured 2-1/2-in. biscuit cutter. Place 2 in. apart on a greased baking sheet. Cover and let rise in a warm place until doubled, about 30 minutes.

Bake at 375° for 11-14 minutes or until lightly browned. Remove to a wire rack. **YIELD:** about 1 dozen.

Poppy Seed Torte

(Pictured above)

PREP: 15 min. + standing **BAKE:** 15 min. + cooling

- 2/3 cup milk
- 1/2 cup poppy seeds
- 1/2 cup butter, softened
- 1 cup sugar
- 2 cups cake flour
- 2 teaspoons baking powder
- 1/4 teaspoon salt
- 3 egg whites

FILLING:
- 1 cup sugar
- 1 cup (8 ounces) sour cream
- 3 egg yolks
- 1 cup chopped walnuts
- 1 teaspoon vanilla extract

MOCHA FROSTING:
- 6 tablespoons butter, softened
- 3 cups confectioners' sugar
- 3 tablespoons baking cocoa
- 3 to 4 tablespoons hot strong brewed coffee

In a bowl, combine milk and poppy seeds; let stand for 1 hour. In a large bowl, cream butter and sugar. Combine flour, baking powder and salt; add to the creamed mixture alternately with the poppy seed mixture.

In another bowl with clean beaters, beat egg whites until soft peaks form; fold into batter. Pour into two greased and floured 9-in. round baking pans. Bake at 350° for 15-20 minutes or until a toothpick inserted near the center comes out clean. Cool for 10 minutes before removing from pans to wire racks.

Featuring an elegant seafood entree as the main course,
this special family-size spread delights everyone at weekly
gatherings around her mother's dinner table.

By Kimberly Laabs, Hartford, Wisconsin

It's a tradition at our house to have dinner together each Sunday. Even now that my brother, sister and I are adults, we still gather at my parents' home in Erin, Wisconsin for one of Mom's incredible meals. It's a special time that our family makes sure to reserve for each other, and we wouldn't have it any other way.

My mom, Sharon Laabs (above), has always made mealtime wonderful...and not just on Sundays. She puts plenty of thought, time and effort into each and every meal she prepares for family and friends.

She loves to entertain, especially at Christmas. When company is coming, Mom will spend the whole day in the kitchen. She'll serve a four-course meal with appetizers, soup or salad, main course and dessert. Everything has to be perfect...right down to the presentation. My mother's dining room table always looks beautiful with a tablecloth, centerpiece, candles and her good dishes.

When it's a celebration—a birthday, graduation, anniversary, etc.—the person who is special that day can put in a menu request with Mom. If it's someone in the family, he or she also gets to eat off the "red plate," which says "You Are Special Today." A few Christmases ago, Mom even gave each of us kids a red plate so we can carry on the tradition with our own families.

My mom's very best meal, I think, is the one my sister, Kristin, chose to have as her birthday dinner: Puff Pastry Salmon Bundles, Comforting Broccoli Casserole, Strawberry Spinach Salad and sweet Ice Cream Cookie Dessert.

The Puff Pastry Salmon Bundles make any menu elegant. The crisp pastry and delicious cucumber sauce are a wonderful combination, and the salmon almost melts in your mouth.

Her Comforting Broccoli Casserole is not only flavorful but nutritious, too. And the Strawberry Spinach Salad is a refreshing, colorful toss with a raspberry vinaigrette.

Our entire family loves dessert and can't wait to see what Mom has prepared as a finishing touch to a meal. Her yummy Ice Cream Cookie Dessert is a real favorite...even during cold winter months.

My mother grew up in Milwaukee and learned to cook from her mom, who was also a wonderful cook. She met my dad, Richard, when they were in the fourth grade! She was a stay-at-home mom when my sister, brother and I were young.

Mom now teaches fourth grade and is assistant principal at an area elementary school. Dad's an executive director of three Lutheran schools.

When Mom cooked for our family of five, she always made too much food—and she still does. Now that our family is larger, though, she can send food home with each of her children.

My sister, Kristin, who's an attorney, is married, as is my brother, Bryan, who's a CPA. He and his wife have a daughter, Calla—my mom's only grandchild. I teach kindergarten at the same school where my mom teaches. It's a privilege to work with her each day and to share her career.

Everyone in our family gets along extremely well. The guys like to golf or attend football games together, while we girls like spending the day at the mall or in the spa. Of course, each week we make a point of joining together for Sunday dinner.

Dinner begins with a prayer and then a big toast to my mom for another wonderful meal.

PICTURED AT LEFT: Puff Pastry Salmon Bundles, Comforting Broccoli Casserole, Strawberry Spinach Salad and Ice Cream Cookie Dessert (recipes are on the next page).

sweet on strawberries

Whether you're preparing the Strawberry Spinach Salad (recipe on page 275), a fresh fruit platter or a classic layered shortcake, strawberries will make your dish a winner. Those little red gems have a sweet, refreshing flavor that folks of all ages love.

Peak season for strawberries occurs in April, May and June. When you're purchasing them fresh, look for berries that are shiny, firm and very fragrant. The berry should be almost completely red, although some whiteness near the cap is acceptable.

Refrigerate unwashed strawberries with the cap on until you're ready to use them. Just before using, wash and hull the berries.

Comforting Broccoli Casserole

(Pictured below and on page 246)

PREP: 20 min. **BAKE:** 30 min.

2 eggs, lightly beaten
1 can (10-3/4 ounces) condensed cream of
   mushroom soup, undiluted
1 medium onion, chopped
1 cup (4 ounces) shredded cheddar cheese
1 cup (4 ounces) shredded Swiss cheese
1/2 cup mayonnaise
2 tablespoons butter, melted
1 package (16 ounces) frozen broccoli cuts, thawed
1 package (10 ounces) frozen chopped broccoli
   (about 3 cups), thawed
1/4 cup dry bread crumbs

In a large bowl, combine the first seven ingredients; fold in broccoli.
Transfer to a greased 1-1/2-qt. baking dish. Sprinkle with bread
crumbs. Cover and bake at 400° for 30-35 minutes or until heated
through. **YIELD:** 8 servings.

EDITOR'S NOTE: Reduced-fat or fat-free mayonnaise is not recommended for this recipe.

purchasing fish

When you need fresh fish fillets or steaks from the market, look for firm flesh that has a moist appearance. Don't
buy fish that appears dried out. Fresh fish should have
a mild, fresh-from-the-ocean smell, not a strong odor.

When purchasing frozen fish, look for packages that are
solidly frozen, tightly sealed and free of freezer burn
and odor.

Puff Pastry Salmon Bundles

(Pictured above)

PREP: 20 min. **BAKE:** 25 min.

2 packages (17.3 ounces *each*) frozen puff pastry,
   thawed
8 salmon fillets (6 ounces *each*), skin removed
1 egg
1 tablespoon water
2 cups shredded cucumber
1 cup (8 ounces) sour cream
1 cup mayonnaise
1 teaspoon dill weed
1/2 teaspoon salt

On a lightly floured surface, roll each puff pastry sheet into a 12-in.
x 10-in. rectangle. Cut each into two 10-in. x 6-in. rectangles. Place
a salmon fillet in the center of each rectangle.
   Beat egg and water; lightly brush over the pastry edges. Bring
opposite corners of pastry over each fillet; pinch seams to seal tightly.
Place seam side down in a greased 15-in. x 10-in. baking pan; brush
with remaining egg mixture.
   Bake at 400° for 25-30 minutes or until pastry is golden brown. In
a small bowl, combine the cucumber, sour cream, mayonnaise, dill
and salt. Serve with bundles. **YIELD:** 8 servings.

Ice Cream Cookie Dessert

(Pictured below)

PREP: 15 min. + freezing

- 1 package (18 ounces) cream-filled chocolate sandwich cookies, crushed, *divided*
- 1/4 cup butter, melted
- 1/2 gallon vanilla ice cream, softened
- 1 jar (16 ounces) hot fudge ice cream topping, warmed
- 1 carton (8 ounces) frozen whipped topping, thawed

In a bowl, combine 3-3/4 cups cookie crumbs and butter. Press into a greased 13-in. x 9-in. dish. Spread with ice cream; cover and freeze until set.

Drizzle fudge topping over ice cream; cover and freeze until set. Spread with whipped topping; sprinkle with remaining cookie crumbs. Cover and freeze for 2 hours or until firm. Remove from the freezer 10 minutes before serving. **YIELD:** 12 servings.

Strawberry Spinach Salad

(Pictured above)

PREP: 20 min. + chilling

- 1/3 cup raspberry vinaigrette
- 1/2 cup sugar
- 1 teaspoon salt
- 1/4 teaspoon prepared mustard
- 1/2 cup canola oil
- 4-1/2 teaspoons poppy seeds
- 1 package (10 ounces) fresh baby spinach
- 1 pint fresh strawberries, sliced
- 1/2 cup coarsely chopped pecans, toasted

In a blender, combine the vinaigrette, sugar, salt and mustard. Cover and process until smooth. While processing, gradually add oil in a steady stream. Stir in poppy seeds. Transfer to a small pitcher or bowl. Refrigerate for 1 hour or until chilled.

Just before serving, toss the spinach, strawberries and pecans in a large salad bowl. Serve with dressing. **YIELD:** 8 servings.

Her mom's German
heritage flavored many
memorable family
Christmas dinners
over the years.

By Rosemarie Forcum, White Stone, Virginia

Some of my happiest memories as a child involve holidays spent with family and wonderful foods.

Although my parents, Katherine (above) and Tobias Ress, met in New Jersey, they were both German immigrants. Some of their siblings also came to America and settled nearby...so our Christmas gatherings were large, with all the aunts, uncles and cousins. What feasts we had!

To me, the ultimate Yuletide menu included Roast Christmas Goose, greens with Mixed Herb Salad Dressing, Creamed Fresh Spinach and Apple Plum Streusel Dessert.

I'll never forget the wonderful aroma of my mother's Roast Christmas Goose, stuffed with apple, orange and lemon. She served this dish alongside flavorful Creamed Fresh Spinach and greens topped with Mixed Herb Salad Dressing.

The festive meal, which also included mashed potatoes and homemade rolls, would end with yummy Apple Plum Streusel Dessert, a coffee cake-like pastry drizzled with icing. Usually, we served it with fresh whipped cream or vanilla ice cream.

My sister and I loved watching our mother in the kitchen and learned how to cook from her. She always fixed wonderful meals for our family.

I inherited my love of cooking from my mom and aunts and still prepare many of Mom's recipes, mostly in winter, since German foods are rich and hearty. Family favorites include goulash, sauerbraten and Wiener schnitzel. At Christmas, Mom's roast goose is often on the menu.

Although it is difficult to get my own children and grandchildren together, when we are, good food like my mom's helps make it a happy and memorable occasion for all.

PICTURED AT LEFT: Roast Christmas Goose, Mixed Herb Salad Dressing, Creamed Fresh Spinach and Apple Plum Streusel Dessert (recipes are on the next page).

Sprinkle the goose cavity with salt and pepper. Place the apple, orange and lemon in the cavity. Place goose breast side up on a rack in a large shallow roasting pan. Prick skin well with a fork. Pour water into pan.

Bake, uncovered, at 350° for 2-1/4 to 3 hours or until a meat thermometer reads 185°. If necessary, drain the fat from the pan as it accumulates. Cover the goose with foil and let stand for 20 minutes before carving. Discard fruit. **YIELD:** 8 servings.

Mixed Herb Salad Dressing

(Pictured below)

PREP/TOTAL TIME: 5 min.

> 6 tablespoons white wine vinegar
> 6 tablespoons canola oil
> 2 tablespoons finely chopped onion
> 1 teaspoon salt
> 1/2 teaspoon *each* dried chives, chervil and tarragon
> 1/2 teaspoon dill weed
Assorted salad greens

In a small bowl, whisk the vinegar, oil, onion and seasonings until blended. Serve with salad greens. **YIELD:** 2/3 cup.

Roast Christmas Goose

(Pictured above)

PREP: 10 min. **BAKE:** 2-1/4 hours + standing

> 1 domestic goose (10 to 12 pounds)
Salt and pepper
> 1 medium apple, peeled and quartered
> 1 medium navel orange, peeled and quartered
> 1 medium lemon, peeled and quartered
> 1 cup hot water

duck, duck, goose

The demand is not high for ducks or geese at supermarkets, so they are usually kept in the frozen food cases. They are often available during the holiday season.

To store, place the frozen goose in a plastic bag to contain any leakage. At home, refrigerate the goose immediately and use within 1 or 2 days. A whole, completely frozen goose will take up to 2 days to thaw completely.

Apple Plum Streusel Dessert

(Pictured below)

PREP: 25 min. **BAKE:** 40 min

- 1/2 cup butter, softened
- 1/2 cup shortening
- 1-1/2 cups sugar
- 4 eggs
- 1 teaspoon almond extract
- 1 teaspoon vanilla extract
- 3 cups all-purpose flour
- 1/2 teaspoon baking powder
- 6 to 7 medium unpeeled plums, thinly sliced
- 5 to 6 medium unpeeled **Golden Delicious** apples, thinly sliced

STREUSEL TOPPING:
- 1/3 cup all-purpose flour
- 1/4 cup packed brown sugar
- 1/4 cup cold butter
- 1/4 cup chopped pecans

GLAZE:
- 1 cup confectioners' sugar
- 1 to 2 tablespoons milk

In a large bowl, cream butter, shortening and sugar. Beat in eggs and extracts until blended. Beat mixture on high speed for 3 minutes. Combine the flour and baking powder; gradually add to creamed mixture. Spread the batter into a greased 15-in. x 10-in. baking pan. Arrange plum and apple slices over batter.

For the streusel, combine the flour and brown sugar. Cut in the butter until the mixture resembles coarse crumbs; stir in pecans. Sprinkle over fruit.

Bake at 350° for 40-45 minutes or until lightly browned. Cool on a wire rack. For the glaze, whisk confectioners' sugar and milk until smooth. Drizzle over streusel. **YIELD:** 16-20 servings.

Creamed Fresh Spinach

(Pictured above)

PREP/TOTAL TIME: 20 min.

- 6 packages (6 ounces *each*) baby spinach
- 1/4 cup butter, cubed
- 1/4 cup all-purpose flour
- 1 cup heavy whipping cream
- 1 cup milk
- 2 tablespoons finely chopped onion

Salt and white pepper to taste

Wash and trim spinach, leaving the water that clings to the leaves. Place in a Dutch oven. Bring to a boil. Reduce heat and steam just until wilted, about 4 minutes. Drain and chop; set aside.

Melt butter in a large saucepan over medium heat. Whisk in the flour until smooth. Gradually add cream and milk. Bring to a boil; cook and stir for 2 minutes or until thickened. Stir in the onion, salt and pepper. Fold in spinach; heat through. **YIELD:** 8 servings.

Taste of Home field editors from across the country are thrilled to share their favorite meals with readers.

editor's meals

Christmas Morning Menu...282
   Christmas Breakfast Casserole • Triple-Cheese Broccoli
   Puff • Hot Curried Fruit • Cider Wassail • Apple-Raisin
   Bundt Cake

Easy and Cheesy Dinner...286
   Hot Cheddar-Mushroom Spread • Golden Squash Soup
   • Simple Sausage Lasagna • Broccoli with Mustard Sauce
   • Caramel-Pecan Cheesecake Pie

Meat-and-Potato Lovers' Meal..290
   Beef Brisket with Mop Sauce • Tossed Salad with Carrot
   Dressing • Grandma's Honey Muffins • Comforting Potato
   Casserole • Poppy Seed Cake

Sunny Lunch in Bloom..294
   Ham on Biscuits • Curried Carrot Soup • Chow Mein
   Chicken Salad • Creamy Lime Sherbet

Lovely Spring Feast of Lamb...298
   Crusty Roast Leg of Lamb • Springtime Asparagus Medley
   • Cracked Pepper Salad Dressing • Banana Citrus Sorbet
   • Strawberry-Banana Angel Torte

Savory Seafood Supper...302
   Chunky Crawfish Spread • Sunday Shrimp Pasta Bake
   • Olive-Cucumber Tossed Salad • Citrus Quencher
   • No-Bake Chocolate Pie

Crown Roast for Christmas..306
   Crown Roast of Pork • Wild Rice Pilaf • Cashew-Peach
   Sweet Potatoes • Devil's Food Caramel Torte

PICTURED CLOCKWISE FROM UPPER LEFT: Ham on Biscuits (page 296), Simple Sausage Lasagna (page 288), No-Bake Chocolate Pie (page 305) and Sunday Shrimp Pasta Bake (page 304).

Christmas Morning Menu

Holiday brunch is a highlight for one field editor and her family.

By Maryellen Hays, Wolcottville, Indiana

We always enjoy a flavorful buffet brunch after our morning church service on Christmas Day. It's so nice to have the family gathered around the table to celebrate this most beautiful of holidays.

Our simple but tasty menu has become an anticipated tradition. It includes Christmas Breakfast Casserole, Triple-Cheese Broccoli Puff, Hot Curried Fruit, Cider Wassail and Apple-Raisin Bundt Cake. This meal works so well for our schedule because much of the food can be prepared ahead of time.

'TWAS THE NIGHT BEFORE CHRISTMAS

Our celebration actually begins on Christmas Eve, when my husband, Ron, and I host a family gathering with a gift exchange and potluck dinner at our home on Big Long Lake, about 45 miles north of Fort Wayne, Indiana. My grandfather built the house we live in, and the property has been in my family since 1927.

During the festivities, we are joined by our daughters, Robin and Heather, and their families, which include grandchildren Anthony, Samantha and Colton and great-granddaughter Gabi. After brunch on Christmas Day, they all move on to celebrate with the other side of their families.

My Christmas Breakfast Casserole is a convenient choice for busy holiday mornings because it's assembled the day before. Light-textured and cheesy, this hearty dish looks and tastes delicious. The bacon in it balances nicely with the other flavors.

Puffy, golden and delicious, Triple-Cheese Broccoli Puff is a lovely side-dish souffle. If you add some diced ham or poultry to the ingredients inside, it easily becomes an entree. Hot Curried Fruit is a comforting, warm accompaniment that's so enjoyable in chilly weather. The recipe came from a cookbook I've had since my days at Indiana State University.

I received the Cider Wassail recipe from a dear friend in Fort Wayne, where we lived for many years. Since it's warm, wonderful and nonalcoholic, we've even served it at church.

It's also perfect for a holiday open house, which we host every other year.

Ron and I enjoy entertaining, whether it be for a few friends, the family or our congregation after church service. We just love the company of people surrounded by warm, comforting food.

I like to cook just about everything, but baking is my specialty. An old-fashioned holiday treat, Apple-Raisin Bundt Cake is very moist, pleasantly spicy and chock-full of raisins and nuts. If you can wait, this cake truly tastes better when baked several days in advance. The extra time allows the flavors to mellow.

A DOWN-HOME COOK

I've often said, "I'm a dump-and-pour cook. If you can't dump and pour it, I can't cook it." What I mean is that I'm not a gourmet cook at all. Plain old home cooking is my style. I use lots of fresh garden produce in season. On almost any road around here, you'll find a fresh-produce stand.

My earliest memories of cooking are from when I was about 4 years old. My wonderful grandmother, Fern Shannon, would lift me onto a kitchen stool that Grandpa made and show me how to make pancakes.

Ron is the family's expert on the grill. He likes to fire up salmon fillets and steaks as well as hamburgers and hot dogs. Now that we spend 2 months each winter in Green Valley, Arizona, he enjoys devoting even more time to outdoor cooking.

Ron retired from a 34-year teaching career in 1994, and I recently retired from my job working for an insurance company. These days, the two of us spend our spare time volunteering at a local county hospital. We also serve as house managers for the Fort Wayne Civic Theatre and are active in our church.

Sharing my favorite recipes as a *Taste of Home* field editor is a lot of fun. I was also thrilled when another *Taste of Home* cook contacted me after a story I wrote about a Mardi Gras party was published in a magazine issue.

It was fun to guide her through planning one of her own parties—from ordering the festive traditional beads to planning the menu.

The next time I fix this brunch, I'll be wondering if some of you readers might be preparing one or more of my recipes for your own celebration. I hope they please your family as much as they do mine.

> **PICTURED AT LEFT:** Christmas Breakfast Casserole, Three-Cheese Broccoli Puff, Hot Curried Fruit, Cider Wassail and Apple-Raisin Bundt Cake (recipes are on the next page).

Triple-Cheese Broccoli Puff

(Pictured below)

PREP: 15 min. **BAKE:** 50 min. + standing

- 1 cup sliced fresh mushrooms
- 1 tablespoon butter
- 1 package (3 ounces) cream cheese, softened
- 6 eggs
- 1 cup milk
- 3/4 cup biscuit/baking mix
- 3 cups frozen chopped broccoli, thawed
- 2 cups (8 ounces) shredded Monterey Jack cheese
- 1 cup (8 ounces) 4% cottage cheese
- 1/4 teaspoon salt

In a small skillet, saute mushrooms in butter until tender; set aside. In a large bowl, beat the cream cheese, eggs, milk and biscuit mix just until combined. Stir in broccoli, cheeses, salt and mushrooms.

Pour into a greased round 2-1/2-qt. baking dish. Bake, uncovered, at 350° for 50-60 minutes or until a knife inserted near the center comes out clean. Let stand for 10 minutes before serving. **YIELD:** 6-8 servings.

Christmas Breakfast Casserole

(Pictured above)

PREP: 10 min. + chilling **BAKE:** 50 min. + standing

- 7 slices white bread, crusts removed and cubed
- 2 cups (8 ounces) shredded cheddar cheese
- 6 eggs
- 3 cups milk
- 1 teaspoon ground mustard
- 1/2 teaspoon salt
- 1/4 teaspoon pepper
- 6 bacon strips, cooked and crumbled

In a greased 11-in. x 7-in. baking dish, combine the bread cubes and cheese. In a large bowl, whisk the eggs, milk, mustard, salt and pepper; pour over bread and cheese. Top with bacon. Cover and refrigerate overnight.

Remove from the refrigerator 30 minutes before baking. Bake, uncovered, at 350° for 50-55 minutes or until a knife inserted near the center comes out clean. Let stand 10 minutes before serving. **YIELD:** 6-8 servings.

Hot Curried Fruit

(Pictured above)

PREP: 10 min. **BAKE:** 35 min.

---

  1 can (20 ounces) unsweetened pineapple chunks
  1 can (16 ounces) pitted dark sweet cherries, drained
  1 can (15-1/4 ounces) pear halves, drained
  1 can (15-1/4 ounces) peach halves, drained
3/4 cup packed brown sugar
1/4 cup butter, melted
  1 teaspoon curry powder
  1 teaspoon ground cinnamon
1/2 teaspoon ground nutmeg

Drain the pineapple, reserving juice. In a greased 2-qt. baking dish, combine the pineapple, cherries, pears and peaches. Combine the brown sugar, butter, curry, cinnamon, nutmeg and reserved juice; pour over fruit.

Cover and bake at 350° for 35-45 minutes or until heated through. **YIELD:** 8 servings.

Cider Wassail

(Pictured on page 282)

PREP/TOTAL TIME: 30 min.

---

  2 quarts apple cider
1-1/2 cups orange juice
3/4 cup pineapple juice
  1 tablespoon brown sugar
1/2 teaspoon lemon juice
  2 cinnamon sticks (3 inches)
Dash ground cinnamon
Dash ground cloves

In a large saucepan, combine all of the ingredients. Bring to a boil. Reduce heat; cover and simmer for 20-30 minutes. Discard cinnamon sticks. Serve hot in mugs. **YIELD:** 10-12 servings (2-1/2 quarts).

Apple-Raisin Bundt Cake

(Pictured below)

PREP: 20 min. **BAKE:** 1 hour + cooling

3/4 cup butter, softened
1-1/2 cups sugar
  1 cup plus 2 tablespoons strawberry jam
3-1/3 cups all-purpose flour
1-1/2 teaspoons baking soda
1-1/2 teaspoons ground nutmeg
3/4 teaspoon _each_ ground allspice, cloves and cinnamon
1-1/2 cups buttermilk
1-3/4 cups raisins
3/4 cup chopped walnuts
3/4 cup chopped peeled apple
GLAZE:
  1 cup confectioners' sugar
  4 teaspoons milk

In a large bowl, cream butter and sugar until light and fluffy. Stir in jam. Combine the flour, baking soda and spices; add into creamed mixture alternately with buttermilk, beating well after each addition. Stir in the raisins, walnuts and apple. Pour into a greased and floured 10-in. fluted tube pan.

Bake at 350° for 1 hour or until a toothpick inserted near the center comes out clean. Cool for 10 minutes before removing from pan to a wire rack. Combine glaze ingredients; drizzle over cake. **YIELD:** 12-16 servings.

Easy and Cheesy Dinner

A few shortcuts don't compromise the rich, satisfying flavor of this editor's delightful dinner.

By Becky Ruff, Monona, Iowa

A resident of northeast Iowa for most of my life, I can't imagine living anywhere else. Many people think of Iowa's landscape as being flat, but in this corner of the state, it's actually very hilly, with scenic bluffs overlooking the mighty Mississippi River.

Although I love to cook home-cooked meals for my clan, I don't always have the time for long, drawn-out preparations. This lasagna menu is one meal that doesn't tie me up for hours and hours in the kitchen. Plus, it's applauded by everyone in my family.

My Hot Cheddar Mushroom Spread, Golden Squash Soup, Simple Sausage Lasagna, Broccoli with Mustard Sauce and Caramel-Pecan Cheesecake Pie are tasty and satisfying yet easy to fix.

A DELICIOUS FIVE-COURSE MEAL

Several years ago, I got together with a group of friends from high school for the weekend, and each of us brought our favorite appetizer to snack on. One of the women made Hot Cheddar Mushroom Spread, and we couldn't get enough of it. She happily shared the recipe for this rich and chunky treat, which I've made many times since for various family holiday get-togethers.

Golden Squash Soup made me change my tune about a wonderful autumn vegetable. My early memories of squash include sitting at the table when I was little while my mom tried to coax me into eating it. Even the addition of butter and brown sugar on top wouldn't do the trick.

I had never been a winter squash-eater until I found this recipe in a newspaper a number of years ago. It sounded interesting, so I tried it. The mellow flavor of the squash combined with the zippy taste of the onions and cheddar cheese made me a squash convert. I think this soup is especially good for fall and winter meals. If I'm in a particular hurry, I simply microwave the squash to speed up the cooking time.

Simple Sausage Lasagna is a dish I created after seeing a recipe in a church cookbook that did not call for pre-cooking the noodles. I have loved lasagna since I can remember, but the traditional preparation was too time-consuming after getting home from work.

Now, even when I do have some extra time on my hands, I still don't cook the noodles first for lasagna. My kids, Tony and Katrina, love this convenient version, and it makes a great dish for family get-togethers or anytime. So, my feeling is, why fix anything else?

Easy but not ordinary, my Broccoli with Mustard Sauce has a unique blend of flavors. Tony loves this sauce on a variety of vegetables, and the only trouble I've ever had with this recipe was not making enough.

An impressive dessert with a pretty layered look, Caramel-Pecan Cheesecake Pie is irresistible and perfect for special meals. I've taken it to potlucks, and I always leave with an empty pie plate. Use your favorite homemade pie crust if you wish. A ready-made frozen crust works well if time is short.

LOVE FOR COOKING STARTED YOUNG

When putting together a yummy dessert like this pie, I think back to when I was about 3 years old. Although just a small child, I would prepare "cakes" for my father to enjoy when he came home from work. They weren't cakes at all, but actually water mixed with every spice I could find in my mom's cupboard! Dad would always smack his lips at this concoction and praise my cooking abilities. To me, it was as if I had made a masterpiece.

As I got older, my parents let me continue experimenting with food and cooking in the kitchen. Ever since, I have retained my love for cooking. And I'm happy to say that my culinary skills have dramatically improved since then!

Besides making wonderful meals for my family, I also work in the dietary department at a residential care facility. I love to cook so much that I look for other food-related opportunities as well. I've helped neighbors and relatives prepare food for large parties. And I've even helped make and serve food for up to 200 people at several of my church's social functions.

The fall season brings tourists (leaf-lookers) to this part of the state to take in the spectacular autumn colors. It's also a time of year when a harvest of rich flavors—like those in this favorite meal of mine—are appreciated. Hope you'll give my recipes a try!

> **PICTURED AT LEFT:** Hot Cheddar-Mushroom Spread, Golden Squash Soup, Simple Sausage Lasagna, Broccoli with Mustard Sauce and Caramel-Pecan Cheesecake Pie (recipes are on the next page).

Hot Cheddar-Mushroom Spread

(Pictured above)

PREP/TOTAL TIME: 25 min.

2 cups mayonnaise
2 cups (8 ounces) shredded cheddar cheese
2/3 cup grated Parmesan cheese
4 cans (4-1/2 ounces *each*) sliced mushrooms, drained
1 envelope ranch salad dressing mix
Minced fresh parsley
Assorted crackers

In a large bowl, combine the mayonnaise, cheeses, mushrooms and dressing mix. Spread into a greased 9-in. pie plate.

Bake, uncovered, at 350° for 20-25 minutes or until cheese is melted. Sprinkle with parsley. Serve with crackers. **YIELD:** 3 cups.

EDITOR'S NOTE: Reduced-fat or fat-free mayonnaise is not recommended for this recipe.

Golden Squash Soup

(Pictured on page 286)

PREP/TOTAL TIME: 30 min.

5 medium leeks (white portion only), sliced
2 tablespoons butter
1-1/2 pounds butternut squash, peeled, seeded and cubed (about 4 cups)
4 cups chicken broth
1/4 teaspoon dried thyme
1/4 teaspoon pepper
1-3/4 cups shredded cheddar cheese
1/4 cup sour cream
2 tablespoons thinly sliced green onion

In a large saucepan, saute leeks in butter until tender. Stir in the squash, broth, thyme and pepper. Bring to a boil. Reduce heat; cover and simmer for 10-15 minutes or until squash is tender. Cool slightly.

In a blender, cover and process squash mixture in small batches until smooth; return to the pan. Bring to a boil. Reduce heat to low. Add cheese; stir until soup is heated through and cheese is melted. Garnish with sour cream and green onion. **YIELD:** 6 servings (about 2 quarts).

Simple Sausage Lasagna

(Pictured below and on page 280)

PREP: 20 min. **BAKE:** 55 min. + standing

1 pound bulk pork sausage
1 jar (26 ounces) spaghetti sauce
1/2 cup water
2 eggs, beaten
3 cups (24 ounces) 4% cottage cheese
1/3 cup grated Parmesan cheese
1 to 2 tablespoons dried parsley flakes
1/2 teaspoon *each* garlic powder, pepper, dried basil and oregano
9 uncooked lasagna noodles
3 cups (12 ounces) shredded part-skim mozzarella cheese

In a large skillet, cook the sausage over medium heat until no longer pink; drain. Stir in spaghetti sauce and water. Simmer, uncovered, for 10 minutes. Meanwhile, in a large bowl, combine eggs, cottage cheese, Parmesan cheese, parsley and seasonings.

Spread 1/2 cup meat sauce into a greased 13-in. x 9-in. x 2-in. baking dish. Layer with three noodles and a third of the cheese mixture, meat sauce and mozzarella cheese. Repeat layers twice.

Cover; bake at 375° for 45 minutes. Uncover; bake 10 minutes longer or until noodles are tender. Let stand for 15 minutes before serving. **YIELD:** 12 servings.

Caramel-Pecan Cheesecake Pie

(Pictured below)

PREP: 15 min. **BAKE:** 35 min. + chilling

- 1 package (8 ounces) cream cheese, softened
- 1/2 cup sugar
- 4 eggs
- 1 teaspoon vanilla extract
- 1 unbaked pastry shell (9 inches)
- 1-1/4 cups chopped pecans
- 1 cup caramel ice cream topping

In a small bowl, beat the cream cheese, sugar, 1 egg and vanilla until smooth. Spread into pastry shell; sprinkle with pecans.

In a small bowl, whisk the remaining eggs; gradually whisk in the caramel topping until blended. Pour over the pecans.

Bake at 375° for 35-40 minutes or until lightly browned (loosely cover with foil after 20 minutes if pie browns too quickly). Cool on a wire rack for 1 hour.

Refrigerate for 4 hours or overnight before slicing. Refrigerate leftovers. **YIELD:** 6-8 servings.

Broccoli with Mustard Sauce

(Pictured above)

PREP/TOTAL TIME: 25 min.

- 2 pounds fresh broccoli florets, cauliflowerets *or* sliced carrots
- 1/2 cup mayonnaise
- 1/3 cup milk
- 1/4 cup grated Parmesan cheese
- 1/4 cup shredded Swiss cheese
- 2 teaspoons lemon juice
- 2 teaspoons prepared mustard

Salt and pepper to taste

Place the broccoli in a steamer basket; place in a large saucepan over 1 in. of water. Bring to a boil; cover and steam for 5-8 minutes or until crisp-tender.

Meanwhile, in a small microwave-safe bowl, combine remaining ingredients. Cover and microwave at 50% power for 2 minutes or until heated through, stirring every 30 seconds. Drain broccoli. Serve with sauce. **YIELD:** 4 servings.

EDITOR'S NOTE: This recipe was tested in a 1,100-watt microwave.

Meat-and-Potato Lovers' Meal

North meets South in this field editor's dinner of tender brisket, tasty sides and a delightful dessert.

By Darlis Wilfer, West Bend, Wisconsin

For those who love to cook—and those who love to eat—I'm sharing a hearty meal that's great for a family gathering or a casual dinner party.

My popular menu features Beef Brisket with Mop Sauce, Comforting Potato Casserole, Tossed Salad with Carrot Dressing, Grandma's Honey Muffins and Poppy Seed Cake. As you will see, I'm not a gourmet cook...I just like to put a different twist on food that people enjoy.

THERE'S NO PLACE LIKE HOME

My husband, Chuck, and I have been married for over 50 years. He's a "meat-and-potatoes" guy, and I am fond of desserts. Three of our five children and their families live nearby, and we get together often for holidays and special occasions. I'm in my glory with a houseful of hungry folks to feed!

Before settling in Georgia, our son Mike and daughter-in-law Sharon lived in Texas. There, we discovered mop sauce. This delicious concoction is traditionally prepared in batches for Texas ranch-style barbecue. The slabs of beef are so large that the sauce is brushed on the meat with a mop!

Beef Brisket with Mop Sauce was quick to gain everyone's approval. "You can make this again, Mom!" they agreed. We just love the zesty flavor of the sauce and think you will, too.

Tossed Salad with Carrot Dressing always draws favorable comments. It tastes so fresh and is easy to mix up. We love going to the farmer's market on Saturdays in summer and fall to buy fresh produce. I like to dress up homegrown lettuce with cut veggies, chow mein noodles, dried cranberries and shredded cabbage.

Comforting Potato Casserole was a dish I first tasted at a wedding reception, and I asked the caterer for the recipe. I make these snazzy potatoes often, as do our daughters, who appreciate that the recipe can be made ahead.

I fondly remember my Grandma Wheeler making her honey muffins. We'd eat them fresh from the oven...nice and warm. Getting the correct measurements for her recipe was quite a challenge because she didn't have them written down.

She used "a pinch of this" and "a handful of that," and knew when there was enough flour because it "felt right."

Deciding which dessert recipe to add to my menu was difficult. I asked the family, and each person had a different suggestion. I chose old-fashioned Poppy Seed Cake. Tender and chock-full of poppy seeds, it has a yummy cream cheese frosting. I got the cake recipe from my longtime friend Mabel, who is of Finnish descent and bakes up a storm.

GENERATIONS OF GREAT COOKS

I'm from a German family in which the grandmothers and mothers took care to pass along cooking lore to their children. My mom, Lorraine, still remembers learning from her mom and grandmother. I'm now passing on those skills and heritage recipes to my children and grandchildren. I especially love to take an old recipe, tweak it to my liking and mix new with old. Usually, they're surprisingly compatible.

Browsing through cookbooks and *Taste of Home* magazines gives me plenty of new ideas. What a privilege it was to have been asked to be one of the magazine's first field editors, in 1993.

I often think of the *Taste of Home* "family" of cooks and the many smiles they have brought to our table year after year. When my family and friends enjoy my cooking, they are also complimenting the many fellow subscribers who have shared their recipes.

My wish is that this meal brings smiles and good eating to you and your family!

PICTURED AT LEFT: Beef Brisket with Mop Sauce, Tossed Salad with Carrot Dressing, Grandma's Honey Muffins, Comforting Potato Casserole and Poppy Seed Cake (recipes are on the next page).

---

about beef brisket

- Beef brisket comes from the breast section behind the foreshank. It's an inexpensive cut of meat that requires slow cooking in order to tenderize the tough tissue.
- When buying a fresh brisket, look for good marbling throughout the meat, not just in one portion. The meat should be a rich, deep color.
- A fresh brisket can be stored in the refrigerator for up to 5 days. If wrapped tightly, it can be frozen for 6 months.
- To give cooked brisket a more tender texture, cut it vertically across the grain into 1/4-in. slices.

Tossed Salad with Carrot Dressing

(Pictured below)

PREP/TOTAL TIME: 25 min.

- 3/4 cup red wine vinegar
- 1 cup sugar
- 2 celery ribs, cut into chunks
- 1 small onion, cut into chunks
- 1 small carrot, cut into chunks
- 1/2 teaspoon salt
- 3/4 cup canola oil

SALAD:

- 8 cups spring mix salad greens
- 2 medium tomatoes, cut into wedges
- 1 medium cucumber, sliced
- 2 green onions, sliced
- 1/2 cup chow mein noodles
- 1/2 cup shredded cheddar cheese
- 1/2 cup dried cranberries

In a blender, combine the first six ingredients; cover and process until smooth. While processing, gradually add oil in a steady stream. Transfer to a bowl or small pitcher; cover and refrigerate until serving.

For the salad, in a large bowl, combine the salad ingredients. Stir dressing and serve with salad. Refrigerate leftover dressing. **YIELD:** 10 servings (3 cups dressing).

Beef Brisket with Mop Sauce

(Pictured above)

PREP: 20 min. **BAKE:** 2 hours

- 1/2 cup water
- 1/4 cup cider vinegar
- 1/4 cup Worcestershire sauce
- 1/4 cup ketchup
- 1/4 cup dark corn syrup
- 2 tablespoons canola oil
- 2 tablespoons prepared mustard
- 1 fresh beef brisket (3 pounds)

In a large saucepan, combine the first seven ingredients. Bring to a boil, stirring constantly. Reduce heat; simmer for 5 minutes, stirring occasionally. Remove from the heat.

Place the brisket in a shallow roasting pan; pour sauce over the top. Cover and bake at 350° for 2 to 2-1/2 hours or until the meat is tender. Let stand for 5 minutes. Thinly slice meat across the grain. **YIELD:** 10-12 servings.

EDITOR'S NOTE: This is a fresh beef brisket, not corned beef.

In a large bowl, combine the soup, sour cream, cheese and onions; stir in potatoes; toss to coat.

Transfer to a greased 2-1/2-qt. baking dish. Bake, uncovered, at 350° for 1-1/2 hours or until potatoes are tender. **YIELD:** 10-12 servings.

Poppy Seed Cake

(Pictured below)

PREP: 20 min. + standing **BAKE:** 25 min. + cooling

- 1/3 cup poppy seeds
- 1 cup milk
- 4 egg whites
- 3/4 cup shortening
- 1-1/2 cups sugar
- 1 teaspoon vanilla extract
- 2 cups all-purpose flour
- 2 teaspoons baking powder

FROSTING:

- 1 package (8 ounces) cream cheese, softened
- 1/2 cup butter, softened
- 1 teaspoon vanilla extract
- 2 cups confectioners' sugar

In a small bowl, soak poppy seeds in milk for 30 minutes. Place egg whites in a large bowl; let stand at room temperature for 30 minutes.

In another large bowl, cream the shortening, sugar and vanilla. Combine the flour and baking powder; add to creamed mixture alternately with poppy seed mixture. Beat egg whites until soft peaks form; fold into batter.

Pour into a greased 13-in. x 9-in. baking dish. Bake at 375° for 25-30 minutes or until a toothpick inserted near the center comes out clean. Cool on a wire rack.

For frosting, in a small bowl, beat the cream cheese, butter and vanilla until smooth. Gradually beat in confectioners' sugar. Spread over cake. Store in the refrigerator. **YIELD:** 12-15 servings.

Grandma's Honey Muffins

(Pictured above)

PREP/TOTAL TIME: 30 min.

- 2 cups all-purpose flour
- 1/2 cup sugar
- 3 teaspoons baking powder
- 1/2 teaspoon salt
- 1 egg
- 1 cup milk
- 1/4 cup butter, melted
- 1/4 cup honey

In a bowl, combine flour, sugar, baking powder and salt. In another bowl, whisk the egg, milk, butter and honey; stir into dry ingredients just until moistened.

Fill greased or paper-lined muffin cups three-fourths full. Bake at 400° for 15-18 minutes or until a toothpick comes out clean. Remove from pan to a wire rack. Serve warm. **YIELD:** 1 dozen.

Comforting Potato Casserole

(Pictured on page 290)

PREP: 10 min. **BAKE:** 1-1/2 hours

- 2 cans (10-3/4 ounces *each*) condensed cream of mushroom soup, undiluted
- 2 cups (16 ounces) sour cream
- 2 cups (8 ounces) shredded part-skim mozzarella cheese
- 5 green onions, sliced
- 1 package (32 ounces) frozen Southern-style hash brown potatoes, thawed

Sunny Lunch in Bloom

Midday meals blossom thanks to a flowery, refreshing menu from this entertaining field editor.

By Betsy Hedeman, Timonium, Maryland

On a beautiful spring or summer afternoon, I love to host a luncheon on my screened porch. Good food and a casual, fresh-air atmosphere are always a treat—whether my group includes my husband, Bill, and me with friends or is a "just us girls" get-together.

On the menu are Curried Carrot Soup, hearty Ham on Biscuits, Chow Mein Chicken Salad and Creamy Lime Sherbet garnished with attractive Candied Flowers.

Curried Carrot Soup is full of flavor and has such a pretty color. The curry is pleasant but not overpowering, and thyme adds another dimension. It's a wonderful starter for our lunch or any menu.

"Remarkably good" is typical of what guests say about Chow Mein Chicken Salad. Crisp lettuce, chow mein noodles and toasted almonds and sesame seeds make it crunchy.

To save time the day of the meal, I prep the ingredients for the chicken salad the night before. A glass pint jar works great for shaking up the dressing.

BRINGING HOME BLUE RIBBONS

For many years, we had a large garden, and I canned pickles, preserves and more. With my creations, I've been fortunate enough to bring home many blue ribbons from the Maryland State Fair.

When State Fair officials asked me to be a food judge, I was delighted. I was still allowed to enter any category that I would not judge.

Other than fair prizes, I've won about 15 food contests—for candy, vegetables, salads and recipes that incorporate Maryland crabmeat. I've also won the Pillsbury Pie Contest twice—with my damson plum and cherry pie recipes.

For my luncheon, I like to serve Ham on Biscuits instead of the typical sandwiches. I use Smithfield Southern cured ham, but whatever kind you like will taste great on the tender homemade biscuits.

Creamy Lime Sherbet is wonderfully smooth and refreshing. While it's a winner all by itself, dressing up the servings with Candied Flowers makes a lovely and elegant finale for a luncheon menu.

My daughters and granddaughters were delighted by and eager to know more about the flowers. To coat the petals with the meringue powder mixture, I use a kid's new paintbrush.

And yes, if you follow the recipe (making sure to use edible flowers that have not been chemically treated), Candied Flowers are edible—delicate and delicious!

NOT "RETIRED" FROM COOKING

I've recently retired from judging and competing at fairs. And Bill and I have moved from our home of 30 years into a retirement community. But I say, once a cook, always a cook!

I quickly broke in the kitchen in our smaller quarters and got involved in soup parties, appetizer challenges and other food events here.

Whenever an issue of *Taste of Home* magazine arrives in the mailbox, I sit right down to read and digest the recipes. I'm still adding new ones to my bread box-size Plexiglas recipe file. I've always said, "If the house ever catches on fire, my recipe box is the first thing I would grab."

I've compiled some of my favorite recipes into a "Granny's Grub" cookbook for my granddaughters. I pulled this popular luncheon menu from my big box as well.

Candied Flowers

(Pictured on page 297)

PREP: 30 min. + standing

- **2 teaspoons meringue powder**
- **2 tablespoons water**
- **40 to 50 edible blossoms *or* flower petals of your choice, such as pansies, edible orchids or rose petals**
- **1-1/4 cups superfine sugar**

In a small bowl, dissolve the meringue powder in the water. Lightly brush over all sides of the flowers to coat completely. Sprinkle with the sugar. Let dry on a waxed paper-lined baking sheet for 1-2 days. Use as a garnish for dessert. **YIELD:** 40-50 candied flowers.

EDITOR'S NOTE: Meringue powder is available from Wilton Industries, Inc. Call 1-800/794-5866 or visit www.tasteofhome.com for a Web site link. Make sure to properly identify flowers before picking. Double-check that the flowers are edible and have not been treated with chemicals.

PICTURED AT LEFT: Ham on Biscuits (recipe is on the next page).

Lovely Spring Feast of Lamb

This creative editor loves to write about food— and to share the secrets of her best-loved recipes.

By Millie Vickery, Lena, Illinois

With all the treasured recipes I've collected over the years, it's impossible to narrow them down to one favorite meal. But this dinner of Crusty Roast Leg of Lamb, Springtime Asparagus Medley, Cracked Pepper Salad Dressing, Banana Citrus Sorbet and Strawberry-Banana Angel Torte is a wonderful way to celebrate the spring season.

These five recipes are among hundreds I've included in my "Cooking with Millie" newspaper column over the years and put together in a cookbook with that same title. I love to try new recipes and adjust them to my taste...to share good recipes with friends...and to entertain.

A FEAST FOR SPECIAL OCCASIONS

Crusty Roast Leg of Lamb is a delightful entree for Easter. It would also be perfect for St. Patrick's Day, since lamb is a traditional favorite of the Irish. With its golden herb crust, this roast makes a beautiful presentation surrounded by apple slices and potatoes on the serving platter.

I grow lots and lots of mint in my little garden and like to serve lamb with mint jelly or mint sauce on the side. Fresh mint also makes a great garnish for any lamb dish, along with pear or apricot halves and red grapes.

For over 50 years, I cooked with joy for my late husband, Eugene "Vic." Although I now live alone, I still love to have family and other guests for dinner. I like to be creative and have fun with food.

My mom, a wonderful cook, was always adding something to her mouthwatering menus for extra color and appeal. Her influence is evident in my eye-catching tossed salad, served with flavorful Cracked Pepper Salad Dressing. It is creamy, delicious and simple to mix up.

Often, I'll start a meal with a salad, then surprise guests with a sorbet refresher before the main course. Banana Citrus Sorbet is a recipe from my friend Adrianne St. George, who gave elegant parties.

A zippy sauce brings out the flavor of the vegetables in Springtime Asparagus Medley. Accented by blue cheese and crunchy almonds, this dish is delicious hot or cold.

When a recipe is easy but it looks like you fussed, it's definitely a keeper. Strawberry-Banana Angel Torte, with its luscious creamy filling and fresh fruit, is one of these desserts.

Of course, you can make the angel food cake from scratch if you have the time and the egg whites. But buying the cake or baking it from a mix gets you off to a quick start.

Over the years, I've won many awards in cooking contests and have given programs on garnishing techniques. I've won many writing awards, too. Currently, I'm typing my husband's last book on the computer. He wrote 10 books after retiring from his practice, including *House Calls: Life of a Country Doctor.* Vic also wrote poetry, including some fun poems about me and my cooking.

NEVER TOO BUSY TO COOK

My life changed dramatically after I lost him. Despite the fact I am often alone, I keep very busy. Recently, I sold the big Victorian home where we lived for decades and moved to an apartment. I still spend much of my time at our vacation home on nearby Apple Canyon Lake.

Whether here or there, you'll often find me in the kitchen, trying a new recipe or making an old favorite. I'm sure you and your family will enjoy the mouth-watering menu here!

PICTURED AT LEFT: Crusty Roast Leg of Lamb, Springtime Asparagus Medley, Cracked Pepper Salad Dressing, Banana Citrus Sorbet and Strawberry-Banana Angel Torte (recipes are on the next page).

---

roasting lamb

The leg of lamb you buy may have a thin, papery white membrane (the fell) covering it, which should be removed before roasting. Do this by cutting and creating a tab of fell to hold onto near the narrow end of the leg. Grab with a paper towel and pull, making sure to pull across, not up. Then trim the fat, which carries a strong flavor that can overpower the meat's delicate flavor. Leave just a few streaks of fat to provide moisture as the lamb cooks.

Place the lamb fat side up on the rack in a shallow roasting pan. Insert a meat thermometer into the thickest muscle, being careful not to let the thermometer rest on a bone or in fat.

Springtime Asparagus Medley

(Pictured below)

PREP/TOTAL TIME: 25 min.

- 1 cup water
- 1-1/2 pounds fresh asparagus, trimmed and cut into 2-inch pieces
- 2 small tomatoes, cut into wedges
- 3 tablespoons cider vinegar
- 3/4 teaspoon Worcestershire sauce
- 1/3 cup sugar
- 1 tablespoon grated onion
- 1/2 teaspoon salt
- 1/2 teaspoon paprika
- 1/3 cup canola oil
- 1/3 cup sliced almonds, toasted
- 1/3 cup crumbled blue cheese, optional

In a large saucepan, bring water to a boil. Add asparagus; cover and cook for 3-5 minutes or until crisp-tender. Drain. Add tomatoes; cover and keep warm.

In a blender, combine vinegar, Worcestershire sauce, sugar, onion, salt and paprika; cover and process until smooth. While processing, gradually add oil in a steady stream. Pour over asparagus mixture; toss to coat.

Transfer to a serving bowl; sprinkle with almonds and blue cheese if desired. Serve warm. **YIELD:** 8-10 servings.

Crusty Roast Leg of Lamb

(Pictured above)

PREP: 20 min. **BAKE:** 2 hours + standing

- 1 large onion, finely chopped
- 1 can (14-1/2 ounces) chicken broth
- 1 boneless leg of lamb (4 to 5 pounds)
- 1 cup soft bread crumbs (about 2 slices)
- 2 tablespoons butter, melted
- 1/2 teaspoon herbes de Provence
- Dash salt and pepper
- 2-1/2 pounds medium potatoes, peeled and cut into wedges
- 1 large tart apple, sliced

Place onion in the bottom of a roasting pan; pour broth over onion. Place leg of lamb on a rack in the roasting pan. Combine the bread crumbs, butter and seasonings; spread over meat. Bake, uncovered, at 325° for 1 hour.

Add the potatoes to the pan; bake 30 minutes longer. Add apple; bake 30 minutes longer or until potatoes are tender and meat reaches desired doneness (for medium-rare, a meat thermometer should read 145°; medium, 160°; well-done, 170°).

Remove the vegetables and apple slices and keep warm. Let roast stand for 10-15 minutes before slicing. **YIELD:** 10 servings.

EDITOR'S NOTE: Look for herbes de Provence in the spice aisle. It is also available from Penzeys Spices. Call 1-800/741-7787 or visit www.penzeys.com.

Place lemon juice and bananas in blender; cover and process until smooth. Add sugar; cover and process until blended. Transfer to a large bowl; stir in water and orange juice.

Fill cylinder of ice cream maker two-thirds full; freeze according to manufacturer's directions. Refrigerate remaining mixture until ready to use. Transfer to a freezer container; freeze for 2-4 hours before serving. May be frozen for up to 1 month. **YIELD:** 2-1/2 quarts.

Strawberry-Banana Angel Torte

(Pictured below)

PREP/TOTAL TIME: 20 min.

  1 **prepared angel food cake (8 inches)**
1/2 **cup sour cream**
1/4 **cup sugar**
1/4 **cup pureed fresh strawberries**
3/4 **cup sliced ripe bananas**
1/2 **cup sliced fresh strawberries**
  1 **cup heavy whipping cream, whipped**
Halved fresh strawberries

Split cake horizontally into three layers; place bottom layer on a serving plate. In a large bowl, combine sour cream, sugar and pureed strawberries; fold in the bananas and sliced strawberries. Fold in the whipped cream.

Spread a third of the filling between each layer; spread remaining filling over top. Cover and refrigerate until serving. Garnish with halved strawberries. **YIELD:** 8-10 servings.

Cracked Pepper Salad Dressing

(Pictured above)

PREP: 15 min. + chilling

  2 **cups mayonnaise**
1/4 **cup water**
1/4 **cup milk**
1/4 **cup buttermilk**
  2 **tablespoons grated Parmesan cheese**
  1 **tablespoon coarsely ground pepper**
  2 **teaspoons finely chopped green onion**
  1 **teaspoon lemon juice**
1/2 **teaspoon garlic salt**
1/2 **teaspoon garlic powder**

In a small bowl, whisk all ingredients until blended. Cover and chill for at least 1 hour. May be stored in the refrigerator for up to 2 weeks. **YIELD:** 2-1/2 cups.

Banana Citrus Sorbet

(Pictured on page 298)

PREP: 10 min. + freezing

1/2 **cup lemon juice**
  3 **medium ripe bananas, cut into chunks**
1-1/2 **cups sugar**
  2 **cups cold water**
1-1/2 **cups orange juice**

Savory Seafood Supper

One of our field editors cooks up a fresh menu that's everyday-simple but company-special.

By Sundra Hauck, Bogalusa, Louisiana

When Thanksgiving, Christmas and New Year's are behind us for yet another year, my husband, Ron, and I are happy for the change of pace.

Although we truly enjoy the rich, traditional food during the holidays, we welcome the basic, simple foods that are the signature "taste of our home."

We've entertained and been entertained plenty, and now we really enjoy just sitting down together for a simple but delicious meal. One of our favorites is this one, featuring Chunky Crawfish Spread, Citrus Quencher, Sunday Shrimp Pasta Bake, Olive-Cucumber Tossed Salad and No-Bake Chocolate Pie.

A SIMPLE MEAL FROM THE BAYOU

Crawfish are my favorite. With Creole seasoning, Chunky Crawfish Spread (pictured on page 304) is just the right touch for conversation and snacking while the main course is finishing up in the oven.

Complementing the rest of the meal with its sweet-tart taste, my sparkling Citrus Quencher is truly refreshing and welcome on hot days. It's so easy to mix up that I serve this sunny beverage year-round.

The Sunday Shrimp Pasta Bake isn't just for Sunday, but it is that good. This delicious dish also serves us well on a Saturday night before a big football game or even during the week, if time allows.

Seafood is plentiful here, so we enjoy it often. Shrimp (or "shrimps," as my 101-year-old mother-in-law, Bertha, calls them) are Ron's favorite.

We often enjoy shrimp and crawfish at the same meal. But if not, I make sure to rotate the two.

The Olive-Cucumber Tossed Salad can be prepped ahead of time and plated up at the last minute. I combine the dressing with the olives and sliced cucumbers in advance. Just before serving, I place the mixture on top of salad greens.

Sometimes dessert has to be served a bit later, as this is a filling meal. But when you bring out the No-Bake Chocolate Pie, no one will turn it down. It's a winner on any occasion.

PICTURED AT LEFT: Sunday Shrimp Pasta Bake, Olive-Cucumber Tossed Salad, Citrus Quencher and No-Bake Chocolate Pie (recipes are on the next page).

Leftovers are not a problem when I prepare this meal for just the two of us. We appreciate these dishes just as much the second time around. If it's too much food for us, I take the leftovers to my workplace the next day and share with co-workers. There's always plenty to go around because I cook "big." It's the way I learned how to cook.

THERE'S ALWAYS TIME FOR A HEARTY MEAL

I work full-time in a medical office, but I still look forward to preparing a nice supper for us. I go into the kitchen, turn on my favorite radio station and cook. After a stress-filled day, I find it to be very relaxing.

Since I work away from home full-time, friends have asked how I manage to find time to cook. I tell them...lists. That's my secret. Lists. It's actually a bit of a joke with those who know me well.

I organize a meal—the menu, the shopping list, even the seating arrangement for special occasions.

The bonus for me is that Ron cleans up. Isn't that just the most wonderful thing of all? I think so!

We were married several years ago. Ron was born in New Orleans and spent most of his life there. He's retired from the U.S. Postal Service.

I'm a Bogalusa native and have a son, a daughter and son-in-law, and two young grandsons. My family loves Ron as if he has been with us always.

My personal cooking pleasures didn't begin until I was an adult. I have come a long way and now am even asked to prepare foods for weddings and showers on occasion. I must admit, however, that I much prefer the simple pleasures of cooking for my husband, family, friends and co-workers.

Ron enjoys his retirement by staying active and spending plenty of time outdoors. He has worked as a nature guide at a local boys' and girls' summer camp and is active in the Knights of Columbus.

I'm a member of the Secular Franciscans (a Roman Catholic fraternity), play in a Po-Ke-No group and enjoy "Eight Is Enough"—a group of ladies who get together several times a year.

Together, Ron and I like what we call "day-tripping." We take jaunts around Louisiana and nearby Mississippi. Often, our destination is Baton Rouge to visit our grandchildren. "The grands" are our hearts, so we visit for any occasion that comes up—from soccer games to birthday party celebrations.

Chunky Crawfish Spread

(Pictured above)

PREP: 20 min. + chilling

1 package (16 ounces) frozen cooked crawfish tails, thawed
1 package (8 ounces) cream cheese, softened
1 medium green pepper, finely chopped
1 medium sweet red pepper, finely chopped
1 small onion, finely chopped
6 garlic cloves, minced
1/2 to 1 teaspoon Creole seasoning
1/2 teaspoon salt
6 to 12 drops hot pepper sauce
Assorted crackers

Chop the crawfish; pat dry. In a small bowl, beat the cream cheese. Add peppers, onion, garlic, Creole seasoning, salt and hot pepper sauce; stir in the crawfish. Cover and refrigerate for at least 2 hours. Serve with crackers. **YIELD:** 3 cups.

crawfish facts

Also known as crayfish or crawdads, crawfish are freshwater crustaceans that are common in France, Scandinavia and also the United States. They are harvested from the waters of the Mississippi Basin and are popular in Louisiana-style cooking. Like lobster, crawfish turn bright red when cooked.

Sunday Shrimp Pasta Bake

(Pictured below and on page 280)

PREP: 30 min. **BAKE:** 25 min.

12 ounces uncooked vermicelli
1 medium green pepper, chopped
5 green onions, chopped
6 garlic cloves, minced
6 tablespoons butter, cubed
2 tablespoons all-purpose flour
2 pounds deveined peeled cooked medium shrimp
1 teaspoon celery salt
1/8 teaspoon pepper
1 pound process cheese (Velveeta), cubed
1 can (10 ounces) diced tomatoes and green chilies, drained
1 can (4 ounces) mushroom stems and pieces, drained
1 tablespoon grated Parmesan cheese

Cook vermicelli according to package directions. Meanwhile, in a large skillet, saute the green pepper, onions and garlic in butter until tender. Gradually stir in the flour until blended. Stir in the shrimp, celery salt and pepper; cook, uncovered, over medium heat for 5-6 minutes or until heated through.

In a microwave-safe bowl, combine the process cheese, tomatoes and mushrooms. Microwave, uncovered, on high for 3-4 minutes or until cheese is melted, stirring occasionally. Add to shrimp mixture. Drain vermicelli; stir into skillet.

Pour into a greased 13-in. x 9-in. baking dish. Sprinkle with Parmesan cheese. Bake, uncovered, at 350° for 25-30 minutes or until heated through. **YIELD:** 8 servings.

EDITOR'S NOTE: This recipe was tested in a 1,100-watt microwave.

Citrus Quencher

(Pictured on page 302)

PREP/TOTAL TIME: 5 min.

- **2 liters lemon-lime soda, chilled**
- **3/4 cup limeade concentrate**
- **1/2 cup orange juice**

In a large pitcher, combine all ingredients. Serve over ice. **YIELD:** 8 servings (2-1/2 quarts).

No-Bake Chocolate Pie

(Pictured below and on page 280)

PREP: 15 min. + chilling

- **7 milk chocolate candy bars (1.55 ounces *each*), chopped**
- **20 large marshmallows**
- **1/2 cup milk**
- **2 cups whipped topping**
- **1 graham cracker crust (9 inches)**

Additional whipped topping, optional

In a large heavy saucepan, combine the candy bars, marshmallows and milk. Cook and stir over low heat until smooth. Remove from the heat; cool. Fold in whipped topping; pour into crust.

Cover and refrigerate for 4 hours or overnight. Garnish with additional whipped topping if desired. **YIELD:** 8 servings.

Olive-Cucumber Tossed Salad

(Pictured above)

PREP: 15 min. + marinating

- **1 cup Italian salad dressing**
- **2 medium cucumbers, peeled, halved, seeded and sliced**
- **1 cup pimiento-stuffed olives, halved**
- **1 teaspoon Creole seasoning**
- **2 packages (10 ounces *each*) ready-to-serve salad greens**

In a large bowl, combine the salad dressing, cucumbers, olives and Creole seasoning. Cover and refrigerate for at least 30 minutes. Just before serving, place the salad greens in a large bowl; add cucumber mixture and toss to coat. **YIELD:** 8 servings.

EDITOR'S NOTE: The following spices may be substituted for 1 teaspoon of Creole seasoning: 1/4 teaspoon *each* salt, garlic powder and paprika; and a pinch each of dried thyme, ground cumin and cayenne pepper.

Crown Roast for Christmas

Elegant pork entree forms the centerpiece of this *Taste of Home* field editor's holiday meal.

By Dianne Bettin, Truman, Minnesota

I love to feed people. And, even though our family has an extremely busy lifestyle, I don't mind taking time out to cook for family, friends and sometimes even strangers!

My husband, Doug, and I have a 350-sow hog operation and grain farm. I have been volunteering with pork producers' organizations for almost 20 years.

So it's no surprise that pork stars on many of my menus. During the holidays and on other special occasions, I enjoy showcasing an elegant yet easy-to-prepare Crown Roast of Pork. Two of my favorite side dishes to serve with the roast are Wild Rice Pilaf and Cashew-Peach Sweet Potatoes. Devil's Food Caramel Torte is a great finish!

A CENTER STAGE ROAST

A crown roast makes Christmas dinner extra special. I order the roast by how many ribs I want—figure on one per person. Just talk to your butcher or grocery store meat manager a few days ahead.

An herb rub accents the pork's flavor. Be sure to use a meat thermometer to guarantee that your roast is done to perfection (see tip at right).

I like to make the Wild Rice Pilaf a day ahead, which allows the rosemary and other flavors time to blend. This make-ahead approach also makes mealtime preparations go smoother the day of the dinner. The rice pilaf reheats well in the microwave. I frequently take it to potlucks—the only bad thing about that is I rarely have any leftovers to bring home for us to enjoy!

I ran across the Cashew-Peach Sweet Potatoes recipe while hunting for variations on the old standby sweet potato bake. I have a vegetable garden and found the recipe one particularly prolific year.

When I cook, I tend to focus on the all-important main meal. The dessert oftentimes is an afterthought. That's why I was thrilled when my sister-in-law, Nicki, showed up at a gathering with scrumptious Devil's Food Caramel Torte. It was definitely one of those recipes I had to add to my collection...and she graciously shared.

I love food and confess that while most people travel to sightsee, I travel to eat! Even when I go to our famous Mall of America here in Minnesota, I spend more time eating than shopping. My favorite stop is a wonderful sushi bar.

NOT JUST A FAMILY AFFAIR

As a member of the National Pork Board—an industry-nominated, government-appointed position—I help promote pork across the country and even overseas. I enjoy cooking new foods that I find on my many travels, especially if they involve pork products! Doug and our children—Tyler and Marisa—are good sports about trying everything I put in front of them.

Doug and I enjoy traveling and camping. Although the farm doesn't give him much free time, he manages to accompany me to some of my out-of-state meetings. We also enjoy time at the lake and around the campfire.

With our youngest off to college, our life will be very different now! I plan to fill some of the void with trying even more new recipes, especially tried-and-true ones from *Taste of Home*.

I hope you'll "pick pork" and consider this menu for your own Christmas dinner!

PICTURED AT LEFT: Crown Roast of Pork, Wild Rice Pilaf, Cashew-Peach Sweet Potatoes and Devil's Food Caramel Torte (recipes are on the next page).

---

dianne's pork pointers

- The old practice of overcooking pork is no longer necessary for food safety. The deliciously improved pork cuts of today are best when left slightly pink in the center, cooked to an internal temperature of 160°.

- I remove my crown roast (and other cuts, too!) from the oven when the meat reaches 150° and let it rest for about 10 minutes before carving. This allows the temperature to continue to rise to 160° while sealing in the wonderful juices.

- New research from the USDA reveals that pork tenderloin contains only 2.98 grams of fat per 3-ounce cooked serving. A 3-ounce cooked skinless chicken breast has 3.03 grams of fat. So when you want to stick to healthy cooking, keep pork in mind!

Wild Rice Pilaf

(Pictured below)

PREP: 1 hour **BAKE:** 25 min.

- 2 cans (14-1/2 ounces *each*) chicken broth
- 3/4 cup uncooked wild rice
- 1 cup uncooked long grain rice
- 1 large onion, chopped
- 2 medium carrots, halved lengthwise and sliced
- 1 garlic clove, minced
- 1/2 teaspoon dried rosemary, crushed
- 1/2 cup butter, cubed
- 3 cups fresh broccoli florets
- 1/4 teaspoon pepper

In a large saucepan, bring broth to a boil. Add the wild rice; reduce heat. Cover and cook for 30 minutes. Add the long grain rice; cook 20-25 minutes longer or until liquid is absorbed and rice is tender.

Meanwhile, in a large skillet, saute the onion, carrots, garlic and rosemary in butter until vegetables are tender. Stir in rice, broccoli and pepper.

Transfer to a greased shallow 2-qt. baking dish. Cover and bake at 350° for 25-30 minutes or until the broccoli is crisp-tender. Fluff with a fork before serving. **YIELD:** 10 servings.

Crown Roast of Pork

(Pictured above)

PREP: 15 min. **BAKE:** 3 hours + standing

- 1 tablespoon dried parsley flakes
- 1 tablespoon canola oil
- 1 teaspoon salt
- 1/2 teaspoon pepper
- 1 pork crown roast (14 ribs and about 8 pounds)

Foil *or* paper frills for rib ends

Combine the parsley, oil, salt and pepper; rub over roast. Place on a rack in a large shallow roasting pan. Cover rib ends with pieces of foil. Bake at 350° for 3 to 3-1/2 hours or until a meat thermometer reads 160°.

Transfer the roast to a serving platter. Let stand for 10-15 minutes. Remove foil pieces. Garnish rib ends with foil or paper frills. Cut between ribs to serve. **YIELD:** 14 servings.

Devil's Food Caramel Torte

(Pictured below)

PREP: 40 min. BAKE: 25 min. + cooling

- 1 package (18-1/4 ounces) devil's food cake mix
- 1 cup buttermilk
- 1/2 cup canola oil
- 3 eggs
- 1 package (7 ounces) milk chocolate turtle candies, chopped, *divided*
- 1 tablespoon baking cocoa
- 1-1/2 cups heavy whipping cream
- 1/3 cup caramel ice cream topping
- 1 can (16 ounces) chocolate frosting

Additional milk chocolate turtle candies, broken, optional

Line two 9-in. round baking pans with waxed paper; grease the paper and set aside. In a large bowl, combine the cake mix, buttermilk, oil and eggs. Beat on low speed for 30 seconds. Beat on medium for 2 minutes. Combine 1 cup candies and cocoa; fold into the batter.

Pour into prepared pans. Bake at 350° for 25-30 minutes or until a toothpick inserted near the center comes out clean. Cool for 10 minutes before removing from pans to wire racks to cool completely. Remove waxed paper.

In a small bowl, beat cream until it begins to thicken. Add caramel topping; beat until stiff peaks form. Fold in remaining candies.

Place one cake layer on a serving plate; spread with chocolate frosting. Top with remaining cake layer; frost top and sides of torte with cream mixture. Garnish with additional candies if desired. Refrigerate until serving. **YIELD:** 12 servings.

Cashew-Peach Sweet Potatoes

(Pictured above)

PREP: 45 min. BAKE: 40 min.

- 6 medium sweet potatoes
- 1/2 cup packed brown sugar
- 1/3 cup coarsely chopped cashews
- 1/2 teaspoon salt
- 1/4 teaspoon ground ginger
- 1 can (15-1/4 ounces) sliced peaches, drained
- 3 tablespoons butter

Place the sweet potatoes in a large saucepan or Dutch oven; cover with water. Bring to a boil. Reduce the heat; cover and cook for 30-45 minutes or just until tender. Drain and cool slightly; peel and cut into cubes.

Combine the brown sugar, cashews, salt and ginger. Place half of the sweet potatoes in an ungreased 11-in. x 7-in. baking dish; top with half of the peaches and brown sugar mixture. Repeat layers; dot with butter.

Cover and bake at 350° for 30 minutes. Uncover; bake 10 minutes longer or until bubbly and heated through. **YIELD:** 10 servings.

The next time you need a meal on the table in a snap, turn to this chapter. Here you'll find several effortless menus that are completely table-ready in just 30 minutes...or less!

meals in minutes

Treat Your Gang to an Italian-Style Supper..312
Shrimp Scampi • Garlic-Almond Green Beans
• Granola Fudge Clusters

Combine Three Favorites for a Fast Lunch 314
Chicken Florentine Panini • Ramen Corn Chowder
• Thousand Island Salad Dressing

Chicken and Veggies Please Families...316
Apricot Honey Chicken • Gingered Cranberry-Carrot Slaw
• Favorite Herbed Potatoes

Skillet Seafood Menu Is Easy and Elegant..318
Pepper-Rubbed Red Snapper • Prosciutto Tortellini
• Frosty Almond Dessert

Quick & Colorful Cuisine Ideal for Summer Cookouts 320
French Onion Burgers • Old Glory Angel Food
• Cranberry Lemonade

Spice Up Dinnertime with Well-Seasoned Dishes 322
Chicken with Paprika Cream • Steamed Broccoli Florets
• Mushroom Bread Wedges

Fix a Pork Chop Supper in a Snap 324
Raspberry Pork Chops • Corn Zucchini Saute
• Cheesecake Waffle Cups

PICTURED CLOCKWISE FROM UPPER LEFT: Pepper-Rubbed Red Snapper and Prosciutto Tortellini (page 319), Cheesecake Waffle Cups (page 325), Apricot Honey Chicken, Gingered Cranberry-Carrot Slaw and Favorite Herbed Potatoes (page 317) and Ramen Corn Chowder (page 315).

Treat Your Gang to an Italian-Style Supper

On evenings when your family's ready for dinner but you're not, an unfortunate, quick solution is often frozen pizza or carry-out chicken.

This fast-to-fix meal, made up of three reader favorites, delivers from-scratch flavor in just 30 minutes. Why not try it out tonight?

Shrimp Scampi, from Lori Packer of Omaha, Nebraska, looks like you fussed but is a snap to prepare. Lemon and herbs enhance the shrimp, and the bread crumbs lend a pleasing crunch. Served over angel hair pasta, this main dish is pretty enough for company.

"Garlic-Almond Green Beans is my family's favorite way to eat this popular vegetable," Genny Monchamp says from Redding, California. "The beans stay so tender and crisp. To speed things up even more, you could use frozen green beans instead of fresh."

Short and sweet, the recipe for yummy Granola Fudge Clusters uses only four ingredients. "I have overheard people say, 'You have to try one of these,' when I serve them at get-togethers," shares Loraine Meyer of Bend, Oregon. "I always double the batch because no one can eat just one."

Shrimp Scampi

PREP/TOTAL TIME: 20 min.

3 to 4 garlic cloves, minced
1/4 cup butter, cubed
1/4 cup olive oil
1 pound uncooked medium shrimp, peeled and deveined
1/4 cup lemon juice
1/2 teaspoon pepper
1/4 teaspoon dried oregano
1/2 cup grated Parmesan cheese
1/4 cup dry bread crumbs
1/4 cup minced fresh parsley
Hot cooked angel hair pasta

In a 10-in. ovenproof skillet, saute the garlic in butter and oil until tender. Stir in the shrimp, lemon juice, pepper and oregano; cook and stir for 2-3 minutes or until shrimp turn pink. Sprinkle with Parmesan cheese, bread crumbs and parsley.

Broil 6 inches from the heat for 2-3 minutes or until the topping is golden brown. Serve over the pasta. **YIELD:** 4 servings.

Garlic-Almond Green Beans

PREP/TOTAL TIME: 20 min.

1 pound fresh green beans
2 garlic cloves, minced
1 tablespoon olive oil
1/4 cup slivered almonds, toasted
Pepper to taste

Place the beans in a large saucepan and cover with water. Bring to a boil; cook, uncovered, for 8-10 minutes or until crisp-tender.

Meanwhile, in a large skillet, cook the minced garlic in oil for 2-3 minutes. Drain the beans. Add beans, slivered almonds and pepper to the skillet; toss to coat. **YIELD:** 4 servings.

Granola Fudge Clusters

PREP/TOTAL TIME: 25 min.

1 cup (6 ounces) semisweet chocolate chips
1 cup butterscotch chips
1-1/4 cups granola cereal without raisins
1 cup chopped walnuts

In a microwave-safe bowl, melt the chocolate and butterscotch chips; stir until smooth. Stir in granola cereal and walnuts.

Drop by tablespoonfuls onto waxed paper-lined baking sheets. Refrigerate for 15 minutes or until firm. **YIELD:** about 2-1/2 dozen.

have a meltdown?

To easily melt chocolate in the microwave, place it in a microwave-safe bowl. Melt semisweet chocolate at 50% power and milk chocolate at 30% power. Stir frequently until the chocolate is melted; do not overheat. If there are large chunks of chocolate, chop them up before microwaving so the chocolate melts evenly.

You can also melt chocolate in a heavy saucepan over low heat; stir until smooth. Even small amounts of water in the mixture can make the chocolate unusable, so be sure all bowls and pots are completely dry.

Combine Three Favorites for a Fast Lunch

What goes together better than a hearty sandwich, hot soup and a salad? Your family will enjoy relaxing with this laid-back, 30-minute menu that works as a satisfying lunch or a light supper.

Chicken Florentine Panini, from Lee Bremson of Kansas City, Missouri, brings an Italian flair to this speedy meal. The grilled sandwich combines chicken with provolone cheese, spinach and red onion.

"Ramen Corn Chowder tastes as good as if it simmered for hours, but it's ready in 15 minutes," says Darlene Brenden of Salem, Oregon. "I thought the original recipe was lacking in flavor, so I jazzed it up with extra corn and bacon bits."

Why buy bottled dressing when you can make delicious, homemade Thousand Island Salad Dressing in a jiffy? This tangy version comes from Elizabeth Montgomery of Taylorville, Illinois.

Chicken Florentine Panini

PREP/TOTAL TIME: 25 min.

- 1 package (6 ounces) fresh baby spinach
- 2 teaspoons olive oil
- 1/4 cup butter, softened
- 8 slices sourdough bread
- 1/4 cup creamy Italian salad dressing
- 8 slices provolone cheese
- 1/2 pound shaved deli chicken
- 2 slices red onion, separated into rings

In a large skillet, saute spinach in olive oil for 2 minutes or until wilted. Butter one side of each slice of bread. Spread the unbuttered side of four slices with the salad dressing; layer with a cheese slice, chicken, spinach, onion and another cheese slice. Top with the remaining bread, buttered side up. Cook in a panini maker or on a griddle until golden brown on both sides. **YIELD:** 4 servings.

Ramen Corn Chowder

(Pictured on page 310)

PREP/TOTAL TIME: 15 min.

- 2 cups water
- 1 package (3 ounces) chicken ramen noodles
- 1 can (15-1/4 ounces) whole kernel corn, drained
- 1 can (14-3/4 ounces) cream-style corn

- 1 cup milk
- 1 teaspoon dried minced onion
- 1/4 teaspoon curry powder
- 3/4 cup shredded cheddar cheese
- 1 tablespoon crumbled cooked bacon
- 1 tablespoon minced fresh parsley

In a small saucepan, bring water to a boil. Break the noodles into large pieces. Add noodles and contents of seasoning packet to water. Reduce heat to medium. Cook, uncovered, for 2-3 minutes or until the noodles are tender.

Stir in the corn, cream-style corn, milk, onion and curry; heat through. Stir in the cheese, bacon and parsley until blended. **YIELD:** 4 servings.

Thousand Island Salad Dressing

PREP/TOTAL TIME: 15 min.

- 1-1/2 cups mayonnaise
- 1/2 cup chili sauce
- 1 hard-cooked egg, chopped
- 2 tablespoons finely chopped celery
- 2 tablespoons finely chopped green pepper
- 2 tablespoons chopped pimiento-stuffed olives
- 1 tablespoon grated onion

In a small bowl, combine all ingredients. Cover and refrigerate until serving. **YIELD:** 2 cups.

all dressed up

Sour cream- and mayonnaise-based salad dressings, like Thousand Island Salad Dressing (recipe above), go well with sturdy greens such as iceberg and romaine lettuce. Delicate greens such as Bibb or Boston lettuce are best with vinegar and oil dressings.

Toss greens with your dressing immediately before serving the salad or place the greens in a salad bowl and pass the dressing at the table. Keep in mind that putting too much dressing on the salad will make it soggy.

Chicken and Veggies Please Families

You just returned home, the clock's ticking and the rest of your family will be walking through the front door any moment now. Don't worry! You won't disappoint them when this appealing, nutritious and quick menu is on the stovetop.

Apricot Honey Chicken from Kathy Hawkins of Gurnee, Illinois boasts a sweet, fruity sauce. There's no need to heat up the oven for this flavorful entree, so you can even enjoy it during the summer. Try the sauce with ham slices as well.

"I saw something similar to Favorite Herbed Potatoes prepared on television and decided to make my own version using the herbs I had on hand," says Naomi Olson of Hamilton, Michigan. "To cut preperation time, I even substituted canned potatoes for fresh ones, and we liked it just as much."

Gingered Cranberry-Carrot Slaw gives this meal a nice tang with cranberries and a sweet-tart pineapple dressing. Genise Krause of Sturgeon Bay, Wisconsin shared the refreshing recipe.

Apricot Honey Chicken

(Pictured on page 310)

PREP/TOTAL TIME: 25 min.

- 4 boneless skinless chicken breast halves (5 ounces *each*)
- 1 tablespoon canola oil
- 3 tablespoons apricot preserves
- 2 tablespoons orange juice
- 4 teaspoons honey

In a large skillet, cook chicken in oil over medium heat for 7-9 minutes on each side or until juices run clear. Combine the preserves, orange juice and honey; pour over chicken. Cook for 2 minutes or until heated through. **YIELD:** 4 servings.

Gingered Cranberry-Carrot Slaw

(Pictured on page 310)

PREP/TOTAL TIME: 10 min.

- 1/2 cup unsweetened pineapple juice
- 2 tablespoons honey
- 1 tablespoon lemon juice
- 1 teaspoon cider vinegar
- 3 cups shredded carrots
- 1/2 cup dried cranberries
- 1 to 2 tablespoons minced fresh gingerroot

In a large bowl, whisk the pineapple juice, honey, lemon juice and vinegar until smooth. Add the carrots, cranberries and ginger; toss to coat. Cover and refrigerate until serving. **YIELD:** 4 servings.

Favorite Herbed Potatoes

(Pictured on page 310)

PREP/TOTAL TIME: 20 min.

- 2 cans (15 ounces *each*) whole potatoes, drained and halved lengthwise
- 1 tablespoon butter
- 1 tablespoon olive oil
- 1-1/2 teaspoons dried parsley flakes
- 1/2 teaspoon dried basil
- 1/2 teaspoon dried thyme
- 1/2 teaspoon rubbed sage
- 1/2 teaspoon dried rosemary, crushed
- 1/2 teaspoon garlic powder
- 1/4 teaspoon paprika
- 1/4 teaspoon pepper

In a large skillet over medium heat, cook potatoes in butter and oil for 6-8 minutes or until browned. Add the remaining ingredients; cook and stir for 2-3 minutes or until well coated. **YIELD:** 4 servings.

surefire success

For a no-fuss supper with loads of tasty appeal, you can't go wrong with this finger-licking combination. To beat the clock, start by assembling Gingered Cranberry-Carrot Slaw. When done, set the dish in the refrigerator to chill while you prepare the rest of the meal.

As the chicken cooks in the oil, brown the potatoes in butter and oil in another skillet. When it's time to flip the chicken over, the potatoes should be just about ready for the seasonings.

Once the potatoes are ready, turn off the heat and cover the skillet to keep them warm. Complete the main course by mixing up the sauce and adding to the chicken, and dinner is served. For extra flair, add a loaf of bread and pick up some ice cream for dessert!

Skillet Seafood Menu Is Easy and Elegant

Rrunning errands, attending after-school events, working late...it all adds up to less time in the kitchen. But you'll need no more than half an hour to put this meal on the table.

"I can prepare Pepper-Rubbed Red Snapper in a flash on a weeknight or when guests visit for dinner," says Windy Byrd of Freeport, Texas.

Scott Jones of Tulsa, Oklahoma whips up Prosciutto Tortellini as a hearty side dish. "I just spruce up frozen pasta with peas, prosciutto and a smooth, cheesy sauce," he says.

For the finale, add five-ingredient Frosty Almond Dessert from Phyllis Schmalz of Kansas City, Kansas.

Pepper-Rubbed Red Snapper

(*Pictured on page 310*)

PREP/TOTAL TIME: 15 min.

- 1/2 **teaspoon onion powder**
- 1/2 **teaspoon garlic powder**
- 1/2 **teaspoon dried thyme**
- 1/2 **teaspoon white pepper**
- 1/2 **teaspoon cayenne pepper**
- 1/2 **teaspoon pepper**
- 1/8 **teaspoon salt**
-   4 **red snapper fillets (8 ounces *each*)**
-   3 **tablespoons butter, melted**

In a small bowl, combine the first seven ingredients. Dip the fish fillets in butter, then rub with spice mixture.

In a large nonstick skillet, cook the fish fillets over medium-high heat for 2-4 minutes on each side or until fish flakes easily with a fork. **YIELD:** 4 servings.

Prosciutto Tortellini

(*Pictured on page 310*)

PREP/TOTAL TIME: 20 min.

-   1 **package (19 ounces) frozen cheese tortellini**
-   1 **tablespoon all-purpose flour**
-   1 **cup half-and-half cream**
- 1/2 **cup shredded part-skim mozzarella cheese**
- 1/2 **cup shredded Parmesan cheese**
- 10 **thin slices prosciutto, chopped**
-   1 **package (10 ounces) frozen peas**
- 1/4 **teaspoon white pepper**

Cook the tortellini according to the package directions. Meanwhile, in a large skillet, combine flour and cream until smooth; stir in the cheeses. Bring to a boil; cook and stir for 2 minutes or until thickened. Reduce heat.

Drain tortellini; add to the cheese sauce. Stir in the prosciutto, peas and pepper. Cook for 5 minutes or until heated through. **YIELD:** 4 servings.

Frosty Almond Dessert

(*Not pictured*)

PREP/TOTAL TIME: 10 min.

-   4 **cups vanilla frozen yogurt**
-   1 **cup ice cubes**
- 1/2 **cup hot fudge ice cream topping**
- 1/4 **teaspoon almond extract**

Whipped topping and baking cocoa, optional

In a blender, place half of the yogurt, ice cubes, fudge topping and extract; cover and process for 1-2 minutes or until smooth. Stir if necessary. Pour into chilled dessert glasses.

Repeat with remaining yogurt, ice, fudge topping and extract. Garnish with whipped topping and baking cocoa if desired. **YIELD:** 4 servings.

defrosting fish

- **REFRIGERATION DEFROSTING.** When defrosting fish or shellfish in the refrigerator, place a tray under the package to catch any liquid or juices and keep the refrigerator clean. Allow 12 or more hours to thaw a 1-pound package.

- **COLD-WATER THAWING.** This is an option that takes less time than refrigeration defrosting but requires more attention. The fish or shellfish must be in a leakproof bag such as its original tightly sealed wrapper. If its package is not leakproof, then place it in a heavy-duty plastic bag.

  Next, submerge the wrapped seafood in cold tap water. Change the water every 30 minutes until the seafood is thawed. For this method of defrosting, allow 1 to 2 hours for every pound.

Quick & Colorful Cuisine
Ideal for Summer Cookouts

When warm summer breezes beckon, even folks who love to cook want to spend less time in the kitchen and more time on the patio or porch. When fresh air builds appetites, a filling, fast-to-fix meal is the order of the day.

The complete-meal menu here consists of favorites from three great cooks and was combined by the *Taste of Home* Test Kitchen staff. Not only is the menu ideal for July Fourth celebrations and weeknight meals alike, but you can have everything ready to serve in just half an hour!

"I created French Onion Burgers one day when I needed to stretch a pound of hamburger," recalls Beth Johnson of Dalton, Ohio. "When we have high school boys help with baling hay, this is one of their favorite foods to enjoy after the work is done."

With its pretty pink blush and tart refreshing flavor, Cranberry Lemonade is sure to satisfy, glass after glass after glass. Darlene Brenden of Salem, Oregon shared this summer thirst-quencher.

Old Glory Angel Food makes a colorful dessert for your Fourth of July celebration. It's easy to assemble, but the triple layers and stars-and-stripes topping look like you fussed.

"One July, we invited a couple over for a backyard barbecue," says Anne Nabbefeld from Greenville, Wisconsin. "The woman had recently become a United States citizen, so I created this cake specifically for her. It was a big hit."

French Onion Burgers

PREP/TOTAL TIME: 20 min.

1 can (4 ounces) mushroom stems and pieces, drained and diced
1 can (2.8 ounces) french-fried onions
1 tablespoon Worcestershire sauce
1/2 teaspoon salt
1 pound ground beef
4 hamburger buns, split
Lettuce leaves and tomato slices

In a large bowl, combine the mushrooms, onions, Worcestershire sauce and salt. Crumble beef over mixture and mix well. Shape into four patties.

Grill, uncovered, over medium heat or broil 4 in. from the heat for 6-9 minutes on each side or until no longer pink. Serve on hamburger buns with lettuce and tomato. **YIELD:** 4 servings.

Old Glory Angel Food

PREP/TOTAL TIME: 20 min.

1 loaf (10-1/2 ounces) angel food cake
1 carton (8 ounces) frozen whipped topping, thawed, *divided*
1 cup quartered fresh strawberries
1 cup fresh blueberries
Additional blueberries and strawberries

Split cake horizontally into thirds. Place bottom layer on a serving platter. Combine 1 cup whipped topping and strawberries; spread over bottom layer. Top with second cake layer.

Combine 1 cup topping and blueberries; spread over second layer. Top with remaining cake layer. Spread with remaining topping. Arrange additional berries over top of cake to form a flag. **YIELD:** 8 servings.

Cranberry Lemonade

PREP: 5 min. **COOK:** 15 min. + chilling

3/4 cup sugar
2/3 cup lemon juice
3 cups cold water
1 cup cranberry juice

In a small saucepan, combine sugar and lemon juice. Cook and stir over medium heat until sugar is dissolved. Stir in the cold water and cranberry juice. Cool; pour into a pitcher. Refrigerate until chilled. Serve over ice. **YIELD:** 4 servings.

patriotic party pizzazz

Give July picnics festive flair with these fun ideas:

- Turn strawberry shortcake into a red, white and blue dessert by adding blueberries and whipped cream.
- Enhance a bowl of fruit punch with strawberries and blueberries. Or freeze the berries in ice cubes and add the cubes to the punch.
- Poke American flag picks into cupcakes spread with red, white or blue frosting or top sugar cookies with red and blue sprinkles.

Spice Up Dinnertime with Well-Seasoned Dishes

Spending time preparing an elaborate meal is no big deal for those who like to cook. But some days, speed is the key ingredient in what you whip up for your hungry family.

The complete menu here is comprised of family favorites from three super cooks. You can have it ready to serve in just 30 minutes.

"Chicken with Paprika Cream is quick to make when you buy boned and skinned chicken breasts," says Marilou Robinson of Portland, Oregon. "Serving it over rice lets you get every last bit of the tasty paprika-flavored cream."

Steamed Broccoli Florets, with a tart mustard vinaigrette, is a delightful fast-to-fix recipe from Peggy Van Arsdale of Crosswicks, New Jersey. "My Aunt Marion was a wonderful cook. I have many recipes from her, including this great one," Peggy says.

Tender sliced mushrooms and a sprinkling of Parmesan cheese dot crisp Mushroom Bread Wedges, made with convenient refrigerated crescent rolls. You can also serve them with soup, chili or a salad. After one bite, they're sure to become staples in your kitchen. Patricia Mele of Apollo, Pennsylvania contributed the recipe.

Chicken with Paprika Cream

PREP/TOTAL TIME: 25 min.

6 boneless skinless chicken breast halves
6 tablespoons butter, *divided*
1 tablespoon canola oil
6 green onions, chopped
1 to 2 tablespoons paprika
2 cups heavy whipping cream
1 teaspoon salt
1/4 teaspoon pepper
Hot cooked rice
Additional chopped green onions, optional

In a large skillet, brown chicken in 1 tablespoon butter and oil over medium heat. Cover and cook for 5-7 minutes or until juices run clear. Remove chicken; keep warm.

In same skillet, saute onions until tender. Reduce heat to medium. Add paprika and remaining butter; heat until butter is melted. Stir in cream, salt and pepper; cook and stir until sauce is thickened, about 4 minutes. Serve with chicken over rice. Garnish with chopped green onions if desired. **YIELD:** 6 servings.

Steamed Broccoli Florets

PREP/TOTAL TIME: 15 min.

1/4 cup sugar
3 tablespoons cider vinegar
2 tablespoons canola oil
2 tablespoons water
1/2 teaspoon prepared mustard
Dash *each* **salt, pepper and ground mustard**
1 pound fresh broccoli florets

In a jar with a tight-fitting lid, combine the sugar, vinegar, oil, water, prepared mustard, salt, pepper and ground mustard; shake well. Set aside. Place broccoli in a steamer basket. Place in a saucepan over 1 in. of water; bring to a boil.

Cover and steam for 5-8 minutes or until crisp-tender. Place in a serving bowl. Shake dressing; drizzle over broccoli and toss to coat. **YIELD:** 6 servings.

Mushroom Bread Wedges

PREP/TOTAL TIME: 25 min.

1 tube (8 ounces) refrigerated crescent rolls
1/2 pound fresh mushrooms, sliced
3 tablespoons butter, melted
1/4 cup grated Parmesan cheese
1/4 teaspoon Italian seasoning

Separate crescent dough into eight triangles and place on a greased 12-in. round pizza pan with points toward the center; seal perforations.

In a small bowl, combine the mushrooms and butter; toss to coat. Spoon mushroom mixture over dough. Sprinkle with Parmesan cheese and Italian seasoning.

Bake at 375° for 15-20 minutes or until crust is golden brown and mushrooms are tender. **YIELD:** 8 servings.

paprika particulars

Paprika is a powder made by grinding dried sweet red peppers. Its flavor can range from mild to hot. Hot paprika is always labeled such; sweet paprika is often just labeled "paprika." Hot paprika is indeed hot—if it's all you have, use sparingly.

Fix a Pork Chop Supper in a Snap

Time isn't always on your side when it comes to getting a decent dinner on the table for a hungry family. You need a meal that's fast, filling and tasty, too.

Our Test Kitchen came up with this quick-to-fix meal using favorite recipes from three great cooks. It's not only delicious...it's also ready to serve in just 30 minutes.

Janette Hutchings of Festus, Missouri covers her succulent Raspberry Pork Chops with a glaze made with mustard, vinegar and jam. Fixed fast in a skillet, these tender chops are simply the best. They're fancy enough for company or perfect for a casual family meal.

Corn Zucchini Saute makes a colorful accompaniment to the pork chops or to any Mexican-style meal. "I've loved this dish since I was a child," says Sylvia Sonnenburg of Ogden, Utah.

"I've found a fun way to serve cheesecake," Janice Greenhalgh from Florence, Kentucky says about her Cheesecake Waffle Cups. The crunchy store-bought "bowls" hold a smooth cream cheese filling that's layered with cherry pie filling. They're a snap to prepare and attractive, too.

Raspberry Pork Chops

PREP/TOTAL TIME: 25 min.

4 boneless pork loin chops (5 ounces *each*)
1 tablespoon canola oil
1/4 cup cider vinegar
1/4 cup seedless raspberry jam
1 tablespoon prepared mustard

In a large skillet, brown pork chops on both sides over medium heat in oil. Stir in the vinegar, jam and mustard. Reduce heat; cover and simmer for 10-15 minutes or until juices run clear.

Remove chops and keep warm. Bring sauce to a boil; cook until liquid is reduced by half, stirring occasionally. Serve with pork chops. **YIELD:** 4 servings.

Corn Zucchini Saute

PREP/TOTAL TIME: 30 min.

3/4 cup chopped sweet onion
3 tablespoons olive oil
2 garlic cloves, minced
3 medium zucchini, quartered lengthwise and sliced
1 plum tomato, seeded and chopped
1 can (15-1/4 ounces) whole kernel corn, drained
1/4 cup water
1 tablespoon dried parsley flakes
1/4 teaspoon salt
1/4 teaspoon pepper
1/2 cup shredded cheddar cheese

In a large skillet, saute the onion in oil until tender. Add the garlic; saute for 1 minute. Add the zucchini and tomato. Cook for 5 minutes, stirring occasionally.

Stir in the corn, water, parsley, salt and pepper. Bring to a boil. Reduce heat; simmer, uncovered, for 10 minutes. Sprinkle with cheese. Cover and cook 2 minutes longer or until cheese is melted. **YIELD:** 4 servings.

Cheesecake Waffle Cups

(Pictured on page 310)

PREP/TOTAL TIME: 10 min.

1 package (8 ounces) cream cheese, softened
1 can (14 ounces) sweetened condensed milk
1/3 cup lemon juice
1 teaspoon vanilla extract
4 waffle bowls
1 cup cherry *or* blueberry pie filling

In a small bowl, beat the cream cheese until smooth. Gradually beat in the milk until smooth. Stir in lemon juice and vanilla. Spoon about 1/3 cup into each waffle bowl; top with 2 tablespoons pie filling. Repeat layers. **YIELD:** 4 servings.

crazy for zucchini

Handle zucchini carefully because they're thin-skinned and easily damaged. The freshest zucchini are firm and heavy squash with a moist stem end and shiny skin. Smaller squash are generally sweeter and more tender.

One medium (1/3 pound) zucchini yields about 2 cups sliced or 1-1/2 cups shredded. Store in a plastic bag in the refrigerator crisper for 4 to 5 days. Zucchini is rich in beta carotene, B vitamins, folic acid, vitamin C and calcium.

Big flavor, low cost. That's what you'll find when you peruse the following menus. These 10 mouthwatering meals are sure to satisfy your family and your pocketbook!

meals on a budget

Feed Your Family for $1.50 a Plate!.................328
  Traditional Meat Loaf • Parmesan Potato Balls
  • Green Bean Salad

Feed Your Family for $1.75 a Plate! 330
  Family-Pleasing Sloppy Joes • German Cukes
  and Tomatoes • Spicy Potato Wedges

Feed Your Family for $1.55 a Plate!................332
  Chinese New Year Skillet • Egg Drop Soup
  • Almond Cookies

Feed Your Family for $1.60 a Plate!................334
  Caraway Pot Roast • Mashed Potato Casserole
  • Fluffy Pineapple Dessert

Feed Your Family for $2.00 a Plate!................336
  Barbecued Ham and Peaches • Three-Fruit
  Salad • Pear-Filled Bundt Cake

Feed Your Family for $2.00 a Plate! 338
  Chicken Spareribs • Cottage Cheese Yeast Rolls
  • Creamed Spinach

Feed Your Family for $2.10 a Plate!................340
  Sausage with Apple Sauerkraut • Crispy Potato
  Cubes • Green Beans with Walnuts

Feed Your Family for $1.10 a Plate!................342
  Tuna Cheese Melts • Radish Potato Salad
  • Cinnamon-Sugar Crisps

Feed Your Family for $1.85 a Plate!................344
  Salmon Chowder • Cracked Pepper Bread
  • Garden Lettuce Salad

Feed Your Family for $1.65 a Plate!................346
  Vegetable Noodle Bake • Green Bean and
  Tomato Salad • Chocolate Ribbon Bars

PICTURED CLOCKWISE FROM UPPER LEFT: Egg Drop Soup (page 333), Barbecued Ham and Peaches and Three-Fruit Salad (page 337), Pear-Filled Bundt Cake (page 337) and Family-Pleasing Sloppy Joes and Spicy Potato Wedges (page 331).

Feed Your Family For $1.50 a Plate!

You can't beat meat loaf when you want to serve your family a satisfying, homey meal any time of the year. You'll take comfort in knowing this flavorful meat loaf menu won't break your grocery budget.

Topped with a sweet sauce, Traditional Meat Loaf tastes so good that you might want to double the recipe so everyone can have seconds. "This meat loaf also freezes well," adds Gail Graham of Maple Ridge, British Columbia.

Mildred Sherrer of Fort Worth, Texas likes the combination of tomato, beans and hard-cooked egg in her Green Bean Salad. And the savory, delicious Parmesan Potato Balls from Pat Habiger of Spearville, Kansas round out this economical menu.

Traditional Meat Loaf

PREP: 15 min. **BAKE:** 1 hour + standing

- 1 egg, lightly beaten
- 2/3 cup milk
- 3 slices bread, crumbled
- 1 cup (4 ounces) shredded cheddar cheese
- 1 medium onion, chopped
- 1/2 cup finely shredded carrot
- 1 teaspoon salt
- 1/4 teaspoon pepper
- 1-1/2 pounds ground beef
- 1/4 cup packed brown sugar
- 1/4 cup ketchup
- 1 tablespoon prepared mustard

In a large bowl, combine first eight ingredients. Crumble beef over mixture and mix well. Shape into a loaf. Place in a greased 9-in. x 5-in. loaf pan.

In a small bowl, combine the brown sugar, ketchup and mustard; spread over the loaf. Bake at 350° for 60-75 minutes or until no pink remains and a meat thermometer reads 160°. Drain. Let stand for 10 minutes before slicing. **YIELD:** 6 servings.

Parmesan Potato Balls

PREP: 45 min. **BAKE:** 15 min.

- 2-1/2 pounds potatoes, peeled and cubed (about 3 large potatoes)
- 2 ounces cream cheese, softened
- 2 tablespoons milk
- 1 tablespoon butter, softened
- 1/4 cup grated Parmesan cheese
- 1 tablespoon chopped green onion
- 2-1/2 teaspoons onion soup mix
- 1/2 teaspoon salt
- 1/8 teaspoon hot pepper sauce
- Dash pepper
- 1 egg, lightly beaten
- 1-1/2 cups crushed cornflakes

Place the potatoes in a large saucepan and cover with water. Bring to a boil. Reduce heat; cover and cook for 15-20 minutes or until tender. Drain.

In a large bowl, mash the potatoes. Beat in the cream cheese, milk and butter until smooth. Stir in the Parmesan cheese, onion, soup mix, salt, hot pepper sauce and pepper. Shape into 1-1/2-in. balls.

Place egg and crushed cornflakes in separate shallow bowls. Dip the potato balls in egg, then roll in the crumbs. Place on ungreased baking sheets.

Bake at 400° for 15-18 minutes or until crisp and golden brown. **YIELD:** 4-1/2 dozen.

Green Bean Salad

PREP: 25 min. + chilling

- 1 pound fresh green beans
- 3 tablespoons olive oil
- 2 tablespoons balsamic vinegar
- 1/2 teaspoon Dijon mustard
- 1/4 teaspoon salt
- 1/8 teaspoon pepper
- 1 medium tomato, seeded and chopped
- 1 small onion, chopped
- 2 tablespoons minced fresh parsley
- 2 teaspoons capers, drained
- 1 hard-cooked egg, chopped

Place beans in a large saucepan and cover with water. Bring to a boil; cook, uncovered, for 8-10 minutes or until crisp-tender. Drain and immediately place beans in ice water. Drain and pat dry. Place in a large bowl.

In a small bowl, whisk the olive oil, balsamic vinegar, mustard, salt and pepper. Pour over the beans and toss to coat. Add the tomato, onion, parsley and capers; gently toss. Cover and refrigerate for at least 2 hours. Just before serving, sprinkle with the egg. **YIELD:** 6 servings.

Feed Your Family
For $1.75 a Plate!

Here's a great way to simplify meals during the laid-back, dog days of summer. Just prepare an all-time-favorite like saucy sloppy joes. They're sure to be popular with the entire family as well as guests.

You'll find that casual dining can be cost-effective as well as satisfying. You can feed your family these saucy beef sandwiches, along with a garden-fresh veggie side dish and spicy spuds, for about $1.75 a plate. Now that's good eating!

"My grandchildren love my Family-Pleasing Sloppy Joes," Patricia Ringle says from Edgar, Wisconsin. "I like this recipe because it can be made ahead of time and can also be put in the slow cooker. I've found it freezes well, too."

Karen Ann Bland of Gove, Kansas adds, "German Cukes and Tomatoes really sparks up a meal and goes fairly well with everything from grilled steak to tuna salad.

"I like to serve it in individual, lettuce-lined glass bowls with a sour cream star piped on top and a sprinkling of dill."

From Keego Harbor, Michigan, Autumn McNamara shares, "When my husband and I barbecue with friends, we always bring Spicy Potato Wedges, and everyone loves them. They're a favorite accompaniment to almost anything we cook on the grill."

With this affordable and tasty menu, everyone will be satisfied and happy. It's a meal that can't be beat!

Family-Pleasing Sloppy Joes

(Pictured on page 326)

PREP: 10 min. **COOK:** 45 min.

> 2 **pounds ground beef**
> 1 **large onion, chopped**
> 1-1/4 **cups ketchup**
> 1/2 **cup water**
> 1 **tablespoon brown sugar**
> 1 **tablespoon white vinegar**
> 1/2 **teaspoon salt**
> 1/2 **teaspoon ground mustard**
> 1/2 **teaspoon chili powder**
> 1/4 **teaspoon ground allspice**
> 8 **sandwich buns, split**

In a Dutch oven, cook the ground beef and chopped onion over medium heat until the meat is completely cooked and no longer pink; drain. Stir in the ketchup, water, brown sugar, white vinegar, salt, ground mustard, chili powder and ground allspice. Bring to a boil. Reduce the heat; simmer, uncovered, for 35-40 minutes or until heated through.

Spoon about 1/2 cup of the meat mixture onto each bun. **YIELD:** 8 servings.

German Cukes and Tomatoes

PREP/TOTAL TIME: 20 min.

> 2 **medium cucumbers, thinly sliced**
> 4 **green onions, thinly sliced**
> 2 **tablespoons minced fresh parsley**
> 1/4 **cup sour cream**
> 2 **tablespoons snipped fresh dill**
> 1 **tablespoon cider vinegar**
> 1/2 **teaspoon salt**
> 1/4 **teaspoon prepared mustard**
> 1/8 **teaspoon pepper**
> 1 **tablespoon milk, optional**
> 3 **small tomatoes, sliced**

In a large bowl, combine the cucumbers, onions and parsley. In a small bowl, combine the sour cream, fresh dill, vinegar, salt, mustard and pepper. Stir in the milk if dressing with a thinner consistency is desired. Pour the dressing over the cucumber mixture and toss to coat. Divide among eight salad plates; top with the tomatoes. **YIELD:** 8 servings.

Spicy Potato Wedges

(Pictured on page 326)

PREP: 15 min. **BAKE:** 30 min.

> 1/4 **cup canola oil**
> 1 **tablespoon chili powder**
> 2 **teaspoons onion powder**
> 2 **teaspoons garlic salt**
> 1 **teaspoon sugar**
> 1 **teaspoon paprika**
> 3/4 **teaspoon salt**
> 1/4 to 1/2 **teaspoon cayenne pepper**
> 3-1/2 **pounds large red potatoes, cut into wedges**

In a large bowl, combine first eight ingredients; add potatoes and toss to coat. Arrange in a single layer on greased baking sheets. Bake at 400° for 30-35 minutes or until the potato wedges are tender and golden brown, turning once. **YIELD:** 8 servings.

Feed Your Family
For $1.55 a Plate!

Celebrate the Chinese New Year with gusto—or enjoy easy-to-make Asian food any time of the year—with this budget menu that lets you feed the whole gang for roughly $1.55 a plate.

Our Test Kitchen put the menu together using tried-and-true recipes from three *Taste of Home* readers, so you know it's delicious!

Chinese New Year Skillet was inspired by a recipe on the back of a rice package in 1957, notes Sherilyn West of Lubbock, Texas. "If you like pork, I guarantee you'll love this recipe," she says. "It satisfies even the heartiest appetites."

Egg Drop Soup is the perfect way to start an Asian meal and requires just five ingredients. "If you want, you can add two minced water chestnuts," says Jenny Haen of Red Wing, Minnesota. "They add a wonderfully crunchy texture to the soup."

Beverly Preston of Fond du Lac, Wisconsin started making Almond Cookies after enjoying similar ones at her favorite Chinese restaurant. "These crisp cookies have wonderful almond flavor," she says. "They're a fitting end to a 'Far East' feast or any meal."

20 minutes or until the meat is tender. Meanwhile, cook the rice according to package directions.

In a small bowl, combine the cornstarch and water until smooth; stir into the pork mixture. Bring to a boil; cook and stir for 2 minutes or until thickened. Stir in the green pepper, tomato, Worcestershire sauce and reserved pineapple; heat through. Serve with rice. **YIELD:** 4 servings.

Egg Drop Soup

(Pictured on page 326)

PREP/TOTAL TIME: 10 min.

---

5 cups chicken broth
1/2 teaspoon sugar
1 egg, lightly beaten
1/3 cup sliced fresh spinach
2 green onions, sliced

In a large saucepan, bring the broth and sugar to a boil over medium heat. Reduce the heat to low. Drizzle the beaten egg into the hot broth. Remove from the heat; stir in the spinach and green onions. **YIELD:** 4 servings.

Chinese New Year Skillet

PREP: 15 min. **COOK:** 25 min.

---

1 pound boneless pork butt roast, cut into 1/2-inch cubes
1 tablespoon canola oil
1 can (20 ounces) unsweetened pineapple tidbits
2 tablespoons white wine vinegar
1 tablespoon sugar
3/4 teaspoon salt
1/4 teaspoon garlic powder
1 cup uncooked long grain rice
1 tablespoon cornstarch
2 tablespoons water
1/2 cup coarsely chopped green pepper
1 medium tomato, cut into wedges
2 tablespoons Worcestershire sauce

In a large skillet, cook pork in oil over medium heat on all sides until pork is lightly browned; drain. Drain pineapple, reserving juice in a 2-cup measuring cup; set pineapple aside.

Add enough water to the juice to measure 1-1/4 cups; then stir into the pork. Add the vinegar, sugar, salt and garlic powder. Bring to a boil, stirring constantly. Reduce the heat; cover and simmer for

Almond Cookies

PREP: 10 min. **BAKE:** 10 min./batch + cooling

---

1 cup shortening
1/2 cup plus 3 tablespoons sugar, *divided*
1/4 cup packed brown sugar
1 egg
1 teaspoon almond extract
2 cups all-purpose flour
1-1/2 teaspoons baking powder
1/8 teaspoon salt
3 tablespoons sliced almonds

In a small bowl, cream the shortening, 1/2 cup sugar and brown sugar. Beat in egg and extract.

Combine the flour, baking powder and salt; gradually add to the creamed mixture and mix well. Shape into 1-in. balls. Roll in the remaining sugar.

Place dough 2 in. apart on ungreased baking sheets. Flatten with the bottom of a glass. Press three almond slices into the center of each cookie.

Bake at 350° for 9-11 minutes or until the edges are lightly browned. Cool for 2 minutes on pan before removing to wire racks. **YIELD:** 3 dozen.

Feed Your Family For $1.60 a Plate!

For low-cost comfort food at its finest, try a menu of Caraway Pot Roast from Violet Beard of Marshall, Illinois. You'll also enjoy the delicious accompaniments of Mashed Potato Casserole from Margaret Lindberg of Richland, Washington and Fluffy Pineapple Dessert from Donna Gaston, Coplay, Pennsylvania.

Caraway Pot Roast

PREP: 10 min. COOK: 2-3/4 hours

- 1 boneless beef chuck roast (3 pounds)
- 2 tablespoons canola oil
- 2 medium onions, sliced
- 2 medium carrots, cut into large chunks
- 1 cup apple cider *or* apple juice
- 1 tablespoon caraway seeds
- 2 garlic cloves, minced
- 3/4 teaspoon salt, *divided*
- 1/2 teaspoon pepper, *divided*
- 2 tablespoons cornstarch
- 1/4 cup cold water
- 1/2 cup sour cream

In Dutch oven, brown roast in oil on all sides over medium-high heat; drain. Combine onions, carrots, cider, caraway, garlic, 1/2 teaspoon salt and 1/4 teaspoon pepper; pour over roast. Bring to boil; reduce heat. Cover; simmer 2 to 2-1/2 hours or until meat is tender.

Remove roast and vegetables; keep warm. Strain pan juices into 2-cup measuring cup. Skim fat; add enough water to measure 2 cups. Return to pot. Combine cornstarch and cold water until smooth; gradually stir into pan juices. Bring to a boil; cook and stir for 2 minutes or until thickened. Remove from the heat; stir in the sour cream and remaining salt and pepper. Serve with roast and vegetables. **YIELD:** 8 servings.

Mashed Potato Casserole

PREP: 30 min. BAKE: 30 min.

- 3 pounds potatoes, peeled and cubed
- 1 package (8 ounces) cream cheese, cubed
- 1 cup (8 ounces) sour cream
- 1/4 cup milk
- 1 small onion, chopped
- 1 teaspoon garlic salt
- 1/2 teaspoon salt
- 2 tablespoons butter, melted
- 1/4 teaspoon paprika

Place the potatoes in a large saucepan and cover with water. Bring to a boil. Reduce heat; cover and simmer until tender. Drain; place potatoes in a large bowl. Add the cream cheese, sour cream, milk, onion, garlic salt and salt; beat until blended.

Transfer to a greased 2-qt. baking dish. Drizzle with butter; sprinkle with paprika. Cover and bake at 350° for 30-35 minutes or until heated through. **YIELD:** 8 servings.

Fluffy Pineapple Dessert

PREP: 25 min. BAKE: 45 min. + cooling

- 1 cup butter, softened
- 1 cup sugar, *divided*
- 7 egg yolks, *divided*
- 1/2 cup sour cream
- 2-1/2 cups plus 3 tablespoons all-purpose flour, *divided*
- 1 teaspoon baking powder
- 1/2 teaspoon salt
- 2 cans (20 ounces *each*) crushed unsweetened pineapple, undrained
- 2 teaspoons vanilla extract

TOPPING:
- 5 egg whites
- 10 tablespoons sugar
- 1 teaspoon vanilla extract
- 1/2 cup finely chopped walnuts

In a large bowl, cream butter and 1/2 cup sugar. Add 3 egg yolks and sour cream; mix well. Combine 2-1/2 cups flour, baking powder and salt; gradually add to yolk mixture. Press into a greased 13-in. x 9-in. baking dish. Bake at 350° for 12-15 minutes or until set and edges are lightly browned.

Meanwhile, in a small saucepan, combine remaining each of sugar, yolks and flour; stir in pineapple. Cook and stir over medium heat until mixture reaches 160° and coats back of a metal spoon. Remove from heat; stir in vanilla. Pour over crust. Bake at 350° for 15 minutes.

For the topping, beat egg whites until soft peaks form. Gradually add the sugar and vanilla, beating until stiff peaks form. Spread over the hot filling, sealing edges to the pan. Sprinkle with walnuts. Bake 15 minutes longer or until golden brown. Cool on a wire rack for 1 hour. Store in the refrigerator. **YIELD:** 16 servings.

Feed Your Family For $2.00 a Plate!

Don't save ham for a special Sunday dinner. At this price, you can ham it up any night of the week! In Chilliwack, British Columbia, Cornelia Whiteway serves Barbecued Ham and Peaches for a main dish that's both economical and irresistible. Because the recipe calls for fully cooked ham that you can easily pick up at the deli, it's quick enough for a convenient weeknight meal. But the entree is also elegant enough for a fancy dinner.

To complete the meal, add the pretty Three-Fruit Salad from Sue Gronholz of Beaver Dam, Wisconsin. Delight everyone at the table with Pear-Filled Bundt Cake from Barbara Sievert of Yorktown, Virginia.

Barbecued Ham and Peaches

(Pictured on page 326)

PREP/TOTAL TIME: 20 min.

- 1/4 **cup ketchup**
- 1 **tablespoon brown sugar**
- 1 **tablespoon cider vinegar**
- 2 **teaspoons Worcestershire sauce**
- 1 **teaspoon canola oil**
- 1/4 **teaspoon pepper**
- 4 **boneless fully cooked ham slices (4 ounces *each*)**
- 1 **can (8-1/2 ounces) sliced peaches, drained**

In a small bowl, combine the ketchup, brown sugar, vinegar, Worcestershire sauce, oil and pepper; brush some of the mixture over ham slices. Place each slice on a greased 12-in. square of heavy-duty foil. Top with peaches; drizzle with remaining ketchup mixture.

Fold foil over ham and peaches and seal tightly. Grill, covered, over medium heat for 5-6 minutes in each side or until heated through. **YIELD:** 4 servings.

Three-Fruit Salad

(Pictured on page 326)

PREP: 10 min. **COOK:** 15 min. + cooling

- 1 **can (20 ounces) pineapple chunks**
- 1/3 **cup sugar**
- 1 **tablespoon cornstarch**
- 1 **tablespoon lemon juice**
- 1/8 **teaspoon salt**
- 2 **eggs, lightly beaten**
- 1 **to 2 small ripe bananas, sliced**
- 1 **cup halved seedless red grapes**
- 1 **cup miniature marshmallows**
- 6 **cups torn lettuce**

Drain pineapple, reserving juice; set pineapple aside. In a small saucepan, combine sugar, cornstarch, lemon juice, salt and reserved juice until smooth. Bring to a boil over medium heat, stirring until sugar is dissolved.

Remove from the heat. Stir a small amount of hot juice mixture into eggs; return all to the pan, stirring constantly. Bring to a gentle boil; cook and stir for 2 minutes. Transfer to a small bowl; cool.

Just before serving, in a bowl, combine the bananas, grapes, marshmallows, pineapple and cooled dressing. Serve over lettuce. **YIELD:** 4 servings.

Pear-Filled Bundt Cake

(Pictured on page 326)

PREP: 25 min. **BAKE:** 35 min. + cooling

- 1/2 **cup butter, softened**
- 1/2 **cup sugar**
- 3 **eggs**
- 1/2 **teaspoon vanilla extract**
- 2 **cups all-purpose flour**
- 1 **teaspoon baking powder**
- 1 **teaspoon baking soda**
- 1/3 **cup orange juice**

FILLING:
- 1/2 **cup packed brown sugar**
- 1/2 **cup diced peeled ripe pear**
- 1/2 **cup sliced almonds**
- 2 **tablespoons all-purpose flour**
- 4-1/2 **teaspoons butter, melted**
- 1/2 **teaspoon ground cinnamon**

GLAZE:
- 1/2 **cup confectioners' sugar**
- 2-1/4 **teaspoons orange juice**

In a large bowl, cream the butter and sugar. Add eggs, one at a time, beating well after each addition. Beat in the vanilla. Combine the flour, baking powder and baking soda; add to the creamed mixture alternately with the orange juice.

Pour half of the batter into a greased 10-in. fluted tube pan. Combine the filling ingredients; sprinkle over batter. Top with remaining batter. Smooth top with a spatula.

Bake at 350° for 35-40 minutes or until a toothpick inserted near the center comes out clean. Cool for 10 minutes before removing from pan to a wire rack. Combine glaze ingredients; drizzle over cake. **YIELD:** 16-20 servings.

Feed Your Family
For $2.00 a Plate!

If real spareribs don't always fit in your budget, try this lip-smacking, economical substitute. Janice Porterfield of Atlanta, Texas turns ordinary chicken thighs into extraordinary Chicken Spareribs with a zippy barbecue-style sauce. You might have to make extras!

You'll also enjoy the two satisfying sides. "I always take my nice and light Cottage Cheese Yeast Rolls to potlucks, where they disappear quickly," says Angie Merriam of Springfield, Ohio.

Using fresh spinach instead of frozen really enhances the flavor of classic Creamed Spinach, shared by Ann Van Dyk of Wrightstown, Wisconsin.

Chicken Spareribs

PREP: 5 min. COOK: 30 min.

    8 bone-in chicken thighs
    2 tablespoons canola oil
    1 cup water
  2/3 cup packed brown sugar
  2/3 cup soy sauce
  1/2 cup apple juice
  1/4 cup ketchup
    2 tablespoons cider vinegar
    2 garlic cloves, minced
    1 teaspoon crushed red pepper flakes
  1/2 teaspoon ground ginger
    2 tablespoons cornstarch
    2 tablespoons cold water

In a Dutch oven, brown the chicken over medium heat in oil in batches on both sides; drain. Return all of the chicken to the pan.

In a large bowl, combine the water, brown sugar, soy sauce, apple juice, ketchup, vinegar, garlic, pepper flakes and ginger; pour over the chicken. Bring to a boil. Reduce the heat; cover and simmer for 20 minutes or until the chicken juices run clear.

Remove the chicken to a platter and keep warm. Combine the cornstarch and water until smooth; stir into cooking juices. Bring to a boil; cook and stir for 2 minutes or until thickened. Serve with the chicken. **YIELD:** 4 servings.

Cottage Cheese Yeast Rolls

PREP: 30 min. + rising BAKE: 10 min./batch

    2 packages (1/4 ounce *each*) active dry yeast
  1/2 cup warm water (110° to 115°)
    2 cups (16 ounces) 4% cottage cheese
    2 eggs
  1/4 cup sugar
    2 teaspoons salt
  1/2 teaspoon baking soda
4-1/2 cups all-purpose flour

In a large bowl, dissolve the yeast in warm water. In a small saucepan, heat the cottage cheese to 110°-115°. Add the cottage cheese, eggs, sugar, salt, baking soda and 2 cups of flour to the yeast mixture; beat until smooth. Stir in enough remaining flour to form a firm dough (dough will be sticky).

Turn onto a floured surface; knead until smooth and elastic, about 6-8 minutes. Place in a greased bowl, turning once to grease top. Cover and let rise in a warm place until doubled, about 1 hour.

Punch the dough down. Turn onto a lightly floured surface; divide into 30 pieces. Shape each piece of dough into a roll by gently rolling the pieces between the palms of your hands. Place 2 in. apart on greased baking sheets. Cover and let the rolls rise until doubled, about 30 minutes.

Bake at 350° for 10-12 minutes or until golden brown. Remove to wire racks. **YIELD:** 2-1/2 dozen.

Creamed Spinach

PREP/TOTAL TIME: 25 min.

  3/4 pound fresh spinach, torn
    2 tablespoons olive oil
    6 tablespoons butter, cubed
  1/4 cup chopped onion
  1/4 cup all-purpose flour
  1/2 teaspoon salt
  1/8 teaspoon ground nutmeg
1-1/2 cups milk

In a Dutch oven, cook the fresh spinach in olive oil for 3 minutes or until wilted. Transfer to a cutting board; chop. Melt cubed butter in the Dutch oven. Add the chopped onion; saute in the butter for 2 minutes or until crisp-tender.

Stir in the flour, salt and ground nutmeg until combined. Gradually whisk in the milk until blended. Bring to a boil; cook and stir for 2 minutes or until thickened. Add the chopped spinach. Reduce the heat to low; cook, uncovered, for 5 minutes or until mixture is heated through. **YIELD:** 4 servings.

Feed Your Family For $2.10 a Plate!

There's no need to scrimp on flavor thanks to this scrumptious (and inexpensive) supper that features Sausage with Apple Sauerkraut. It was created by Carolyn Schmeling of Brookfield, Wisconsin, who based her recipe variation on a traditional sausage and sauerkraut dish. With just the right touch of caraway and fennel seeds, the sauerkraut is wonderfully sweet. For some extra tang, drizzle on some mustard.

"My mother used to serve Crispy Potato Cubes when I was growing up, and she included the recipe in a cookbook she made for me when I got married," says Jenelle Piepmeier of Severna Park, Maryland. "They fill the kitchen with a heavenly aroma."

Barbara Carlucci of Orange Park, Florida developed Green Beans with Walnuts in her kitchen and has prepared it many times. "It requires just 15 minutes," she says. "The sauce is yummy not only on green beans but also on fresh or frozen broccoli."

Sausage with Apple Sauerkraut

PREP: 10 min. COOK: 35 min.

- 1 medium sweet onion, sliced
- 3 tablespoons butter
- 2 medium apples, peeled and shredded
- 1 tablespoon lemon juice
- 1 can (8 ounces) sauerkraut, rinsed and well drained
- 1/2 cup unsweetened apple juice
- 1 teaspoon caraway seeds
- 1/2 teaspoon fennel seeds, crushed
- 1 package (16 ounces) smoked Polish sausage

In a large skillet, saute the onion in butter for 15 minutes or until lightly browned.

In a large bowl, toss the apples with lemon juice. Add the apples, sauerkraut, apple juice, caraway and fennel seeds to the onion. Bring to a boil. Reduce heat; cover and simmer for 15 minutes. Meanwhile, heat the sausage according to package directions; cut into slices. Serve with sauerkraut. **YIELD:** 4 servings.

Crispy Potato Cubes

PREP: 10 min. BAKE: 35 min.

- 1/3 cup all-purpose flour
- 3/4 teaspoon salt
- 1/2 teaspoon dried thyme
- 1/2 teaspoon dried marjoram
- 1/8 teaspoon pepper
- 5 medium potatoes, peeled and cut into 1-inch cubes
- 1/4 cup butter, melted
- 1 garlic clove, minced
- 1 bay leaf

In a large resealable plastic bag, combine the flour, salt, thyme, marjoram and pepper. Add the potatoes; seal bag and shake to coat. Pour the butter into a 13-in. x 9-in. baking dish; stir in the garlic. Add the potatoes and bay leaf.

Cover and bake at 450° for 20 minutes. Uncover and stir; bake 15-20 minutes longer or until the potatoes are lightly browned and tender. Discard bay leaf. **YIELD:** 4 servings.

Green Beans with Walnuts

PREP/TOTAL TIME: 15 min.

- 1 package (16 ounces) frozen cut green beans
- 1/4 cup chopped walnuts, _divided_
- 1/4 cup teriyaki sauce
- 2 tablespoons butter, cubed

In 1-1/2-qt. microwave-safe dish, combine the beans, 2 tablespoons walnuts, teriyaki sauce and butter. Cover and microwave on high for 3 minutes; stir. Cook 5-6 minutes longer or until beans are tender. Sprinkle with remaining walnuts. **YIELD:** 4 servings.

EDITOR'S NOTE: This recipe was tested in a 1,100-watt microwave.

meal planning on a budget

Remember these tips when planning menus and before heading to the grocery store:

- Keep your pantry well stocked with staples and use those items before stocking up on more.
- Plan your grocery list according to what's on sale. Stock up on staple items when prices are low.
- To stretch your hard-earned dollars, shop at more than one grocery store, including discount chains.
- Throwing food away is like tossing money down the disposal. So plan your leftovers...or only make enough to avoid having any extras.

Feed Your Family for $1.10 a Plate!

Looking for ways to save on your grocery bill while still serving your family delicious and nutritious meals? Leave it to our readers to come up with some taste-tempting solutions!

Our Test Kitchen home economists have put together this satisfying meal with recipes from three great cooks. It makes a filling lunch or a light summer supper...at just $1.10 per person.

For her Tuna Cheese Melts, Bernadine Dirmeyer of Harpster, Ohio dresses up a typical tuna sandwich with American cheese and rye bread spread with a mixture of sour cream and garlic salt. Cooked in a skillet, this sandwich oozes with flavor and comfort.

Radish Potato Salad from Lydia Garcia of Hanover, Pennsylvania is well coated with a scrumptious and creamy dill dressing. This summery salad, made with radish slices and chopped eggs, is not only pretty but easy to prepare, too.

"Cinnamon-Sugar Crisps are a favorite with children...and adults, too," says Kim Marie Van Rheenen of Mendota, Illinois. These sweet and spicy refrigerator cookies go great with a cup of coffee or a glass of milk. You won't be able to eat just one!

Tuna Cheese Melts

PREP/TOTAL TIME: 25 min.

- 1/2 cup sour cream
- 1/2 teaspoon garlic salt
- 8 slices rye *or* white bread
- 1 can (6 ounces) tuna, drained and flaked
- 2 tablespoons mayonnaise
- 4 slices process American cheese
- 4 tablespoons butter, *divided*

In a small bowl, combine sour cream and garlic salt; spread on one side of each slice of bread. In another small bowl, combine the tuna and mayonnaise; spread on four slices of bread. Top with cheese and remaining bread; gently press together.

Melt 2 tablespoons butter in a large skillet over medium heat. Add two sandwiches; toast sandwiches until bread is lightly browned on both sides and cheese is melted. Repeat with remaining butter and sandwiches. **YIELD:** 4 servings.

Radish Potato Salad

PREP: 30 min. + chilling

- 5 medium red potatoes (about 1-1/2 pounds)
- 1 cup sliced radishes
- 2 hard-cooked eggs, chopped
- 3/4 cup mayonnaise
- 3 tablespoons minced fresh dill
- 2 tablespoons cider vinegar
- 1 tablespoon sugar
- 1/4 teaspoon salt

Dash pepper

Place potatoes in a saucepan and cover with water. Bring to a boil. Reduce heat; cover and cook for 15-20 minutes or until tender. Drain and cool.

Peel and cube the potatoes; place in a large bowl. Add the radishes and eggs.

In a small bowl, combine the mayonnaise, dill, vinegar, sugar, salt and pepper. Pour over the potato mixture; gently toss to coat. Cover and refrigerate for at least 1 hour. **YIELD:** 4 servings.

Cinnamon-Sugar Crisps

PREP: 30 min. + chilling **BAKE:** 15 min.

- 3/4 cup butter, softened
- 1/3 cup sugar
- 1/3 cup packed brown sugar
- 1 egg
- 1 teaspoon vanilla extract
- 1-3/4 cups all-purpose flour
- 1 teaspoon ground cinnamon
- 1/4 teaspoon salt
- 2 tablespoons colored sprinkles

In a large bowl, cream the butter, sugar and brown sugar together until light and fluffy. Beat in the egg and vanilla extract. Combine the flour, cinnamon and salt; gradually add to the creamed mixture and mix well.

Shape the dough into a 12-in. roll; wrap in plastic wrap. Refrigerate for 2 hours or until firm.

Unwrap and cut into 1/2-in. slices. Place 2 in. apart on ungreased baking sheets. Decorate with sprinkles.

Bake at 350° for 10-12 minutes or until lightly browned. Remove to wire racks to cool. **YIELD:** 3-1/2 dozen.

Feed Your Family for $1.85 a Plate!

Grocery budget a little tight? Don't worry! You can still enjoy foods that are satisfying and full of flavor.

Three frugal cooks prove it with this mouthwatering meal that's perfect for a springtime luncheon or a light supper. Our Test Kitchen home economists estimate the total cost of this meal at about $1.85 per setting.

Canned salmon and frozen peas streamline the preparation of hearty Salmon Chowder from Pat Waymire of Yellow Springs, Ohio. Shredded Swiss and cheddar cheeses, along with cauliflower and dill weed, add flavor to this appealing stovetop dish.

"I love my bread machine and am always trying new recipes in it," says Joy McMillan from The Woodlands, Texas. "Cracked Pepper Bread is one of my successes. When it's baking in the oven, the whole kitchen smells wonderful." Basil, garlic, chives and Parmesan cheese give this tall tender loaf a real Italian flavor.

Bernice Morris from Marshfield, Missouri dresses up her Garden Lettuce Salad with tomatoes, radishes, green onions, crisp bacon, hard-cooked eggs and a creamy homemade dressing. "It's a nice change from our usual wilted lettuce salad," she says. "It's also good with fried chicken and mashed potatoes or with a barbecue dinner."

Salmon Chowder

PREP/TOTAL TIME: 20 min.

- 1 cup thinly sliced green onions
- 2 celery ribs, thinly sliced
- 2 tablespoons butter
- 2 tablespoons all-purpose flour
- 1/2 teaspoon salt
- 1/2 teaspoon dill weed
- 4 cups milk
- 2 cups cauliflowerets, cooked
- 1 can (14-3/4 ounces) salmon, drained, skin and bones removed
- 1 package (10 ounces) frozen peas, thawed
- 1/2 cup shredded Swiss cheese
- 1/2 cup shredded cheddar cheese

In a large saucepan, saute onions and celery in butter until tender. Stir in the flour, salt and dill until blended. Gradually add milk. Bring to a boil; cook and stir for 2 minutes or until thickened. Add cauliflower, salmon and peas; heat through. Stir in the cheeses until melted. Serve immediately. **YIELD:** 8 servings.

Cracked Pepper Bread

PREP: 10 min. **BAKE:** 3 hours

- 1-1/2 cups water (70° to 80°)
- 3 tablespoons olive oil
- 3 tablespoons sugar
- 2 teaspoons salt
- 3 tablespoons minced chives
- 2 garlic cloves, minced

1 teaspoon garlic powder
1 teaspoon dried basil
1 teaspoon cracked black pepper
1/4 cup grated Parmesan cheese
4 cups bread flour
2-1/2 teaspoons active dry yeast

In bread machine pan, place all ingredients in order suggested by manufacturer. Select basic bread setting. Choose crust color and loaf size if available. Bake according to bread machine directions (check dough after 5 minutes of mixing; add 1 to 2 tablespoons of water or flour if needed). **YIELD:** 1 loaf (2 pounds, 16 slices).

Garden Lettuce Salad

PREP/TOTAL TIME: 15 min.

5 cups torn leaf lettuce
2 medium tomatoes, chopped
3 hard-cooked eggs, sliced
3/4 cup sliced radishes
4 bacon strips, cooked and crumbled
3 green onions, sliced

DRESSING:
3/4 cup mayonnaise
1 tablespoon red wine vinegar
1 teaspoon lemon-lime soda
1/2 teaspoon salt
1/2 teaspoon sugar

In a salad bowl, toss the lettuce, tomatoes, hard-cooked eggs, radishes, bacon and onions. In a small bowl, whisk together the dressing ingredients. Serve with salad. **YIELD:** 6 servings.

Feed Your Family for $1.65 a Plate!

Eating well at today's prices isn't impossible. The frugal yet flavorful meal here combines recipes from three creative cooks. Our Test Kitchen staff estimates the total cost at about $1.65 per serving.

Traditional lasagna fixin's (minus the meat) make up the ingredient list for Vegetable Noodle Bake, a satisfying casserole shared by Dixie Terry of Goreville, Illinois. The egg noodles are a great substitute for the usual lasagna noodles. "If you're out of hamburger, serve this dish and no one will even notice it's meatless because it's so tasty," Dixie assures.

Potato, tomato and onion complement the fresh green beans in colorful Green Bean Salad. A subtle oil-and-vinegar dressing lends fresh herb flavor to the wonderful mix. The recipe comes from the kitchen of Sarah Maranto of Bakersfield, California.

No one will be able to eat just one of Gail Wiese's yummy Chocolate Ribbon Bars, full of butterscotch, peanut butter and chocolate flavor. "Over the years I've accumulated quite a few terrific recipes from my co-workers, and this one is so easy to prepare," says Gail from her home in Athens, Wisconsin.

Vegetable Noodle Bake

PREP: 15 min. **BAKE:** 20 min.

- 1 can (14-1/2 ounces) diced tomatoes, drained
- 3/4 cup canned tomato puree
- 1/3 cup chopped onion
- 1-1/4 teaspoons dried oregano
- 1/4 teaspoon garlic powder
- 1/4 teaspoon salt
- 1/8 teaspoon pepper
- 2-1/2 cups uncooked medium egg noodles
- 1/2 cup 4% cottage cheese
- 1 package (10 ounces) frozen chopped spinach, thawed and squeezed dry
- 1/3 cup shredded American cheese

In a large saucepan, combine the diced tomatoes, tomato puree, onion, dried oregano, garlic powder, salt and pepper. Bring to a boil. Reduce heat; simmer, uncovered, for 15 minutes.

Meanwhile, cook noodles according to package directions; drain. Spread 1/3 cup tomato mixture in a greased, shallow 2-qt. baking dish. Top with half of the noodles. Spread with cottage cheese; top with spinach. Drizzle with 1/2 cup tomato mixture; top with remaining noodles and tomato mixture. Sprinkle with American cheese. Cover and bake at 350° for 20-25 minutes or until cheese is melted. **YIELD:** 4 servings.

Green Bean and Tomato Salad

PREP: 15 min. **COOK:** 15 min.

- 1 medium potato, peeled
- 1/2 pound fresh green beans, cut into 2-inch pieces
- 1 medium tomato, cubed
- 1/2 small red onion, sliced and separated into rings
- 2 tablespoons red wine vinegar
- 2 tablespoons canola oil
- 2 tablespoons minced fresh oregano

2 tablespoons minced fresh parsley
1/8 teaspoon salt

Place potato in a saucepan and cover with water. Bring to a boil; reduce heat; cover and simmer for 15-20 minutes or until tender. Drain and cool; cut into cubes.

Meanwhile, place the green beans in a saucepan and cover with water. Bring to a boil; reduce heat. Cook, uncovered, for 6-8 minutes or until crisp-tender. Drain and then cool.

In a large serving bowl, combine the beans, potato, tomato and onion. In a jar with a tight-fitting lid, combine remaining ingredients; shake well. Pour over bean mixture; toss to coat. **YIELD:** 4 servings.

Chocolate Ribbon Bars

PREP: 20 min. + chilling

1 package (10 to 11 ounces) butterscotch chips
1 cup peanut butter

8 cups crisp rice cereal
2 cups (12 ounces) semisweet chocolate chips
1/4 cup butter, cubed
2 tablespoons water
3/4 cup confectioners' sugar

In a large microwave-safe bowl, combine the butterscotch chips and peanut butter and melt; stir together until smooth. Gradually stir in the crisp rice cereal until it is well coated. Press half of the mixture into a greased 13-in. x 9-in. pan; set the remaining mixture aside.

In another large microwave-safe bowl, melt semisweet chocolate chips and butter. Stir in water until blended. Gradually add the confectioners' sugar, stirring until smooth.

Spread over cereal layer. Cover and refrigerate for 10 minutes or until chocolate layer is set. Spread remaining cereal mixture over the top. Chill before cutting. **YIELD:** 2 dozen.

EDITOR'S NOTE: Reduced-fat or generic brands of peanut butter are not recommended for this recipe.

From **breezy** spring days to chilly winter evenings, there are countless ways to celebrate throughout the year.

seasons of good taste

Peeps Sunflower Cake 350

Strawberry Pretzel Dessert.............................350

Pickled Baby Carrots 351

Stuffed Ham with Raisin Sauce 351

Overnight Asparagus Strata 352

Almond-Butter Cookie Bouquet.................352

Minted Lamb and Veggie Kabobs 353

Spring Breeze Cheesecake Pie......................353

Butterfly Cheese Sandwiches.........................354

Ladybug Cake...354

Tomato-Cucumber Mozzarella Salad..........355

Rustic Roasted Vegetable Tart.......................355

Corn Fritters with Caramelized
  Onion Jam...356

Spicy Zucchini Quesadillas.............................356

Blackberry Crisp 357

Peaches & Cream Tart....................................357

Russian Cream 358

Golden Corn Quiche......................................358

Ultimate Caramel Apples................................359

Apple-Cherry Pork Chops 359

Turkey with Sausage-Corn Bread
  Stuffing...360

Rice-Stuffed Acorn Squash 360

Wicked Witch Cupcakes 361

Cranberry Walnut Tart....................................362

Spiced Squash Muffins 362

Beef Rib Roast...363

Coconut Snowmen...363

Spinach and Sausage Pork Loin 364

Italian Herb Muffins 364

Brussels Sprouts with Water Chestnuts......365

Festive White Chocolate Cheesecake........365

Peanut Butter Christmas Mice 366

Spicy Seafood Bisque 366

Crab and Brie Strudel Slices...........................367

Lemon Cream Puffs 367

PICTURED CLOCKWISE FROM UPPER LEFT: Rustic Roasted Vegetable Tart (page 355), Minted Lamb and Veggie Kabobs (page 353), Festive White Chocolate Cheesecake (page 365) and Ultimate Caramel Apples (page 359).

spring has sprung!

Strawberry Pretzel Dessert

(Pictured below)

PREP: 15 min. + chilling

I love the sweet-salty taste of this pretty layered dessert. Sliced strawberries and gelatin top a smooth cream cheese filling and crispy pretzel crust.

—Wendy Weaver, Leetonia, Ohio

- 1/3 cup crushed pretzels
- 2 tablespoons butter, softened
- 2 ounces cream cheese, softened
- 1/4 cup sugar
- 3/4 cup whipped topping
- 2 tablespoons plus 1-1/2 teaspoons strawberry gelatin powder
- 1/2 cup boiling water
- 1 cup sliced fresh strawberries

In a bowl, combine pretzels and butter. Press onto the bottom of two 10-oz. greased custard cups. Bake at 375° for 6-8 minutes or until set. Cool on a wire rack.

In a small bowl, combine the cream cheese and sugar. Fold in the whipped topping. Spoon over crust. Refrigerate for 30 minutes.

Meanwhile, in a bowl, dissolve gelatin in boiling water. Cover and refrigerate for 20 minutes or until slightly thickened. Fold in the strawberries. Carefully spoon over filling. Cover and refrigerate for at least 3 hours. **YIELD:** 2 servings.

Peeps Sunflower Cake

(Pictured above)

PREP: 15 min. **BAKE:** 30 min. + cooling

The inspiration for this cake came from one of my favorite flowers. The yellow Peeps make for attractive petals, and the chocolate chips resemble the seeds in the center. It's really easy to make but looks impressive.

—Bethany Eledge, Cleveland, Tennessee

- 1 package (18-1/4 ounces) yellow cake mix
- 2 cans (16 ounces *each*) chocolate frosting
- 19 yellow chick Peeps candies
- 1-1/2 cups semisweet chocolate chips

Prepare and bake cake according to the package directions, using two greased and waxed paper-lined 9-in. round baking pans. Cool for 10 minutes before removing from pans to wire racks to cool completely; carefully remove waxed paper.

Level tops of cakes. Spread frosting between layers and over the top and sides of cake.

Without separating Peeps and curving slightly to fit, arrange chicks around edge of cake for sunflower petals. For sunflower seeds, arrange chocolate chips in center of cake. **YIELD:** 12 servings.

Pickled Baby Carrots

(Pictured above)

PREP: 20 min. + chilling

With mild herb flavor and crunchy texture, these baby carrots make a delightful addition to an appetizer tray or a casual meal. Plan ahead because they need to chill for several hours.

—*Audrey Cremer, Harmony, Minnesota*

> 2 **pounds fresh baby carrots**
> 2/3 **cup white wine vinegar**
> 1/2 **cup honey**
> 2 **tablespoons mustard seed**
> 2 **tablespoons dill weed**
> 1 **teaspoon salt**

Place 1 in. of water in a large saucepan; add carrots. Bring to a boil. Reduce the heat; cover and simmer for 5-6 minutes or until crisp-tender. Drain.

In a large bowl, combine the remaining ingredients. Stir in carrots. Cover and refrigerate for 8 hours or overnight, stirring several times. Serve with a slotted spoon. **YIELD:** 8-10 servings.

Stuffed Ham with Raisin Sauce

(Pictured at right)

PREP: 30 min. **BAKE:** 1-3/4 hours

This eye-catching ham makes a great centerpiece for a holiday dinner, but I've served it most often for brunch. It always draws rave reviews.

—*Jeanne Miller, Big Sky, Montana*

> 1 **boneless fully cooked ham (6 to 7 pounds)**
> 1 **large onion, chopped**
> 1/4 **cup butter, cubed**
> 2 **cups corn bread stuffing mix**
> 1-1/2 **cups chopped pecans, toasted**
> 1/2 **cup minced fresh parsley**
> 1/4 **cup egg substitute**
> 2 **tablespoons prepared mustard**
> 1/2 **cup honey**
> 2 **tablespoons orange juice concentrate**
> **RAISIN SAUCE:**
> 1/2 **cup packed brown sugar**
> 2 **tablespoons all-purpose flour**
> 1/2 **teaspoon ground mustard**
> 1/2 **cup raisins**
> 1-1/2 **cups water**
> 1/4 **cup cider vinegar**

Using a sharp thin-bladed knife and beginning at one end of the ham, carefully cut a 2-1/2-in. circle about 6 in. deep; remove the cutout. Cut a 1-1/2-in. slice from the end of removed piece; set aside. Continue cutting a 2-1/2-in. tunnel halfway through ham, using a spoon to remove pieces of ham (save for another use). Repeat from opposite end of ham, cutting and removing ham until a tunnel has been cut through entire length of ham.

In a skillet, saute the onion in butter until tender. In a large bowl, combine stuffing mix, pecans, parsley, egg substitute and mustard. Stir in onion. Stuff ham; cover end openings with reserved ham slices. Place in a shallow roasting pan.

Bake, uncovered, at 325° for 1-1/4 hours. In a small saucepan, combine honey and orange juice concentrate; cook and stir for 1-2 minutes or until blended. Brush over ham. Bake 30 minutes longer or until a meat thermometer reads 140°.

For sauce, combine the brown sugar, flour, mustard and raisins in a saucepan. Gradually add water and vinegar. Bring to a boil; cook and stir for 1-2 minutes or until thickened. Serve with ham. **YIELD:** 12-14 servings.

Overnight Asparagus Strata

(Pictured below)

PREP: 15 min. + chilling **BAKE:** 40 min. + standing

I've made this tasty egg dish for breakfast and brunch. With its English muffin crust, this is not your run-of-the-mill strata. Friends always ask for the recipe.

—Lynn Licata, Sylvania, Ohio

- 1 pound fresh asparagus, trimmed and cut into 1-inch pieces
- 4 English muffins, split and toasted
- 2 cups (8 ounces) shredded Colby-Monterey Jack cheese, *divided*
- 1 cup diced fully cooked ham
- 1/2 cup chopped sweet red pepper
- 8 eggs
- 2 cups milk
- 1 teaspoon salt
- 1 teaspoon ground mustard
- 1/4 teaspoon pepper

In a large saucepan, bring 8 cups of water to a boil. Add the asparagus; cover and cook for 3 minutes. Drain and immediately place the asparagus in ice water. Drain and pat dry.

Arrange six English muffin halves, cut side up, in a greased 13-in. x 9-in. baking dish. Fill in spaces with remaining muffin halves. Sprinkle with 1 cup cheese, asparagus, ham and red pepper. In a bowl, whisk the eggs, milk, salt, mustard and pepper; pour over muffins. Cover and refrigerate overnight.

Remove from the refrigerator 30 minutes before baking. Sprinkle with remaining cheese. Bake, uncovered, at 375° for 40-45 minutes or until a knife inserted near the edge comes out clean. Let stand for 5 minutes before cutting. **YIELD:** 6-8 servings.

Almond-Butter Cookie Bouquet

(Pictured above)

PREP: 2 hours + chilling **BAKE:** 10 min./batch + cooling

I insert cute cookie pops into a block of foam fitted into a basket or bowl and cover the foam with cellophane to make a great centerpiece or hostess gift.

—Krissy Fossmeyer, Huntley, Illinois

- 1-1/4 cups butter, softened
- 1-3/4 cups confectioners' sugar
- 2 ounces almond paste
- 1 egg
- 1/4 cup milk
- 1 teaspoon vanilla extract
- 4 cups all-purpose flour
- 1/2 teaspoon salt
- Wooden skewers *or* lollipop sticks
- **ICING:**
- 1 cup confectioners' sugar
- 4 teaspoons evaporated milk
- Food coloring of your choice

In a large bowl, cream butter and confectioners' sugar until light and fluffy; add almond paste. Beat in egg, milk and vanilla. Combine the flour and salt; gradually add to the creamed mixture. Cover and refrigerate for 1 hour.

On a lightly floured surface, roll out dough to 1/4-in. thickness. Cut out with floured 3-in. cookie cutters. Place 1 in. apart on ungreased baking sheets. Insert sticks. Bake at 375° for 7-8 minutes or until firm. Let stand 2 minutes before removing to wire racks to cool.

In a bowl, whisk confectioners' sugar and milk. Divide into small bowls; tint with food coloring. Gently spread icing over cookies. Decorate with other colors of icing if desired. **YIELD:** about 2-1/2 dozen.

Minted Lamb and Veggie Kabobs

(Pictured below and on page 348)

PREP: 30 min. + marinating **GRILL:** 10 min.

Mint leaves give these lamb kabobs an enticing flavor and aroma. Served with brown rice, the eye-catching meat and vegetable skewers look and taste special enough to dish up for company.

—Michael Rose, Grand Prairie, Texas

   3 **tablespoons olive oil**
   2 **tablespoons lemon juice**
   4 **garlic cloves, minced**
   2 **teaspoons dried basil**
   1 **teaspoon dried oregano**
   1 **teaspoon pepper**
1/2 **teaspoon salt**
1/2 **teaspoon dried thyme**
   1 **pound boneless leg of lamb, cut into 1-inch cubes**
   1 **medium sweet red pepper, cut into 1-inch pieces**
   1 **medium sweet yellow pepper, cut into 1-inch pieces**
   1 **medium zucchini, cut into 1/4-inch slices**
   1 **small red onion, cut into chunks**
 16 **medium fresh mushrooms**
   1 **cup fresh mint leaves**
Hot cooked brown rice

In a large resealable plastic bag, combine oil, lemon juice, garlic, basil, oregano, pepper, salt and thyme; add lamb. Seal bag and turn to coat; refrigerate for 30 minutes.

On eight metal or soaked wooden skewers, alternately thread the lamb and vegetables with mint leaves.

Grill, covered, over medium heat for 4-5 minutes on each side or until meat reaches desired doneness and vegetables are tender. Serve with rice. **YIELD:** 4 servings.

Spring Breeze Cheesecake Pie

(Pictured above)

PREP: 30 min. + chilling **COOK:** 15 min. + cooling

I combined two of my favorite foods, cheesecake and rhubarb, to come up with this mouthwatering dessert. It's so creamy and colorful, everyone who tries it loves it.

—Deanna Taylor, Ainsworth, Nebraska

   1 **package (8 ounces) cream cheese, softened**
1/3 **cup sugar**
   1 **cup (8 ounces) sour cream**
   2 **teaspoons vanilla extract**
   1 **carton (8 ounces) frozen whipped topping, thawed**
   1 **graham cracker crust (9 inches)**
TOPPING:
   3 **cups chopped fresh *or* frozen rhubarb**
1/3 **cup sugar**
1/8 **teaspoon ground cinnamon**
   1 **tablespoon cornstarch**
   2 **tablespoons cold water**

In a small bowl, beat cream cheese until smooth. Gradually beat in sugar. Add sour cream and vanilla; mix well. Set aside 1/2 cup whipped topping for garnish; cover and refrigerate. Beat 1/2 cup whipped topping into cream cheese mixture; fold in remaining whipped topping. Spoon into the crust. Cover and refrigerate for at least 2 hours.

For topping, in a large saucepan, bring the rhubarb, sugar and cinnamon to a boil. Reduce heat; simmer, uncovered, for 5-8 minutes or until rhubarb is tender. In a small bowl, combine cornstarch and cold water until smooth. Gradually stir into rhubarb mixture. Return to a boil; cook and stir for 1-2 minutes or until thickened. Cool to room temperature.

Cut pie into slices; top with rhubarb sauce and reserved whipped topping. **YIELD:** 6-8 servings.

summer livin' is easy

In a small bowl, beat cream cheese, milk, garlic powder and onion powder until smooth; set side 1/4 cup. Spread 1 tablespoon of remaining cream cheese mixture over each slice of bread. Top each with a cheese slice. Cut out each sandwich with a butterfly-shaped cookie cutter.

Cut 12 olives in half lengthwise; place two halves, cut side down, in the center of each sandwich for butterfly body. Cut remaining whole olives into slices; place two on each wing. Set olive ends aside.

Cut a small hole in the corner of a pastry or plastic bag; insert a small start tip. Fill bag with reserved cream cheese mixture. Pipe star on each olive slice; pipe two stars on front of each butterfly body for eyes. Cut olive ends into small pieces; place on eyes. **YIELD:** 1 dozen.

Ladybug Cake

(Pictured at left, top)

PREP: 15 min. **BAKE:** 1 hour + cooling

This cute chocolate dessert stole the show at my son's bug-themed birthday party. It was really easy to make. I baked the batter in a bowl, tinted the frosting a vivid red with paste food coloring and decorated the cake with licorice and gumdrops.

—Lenore Walters

   1 package (18-1/4 ounces) chocolate cake mix
1-1/4 cups water
   1/3 cup canola oil
   3 eggs
   1 tablespoon mayonnaise
1-1/3 cups vanilla frosting
Red paste food coloring
   2 large white gumdrops
   3 large black gumdrops
   1 rope black licorice
   1 shoestring black licorice

In a large bowl, beat the cake mix, water, oil, eggs and mayonnaise on low speed for 30 seconds. Beat on medium for 2 minutes. Pour into a greased and floured 2-qt. ovenproof bowl.

Bake at 350° for 60-70 minutes or until a toothpick inserted near the center comes out clean. Cool for 10 minutes before removing from bowl to a wire rack to cool completely. Place on a serving plate.

In a small bowl, combine the frosting and food coloring. Spread over cake. For eyes, flatten the white gumdrops and shape into ovals; place on ladybug. Cut the black gumdrops horizontally into three slices; discard tops. Slightly flatten slices; place two on white gumdrops for pupils, securing with a toothpick if necessary. Arrange the remaining slices on body for spots, pressing down gently.

Cut rope licorice into six pieces; insert into cake for legs. Cut a small piece from the shoestring licorice; add for mouth. **YIELD:** 12-16 servings.

Butterfly Cheese Sandwiches

(Pictured above, bottom)

PREP/TOTAL TIME: 30 min.

These adorable little sandwiches are easy to make and are perfect for a child's birthday party.

—Lenore Walters, Oklahoma City, Oklahoma

   1 package (8 ounces) cream cheese, softened
   2 tablespoons milk
   1/2 teaspoon garlic powder
   1/2 teaspoon onion powder
   12 slices white bread
   12 slices American cheese
   22 pitted ripe olives

Tomato-Cucumber Mozzarella Salad

(Pictured above)

PREP: 20 min. + chilling

I used fresh mozzarella for the first time some years ago and loved it. I wanted to incorporate it into as many dishes as possible and came up with this garden-fresh salad. It has quickly become a mainstay at my house.

—Jennifer Klann, Corbett, Oregon

- 1/3 cup olive oil
- 2 tablespoons red wine vinegar
- 2 tablespoons balsamic vinegar
- 1 teaspoon sugar
- 1/2 teaspoon salt
- 1/2 teaspoon dried oregano
- 1/4 teaspoon pepper
- 3 medium tomatoes, chopped
- 1 English cucumber, quartered and cut into 1/4-inch slices
- 1 small green pepper, chopped
- 1/4 cup thinly sliced onions
- 12 pitted Greek olives, sliced
- 2 tablespoons minced fresh parsley
- 1 tablespoon minced fresh basil
- 4 ounces fresh mozzarella cheese, cubed

In a jar with a tight-fitting lid, combine the first seven ingredients; shake well.

In a large bowl, combine the tomatoes, cucumber, green pepper, onions, olives, parsley and basil. Drizzle with dressing; toss to coat. Cover and refrigerate for at least 15 minutes. Just before serving, stir in cheese. Serve with a slotted spoon. **YIELD:** 8 servings.

Rustic Roasted Vegetable Tart

(Pictured below and on page 348)

PREP: 45 min. **BAKE:** 20 min.

No one will miss the meat in this appealing tart. The flaky, rustic-style crust holds an assortment of flavorful veggies simply seasoned with garlic and olive oil. It's guaranteed to make an impression on everyone.

—Marie Rizzio, Interlochen, Michigan

- 1 small eggplant, cut into 1-inch pieces
- 1 large zucchini, cut into 1/4-inch slices
- 4 plum tomatoes, chopped
- 1 medium sweet red pepper, cut into 1-inch pieces
- 4 tablespoons olive oil, *divided*
- 4 garlic cloves, minced
- 1/2 teaspoon salt
- 1/8 teaspoon pepper
- 1 sheet refrigerated pie pastry
- 1 tablespoon cornmeal
- 2 tablespoons shredded Parmesan cheese

Minced fresh basil, optional

In a large bowl, combine vegetables, 3 tablespoons olive oil, garlic, salt and pepper. Transfer to an ungreased 15-in. x 10-in. x 1-in. baking pan. Bake at 450° for 25-30 minutes or until the vegetables are tender and the moisture has evaporated, stirring every 10 minutes.

On a lightly floured surface, roll pastry into a 13-in. circle. Sprinkle cornmeal over a greased 14-in. pizza pan; place pastry on prepared pan. Spoon the vegetable mixture over pastry to within 1-1/2 in. of edges. Fold up the edges of the pastry over filling, leaving center uncovered. Brush the pastry with remaining oil.

Bake at 450° for 20-25 minutes or until crust is golden brown. Sprinkle with Parmesan cheese. Cut into wedges. Garnish with basil if desired. **YIELD:** 8 servings.

Corn Fritters with Caramelized Onion Jam

(Pictured below)

PREP: 30 min. **COOK:** 15 min.

A friend's husband, who's a chef, frequently made light and fluffy corn fritters, accompanied by a perfect sweet-tart jam. This recipe is my own version. I serve them with soups and barbecued chicken or pork.

—*Kim Cupo, Albany, Georgia*

- 1 large sweet onion, halved and thinly sliced
- 1 tablespoon olive oil
- 2 teaspoons balsamic vinegar
- 1/3 cup apple jelly
- 1/3 cup canned diced tomatoes
- 1 tablespoon tomato paste
- 1/8 teaspoon curry powder
- 1/8 teaspoon ground cinnamon

Dash salt and pepper

FRITTERS:

- 2 cups biscuit/baking mix
- 1 can (11 ounces) gold and white corn, drained
- 2 eggs, lightly beaten
- 1/2 cup milk
- 1/2 cup sour cream
- 1/2 teaspoon salt

Oil for frying

In a small skillet, saute onion in oil until golden brown. Add vinegar; cook and stir for 2-3 minutes. Set aside.

In a small saucepan, combine the jelly, tomatoes, tomato paste, curry, cinnamon, salt and pepper. Cook over medium heat for 5-7 minutes or until heated through. Add onion mixture. Cook and stir for 3 minutes; set aside and keep warm.

For the fritters, combine the baking mix, corn, eggs, milk, sour cream and salt just until combined.

In a deep-fat fryer or electric skillet, heat oil to 375°. Drop batter by heaping tablespoonfuls into hot oil; fry for 1-1/2 minutes on each side or until golden brown. Drain on paper towels. Serve warm with jam. **YIELD:** 2 dozen fritters (3/4 cup jam).

Spicy Zucchini Quesadillas

(Pictured above)

PREP/TOTAL TIME: 15 min.

My family loves Mexican food, so I created this easy recipe one summer when our garden was bursting with zucchini. For milder quesadillas, use Monterey Jack instead of pepper Jack cheese. If you want them spicier, add some red pepper flakes.

—*Linda Taylor, Lenexa, Kansas*

- 1 large onion, chopped
- 1/2 cup chopped sweet red pepper
- 1 teaspoon plus 2 tablespoons butter, softened, *divided*
- 2 cups shredded zucchini
- 2 tablespoons taco seasoning
- 8 flour tortillas (7 inches)
- 8 ounces pepper Jack cheese, shredded

Salsa, sour cream and pickled jalapeno pepper slices

In a large skillet, saute onion and red pepper in 1 teaspoon butter for 3 minutes. Stir in zucchini and taco seasoning; saute 3-4 minutes longer or until vegetables are tender. Remove from the heat.

Spread the remaining butter over one side of each tortilla. Place tortillas butter side down on a griddle. Sprinkle about 1/4 cup cheese and 1/4 cup zucchini mixture over half of each tortilla; fold over.

Cook over low heat for 1-2 minutes on each side or until cheese is melted. Serve with salsa, sour cream and jalapenos. **YIELD:** 4 servings.

Blackberry Crisp

(Pictured below)

PREP: 15 min. **BAKE:** 20 min.

I adapted this comforting dessert from a recipe given to me by my mother-in-law. When I make this for my kids, there are never any leftovers!

—Marliss Lee, Independence, Missouri

- 2 cups fresh *or* frozen blackberries
- 2 tablespoons sugar
- 1 teaspoon cornstarch
- 1-1/2 teaspoons water
- 1/2 teaspoon lemon juice
- 1/2 cup quick-cooking oats
- 1/4 cup all-purpose flour
- 1/4 cup packed brown sugar
- 1/2 teaspoon ground cinnamon
- 1/4 cup cold butter

Vanilla ice cream

Place blackberries in a greased 1-qt. baking dish. In a small bowl, combine the sugar, cornstarch, water and lemon juice until smooth. Pour over berries. Combine the oats, flour, brown sugar and cinnamon; cut in butter until crumbly. Sprinkle over berries.

Bake, uncovered, at 375° for 20-25 minutes or until the filling is bubbly. Serve warm with ice cream. **YIELD:** 2 servings.

Peaches & Cream Tart

(Pictured above)

PREP: 30 min. **BAKE:** 15 min. + cooling

Fresh peach slices and big, juicy raspberries crown this beautiful tart and are complemented by an almond-flavored cream filling and macaroon crust. It's the perfect dessert to serve to guests during peach season.

—Brenda Harmon, Hastings, Minnesota

- 2 cups crumbled soft macaroon cookies
- 1 cup ground pecans
- 3 tablespoons butter, melted
- 1/2 cup heavy whipping cream
- 1 package (8 ounces) cream cheese, softened
- 1/3 cup sugar
- 2 teaspoons orange juice
- 1 teaspoon vanilla extract
- 1/4 teaspoon almond extract
- 4 medium peaches, peeled and sliced *or* 3 cups frozen unsweetened sliced peaches, thawed
- 2 tablespoons lemon juice
- 1/2 cup fresh raspberries
- 1/4 cup apricot preserves
- 2 teaspoons honey

In a food processor, combine the crumbled cookies, pecans and butter; cover and process until blended. Press onto the bottom and up the sides of an ungreased 11-in. fluted tart pan with removable bottom.

Place pan on a baking sheet. Bake at 350° for 12-14 minutes or until golden brown. Cool completely on a wire rack.

In a small bowl, beat cream until soft peaks form; set aside. In another small bowl, beat cream cheese and sugar until smooth. Beat in orange juice and extracts. Fold in whipped cream. Spread over crust.

In a small bowl, combine peaches and lemon juice. Arrange peaches and raspberries over filling.

In a small saucepan, combine preserves and honey. Cook and stir over low heat until melted; strain. Brush over the fruit. Store in the refrigerator. **YIELD:** 10 servings.

Russian Cream

(Pictured above)

PREP: 20 min. + chilling

What a pretty parfait! Layered with fresh raspberries, it's a summertime treat. I'm a busy veterinarian, so I like making this sweet treat for my family because it comes together quickly.
—*Barbara Ulrich, Newark Valley, New York*

- 1 envelope unflavored gelatin
- 1/2 cup cold water
- 1 cup heavy whipping cream
- 3/4 cup sugar
- 1 cup (8 ounces) sour cream
- 1/2 teaspoon vanilla extract
- 1 package (10 ounces) frozen sweetened raspberries, thawed

Fresh raspberries and mint sprigs, optional

In a small saucepan, sprinkle gelatin over cold water; let stand for 1 minute. Bring to a boil; cook and stir until gelatin is dissolved. Remove from the heat; set aside.

In another saucepan, heat the whipping cream and sugar over medium heat until sugar is dissolved and mixture is lukewarm. Remove from heat; stir in the gelatin mixture until completely dissolved. Cover and refrigerate for 30 minutes or until slightly thickened.

Stir in the sour cream and vanilla. In each of four parfait glasses, place a scant 1/4 cupful of cream mixture; top each with a rounded tablespoonful of raspberries. Repeat the layers. Top each with a scant 1/4 cup of the cream mixture.

Cover and refrigerate for 3 hours or until set. Just before serving, garnish with fresh raspberries and mint if desired. **YIELD:** 4 servings.

Golden Corn Quiche

(Pictured below)

PREP: 20 min. **BAKE:** 35 min. + standing

I serve cut-up fresh fruit with this comforting quiche, which my vegetarian son really enjoys. You could also pair it with a slice or two of ham. Try it for brunch or dinner.
—*Donna Gonda, North Canton, Ohio*

- 1 unbaked pastry shell (9 inches)
- 1-1/3 cups half-and-half cream
- 3 eggs
- 3 tablespoons butter, melted
- 1/2 small onion, cut into wedges
- 1 tablespoon all-purpose flour
- 1 tablespoon sugar
- 1 teaspoon salt
- 2 cups frozen corn, thawed

Line unpricked pastry shell with a double thickness of heavy-duty foil. Bake at 375° for 5 minutes. Remove foil; bake 5 minutes longer.

In a blender, combine the cream, eggs, butter, onion, flour, sugar and salt; cover and process until blended. Stir in corn; pour into crust.

Bake for 35-40 minutes or until a knife inserted near the center comes out clean. Let stand for 10 minutes before cutting. **YIELD:** 8 servings.

fall is flavorful!

In a small microwave-safe bowl, microwave white chocolate at 50% power for 1-2 minutes or until melted; stir until smooth. Transfer to a small heavy-duty resealable plastic bag; cut a small hole in a corner of bag. Drizzle over apples. Repeat with semisweet chocolate. Sprinkle tops with remaining pistachios if desired. Chill until set. **YIELD:** 6 servings.

Apple-Cherry Pork Chops

(Pictured below)

PREP/TOTAL TIME: 30 min.

You'll never want pork chops any other way once you try this recipe. I season the juicy chops with a fragrant herb rub and serve them with a scrumptious apple and cherry sauce.

—*Doris Heath, Franklin, North Carolina*

  2 **boneless pork loin chops (1/2 inch thick and 5 ounces *each*)**
1/4 **teaspoon dried thyme**
1/8 **teaspoon salt**
  1 **tablespoon olive oil**
2/3 **cup apple juice**
  1 **small apple, sliced**
  2 **tablespoons dried cherries *or* cranberries**
  2 **tablespoons chopped onion**
  1 **teaspoon cornstarch**
  1 **tablespoon cold water**

Rub the pork chops with thyme and salt. In a skillet, cook pork in oil for 3-4 minutes on each side or until the juices run clear. Remove and keep warm.

In the same skillet, combine the apple juice, apple, cherries and onion. Bring to a boil.

In a small bowl, combine cornstarch and water until smooth; stir into skillet. Bring to a boil; cook and stir for 1-2 minutes or until thickened. Spoon over pork chops. **YIELD:** 2 servings.

Ultimate Caramel Apples

(Pictured above and on page 348)

PREP: 45 min. **COOK:** 25 min. + chilling

I have such a sweet tooth that I've been known to make a dessert just to satisfy my craving. One day when I was in the mood for caramel, I came up with these fun treats.

—*Clarissa Loyd, Mineral Wells, Texas*

  6 **medium Red Delicious apples**
  6 **Popsicle sticks**
  1 **cup sugar**
  1 **cup light corn syrup**
1/4 **cup water**
Pinch baking soda
1/4 **cup butter, cubed**
1/4 **cup heavy whipping cream**
1/2 **cup shelled pistachios, chopped, *divided***
  3 **squares (1 ounce *each*) white baking chocolate, chopped**
  3 **squares (1 ounce *each*) semisweet chocolate, chopped**

Line a baking sheet with waxed paper and grease the paper; set aside. Wash and thoroughly dry apples. Insert a Popsicle stick into each; place on prepared pan. Chill.

In a large heavy saucepan, combine the sugar, corn syrup and water; bring to a boil over medium heat, stirring occasionally. Stir in baking soda. Stir in butter until melted; gradually add cream, stirring constantly. Cook and stir until a candy thermometer reads 242° (firm-ball stage). Remove from heat and cool to 200°.

Place 1/4 cup pistachios in a shallow dish. Dip apples into caramel mixture until completely coated, then dip the bottom of each in pistachios. Return to baking sheet; chill.

Turkey with Sausage-Corn Bread Stuffing

(Pictured above)

PREP: 1 hour + cooling **BAKE:** 3-3/4 hours + standing

Complement your bird with savory stuffing. I've made this recipe for many potlucks and church suppers, and everyone raves about it...even those who usually don't like stuffing.

—June Kathrein, Delta, Colorado

- 2-1/2 cups yellow cornmeal
- 1-1/2 cups all-purpose flour
- 1/4 cup sugar
- 6 teaspoons baking powder
- 1-1/2 teaspoons salt
- 2 eggs
- 2 cups milk
- 6 tablespoons canola oil

STUFFING:
- 1 pound bulk sage pork sausage
- 1 bunch celery, chopped
- 2 medium onions, chopped
- 1 cup chopped fresh mushrooms
- 1/2 cup chopped sweet red pepper
- 1/2 cup butter, cubed
- 1 can (49-1/2 ounces) chicken broth

- 2 to 3 tablespoons rubbed sage
- 1 tablespoon poultry seasoning
- 1/2 teaspoon pepper
- 1 turkey (14 to 16 pounds)

Additional butter, melted

In a large bowl, combine first five ingredients. Combine eggs, milk and oil; stir into dry ingredients just until moistened. Pour into a greased 13-in. x 9-in. baking pan. Bake at 425° for 18-20 minutes or until a toothpick comes out clean. Cool on a wire rack.

In a Dutch oven, cook sausage over medium heat until no longer pink; drain and set aside. In the same pan, saute the celery, onions, mushrooms and red pepper in butter until tender. Stir in the broth, seasonings and sausage. Bring to a boil. Reduce the heat; simmer, uncovered, for 10 minutes. Remove from the heat. Cut corn bread into 1/2-in. cubes; fold into sausage mixture.

Just before baking, loosely stuff the turkey. Place the remaining stuffing in a greased 13-in. x 9-in. baking dish; cover and refrigerate. Remove from the refrigerator 30 minutes before baking.

Skewer turkey openings; tie drumsticks together with kitchen string. Place breast side up on a rack in a roasting pan. Brush with melted butter. Bake, uncovered, at 325° for 3-3/4 to 4-1/2 hours or until a meat thermometer reads 180° for the turkey and 165° for the stuffing, basting occasionally with pan drippings (cover loosely with foil if turkey browns too quickly).

Bake additional stuffing, covered, for 45-50 minutes. Uncover; bake 10 minutes longer or until lightly browned. Cover the turkey with foil and let stand for 20 minutes before removing stuffing and carving. **YIELD:** 12 servings (16 cups stuffing).

Rice-Stuffed Acorn Squash

(Pictured above right)

PREP: 45 min. **BAKE:** 20 min.

We often make this side dish in the fall, after harvesting fresh squash from our garden. A hint of Asian flavor offers a different, unexpected accent. I especially enjoy the pleasant taste combination of mozzarella and ginger.

—Lydia Garcia, Gettysburg, Pennsylvania

- 2 large acorn squash
- 3/4 cup uncooked long grain rice
- 1-1/2 cups water
- 2 tablespoons soy sauce
- 1 medium onion, chopped
- 1/4 cup butter, cubed
- 2 medium tart apples, peeled and chopped
- 1 cup (4 ounces) shredded part-skim mozzarella cheese
- 1/2 cup chopped walnuts
- 1/2 cup half-and-half cream
- 1/4 cup balsamic vinegar
- 3 tablespoons honey
- 3 teaspoons minced fresh gingerroot
- 1 teaspoon curry powder

WITCH HATS:
    1 can (16 ounces) vanilla frosting
    2 teaspoons milk
Assorted food coloring of your choice
    12 to 16 ice cream sugar cones
Fruit Roll-Ups, licorice and assorted candies of choice

In a large bowl, cream butter and sugar until light and fluffy. Add eggs, one at a time, beating well after each addition. Combine the flour, cocoa, baking soda, baking powder and salt; add to creamed mixture alternately with milk. Beat just until combined.

    Fill paper- or foil-lined muffin cups two-thirds full. Bake at 350° for 18-22 minutes or until a toothpick comes out clean. Cool for 10 minutes before removing from pan to a wire rack to cool completely. Tint frosting green; frost cupcakes. For hats, combine frosting and milk; tint with food coloring. Frost ice cream cones. Using small cookie cutters, cut out shapes from Fruit Roll-Ups; arrange on hats. Add licorice for hair and candies for faces. Place a hat on each witch. **YIELD:** about 1 dozen.

EDITOR'S NOTE: Chocolate frosting and jimmies may also be used to decorate witch hats.

Cut the squash in half; remove the seeds. Place cut side down in a greased 13-in. x 9-in. baking dish. Cover and bake at 350° for 40-45 minutes or until tender.

    Meanwhile, in a large saucepan, bring rice, water and soy sauce to a boil. Reduce the heat; cover and simmer for 15-18 minutes or until the liquid is absorbed and rice is tender.

    In a large skillet, saute onion in butter until almost tender. Add apples; saute for 3 minutes. Remove from the heat; stir in the cooked rice, cheese, walnuts, cream, vinegar, honey, ginger and curry.

    Turn the squash over; stuff with rice mixture. Bake, uncovered, for 20-25 minutes or until heated through. **YIELD:** 4 servings.

Wicked Witch Cupcakes

(Pictured at right)

PREP: 1-1/4 hours **BAKE:** 20 min. + cooling

More fun than frightening, these whimsical witches cast their spell on every sweet tooth. Everyone will be delighted with the pointy-hat cupcake characters.

—Joan Antonen, Arlington, South Dakota

    1/2 cup butter, softened
    1 cup sugar
    2 eggs
1-1/2 cups all-purpose flour
    1/2 cup baking cocoa
    1 teaspoon baking soda
    1/2 teaspoon baking powder
    1/2 teaspoon salt
1-1/4 cups milk
    1 can (16 ounces) vanilla frosting
Green food coloring

Place flour, butter and sugar in a food processor; cover and process until mixture resembles coarse crumbs. Add the egg yolks, water, lemon juice and peel; cover and process until the dough forms a ball. Divide the dough in half; wrap in plastic wrap. Refrigerate for 1 hour or until firm.

For the filling, in a small saucepan, bring the sugar, butter and water to a boil; cook and stir for 1 minute. Cook, without stirring, until mixture turns a golden amber color, about 7 minutes.

Remove from the heat; gradually stir in cream. Return to heat; stir in honey and salt until smooth. Stir in walnuts and cranberries. Bring to a boil. Reduce heat; simmer, uncovered, for 5 minutes. Remove from the heat; cool to room temperature.

On a lightly floured surface, roll out one portion of the dough into an 11-in. circle. Transfer to an ungreased 9-in. fluted tart pan with a removable bottom; trim pastry even with edge. Add the filling. Roll out remaining dough to fit top of tart; place over filling. Trim and seal edges. Cut slits in pastry.

Brush with egg white; sprinkle with coarse sugar. Bake at 400° for 20-25 minutes or until filling is bubbly. Cool on a wire rack. **YIELD:** 10-12 servings.

Spiced Squash Muffins

PREP: 20 min. **BAKE:** 15 min.

When I created these moist muffins one day with our garden-fresh squash, my three-year-old son kept asking for more. That batch disappeared quickly...and so did the second one!
—*TaeRee Glover, Nelson, Nebraska*

- 2 cups all-purpose flour
- 1/3 cup packed brown sugar
- 2 teaspoons baking powder
- 1 teaspoon ground cinnamon
- 1/2 teaspoon salt
- 1/4 teaspoon ground ginger
- 1/4 teaspoon ground nutmeg
- 2 eggs, beaten
- 3/4 cup mashed cooked butternut squash
- 3/4 cup light corn syrup
- 1/4 cup butter, melted
- 1/4 cup canola oil
- 1 teaspoon vanilla extract

TOPPING:
- 1/2 cup packed brown sugar
- 1 teaspoon ground cinnamon
- 4 teaspoons cold butter

In a large bowl, combine the first seven ingredients. In another bowl, combine the eggs, squash, corn syrup, butter, oil and vanilla; stir into the dry ingredients just until moistened.

Fill greased or paper-lined muffin cups three-fourths full. In a small bowl, combine brown sugar and cinnamon; cut in the butter until crumbly. Sprinkle over batter.

Bake at 400° for 15-20 minutes or until a toothpick comes out clean. Cool for 5 minutes before removing from pan to a wire rack. Serve warm. **YIELD:** 1 dozen.

Cranberry Walnut Tart

(Pictured above)

PREP: 30 min. + chilling **BAKE:** 20 min. + cooling

Both attractive and delicious, this flaky tart combines a tender golden brown crust with a sweet filling that might remind you of baklava. It's a holiday favorite at our house.
—*Patricia Harmon, Baden, Pennsylvania*

- 2-1/2 cups all-purpose flour
- 1 cup cold butter, cubed
- 1/4 cup sugar
- 2 egg yolks
- 3 tablespoons cold water
- 1 tablespoon lemon juice
- 1/2 teaspoon grated lemon peel

FILLING:
- 1 cup sugar
- 1/4 cup butter, cubed
- 1/4 cup water
- 2/3 cup heavy whipping cream
- 3 tablespoons honey
- 1/2 teaspoon salt
- 2 cups chopped walnuts
- 1/2 cup dried cranberries
- 1 egg white, beaten
- 1 teaspoon coarse sugar

winter celebrations

Beef Rib Roast

(Pictured above)

PREP: 15 min. **BAKE:** 2 hours + standing

My mom, Elizabeth, topped beef roast with bacon and onion. Whenever I prepare it, I can't help but reminisce about the wonderful things she did for her children.

—Betty Abel Jellencich, Utica, New York

 1 **bone-in beef rib roast (4 to 5 pounds)**
 1 **garlic clove, minced**
 1 **teaspoon salt**
1/2 **teaspoon pepper**
 1 **small onion, sliced**
 6 **to 8 bacon strips**

Place roast, fat side up, on a rack in a shallow roasting pan. Rub with garlic, salt and pepper; top with onion and bacon.

Bake, uncovered, at 325° for 2-3 hours or until the meat reaches desired doneness (for medium-rare, a meat thermometer should read 145°; medium, 160°; well-done, 170°).

Transfer to warm serving platter. Let stand for 10-15 minutes before slicing. **YIELD:** 10-12 servings.

Coconut Snowmen

(Pictured below)

PREP: 4 hours + chilling

My mom made her basic coconut candy recipe for years, but I took it a step further and created jolly snowman heads. These cute little treats are worth the extra effort because they're always a big hit!

—Donell Mayfield, Rio Rancho, Minnesota

  4 **cups flaked coconut, coarsely chopped**
3-3/4 **cups confectioners' sugar**
 2/3 **cup sweetened condensed milk**
 1/4 **cup butter, softened**
1-1/2 **cups vanilla *or* white chips**
  2 **packages (11-1/2 ounces *each*) milk chocolate chips**
  1 **package (10-1/2 ounces) large marshmallows**
Black, orange and red decorator icing
Green leaf-shaped decorator candies

In a large bowl, combine coconut, confectioners' sugar, milk and butter. Shape into 1-1/4-in. balls; place on waxed paper-lined baking sheets. Loosely cover and chill for 1-1/4 hours or until firm.

In a microwave-safe bowl, melt vanilla chips; stir until smooth. Dip balls in melted chips; place on waxed paper-lined baking sheets. Chill until firm, about 15 minutes. Set aside remaining melted vanilla chips.

Melt the chocolate chips; stir until smooth. For hats, dip each marshmallow in chocolate; place on a waxed paper-lined baking sheet, allowing excess to drip down. Swirl the marshmallows in chocolate on waxed paper to create hat brims. Chill until firm, about 15 minutes.

Level the top of coated coconut balls. Attach marshmallows hats, using reserved melted vanilla chips. With black icing, add eyes and a mouth to each face; with orange icing, add a nose. Use red icing and leaf candies for holly on hats. Store in an airtight container. **YIELD:** 4 dozen.

Spinach and Sausage Pork Loin

(Pictured above)

PREP: 20 min. **BAKE:** 2 hours + standing

Two of our children live relatively close, and we invite them frequently for an evening meal. They seem to enjoy the fact that Dad has done the cooking. This special roast has been one of our favorites for years.

—Ed Leland, Van Wert, Ohio

- 1 package (10 ounces) frozen chopped spinach, thawed and squeezed dry
- 1 egg, beaten
- 1/2 cup slivered almonds, toasted
- 1/4 cup dry bread crumbs
- 2 tablespoons minced fresh parsley
- 1 tablespoon onion soup mix
- 4 garlic cloves, minced
- 1 teaspoon dried thyme, *divided*
- 1 teaspoon pepper
- 1/2 pound bulk Italian sausage
- 1 boneless pork loin roast (about 3 pounds)
- 1 tablespoon olive oil

In a large bowl, combine 1/2 cup spinach, egg, almonds, bread crumbs, parsley, soup mix, garlic, 1/2 teaspoon thyme and pepper. Crumble sausage over mixture and mix well. (Save the remaining spinach for another use.)

Make a lengthwise slit down the center of the roast to within 1/2 in. of bottom. Open roast so it lies flat; cover with plastic wrap. Flatten slightly. Spread sausage mixture over meat. Close and tie several times with kitchen string; secure ends with toothpicks. Place the fat side up on a rack in a shallow roasting pan. Brush with oil; sprinkle with remaining thyme.

Bake, uncovered, at 350° for 2 to 2-1/2 hours or until a meat thermometer inserted into roast and sausage mixture reads 160°. Let stand for 10-15 minutes. Remove string and toothpicks before slicing. **YIELD:** 10 servings.

Italian Herb Muffins

(Pictured below)

PREP: 20 min. **BAKE:** 15 min.

While preparing spaghetti for dinner one day, I realized I was out of bread as an accompaniment and thought, "Why not make an herb muffin instead?" I created this recipe, and it was a hit.

—Cyndee Page, Reno, Nevada

- 2 cups all-purpose flour
- 2 tablespoons grated Parmesan cheese
- 1 tablespoon sugar
- 1 tablespoon Italian seasoning
- 3 teaspoons baking powder
- 1 teaspoon salt
- 1 egg
- 3/4 cup milk
- 1/2 cup canola oil
- 1/4 cup butter, softened
- 1/2 teaspoon garlic powder

In a bowl, combine flour, Parmesan cheese, sugar, Italian seasoning, baking powder and salt. In another bowl, whisk the egg, milk and oil; stir into dry ingredients just until moistened.

Fill greased or paper-lined muffin cups three-fourths full. Bake at 400° for 15-20 minutes or until a toothpick comes out clean. Cool for 5 minutes before removing from pan to a wire rack.

In a small bowl, combine the butter and garlic powder. Serve with warm muffins. **YIELD:** 10 muffins.

Brussels Sprouts with Water Chestnuts

(Pictured above)

PREP/TOTAL TIME: 30 min.

This reliable recipe dates back to the 1970s. A dash of nutmeg adds interest to the fast-to-fix combination of tender brussels sprouts and crunchy water chestnuts.

—*Ruth Peterson, Jenison, Michigan*

> 1 pound fresh brussels sprouts
> 3 tablespoons butter
> 1/2 cup sliced water chestnuts
> 1/4 teaspoon salt
> **Dash pepper and ground nutmeg**

Remove any loose leaves and trim the stem ends of the brussels sprouts. Cut an "X" in the core end of each with a sharp knife.

Place sprouts in a steamer basket; place in a large saucepan over 1 in. of water. Bring to a boil; cover and steam for 8-10 minutes or until crisp-tender.

In a large skillet, melt the butter. Add the water chestnuts, salt, pepper and nutmeg; heat through. Stir in the brussels sprouts. **YIELD:** 6 servings.

Festive White Chocolate Cheesecake

(Pictured at right and on page 348)

PREP: 30 min. BAKE: 35 min. + chilling

A buttery shortbread crust, creamy white chocolate filling and tangy cranberry-raspberry sauce add up to one mouthwatering dessert. Top with sweetened whipped cream and berries, you have a real showstopper.

—*Mary Alice Graves, Kempton, Indiana*

> 2 cups crushed shortbread cookies
> 1/4 cup butter, melted
> **FILLING:**
> 2 packages (8 ounces *each*) cream cheese, softened
> 1 cup vanilla *or* white chips, melted and cooled
> 2/3 cup sour cream
> 3/4 cup sugar
> 1 tablespoon grated orange peel
> 1 teaspoon vanilla extract
> 3 eggs, lightly beaten
> **SAUCE:**
> 1 cup whole-berry cranberry sauce
> 1/2 cup seedless raspberry jam
> 1/2 teaspoon grated orange peel
> **TOPPING:**
> 2 cups heavy whipping cream
> 1/4 cup confectioners' sugar

In a small bowl, combine cookie crumbs and butter. Press onto the bottom of a greased 9-in. springform pan; set aside.

For the filling in a large bowl, beat cream cheese, chips, sour cream, sugar, orange peel and vanilla until smooth. Add eggs; beat on low speed just until combined. Pour over crust. Place pan on a baking sheet.

Bake at 350° for 35-40 minutes or until center is almost set. Cool on a wire rack for 10 minutes. Carefully run a knife around edge of pan to loosen; cool 1 hour longer. Refrigerate overnight.

In a small saucepan, combine sauce ingredients. Cook and stir over medium heat until blended. Cool.

Just before serving, remove sides of springform pan. Spoon sauce over cheesecake to within 1 in. of edges. In a small bowl, beat cream and confectioners' sugar until stiff peaks form. Pipe over sauce. Refrigerate leftovers. **YIELD:** 12 servings.

2 tablespoons green and red M&M's miniature baking bits
4 teaspoons miniature semisweet chocolate chips
Cake decorator holly leaf and berry candies
60 to 66 pieces red shoestring licorice (2 inches *each*)

In a large bowl, cream the peanut butter, butter, sugar and brown sugar. Beat in the egg and vanilla. Combine the flour and baking soda; gradually add to the creamed mixture. (Dough will be soft.) Refrigerate for 1 hour or until easy to handle.

Roll into 1-in. balls. Place 2 in. apart on ungreased baking sheets. Pinch each ball at one end to taper. Insert two peanut halves in the center of each ball for ears. Add one M&M baking bit for nose and two chocolate chips for eyes. Arrange holly and berry candies in front of one ear.

Bake at 350° for 8-10 minutes or until set. Gently insert one licorice piece into each warm cookie for tail. Remove to wire racks to cool completely. **YIELD:** about 5 dozen.

EDITOR'S NOTE: Reduced-fat or generic brands of peanut butter are not recommended for this recipe.

Peanut Butter Christmas Mice

(*Pictured above*)

PREP: 30 min. **BAKE:** 10 min./batch + cooling

With their red licorice tails, candy noses and peanut ears, these chewy "mice" were always a hit at classroom parties. My children are in their teens now, but they still ask me to make these cookies for the holidays.

—*Nancy Rowse, Bella Vista, Arkansas*

1 cup creamy peanut butter
1/2 cup butter, softened
1/2 cup sugar
1/2 cup packed brown sugar
1 egg
1 teaspoon vanilla extract
1-1/2 cups all-purpose flour
1/2 teaspoon baking soda
1/2 cup peanut halves

Spicy Seafood Bisque

PREP/TOTAL TIME: 30 min.

This spicy soup, featuring shrimp, crabmeat and tomatoes, gets its zip from hot pepper sauce and cayenne pepper. It's easy to prepare and dresses up any meal.

—*Kevin Weeks, North Palm Beach, Florida*

1/2 cup chopped onion
1/2 cup chopped celery
2 tablespoons butter
4 cups chicken broth
3 cups tomato juice
1 can (14-1/2 ounces) diced tomatoes, undrained
1 tablespoon Worcestershire sauce
1 teaspoon seafood seasoning
1 teaspoon dried oregano
1/2 teaspoon garlic powder
1/2 teaspoon hot pepper sauce
1/4 teaspoon cayenne pepper
1 bay leaf
1/2 cup uncooked small shell pasta *or* elbow macaroni
1 pound uncooked medium shrimp, peeled and deveined
1 can (6 ounces) crabmeat, drained, flaked and cartilage removed

In a large saucepan, saute onion and celery in butter until tender. Add the broth, tomato juice, tomatoes, Worcestershire sauce and seasonings; bring to a boil. Reduce the heat; cover and simmer for 20 minutes.

Discard bay leaf. Add pasta to the soup; cook, uncovered, until tender. Add shrimp and crab; simmer 5 minutes longer or until the shrimp turn pink. **YIELD:** 10-12 servings (about 3 quarts).

Crab and Brie Strudel Slices

(Pictured above)

PREP: 45 min. **BAKE:** 20 min.

Mouthwatering Brie, succulent crab and a hint of pear make this wintry appetizer a favorite.

—*Jennifer Pfaff, Indianapolis, Indiana*

- 1/2 **pound fresh crabmeat**
- 6 **ounces Brie *or* Camembert cheese, rind removed and cut into 1/4-inch cubes**
- 2-1/2 **cups finely chopped peeled ripe pears**
- 1/2 **cup thinly sliced green onions**
- 1/2 **cup diced fully cooked ham**
- 2 **teaspoons lemon juice**
- 1 **garlic clove, minced**

Dash pepper

- 14 **sheets phyllo dough (14 inches x 9 inches)**
- 3/4 **cup butter, melted**

In a large bowl, combine the first eight ingredients; set aside.

Place a piece of plastic wrap larger than a sheet of phyllo on a work surface. Place one phyllo sheet on plastic wrap; brush with butter. (Keep remaining phyllo covered until ready to use.) Repeat six times. Spread half of crab filling to within 1 in. of edges. Fold the two short sides over filling. Using the plastic wrap to lift one long side, roll up jelly-roll style.

Transfer to a greased 15-in. x 10-in. x 1-in. baking pan; discard the plastic wrap. Brush top with butter; score the top lightly at 1-in. intervals. Repeat with remaining phyllo, butter and filling.

Bake at 375° for 20-25 minutes or until golden brown. Let stand for 5 minutes. Cut into slices along scored lines. **YIELD:** 2 dozen.

Lemon Cream Puffs

(Pictured below)

PREP: 20 min. + cooling **BAKE:** 30 min.

The fluffy filling for these light crisp shells has a delectable citrus flavor. They are a special treat for get-togethers.

—*Doreen Martin, Kitimat, British Columbia*

- 1/2 **cup water**
- 1/4 **cup butter, cubed**
- 1/2 **cup all-purpose flour**
- 2 **eggs**

LEMON FILLING:

- 1 **egg, beaten**
- 1/3 **cup sugar**
- 3 **tablespoons lemon juice**
- 2 **tablespoons butter, cubed**
- 1 **cup heavy whipping cream**
- 2 **teaspoons sugar**

Confectioners' sugar

In a saucepan, bring water and butter to a boil. Add flour all at once, stirring until a smooth ball forms. Remove from the heat; let stand for 5 minutes. Add the eggs, one at a time, beating well after each addition. Continue beating until mixture is smooth.

Drop by rounded tablespoonfuls 3 in. apart onto greased baking sheets. Bake at 400° for 30-35 minutes or until golden brown. Remove to wire racks. Immediately split puffs and remove tops; discard soft dough from inside. Set puffs and tops aside to cool. For the filling, in a small heavy saucepan, combine the egg, sugar, lemon juice and butter. Bring to a boil over medium heat; cook and stir for 5-7 minutes or until mixture is thick enough to coat a metal spoon.

Remove from the heat. Cool quickly by placing pan in a bowl of ice water; stir for 2 minutes. Transfer to a bowl; press plastic wrap onto surface of filling. Chill for 1 hour or until partially set.

In a bowl, beat cream and sugar until stiff peaks form; fold into lemon mixture. Fill cream puffs; replace tops. Dust with confectioners' sugar. **YIELD:** 10 servings.

CANDIES (continued)
Coconut Snowmen, 363
Cookie Dough Truffles, 148
Elegant Dipped Cherries, 149
Granola Fudge Clusters, 313
Homemade Peanut Butter Cups, 158

CARAMEL
Caramel Chocolate Trifle, 191
Caramel Fruit Dip, 14
Caramel-Pecan Apple Pie, 183
Caramel-Pecan Cheesecake Pie, 289
Chocolate Pecan Ice Cream Torte, 162
Devil's Food Caramel Torte, 309
Ultimate Caramel Apples, 359

CARROTS
Apple and Carrot Slaw, 209
Candied Carrots, 258
Carrot Cheesecake, 180
Carrot Zucchini Fritters, 20
Chocolate Carrot Cake, 178
Curried Carrot Soup, 296
Fried Shoestring Carrots, 68
Gingered Cranberry-Carrot Slaw, 317
Layered Carrot Cake, 162
Onion-Bacon Baby Carrots, 74
Party Carrots, 77
Pickled Baby Carrots, 351
Roasted Carrot Dip, 11
Sunny Carrot Salad, 29
Sunshine Sweet Rolls, 125
Sweet Herbed Carrots, 238
Tossed Salad with Carrot Dressing, 292

CASSEROLES
Main Dishes
Asparagus Sausage Crepes, 85
Biscuit-Topped Lemon Chicken, 222
Broccoli Chicken Supreme, 228
Butternut Turkey Bake, 89
Cheddar Ham Strata, 223
Cheese Enchiladas, 224
Christmas Breakfast Casserole, 284
Corn Tortilla Chicken Lasagna, 221
Creamy Ham and Macaroni, 87
Crescent-Topped Turkey Amandine, 117
Deluxe Breakfast Bake, 228
Fiesta Lasagna, 98
Meatless Mexican Lasagna, 106
Meaty Pasta Casseroles, 218
Onions Neptune, 211
Overnight Asparagus Strata, 352
Reuben Crescent Bake, 119
Scalloped Potatoes and Ham, 216
Simple Sausage Lasagna, 288
Spicy Nacho Bake, 93
Spiral Pepperoni Pizza Bake, 226

Sunday Shrimp Pasta Bake, 304
Turkey Enchiladas, 107
Vegetable Noodle Bake, 346
Side Dishes
Cashew-Pecan Sweet Potatoes, 309
Cheesy Noodle Casserole, 67
Comforting Broccoli Casserole, 274
Comforting Potato Casserole, 293
Corn Pudding, 258
Crispy Potato Cubes, 341
Double Corn Dressing, 73
Duo Tater Bake, 65
Loaded Red Potato Casserole, 79
Mac and Cheese for a Bunch, 214
Mashed Potato Casserole, 335
Mexicorn Grits, 70
Onion-Bacon Baby Carrots, 74
Party Carrots, 77
Pearl Onion Broccoli Bake, 64
Swiss-Almond Floret Bake, 80
Tortellini Spinach Casserole, 225
Triple-Cheese Broccoli Puff, 284
Wild Rice Pilaf, 309

CAULIFLOWER
Crunchy Floret Salad, 266
Swiss-Almond Floret Bake, 80

CHEESE
Breads
Berry Cheesecake Muffins, 127
Cheddar Loaves, 135
Cheddar Skillet Corn Bread, 125
Cottage Cheese Yeast Rolls, 339
Feta and Chive Muffins, 135
Parmesan Breadsticks, 136
Vegetable & Cheese Focaccia, 138
Cheesecakes
Carrot Cheesecake, 180
Cinnamon Apple Cheesecake, 179
Festive White Chocolate
    Cheesecake, 365
Layered Mocha Cheesecake, 170
Lemony White Chocolate
    Cheesecake, 169
Mascarpone Cheesecake, 172
Peanut Butter Cup Cheesecake, 182
Rhubarb Swirl Cheesecake, 164
Strawberry Swirl Cheesecake, 174
Cookies and Brownies
Berry-Cream Cookie Snaps, 147
Creamy Cashew Brownies, 145
Tiramisu Brownies, 159
Desserts
Cheesecake Waffle Cups, 325
Chocolate-Covered Cheesecake
    Squares, 194
Lemon Cheesecake Dessert, 201

Peaches 'n' Cream Cups, 204
Strawberry Cheesecake Ice Cream, 199
Tiramisu Cheesecake Dessert, 197
Main Dishes
Bacon-Cheese Topped Chicken, 109
Cheddar Ham Strata, 223
Cheese Enchiladas, 224
Creamy Ham and Macaroni, 87
Cube Steaks Parmigiana, 110
Meatless Mexican Lasagna, 106
Mozzarella-Stuffed Meatballs, 102
Pies and Tarts
Berry Cheesecake Pie, 184
Butternut Cream Pie, 168
Caramel-Pecan Cheesecake Pie, 289
Cream Cheese Blueberry Pie, 167
Peaches & Cream Tart, 357
Raspberry Patch Cream Pie, 171
Spring Breeze Cheesecake Pie, 353
Salads
Apple-Brie Spinach Salad, 31
Chunky Blue Cheese Dressing, 33
Tomato-Cucumber Mozzarella
    Salad, 355
Sandwiches
Blue Cheese Clubs, 47
Butterfly Cheese Sandwiches, 354
Swiss Tuna Melts, 48
Tuna Cheese Melts, 342
Side Dishes
Cheese-Stuffed Potatoes, 236
Cheesy Noodle Casserole, 67
Cherry Tomato Mozzarella Saute, 77
Mac and Cheese for a Bunch, 214
Parmesan Potato Balls, 329
Peas in Cheese Sauce, 74
Prosciutto Tortellini, 319
Swiss-Almond Floret Bake, 80
Tortellini Spinach Casserole, 225
Triple-Cheese Broccoli Puff, 284
Snacks and Beverages
Blue Cheese Deviled Eggs, 226
Crab and Brie Strudel Slices, 367
Hot Cheddar-Mushroom Spread, 288
Lemon Cream-Stuffed Grapes, 16
Par-Cheesy Pizza, 17
Pineapple Cheese Ball, 12
Rhubarb Cheesecake Smoothies, 13
Savory Ham Cheesecake, 10
Three-Cheese Pesto Pizza, 23
Soups
Cheeseburger Paradise Soup, 54
Cheesy Corn Chowder, 54

CHEESECAKES
Carrot Cheesecake, 180
Chocolate-Covered Cheesecake
    Squares, 194

Cinnamon Apple Cheesecake, 179
Festive White Chocolate Cheesecake, 365
Layered Mocha Cheesecake, 170
Lemony White Chocolate
    Cheesecake, 169
Mascarpone Cheesecake, 172
Peanut Butter Cup Cheesecake, 182
Rhubarb Swirl Cheesecake, 164
Strawberry Swirl Cheesecake, 174

CHERRIES

Apple-Cherry Pork Chops, 359
Cappuccino Cherry Trifle, 192
Cheesecake Waffle Cups, 325
Cherry Chocolate Bark, 159
Cherry Gingerbread Cupcakes, 179
Cherry Ice Cream Cake, 204
Door County Cherry Biscotti, 156
Elegant Dipped Cherries, 149
Fresh Cherry Pie, 165
Raspberry Cherry Pie, 166

CHICKEN

Main Dishes
Apricot Honey Chicken, 317
Asian Chicken Thighs, 96
Bacon-Cheese Topped Chicken, 109
Biscuit-Topped Lemon Chicken, 222
Brined Roasting Chicken, 91
Broccoli Chicken Supreme, 228
Chicken and Asparagus Kabobs, 90
Chicken & Tomato Risotto, 113
Chicken Pepper Stir-Fry, 105
Chicken Spareribs, 339
Chicken with Paprika Cream, 323
Corn Tortilla Chicken Lasagna, 221
Creamed Chicken over Biscuits, 114
Down-Home Chicken, 262
Forgotten Jambalaya, 208
Grilled Raspberry Chicken, 103
Honey-Mustard Chicken, 238
Old-Fashioned Chicken Potpie, 102
Orange Chicken with Sweet
    Potatoes, 84
Pecan Chicken with Chutney, 97
Spinach Crab Chicken, 111
Sunday Chicken Stew, 106
Thai Chicken Fettuccine, 119
Tropical Lime Chicken, 116
Salads
Chow Mein Chicken Salad, 297
Crispy Chicken Strip Salad, 30
Special Sesame Chicken Salad, 36
Summer Chicken Salad, 35
Sandwiches
Buffalo Chicken Wraps, 57
Chicken Broccoli Calzones, 61
Chicken Florentine Panini, 315

Snacks
Buffalo Chicken Dip, 223
Chicken Fingers with Lemon Sauce, 10
Chicken Pom-Poms, 16
Chicken Potstickers, 25
Hot Wings, 23
Prosciutto Chicken Kabobs, 12
Soups
Chicken Asparagus Soup, 60
Chicken Soup with Potato
    Dumplings, 56
Colorful Chicken and Squash Soup, 50
Lemony Chicken Soup, 49
White Bean Chicken Chili, 59

CHILI

Black Bean and Pumpkin Chili, 51
Colony Mountain Chili, 48
Spicy Pork Chili, 217
White Bean Chicken Chili, 59

CHOCOLATE

Bars and Brownies
Almond Truffle Brownies, 157
Chocolate Pecan Bars, 147
Chocolate Ribbon Bars, 347
Coffee and Cream Brownies, 150
Creamy Cashew Brownies, 145
Frosted Cookie Brownies, 154
Irish Mint Brownies, 152
Peanut Butter Blondies, 156
Peanut Lover's Brownies, 219
Tiramisu Brownies, 159
Beverages
Cinnamon Mocha Coffee, 19
Cocoa for a Crowd, 11
Breads
Rich Coffee Cake, 128
White Chocolate Macadamia
    Muffins, 129
Cakes and Cupcakes
Chocolate Carrot Cake, 178
Classic Red Velvet Cake, 185
Devil's Food Caramel Torte, 309
Elegant Chocolate Torte, 166
Ladybug Cake, 354
Layered Mocha Cheesecake, 170
Lemony White Chocolate
    Cheesecake, 169
Mocha Nut Torte, 163
Peanut Butter Chocolate Cupcakes, 216
Peanut Butter Cup Cheesecake, 182
Peeps Sunflower Cake, 350
Poppy Seed Torte, 271
Special Mocha Cupcakes, 176
Summer Celebration Ice Cream
    Cake, 173

Texas Chocolate Cupcakes, 185
Valentine Cakes, 236
Wicked Witch Cupcakes, 361
Candies
Cherry Chocolate Bark, 159
Chocolate Pretzels, 155
Coconut Snowmen, 363
Cookie Dough Truffles, 148
Elegant Dipped Cherries, 149
Granola Fudge Clusters, 313
Homemade Peanut Butter Cups, 158
Cookies
Chocolate Heart Cookies, 146
Chocolate Mint Dreams, 144
Coconut Pecan Cookies, 146
Delicate Mint Thins, 143
Door County Cherry Biscotti, 156
Hazelnut-Espresso Sandwich
    Cookies, 154
Meringue Fudge Drops, 153
Pinwheels and Checkerboards, 149
Desserts
Banana Split Brownie Pie, 202
Cappuccino Cherry Trifle, 192
Caramel Chocolate Trifle, 191
Cherry Ice Cream Cake, 204
Chocolate Chip Mousse, 188
Chocolate-Covered Cheesecake
    Squares, 194
Chocolate Ice Cream Sandwiches, 193
Chocolate Pecan Ice Cream Torte, 162
Frosty Almond Dessert, 319
Ice Cream Cookie Dessert, 275
Minty Ice Cream Shamrocks, 242
Mixed Nut Chocolate Tart, 202
Peanut Butter Pudding Dessert, 213
Praline Chocolate Dessert, 189
Rich Hot Fudge Sauce, 195
Rocky Road Ice Cream, 190
Strawberry Puff Pastry Dessert, 195
White Chocolate Berry Dessert, 196
Pies
Frosty Mocha Pie, 165
Frozen Peanut Parfait Pies, 175
Frozen Strawberry Pie, 182
Fudgy Nut Coffee Pie, 181
No-Bake Chocolate Pie, 305
Snacks
Chocolate Wheat Cereal Snacks, 22
Double Chocolate Fondue, 22

CHOWDER

Asparagus Leek Chowder, 54
Cheesy Corn Chowder, 54
Golden Seafood Chowder, 57
Ramen Corn Chowder, 315
Salmon Chowder, 344

CINNAMON
Cinnamon Apple Cheesecake, 179
Cinnamon Mocha Coffee, 19
Cinnamon-Raisin Soft Pretzels, 198
Cinnamon-Sugar Rhubarb Cake, 225
Mini Maple Cinnamon Rolls, 139
Pretty Pumpkin Cinnamon Buns, 130
Vanilla Cinnamon Rolls, 134

COCONUT
Coconut Pecan Cookies, 146
Coconut Pecan Cupcakes, 210
Coconut Snowmen, 363
Lemon Coconut Cake, 174

CONDIMENTS & GARNISHES
(also see Salsa)
Baked Cranberry Sauce, 74
Candied Flowers, 295
Dilly Pickled Asparagus, 66
Garlic-Pepper Rub, 78
Mango Cranberry Sauce, 78
Orange Rhubarb Spread, 71
Pickled Baby Carrots, 351
Salsa for a Crowd, 229
So-Sweet Squash Pickles, 68
Tangy Rhubarb Chutney, 73

COOKIES (also see Bars & Brownies)
Almond-Butter Cookie Bouquet, 352
Almond Cookies, 333
Almond Sugar Cookies, 151
Berry-Cream Cookie Snaps, 147
Butterscotch Eggnog Stars, 148
Chewy Apple Oatmeal Cookies, 157
Chocolate Heart Cookies, 146
Chocolate Mint Dreams, 144
Cinnamon-Sugar Crisps, 343
Coconut Pecan Cookies, 146
Delicate Mint Thins, 143
Dipped Pecan Spritz, 155
Door County Cherry Biscotti, 156
Frosted Rhubarb Cookies, 153
Gingerbread Boy Cookies, 263
Hazelnut-Espresso Sandwich Cookies, 154
Iced Pumpkin Cookies, 142
Lavender Cookies, 145
Lemon Tea Cookies, 143
Meringue Fudge Drops, 153
Nice and Soft Sugar Cookies, 152
Peanut Butter Christmas Mice, 366
Pinwheels and Checkerboards, 149
Ranger Cookies, 158
Rhubarb Cranberry Cookies, 215
Slice and Bake Lemon Gems, 150

CORN & GRITS
Cheddar Skillet Corn Bread, 125
Cheesy Corn Chowder, 54

Corn Fritters with Caramelized Onion
    Jam, 356
Corn Pudding, 258
Corn Zucchini Saute, 325
Double Corn Dressing, 73
Fresh Corn Medley, 72
Golden Corn Quiche, 358
Grilled Corn Dip, 15
Grilled Corn Salsa, 66
Mexicorn Grits, 70
Poached Corn, 262
Ramen Corn Chowder, 315
Smoky Grilled Corn, 74
Tomato and Corn Risotto, 69
Tomato Corn Salad, 31

CORN BREAD & CORNMEAL
Blueberry Cornmeal Cobbler, 192
Cheddar Skillet Corn Bread, 125
Corn Pudding, 258
Cornmeal Ham Cakes, 95
Salmon with Polenta, 99
Tamales, 212
Turkey with Sausage-Corn Bread
    Stuffing, 360

CRANBERRIES
Baked Cranberry Sauce, 74
Colorful Turkey Salad Cups, 34
Cran-Apple Crisp, 222
Cranberry Gelatin Squares, 221
Cranberry Ham Loaf, 104
Cranberry Lemonade, 321
Cranberry-Topped Lemon Tarts, 194
Cranberry Walnut Tart, 362
Cranberry Zucchini Wedges, 176
Festive Rice Salad, 218
Festive White Chocolate Cheesecake, 365
Gingered Cranberry-Carrot Slaw, 317
Mango Cranberry Sauce, 78
Pumpkin Scones with Berry Butter, 134
Rhubarb Cranberry Cookies, 215
Spiral Ham with Cranberry Glaze, 84
Sunrise Slushies, 24
Very Berry-licious Smoothies, 17

CREPES & PANCAKES
Asparagus Sausage Crepes, 85
Buckwheat Brunch Crepes, 88
Cornmeal Ham Cakes, 95
Pecan Apple Pancakes, 89
Strawberry Crepes, 188

CRISPS & COBBLERS
Apple Crumble, 198
Blackberry Crisp, 357

Blueberry Cornmeal Cobbler, 192
Cran-Apple Crisp, 222
Double-Berry Crisp, 199
Mom's Apple Crisp, 267
Peach Rhubarb Crisp, 197
Raspberry Pear Crisp, 198
Toffee Apple Crunch, 245

CUCUMBERS
Crunchy Cucumber Rounds, 8
German Cukes and Tomatoes, 331
Olive-Cucumber Tossed Salad, 305
Steaks with Cucumber Sauce, 101
Tomato-Cucumber Mozzarella Salad, 355

CUPCAKES
Cherry Gingerbread Cupcakes, 179
Coconut Pecan Cupcakes, 210
Peanut Butter Chocolate Cupcakes, 216
Pineapple Upside-Down Cupcakes, 181
Raspberry Peach Cupcakes, 183
Special Mocha Cupcakes, 176
Texas Chocolate Cupcakes, 185
Walnut Banana Cupcakes, 177
Wicked Witch Cupcakes, 361

DEEP-FRIED RECIPES
Carrot Zucchini Fritters, 20
Chicken Fingers with Lemon Sauce, 10
Corn Fritters with Caramelized Onion
    Jam, 356
Fried Shoestring Carrots, 68
Mom's Fried Fish, 266
Pork and Shrimp Spring Rolls, 8

**DESSERTS (also see Bars & Brownies;
Cakes; Cheesecakes; Cupcakes;
Cookies; Crisps & Cobblers; Ice
Cream & Toppings; Pies & Tarts)**
Apple Dumplings, 205
Apple Pizza, 200
Apple Plum Streusel Dessert, 279
Baked Bananas in Orange Sauce, 241
Cappuccino Cherry Trifle, 192
Caramel Chocolate Trifle, 191
Cheesecake Waffle Cups, 325
Chocolate Chip Mousse, 188
Cinnamon-Raisin Soft Pretzels, 198
Fluffy Pineapple Dessert, 335
Gingerbread Pudding Cake, 201
Grandmother's Bread Pudding, 190
Ladyfinger Lemon Torte, 191
Lemon Cheesecake Dessert, 201
Lemon Cream Puffs, 367
Lemon Rice Pudding Brulee, 205
Mixed Fruit Shortcakes, 233

Mixed Nut Chocolate Tart, 202
Peaches 'n' Cream Cups, 204
Peanut Butter Pudding Dessert, 213
Praline Chocolate Dessert, 189
Pumpkin Rice Pudding, 189
Raisin Pecan Baklava, 196
Raspberry Squares, 255
Russian Cream, 358
Strawberry Pretzel Dessert, 350
Strawberry Puff Pastry Dessert, 195
Strawberry Tartlets, 200
Tiramisu Cheesecake Dessert, 197
Ultimate Caramel Apples, 359
Vanilla Pudding Dessert, 224
White Chocolate Berry Dessert, 196

DIPS (also see Salsa)
A Touch of Greek Dip, 9
Buffalo Chicken Dip, 223
Caramel Fruit Dip, 14
Cowboy Beef Dip, 19
Dilly Zucchini Dip, 220
Double Chocolate Fondue, 22
Grilled Corn Dip, 15
Roasted Carrot Dip, 11
Tex-Mex Dip, 224

EGGS
Asparagus Crab Omelets, 107
Bacon-Egg English Muffin, 234
Blue Cheese Deviled Eggs, 226
Cheddar Ham Strata, 223
Christmas Breakfast Casserole, 284
Deluxe Breakfast Bake, 228
Egg Drop Soup, 333
Golden Corn Quiche, 358
Mini Sausage Quiches, 18
Overnight Asparagus Strata, 352
Pepperoni Spinach Quiche, 101
Triple-Cheese Broccoli Puff, 284

ENCHILADAS & QUESADILLAS
Cheese Enchiladas, 224
Shrimp Quesadillas, 118
Spicy Zucchini Quesadillas, 356
Turkey Enchiladas, 107

FISH & SEAFOOD
Main Dishes
    Asparagus Crab Omelets, 107
    Caesar Orange Roughy, 120
    Crab-Stuffed Sole, 116
    Curried Shrimp and Apples, 112
    Forgotten Jambalaya, 208
    Lime Shrimp with Asparagus, 98
    Macadamia-Crusted Tilapia, 99
    Mom's Fried Fish, 266

Pepper-Rubbed Red Snapper, 319
    Puff Pastry Salmon Bundles, 274
    Salmon with Polenta, 99
    Shrimp Pasta Primavera, 95
    Shrimp Quesadillas, 118
    Shrimp Scampi, 313
    Spinach Crab Chicken, 111
    Sunday Shrimp Pasta Bake, 304
Salads and Dressings
    Garlic Anchovy Salad Dressing, 42
    Greek Seafood Salad, 35
    Green Goddess Salad Dressing, 28
    Waldorf Tuna Salad, 41
Sandwiches
    Mini Chicken Salad Croissants, 210
    Shrimp Salad Croissants, 60
    Swiss Tuna Melts, 48
    Tuna Cheese Melts, 342
Snacks
    Chunky Crawfish Spread, 304
    Crab and Brie Strudel Slices, 367
    Onions Neptune, 211
    Pork and Shrimp Spring Rolls, 8
    Shrimp Toast Cups, 21
    Shrimp Wrapped in Bacon, 24
    Warm Asparagus-Crab Spread, 15
Soups
    Golden Seafood Chowder, 57
    Salmon Chowder, 344
    Spicy Seafood Bisque, 366

FOWL & GAME
Hens with Apricot Rice Stuffing, 250
Holiday Game Hens, 245
Pineapple-Stuffed Cornish Hens, 104
Roast Christmas Goose, 278

FRENCH TOAST
Apple-Stuffed French Toast, 85
Fruity French Toast, 234

FRUIT (also see specific kinds)
Blackberry Crisp, 357
Caramel Fruit Dip, 14
Colorful Turkey Salad Cups, 34
Fresh Fruit Tarts, 175
Fruit and Nut Stollen, 130
Fruit and Nut Tossed Salad, 37
Fruit-Nut Pumpkin Bread, 132
Fruit Salad Dressing, 39
Grapefruit Lettuce Salad, 245
Hint of Mint Fruit Salad, 213
Holiday Spiral Ham, 258
Hot Curried Fruit, 285
Lemon Cream-Stuffed Grapes, 16
Mixed Fruit Shortcakes, 233

Poppy Seed Fruit Salad, 41
Special Sesame Chicken Salad, 36
Three-Fruit Salad, 337
Watermelon Basket, 214

GRILLED & BROILED
Main Dishes
    Barbecued Ham and Peaches, 337
    Chicken and Asparagus Kabobs, 90
    Grilled Asparagus Pizzas, 94
    Grilled Raspberry Chicken, 103
    Maple-Glazed Ribs, 96
    Minted Lamb and Veggie Kabobs, 353
    Salisbury Steak, 241
    Steaks with Cucumber Sauce, 101
    Sweetheart Steaks, 237
    Tropical Lime Chicken, 116
Salads
    Apple-Brie Spinach Salad, 31
    Grilled Apple Tossed Salad, 32
    Grilled Steak Caesar Salad, 34
    Grilled Three-Potato Salad, 41
Sandwiches
    Firecracker Burgers, 59
    French Onion Burgers, 321
Side Dishes
    Curried Butternut Squash Kabobs, 71
    Grilled Asparagus Medley, 72
    Grilled Corn Salsa, 66
    Smoky Grilled Corn, 74
Snacks
    Grilled Corn Dip, 15
    Prosciutto Chicken Kabobs, 12

GROUND BEEF
Main Dishes
    Cube Steaks Parmigiana, 110
    Dad's Swedish Meatballs, 86
    Fiesta Lasagna, 98
    Meat Loaf Wellington, 103
    Meaty Pasta Casseroles, 218
    Mozzarella-Stuffed Meatballs, 102
    Prosciutto-Stuffed Meat Loaf, 108
    Salisbury Steak, 241
    Spicy Nacho Bake, 93
    Stuffed Squash for Two, 100
    Sweet and Tender Cabbage Rolls, 113
    Taco Meat Loaves, 115
    Traditional Meat Loaf, 329
Salad
    Crowd-Pleasing Taco Salad, 39
Sandwiches
    Family-Pleasing Sloppy Joes, 331
    Firecracker Burgers, 59
    French Onion Burgers, 321

GROUND BEEF (continued)

Sandwiches
Meat Loaf Gyros, 114
Meatball Calzones, 229
Pizza Meatball Subs, 52

Snacks
Cowboy Beef Dip, 19
Party Meatballs, 9

Soups
Cheeseburger Paradise Soup, 54
Italian Wedding Soup, 52

HAM & PROSCIUTTO
Apple and Prosciutto Sandwiches, 49
Artichoke Ham Puffs, 118
Barbecued Ham and Peaches, 337
Cheddar Ham Strata, 223
Cornmeal Ham Cakes, 95
Cranberry Ham Loaf, 104
Creamy Ham and Macaroni, 87
Deluxe Breakfast Bake, 228
Grilled Asparagus Pizzas, 94
Ham Bundles, 220
Ham on Biscuits, 296
Hawaiian Ham Salad, 34
Holiday Spiral Ham, 258
Home Run Slugger Sub, 58
Pretty Penne Ham Skillet, 93
Prosciutto Chicken Kabobs, 12
Prosciutto-Stuffed Meat Loaf, 108
Prosciutto Tortellini, 319
Savory Ham Cheesecake, 10
Scalloped Potatoes and Ham, 216
Spiral Ham with Cranberry Glaze, 84
Stuffed Ham with Raisin Sauce, 351
Waldorf Stuffed Ham, 91

HONEY & MAPLE SYRUP
Apricot Honey Chicken, 317
Grandma's Honey Muffins, 293
Honey-Mustard Chicken, 238
Honey-Oat Pan Rolls, 132
Honey Pecan Pie, 168
Maple Pumpkin Pie, 184
Maple Walnut Rolls, 124
Mini Maple Cinnamon Rolls, 139
Vermont Honey-Wheat Bread, 124

ICE CREAM & TOPPINGS
Banana Citrus Sorbet, 301
Banana Split Brownie Pie, 202
Blond Brownies a la Mode, 142
Butter Pecan Ice Cream, 193
Cherry Ice Cream Cake, 204
Chocolate Ice Cream Sandwiches, 193
Chocolate Pecan Ice Cream Torte, 162
Creamy Lime Sherbet, 297

Fluffy Lemon Squares, 203
Frosty Almond Dessert, 319
Fudgy Nut Coffee Pie, 181
Ice Cream Cookie Dessert, 275
Minty Ice Cream Shamrocks, 242
Peach Ice Cream, 193
Rhubarb Cheesecake Smoothies, 13
Rich Hot Fudge Sauce, 195
Rocky Road Ice Cream, 190
Strawberry Cheesecake Ice Cream, 199
Summer Celebration Ice Cream Cake, 173
Three-Fruit Sundae Sauce, 203

LAMB
Crusty Roast Leg of Lamb, 300
Meat Loaf Gyros, 114
Minted Lamb and Veggie Kabobs, 353
Rosemary Leg of Lamb, 111

LEMON & LIME
Almond-Lemon Pound Cake, 238
Banana Citrus Sorbet, 301
Biscuit-Topped Lemon Chicken, 222
Chicken Fingers with Lemon Sauce, 10
Citrus Quencher, 305
Cranberry Lemonade, 321
Cranberry-Topped Lemon Tarts, 194
Creamy Lime Sherbet, 297
Fluffy Lemon Squares, 203
Green Beans in Lemon Chiffon Sauce, 80
Ladyfinger Lemon Torte, 191
Lemon Cheesecake Dessert, 201
Lemon Chiffon Cake, 172
Lemon Coconut Cake, 174
Lemon Cream Puffs, 367
Lemon Cream-Stuffed Grapes, 16
Lemon Pound Cake Muffins, 129
Lemon Rice Pudding Brulee, 205
Lemon Tea Cookies, 143
Lemonade Icebox Pie, 169
Lemonade Meringue Pie, 171
Lemony Chicken Soup, 49
Lemony White Chocolate
   Cheesecake, 169
Pecan Lemon Loaf, 133
Red Cream Soda Punch, 227
Sensational Slush, 9
Slice and Bake Lemon Gems, 150
Sparkling Ginger Lemonade, 14
Sweetheart Punch, 20
Tossed Salad with Lemon Vinaigrette, 215
Tropical Lime Chicken, 116

MARSHMALLOWS
Cherry Chocolate Bark, 159
Coconut Snowmen, 363
Frosted Cookie Brownies, 154
No-Bake Chocolate Pie, 305
Rocky Road Ice Cream, 190
Three-Fruit Salad, 337

MEAT LOAVES & MEATBALLS
Cranberry Ham Loaf, 104
Dad's Swedish Meatballs, 86
Meat Loaf Gyros, 114
Meat Loaf Wellington, 103
Meatball Calzones, 229
Meatballs in Plum Sauce, 209
Mozzarella-Stuffed Meatballs, 102
Party Meatballs, 9
Pizza Meatball Subs, 52
Prosciutto-Stuffed Meat Loaf, 108
Taco Meat Loaves, 115
Traditional Meat Loaf, 329

MEAT PIES & PIZZAS
Chicken Broccoli Calzones, 61
Giant Calzone, 100
Grilled Asparagus Pizzas, 94
Meatball Calzones, 229
Mini Sausage Quiches, 18
Old-Fashioned Chicken Potpie, 102
Par-Cheesy Pizza, 17
Pepperoni Spinach Quiche, 101
Pizza Margherita, 110
Three-Cheese Pesto Pizza, 23
Turkey Potpies, 112

MICROWAVE RECIPES
Asparagus with Mustard Sauce, 77
Black Bean Burgers, 56
Crab-Stuffed Sole, 116
Granola Fudge Clusters, 313
Green Beans with Walnuts, 341
Homemade Peanut Butter Cups, 158
Lime Shrimp with Asparagus, 98
Rustic Squash Tarts, 70
Spaghetti Squash with Red Sauce, 108
Thai Chicken Fettuccine, 119
Toffee Apple Crunch, 245
Tomato Rice Pilaf, 241

MINT
Chocolate Mint Dreams, 144
Delicate Mint Thins, 143
Irish Mint Brownies, 152
Minted Lamb and Veggie Kabobs, 353
Minty Ice Cream Shamrocks, 242

MUFFINS
Almond Berry Muffins, 137
Apple Streusel Muffins, 227
Berry Cheesecake Muffins, 127
Feta and Chive Muffins, 135
Grandma's Honey Muffins, 293
Irish Soda Muffins, 242
Italian Herb Muffins, 364
Lemon Pound Cake Muffins, 129

Spiced Squash Muffins, 362
Walnut Raspberry Muffins, 138
White Chocolate Macadamia Muffins, 129

MUSHROOMS
Hot Cheddar-Mushroom Spread, 288
Mushroom Bread Wedges, 323
Mushroom Tomato Bisque, 61
Turkey with Mushrooms and Cream, 270

MUSTARD
Asparagus with Mustard Sauce, 77
Broccoli with Mustard Sauce, 289
Mustard-Sour Cream Salad Dressing, 29

NUTS & PEANUT BUTTER
Breads
Almond Berry Muffins, 137
Fruit and Nut Stollen, 130
Fruit-Nut Pumpkin Bread, 132
Maple Walnut Rolls, 124
Pecan Lemon Loaf, 133
Special Banana Nut Bread, 132
Walnut Raspberry Muffins, 138
White Chocolate Macadamia
  Muffins, 129
Cakes and Cupcakes
Almond-Lemon Pound Cake, 238
Banana Nut Cake, 167
Coconut Pecan Cupcakes, 210
Peanut Butter Chocolate Cupcakes, 216
Peanut Butter Cup Cheesecake, 182
Walnut Banana Cupcakes, 177
Candies
Cherry Chocolate Bark, 159
Granola Fudge Clusters, 313
Homemade Peanut Butter Cups, 158
Cookies and Bars
Almond Cookies, 333
Almond Sugar Cookies, 151
Almond Truffle Brownies, 157
Chocolate Pecan Bars, 147
Coconut Pecan Cookies, 146
Creamy Cashew Brownies, 145
Dipped Pecan Spritz, 155
Glazed Peanut Butter Bars, 151
Hazelnut-Espresso Sandwich
  Cookies, 154
Peanut Butter Blondies, 156
Peanut Butter Christmas Mice, 366
Peanut Lover's Brownies, 219
Rustic Nut Bars, 144
Desserts
Butter Pecan Ice Cream, 193
Chocolate Pecan Ice Cream Torte, 162
Frosty Almond Dessert, 319

Mixed Nut Chocolate Tart, 202
Mocha Nut Torte, 163
Peanut Butter Pudding Dessert, 213
Praline Chocolate Dessert, 189
Raisin Pecan Baklava, 196
Rocky Road Ice Cream, 190
Main Dishes
Crescent-Topped Turkey Amandine, 117
Macadamia-Crusted Tilapia, 99
Pecan Apple Pancakes, 89
Pecan Chicken with Chutney, 97
Pies and Tarts
Caramel-Pecan Apple Pie, 183
Caramel-Pecan Cheesecake Pie, 289
Cranberry Walnut Tart, 362
Frozen Peanut Parfait Pies, 175
Fudgy Nut Coffee Pie, 181
Honey Pecan Pie, 168
Salads
Cashew-Pear Tossed Salad, 211
Fruit and Nut Tossed Salad, 37
Hazelnut Vegetable Salad, 270
Pecan-Pear Green Salad, 29
Side Dishes
Cashew-Pecan Sweet Potatoes, 309
Garlic-Almond Green Beans, 313
Green Beans with Walnuts, 341
Snacks
Roasted Cumin Cashews, 22
Spiced Orange Pecans, 12

OATMEAL
Chewy Apple Oatmeal Cookies, 157
Honey-Oat Pan Rolls, 132
Ranger Cookies, 158

ONIONS & LEEKS
Asparagus Leek Chowder, 54
Corn Fritters with Caramelized Onion
  Jam, 356
French Onion Burgers, 321
Onion-Bacon Baby Carrots, 74
Onions Neptune, 211
Orange and Red Onion Salad, 250
Pearl Onion Broccoli Bake, 64
Poppy Seed Onion Bread, 131

ORANGE
Baked Bananas in Orange Sauce, 241
Banana Citrus Sorbet, 301
Broccoli with Orange Sauce, 71
Citrus Quencher, 305
Orange and Red Onion Salad, 250
Orange Chicken with Sweet Potatoes, 84
Orange Gelatin Pretzel Salad, 33

Orange-Glazed Acorn Squash, 75
Orange-Rhubarb Breakfast Bread, 126
Orange Rhubarb Spread, 71
Red Cream Soda Punch, 227
Spiced Orange Pecans, 12
Sunrise Slushies, 24
Sweetheart Punch, 20
Three-Fruit Sundae Sauce, 203

OVEN ENTREES (also see Casseroles; Meat Loaves & Meatballs; Meat Pies & Pizzas; Microwave Recipes; Slow Cooker Recipes)
Beef and Ground Beef
Beef Brisket with Mop Sauce, 292
Beef Rib Roast, 363
Braised Short Ribs, 109
Brisket in a Bag, 121
Cube Steaks Parmigiana, 110
Meat Loaf Gyros, 114
Meat Loaf Wellington, 103
Prosciutto-Stuffed Meat Loaf, 108
Stuffed Squash for Two, 100
Tenderloin in Puff Pastry, 92
Traditional Meat Loaf, 329
Chicken
Bacon-Cheese Topped Chicken, 109
Brined Roasting Chicken, 91
Honey-Mustard Chicken, 238
Spinach Crab Chicken, 111
Fish and Seafood
Caesar Orange Roughy, 120
Macadamia-Crusted Tilapia, 99
Puff Pastry Salmon Bundles, 274
Fowl and Game
Hens with Apricot Rice Stuffing, 250
Holiday Game Hens, 245
Pineapple-Stuffed Cornish Hens, 104
Roast Christmas Goose, 278
Lamb
Crusty Roast Leg of Lamb, 300
Meat Loaf Gyros, 114
Rosemary Leg of Lamb, 111
Pork, Ham and Sausage
Cranberry Ham Loaf, 104
Crown Roast of Pork, 308
Holiday Spiral Ham, 258
Pork Tenderloin with Stuffing, 254
Spinach and Sausage Pork Loin, 364
Spiral Ham with Cranberry Glaze, 84
Stuffed Ham with Raisin Sauce, 351
Stuffed Pork Tenderloin, 233
Waldorf Stuffed Ham, 91
Turkey
Rolled-Up Turkey, 120
Turkey with Sausage-Corn Bread
  Stuffing, 360

SALADS & DRESSINGS (continued)

Vegetable Salads
Green Bean and Tomato Salad, 346
Hazelnut Vegetable Salad, 270
Sunny Carrot Salad, 29
Tomato Corn Salad, 31
Tomato-Cucumber Mozzarella
    Salad, 355
Zucchini Apple Salad, 254

SALSA
Salsa for a Crowd, 229
Asparagus Salsa, 23
Grilled Corn Salsa, 66

SANDWICHES

Cold Sandwiches
Black Bean Burgers, 56
Blue Cheese Clubs, 47
Butterfly Cheese Sandwiches, 354
Home Run Slugger Sub, 58
Mini Chicken Salad Croissants, 210
Shrimp Salad Croissants, 60
Turkey Muffuletta, 46
Zesty Vegetarian Wraps, 60

Hot Sandwiches
Apple and Prosciutto Sandwiches, 49
Buffalo Chicken Wraps, 57
Chicken Broccoli Calzones, 61
Chicken Florentine Panini, 315
Cuban Pork Sandwiches, 55
Family-Pleasing Sloppy Joes, 331
Firecracker Burgers, 59
French Onion Burgers, 321
Ham on Biscuits, 296
Meat Loaf Gyros, 114
Pizza Meatball Subs, 52
Shredded Beef and Slaw Sandwiches, 215
Swiss Tuna Melts, 48
Tuna Cheese Melts, 342

SAUSAGE & PEPPERONI

Main Dishes
Asparagus Sausage Crepes, 85
Cranberry Ham Loaf, 104
Forgotten Jambalaya, 208
Giant Calzone, 100
Meaty Pasta Casseroles, 218
Pepperoni Spinach Quiche, 101
Prosciutto-Stuffed Meat Loaf, 108
Sausage with Apple Sauerkraut, 341
Simple Sausage Lasagna, 288
Spinach and Sausage Pork Loin, 364
Spiral Pepperoni Pizza Bake, 226
Turkey with Sausage-Corn Bread
    Stuffing, 360

Sandwiches
German Potato Salad with Sausage, 76
Home Run Slugger Sub, 58

Snacks
Mini Sausage Quiches, 18
Par-Cheesy Pizza, 17
Smoky Jalapenos, 21

Soups
Colony Mountain Chili, 48
Italian Wedding Soup, 52
Minestrone with Italian Sausage, 51

SEAFOOD (see Fish & Seafood)

SIDE DISHES (also see Casseroles; Condiments; Salads & Dressings)

Beans
Baked Garlic Green Beans, 233
Garlic-Almond Green Beans, 313
Green Beans in Lemon Chiffon
    Sauce, 80
Green Beans with Walnuts, 341
Slow-Cooked Bean Medley, 64

Miscellaneous
Corn Fritters with Caramelized Onion
    Jam, 356
Hot Curried Fruit, 285
Rustic Roasted Vegetable Tart, 355
Rustic Squash Tarts, 70

Pasta
Creamy Vegetable Bow Tie Toss, 78
Crumb-Coated Spaetzle, 72
Gnocchi with Thyme Butter, 76
Prosciutto Tortellini, 319

Potatoes
Cheese-Stuffed Potatoes, 236
Favorite Herbed Potatoes, 317
German Potato Salad with Sausage, 76
German-Style Mashed Potatoes, 67
O'Larry's Skillet Potatoes, 81
Parmesan Potato Balls, 329
Parsley Red Potatoes, 267
Spicy Potato Wedges, 331

Rice and Barley
Springtime Barley, 65
Tomato and Corn Risotto, 69
Tomato Rice Pilaf, 241

Vegetables
Asparagus with Mustard Sauce, 77
Bacon Squash Saute, 250
Broccoli with Mustard Sauce, 289
Broccoli with Orange Sauce, 71
Brussels Sprouts with Water
    Chestnuts, 365
Candied Carrots, 258
Cherry Tomato Mozzarella Saute, 77
Corn Zucchini Saute, 325
Creamed Fresh Spinach, 279
Creamed Spinach, 339
Curried Butternut Squash Kabobs, 71
Fresh Corn Medley, 72
Fried Shoestring Carrots, 68
Grilled Asparagus Medley, 72
Herbed Tomatoes and Green Beans, 75
Maple-Ginger Root Vegetables, 69
Orange-Glazed Acorn Squash, 75
Parsnip Pancakes, 255
Peas in Cheese Sauce, 74
Peppery Parsnip Fries, 81
Poached Corn, 262
Ribboned Vegetables, 66
Rice-Stuffed Acorn Squash, 360
Roasted Squash Medley, 67
Smoky Grilled Corn, 74
Spaghetti Squash Supreme, 79
Springtime Asparagus Medley, 300
Steamed Broccoli Florets, 323
Sweet & Sour Brussels Sprouts, 81
Sweet Herbed Carrots, 238

SKILLET & STOVETOP SUPPERS

Beef and Ground Beef
Asian Pot Roast, 115
Asparagus Beef Stir-Fry, 121
Caraway Pot Roast, 335
Curried Beef with Dumplings, 94
Dad's Swedish Meatballs, 86
Indiana Swiss Steak, 97
Thai Beef Stir-Fry, 86

Chicken
Apricot Honey Chicken, 317
Asian Chicken Thighs, 96
Chicken & Tomato Risotto, 113
Chicken Pepper Stir-Fry, 105
Chicken Spareribs, 339
Chicken with Paprika Cream, 323
Creamed Chicken over Biscuits, 114
Down-Home Chicken, 262
Pecan Chicken with Chutney, 97

Fish and Seafood
Curried Shrimp and Apples, 112
Pepper-Rubbed Red Snapper, 319
Salmon with Polenta, 99
Shrimp Pasta Primavera, 95
Shrimp Quesadillas, 118
Shrimp Scampi, 313

Meatless
Savory Pumpkin Ravioli, 117
Vegetarian Pasta Sauce, 89

Pork, Ham and Sausage
Apple-Cherry Pork Chops, 359
Artichoke Ham Puffs, 118
Butterflied Pork Chop Dinner, 105
Chinese New Year Skillet, 333

Pretty Penne Ham Skillet, 93
Raspberry Pork Chops, 325
Sausage with Apple Sauerkraut, 341
Turkey
  Next Day Turkey Primavera, 107
  Turkey Chop Suey, 121
  Turkey with Mushrooms and
    Cream, 270

SLOW COOKER RECIPES
Bavarian Pork Loin, 88
Black Bean and Pumpkin Chili, 51
Colony Mountain Chili, 48
Corned Beef Supper, 242
Forgotten Jambalaya, 208
German Potato Salad with Sausage, 76
Orange Chicken with Sweet Potatoes, 84
Pot Roast with Gravy, 87
Slow-Cooked Bean Medley, 64
Slow-Cooked Pork and Beans, 219
Sunday Chicken Stew, 106
Sweet and Tender Cabbage Rolls, 113
Tasty Pork Ribs, 90
Vegetarian Stuffed Peppers, 92

SOUPS (also see Chili; Chowder)
Cheeseburger Paradise Soup, 54
Chicken Asparagus Soup, 60
Chicken Soup with Potato Dumplings, 56
Chunky Taco Soup, 48
Colorful Chicken and Squash Soup, 50
Curried Carrot Soup, 296
Danish Turkey Dumpling Soup, 58
Egg Drop Soup, 333
Garlic Butternut Bisque, 50
Gingered Butternut Squash Soup, 47
Golden Squash Soup, 288
Hearty Beef Vegetable Soup, 53
Italian Wedding Soup, 52
Land of Enchantment Posole, 55
Lemony Chicken Soup, 49
Minestrone with Italian Sausage, 51
Mushroom Tomato Bisque, 61
Roasted Yellow Pepper Soup, 53
Southwestern Turkey Soup, 46
Spanish Gazpacho, 46
Spicy Seafood Bisque, 366

SPINACH
Apple-Brie Spinach Salad, 31
Berry Spinach Salad, 275
Chicken Florentine Panini, 315
Creamed Fresh Spinach, 279
Creamed Spinach, 339
Fruit and Nut Tossed Salad, 37
Hot Spinach Spread with Pita Chips, 17
Pepperoni Spinach Quiche, 101

Special Sesame Chicken Salad, 36
Spinach and Sausage Pork Loin, 364
Spinach Crab Chicken, 111
Strawberry Spinach Salad, 43
Tortellini Spinach Casserole, 225
Warm Asparagus Spinach Salad, 40

SPREADS
Chunky Crawfish Spread, 304
Hot Cheddar-Mushroom Spread, 288
Hot Spinach Spread with Pita Chips, 17
Pineapple Cheese Ball, 12
Savory Ham Cheesecake, 10
Warm Asparagus-Crab Spread, 15

SQUASH (also see Zucchini)
Bacon Squash Saute, 250
Butternut Cream Pie, 168
Butternut Squash Cake Roll, 164
Butternut Turkey Bake, 89
Colorful Chicken and Squash Soup, 50
Curried Butternut Squash Kabobs, 71
Garlic Butternut Bisque, 50
Gingered Butternut Squash Soup, 47
Golden Squash Soup, 288
Orange-Glazed Acorn Squash, 75
Rice-Stuffed Acorn Squash, 360
Roasted Squash Medley, 67
Rustic Squash Tarts, 70
So-Sweet Squash Pickles, 68
Spaghetti Squash Supreme, 79
Spaghetti Squash with Red Sauce, 108
Spiced Squash Muffins, 362
Stuffed Squash for Two, 100

STRAWBERRIES
Almond Berry Muffins, 137
Asparagus Berry Salad, 28
Banana Split Brownie Pie, 202
Berry Banana Smoothies, 234
Berry Pinwheel Cake, 170
Berry-Cream Cookie Snaps, 147
Berry Spinach Salad, 275
Frozen Strawberry Pie, 182
Fruity French Toast, 234
Old Glory Angel Cake, 321
Rhubarb Cheesecake Smoothies, 13
Sensational Slush, 9
Strawberry-Banana Angel Torte, 301
Strawberry Cheesecake Ice Cream, 199
Strawberry Crepes, 188
Strawberry Popovers, 136
Strawberry Pretzel Dessert, 350
Strawberry Puff Pastry Dessert, 195
Strawberry Shortbread Pie, 163
Strawberry Spinach Salad, 43
Strawberry Swirl Cheesecake, 174

Strawberry Tartlets, 200
Summer Chicken Salad, 35
Sunrise Slushies, 24
Sweetheart Punch, 20
Three-Fruit Sundae Sauce, 203
Vanilla Pudding Dessert, 224
Very Berry-licious Smoothies, 17
White Chocolate Berry Dessert, 196

SWEET POTATOES
Butterflied Pork Chop Dinner, 105
Cashew-Pecan Sweet Potatoes, 309
Duo Tater Bake, 65
Grilled Three-Potato Salad, 41
Orange Chicken with Sweet Potatoes, 84

TOMATOES
Asparagus Salsa, 23
Cherry Tomato Mozzarella Saute, 77
Chicken & Tomato Risotto, 113
Chunky Taco Soup, 48
Fiesta Lasagna, 98
Garden-Fresh Bruschetta, 13
German Cukes and Tomatoes, 331
Green Bean and Tomato Salad, 346
Herbed Tomatoes and Green Beans, 75
Meaty Pasta Casseroles, 218
Mozzarella-Stuffed Meatballs, 102
Mushroom Tomato Bisque, 61
Pizza Margherita, 110
Salsa for a Crowd, 229
Simple Sausage Lasagna, 288
Spaghetti Squash with Red Sauce, 108
Springtime Asparagus Medley, 300
Tomato and Corn Risotto, 69
Tomato Corn Salad, 31
Tomato-Cucumber Mozzarella
  Salad, 355
Tomato Focaccia, 131
Tomato Rice Pilaf, 241

TURKEY
Black Bean and Pumpkin Chili, 51
Blue Cheese Clubs, 47
Butternut Turkey Bake, 89
Colorful Turkey Salad Cups, 34
Crescent-Topped Turkey Amandine, 117
Danish Turkey Dumpling Soup, 58
Mini Hot Browns, 14
Next Day Turkey Primavera, 107
Roasted Vegetable Turkey Pinwheels, 25
Rolled-Up Turkey, 120
Southwestern Turkey Soup, 46
Turkey Chop Suey, 121
Turkey Muffuletta, 46
Turkey Potpies, 112

TURKEY (continued)
Turkey with Mushrooms and
    Cream, 270
Turkey with Sausage-Corn Bread
    Stuffing, 360

VEGETABLES (also see specific kinds)
Artichoke Ham Puffs, 118
Creamy Vegetable Bow Tie Toss, 78
Hazelnut Vegetable Salad, 270
Hearty Beef Vegetable Soup, 53
Maple-Ginger Root Vegetables, 69
Meatless Mexican Lasagna, 106
Minted Lamb and Veggie Kabobs, 353
Mostaccioli Veggie Salad, 38
Next Day Turkey Primavera, 107
Ribboned Vegetables, 66
Roasted Vegetable Turkey Pinwheels, 25
Rustic Roasted Vegetable Tart, 355
Shrimp Pasta Primavera, 95
Southwestern Rice Salad, 30
Spanish Gazpacho, 46
Turkey Potpies, 112
Vegetable & Cheese Focaccia, 138
Vegetable Noodle Bake, 346
Vegetarian Pasta Sauce, 89
Zesty Vegetarian Wraps, 60

WONTON WRAPPERS
Pork and Shrimp Spring Rolls, 8
Strawberry Tartlets, 200

YEAST BREADS (also see Rolls &
Breadsticks; Bread Machine Recipes)
Black Raspberry Bubble Ring, 127
Cheddar Loaves, 135
Cinnamon-Raisin Soft Pretzels, 198
Cracked Pepper Bread, 344
Five-Topping Bread, 129
Fruit and Nut Stollen, 130
Maple Walnut Rolls, 124
Tomato Focaccia, 131
Tricolor Braid, 126
Vermont Honey-Wheat Bread, 124

ZUCCHINI
Carrot Zucchini Fritters, 20
Corn Zucchini Saute, 325
Cranberry Zucchini Wedges, 176
Dilly Zucchini Dip, 220
Spicy Zucchini Quesadillas, 356
Zucchini Apple Salad, 254

cooking terms

Here's a quick reference for some of the cooking terms used in *Taste of Home More Classic Recipes*.

BASTE: To moisten food with melted butter, pan drippings, marinades or other liquid to add more flavor and juiciness.

BEAT: A rapid movement to combine ingredients using a fork, spoon, wire whisk or electric mixer.

BLEND: To combine ingredients until just mixed.

BOIL: To heat liquids until bubbles form that cannot be "stirred down." In the case of water, the temperature will reach 212°.

BONE: To remove all meat from the bone before cooking.

CREAM: To beat ingredients together to a smooth consistency, usually in the case of butter and sugar for baking.

DASH: A small amount of seasoning, less than 1/8 teaspoon. If using a shaker, a dash would comprise a quick flip of the container.

DREDGE: To coat foods with flour or other dry ingredients. Most often done with pot roasts and stew meat before browning.

FOLD: To incorporate several ingredients by careful and gentle turning with a spatula. Used generally with beaten egg whites or whipped cream when mixing into the rest of the ingredients to keep the batter light.

JULIENNE: To cut foods into long thin strips much like matchsticks. Used most often for salads and stir-fry dishes.

MINCE: To cut into very fine pieces. Used often for garlic or fresh herbs.

PARBOIL: To cook partially, usually used in the case of chicken, sausages and vegetables.

PARTIALLY SET: Describes the consistency of gelatin after it has been chilled for a small amount of time. Mixture should resemble the consistency of egg whites.

PUREE: To process foods to a smooth mixture. Can be prepared in an electric blender, food processor, food mill or sieve.

SAUTE: To fry quickly in a small amount of fat, stirring almost constantly. Most often done with onions, mushrooms and other chopped vegetables.

SCORE: To cut slits partway through the outer surface of foods. Often used with ham or flank steak.

STIR-FRY: To cook meats and/or vegetables with a constant stirring motion in a small amount of oil in a wok or skillet over high heat.

alphabetical recipe index

A

A Touch of Greek Dip, 9
Almond Berry Muffins, 137
Almond-Butter Cookie Bouquet, 352
Almond Cookies, 333
Almond-Lemon Pound Cake, 238
Almond Sugar Cookies, 151
Almond Truffle Brownies, 157
Apple and Carrot Slaw, 209
Apple and Prosciutto Sandwiches, 49
Apple-Brie Spinach Salad, 31
Apple-Cherry Pork Chops, 359
Apple Crumble, 198
Apple Dumplings, 205
Apple Pizza, 200
Apple Plum Streusel Dessert, 279
Apple-Raisin Bundt Cake, 285
Apple Streusel Muffins, 227
Apple-Stuffed French Toast, 85
Applesauce-Raspberry Gelatin Mold, 43
Apricot Honey Chicken, 317
Artichoke Ham Puffs, 118
Asian Chicken Thighs, 96
Asian Pot Roast, 115
Asparagus Beef Stir-Fry, 121
Asparagus Berry Salad, 28
Asparagus Brunch Packets, 18
Asparagus Crab Omelets, 107
Asparagus-Fennel Pasta Salad, 42
Asparagus Leek Chowder, 54
Asparagus Salsa, 23
Asparagus Sausage Crepes, 85
Asparagus with Mustard Sauce, 77

B

Bacon-Cheese Topped Chicken, 109
Bacon-Egg English Muffin, 234
Bacon Squash Saute, 250
Baked Bananas in Orange Sauce, 241
Baked Cranberry Sauce, 74
Baked Garlic Green Beans, 233
Balsamic Vinegar Dressing, 32
Banana Citrus Sorbet, 301
Banana Cream Pie, 251
Banana Nut Cake, 167
Banana Split Brownie Pie, 202
Barbecued Ham and Peaches, 337
Bavarian Pork Loin, 88
Beef Brisket with Mop Sauce, 292

Beef Rib Roast, 363
Berry Banana Smoothies, 234
Berry Cheesecake Muffins, 127
Berry Cheesecake Pie, 184
Berry-Cream Cookie Snaps, 147
Berry Pinwheel Cake, 170
Berry Spinach Salad, 275
Biscuit-Topped Lemon Chicken, 222
Black Bean and Pumpkin Chili, 51
Black Bean Burgers, 56
Black Raspberry Bubble Ring, 127
Blackberry Crisp, 357
Blond Brownies a la Mode, 142
Blue Cheese Clubs, 47
Blue Cheese Deviled Eggs, 226
Blueberry Cornmeal Cobbler, 192
Braised Short Ribs, 109
Brined Roasting Chicken, 91
Brisket in a Bag, 121
Broccoli Chicken Supreme, 228
Broccoli with Mustard Sauce, 289
Broccoli with Orange Sauce, 71
Brown Rice Lentil Salad, 38
Brussels Sprouts with Water
    Chestnuts, 365
Buckwheat Brunch Crepes, 88
Buffalo Chicken Dip, 223
Buffalo Chicken Wraps, 57
Butter Pecan Ice Cream, 193
Butterflied Pork Chop Dinner, 105
Butterfly Cheese Sandwiches, 354
Butternut Cream Pie, 168
Butternut Squash Cake Roll, 164
Butternut Turkey Bake, 89
Butterscotch Eggnog Stars, 148

C

Caesar Orange Roughy, 120
Candied Carrots, 258
Candied Flowers, 295
Cappuccino Cherry Trifle, 192
Caramel Chocolate Trifle, 191
Caramel Fruit Dip, 14
Caramel-Pecan Apple Pie, 183
Caramel-Pecan Cheesecake Pie, 289
Caraway Pot Roast, 335
Carrot Cheesecake, 180
Carrot Zucchini Fritters, 20
Cashew-Pear Tossed Salad, 211

Cashew-Pecan Sweet Potatoes, 309
Cheddar Ham Strata, 223
Cheddar Loaves, 135
Cheddar Skillet Corn Bread, 125
Cheese Enchiladas, 224
Cheese-Stuffed Potatoes, 236
Cheeseburger Paradise Soup, 54
Cheesecake Waffle Cups, 325
Cheesy Corn Chowder, 54
Cheesy Noodle Casserole, 67
Cherry Chocolate Bark, 159
Cherry Gingerbread Cupcakes, 179
Cherry Ice Cream Cake, 204
Cherry Tomato Mozzarella Saute, 77
Chewy Apple Oatmeal Cookies, 157
Chicken and Asparagus Kabobs, 90
Chicken & Tomato Risotto, 113
Chicken Asparagus Soup, 60
Chicken Broccoli Calzones, 61
Chicken Fingers with Lemon Sauce, 10
Chicken Florentine Panini, 315
Chicken Pepper Stir-Fry, 105
Chicken Pom-Poms, 16
Chicken Potstickers, 25
Chicken Soup with Potato Dumplings, 56
Chicken Spareribs, 339
Chicken with Paprika Cream, 323
Chinese New Year Skillet, 333
Chocolate Carrot Cake, 178
Chocolate Chip Mousse, 188
Chocolate-Covered Cheesecake
    Squares, 194
Chocolate Heart Cookies, 146
Chocolate Ice Cream Sandwiches, 193
Chocolate Mint Dreams, 144
Chocolate Pecan Bars, 147
Chocolate Pecan Ice Cream Torte, 162
Chocolate Pretzels, 155
Chocolate Ribbon Bars, 347
Chocolate Wheat Cereal Snacks, 22
Chow Mein Chicken Salad, 297
Christmas Breakfast Casserole, 284
Christmas Morning Croissants, 137
Chunky Apple Cake, 208
Chunky Blue Cheese Dressing, 33
Chunky Crawfish Spread, 304
Chunky Taco Soup, 48
Cider Wassail, 285
Cinnamon Apple Cheesecake, 179
Cinnamon Mocha Coffee, 19

Cinnamon-Raisin Soft Pretzels, 198
Cinnamon-Sugar Crisps, 343
Cinnamon-Sugar Rhubarb Cake, 225
Citrus Quencher, 305
Classic Red Velvet Cake, 185
Cocoa for a Crowd, 11
Coconut Pecan Cookies, 146
Coconut Pecan Cupcakes, 210
Coconut Snowmen, 363
Coffee and Cream Brownies, 150
Colony Mountain Chili, 48
Colorful Chicken and Squash Soup, 50
Colorful Turkey Salad Cups, 34
Comforting Broccoli Casserole, 274
Comforting Potato Casserole, 293
Cookie Dough Truffles, 148
Corn Fritters with Caramelized Onion
    Jam, 356
Corn Pudding, 258
Corn Tortilla Chicken Lasagna, 221
Corn Zucchini Saute, 325
Corned Beef Supper, 242
Cornmeal Ham Cakes, 95
Cottage Cheese Yeast Rolls, 339
Cowboy Beef Dip, 19
Crab and Brie Strudel Slices, 367
Crab-Stuffed Sole, 116
Cracked Pepper Bread, 344
Cracked Pepper Salad Dressing, 301
Cran-Apple Crisp, 222
Cranberry Gelatin Squares, 221
Cranberry Ham Loaf, 104
Cranberry Lemonade, 321
Cranberry-Topped Lemon Tarts, 194
Cranberry Walnut Tart, 362
Cranberry Zucchini Wedges, 176
Cream Cheese Blueberry Pie, 167
Creamed Chicken over Biscuits, 114
Creamed Fresh Spinach, 279
Creamed Spinach, 339
Creamy Cashew Brownies, 145
Creamy Ham and Macaroni, 87
Creamy Lime Sherbet, 297
Creamy Vegetable Bow Tie Toss, 78
Crescent-Topped Turkey Amandine, 117
Crispy Chicken Strip Salad, 30
Crispy Potato Cubes, 341
Crowd-Pleasing Taco Salad, 39
Crown Roast of Pork, 308
Crumb-Coated Spaetzle, 72
Crumbleberry Pie, 178
Crunchy Cucumber Rounds, 8
Crunchy Floret Salad, 266
Crusty Roast Leg of Lamb, 300
Cuban Pork Sandwiches, 55
Cube Steaks Parmigiana, 110
Curried Beef with Dumplings, 94
Curried Butternut Squash Kabobs, 71
Curried Carrot Soup, 296
Curried Shrimp and Apples, 112

D

Dad's Swedish Meatballs, 86
Danish Turkey Dumpling Soup, 58
Delicate Mint Thins, 143
Deluxe Breakfast Bake, 228
Devil's Food Caramel Torte, 309
Dilly Pickled Asparagus, 66
Dilly Potato Salad, 37
Dilly Zucchini Dip, 220
Dipped Pecan Spritz, 155
Door County Cherry Biscotti, 156
Double-Berry Crisp, 199
Double Chocolate Fondue, 22
Double Corn Dressing, 73
Down-Home Chicken, 262
Duo Tater Bake, 65

E

Egg Drop Soup, 333
Elegant Chocolate Torte, 166
Elegant Dipped Cherries, 149

F

Family-Pleasing Sloppy Joes, 331
Fancy Bean Salad, 42
Favorite Herbed Potatoes, 317
Festive Rice Salad, 218
Festive White Chocolate Cheesecake, 365
Feta and Chive Muffins, 135
Fiesta Lasagna, 98
Firecracker Burgers, 59
Five-Topping Bread, 129
Fluffy Lemon Squares, 203
Fluffy Pineapple Dessert, 335
Forgotten Jambalaya, 208
Freezer Coleslaw, 263
French Onion Burgers, 321
Fresh Cherry Pie, 165
Fresh Corn Medley, 72
Fresh Fruit Tarts, 175
Fried Shoestring Carrots, 68
Frosted Cookie Brownies, 154
Frosted Rhubarb Cookies, 153
Frosty Almond Dessert, 319
Frosty Mocha Pie, 165
Frozen Peanut Parfait Pies, 175
Frozen Strawberry Pie, 182
Fruit and Nut Stollen, 130
Fruit and Nut Tossed Salad, 37
Fruit-Nut Pumpkin Bread, 132
Fruit Salad Dressing, 39
Fruity French Toast, 234
Fudgy Nut Coffee Pie, 181

G

Garden-Fresh Bruschetta, 13
Garden Lettuce Salad, 345

Garlic-Almond Green Beans, 313
Garlic Anchovy Salad Dressing, 42
Garlic Butternut Bisque, 50
Garlic-Pepper Rub, 78
German Cukes and Tomatoes, 331
German Potato Salad with Sausage, 76
German-Style Mashed Potatoes, 67
Giant Calzone, 100
Gingerbread Boy Cookies, 263
Gingerbread Pudding Cake, 201
Gingered Butternut Squash Soup, 47
Gingered Cranberry-Carrot Slaw, 317
Glazed Peanut Butter Bars, 151
Gnocchi with Thyme Butter, 76
Golden Corn Quiche, 358
Golden Seafood Chowder, 57
Golden Squash Soup, 288
Grandma's Honey Muffins, 293
Grandmother's Bread Pudding, 190
Granola Fudge Clusters, 313
Grapefruit Lettuce Salad, 245
Greek Seafood Salad, 35
Green Bean and Tomato Salad, 346
Green Bean Salad, 329
Green Beans in Lemon Chiffon Sauce, 80
Green Beans with Walnuts, 341
Green Goddess Salad Dressing, 28
Grilled Apple Tossed Salad, 32
Grilled Asparagus Medley, 72
Grilled Asparagus Pizzas, 94
Grilled Corn Dip, 15
Grilled Corn Salsa, 66
Grilled Raspberry Chicken, 103
Grilled Steak Caesar Salad, 34
Grilled Three-Potato Salad, 41

H

Ham Bundles, 220
Ham on Biscuits, 296
Hawaiian Ham Salad, 34
Hazelnut-Espresso Sandwich Cookies, 154
Hazelnut Vegetable Salad, 270
Hearty Beef Vegetable Soup, 53
Hens with Apricot Rice Stuffing, 250
Herbed Popovers, 139
Herbed Tomatoes and Green Beans, 75
Hint of Mint Fruit Salad, 213
Holiday Game Hens, 245
Holiday Spiral Ham, 258
Home Run Slugger Sub, 58
Homemade Peanut Butter Cups, 158
Honey-Mustard Chicken, 238
Honey-Oat Pan Rolls, 132
Honey Pecan Pie, 168
Hot Cheddar-Mushroom Spread, 288
Hot Curried Fruit, 285
Hot Spinach Spread with Pita Chips, 17
Hot Wings, 23

I

Ice Cream Cookie Dessert, 275
Iced Pumpkin Cookies, 142
Indiana Swiss Steak, 97
Irish Mint Brownies, 152
Irish Soda Muffins, 242
Italian Herb Muffins, 364
Italian Wedding Soup, 52

L

Ladybug Cake, 354
Ladyfinger Lemon Torte, 191
Land of Enchantment Posole, 55
Lavender Cookies, 145
Layered Carrot Cake, 162
Layered Mocha Cheesecake, 170
Layered Summertime Salad, 217
Lemon Cheesecake Dessert, 201
Lemon Chiffon Cake, 172
Lemon Coconut Cake, 174
Lemon Cream Puffs, 367
Lemon Cream-Stuffed Grapes, 16
Lemon Pound Cake Muffins, 129
Lemon Rice Pudding Brulee, 205
Lemon Tea Cookies, 143
Lemonade Icebox Pie, 169
Lemonade Meringue Pie, 171
Lemony Chicken Soup, 49
Lemony White Chocolate
    Cheesecake, 169
Lime Shrimp with Asparagus, 98
Loaded Red Potato Casserole, 79

M

Mac and Cheese for a Bunch, 214
Macadamia-Crusted Tilapia, 99
Mango Cranberry Sauce, 78
Maple-Ginger Root Vegetables, 69
Maple-Glazed Ribs, 96
Maple Pumpkin Pie, 184
Maple Walnut Rolls, 124
Mascarpone Cheesecake, 172
Mashed Potato Casserole, 335
Meat Loaf Gyros, 114
Meat Loaf Wellington, 103
Meatball Calzones, 229
Meatballs in Plum Sauce, 209
Meatless Mexican Lasagna, 106
Meaty Pasta Casseroles, 218
Meringue Fudge Drops, 153
Mexicorn Grits, 70
Minestrone with Italian Sausage, 51
Mini Chicken Salad Croissants, 210
Mini Hot Browns, 14
Mini Maple Cinnamon Rolls, 139
Mini Sausage Quiches, 18
Minted Lamb and Veggie Kabobs, 353

Minty Ice Cream Shamrocks, 242
Mixed Fruit Shortcakes, 233
Mixed Herb Salad Dressing, 278
Mixed Nut Chocolate Tart, 202
Mocha Nut Torte, 163
Mom's Apple Crisp, 267
Mom's Fried Fish, 266
Mostaccioli Veggie Salad, 38
Mozzarella-Stuffed Meatballs, 102
Mushroom Bread Wedges, 323
Mushroom Tomato Bisque, 61
Mustard-Sour Cream Salad Dressing, 29

N

Napa Cabbage Slaw, 40
Next Day Turkey Primavera, 107
Nice and Soft Sugar Cookies, 152
No-Bake Chocolate Pie, 305

O

O'Larry's Skillet Potatoes, 81
Old-Fashioned Chicken Potpie, 102
Old Glory Angel Cake, 321
Olive-Cucumber Tossed Salad, 305
Onion-Bacon Baby Carrots, 74
Onions Neptune, 211
Orange and Red Onion Salad, 250
Orange Chicken with Sweet Potatoes, 84
Orange Gelatin Pretzel Salad, 33
Orange-Glazed Acorn Squash, 75
Orange-Rhubarb Breakfast Bread, 126
Orange Rhubarb Spread, 71
Overnight Asparagus Strata, 352

P

Par-Cheesy Pizza, 17
Parker House Dinner Rolls, 128
Parmesan Breadsticks, 136
Parmesan Potato Balls, 329
Parsley Red Potatoes, 267
Parsnip Pancakes, 255
Party Carrots, 77
Party Meatballs, 9
Peach Ice Cream, 193
Peach Rhubarb Crisp, 197
Peaches 'n' Cream Cups, 204
Peaches & Cream Pie, 180
Peaches & Cream Tart, 357
Peanut Butter Blondies, 156
Peanut Butter Chocolate Cupcakes, 216
Peanut Butter Christmas Mice, 366
Peanut Butter Cup Cheesecake, 182
Peanut Butter Pudding Dessert, 213
Peanut Lover's Brownies, 219
Pear-Filled Bundt Cake, 337
Pearl Onion Broccoli Bake, 64
Peas in Cheese Sauce, 74

Pecan Apple Pancakes, 89
Pecan Chicken with Chutney, 97
Pecan Lemon Loaf, 133
Pecan-Pear Green Salad, 29
Peeps Sunflower Cake, 350
Pepper-Rubbed Red Snapper, 319
Pepperoni Spinach Quiche, 101
Peppery Parsnip Fries, 81
Pickled Baby Carrots, 351
Pineapple Cheese Ball, 12
Pineapple Sour Cream Pie, 259
Pineapple Upside-Down Cupcakes, 181
Pineapple-Stuffed Cornish Hens, 104
Pinwheels and Checkerboards, 149
Pizza Margherita, 110
Pizza Meatball Subs, 52
Poached Corn, 262
Poppy Seed Cake, 293
Poppy Seed Fruit Salad, 41
Poppy Seed Onion Bread, 131
Poppy Seed Torte, 271
Pork and Shrimp Spring Rolls, 8
Pork Tenderloin with Stuffing, 254
Pot Roast with Gravy, 87
Praline Chocolate Dessert, 189
Pretty Penne Ham Skillet, 93
Pretty Pumpkin Cinnamon Buns, 130
Prosciutto Chicken Kabobs, 12
Prosciutto-Stuffed Meat Loaf, 108
Prosciutto Tortellini, 319
Puff Pastry Salmon Bundles, 274
Pull-Apart Bacon Bread, 133
Pumpkin Rice Pudding, 189
Pumpkin Scones with Berry Butter, 134

R

Radish Potato Salad, 342
Rainbow Pepper Appetizers, 24
Raisin Pecan Baklava, 196
Ramen Corn Chowder, 315
Ranger Cookies, 158
Raspberry Cherry Pie, 166
Raspberry Patch Cream Pie, 171
Raspberry Peach Cupcakes, 183
Raspberry Pear Crisp, 198
Raspberry Pork Chops, 325
Raspberry Squares, 255
Raspberry Vinaigrette, 28
Red Cream Soda Punch, 227
Red Potato Salad, 212
Reuben Crescent Bake, 119
Rhubarb Cheesecake Smoothies, 13
Rhubarb Cranberry Cookies, 215
Rhubarb Swirl Cheesecake, 164
Rhubarb Upside-Down Cake, 173
Ribboned Vegetables, 66
Rice-Stuffed Acorn Squash, 360
Rich Coffee Cake, 128

Rich Hot Fudge Sauce, 195
Roast Christmas Goose, 278
Roasted Carrot Dip, 11
Roasted Cumin Cashews, 22
Roasted Squash Medley, 67
Roasted Vegetable Turkey Pinwheels, 25
Roasted Yellow Pepper Soup, 53
Rocky Road Ice Cream, 190
Rolled-Up Turkey, 120
Rosemary Leg of Lamb, 111
Russian Cream, 358
Rustic Autumn Fruit Tart, 177
Rustic Nut Bars, 144
Rustic Roasted Vegetable Tart, 355
Rustic Squash Tarts, 70

S

Salisbury Steak, 241
Salmon Chowder, 344
Salmon with Polenta, 99
Salsa for a Crowd, 229
Sausage with Apple Sauerkraut, 341
Savory Ham Cheesecake, 10
Savory Pumpkin Ravioli, 117
Scalloped Potatoes and Ham, 216
Sensational Slush, 9
Shredded Beef and Slaw Sandwiches, 215
Shrimp Pasta Primavera, 95
Shrimp Quesadillas, 118
Shrimp Salad Croissants, 60
Shrimp Scampi, 313
Shrimp Toast Cups, 21
Shrimp Wrapped in Bacon, 24
Simple Sausage Lasagna, 288
Slice and Bake Lemon Gems, 150
Slow-Cooked Bean Medley, 64
Slow-Cooked Pork and Beans, 219
Smoky Grilled Corn, 74
Smoky Jalapenos, 21
So-Sweet Squash Pickles, 68
Southwestern Rice Salad, 30
Southwestern Turkey Soup, 46
Spaghetti Squash Supreme, 79
Spaghetti Squash with Red Sauce, 108
Spanish Gazpacho, 46
Sparkling Ginger Lemonade, 14
Special Banana Nut Bread, 132
Special Mocha Cupcakes, 176
Special Sesame Chicken Salad, 36
Spiced Orange Pecans, 12
Spiced Squash Muffins, 362
Spicy Nacho Bake, 93
Spicy Pork Chili, 217
Spicy Potato Wedges, 331
Spicy Seafood Bisque, 366
Spicy Zucchini Quesadillas, 356
Spinach and Sausage Pork Loin, 364
Spinach Crab Chicken, 111

Spiral Ham with Cranberry Glaze, 84
Spiral Pepperoni Pizza Bake, 226
Spring Breeze Cheesecake Pie, 353
Springtime Asparagus Medley, 300
Springtime Barley, 65
Steaks with Cucumber Sauce, 101
Steamed Broccoli Florets, 323
Strawberry-Banana Angel Torte, 301
Strawberry Cheesecake Ice Cream, 199
Strawberry Crepes, 188
Strawberry Popovers, 136
Strawberry Pretzel Dessert, 350
Strawberry Puff Pastry Dessert, 195
Strawberry Shortbread Pie, 163
Strawberry Spinach Salad, 43
Strawberry Swirl Cheesecake, 174
Strawberry Tartlets, 200
Stuffed Ham with Raisin Sauce, 351
Stuffed Pork Tenderloin, 233
Stuffed Squash for Two, 100
Summer Celebration Ice Cream Cake, 173
Summer Chicken Salad, 35
Sunday Chicken Stew, 106
Sunday Shrimp Pasta Bake, 304
Sunny Carrot Salad, 29
Sunrise Slushies, 24
Sunshine Sweet Rolls, 125
Sweet & Sour Brussels Sprouts, 81
Sweet and Tender Cabbage Rolls, 113
Sweet Herbed Carrots, 238
Sweet Milk Dinner Rolls, 139
Sweet Pea Salad, 226
Sweetheart Punch, 20
Sweetheart Steaks, 237
Swiss-Almond Floret Bake, 80
Swiss Tuna Melts, 48

T

Taco Meat Loaves, 115
Tamales, 212
Tangy Rhubarb Chutney, 73
Tasty Pork Ribs, 90
Tenderloin in Puff Pastry, 92
Texas Chocolate Cupcakes, 185
Tex-Mex Dip, 224
Thai Beef Stir-Fry, 86
Thai Chicken Fettuccine, 119
Thousand Island Salad Dressing, 315
Three-Cheese Pesto Pizza, 23
Three-Fruit Salad, 337
Three-Fruit Sundae Sauce, 203
Tiramisu Brownies, 159
Tiramisu Cheesecake Dessert, 197
Toffee Apple Crunch, 245
Tomato and Corn Risotto, 69
Tomato Corn Salad, 31
Tomato-Cucumber Mozzarella Salad, 355
Tomato Focaccia, 131

Tomato Rice Pilaf, 241
Tortellini Spinach Casserole, 225
Tossed Salad with Carrot Dressing, 292
Tossed Salad with Lemon Vinaigrette, 215
Traditional Meat Loaf, 329
Tricolor Braid, 126
Triple-Cheese Broccoli Puff, 284
Tropical Lime Chicken, 116
Tuna Cheese Melts, 342
Turkey Chop Suey, 121
Turkey Enchiladas, 107
Turkey Muffuletta, 46
Turkey Potpies, 112
Turkey with Mushrooms and Cream, 270
Turkey with Sausage-Corn Bread
    Stuffing, 360

U

Ultimate Caramel Apples, 359

V

Valentine Cakes, 236
Vanilla Cinnamon Rolls, 134
Vanilla Pudding Dessert, 224
Vegetable & Cheese Focaccia, 138
Vegetable Noodle Bake, 346
Vegetarian Pasta Sauce, 89
Vegetarian Stuffed Peppers, 92
Vermont Honey-Wheat Bread, 124
Very Berry-licious Smoothies, 17

W

Waldorf Stuffed Ham, 91
Waldorf Tuna Salad, 41
Walnut Banana Cupcakes, 177
Walnut Raspberry Muffins, 138
Warm Asparagus-Crab Spread, 15
Warm Asparagus Spinach Salad, 40
Watermelon Basket, 214
White Bean Chicken Chili, 59
White Chocolate Berry Dessert, 196
White Chocolate Macadamia Muffins, 129
Wicked Witch Cupcakes, 361
Wild Rice Pilaf, 309

Y

Yummy Yeast Rolls, 271

Z

Zesty Snack Mix, 22
Zesty Vegetarian Wraps, 60
Zucchini Apple Salad, 254